MEXICO
1994

1994 FIELDING TITLES

Fielding's Australia 1994

Fielding's Belgium 1994

Fielding's Bermuda/Bahamas 1994

Fielding's Brazil 1994

Fielding's Britain 1994

Fielding's Budget Europe 1994

Fielding's Caribbean 1994

Fielding's Europe 1994

Fielding's Far East 1994

Fielding's France 1994

Fielding's The Great Sights of Europe 1994

Fielding's Hawaii 1994

Fielding's Holland 1994

Fielding's Italy 1994

Fielding's Mexico 1994

Fielding's Scandinavia 1994

Fielding's New Zealand 1994

Fielding's Spain & Portugal 1994

Fielding's Switzerland & the Alpine Region 1994

Fielding's Worldwide Cruises 1994

Fielding's Shopping Europe 1994

Fielding Travel Guides

MEXICO 1994

The Most In-depth Guide to the Culture and Mysteries of Mexico

by
Lynn V. Foster
and
Lawrence Foster

Fielding Worldwide, Inc.
308 South Catalina Avenue
Redondo Beach, California 90277 U.S.A.

Fielding's Mexico 1994

Published by Fielding Worldwide, Inc.

Text Copyright @1994 Lynn V. Foster & Lawrence Foster

Icons & Illustrations Copyright ©1993 FWI

Photo Copyrights ©1993 to Individual Photographers

FIELDING WORLDWIDE INC.

PUBLISHER AND CEO	**Robert Young Pelton**
DIRECTOR OF PUBLISHING	**Paul T. Snapp**
CO-DIR. OF ELECTRONIC PUBLISHING	**Tony E. Hulette**
CO-DIR. OF ELECTRONIC PUBLISHING	**Larry E. Hart**
PRODUCTION SUPERVISOR	**Michael Rowley**
PRODUCTION MANAGEMENT	**Beverly Riess**
EDITORIAL MANAGER	**Wink Dulles**
OFFICE MANAGER	**Christy Donaldson**

EDITORS

Linda Charlton	**Kathy Knoles**
Tina Gentile	**Evelyn Lager**
Loretta Rooney Hess	**Jane M. Martin**
Dixie Hulette	**Peggy Plendl**
Ann Imberman	**Jeanne-Marie Swann**
Forrest Kerr	**Gladis R. Zaimah**

PRODUCTION

Norm Imberman	**Harold Pierson**
Bryan Kring	**Kip Riggins**
Lyne Lawrence	**Munir Shaikh**
Chris Medeiros	**Chris Snyder**
	Lillian Tse

COVER DESIGNED BY	**Pelton & Associates, Inc.**
COVER PHOTOGRAPHERS — Front Cover	**Craig Aurness/Westlight**
Background Photo, Front Cover	**Dallas and John Heaton/Westlight**
Back Cover	**Dallas and John Heaton/Westlight**
INSIDE PHOTOS	**Edelman Public Relations & Peter Foster**
MAPS	**Geosystems**

Inquiries should be addressed to: Fielding Worldwide, Inc., 308 South Catalina Ave., Redondo Beach, California 90277 U.S.A., Telephone (310) 372-4474, Facsimile (310) 376-8064, 8:30 a.m. - 5:30 p.m. Pacific Standard Time.

ISBN 1-56952-016-X

Printed in the United States of America

Dedication

To Manuel of Gavillera, Salvador of Jalisco, and Baleria of Maconda
for sharing their Mexico with us.

Letter from the Publisher

In 1946, Temple Fielding began the first of what would be a re-markable new series of well-written, highly personalized guide books for independent travelers. Temple's opinionated, witty, and oft-imitated books have now guided travelers for almost a half-century. More important to some was Fielding's humorous and direct method of steering travelers away from the dull and the insipid. Today, Fielding Travel Guides are still written by experienced travelers for experienced travelers. Our authors carry on Fielding's reputation for creating travel experiences that deliver insight with a sense of discovery and style.

Lynn and Larry Foster bring a true passion to their writing in this charming and warm guide to the enchanted land "south of the border." The Fosters call Mexico their home much of the year, and the reasons become obvious as you digest the pages and absorb their unmatched insight into this very special and diverse country. Wherever you choose to explore, the Foster's cultural and emotional empathy will help make your Mexico experience truly unforgettable.

In 1994, the concept of independent travel has never been bigger. Our policy of *brutal honesty* and a highly personal point of view has never changed; it just seems the travel world has caught up with us.

Enjoy your Mexico adventure with Lynn and Larry Foster and Fielding.

Robert Young Pelton
Publisher and CEO
Fielding Worldwide, Inc.

ACKNOWLEDGMENTS

Thanks inadequately express our gratitude to those who have encouraged and assisted us throughout the preparation of this new edition of our book. Christine Sonnhalter, Carlota and Phil Bragar, and Dan and Genevieve Hartman have sacrificed their time to double check items for us.

Travel to gather the most current information for this edition was made possible by the generous assistance of:

The Secretary of Tourism, Pedro Joaquin Caldwell and his able staff in New York and at the Ministry of Tourism in Mexico City;

Continental Airlines.

ABOUT THE AUTHORS

Lynn and Lawrence Foster

Lawrence Foster, who has a Ph.D. in philosophy from the University of Pennsylvania, is the former Director of the Law and Justice Program and the current chairman of the philosophy department at the University of Massachusetts, Boston.

Lynn Foster, who has a Ph.D. in philosophy from Brandeis University, has also studied at Harvard and the Sorbonne, and has taught at Smith, Mt. Holyoke, and the University of Massachusetts at Amherst and in Boston. For more than fifteen years the Fosters have traveled in Mexico by bus, train, car, Land Rover, and canoe-exploring hidden ruins and remote villages as well as major cities. In addition, they have lived in Mexico City and Oaxaca. Both have studied Mesoamerican archaeology at Harvard University and in Mexico and are members of the Society for American Archaeology. Lynn has also studied Maya hieroglyphics at the University of Texas and has lectured in Mexico on the Maya civilization. They are godparents to a Mixteca Indian boy. The Fosters live in Boston.

SPECIAL BULLETIN

In 1993 the value of the peso was changed from three-thousand pesos to one U. S. dollar to approximately three new pesos. New currency is gradually being introduced; the bills and larger coins (those worth 5 and 10 new pesos certainly aren't the small change they appear to be) are marked "nuevos pesos," or new pesos. During the transition, there surely will be confusion in prices and currency over old and new pesos—don't hesitate to ask for clarification.

Fielding Rating Icons

The Fielding Rating Icons are highly personal and awarded to help the besieged traveler choose from among the dizzying array of activities, attractions, hotels, restaurants and sights. The awarding of an icon denotes unusual or exceptional qualities in the relevant category. We encourage you to create your own icons in the margin to help you find those special places that make each trip unforgettable.

Fielding Selection	Author Selection	Money Saver	Expensive	Quality	Warning
Homey	Luxurious	Rustic	Simple	Scenic	Business
Great Scenery	Picturesque	Beaches & Resorts	Spectacular Cuisine	Romantic	Relaxing
Museum/ Art Gallery	Artistically Important	Architecturally Interesting	History	Book Reference	Musically Interesting
Shopping	Festivals	Nightlife	Wine Tasting	Crafts	etc.
Cycling	Hiking	Golf	Tennis	Strolling	Horseback Riding
Cross-country Skiing	Downhill Skiing	Deep-sea Fishing	Fresh-water Fishing	Snorkeling & Diving	Sailing
Arrival & Departure	By Bus/Local Transportation	By Air	By Road	By Water	By Rail

TABLE OF CONTENTS

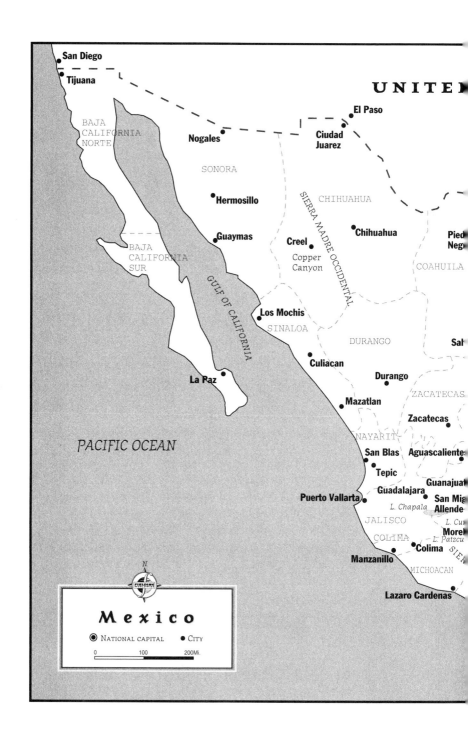

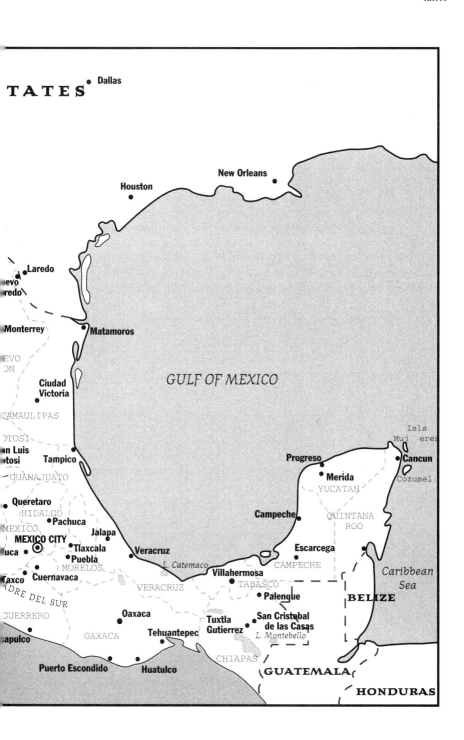

INTRODUCTION

On Route to Puebla

While Mexico shares the North American continent, its heritage is more properly part of Latin America to the south. Conveniently near for travel, Mexico is as exotic as countries continents away. As Spain's wealthiest colony in the Americas, Mexico has an architectural richness that vies with Europe. As the land of great Indian civilizations, it offers ruins as fascinating as, if less familiar than, those in Greece. And as a modern nation, its distinctive culture, involving an enchanting blend of Indian and Spanish music, dance, cuisine, handcrafts, and arts, is unparalleled.

A LAND OF CONSTANT DISCOVERY

Much of Mexico comes as a delightful surprise to the first-time visitor—especially the friendliness of its people, the excellence of its accommodations, and its reasonable prices. Travel becomes easier each year as Mexico opens new roads to formerly isolated villages and builds modern airports where thatched-roof structures once stood. Still, Mexico remains so different from what most North Americans are used to that a good guidebook is important for understanding this traditional land.

Year after year, we have traveled in Mexico with yet another guidebook. These books usually provided acceptable information on hotels and restaurants but deserted us at major sights—such as the Yucatán ruins of Chichen Itza—giving too little information and the advice to buy a special guidebook. We found ourselves burdened with a suitcase of books—one or more on ruins, the same for history, plus a few guidebooks specializing in shopping, budget hints, and the like. Our aching arms and fascination with Mexico led us to write this all- in-one Fielding Guide based on our own travels and research. Combining comprehensive and up-to-date practical information with extensive supplements on sightseeing, ancient civilizations, history, and culture, this guide offers all travelers—from deluxe to budget class—the information so essential for fully enjoying Mexico.

A GUIDE TO FIELDING'S MEXICO

Fielding's Mexico coincides with the northern limits of ancient Indian civilizations and Spanish colonial cities, if not with the border now shared with the United States. It encompasses Mexico's most famous resorts and most spectacular cities and ruins. In addition to these major sights, it describes less frequented points of interest for the more adventurous traveler, including some of the most traditional Indian villages. The extreme north toward the U.S. border and the peninsula of Baja California hold few traces of traditional Mexico and offers mostly a barren landscape dotted with modern cities showing as much U.S. influence as Mexican. The few sights to see in this northern expanse—for example, Copper Canyon—are covered in the section "Land Routes into Mexico." The fishing and camping facilities of Baja California are not covered at all.

HOW TO USE THIS GUIDE

Introductory chapters are provided for practical travel information, itineraries, Mexican culture, ancient Mexico, and Mexican history.

Because we have tried to put as much information as feasible in the regional chapters where it is most convenient for the traveler, these opening chapters provide overviews rather than regional details and variations. Each regional chapter contains an introduction to local geography, ancient cultures, important historical events, and contemporary cultures and should be used as a supplement to the introductory chapters. Travel sections on major cities, sights, and resorts follow the regional introductions. Each travel section begins with a thumbnail outline of tourist sights and facilities called the **"Key"** and a **"Directory"** of local offices and services you might need during your trip. Most of the travel section is an elaboration of the information contained in the Key, including *sightseeing, excursions, shopping, accommodations, regional cuisine and restaurants, and entertainment.* These sections end with advice on getting to and from the area. Also, where pertinent, special **on-the-road** sections describe sights to visit en route between two major tourist areas. The **"Hotel Quick-Reference Tables"** list hotel phone numbers for making your own reservations, as well as prices. **Recommended readings**, a **Spanish glossary**, and **road signs** are included. The **Index** is useful for looking up places and information not listed in the **Contents**.

PRICES

Originally, we intended to include prices in pesos throughout this guide, but over the years we found that sudden devaluations of the peso made this imprudent. While the peso rate has been relatively stableduring 1991-93 (and as this book goes to press is valued at 3.08 new pesos to one U.S. dollar), there is an additional problem in quoting prices for the next year in that Mexico is experiencing an annual inflation rate of over 15%. In order to give you the least misleading price indications, we decided to give price categories based on U.S. dollars. The peso may be devalued again, which would make prices cheaper than we list, or, more likely, inflation in Mexico might increase them. We expect, but cannot guarantee, that a combination of devaluation and inflation will keep our price categories accurate and make our hotel prices more accurate than if we listed them in pesos. However, since the government no longer sets hotel prices, even our best efforts to provide accurate prices may fail. We can only say that the prices are the most up-to-date at press time.

RESTAURANT PRICE CATEGORIES

The following price categories are based on dinner for two including tax (10%), but excluding tip and beverage and are quoted in U.S. dollars:

Expensive	$50 and up
Moderately expensive	$40-49
Moderate	$30-39
Inexpensive	less than $30

HOTEL PRICE CATEGORIES

The following price categories are based on a room for two including tax (10%) and are quoted in U.S. dollars:

Resort Expensive	$175 and up
Very Expensive	$130-174
Expensive	$95-129
Moderate	$60-94
Inexpensive	$35-59
Budget	less than $35

We list restaurants and hotels according to the above price categories. For hotels, we also give telephone numbers and specific prices. For easy reference, we provide a complete list of hotel telephone numbers and rates in the "**Hotel Quick-Reference Tables**" located at the end of this book. Unless otherwise noted, rates are for a standard double room on the European Plan, without meals. A range of prices indicates that the rooms vary in amenities, size, location or view. Where **CP (Continental Plan)** is noted, breakfast is included; **AP (American Plan)** includes breakfast, lunch and dinner; **MAP (Modified American Plan)** includes breakfast and either lunch or dinner. We use categories such as "expensive" and "budget" for want of better comparative words, because expensive hotels and restaurants certainly are not high priced relative to U.S. standards and many budget hotels and restaurants provide good facilities. These categories are simply ways of informing you about prices at one place relative to prices in other Mexican establishments so you can select a hotel or restaurant within your travel budget.

You will find, to your delight, that expensive Mexican hotels and restaurants, except at the biggest resorts, are priced below expensive establishments in the United States. And traveling moderately in

Mexico is traveling quite well. Two people selecting their hotels and meals from our moderate categories can expect to spend an average of $130 U.S. daily, or $65 per person for lodging and three meals. Although highway tolls can match and even exceed those in the U.S., other items such as bus or taxi travel carry far lower prices than at home. Overall, prices in Mexico are reasonable and sometimes surprisingly low, making a trip to Mexico affordable even for those travelling on a tight budget.

HOTEL RATINGS

We use a **star (★)** and **check (√)** system to rate hotels. The stars reflect numerous considerations such as the size and furnishings of rooms, the quality of its view and lighting, the size and attractiveness of the bathrooms, and, of course, cleanliness. The amenities of a hotel are important too, such as whether it has restaurants, bars, swimming pool, tennis courts or other sports facilities, and laundry or room service. The overall attractiveness and maintenance of a hotel also enter significantly into the allotment of stars, as does the quality of its service. Finally, the stars reflect our subjective judgment on the hotels' overall quality and ambience. All of these factors, many intangible, enter into our final awarding of stars to guide your hotel selection.

★★★★★ A truly exceptional hotel that has the qualities of a four-star hotel plus some striking feature that makes it even more outstanding. The hotel excels in architecture, service, ambience, or some other important characteristic that makes it one of the select few.

★★★★ A luxury hotel with all the amenities, including quality service.

★★★ A first-class, comfortable hotel with most amenities including a restaurant and bar.

★★ A recommended hotel above our minimum requirements that often has a restaurant and/or bar and some special feature to distinguish it from a one-star hotel.

★ An acceptable hotel, meeting our minimum standards. Often these hotels are plain yet provide decent accommodations and a few services.

NO STAR-After reading our description of such a hotel, you may find it acceptable to you, particularly if you are traveling on a tight budget and starred hotels in the budget category are not available.

√   The check reflects our judgment that the hotel is a particularly good buy in its price category. Although hotel prices are generally below prices for comparable hotels in the United States, some stand out among the rest as an exceptional value.

Hotels are grouped into price categories, starred, checked, and described. Within price categories, the order of the hotels reflects our judgment of relative quality. If you are traveling on a moderate budget, you can read the descriptions, check the star ratings, and if you are still undecided, you can just select the first hotel listed under the "moderate" category. Since preferences for hotels vary, read the descriptions to make sure you are selecting a hotel suitable to your tastes.

UPDATES

We have made enormous efforts to provide the most up-to-date and accurate information, but between our visit and yours, hotels may change management and restaurants their chefs. While we cannot be responsible for the inaccuracies that must result from these constant changes in the tourism industry, we will make an ongoing effort to keep abreast of them. Your comments and suggestions would be most welcome and helpful. Write to Lynn and Lawrence Foster:

c/o *Fielding Worldwide, Inc.,*
308 South Catalina Avenue,
Redondo Beach, CA 90277.

PRACTICAL TRAVEL INFORMATION

Cozumel

As comfortable and easy as it is to travel through Mexico, it still is a foreign country requiring some special adjustments and advance planning for your trip to go as smoothly as you would like. Deluxe and first-class travelers will find their hotels convenient for arranging tours, renting cars, placing telephone calls, and the like, whereas budget travelers will have to rely more on themselves for making arrangements from bus reservations to seeking out a post office to buy stamps. Although the practical information contained in this chapter should be useful to all travelers, much of the detail here and in the directories to major cities in this book will be most critical for those making their own arrangements.

SPECIAL TIPS

Whatever your style of travel, you will be interacting with Mexicans throughout your trip. They can make your trip more pleasurable than you could possibly dream if you remain sensitive to some of their customs and attitudes. Courtesy is an essential ingredient of the Mexican character. Even if you can't speak Spanish, a *gracias* or a *muy amable* ("very kind of you") here and there is always in order. In response, you won't receive a mere "you're welcome," but rather "it is nothing" (*de nada*), or "in order to serve you" (*para servirle*), or occasionally an astonishing "at your feet" (*a sus pies*). Also, Mexicans, like all Latin Americans, consider themselves Americans. For this reason, it is best for U.S. citizens to state their nationality as North American and to say they are from the United States, not from America.

The *mañana* mentality is only too well known, yet just as often misunderstood. True, you may find yourself waiting in a bank line while a clerk socializes with a customer, or you may find a small museum or shop closed when it should be open. Neither occurance is due to laziness or fuzzy-headedness but to the Mexican's warmth toward other people. A Mexican would consider it rude to cut off a customer so the bank line moves faster. And better to open the shop late than not to assist some lost tourist to find his or her destination. There's a Mexican saying that North Americans live to work, but Mexicans work to live. The only way to cope with this difference is to schedule your trip to allow for some delays. A little patience and humor, a few smiles and some flattery are bound to be most generously returned.

CLIMATE

In some areas of Mexico you may need a sweater most evenings (Mexico City, San Cristobal de las Casas, and Patzcuaro). Even these coolest spots become comfortably warm during the day. We begin with the "chilly" areas because Mexico is most often thought of as hot and humid. In fact, most of the country is neither tropical nor cold, but temperate and springlike year-round. In general, Mexico has a dry (November-April) and rainy (May-October) season, but some rain can occur during the dry season, and the rainy season seldom presents travel problems as storms usually are torrential yet brief. Resorts, however, should be avoided during the rainiest months of June and September. Temperatures are slightly cooler in the winter months (December and January are the "coldest"), and the end of the dry season (May) can be the hottest time of the year in the highlands. The temperatures in Mexico vary with altitude from the hot lowland coastal areas to the pine-forested mountain regions. The sea-level resort areas are tropical and summerlike all year, with their humidity and temperature increasing during the summer months (average annual temperature about 80°F). Most cities are situated in the mountains with an altitude between 4000-6000 feet, and they have milder, subtropical weather with slightly warmer than spring temperatures all year (average 66°F). Mexico City and other cities situated over 7000 feet above sea level have cooler temperatures than the subtropics (average 60°F). In planning your trip, check the Key to the cities you will be visiting to know the weather you will encounter. If you are driving into Mexico, realize the northern area has a climate most similar to Texas, with frost and even occasional snow in the winter.

WHEN TO TRAVEL

In general, Mexico's tourism is greatest from December to April and during the summer months, but information about local seasons is included in the accommodations section for each city. You should try to have reservations well in advance of any of these popular times, especially Christmas to January 6, the week before Easter, and July through August (times when Mexican families and Europeans go on holiday) as well as during the February and March school breaks in the U.S.A. If you travel off-season, you may be able to obtain less expensive hotel rates. During special fiestas (as opposed to bankers' holidays), a town can be transformed by special entertainments, lively crowds, and traditional religious processions. We list some of the more popular of these fiestas in the Keys to cities so you can try to include some of them on your itinerary.

NATIONAL HOLIDAYS

Businesses usually close during holidays, so if you are planning a shopping spree in one particular town make sure you are there when the shops will be open. Often you will find shops closed early the day before a holiday. The weeks before Christmas and New Year's are often celebrated quite intensely and wonderfully (it's a particularly gay time to be in Mexico), but the shops stay open. The week before Easter is a time of many local celebrations, although in the non-resort areas of Mexico you may find things quiet because everyone has gone to the beach. In addition to the following holidays, check the Key before each city for special fiestas: January 1, January 6 (the Day of the Three Kings), February 5 (Constitution Day), March 21 (Benito Juarez' Birthday), May 1 (Labor Day), May 5 (Battle of Puebla), September 1 (President's message to the nation), September 16 (Independence Day), October 12 (Day of the Race or Columbus Day), November 20 (Anniversary of the Revolution), December 12 (Festival of the Virgin of Guadalupe), and December 25.

CLOTHING

If you plan a wardrobe just as you would for different settings at home, you won't go wrong—with a few exceptions. You won't want to bring easily wrinkled clothes or delicate fabrics that need special care at your favorite dry cleaners. Bring along at least one pair of comfortable, thick-soled walking shoes for city sightseeing, and the soles should be suitable for climbing steep pyramids at ruins (where constricting straight skirts and tight slacks can hamper your movements). Shorts are perfectly fine for resorts but unacceptable elsewhere. Miniskirts are fine at resorts and fashion-conscious cities like the capital but inappropriate for crowded markets and traditional villages. For the tropics, you may want to take a sun hat.

While you will have difficulty discovering a restaurant in the tropics or at resorts requiring men to wear a tie and jacket, some of the better restaurants in highland cities are more formal. On the whole, dress can be as informal in the highlands as in the tropics (if not as flamboyant), but by bringing a tie and a sports jacket (you might need it anyway against a chilly evening), you can guarantee your admission to any place that appeals to you. Similarly, women should be prepared with something more elegant than slacks in both the highlands and tropics.

Variations in climate need to be considered too. During the rainy season, bring an umbrella or raincoat. (We always do but seem never to have them with us when it rains—like Mexicans we take shelter until the usually brief storm passes.) For any season and destination, bring at least one lightweight sweater or jacket in case night air or sudden dampness from rain gives you a slight chill and, yes, a bathing suit, in case a swimming pool beckons you. For the tropics, the coolest of lightweight clothing is appropriate. For the subtropics, your lightweight clothing may serve during sunny afternoons, but clothing more appropriate for spring weather will be needed at other times (lightweight knits, long-sleeved shirts, etc.). For the higher altitudes like Mexico City, you definitely should be prepared to dress for the chill of a fall day during winter. Gabardine-weight or lightweight corduroys are in order, along with a heavy sweater. If you are traveling extensively in Mexico, you will descend and ascend mountains and change altitude often. The lightest way to travel is to layer your clothes, peeling off your pullover sweater, your long-sleeved shirt, and finally stripping to short sleeves as you descend into the tropics.

OTHER ITEMS TO TAKE

Mexico is a land of color, so if you bring your camera, also bring color film (you're allowed to bring in 12 rolls) unless you are unusually creative with black and white. Film costs more in Mexico, but if you run out, Mexican shops can supply most of whatever you need. The sun is brilliant here, so buy your film accordingly. Kodachrome 64 and Kodacolor 100 are good all-purpose films. In traditional parts of Mexico, the people sometimes dislike—and even are fearful of—having their pictures taken. At the very least, be discreet (or ask permission).

Insect repellent and suntan lotion usually cost more in Mexico than at home. Toothpaste, shampoos, and medicines are available but maybe not your particular brand. Bring them with you.

You never know when you might need thread and needle, safety pins, facial tissue (for wiping your hands, for poorly supplied public bathrooms, and so on, not just for the sniffles), Band-Aids and an antiseptic cream. All these supplies are available in Mexico, but a store may not be nearby when you need them. If you are traveling budget class, bring an extra towel (especially if you're going to the beach), a few hangers, and maybe even a bar of soap.

If you're a restless sleeper or particularly sensitive to noise, you may find earplugs your salvation during Mexican nights, filled as they are with the sounds of truck gears grinding, roosters crowing, and revelers serenading.

A Swiss Army knife can be useful, particularly for a picnic or snack while traveling. And binoculars are good not only for birdwatching, but also for looking at inaccessible carvings on ruins and churches. Sunglasses are essential if you are driving.

Your hair dryer or electric razor can usually operate on Mexican current, yet in a few small towns they may not. Bring a safety razor, just in case. Also, the new plugs (with different size prongs) require an adapter to fit into Mexican sockets. Coin laundries are difficult to find, but any hotel can make arrangements for laundry and dry cleaning. But you may still want to wash a few items by hand, so bring a flat disk stopper (it will work with any drain) and some detergent.

Finally, books in English can be bought in major cities and resorts, but not necessarily the one you were dying to read during your vacation. And because they are imported, they cost more than at home. It's best to bring reading materials with you, but just in case you run out, we list bookshops, when they exist, in the city Directories.

HEALTH TIPS

No inoculations are necessary for entering Mexico, though you should check with your doctor for his or her recommendations. We recommend a tetanus shot if yours is out of date. We also suggest you consider wearing an ID tag provided by Medic Alert International (Box 1009, Turlock, CA 95381; ☎ 800-ID-ALERT; fee) if you suffer from epilepsy, diabetes, allergies to ordinary medications, heart disease, or other such hidden medical conditions.

Moctezuma's revenge, as we know it, or *turista*, as Mexicans call it, is the greatest health concern of most tourists. This affliction of diarrhea sometimes accompanied by fever can last a few days and require complete bed rest. It usually results not from dirty water or dirty anything but from exposure to bacteria different from those at home. (Mexicans visiting the United States are similarly affected by our bacteria.) There is no guaranteed method for preventing it. We have seen the most cautious traveler get *turista* and the least cautious emerge unscathed. The absolutely safest thing to do is to limit your drinking water to that found bottled. Many first-class hotels have purified water (*agua purificada*) in their taps, but you may want to be conservative and use it only for brushing your teeth. Budget hotels provide agua purificada to you in bottles or carafes. A further precaution is not to take a chance on ice cubes and to request beverages *sin hielo*. (Most pricier establishments use purified water for everything, but ask to make sure.) If you are craving a glass of cold water, try a chilled bottle of Mexico's good mineral water (called *agua mineral*, and *sin gas* if you don't want it carbonated). The standard advice also warns you to avoid salads and unpeeled raw vegetables and fruit, but again you might want to use your judgment as to the kind of restaurant you're eating in. However, you definitely should follow these guidelines in markets and provincial areas. At high altitudes, overexhaustion and overindulgence in food or drink may contribute to your susceptibility. Treatment depends on the intensity of your ailment. Many people swear that advance daily doses of chewable Pepto-Bismal will prevent illness, but for serious attacks you should stay in bed, restrict yourself to a diet of tea, and take whatever drug your doctor recommends. (Some, like *Lomotil* and *Vibramicin*, are available over the counter in Mexico.) Your hotel can arrange for a doctor if you become concerned about your condition. Mexican doctors are expert in treating this illness. Once you're out of bed, stay on a bland diet until you feel completely well.

In the last few years cholera has broken out in the rural areas of Mexico, and it will take until at least 1996 to eradicate it. Medical experts recommend simple preventive measures similar to the ones above for avoiding *turista*: Namely, avoid raw foods. In particular, you should avoid raw fish, found most often in Mexican restaurants in the form of *ceviche*. (Most restaurants have either stopped serving ceviche or now cook the fish before marinating it for the fish cocktail.)

The high altitude of many cities has a variety of effects on people. Some are elated by it, others don't notice it at all, but most people feel tired more quickly than usual (especially climbing steps) and experience some dizziness. Although these feelings pass in a day or two as your body becomes accustomed to the new environment, consider taking a nap during the afternoon and be prudent initially in your enjoyment of food and drink. Altitude problems are most likely to affect you in Mexico City, Toluca, Puebla, Patzcuaro, and San Cristobal de las Casas because they are all over 7000 feet above sea level. People with heart problems should seek a doctor's advice before traveling to these areas.

If you have a chronic medical problem that might require attention, you should discuss your travel plans with your doctor. **The International Association for Medical Assistance to Travelers** (*IAMAT, 417 Center St., Lewiston, NY 14092*; donation) can provide listings of English-speaking physicians for a number of Mexican towns if you write them a few months before departure. However, if you suddenly find yourself in need of a doctor, any hotel can help you—even budget hotels in provincial towns can call a doctor (who often will speak at least some English) or put you in a taxi for the nearest clinic. But if you find yourself without access to help, ask for the hospital (os-pee-TAHL) or ISSTE (EES-tay), part of an extensive network of government clinics. If more care is needed or you have a **medical emergency,** contact the nearest consular agent. (See "Emergencies" below.)

MEDICATION

For medication, every town has at least one pharmacy and usually more. They may not provide you with the exact brand you are used to, but they can usually find an equivalent. Most drugs, even penicillin, don't require prescriptions in Mexico, so check a pharmacy before going to the doctor if you know exactly what you need. In most towns, pharmacies take turns staying open all night to handle emergencies. Your hotel or the ISSTE clinic should be able to tell you which one is open.

Recently, the U.S. Food and Drug Administration issued a warning about the dangers of lead poisoning resulting from the use of ceramics that have been improperly produced. Many lovely ceramics sold in the U.S.A., as well as Mexico and the rest of the world, are coated with lead glazes. For a piece of ceramic ware to be safe for food storage and use, the lead glaze has to be heated or fired to a high enough temperature for a sufficient amount of time. Unfortunately, there is no way to tell merely by looking whether the ceramic piece that you desperately want to buy has a glaze that contains lead, and if it does, whether it has been fired properly. To be extra safe, you shouldn't use ceramic ware for storing food, especially food such as fruit juice, with a high acidic content. The acid tends to increase the amount of lead released into the food.

MONEY

At the time this book is going to press, 3.08 new Mexican pesos, or 3080 old Mexican pesos are equivalent to one U.S. dollar, but the exchange rate is fluctuating. Pesos come in many denominations, both in coins and paper bills. The old peso is worth a mere fraction of a penny; the *nuevo peso*, or new peso (abbreviated as N. or N. P.), 33 cents, so be careful with those new five- and ten-peso coins.

It is important to note that Mexico uses the dollar sign for its peso. Don't get confused. Normally, unless a sign states a price is in U.S. dollars, the amount is in pesos.

MONEY EXCHANGES

In most cities and resorts, cash can be obtained from the **24-hour ATMs** (*caja permanente*) at Banamex, Mexico's largest bank, through Cirrus on your own bank card. The fee per transaction (the maximum withdrawal permitted is the same as at your bank ATM) usually is minimal (unlike Cirrus on credit cards), especially when balanced against the excellent exchange rates of international banking. So far we have seen in Mexico little sign of Cirrus' competitors like Plus. If your bank card is linked with Cirrus, then make sure you get a 4-digit PIN access code before leaving on your trip and you'll avoid long bank and cambio lines. Even if you do have Cirrus, we still recommend that you travel with some **traveler's checks** (passport or photo I.D. required to cash them) in case you can't find a Cirrus ATM (not all banks have them), credit cards, and a small amount of dollars (for border fees or small exchanges in shops). It is next to impossible to cash personal checks here. Without Cirrus, change some of your traveler's checks into pesos upon arrival in Mexico and then keep changing more as you need money. Usually the best rates are in banks, but with the scramble for dollars, some resort hotels and money exchanges (cambio de moneda) are outbidding them. Banks are usually open 9 a.m.-1:30 p.m., Monday-Friday; cambios have longer hours. We have seen some people operate with only dollars in the large resorts, but you inevitably will encounter difficulties elsewhere in Mexico. While you can convert all the pesos back into dollars, not all banks or cambios can do this for you.

EMERGENCY MONEY

If you are running short of money, American Express accepts personal checks from its cardholders toward the purchase of a limited amount of traveler's checks. Their offices can be found in many of Mexico's major cities (listed later under city directories). PIN access to cash, offered by many credit cards, is too limited in availability in Mexico to be useful. However, bank cash cards, such as Cirrus, can be useful, even though the fees usually are heftier than for traveler's checks. Check with your bank for a listing of affiliates within Mexico. If you are still in a cash bind, somewhat pricey arrangements can be made for cabling money, either through American Express moneygrams (☎ 800-543-4080 in U.S.), or to a bank through Western Union (☎ 800-325-4176). In an emergency, money can be sent to embassies and consulates (☎ 202-647-5225 for Citizens Emergency Center, U.S. State Department; fee).

Mexico has no restrictions as to the amount of dollars you take into the country, but the United States requires that you file a report to the U.S. Customs Service if you are carrying more than $5000 (in cash, traveler's checks, bank drafts, etc.) in or out of the U.S.

LANGUAGE

Spanish is the language of Mexico, yet it is a Spanish spoken without the lisp of Spain and enriched with place names derived from native Indian languages. (Although an estimated 13 percent of Mexicans still speak Indian dialects among themselves, the majority of these people are bilingual in Spanish.) Even if you don't know Spanish at all, you will be able to get along in Mexico surprisingly well. Mexicans are thrilled by anyone attempting to honor them by speaking their language, so they encourage you and make you feel fluent when you can barely pronounce the simplest phrase (except in deluxe establishments where they are trained to speak English with you).

If you speak no Spanish, you will get along in first-class resorts with no difficulty and will be surprised at the numbers of Mexicans elsewhere who can rescue you with a few words of English. But you should make a small effort in Spanish to facilitate your communication with waiters, taxi and bus drivers, vendors in Indian markets, etc. Knowing how to say "where?" (*donde*), "how much?" (*cuanto*), and "I would like" (*quisiera*) will get you through many situations, as will "please" (*por favor*). A small Spanish-English dictionary or phrase book to supplement the Spanish Glossary at the end of this guide will help. And carrying a small pad of paper and a pen for others to write down numbers will help you understand the price of a cab or a *piñata*.

FOOD

You need not be concerned about Mexico's reputation for fiery, hot food. Most of the food, although flavorful, is mild. Hot sauce is placed on the side to be used if desired. If you are reluctant to try Mexican food, don't fret. Even in the most rural area you still will be able to eat eggs, roast chicken, and a variety of soups including rich chicken broth called *caldo de pollo*. International restaurants can be found in most cities, and seafood is plentiful. Fruits and vegetables are succulent. But if you are willing to experiment, you will have some exceptional meals of Mexican food. (See chapter on Mexican Ways for an introduction to Mexican cuisine and "Eating Out" for each city for regional specialties.)

Although Mexicans appear to eat continuously, the main meal (*comida*) is taken in the afternoon, usually between 1 and 4 p.m., when restaurants often feature a fixed-price meal of several courses (*comida corrida or menu turistico*). While Mexicans often just have a light snack and cup of hot chocolate in the evening, a late dinner is warranted for special occasions (*cena*). You can get a full-course dinner (all dishes a la carte) at most restaurants. The popular hour for a cena is around 9 p.m., but restaurants open much earlier and many stay open throughout the day. Breakfast (*desayuno*) is served throughout the morning. In all but the most elegant restaurants, food is served very quickly, but the check almost never appears until you ask for it. (Mexicans like to linger over their meals.) To request a check without speaking a word of Spanish, do as Mexicans do—raise your hand and make a motion as if you are writing out the bill or signing your name. If you prefer to practice your Spanish, say, "*La cuenta, por favor.*"

Restaurant prices are extremely reasonable, except at some tourist restaurants in the major resorts. Dishes that may not be affordable at home, like Chateaubriand, may well be within your means in Mexico; elegance that you never would think of enjoying elsewhere will be affordable for at least one splurge.

HOTELS

Whatever your travel style, you will be pleased with Mexico's offerings and prices. To decide on a hotel, look through "Accommodations" in the areas you plan to visit and select a hotel that best suits your tastes and budget. (Also see "How to Use This Guide" in the Introduction.) Travel agents usually can make reservations for you for most first-class hotels and even for many moderately priced hotels. Some of these hotels, especially those operated by chains, have toll-free 800 numbers that you can call from most states in the U.S. for reservations. We have listed these numbers under the hotel descriptions although we have found that sometimes prices are lower when arranged directly within Mexico. If your travel agent can't book the less expensive hotels for you, follow the recommendations in "Traveling on a Budget," below. The Mexican government's star-rating system is currently based on reports by the hotels themselves and does not coincide with the system used in this book. Prices are set by the government.

CAMPING

Mexico has many national parks but few facilities for tent campers. Facilities for recreational vehicles are far more plentiful, making it feasible to travel through Mexico in your trailer or van. Some RV campgrounds are listed under accommodations, but you will require a more comprehensive listing to travel through Mexico. You might want to contact Sanborn Tours (☎ 800-531-5440) for their listings, or consider a tour with Point South R.V. Tours (☎ 800-421-1394). VILLAS Two agencies advertise villas and condominiums for rent in major resort areas like Acapulco, Cancún, and Puerto Vallarta. While we are unfamiliar with these firms, they may provide just the vacation opportunity you have been looking for. For more information, call:

Travel   Resources,   ☎ 800-327-5039   or   Creative   Leisure,
☎ 800-4-CONDOS.

HOSTELS

The Mexican National Youth Council (CREA) operates hostels in
a number of tourist areas, but they are primarily utilized by the very
young and are quite restrictive. CREA also sponsors some very economical package tours. For more information on locations and costs,
write: Agencia Nacional de Turismo Juvenil, Glorieta Metro Insurgentes, Local CC-11, 06600 Mexico D.F., Mexico, or call
☎ 525-25-48 in Mexico City.

SPORTS FACILITIES

Caribbean and Pacific resorts certainly offer the most in the way of
watersports—windsurfing, snorkeling, scuba diving, waterskiing,
parachute rides over the sea, and deep-sea fishing, but other areas
offer their share of sports as well. Highland spas often feature golf,
horseback riding, and tennis. Urban areas like Guadalajara and Mérida have golf and tennis facilities. Check the Keys and Directories to
cities to learn which sports are available. Many hotels throughout
Mexico have swimming pools, and some have tennis courts. (Check
hotel descriptions.) Of all these sports, only fishing is regulated.
Spear fishing is often restricted, and catching lobster, shrimp, aba-
lone, oysters, sea turtles, and a few other species is prohibited. When
you arrange for your fishing license at a resort or seaport, ask for an
up-to-date list of prohibited species.

TOURS

Perhaps because Mexico is such an easy country to travel in, few
guided tours operate from outside the country. Often, travelers who
don't want to bother making their own arrangements fly into Mexico and there hook up with tours. And even more frequently, tourists
simply travel on their own. This book provides enough information
for you to travel independently, but local tour facilities are listed in
the directory of each city. Tours vary from hiring your own chauffeur-driven car to small groups in a van to large bus groups, all of
which are more expensive than traveling on your own (unless you're
renting a car). However, discounted package tours are available from
Mexicana and Aeromexico airlines. Because these packages (called
VHI, VTP, or VTI) are designed to enable Mexicans to enjoy their
country, they can be booked only through travel agencies within
Mexico.

The standard tour from outside Mexico used to include Mexico
City, Taxco, and Acapulco. Now the popularity of Yucatán has creat-

ed tour opportunities that combine Maya ruins with a stay at a resort like Cancún. Other tours are available; most include a package arrangement of at least land transportation, hotels, and some meals. To know what's available, contact your travel agent or a tour operator such as Sanborn Tours, ☎ 800-531-5440.

Special-interest tours are also available. Borderland Tours (☎ 800-525-7753; 2555 W. Calle Padilla, Tucson, AZ 85745) sponsors nature tours as does Questers (☎ 800-468-8668; 257 Park Ave. S., Dept ITN, NY, NY 10010), and some museums and travel agents sponsor tours of ruins with archaeologists as your guides. Among the most demanding tours is a trek to El Triunfo rain forest in Chiapas (Field Guides, Inc., Box 16072 A, Austin, TX 78716; ☎ 512-327-4953). Just as adventurous—with rides through rapids on the Usuamacinta River to Maya ruins—is the tour offered by the Foundation for Latin American Anthropological Research (write Nicholas Hellmuth, Brevard Community College, 1519 Clearlake Rd., Cocoa, FL 32922). Other scholarly tours can be found through advertisements in magazines such as Archaeology and Smithsonian. Michael Edwards (at Edwards Travel Service, 8 S. Tulane St., Princeton, NJ 08542; ☎ 800-669-9692, or, locally, ☎ 609-924-4443) specializes in Mexican travel and designs individualized itineraries that focus not just on the major sights but also on your interests, be they flower festivals or traditional Indian ceremonies.

Travel agencies often purchase blocks of hotel rooms and airplane seats to create a package deal that you as an individual traveler can buy into. Package trips are plentiful to first-class resorts and Mexico City but difficult to arrange for other destinations. Since these packages often offer a week in a hotel at not much more than the cost of the flight alone, they are well worth investigating if you don't plan to travel within Mexico. Prices vary with the cost of the hotel and the season, the summer off-season at resorts being cheaper than the winter season. Comparison shop among these packages by checking the travel section in the Sunday paper of the nearest city with a busy international airport, or consult a travel agent.

TRAVELING ON A BUDGET

In many ways, traveling through Mexico on a tight budget can be more rewarding than luxurious trips. You can eat, sleep, and travel as many Mexicans do, and in the process come in contact with more Mexicans and fewer tourists—or more accurately, fewer non Mexican tourists. The vast majority of tourists in Mexico are Mexicans, many traveling on a tight budget also. As a result, tourist facilities abound for the budget traveler. The trick is to know *how* to travel economically and *where* to find the best buys.

Throughout the book we have listed the best of the budget and inexpensive hotels and restaurants we have encountered on our travels. As Mexicans well know, even at the fanciest and most expensive resorts, the budget-minded traveler can find economical accommodations and meals, especially during the summer when Mexican travel agencies offer discounted packages. And, of course, accommodations are less expensive if you have a traveling companion or two to share the cost of a room. The cheaper hotels normally cannot be reserved through a travel agent, and you will have to book them yourself. The safest procedure is to write well in advance of your visit (a letter to Mexico can take anywhere from 5 days to 3 weeks), in Spanish if possible, and send a money order to serve as a deposit. The equivalent of a one-night stay is generally adequate to reserve a room. The letter should be sent by registered mail with a return receipt requested. If you know your precise itinerary, you can follow this procedure for all of your hotels. On the other hand, if you plan to travel more casually, you can try your luck without reservations. In the off-season, at least, we have never had problems finding acceptable hotels without reservations, and we have found the rates are often lower than the official ones quoted with reservations. During fiestas and the high seasons, however, it is advisable to reserve well in advance, so check the information under "Accommodations" for each city to know when to reserve.

A procedure we have followed with success is to reserve a hotel by mail for our first destination. After our arrival and once we know when we are moving on to the next city, we telephone ahead to the next hotel for reservations. If you do not speak Spanish, you can ask the hotel clerk to call for you.

EATING ECONOMICALLY

To eat economically, have your main meal in the afternoon when you can find a *comida corrida*, a fixed-priced full-course meal offered at inexpensive (as well as expensive) restaurants throughout the country. This usually is so filling that you won't want more than a snack later in the evening. For breakfast you can save money by buying fruit at a market, cheese and other items from grocery stores (some are listed in Directories to cities), and fresh orange juice at a street stand (often at half the price of juice in restaurants). Bread or pastry bought at a bakery (*panaderia or pasteleria*) will be cheaper than at a hotel. If you don't want to make your own breakfast in this fashion, check the restaurant recommendations under "Eating Out" in the city you are visiting for a low-priced restaurant. Big coffee drinkers should note that the more inexpensive restaurants generally charge per cup (and frequently serve instant coffee), but the more expensive restaurants, especially those in hotels, often provide unlimited coffee for the price of a cup.

If possible, stick to Mexican food. You will find eating tacos a lot cheaper (and tastier, we think) than hamburgers. *Molletes*, grilled open-face Mexican rolls topped with melted cheese and refried beans (or various meats, if you wish), are particularly economical, nutritious, and filling. They are fine for breakfast, lunch, or snacks. Alcoholic beverages add a lot to the cost of any meal, but beer is cheaper than wine. If you drink beer or wine, stick with the domestic variety. Due to taxes, imported wines and beers carry higher prices. Imported liquor—scotch, bourbon, or rye—will cost you, too. Mexico makes rum, vodka, gin, and, of course, tequila and mezcal, which are cheaper. The least expensive of meals are served in the market, but they will seldom meet your standards of cleanliness and can be risky. The safest item to eat is soup, well-simmered and usually quite flavorful.

FREE ENTERTAINMENT

Free entertainment is provided by many cities in their parks and squares. Throughout the book we have listed the parks and squares with free concerts, and you may find them as enjoyable as places with more formal entertainment. Even without concerts, the parks and squares are intriguing just for people watching. For the price of a beer or soft drink, you can sit for hours in a sidewalk cafe and watch the life of a town displayed before you. Or nurse a drink in one of the many bars with live entertainment. In large cities like Mexico City and Guadalajara, some restaurants and bars have a musical group in residence. They perform when hired by a patron of the restaurant. If you are lucky, another table will pay for your entertainment. Admission fees to concerts are well below prices at home.

PUBLIC TRANSPORTATION

When traveling within a city, take public transportation. Buses, subways, and collective vans are inexpensive. Between cities, buses provide the most efficient and economical transportation. If you are adventurous, you can save even more money by taking second-class rather than first-class buses when you have the time. Here you will surely travel with the people, and you will have a memorable, if uncomfortable, experience.

Try to sightsee on your own rather than on organized tours. For example, you can easily visit on your own the pyramids of Teotihuacan outside of Mexico City or the Maya ruins of Chichen Itza outside of Mérida. And the information provided in this book about these sites and others is usually of greater depth and accuracy than what you will get from a tour guide. Sound-and-light shows in Spanish often are half the cost of those in English. Given the pricey fees at some monuments and museums, you may want to take advantage of Sunday's free admission.

Hotels, restaurants, entertainment, and public transportation cost considerably less in Mexico than in the United States or Canada. By exercising care, following our tips, selecting our recommended inexpensive or budget hotels and restaurants, and utilizing our sightseeing information, you can experience the wonders of Mexico well below the cost of travel elsewhere in North America.

WOMEN TRAVELING ALONE

It is safe for you to travel alone, but common sense will lead you to avoid *cantinas* (unescorted women were prohibited until recently) and other very local spots where your presence will be misinterpreted. You may find some nightclubs barring your admission as well. Apart from these few pitfalls, your solitude will attract the concern of many Mexicans who may offer to share their lunch with you on a bus or make a special effort to see that you are comfortable. Although Mexican men may approach you with flattering words and invitations, fortunately, pinching is not part of their repertoire. To be left alone, avoid making eye contact, talking, or smiling—any one of which will be considered an encouragement.

TRAVELING WITH DISABILITIES

Many of the old hacienda-style hotels in Mexico are without elevators or ramps. The pitted sidewalks can be difficult for those without 20/20 vision if they don't take care. The traffic lights don't have auditory signals, nor do most elevators. If you have a disability, you might want to consult a travel expert or join a tour that has been planned with your comfort in mind. The Information Center for Individuals with Disabilities in Massachusetts (ICID, Fort Point Place, First Floor, 27-43 Wormwood St., Boston MA 02210; ☎ 617-727-5540; 11a.m.-4p.m.) publishes useful materials, including a list of travel agencies. Fee for out-of-state residents.

EMERGENCIES

Embassies and consular agents should be contacted for such emergencies as lost passports or tourist cards, medical difficulties or accidents, or if you find that your car is unable to make the requisite return trip out of Mexico. The U.S., Canadian, and British Embassies (all with 24-hour emergency contact service) are listed under the Mexico City directory. In addition, the following consular services are listed under the appropriate directories: U.S. consuls in Acapulco, Cancún, Guadalajara, Mazatlan, Mérida, Oaxaca, Puerto Vallarta, San Luis Potosi, San Miguel Allende, and Veracruz; Canadian consuls in Acapulco, Cancún, Guadalajara, Mazatlan, Oaxaca, and Puerto Vallarta; and British consuls in Acapulco, Guadalajara, Mérida, Oaxaca, and Veracruz. These countries also have consuls in border cities; all of them in Tijuana, Britain and the U.S. in Ciudad Juarez, and the U.S. only in Hermosillo, Nuevo Laredo, and Matamoros. If you can't reach the local authorities, try your embassy's line or the bilingual, Mexican government service (☎ area code 5, 240-0123), both in Mexico City.

TIPPING

In general, you should tip the same at restaurants as you do at home—15% before tax is the normal tip, depending on the quality of service. Tips for bellhops and maids should vary with the quality of the establishment, as expectations will differ between an inexpensive hotel and a deluxe one. On the average, give about $1 U.S. for each bag to a bellhop and $1 U.S. for each day to a maid. An adult car watcher receives 50¢ U.S., and children who just happen along usually will be happy with 10¢ U.S. or so. Tour guides should be tipped between $1 and $2 U.S. It is not necessary to tip shoeshiners, although it is an acceptable practice. Taxi drivers don't receive tips unless they perform a special service for you, or if they have not used their meter and you want to express your gratitude. Ushers and washroom attendants receive small gratuities in Mexico, but again the amount depends on the kind of establishment you are in.

BARGAINING

Mexico is a shoppers' delight with items ranging from elegant designer clothes, leather, and jewelry, through fine Indian weavings and ceramics, to inexpensive paper flowers, pinatas, and the like. You can find all these items in shops where the prices are fixed, and nearly every town has at least a small market where you can find some local craft; in some towns, such as Oaxaca, market shopping might be one of the main reasons you are there. Bargaining at markets is a necessity. If you are hesitant about bargaining, look at prices in a few shops first to gain confidence about a reasonable price in the market. A good rule of thumb is to offer vendors two-thirds of their asking prices. Then the two of you, quite somberly, will lower and raise your prices until you reach an agreed-upon price in the middle. This negotitation doesn't always work, of course. The vendor may be reluctant to reduce his price to this ideal compromise and will indicate as much by giving you only a small reduction in his second asking price. If you don't want to pay more than the compromise price, raise yours by the same small increment and feel your way through the bargaining. Once you have offered a price, you should be willing to buy if that price is accepted. You may walk away from a bargaining session only to find the vendor racing after you to offer the item at a price previously rejected. If that happens, you've won, and you should most certainly buy. Carry small bills with you to the markets so you can pay as close to the exact amount as possible. After protesting a price during bargaining, it is embarrassing to pull out a huge peso bill. (There may not be enough change for it, either.) Most importantly, if an article enchants you, buy it. You may never see another like it.

MORDIDAS

Mordidas (literally meaning "bites"), or bribes, are practically customary in certain situations. If you fly into Mexico and never drive a car in the country, you probably never will encounter the bribe problem with officialdom. Otherwise, if you don't speak a word of Spanish, you may wonder why a border official or policeman is taking so long looking over your papers. Usually, the delay will stop with a request for a small fee (often about $2 U.S.). At the border, this is most likely to occur if you aren't dressed neatly and conservatively. When driving, you are most likely to be stopped in Mexico City. Our advice is to grin and bear it.

BEGGARS

Because Mexico has no unemployment insurance program and no welfare payment system, the country's current economic ills have forced many more women and children into quiet begging outside churches, at sidewalk cafes, and on street corners. The economy has led also to an increase in street activities, with more children than ever selling Chiclets and trinkets or offering to watch your car, with more makeshift musical groups strolling through buses between stops or suddenly serenading you under your window, and with more women selling fruit or tamales wherever they may find a customer.

CRIME

No country is crime-free, yet Mexican crime rates are low. Theft is the most common problem encountered by tourists. In crowded places like buses and markets, guard against pickpockets by keeping your money in a front, not rear, pocket and by holding your shoulder bag securely—or better yet, wear a money belt or necklace pouch. Lock up your car, and when you can, put it into a lot or garage. Never leave belongings on the seat of a car, bus, or train. At beaches, don't leave valuables unattended. Many hotels provide safety deposit boxes for your valuables; a fee will be charged to your bill only if you fail to return the key.

Maybe we have had exceptionally good luck in our many years in Mexico. We have experienced no theft and many instances of people going out of their way to return forgotten items to us. There are, of course, incidents of violent crime, so use your common sense about where you walk at night. And with the Mexican economy as depressed as it is, you should take some ordinary precautions like the ones above, and those under "Driving Tips" below.

In case of an emergency, contact the nearest consulate (see "Emergencies").

LEGAL SYSTEM

The Mexican legal system is based on the Napoleonic Code which, unlike our legal system, presumes your guilt until evidence to the contrary is presented. Long stays in jail awaiting trial are not unusual. The only way you inadvertently might become involved in this system is if you have a car accident. You could face confinement in jail, especially if you do not have Mexican automobile insurance to prove your ability to pay damages. (See "Emergencies," above.) In fact, many Mexicans believe it's wiser to leave the scene of a minor accident rather than deal with the police. Parking violations may be handled on the spot if you are lucky enough to be present. If not, you will have to go to the police station to get your license plates back because they are removed when a car is parked illegally. Therefore, park your car legally. The Mexican government is a tough enforcer of its drug laws, and no special consideration is given to foreigners. Be warned.

COMPLAINTS

The Departamento de Quejas in Mexico City is the right place to lodge any complaints you have about restaurant services, hotels, guides, car rentals, and travel agencies that operate in Mexico. Drop by or write the first-floor office of Orientacion, Informacion y Quejas at the Departamento at Secretaria de Turismo, Av. Presidente Mazaryk 172, Mexico 11550, DF, Mexico. Or call the 24-hour, English-speaking operators at ☎ (5) 50-0123.

NEWSPAPERS

Mexico publishes a daily newspaper in English called *The News.* You can buy it at newsstands in all major cities and resorts. The large hotels sell U.S. newspapers (sometimes a few days old).

MAIL

The postal system is erratic, particularly in regard to postcards. To improve the chances that your cards and letters will reach their destination, send them in airmail envelopes and post them in cities with airports. MEXPOST is Mexico's equivalent to Express Mail and is coordinated with the U. S. Postal Service for expedited, if not rapid, international mail delivery. Although MEXPOST is affordable compared to the unbelievably high rates charged by the private express mail companies (FedEx, DHL, etc.) that operate in some Mexican cities, we also have found it to be slower. You can buy stamps and post your mail either through your hotel desk or the post office. Post office addresses are listed in the Directories included in each city section of this book.

To receive mail, you can use hotel addresses where you have a reservation (the envelope should always be marked with "Favor de retener hasta llegada") or a general delivery system to the main post office of the cities you plan to visit. After your name, the letter should be addressed: a/c Lista de Correos, city, state, Mexico. Take identification with you in order to pick up your mail. If you use American Express traveler's checks or credit cards, their offices in Mexico City, Guadalajara, Acapulco, Taxco, Oaxaca, and other towns (see Directory under destination chapters) will hold mail for you.

You can mail packages to the United States (see "U.S. Customs," below), but the cost can be exorbitant. It is best to have a store make arrangements for you; otherwise, you will find yourself spending vacation time seeking the right post office and going through the tedium of customs. Be concerned about breakage and loss before deciding to mail an item.

TELEGRAMS AND FAX

Domestic telegrams are usually reliable. International telegrams usually arrive but are more expensive. (A night letter or *mensaje nocturno* is the least expensive.) Telegrams can be sent in English as well as Spanish from the offices listed in the Directories of the city sections or from many hotels. *Faxes are more reliable and even easier to send* as public services are available in cities at many pharmacies and stationers. Prices are comparable to those in the U.S.A.

TELEPHONE

The most convenient place to make your calls is from your hotel, and some allow phone calls without any extra charge. However, every city has a *Larga Distancia* office where operators place calls for you and some of these offices also charge fees. You can try to place a call yourself from a pay phone: A few high-tech ones, called Ladatel, are found near the zócalos of provincial cities, at airports and bus stations, and permit up to ten 1000-old peso coins—enough for a brief direct-dial call to the U.S. or Canada, and any change will be returned. On some, you must push a button for the dial tone after inserting coins. Other Ladatel phones accept only credit cards or reusable magnetic change cards, or "tarjetas Ladatel," purchased in amounts from 5 to 50 new pesos. However, most pay phones can't be used for long-distance calls, and those that can be so used often allow only collect calls. To make a collect call, dial 09 for the international operators, all of whom speak English. You may experience delays in reaching the operator from pay phones, but collect calls are worth the effort as they avoid the 50% tax on international calls if not the telephone company's surcharge (levied whether there's an answer or not). Some small town switchboards don't permit collect calls. To make a direct rather than a collect call to Canada or the U.S., dial 95 before the area code and number. The call will go through without an operator. For long-distance calls within Mexico, dial 91 plus the *clave* (see the Hotel Appendix for these area codes) and the number, or call the operator for assistance (02). International calls are extremely expensive, but you can save yourself some of the expense if you have an AT&T calling card. (Other phone companies do not yet have this dial direct service from Mexico.) By dialing **01 on a push button phone or ☎ 95-800-462-4240 on a rotary, you can connect with a U. S. operator and charge your call at U. S. rates.

To make a local call from a pay phone, be aware that many such phones connect you with your party and then require that you push a button in order to communicate. (This push deposits the coin into the phone box.) Depending on their vintage, pay phones vary in the coins they accept; usually the old 100-peso coin will work.

TIME ZONES

Mexico never operates on daylight savings time, and most of the country is on central time, except for the states of Nayarit, Sinaloa, and Sonora, where Pacific standard time is in effect.

MEASUREMENTS

The metric system is used in Mexico, so prices are not for miles but kilometers (0.62 mile), not for pounds but kilos (2.2 pounds), not for quarts but liters (1.03 quarts), and not for feet but meters (3.3 feet).

CREDIT CARDS

First-class hotels and restaurants, car rental agencies, airlines, and many shops honor major credit cards; gasoline stations do not. American Express cardholders may find a backup necessary, as VISA and MasterCard are more widely accepted.

EXPRESSIONS TO WATCH FOR

Water taps in Mexico may confuse you, but just check for the "C," which stands for *caliente* ("hot"), even when U.S. fixtures are used with their telltale "C"s and "H"s. ("Cold" in Spanish is *frío*.) *Zócalo* is interchangeable with main square or plaza. *Malecón* is an ocean or river front drive. *Mexico* almost always refers to the capital city, not the country. *Planta Baja*, or PB, is the first floor in Mexico, making their floor numbered "1" our second floor. *Gringo*, the Mexican word for us, is not used as an insult. In fact, if a Mexican feels comfortable enough to use gringo with you, take it as a compliment. *Caballeros* and *Damas* most often mark bathroom (*sanitario*) doors but be careful with *Senores* (men) and *Senoras* (women). Dates in museums can mislead: A.C. is B.C. and D.C. is A.D. Hand gestures similar to ours for "go away" mean "come here."

TAXES

Check to see whether the prices at hotels, restaurants, and shops already include a 10 percent tax (called I.V.A.).

If your airline ticket doesn't include the U. S. $12 departure tax, expect to pay it at the airport.

TRANSPORTATION IN MEXICO

Means of transportation in, around, and between cities are described under each city and its excursions, so once you get to your first destination in Mexico you will be able to choose among the numerous options of getting around.

DOMESTIC FLIGHTS

Mexicana and Aeromexico airlines are the major domestic carriers in Mexico. Most cities have airports and most receive some service from these major carriers. However, the major carriers offer only limited connections among the smaller cities, resulting in lots of backtracking to Mexico City in order to go anywhere else in the country. Fortunately regional airlines, often with smaller turbo jets, have been filling in the service gaps, particularly Aeromar, with service in the critical central region, and Aerocaribe, with connections in the Yucatán Peninsula and the Southeast. Reservations for both these airlines can be made in the United States via Mexicana. Another regional airline is Aero California; it flies its DC-9s among many northern cities and includes some international flights from near the border. And there are other, much smaller airlines. We include the latest information at press time in the "Directories" and "Getting To and From" sections of cities, but you would be wise to check for the most up-to-date information with a travel agent as the regional situation is in flux.

Note: Since overbooking can be a problem on any of the carriers, you must arrive at the airport one hour before departure to ensure that you get on your flight. Some airports charge a departure tax for domestic flights. Collect and recheck your baggage with each change of plane to lessen chances of loss.

CAR RENTALS

International and local rental agencies operate in most cities, both at the airports and in town. To indicate their availability, we have listed a few agencies in the city Directories. The cost of a car rental varies from city to city, but it always costs more than in the U.S., often prohibitively more. (For a day trip it sometimes is actually cheaper to hire a taxi.) If you need a car rental, reserve a car in the U.S. *before* your departure to get the best rates; recently we've found Avis to have the lowest rates, but ask your travel agent to search for the best deal. And remember, you may find the luxury of a chauffeur-driven car, namely a taxi or tour, is cheaper for a short excursion than a rental car.

Car insurance varies from company to company in price and coverage, but the deductible for collision alone can add US $5 to $10 a day. If your credit card provides coverage (usually up to 15 days per rental contract), avoid these charges by waiving collision damage and charging the rental on that card. In case of theft you are required to pay a hefty amount, generally about 10 percent of the value of the car. For this reason alone, whenever possible you should park in a guarded parking lot. To rent a car, you'll need a tourist card, your driver's license, and credit card (or cash deposit). If you drop a rental car off at another location, there is an exorbitant extra charge. Make sure you're covered by Mexican insurance (you can land in jail without it), and check "Driving Tips" below.

DELUXE BUSES

In 1991 many first-class bus companies added an entire new line of buses with quality suspension, airline-style seats, half-bathrooms, videos, and air conditioning. The service—called "Uno" by ADO, "Express," "Ejecutivo," and whatever by others—includes speed (nonstop Acapulco to Mexico City, direct to Mérida and Puebla from Villahermosa, etc.), special reservation modules in bus terminals, and sometimes even stewards and boxed meals. The price is usually about twice that of first-class yet certainly less than a car rental or flight. The service is still expanding, so check locally about routes and availability.

FIRST-CLASS (PRIMERA CLASE) BUSES

Efficient, comfortable, and inexpensive, Mexican buses connect all cities. If you can, reserve your seat at least a day in advance and ask for the most direct (*directo*) route. Bring a sweater in case the air conditioning is working only too well. On long-distance trips, you might want to bring your own snack in case you don't like the restaurant where the bus stops. Also, bus station bathrooms vary in cleanliness and supplies, so bring your own tissues.

SECOND-CLASS (SEGUNDA CLASE) BUSES

In a few instances, the second-class system can approach first class in comfort but never in efficiency. These buses make more stops and seldom have reserved seats. However, they do run more frequently than, and go to towns not served by, first class. In fact, you probably can get to almost any village in Mexico by taking a series of second-class (or even third-class) buses. You may share your travels with chickens and the like, and you may find the bus too small to stand in, but you'll probably never be bored. Just remember, you need time to travel second-class.

TRAINS

During the 1980s the Mexican National Railways (known as *Ferrocarriles Nacionales de Mexico*, or FNM, in Mexico) undertook the renovation of its first-class and pullman cars on certain trains. The result to date has delighted train buffs, providing them with the means to travel in comfort, if not in luxury, from the border to the Pacific

Coast or Mexico City (see below, "Getting to Mexico") and to link up with many of the major tourist areas. (Check the "Getting To and From" section under your destination.) Some find the overnight service, say from Mexico City to Veracruz or Mexico City to Guadalajara, a comfortable and inexpensive substitute for a hotel. Others find the day service convenient, say from Mexico City to San Miguel de Allende, because it avoids the hassle of getting to the bus terminals on the edge of the capital.

The improved, air-conditioned service is available only on some specially named trains and only in their star service class (*servicio estrella*) also called *primera especial.* It includes reclining seats with snacks or a boxed, inedible meal included in the price and/or pullman roomettes (*dormitorios*) for overnight trains (extra fee) on which there are also dining cars. The price is inexpensive. However, trains remain the slowest form of transportation and those without *servicio estrella* service are even slower (and often without any comforts, especially in second-class). You might want to travel only on those trains with Star Service, or at the very least, *primera especial* (special first class). Apart from buying your ticket at the train station (and perhaps finding no available seats, especially at Christmas, the week before Easter, and July/August holidays), you can reserve from within the U.S.A. in advance (15 to 30 days recommended, depending on season) through Mexico By Rail (☎800-228-3225) or through your travel agent. Within Mexico, local travel agents often will make arrangements. However, these reservations can double the cost.

TAXIS

Taxis are very affordable for most travelers, although certainly not as cheap as local buses. Few taxis operate with meters, yet they do have set rates—which may not be easy to determine except at airports. Our best advice, which we shall remind you of occasionally, is to establish the fare before getting into a cab. Doing this not only avoids brutal surprises but also can actually reduce the fare. (We've experimented.) Whether one driver charges you more than another is no cause for gringo alarm. Nothing personal is meant, nor is any discrimination going on—Mexicans suffer from the same whims of drivers. Sometimes you can bargain, but you can find yourselves spending considerable time waiting for a taxi to come with the rate you consider fair.

COLLECTIVE VANS

Colectivos or *combis* operate from most airports into the cities. They have set fares and provide transportation right to your hotel. Some cities have *combis* and shared cabs operating along set routes. They are cheaper than taxis and more expensive than buses. When such service is available, we note so in the following chapters.

GETTING TO MEXICO

For most travelers on vacation, flying into Mexico is sensible. Land transportation requires that you travel at least 900 miles from the U.S. border before reaching Mexico City, and too few of those miles will take you into areas worthy of sightseeing. Once you add the cost of your meals and hotels to your transportation, you probably will spend more money than you would if you simply took a plane. But in case you prefer to reach central Mexico by land, various routes are given subsequently.

AIR

Flights can be arranged on major international carriers like Continental, American, Air Canada, and others including Mexicana and Aeromexico. They fly out of major U.S. and Canadian cities into Mexico City, Mérida, Guadalajara, and first-class resorts on the Caribbean and Pacific coasts. Excursion and special promotional rates seem to change each month. To keep abreast of the best deals, check the ads in your newspaper's Sunday travel section or consult a travel agent. Basically, package deals restrict you to one city, so if you plan to travel around you won't find them convenient. Excursion rates offer more flexibility yet usually require that you book your flight a certain amount of time in advance of your trip, and they restrict you to 7 to 21 days of travel. Sometimes the Mexican airlines offer special discounts on their domestic flights if you book your international flight with them.

Practical Tips

• *Nearly all the international airlines require that you reconfirm your return flight within 72 hours of departure. If you forget, and the plane is overbooked, you may find yourself without a reservation.*

• *Mexico charges a departure tax on international flights.*

• *If you live near the border, you can save money by crossing the border to Tijuana, Mexicali, Cuidad Juarez, Nuevo Laredo, or Matamoros and taking a Mexican domestic flight to your destination.*

TRAIN

Most trains from the border have been renovated. Although *the comfort level may not be quite what you'd like*—in fact, the long journey from Nogales to Mazatlan and then to Guadalajara (25 hours) does not include sleeping cars—*Servicio Estrella* ("Star Service"), also known as *primera especial,* on these trains now includes reclining seats, food service, air conditioning, and, sometimes, even Pullman roomettes (*a camarin* is a squeeze for two, the *alcoba* ample; both have private half-baths) for overnight trips. From Juarez, the *Division del Norte* train offers this renovated service en route to Mexico City (36 hours), passing through Zacatecas and Queretaro. Also from Juarez, the *Rapido de la Frontera* takes you to Chihuahua, where you can overnight for the next morning's departure of the *Chihuahua Pacifico,* a terrific train ride that winds through the Copper Canyon to Los Mochis, near the Pacific. (For details, see chapter on *Land Routes into Mexico.)* Another important train into Mexico is *El Regiomontano,* leaving from Nuevo Laredo each afternoon and arriving in Mexico City approximately 18 hours later (1184 km, 735 m). Other border trains feed into the Regiomontano: *El Tamaulipeco* from Matamoros (5 hours) and Reynosa (3 hours) to Monterrey (then 14 hours to Mexico City); *El Coahuilense* from Piedras Negras to Saltillo (7 hours), then on to Mexico City (12 hours). Of course there can be delays due to connections and other complications. Although it can double the price, it's easiest to make advance reservations in the U.S. through Mexico By Rail (☎ 800-228-3225). Otherwise, reserve directly through Ferrocarriles Nacionales de Mexico (International Passengers, Buena Vista Station, 06358 Mexico, D.F.; ☎ [5] 547-8972).

BUS

Once you cross the border, you will need to change to a Mexican bus (unless you're on a tour). In some instances, however, Greyhound can book you straight through so you won't need to purchase new tickets. (They have offices in Mexico City where you can reserve a return trip; otherwise, check with Mexican travel agencies.)

The car routes in *Land Routes into Mexico* can be used as guidelines for planning your bus trip into traditional Mexico. To break up the especially long bus trips, get a ticket to an interim point so you can stretch your legs a while before picking up another bus to your final destination. Although you can arrange bus transportation from Tijuana or Mexicali, it is faster to travel in the U.S. to Nogales before crossing the border. From Matamoros, you can arrange a bus to Mexico City, but will have more difficulty getting to Veracruz.

Practical Tip

For long trips within Mexico, check out the availability of the new deluxe bus service.

CAR

Of the main routes into Mexico, all except one requires at least one overnight stay before you reach a major tourist destination. These routes are described in *Land Routes into Mexico*. Before leaving for Mexico, check the sections on "Border Regulations and Customs" and "Driving Tips" below. If you need to spend the night near the border, try crossing into Mexico (particularly at El Paso, Laredo, and Brownsville), where you can get better rates at hotels and then an early start in the morning with customs behind you.

CRUISES

Many luxury liners stop at Pacific and Caribbean resorts on their cruises. Check with a travel agent for information.

DRIVING TIPS

We have driven extensively in Mexico without incident, but we have driven as if a herd of cattle might await us around every turn. Only a few herds have blocked our way. More often it's a dog, or a bull looming very large; and once, in a remote region, we encountered a family picnicking on the road. Driving here is not exactly as uncomplicated as going to your local supermarket, but it's more interesting and just as safe if you make a few adjustments. The most important adjustment is to schedule your trip to allow much more time to cover set distances than you would at home.

1. As this book goes to press, there are no U.S. State Department travel advisories for Mexico, but there are for Guatemala. So you probably won't want to plan a drive into Guatemala from Mexico without checking first with the State Department (☎ 202-647-5225 for 24-hour, touch-tone-operated tape). In Mexico, some robberies have occurred in past years, so special caution is recommended if you're driving in isolated areas. You might avoid driving alone and you should not travel at night or sleep in your car at the side of the road.

2. Road maps can be bought in Mexico, but you might prefer traveling with one with explanations in English. Many automobile clubs as well as Sanborn's (☎ 512-686-3601) have maps of Mexico, and some provide members with trip-tiks that indicate the locations of gasoline stations.

3. Familiarize yourself with the road signs listed at the end of this guide; they can be essential to understanding the condition of a road.

4. Toll ("cuota") roads in Mexico are usually quite decent, and in most instances worth the high cost (higher than in U.S.) when you want to make good time. A few of the new superhighways, however, can be as expensive as flying. (See the Acapulco chapter.) Most roads are two lanes and lesser ones don't have shoulders. The Sierra Madre mountains often require a good deal of ascending and descending in addition to just going forward. When you travel in highland areas, expect a trip to take longer than you would estimate by just looking at a map.

5. If you are driving your own car in Mexico, make sure it is in excellent condition so you don't have to concern yourself with repairs. Just in case, bring along a few spare parts (for example, a fan belt, a good spare tire, and some extra hoses). Check with your car dealer for listings in Mexico to make sure you will be able to get parts when you need them. (We know no Toyota parts are available, not even oil filters.) In highland areas, you may need extra water for your radiator, and you may need to make an adjustment to your carburetor to allow greater intake of oxygen. A flashlight can always come in handy.

6. If you are not on a toll highway, it can be difficult to pass in mountainous regions, yet you might find yourself behind trucks grinding their gears up a mountain. No matter what you see others doing in this situation, settle back until you have a safe opportunity to pass. Sometimes the truck driver will wave you on or put on a turn signal to indicate it's safe for you to pass. Whether you want to rely on this advice is up to you—just make sure the driver isn't indicating a left turn!

7. Accidents or breakdowns are indicated by branches or rocks being placed on the road. Sometimes vehicles coming toward you will flash their lights to indicate a problem ahead. This procedure is followed most in the mountains where a forewarning can be important to your slowing down in time. Salute to express "gracias" for the warning (or return a flash of your headlights).

8. *Topes*, or metal and cement humps in the road to force you to slow down, are placed before and after most villages. Sometimes there can be a whole series of them. Usually, but not always, you are given advance warning by signs with a drawing of a few humps, or signs announcing *Topes, Tumulos, Vibradores, or Bordos*.

9. You may be fortunate enough to drive over roads in good condition, but more often than not part of a road will be under repair and you will drive over potholes, pavement that feels like corrugated iron, or just dirt. Summer rains worsen conditions, causing rock slides on the mountainous roads connecting the highlands and coasts—then it's best to opt for the wider toll roads when available. Or at least ask locally about conditions.

10. *Never drive outside of cities at night* because of the animals, people, potholes, and topes, as well as precipitous mountain curves you won't be able to see.

11. The Ministry of Tourism sponsors an emergency highway service called the "Green Angels." Radio-equipped, green-and-orange trucks cruise the major tourist roads from 8 a.m.-9 p.m. (except Tuesday morning), providing free advice and service. The drivers are not only bilingual, but they are also trained mechanics. There is a charge for parts.

12. The Mexican government controls the petroleum industry in Mexico, including the sale of gasoline. All stations are government controlled, too, and called Pemex. If you fill up in town before going on a road trip, you will find the stations adequately spaced along the roads. Try to keep your tank at least half full, especially if you use unleaded gas, which sometimes is hard to obtain in remote areas. Unleaded 87-octane gas is called Magna Sin (in green pumps); leaded 81-octane gas is called Nova Plus (in blue pumps); and diesel fuel is sold at some stations. The octane may not be what your car is used to, and it's a bit costly besides. (The price of gas increases often in Mexico, so we can't predict how much you will pay, but at the time this book is going to press it costs about U.S.$1.50 for a gallon of Nova, U.S.$1.70 for Magna.) Gas is sold in liters not gallons (there are 3.8 liters to one U.S. gallon). Pemex stations don't have repair shops; for that you will need to ask in town for a *mecanico*.

13. Speed limits on some toll roads may be as high as 110 km per hour (68 mph), but more often they are about 60 mph. Many of the two-lane roads have limits of no more than 40 km per hour (25 mph).

ENTRY REQUIREMENTS AND CUSTOMS
MEXICAN DOCUMENTS

U.S. and Canadian citizens need only a tourist card (see below) and proof of citizenship to enter Mexico for a vacation period of no more than 180 days. The safest documents for both entry into Mexico and re entry into your own country are: a valid passport (the best form of identification in any foreign country, particularly for cashing traveler's checks), or an official birth certificate with a raised seal plus a photo ID. Naturalized Canadian citizens must use a passport, but U.S. naturalized citizens may substitute their certified naturalization papers. Children traveling with anyone other than both their parents should have notarized permission from the parents not accompanying them. Death, divorce, and guardianship certificates can replace the permission when applicable. Parents with different surnames should carry the child's birth certificate to avoid any bureaucratic confusion.

Tourist cards are free, and they can be obtained in advance of your trip. Mexican consulates can provide them, as can most travel agencies and airlines operating to Mexico. (For a listing of consulates, write Mexican Government Tourist Office at 405 Park Ave., Suite 1002, New York, NY 10022 or 10100 Santa Monica Blvd., Suite 224, Los Angeles, CA 90067.) Your tourist card admits you for 90 days, and it can be renewed for another 90 days at an office of the

Mexican Department of Interior upon proof of economic solvency during the rest of your stay. *Mexican law requires that you carry your tourist card with you at all times.*

If you are driving into Mexico, you will need to acquire a **car permit** when reaching the border, which will also serve as your tourist card. You need the same proof of your citizenship plus proof of car ownership (registration will do best). Recreational vehicles must follow the same procedures, but if you are traveling with two vehicles—a car plus a trailer—the permit will be issued only to two travelers, not to just one person. (You will need a notarized letter from the owner to the traveling companion authorizing use.) These permits are good for 90 days, and, like the tourist cards, they can be renewed. It is illegal to sell your vehicle or to leave it in Mexico, and you will be unable to leave Mexico without it. In case your vehicle breaks down or cannot be removed, notify your embassy. (See "Emergencies," above.) A valid U.S. or Canadian driver's license. *Mexican automobile insurance*, as well as at least two months of U.S. insurance (including theft, third party liability, and comprehensive) are essential. Agencies like AAA and Sanborn's are available at U.S. border towns to advise you on insurance and to sell you a temporary policy for your trip.

Note: There are random document checkpoints about 15 miles in from the border. You need stop only if the light is red.

MEXICAN CUSTOMS

A good rule of thumb is to bring only what you can use during the trip. Extra hair dryers, radios, or quantities of the same item will appear to be for the purpose of resale in Mexico (which is illegal). Each person is permitted one still and one portable 8-mm movie camera and up to 12 rolls of film. Adults may bring one carton of cigarettes, 50 cigars, and one liter of alcoholic beverage.

Firearms are prohibited except under strict regulations for hunters. (Contact a Mexican consulate months in advance to learn about licensing and permit restrictions.) Narcotic or habit-forming drugs should be carried only with a letter from your physician prescribing their use and only in amounts for personal use. You cannot bring in fruits and plants.

Pets may be brought into Mexico—either a dog or a cat and up to four canaries(!)—but you must have a veterinarian's certificate issued no more than 72 hours before your arrival stating that the animal is healthy, and a vaccination certificate showing that the animal has been inoculated against rabies, hepatitis, pip, and leptospirosis. Fur-

ther, a Mexican consul must stamp these papers. (After 30 days, the
U.S. will require the inoculation certificate for rabies upon your return.)

U.S. CUSTOMS

All U.S. residents are exempted from paying duty on items with a
combined retail value of up to U.S.$400 as long as they have not
made other such claims within 30 days and as long as the articles are
for personal use (not for resale). Families may pool their exemptions
by filling out only one customs form. You may include within your
exemption 200 cigarettes and 100 cigars. If you are over 21 and your
home state has no more restrictive laws, you may include one liter of
alcohol in your exemption. (Reentering by the Texas border results
in a state tax being imposed on any imported alcohol.) A flat rate of
10 percent duty is imposed on the first U.S.$1000 in excess of your
exemption. If you have previously claimed your 30-day exemption,
you may still bring in U.S.$25 worth of goods. Keep your sales slips

available in case officials request them. If you are a big shopper and
expect to exceed your exemption, write the U.S. Customs Service,
Washington, DC 20229, for information on GSP. Many silver and
handcrafted items fall under the tax exemptions permitted by GSP
(Generalized System of Preferences), so that you may avoid paying
duty even on purchases in excess of U.S.$400.

Many articles are restricted by the U.S.A. Pre-Hispanic Indian artifacts are illegal to bring into the U.S. (and just as illegal to remove
from Mexico). And avoid buying Cuban cigars or tobacco, as they
are not permitted in the U.S. unless purchased in Cuba. Lottery
tickets and fireworks are prohibited. Products made with any part of
an endangered species cannot be imported. Before losing your tortoiseshell or black coral jewelry, your crocodile belt, or jaguar pelt
wallet to customs, call for a copy of the World Wildlife Fund's bro-
chure "Buyer Beware" (☎ 800-634-4444 outside Washington,
DC). The U.S. also restricts the import of animals, meat, plants, and
fruit, so if you want to bring home parrots or wild orchids, write the
U.S. Department of Agriculture, Washington, DC 20250, for their
pamphlet. Prescription drugs should be accompanied with their prescriptions to avoid delays at the border.

Try to bring all your purchases with you. Packages sent to your
home are not covered by the U.S.$400 exemption, so you will have
to pay duty. You may send unsolicited gifts to friends without duty
being charged if the value is no more than U.S.$50. Only one pack-
age can be received at one address without duty being charged.

Write on the package clearly: "Unsolicited Gift of Value Less than U.S.$50." Unless you are certain of exceeding your exemption with these gifts, it is safer to carry them with you rather than take the chance of loss or damage through the mail.

CANADIAN CUSTOMS

Canadian citizens who remain out of Canada for at least seven days may receive an exemption on duty for personal goods with a value not exceeding C.$300. This exemption will be received upon written declaration, but only once each calendar year. In addition, an unlimited number of C.$100 exemptions can be claimed once each calendar quarter after absences of at least 48 hours and an unlimited number of C.$20 exemptions can be declared after absences of at least 24 hours. However, these exemption categories cannot be combined after a single trip. You may bring in 50 cigars, 200 cigarettes, and 1.1 liters of liquor or wine, or 8.5 liters of beer except under the C.$20 exemption. The first C.$300 in excess of your exemption will be taxed at only 20% of regular duty rates (alcohol and cigarettes not included). Families cannot pool their exemptions.

Carry your purchases with you, as any packages mailed will be subject to duty. Gifts to friends can be sent duty-free as long as they are marked as unsolicited gifts and have a value of no more than C.$40. For restricted or prohibited articles, check with Revenue Canada (MacKenzie Ave., Ottawa, Ont., K1A 0L5) for their brochure, "I Declare." Under Mexican law, no pre-Hispanic Indian artifacts may be removed from Mexico.

All these amounts are quoted in Canadian dollars.

ITINERARIES

Quetzalcoatl Temple, Pyramids of Teotihuacan

Mexico offers so many sights in so many regions that the most difficult task of your trip may be selecting an itinerary. By browsing through the Keys and introductory paragraphs to the city travel sections, you can quickly get an idea of the places that might interest you most. If you already know your primary destination but wish to supplement it with some other sights, look up the region you're planning to visit or even the key to your destination. For example, the Key to Acapulco indicates the convenience of visiting Taxco and Mexico City from there, and the Key to Oaxaca indicates the proximity of the Pacific Coast resorts of Puerto Escondido and Huatulco.

On your first trip, you might want to visit the most frequented tourist spots, saving the lesser known excursions and sights for later trips. The following itineraries incorporate the most popular tourist spots, along with a sampling of colonial Mexico, its ruins and markets. For those who wish to spend more time at a resort or spa, it is simple enough to eliminate part of an itinerary, substituting your resort time for sightseeing.

MINI-VACATIONS

If you just have four or five days to escape work, you won't be able to travel much, but you can enjoy yourself at a single destination. There are direct flights into the major beach resorts of the Caribbean and Pacific where you swim, snorkle, or fish year-round. And the direct flights into Mexico City can put you in easy reach of most highland resorts and spas (listed below) where you can enjoy a bit of sightseeing along with tennis, golf, or even horseback riding.

ONE-WEEK TRIPS

1. The most popular one-week trip must include the Caribbean resort of **Cancún** with some excursions down the East Coast to the **ruins of Tulum** or inland to **Chichén Itzá**.

2. **Mexico City and the pyramids at Teotihuacan** (4 days), and a flight to **Oaxaca** for the weekend (3 days).

3. A tour of **Maya ruins** starting at **Mérida** (1 day) can include **Chichen Itza** (2 days), **Uxmal** and vicinity (1-2 days), and a quick flight from Mérida to **Villahermosa** for a visit to museums and nearby ruins of **Palenque** (2 days, but 3 days by bus).

4. Mexico City and the pyramids at Teotihuacan (4 days) can be combined with any number of Mexico City excursions like **Taxco** (2 days) and **Puebla** (1 day), or with a flight to Morelia and nearby **Pátzcuaro** (3 days), or a land trip to Silver Cities such as **Querétaro** and **San Miguel de Allende**.

5. Relax at a resort for 4 days; then take several days to sightsee. Pacific Coast resorts, such as **Puerto Vallarta** or **Acapulco**, can be combined with a flight to Mexico City, Oaxaca, or Guadalajara. Caribbean resorts, such as **Cozumel** or the East Coast, can be combined with a trip through **Yucatán** or even a visit to the **ruins of Palenque**.

TWO-WEEK TRIPS

6. **Mexico City and pyramids at Teotihuacan** (5 days), land trip to the **Silver Cities** (4 days, or more if you stay at a resort or spa along the way) via **Tepotzotlan** and **Tula** to **San Miguel de Allende** and **Guanajuato** with return to Mexico City. Fly to **Oaxaca** for a long weekend (4 days, or by bus, 5 days).

7. Trip 3 can be modified to include Oaxaca and some time at the beach by flying to Oaxaca for a long weekend (4 days, or 5 by bus) from Villahermosa and returning home via Mexico City. If you want a resort on the Caribbean, plan your beach stay to follow a tour of the ruins at **Chichén Itzá**. If rustic **Puerto Escondido** and developing **Huatulco** sound ideal to you, visit one of them after touring Oaxaca.

THREE-WEEK TRIPS

8. Trip 6 can be extended by continuing from **Guanajuato** to **Morelia** and **Pátzcuaro** before returning to Mexico City (add 3 days). From Oaxaca, fly to Mérida for a visit to the ruins of **Chichén Itzá** and **Uxmal** (4 days).

SPECIAL INTERESTS

In addition to the above trips, many other areas of Mexico may be explored if you have a special interest. Arrange a trip that most suits you by considering the following highlighted areas.

HIGHLAND RESORTS AND SPAS

If you want a relaxing vacation, but not one on the Caribbean or Pacific, consider arranging your sightseeing around an extended stay at one of Mexico's excellent highland resorts or spas. These resorts are usually conveniently located near major tourist areas and, more often than not, offer **golf**, **horseback riding**, **tennis**, and other sports in addition to extraordinary ambience and magnificent gardens. The spas also provide a chance to bathe in **hot mineral springs** and sometimes offer **massage and health programs**.These resorts are described under "Mexico City Excursions," and in sections on San Miguel de Allende, Taxco, Morelia, Guadalajara, Tequisquiapan, Uruapan, and Cuernavaca.

BEACHCOMBING

In addition to the major Pacific and Caribbean resorts, Mexico has many isolated, undeveloped beaches for those who want to get away from it all. One of the most fascinating areas to explore is the **East Coast of Quintana Roo**, where development has not yet eliminated the pristine beaches south of Tulum or even some of the thatched hammock shelters on the beaches near **Akumal**. The opening of MEX 200 along the Pacific Coast has made more beaches accessible outside of the major resorts (see "Costa de Oro" especially). The Gulf Coast beaches, both in Veracruz and Yucatán, are less beautiful but provide an authentic Mexican experience along with your beach enjoyment.

MAYA "RUIN-A-MANIA"

If you fly into Mérida and rent a car, you can visit most Maya ruins described in this book in two weeks of determined travel. From Mérida, visit **Chichén Itzá,** then continue to Coba on the new Nuevo X-Can road. Visit **Tulum** before continuing to Chetumal or Bacalar for an overnight stay. Take a day for excursions to ruins outside **Chetumal** before setting off for **Palenque.** From Palenque charter a plane or van to **Bonampak** and **Yaxchilán** before continuing to **Villahermosa** for museums and a trip to **Comalcalco.** If you still are determined, drive straight to Campeche for the night. Next day, visit **Edzna, Kabah**, and **Uxmal.** In the morning, visit other ruins near Uxmal before continuing to Mérida via Mayapan. Another day for **Dzibilchaltún** and you'll be done. We know people who have made this tour, but we don't recommend it. Leave some ruins for another trip and enjoy yourself by a pool or on Caribbean and Gulf Coast beaches for a few days.

OTHER RUINS

A total of 155 ancient ruins, out of the 10,000 known to exist, are open to the public. These ruins can be found in all the areas with traditional Indian cultures (see below), but the Central Valley around Mexico City and Oaxaca have the largest concentrations of important ruins in addition to the Maya ones in the Yucatán Peninsula and Chiapas described above.

COLONIAL CITIES

It's difficult to find any town devoid of buildings from Mexico's colonial period, but the following ones are among the most interesting: all of the Silver Cities, **Morelia, Pátzcuaro, Taxco, Oaxaca, San Cristóbal de las Casas, Puebla**, and **Mexico City**.

INDIAN CULTURE

Regions with large Indian populations provide the best markets, the most traditional fiestas and crafts. **Oaxaca, Pátzcuaro, San Cristóbal de las Casas, Yucatán**, and the seldom visited **Sierra de Puebla** regions count among the most important of these areas.

MURAL ART

Many towns have the interior of their municipal or state palaces painted in the tradition made famous by Rivera, Orozco, Siqueiros, and O'Gorman. But murals by the masters themselves are concentrated in **Mexico City** and nearby **Chapingo**, and in **Cuernavaca** as well as **Guadalajara**.

NATURE

The train ride through **Copper Canyon** (see Index), the 4-wheel drive up to the **Monarch butterfly sanctuary** of Angangueo (see Index), boat trips through the **rapids of the Usumacinta** (see Tours), and **snorkeling** or **diving** in the Caribbean offer excellent and diverse opportunities to sample Mexico's natural beauty.

LAND ROUTES INTO MEXICO

Copper Canyon

In this chapter we describe the traditional routes into Mexico from the northern border with the United States. Most routes require at least one overnight stay before you reach a major tourist destination. With the exception of the Copper Canyon, these routes are described as if you would like to get through them as quickly as possible. Each route ends with a city or resort that is described later in this guide, where you can find further driving information. The Barranca del Cobre (Copper Canyon), however, is a desirable destination in and of itself, hardly a part of Mexico to rush through for those who enjoy the outdoors. And, too, it is not a driving route at all, but rather a train trip for you and your car that just happens to provide a fascinating link between the U.S. border and the Pacific Coast. We begin at the Copper Canyon, exploring it with pleasure before getting on with the description of other routes. Remember to check "Customs" and "Driving Tips" before setting out with your car. And if you need to spend the night near the border, try crossing into Mexico (particularly at El Paso, Laredo, and Brownsville), where you can get better rates at hotels and then an early start in the morning with customs behind you.

BARRANCA DEL COBRE (COPPER CANYON)

As a land trip into Mexico, the canyon route between Chihuahua and the Pacific near Los Mochis is simply beautiful. And the driving, except for the monotonous stretch between El Paso and Chihuahua (see below, "El Paso to Zacatecas"), is unusually easy, since it must be left to the Chihuahua al Pacifico train conductor. Not until 1961 did this route become passable by more than a mule. By then, it had taken almost 50 years to complete the **39 bridges** that skim over rivers and gorges and the **86 tunnels** that burrow into the rugged sierra along the 650-km (403-m) swath of track. The train crosses the homeland of the Tarahumara Indians, spanning the deep barrancas where they have retreated from centuries of encroachment since the arrival of Spanish missionaries in 1611; it dips from an 8,000-foot plateau of Ponderosa pines down to sub-tropical apple orchards, then tropical banana palms, before following El Fuerte river toward the Sea of Cortés for its arrival at Los Mochis. As a route on the way to other destinations, the Chihuahua al Pacifico train is a delightful bonus. Yet it is easy to overstate its pleasures. The scenery can be breathtaking between Creel and Bahuichivo; more often it's simply lovely, and sometimes even unmemorable. The engineering required to build the train, such as U-turns inside mountains, can be more dramatic in the reading than in reality. It is a lengthy trip: scheduled for 13 hours, it often takes longer. The only break is the 20-minute stop at the magnificent lookout of **Divisadero**, about midway. Is it worthwhile? Absolutely, but one-way, rather than round-trip will do. And even then we recommend breaking the trip up with an overnight in Divisadero or Creel.

Although the train adds to the adventure and feeling of isolation, it is the Copper Canyon itself that is worthy of a special journey. The maze of barrancas and rivers forming what is simply called the

"Copper Canyon" covers 25,000 square miles, and sometimes plummets one-and-a-half times deeper than the Grand Canyon, down from the hawks and pines of the uplands, to the parrots and wild orchids below. Larger and younger than the Grand, these barrancas are greener and often narrower, without so many geological strata. Inhabited for millennia, the canyons hold painted caves as well as old Spanish missions and abandoned silver mines. They remain home to the colorfully dressed, semi-nomadic **Tarahumara**, who herd their flocks of sheep and goats among valleys of volcanic rocks that are wind-carved into free-standing sculptures of turtles, teetering mushrooms, and elephants. And where 25,000 visitors a day may check out the Grand Canyon, here there are fewer than 200,000 in a year to share your hikes, horseback trips, or tours to canyon view points, **hot springs**, abandoned Spanish churches, and waterfalls (Basaseachic Falls has a drop of more than 1000 feet).

WHERE TO STAY

Spending time in the canyons is easy, especially if you don't require fancy accommodations and cuisine. The few lodges here are rustic, but offer the companionability of sitting in front of the fireplace on a cool night while listening to the strumming of a Mexican guitarist. All have guides and hiking tours for visiting the canyons; all have English-speaking staff. Not all have electricity.

Creel, the largest village in the canyons and the heart of the Tarahumara community, is the only tourist stop large enough to have restaurants and shops (visit Mission Crafts, where the profits on Tarahumara weavings and musical instruments go to the local hospital; closed 1-3 p.m.) There are several small hotels (write them at Creel, Chih., Mexico) on the main street ranging from the hostel-like ambience of **Margarita's** *(Lopez Mateos 11* ☎ *[145] 6-00-45; budget)* to the ★**Parador de la Montana** *(Lopez Mateos 47* ☎ *[145] 6-00-75; $65)* with 55 carpeted rooms and a big TV screen in the lounge and restaurant. Next door, the ★**Cascada Inn** *(Lopez Mateos 49* ☎ *[145] 6-01-51; $118)* offers a heated pool along with its 30 carpeted rooms. Our favorite place, ★**Copper Canyon Sierra Lodge**, *(reserve in U.S. 1100 Owendale, Suite G, Troy MI 48083; call toll-free,* ☎ *800-776-3942; $130 AP and transport from train)* is found 13 miles outside the village, in a tranquil setting next to the Cusarare creek on Tarahumara land. The log-cabin style architecture here includes 26 rooms with kerosene lamps only for light, wood-burning stoves for heat, yet private baths with hot water. The star is for canyon ambience, not the lack of utilities. The hike-and-van-tour offerings are extensive, ranging from an easy hike to a nearby waterfall to a dramatic drive to their other lodge, the renovated 19th-century hacienda and gardens now called the **Copper Canyon Riverside Lodge**, deep inside the canyon at the former mining town of Batopilas as well as 6-to 9-day camping trips, for which you need to reserve in advance.

Divisadero is no more than a train stop in Tarahumara county, but the reason for the halt is the stupendous view over three canyons. There are three hotels near here, but only the ★ **Cabanas Divisadero Barrancas** *(reserve at Apartado Postal 661, Chihuahua* ☎ *[14] 12-33-62; $140 AP)* is right on the rim, its glass-walled lobby framing the mesmerizing sight. The 55 rooms vary; all are clean, and about half have balconies with canyon views. The star is for the setting, not the erratic supply of hot water. There are rim hikes and horseback riding, and more difficult overnight descents into the canyons.

The pleasant village of **Cerocahui** is 10 miles on a dirt road from the Bahuichivo train stop. Here the ★ **Hotel Mision** *(contact Viajes Flamingo, Apartado 1034, Los Mochis, Sin.* ☎ *[681] 2-16-13; $150 with AP and train transfer)* offers decent lodgings in its 30 rooms heated by wood stoves and with tiled baths and hot water. Horseback riding is available along with tours to old missions, waterfalls, and the awesome view over Urique canyon from Cerro El Gallego.

ARRIVING

To pick up the train, you must overnight in either Los Mochis or Chihuahua (see "Index" for listings in those cities). These cities can be reached by air (Aeromexico flies to Los Mochis from Tucson and Mexico City, for example, and to Chihuahua from Mexico City; Aero Leo Lopez [in U.S., ☎ 915-778-1022] flies to Chihuahua from El Paso and Los Mochis); by train (in Chihuahua you need to change train stations and in Los Mochis you need to transfer trains at Sufragio); by bus or car on the routes below. If you aren't interested in the train, you can drive from Chihuahua to Creel, or however far progress has been made on the road from Creel to San Rafael, beyond Divisadero—but to date, you cannot get through the canyons except by train.

TRAIN ARRANGEMENTS

There are three separate trains through the canyon for first-and second-class passenger service and for freight. The train recommended for tourists is the primera especial (special first class) that traverses the canyons in daylight and offers reserved reclining seats (from Chihuahua, the best views in the canyon are on the left side), a boxed breakfast and dining car (you might bring your own fruit or favorite snack, and bottled water) air conditioning, and somewhat clean windows (make sure you occasionally stand between cars for clearer views and photograph-taking) and bathrooms (bring tissues). This train leaves Chihuahua at 7 a.m. daily and returns from Los Mochis at the same time. (Note: The train operates on Central time, but Los Mochis is on Pacific time, making the departure locally 6 a.m.) Some trains transport your car for a fee (contact the railroad), while special arrangements can be made for piggybacking your RV. (Contact *Point South RV Tours,* 11313 Edmonson Ave., Moreno Valley, CA 92360; or call toll-free, ☎ 800-421-1391). While you can make the least expensive train reservations yourself by writing directly to: *Jefe, Ferrocarril de Chihuahua al Pacifico* (Apartado 46, Chihuahua, Chih.), *Mexico-by-Rail,*

(☎ 800-228-3225 in U.S.) can do it for you. Many tour agencies and nature groups offer packages into the canyon. *Sanborn Tours* (P.O. Drawer 749, Bastrop, TX 278602; or call toll-free ☎ 800-531-5440), not only has tours departing on almost a weekly basis, but their one-way train trip with additional nights in the canyon is reasonably priced. For other options, such as the deluxe trains of *Sierra Madre Express*, (☎ 800-666-0346), check with a travel agent.

SEASONS AND FESTIVALS

The canyons can be visited and explored year-round, but *they are most in demand during the Tarahumara festivals of Holy Week*, when the Indians play a form of stick ball, running for three days and over 100 miles non-stop. Then you need to reserve almost a year in advance. The fall, richly verdant after summer, and the orchards laden with fruit, is the next most popular season, although the flowers of spring attract many as well. Creel and Divisadero are located at around 7,600 feet, Cerocahui at 5,000, which means that summer temperatures there are benign, while those on the canyon floors can be stifling; winter there can dust the canyon with snow and drop to freezing at night, though afternoons are balmy and the canyon bottoms, where many Tarahumara retreat, are pleasantly warm.

NOGALES TO MAZATLAN

MEX 15 is the most convenient route for those traveling from the western part of the United States. It covers 1230 km (763 m) and may require two overnight stays before reaching Mazatlán. This road is four lanes for much of the way, but between Nogales and Guaymas it is curvy on its drop to the coast. From Mazatlán the 7 hours to Guadalajara will be shortened with the completion of MEX 15D. From Guadalajara it's another full day to Mexico City. **WARNING**: Highway robberies are not uncommon day or night along MEX 15 between Los Mochis and Mazatlan. The problem is worse on little used Superhighway 1 in the same area.

Try to cross the border early enough to reach **Guaymas** (WHY–mahs) on your first day (430 km, 266 m). This trip is desert-hot during the summer and not scenic any time. If you get delayed, you'll find moderately priced motel accommodations on the highway near Hermosillo. At Guaymas, at least you'll be on the Pacific, if not at one of Mexico's most fashionable resorts, even though there is a Club Med.

WHERE TO STAY

Hotel Playa de Cortes ★★
located about 3 km (2 m) off MEX 15 on Bocochibampo Bay. Its 135 air-conditioned units include access to the beach, a pool, restaurant, and parking. *Moderate*

Del Puerto Motel

(Calle 19 and Yanez) with air conditioning and parking. About 11 km (7 m) before town, turn off for San Carlos Bay to the Teta Kawi Trailer Park with 132 sites and hookups.   *Inexpensive*

Guaymas is a fishing port, so try the seafood at the *Restaurant Del Mar* (Serdan and Calle 17; moderate).

From Guaymas to Mazatlán it's a little less than 800 km (496 m). You may not want to travel to Mazatlán in one day, so consider a detour to the 18th-century colonial silver city of **Alamos** (55 km, 34 m, off MEX 15 at Navojoa) and an overnight in **Los Mochis**. Los Mochis is where you can catch the train through the spectacular Copper Canyon (see above). From nearby Topolobampo Bay, Los Mochis also is connected to La Paz by car ferry and hydrofoil service across the Sea of Cortes. Although an important crossroads, Los Mochis itself is of no touristic interest, yet facilities are good.

Hotel Santa Anita

(Leyva at Hidalgo, ☎ *[681] 5-70-46; $84)* is a bustling commercial hotel, full of locals and Copper Canyon tourists alike. Located in the heart of town, within walking distance of the bus terminal and with vans to the train, the hotel offers 135 well-maintained, carpeted, a/c rooms. Tour arrangements into the canyon; and access to a pool. Good restaurant (opens 4:30 a.m. for train departures); bar and disco. Parking. Write Apartado 159.

El Dorado

(Leyva and Valdez, ☎ *[681] 5-11-11; $52)* is more motel-like and not quite so central, but its 90 rooms have a/c and there's a restaurant, pool, and parking. If the lure of Copper Canyon hasn't taken you on a detour, the next day you'll find Mazatlán 435 km (270 m), or about 5 hours, away.

Just around the corner from the Santa Anita is El Farallon (Obregón at Flores; moderate), a surprisingly good seafood restaurant with stuffed fish filet and smoked marlin machaca.

EL PASO TO ZACATECAS

MEX 45 is the most convenient entry point from southwestern United States into the central highlands of Mexico (the Mexican border town is Ciudad Juárez). It traverses 1225 km (760 m) to **Zacatecas**, which brings you to the region of the Silver Cities. From Zacatecas to Mexico City, it is another 596 km (370 m) via San Luis Potosí, a trip that can be completed in one day if you plan to bypass the fine tourist attractions in this region. From Zacatecas, it is only 312 km (193 m) to Guadalajara. The most northern stretch of this route is subject to snow, especially in January, and dust storms in the dry season.

The 4-lane, toll road MEX 45D enables you to complete the drive from Ciudad Juárez to **Chihuahua** (375 km, 233 m) in under 4-1/2 hours.

Chihuahua has a pleasant downtown and good facilities, making it a valuable stopping point on a long journey south. For those planning a trip into the Copper Canyon (see above), it is essential to overnight. While here visit the Quinta Gameros (Bolivar 401; open Tues.-Sun. 10 a.m.-2 p.m., 4-7 p.m.; fee), a turn-of-the-century mansion spendidly furnished in the art nouveau style; and the Museo de la Revolución (Calle 10 Nte. 3014; open 9 a.m.-1 p.m., 3-7 p.m. daily; fee), located in Pancho Villa's home and furnished with photographs and memorabilia, including the bullet-ridden Dodge he was driving when assassinated. Also, the 18th-century cathedral (near Juarez at Independencia) has a handsomely carved facade. There are numerous hotels, including motels on the MEX 45 entry road.

WHERE TO STAY

Victoria ★

(Juárez at Colón; $60), is our preference despite its tragically poor maintenance—tragic, we say, because the hand-painted tiled walls of the lobby and the lovely hacienda-style garden and pool are among the sights of the city. If the old-fashioned ambience of this 40s hotel is enough to compensate for the often poor state of the 125 rooms (shop around, some are better than others), then this is the place for you. The location is right, too, next to the strip of better restaurants. Disco. Parking. Write Apartado 19.

San Francisco Mision Park Inn ★★★

(Victoria 409, ☎ *[14] 16-75-55; in U. S.,* ☎ *800-648-7818; $80)*, is a commercial first-class hotel located between the cathedral and the market. Its 140 a/c rooms have modern tiled baths, clean carpets, TVs, and all that is lacking at the Victoria. Restaurant, bar, and disco, parking. For dining, there's *Chihuahua Charlie's* (Juárez 3329; moderately expensive) for steak and seafood near the Victoria, and *Trastevere* (moderate and hearty) across from the San Francisco for Italian and Mexican. For city tours or Copper Canyon arrangements, contact Rojo y Casavantes (Guerrero 1207; ☎ [14] 15-46-36).

On your second day continue south, part of the way on a four-lane road, to **Gómez Palacio/Torreón** (470 km, 291 m). Along the way, MEX 45 branches at Ciudad Jiménez for Durango (260 km, 161 m and then through the mountains to Mazatlán on the coast, an additional 6 hours). Unless you are on your way to Mazatlán, follow MEX 49 to Gómez Palacio, where you'll be in a good position to reach Zacatecas the next day (380 km, 236 m). At Gómez Palacio Mex 49 south carries you to the moderate. ★★**Posada del Rio** (Madero at Juárez), with 85 a/c rooms, restaurant, pool, and parking, then continues to Zacatecas.

EAGLE PASS TO SAN LUIS POTOSÍ

MEX 57 provides the most level and easiest access road into Mexico and joins the route from Laredo (see below) at Saltillo. Opposite Eagle Pass is the Mexican town of Piedras Negras. From Eagle Pass to Mexico City it is

1345 km (834 m). While you will need to overnight before reaching Mexico City, you will reach the Silver City sightseeing region starting at San Luis Potosí (890 km, 552 m) or San Miguel de Allende early on the second day. Depending on when you leave Piedras Negras, you probably will want to overnight in either **Saltillo** (445 km, 276 m) or **Matehuala** (260 km, 161 m, from Saltillo). Saltillo offers a good climate at its altitude of just over 5,000 feet and has a lovely Alameda park for strolling. On MEX 57, you will find excellent accommodations, ★★★**Camino Real Saltillo,** expensive with all services. If you are on a tight budget, Matehuala offers you the best option, with the moderate, ★★**Las Palmas Motel** offering parking, a pool, a restaurant, and a/c rooms as well as RV sites (near the entrance road on MEX 57 to Matehuala). If you find yourself stalled here, check out the ghost mining town of **Real de Catorce**, a day's excursion from Matehuala.

LAREDO TO SAN LUIS POTOSÍ

Laredo is the most convenient border crossing for those traveling from the north and east. After crossing to the Mexican town of **Nuevo Laredo**, it is only 14 hours or 1223 km (758 m) to Mexico City. The fastest route is to follow MEX 85 to Monterrey; then MEX 40 to Saltillo, where you can hook up with MEX 57 described just above. Saltillo is only 323 km (200 m) from the border, or about 3-1/2 hours. If you get an early start at the border and are willing to drive for about 10 hours, you can reach San Luis Potosí and the Silver Cities region on your first day—especially once the toll road to **Monterrey** (MEX 85D) is completed, saving you an hour.

MEX 85 at Monterrey also leads to Mexico City, *but while parts of this route are scenic, the trip is more arduous and offers fewer major tourist attractions.* If you are heading for the Gulf Coast, take MEX 85 to just south of Ciudad Mante (425 km, 264 m), and turn onto MEX 80 to Tampico (159 km, 99 m). For more information on the Gulf Coast route from Tampico, see below.

BROWNSVILLE TO VERACRUZ

Because the U.S. roads leading to the border at Brownsville-Matamoros and MEX 180 are inferior to the others already discussed, this route is seldom used. MEX 180/101 splits to become MEX 101, which continues to MEX 57 and San Luis Potosí (see above) after 520 km (322 m), making for a short route into central Mexico. However, MEX 180 is most convenient if you are heading to Veracruz (983 km, 609 m) or Yucatán. Because of the lack of facilities along this road until you get to Tampico, it is best to overnight in Matamoros and get an early start for your trip. *During the summer, this area can be subject to torrential storms.* When we drove this route during hurricane warnings, some villages were flooded and parts of the road were not in tip-top condition. Still, we would have made the 700-km (434-m) trip to **Tuxpán** before nightfall if we had not encountered delays with the ferry at **Tampico**. Now MEX 180 bridges the river itself (toll).

But if you arrive late at Tampico (500 km, 310 m, from Brownsville), you can always make a decision to spend the night here. ★ ★ **Camino Real Motor Hotel** on MEX 80/180 borders on the expensive category but is a full-service hotel; ★ **Impala**, with a garage, near the zócalo, inexpensive. Tuxpán is a picturesque fishing town with a good beach. By spending the night here you can quickly reach Papantla (56 km, 35 m) the next morning in time to visit the ruins of El Tajin before continuing your journey to Veracruz on well-paved roads (see "Central Gulf Coast" chapter). Following MEX 180 across the toll bridge at Tuxpán, turn left for the ★ ★ **Hotel Tajin** with comfortable rooms, pool, and tennis at moderate to expensive prices. In Tuxpán, the main street of Juárez offers a number of inexpensive yet adequately modernized hotels with air-conditioned rooms (like the Reforma at #25), while just a few blocks away is the newer ★ **Sara** (Garizurieta 44; inexpensive) with large a/c rooms and pool. All have restaurants, but you might try the inexpensive seafood at Del Puerto (Juárez 44).

ANCIENT MEXICO

Here were the remains of a cultivated, polished, and peculiar people,
who had passed through all the stages incident to the rise and fall of
nations; reached their golden age, and perished, entirely unknown.

John L. Stephens, 1841

Thinking he had reached Asia, Columbus called the peoples of the Caribbean "Indians." He died without realizing that he had chanced upon a far greater discovery. An "entirely unknown" land lay nearby, populated by millions of people and adorned with glistening cities. As Europeans realized the discovery was of an unexpected new world, they imagined it as a land of all possibilities—the place of legendary Amazonas or the fountain of youth. But the origins of the "Indians" became the issue that captured their imaginations most. After all, everyone descended from Adam and Eve, so the Indians and their civilization must have roots in the Old World.

NEW WORLD CULTURES

There was no lack of theories, no lack of response to the romance of explaining the origin of the New World cultures. Over the centuries, debate involved presidents, doctors, leaders of the world's religions, scientists, and just plain kooks. The Indians, it was proposed, were survivors of the lost continents of Mu or Atlantis, or perhaps the descendants of the Lost Tribes of Israel, or even the survivors of Alexander's shipwrecked fleet in the 4th century. Maybe they were Phoenicians, Africans, Chinese, or even early Welsh or Irish. Or perhaps the New World was the land of Noah before the flood or an outpost of ancient Egypt. The intensity of the debate led to 19th-century adventurers exploring Mexico, risking malaria for the glory of discovering proof for their pet theories; and it led to sacrifices like that of Lord Kingsborough who spent his fortune arguing the Lost Tribes of Israel position and, as a result, died in a debtors prison. In the 20th century, the intensity may have subsided, but the debates continue, often becoming the material for best-sellers like *The Chariots of the Gods* with its modern-style voyagers from outer space.

As fabulous as it might be to envision Alexander's lost troops embarking on the shores of the New World or space ships landing in Mexico (but forgetting to leave more than a Stone Age technology), the relatively new science of archaeology has produced much information on Mexico's ancient past—and that information provides little support for earlier conjectures. New discoveries and radiocarbon dating have pushed the antiquity of Mexican civilization further and further back into time (to 1200 B.C., according to present scholarship), disqualifying most Old World cultures from having civilized the New World. Those civilizations of sufficient antiquity to have contributed to Mexico's earliest civilization—like Egypt and China —lacked ships sophisticated enough to survive repeated transoceanic travel. Still, if foreign peoples somehow brought themselves to the New World, they left surprisingly little in the way of evidence for their presence. The plants and animal life of the New World show no imports whatsoever—except the coconut, which is known to be capable of floating across the Pacific Ocean and seeding itself. Indian languages are completely distinctive from those of other parts of the world. And no Phoenician coins, no Chinese vases, no artifacts from other civilizations have turned up in excavations.

THE BIG GAME HUNTERS

With no direct evidence for foreign contact in Mexico, we should look to the Indians themselves to understand their origins and civilizations. Fortunately, archaeologists do have an explanation of how the Americas were peopled, even if they can't exactly pinpoint when the Indians started to arrive. The Ice Age created a land bridge from Siberia to Alaska where the Bering Straits now are. Somewhere between 50,000 and 10,000 years ago, bands of nomadic Asians crossed this strip of land while hunting mammoths and mastodons and entered the Americas. (By at least 11,000 years ago some of them reached the tip of South America.) As the Ice Age ended, melting ice submerged much land, including the "bridge" from Siberia, and the migrations halted. The big game hunters, equipped with only the rudiments of culture, were in the Americas to stay. Over the millennia, they were forced to adapt to a radically changed environ-

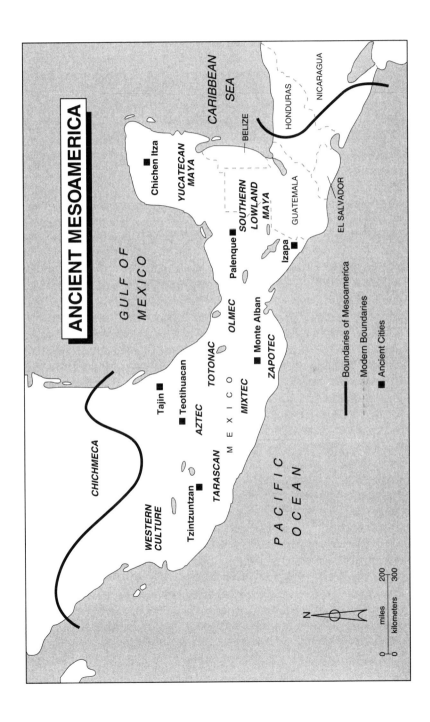

ANCIENT MESOAMERICA

GULF OF MEXICO

CARIBBEAN SEA

PACIFIC OCEAN

CHICHMECA

WESTERN CULTURE

TARASCAN

AZTEC

TOTONAC

MIXTEC

OLMEC

ZAPOTEC

MEXICO

Tzintzuntzan

Tajin

Teotihuacan

Monte Alban

Palenque

Izapa

SOUTHERN LOWLAND MAYA

YUCATECAN MAYA

Chichen Itza

BELIZE

GUATEMALA

HONDURAS

NICARAGUA

EL SALVADOR

Boundaries of Mesoamerica
Modern Boundaries
■ Ancient Cities

N

miles 200
kilometers 300
0
0

ment—one bereft of their original prey—and eventually they created
the civilization of ancient Mexico.

MESOAMERICA

*But for written records, Egyptian, Grecian and Roman remains
would be as mysterious as the ruins of America.*

John L. Stephens, 1843

Mexico contains the ruins of about 10,000 ancient cities (155 sites
are open to the public), yet the civilization that evolved here was
even larger, extending south into Guatemala, Belize, El Salvador,
and parts of Honduras. In the north, this civilization usually spread
no more than 300 miles above the Central Valley of Mexico City,
where arid lands prevented agriculture and settled, civilized life. Because the borders of this ancient civilization defy any current political designation, the area is called Mesoamerica.

While the Spanish left a wealth of records on the Aztecs and a few
on other groups like the Maya, the peoples they encountered were
the last representatives of a civilization that had endured from 1200
B.C. During those thousands of years before the Spanish, magnificent cities had flourished, most intensely in the Classic period (A.D.
250-900), and were abandoned for reasons no written history now
records. While Mesoamerica was the only civilization of the Americas to develop and use writing, most of their texts were recorded in
bark paper or deerskin books that were destroyed by the elements
and time. Most of those that did survive the Conquest were destroyed by Spanish friars in their effort to wean the Indians from heathen ways. With few books remaining and only brief texts surviving
on stone sculptures, archaeologists have had the awesome task of
"making dead men tell tales" from pottery fragments, plants, bones,
and stone monuments. With no voice to speak, Mesoamerican civilization has taken on a cloak of mystery that archaeologists gradually
are unraveling through painstaking effort.

SHARED TRAITS

Even before the first civilization of the Olmec blossomed in 1200
B.C. along the tropical rivers of the Gulf Coast region, the mountainous valleys and lowland tropics of Mexico were populated by
people living off agriculture, hunting of deer, peccary, and fish, and
who had pottery, tools made of obsidian (volcanic glass), and limited
ceremonial architecture. Later, they traded with various regions for
the goods their own environment couldn't provide. The lowlands

CHRONOLOGY OF ANCIENT MEXICO

	PRE-CLASSIC PERIOD			PROTO-CLASSIC PECIOD	CLASSIC PERIOD		POST-CLASSIC PERIOD	
	1200 B.C.	900 B.C.	500 B.C.	100 B.C.	250 A.D.	600 A.D.	900 A.D.	1200 A.D. — 1520 A.D.
CENTRAL MEXICO	Tlatilco		Cuicuilco	Teotihuacan		Xochicalco	Toltec	Aztec
OAXACA	San Jose Magote		Monte Alban I	Monte Alban II	Monte Alban III	Monte Alban IV		Mixtec
GULF COAST	Olmec / San Lorenzo	La Venta	Tres Zapotes		El Tajin			Zempoala
CHIAPAS	Chiapa de Corzo			Izapa		Palenque		
YUCATÁN MAYA	Dzibilchaltun			Loltun	Uxmal Edzna Coba Kohunlich		Chichen Itza	Tulum Mayapan
MICHOACAN MEXICO WEST		Guerrero Olmec	Chupicuaro	Shaft Tombs				Tarascan

always needed obsidian and often stone; the highlands salt, sea and tropical food products, and cotton. They even traded for exotic items like jade, their most precious item of all; cacao (chocolate beans), which eventually was used for currency; and colorful bird feathers, especially those from the quetzal, for headdresses and adornments. Trade for these products intensified during later centuries and continued until the Conquest, when we get Spanish descriptions of the powerful Pochteca merchants of the Aztecs and the seafaring traders of the Maya.

Most likely, trade throughout Mesoamerica, along routes covering untold miles, accounts for the shared characteristics unique to this civilization—for example, its diet of corn, beans, and squash, its ritual ball game, its calendar, writing, and astronomy, and its religious beliefs that dominated all aspects of life and art. Today, impressive ruined cities and museum collections eloquently record this civilization's accomplishments in architecture, city planning, ceramics, painting, and lapidary work. Jade was finely polished and intricately carved; cities were constructed with temples raised on stepped pyramids and carefully arranged around open courtyards. Yet these enduring expressions of the ancient past were accomplished with a Stone Age technology. Metallurgy was unknown before A.D. 900 and, even then, gold, silver, and bronze were used for ornament, rarely for tools and weapons. Obsidian made the hardest, sharpest tools, but it could not cut a hard stone like jade (which was polished and carved through sand and rope abrasion). Further, Mesoamerica had no draft or pack animals to aid in constructing cities. For this reason, perhaps, the wheel was never developed for practical purposes, only for toys. Even the potter's wheel wasn't used for shaping the most refined ceramics of this culture. Overcoming the limitations of their Stone Age technology, the ancients produced exceptional works of world art and excelled in the building of massive, but harmoniously arranged, cities with sacred precincts of pyramids and open plazas. Yet Mesoamerica's accomplishments and contributions to the world are not limited to art.

DIET

We find it difficult to imagine Italians without their tomatoes, the Swiss without their chocolate, and the world without corn and turkey, yet it took the discovery of the New World for these items to be introduced to shores beyond America. While beans, squash, chiles, and corn ground into flour formed the basic diet for most Mesoamericans, venison, turkey, dog(!), and fish supplemented it. Chocolate was so valuable—it was also used as money—that only the elite drank it (with a trace of that very Mexican flavoring, vanilla). Honey, made by the stingless bees of Yucatán, was the only sweetener known. The most popular crop discovered in Mexico had nothing to do with diet, but it was distributed and grown around the world in less than a century. We call it tobacco.

BALL GAME

The Mesoamerican ball game so fascinated the Spaniards that Cortes took two teams of Aztec ballplayers to Spain when he first returned to report to Charles V. At that time, Europe had few team sports played competitively, and certainly none played with the amazing American rubber ball, which Friar Diego Duran struggled to describe in 1579:

> *The material that the ball was made of was called ollin...which is the resin of a certain tree. When cooked it becomes stringy....Jumping and bouncing are its qualities, upward and downward, to and from. It can exhaust the pursuer running after it before he can catch up.*

Called "hipball," the game was played on stone courts located in the central ceremonial precinct of each city; the game consisted in keeping a heavy, solid-rubber ball in the air without the use of hands, feet, or head. Teams scored points by preventing the ball from sailing over the wall and by not allowing the ball to bounce on the floor of the court. To protect them against the heavy ball and cement floor, players wore kneepads, hip belts called "yokes," and sometimes face masks and helmets. In some areas, they could win the game by hitting the ball through stone rings with openings barely large enough for the ball to pass. So rare was this feat that players who accomplished it were rewarded with all the jewelry belonging to the spectators. According to Spanish accounts, so intense was the gambling among spectators that rulers even settled border disputes based on the outcome of a game.

Exactly when and where the game of hipball originated is not known, although it is suspected to have begun in the Gulf Coast region where rubber is found. The popularity of the game spread beyond Mesoamerica to Arizona, Haiti, and northern South America. Unlike our sports, the Mesoamerican game had religious significance and, sometimes, was accompanied by human sacrifice of the losing captain. It is said that Toltec kings played the rain gods for a plentiful harvest, and symbols of agricultural fertility often accompany portrayals of the game. Many ball courts are aligned with the setting sun, leading some archaeologists to speculate that the ball represented the sun and the game a sacred ceremony to keep it moving across the sky.

Other ball games were played in Mesoamerica, but none were as prevalent or as important as hipball. At Teotihuacan, a painting shows a version of stick ball; in Nayarit, ceramic figurines with club in hand, pose in perfect baseball stance. The Tarascans played a form of hockey at night with a ball of slow-burning roots that showered sparks when hit. Handball was played by the Aztecs, Yucatecan Maya, as well as other cultures. While the ancient rules have been lost, the American affection for team sports seems to have spread around the world.

CALENDARS AND COMPUTATIONS

...It is a marvel to see the freedom with which they know how to count and understand things.

Friar Diego de Landa , 1566

All Mesoamerican cultures computed time based on calendars, and all used a numerical system that usually was composed of a bar sign for numeral five and a dot for the numeral one. But the Maya showed themselves to have a particular affinity for this field. They may have had one of the earliest concepts of zero in the world, a concept that not even the Romans had. And they used a positional system of numbers like the decimal system, only theirs was based on 20 not 10. They computed time millions of years into the past, and occasionally thousands into the future. They knew the true length of the solar year before Europeans, and they recorded time in a system called the Long Count, which was as accurate as our Gregorian calendar of today. The earliest known date in this system is recorded on a stone monument from 31 B.C. The system may have evolved long before then when, perhaps, dates were recorded on more perishable materials like wood or bark paper. Translations of Long Count dates enable archaeologists to establish that a monument was erected, say, on January 10, A.D. 777. Unfortunately, for our understanding of the past, the system was not used throughout Mesoamerica, and the Maya stopped using it around A.D. 900.

All Mesoamerican cultures used a dating system called the Calendar Round, a system of greater antiquity—perhaps from before 1200 B.C.—than the Maya Long Count. This calendar guided the ancients in their agriculture and ceremonies, but it also forecast omens for each day. The importance of the calendar in the Indians' lives can be gleaned from a priest's concern:

> *Used in antiquity by all the Indian nation in heathen times both in their feasts and ceremonies and on other occasions during the year when they sowed and reaped [and] observed the days upon which children were born so as to understand the fates and destinies under which they were brought forth. This is described here in order to instruct the priesthood for...the dissemination of the Holy Catholic Faith, and the extirpation of the ceremonies and rites of the past.*

Friar Diego Duran, 1579

The Calendar Round was actually an intermeshing of two calendars: the 260 sacred count and the solar-year calendar. The solar year calendar contained 360 days plus five unlucky days at the end, which required great penance and fasting. Children born on one of these five days were considered unfortunate. Although the intermeshing of the two calendars was such that no date was repeated for 52 years, today it is difficult to determine when any particular date occurred within this system since the information supplied is more like the two-digit '42 than the full date 1842. We might understand the significance the ancients attached to the end of a 52-year cycle by comparing it with our century, when we celebrate the coming of a new era. But instead of a joyous New Year's Eve celebration, the Aztecs extinguished all fires, broke all pottery, and spent the night anxiously awaiting a sign that the gods would allow the Calendar Round to begin anew and the world to continue.

ASTRONOMY

> *The heavens touched nearly every aspect of their culture; consequently, we find ancient astronomy woven into myth, religion and astrology. So great was the reliance of the ancients upon the sun and moon that they deified them.*

Anthony F. Aveni, 1980

The sophistication of Mesoamerican calendars and computation of time was based on an equally sophisticated study of celestial events. Without the aid of refined instruments, the ancients knew not only the length of the solar year but the length of the lunar month and the Venus year. They predicted eclipses with extraordinary accuracy. For them, the universe was layered with 13 levels above the earth— where the moon traveled in one level, and above this the clouds, stars, and sun, and in the uppermost layer, the creator god. Below the earth were the nine levels of the evil underworld where death ruled. This view of the cosmos precluded an understanding of the rotation of planets that could have assisted them in making their calculations. Nonetheless, their calculations resulted in remarkable precision—a lunar cycle only seven minutes off modern values and a Venus cycle with only a 2-hour margin of error over nearly 500 years.

THE PATH OF THE SUN

Some ancient observatories have been discovered, the most famous being the Caracol at the ruins of Chichen Itza. More often a complex of buildings was used to sight the path of the sun, or the doorway of a building was aligned with a hill to mark the rising or setting of stars and planets. The entire great city of Teotihuacan was laid out on a grid plan oriented to the heliacal rising of the Pleiades, an event that forecast one of the sun's zenith passages across the sky. In fact, most Mesoamerican cities were not aligned with true north or south, but rather with an important celestial event. One of the most dramatic alignments can be observed at Chichen Itza during the equinoxes, when the setting sun illuminates the serpent balustrade of the Castillo, transforming it into an undulating snake.

The purpose of Mesoamerican astronomy most definitely was religious: to predict the behavior of the gods and their impact on the universe. Eclipses and the rising of Venus were fearsome times when evil could beset the world if proper steps were not taken. The first annual zenith passage of the sun marked the beginning of the ancients' planting season, an event so important that other stars, like the Pleiades, were studied to predict it. Solemn religious rituals accompanied the occurrence of the zenith passage; these rituals were so ingrained that after the Conquest, King Philip of Spain ordered that dates for the sun's zenith passage be collected for each town in Mexico so that Indian solar-cult ceremonies could be prevented. So strong were traditions, though, that today the ancient solar calendar still governs rituals of Maya in the state of Chiapas.

RELIGION

The gods were so honored and revered by the natives that any offense against them was paid for with one's life. They held the gods in more fear and reverence than we show to our own God.

Friar Diego Duran, 1576-1579

The ancients lived in a universe animated by many gods—the sun, moon, Venus (the famous god Quetzalcoatl), rain, wind, earth, and fire were among the most important. This universe was perceived to be under the constant threat of destruction. Four worlds had existed before the one the ancients lived in, and each had suffered cataclysmic destruction: the first, by devouring jaguars; the second, by hurricanes; the third, by volcanic eruptions; and the fourth, by floods. The fifth world was to be destroyed as well, but by earthquakes. The only question was when. The cycles of death and rebirth repeated themselves in personal lives (for there was always the chance of an afterlife), in the life-giving cycle of the sun that set each night into the dangerous underworld where it struggled to be reborn the next day, and in the alternation of the cropless dry season and the fertile wet season of each year.

The ancients had much to fear. Unless they propitiated the gods and performed ceremonies to avert disaster, the rains could fail, the sun could set never to rise again, and earthquakes could destroy all. Although religious ceremonies were often gay, filled with dancing and music, they also involved personal sacrifices ranging from fasting and bloodletting (*"You are to pierce your tongue...with a maguey thorn and through the same hole you will pass twigs..."*—Sahagun) to death in the form of human sacrifice. All ancient Mesoamericans, not just the Aztecs, practiced human sacrifice to some degree, even to the point of conducting war only to gather captives for sacrifices. Without human sacrifice, the ancients believed the sun would die and the cosmos would end.

REGIONAL CULTURES

Despite the important similarities among cultures throughout ancient Mesoamerica, their diversity is even more striking. Temporal horizons differ from the earliest Olmec civilization with its massive stone sculptures, to the Classic period with its monumental religious centers, to the increasingly secular and militaristic cultures of the Post-Classic period. Even within the temporal horizons, there are great regional variations because at no time did any one culture control all of Mesoamerica. The greatest contrasts can be found between the highland and lowland cultures. Highland cultures like the Aztecs and their predecessors at Teotihuacan tended toward large centralized states, while the lowland cultures had more numerous, but smaller, cities. For example, at the height of Teotihuacan only a few other important sites shared the central highland area, but during the same period in the lowland Maya area there were approximately 300 centers. The art styles of these two areas also reflect their differences. The highland style is rectilinear and stylized with repetitive ritualistic scenes; the lowland style is softer, more naturalistic, and highly individualistic. So distinctive are these styles that everyone seems to choose between them, either favoring the human portraits of the lowlands or the power expressed in highland art. Even within the highland and lowland regions there is so much diversity that the visitor to many ruins is rewarded each time with something striking and new.

The cultural diversity of Mexico can be bewildering until one travels through the country visiting ruins and museums. For this reason, the development of various cultures and their special characteristics are discussed in the regional chapters where, after you sample the local sights, the descriptions will make more sense. For example, the Mixtecs and Zapotecs are discussed under Oaxaca; the Toltecs and Aztecs under Central Mexico; the Tarascans under Michoacan; the Olmec, Central Gulf Coast; the southern lowland Maya, Chiapas; and the northern lowland Maya, the Yucatán and Quintana Roo. For further information, check the headings listed for the individual cultures, like "Aztec" or "Mixtec."

MEXICAN HISTORY

Diego Rivera mural, National Palace, Mexico City

Events throughout Mexican history have caught the imagination of people around the world. The drama of the encounter between the Old and New Worlds embodied in the Spanish conquest of the **Aztecs** still nurtures best-sellers; the tragic figures of **Emperor Maximilian** and his wife Carlota have inspired romantic novels; and the quiet dignity of the peasant rebel **Emiliano Zapata** has been immortalized in Hollywood movies. Mexico, too, is inspired by its history and takes pride in those heroes and martyrs who symbolize national aspirations and the uniqueness of its culture. Yet Mexico's perspective on historical events may surprise many. **Cortes** may be a hero in Spain, but in Mexico he is viewed as an interloper and destroyer of ancient civilizations. Not one statue commemorates him in all the land, although many commemorate the heroism of Aztec rulers who fought him. While Maximilian is considered a kindly figure and is tolerated, he, too, was a foreigner on Mexican soil. The real Mexican hero is **Benito Juárez**, who defeated the French and had Maximilian assassinated. Maximilian may have constructed the elegant avenue of the Reforma in Mexico City, but it is named after the Reforms instituted by Juárez. Emiliano Zapata, however, is a true Mexican hero, symbolizing the progress made in Mexico's Revolution of 1910. His statues can be found in most towns, and his white-clad figure can be identified in hundreds of historic murals that adorn the walls of Mexico's public buildings.

Any traveler in Mexico is constantly reminded of its heroes and history. Ruins of pre-Hispanic civilizations are everywhere, as are the towns neatly arranged by the Spaniards. Street names in the smallest town attempt to record as much history as possible, even to the point of adding a new hero's name to each block—a practice confusing to the traveler but pleasing to local residents. The following summary of Mexican history, along with the regional background sections, is offered with a Mexican perspective in the hope that it will help you better enjoy your travels through this proud country.

CONQUEST

13 August 1521, Tlatelolco—heroically defended by Cuauhtemoc—fell under the power of Hernan Cortes. It was neither a triumph nor a defeat; it was the painful birth of the mestizo nation that is Mexico today.

Plaque on Aztec ruins at Tlatelolco

Ever since Columbus' voyage across the Atlantic in search of a new route to India, Spain had a foothold in the Caribbean—at Cuba, Hispaniola (now Haiti and the Dominican Republic), and other islands. Those islands failed to yield much wealth to Spain and her soldiers of fortune, so Spaniards continued to explore, looking for the fabulous wealth that would reward their efforts. In 1502, Columbus reported seeing a canoe filled with magnificent goods sailing from what is now Honduras to an unknown land called Yucatán. While he didn't live to discover this land himself, other expeditions did find the Yucatán and even ventured to modern-day Veracruz where they learned about the wealthy Aztecs who lived by a lake in the mountains. This news spread rapidly through the Spanish-held islands, leading to the fateful expedition of **Hernan Cortes**. Cortes and his 550 men, 16 horses, attack dogs, and cannon reached the port of Veracruz in 1519. In the next 30 years, they successfully conquered not only the Aztec nation but all of Mexico and Guatemala as well (see chapter on Mexico City).

As well known as these historical facts are, it remains difficult to comprehend how so few individuals conquered so foreign a territory occupied by millions upon millions of people. It is just as hard to fathom the sheer bravado of these conquistadors in undertaking such a mission at all. Cortes, as the leader of the expedition, was crucial to its success. His first action was to destroy the Spanish ships at Veracruz so there could be no thought of retreat. His second step was to inform his men that one ship remained for those who wanted to leave. Then he carefully noted those who showed interest in fleeing—because, in fact, there was no ship. All his men found themselves in a do-or-die situation. And Cortes proved himself to have the cunning, decisiveness, and determination that were to lead them to victory.

SPANISH WEAPONS

The Spaniards were greatly aided by their weapons, which gave them an advantage over the Indians somewhat akin to a nuclear bomb in a conventional war. Against Spanish cannons, the Indians had only their superior numbers. Against Spanish guns, they had arrows; against the steel of Spanish swords, they had obsidian spears. Even Spanish horses and war dogs (greyhounds and mastiffs weighing up to 200 pounds whose yellow eyes "flash fire") horrified the Indians who had seen nothing like them before. One Aztec's impression has been recorded in The Broken Spears:

> These "stags," these "horses," snort and bellow. They sweat a very great deal, the sweat pours from their bodies in streams. The foam from their muzzles drips onto the ground. It spills out in fat drops... They make a loud noise when they run; they make a great din, as if stones were raining on the earth. Then the ground is pitted and scarred where they set down their hooves. It opens wherever their hooves touch it.

Despite the bravery and superior weapons of the Spaniards, their victory resulted from a good deal of luck. Based on Cortes' reports to Spain, so brave were the Indians—willing to hurl themselves in front of cannons and guns on suicide missions—so great were their numbers, they should eventually have repelled their invaders. But the conquistadors fought with the aid of thousands of Indian allies. Cortes was able to form these alliances because he had the good fortune of having translators. Before reaching Veracruz, he had learned of a shipwrecked Spaniard living in Yucatán. Rescuing this individual, **Jeromino de Aguilar**, provided him with one link in his translation chain—from Mayan to Spanish. Still within Maya territory, the Spaniards received a gift of 20 maidens, one of whom was originally from Veracruz. Known as **Malinche**, she spoke Mayan as well as Nahuatl, the language of the Aztecs and central Mexican area. (Malinche has a position in Mexican history comparable to that of Benedict Arnold in ours. Her name is a common Mexican word meaning "traitor." The Spaniards called her Marina.) When Cortes arrived at Veracruz, he therefore brought with him the ability to communicate with the Indians, first through Malinche in Nahuatl, who then translated into Mayan for Aguilar, who then spoke in Spanish to Cortes. Through his interpreters, Cortes learned of the Aztecs' enemies and formed alliances with them that were critical to the success of the Spanish Conquest.

AZTEC KING MOCTEZUMA II

Another aspect of the Spaniards' exceptional good luck was that they arrived during the reign of the Aztec king **Moctezuma II**. All Aztec rulers had been men of action, warlike and often ruthless in their resolution to create and maintain the empire—all, that is, except Moctezuma. He was a reflective man, often considering the subtleties of a situation so much that he became indecisive. In the case of the Spaniards, he was unable to judge whether these strangers, "their skin white, as if it were made of lime," were enemies to be defeated or representatives of gods to be honored. Pending his final decision, he ordered his people to offer the Spaniards hospitality and showered them with gifts of gold and gems, only making the Europeans greedier and more determined. By the time the conquistadors arrived at the Aztec capital of **Tenochtitlan**, they had barely been tested in battle but had arranged alliances with the Aztecs' enemies. Once the Aztecs did fight, the Spaniards were nearly destroyed. Only the support of Indian allies allowed the Spanish to survive and, eventually, to defeat the mightiest kingdom in ancient Mexico. Other battles lay ahead in other parts of Mexico, but the Conquest was for all intents and purposes a foregone conclusion with the fall of Tenochtitlan. As Cortes wrote to Charles V of Spain:

> *...I am desirous that your Majesty should know of matters concerning this land which is so great and marvelous that...your Majesty may well call himself Emperor of it with no less reason and title than he now does of Germany, which by the Grace of God your Majesty possesses.*

The land of the Aztecs and Mayas had become the first great New World province and was called New Spain.

COLONIAL PERIOD (1521-1810)

Mexico was conquered by individual soldiers of fortune seeking "to serve God and the King and also to get rich," but it was the Spanish bureaucracy that was to govern the new colony. Spain's task was awesome. It was not possible simply to overwhelm the new land by sending settlers when Spain's own population was less than 8 million in 1519, whereas the population of central Mexico alone has been estimated at 20 million. (The Spanish Crown's total eventual possessions in the New World were 40 times the size of Spain.) Even communication between the mother country and the colony was minimal. The Spanish galleon, providing the only trade beween the two, sailed only once a year, and its arrival was always subject to the whims of French and English pirates.

CONVERSION TO CHRISTIANITY

Spain's progress in Mexico during the first half of the 16th century was remarkable and in some ways admirable. While the Crown issued a slew of regulations governing nearly every aspect of life (including the layout of all towns into main plazas and grid streets, which still is the hallmark of Mexican villages), economic activity bustled with the arrival of all manner of Old World animals and plants—horses and cattle, citrus trees and wheat. In the Pacific, Manila was discovered, and a trade route with the Orient was established via Acapulco. Franciscan, Dominican, and Augustinian friars arrived to educate and convert the Indians to Christianity, and by 1537 the Church claimed to have converted 9 million.

The colonial history of Mexico is inseparable from the role of the Church. Spain's interference in the New World was considered justified by the need to convert heathens to Christianity. Spain assumed this role with the blessing of the pope and a good deal of idealism. It was hoped that through education and protective laws the Indians would mature into loyal Spanish subjects equal to her other citizens. The first friars approached their responsibilities with enthusiasm, often traveling to the remotest corners of the empire to bring Christianity and solace to the defeated Indians. They investigated the land and its peoples and produced scholarly studies that have provided the modern world with a wealth of information on ancient beliefs. They also founded schools for the education of Indians. In **Tlatelolco**, the Church founded a college for teaching Indian nobles Latin and theology. Soon the capable Indians were instructing sons of the conquistadors in Latin and writing their own books on the history of their people.

12,000 CHURCHES

While the institution of the Inquisition in the latter part of the 16th century had a chilling effect on the friars' scholarship and the intellectual life of the colony, the importance of the Church still left the most lasting imprint on Mexico. In three centuries, 12,000 churches were constructed in New Spain. Over the years, they reflected changing European styles—from Renaissance, baroque, rococo, to neoclassical. But this imprint had Mexican variations as Indian sculptors and painters infused the architecture with their own innovations. The 18th-century Churrigueresque style, with its wealth of ornamentation more exuberant than baroque, and beyond even rococo, can only be described as Mexican. The local materials of the country created regional differences that today give cities their distinctive character—the capital with its reddish volcanic stone contrasting with white limestone trim; Oaxaca's pale green; Guanajuato and San Miguel with their rose tones; and Puebla, brilliant in hand-painted tiles. This architectural legacy pervades the smallest village and the largest city in Mexico today.

Unfortunately, the friars' initial idealism and respect for the Indians was not to last as long as their churches. Economic demands created practices that enslaved the Indians. During the 16th century, millions of Indians died. Some died from abuse, some from social dislocation, but most died from European diseases—smallpox, measles, and typhoid—for which they had no immunity. In one of the most catastrophic population declines in world history, only one and a half million Indians survived in central Mexico in 1610 compared to 20 million in 1519. More conservative estimates consider the decline throughout Mexico to have been at least 80%. As the numbers of Spaniards increased in proportion to the Indian population, the demands on the Indians for labor and tribute grew to abusive proportions.

The survival of the colony depended on Indian labor—for church construction, farming and mining. Spaniards certainly didn't expect to work—because they had come to the New World to become gentlemen of leisure. Thus, whatever endeavor Spaniards embarked upon, Indians became their unwilling companions, often beaten and locked up so they couldn't escape their forced labor.

> *It is the custom for all owners of haciendas, workshops, estancias, and drovers to sell their workers along with their establishments.—What? Are these Indian workers free or slave?*

Jeronimo de Mendieta, 1595-1596

(as translated by Stein and Stein)

Needing Indians only to support them and produce their profits, the Spaniards had no interest in their treatment as human beings, nor in their preparation to become loyal Spanish subjects. The college at Tlateloco was closed, and most of the early schools were converted into schools for "whites." By the end of the 18th century, there were only ten primary schools in all of Mexico. Kindly friars were replaced by priests who charged fees for marriages and baptisms, exacting their own tribute from the Indian population. The clergy grew wealthy from their fees and land holdings yet returned nothing in the way of care to the Indians. Most villages saw a priest once or twice a year, if that.

> *The color, the ignorance, and the misery of the Indians put them at an infinite distance from the Spaniards.*

Manuel Abad y Queipo to Charles IV
(as translated by Charles Cumberland)

Spain's economic policies exploited not only the Indians, but the entire nation. Everything was overregulated, overtaxed, and monopolized by the mother country. While this benefited Spain, it did little to develop the colony itself. Trade with other nations was banned, and the colony was forbidden to grow items that competed with Spain. Those items that were allowed were mostly raw products that were sent to Spain to be converted into finished goods and then sold back to the colony at outrageously high prices. Such practices prevented the development of Mexico's self-sufficiency and manufacturing capability.

By the end of the 18th century, Mexico was the most prosperous of Spain's holdings. Her taxes, silver, cochineal dye, sugar, tobacco, and other goods constituted three-quarters of all of Spain's profits from her colonies. Most of these profits went directly to Spain or to less prosperous colonies to pay for their administration. Little was invested in New Spain itself. Mexico's roads, bridges, and ports were next to nonexistent. Commerce was so hindered that agricultural surpluses in one part of Mexico couldn't be sent to a nearby area that was subject to drought. And, upon Independence, Mexico found herself bereft of basic structures for economic survival.

> *The world's trade flourishes at the expense of the peoples of America and their immense labors, but the riches they draw from the bosom of the fertile earth are not retained.*

Memoir to Viceroy of Mexico, 1723
(as translated by Stein and Stein)

By the end of the colonial period, Mexican society was stratified according to race. At the very bottom of society were the Indians, constituting over half of Mexico's 6 million people. Next were the mestizos, those of mixed Indian and Spanish ancestry who were denied the privilege of white society and prevented from living in Indian communities. Many mestizos became ranchers in remote parts of the country; a few were allowed into the lower echelons of the clergy; others became foremen and skilled laborers; and many were simply homeless and half-naked beggars and bandits. Next came the approximately one million creoles, white Spaniards born in Mexico who, for that reason, were suspected of disloyalty and racial taint. Creoles were quite wealthy, yet they were prevented from holding the most responsible positions in government and the Church. At the very highest echelon of society were the peninsulars, born in Spain and of undoubted white parentage and loyalty to the mother country. They were denied nothing.

In the 20th century, Mexico was to become a truly mestizo country, where the whitest of skin would still boast of Indian blood. But as Mexico entered the 19th century, it seethed with discontent and divisiveness. Creoles were angry at the arrogance of the peninsulars; Indians and mestizos patiently awaited their moment for revenge. Spain's legacies of racism and underdevelopment were to plague Mexico for the century to come.

INDEPENDENCE (1810-1822)

Inspired by the American and French Revolutions, Mexicans dreamed of their own independence and enlightened political and social policies. Creoles dominated the commercial and social life of Mexican cities. Enriched by their farms and mines, the creoles believed they would be wealthier without Spain's monopolies and taxation policies. They wanted to govern their own country but were prevented by Spain from doing so. As the creoles agitated for reforms, Spain grew more conservative, fearful that any change would precipitate a revolution. Its conservative policies backfired. On September 16, 1810, the priest of a small parish, **Father Hidalgo**, proclaimed Mexico's independence from Spain with the support of the creole population (see Silver Cities chapter).

Hidalgo's parishioners were mestizos and Indians who had their own grievances against Spain. Degraded for the color of their skin and practically enslaved by both peninsulars and creoles, they wanted their own land and an end to their political oppression. Hidalgo's call to battle galvanized them into action. While the creoles had started the revolution, the massive armies of mestizos and Indians soon set their own course. They fought battles throughout the north and won them, yet in the course of these fights they massacred many peninsulars, and even creoles. They expropriated haciendas—of both peninsulars and creoles. Royalists fought back with equal ferocity and brutality, and they soon were joined by frightened creoles. By 1811, the original creole leaders of independence such as Hidalgo had been shot and others had recanted their positions. The masses were now on their own.

A new leader emerged, who by 1813 had overtaken most of Mexico. **Jose Maria Morelos** was a mestizo priest recruited to the cause by Father Hidalgo. Unlike Father Hidalgo, however, he was a military and political genius. With the assistance of generals who ranged from students and peasants to Indian chieftains such as Julian I, emperor of the Huasteca, fighters were organized into effective guerrilla bands that the Royalists had difficulty combating. At one point, only Mexico City, Puebla, and Veracruz remained outside Morelos' control of the south of Mexico. To govern the freed territory, Morelos called a constitutional convention where he espoused universal suffrage, representational government, racial equality, and the distribution of unused lands to those who would work them.

> *Spirits of Moctezuma, Cacamitzin, Cuahtemoc Xicotencatl, Calzontzin! Take pride in this august assembly and celebrate this happy moment in which your sons have congregated to avenge your insults! After August 12, 1521, comes September 8, 1813! The first date tightened the chains of our slavery in Mexico-Tenochtitlan; the second broke them forever…We are therefore going to restore a Mexican Empire.*

Jose Maria Morelos, 1813
(as translated by Charles Cumberland)

While Morelos' proposals were in the spirit of the French Revolution and later liberal reforms in Europe under Napoleon, most creoles and all peninsulars in Mexico were horrified, believing such reforms threatened their positions in society. Unfortunately for Morelos and the thousands who followed him, the Spanish Royalist forces grew increasingly successful against them. Morelos was executed in 1815, and by 1816 most of the remaining leaders had suffered so many defeats that they had retreated to inaccessible parts of the country, no longer able to fight.

In 1820, the creoles again agreed independence was necessary. Spain, under Napoleon, had instituted a liberal constitutional government that set about doing in Spain some of the very things espoused by Morelos. In fear that such reforms would be passed from the mother country to its colony, the creoles staged a coup. In 1822,

Mexico finally gained its independence from Spain, but with none of the social reforms hoped for by the masses who had fought in the war.

YEARS OF CHAOS (1822-1867)

Mexican hopes that independence would bring a modernized economy, democratic government, and social equality were not realized in the next century. Spaniards were replaced by the creoles in government, and the Spanish crown was replaced by Mexico's very own **Emperor Iturbide**. Mexico's social problems remained the same as in preceding centuries, and its economy was completely devastated. Years of civil strife destroyed the haciendas and ruined the silver mines. Men who had fought in the armies returned to their homes to find no work. Nearly 20% of the adult male population had absolutely no income. These problems were further compounded by foreign invasions and political chaos.

Emperor Iturbide survived in office a mere 11 months before a military coup by **Santa Anna** set the pace for the years to come. While Santa Anna himself was to be president 11 times, there were a total of 56 different governments formed in the next 40 years. The government, unable to address economic concerns amid such turmoil, was bankrupt. Mexico's internal weakness attracted foreign intervention: Spain, still hopeful of regaining its largest colony, sent expeditions against it and, in 1829, invaded; France captured Veracruz in 1838 with the excuse that the Mexican government owed money to one of its pastry chefs; and the United States agitated to take over the northern part of the country. France finally installed in Mexico City its own choice of monarch, the **Emperor Maximilian**. By 1850, Mexico had lost half its territory to the United States, faced a civil war over the role of the Church in government, and had had to contend with an invasion from France. Not until 1867 was Mexico able peacefully to implement some of the goals of the new republic.

AMERICAN INTERVENTION

While most schoolchildren in the United States are taught about the heroism of Davy Crockett and Jim Bowie at The Alamo and the atrocities committed by Santa Anna, less attention is paid to the subsequent invasion of Mexico by U.S. troops. After Mexico tried to retain control of Texas in the battle of **The Alamo** in 1836, its president Santa Anna was captured by **Sam Houston**. To regain his freedom, Santa Anna agreed to grant Texas independence from Mexico. While

Mexicans were outraged by Santa Anna's singularly self-serving act, Texas remained independent as the Lone Star Republic until the United States voted to annex it in 1845. Mexico, still bankrupt and in political turmoil, tried initially to avoid a confrontation and agreed to negotiate with the United States on the status of Texas. But the United States was in an expansionist mood and had re-defined Texan territory to include most of New Mexico, Colorado, and California. Unwilling to lose so much territory, Mexico sent troops to secure it. Claiming its territory had been invaded, the United States declared war and sent troops to battle along its newly defined borders in the west.

These battles were won easily by the Americans, but the Mexicans were still unwilling to sign a treaty. More troops were sent to capture Mexico City itself. Americans landed in **Veracruz**, where they set about barbarously shelling everyone in the port city, killing twice as many civilians—including women and children—as soldiers. After this victory, the U.S. forces headed toward Mexico City where the last battle of this invasion was fought in **Chapultepec Park.** After 2000 Mexicans and 700 Americans were killed, only the military col-lege at Chapultepec Castle remained to be conquered for total American victory. On September 13, 1847, a thousand Mexican sol-diers and cadets died in battle rather than surrender. A treaty was signed that granted the United States Mexico's territory above the Rio Grande—half of the original Mexico. In return, Mexico received $18 million—less than half its annual budget. The loss of territory was devastating, yet that territory had never been densely settled or strongly controlled by Mexico. The humiliation of the invasion and defeat by the United States, a neighbor Mexico had admired and hoped to emulate in its development, was far more serious. Today, Mexico remembers the heroism of the young cadets (known as **"Ninos Heroes"**) every September 13th. They are immortalized in street names and monuments throughout Mexico, but no monu-ment is more impressive than the one erected near Chapultepec Cas-tle in Mexico City where it is said one of the cadets fell to his death, wrapped in a Mexican flag.

REFORM PERIOD (1855-1861)

The Reform Period is mostly associated with Mexico's revered president, **Benito Juarez**. Raised and educated by a Franciscan priest, Juarez best exemplifies the conflicts that existed in Mexico between devout Catholic citizens and their political concerns about the Church—concerns that were to result in civil war during this period.

Juarez was a pure Zapotec Indian, born in a Oaxacan village and orphaned at the age of three. At the age of 12, speaking no Spanish, he walked 47 miles to the city of Oaxaca to seek work. Fortunate enough to be taken in by the friar, he received education and sustenance in exchange for household chores. Despite his devotion to the generous friar and despite his Catholic unbringing, Juarez later used his education in law and his political career to control the role of the Church in Mexican politics.

The Church owned half the real property in Mexico, most of which lay fallow and outside the Mexican economy; its ample income was at least five times larger than the government's. Wealthier than the state, the Church was also more powerful, with total control of education, registry functions of recording births and deaths, and controlling marriages and burials. Yet, the Church used its wealth and power against every attempt at political and social change in Mexico and even failed adequately to perform its mandated functions. Such was the Church's attitude toward education that fewer than 5% of school-age children attended school. In performing the sacraments, the Church charged such high fees (five months of a peasant's income for baptism or last rites) that few could receive them, and some couldn't even be buried.

In some ways, the United States invasion of Mexico precipitated the Reform Period. The Church had refused to lend the government funds to fight the invading Americans, proving itself disloyal in the eyes of many. The invasion contributed to the patriotism of a growing middle class of doctors, lawyers, and writers—including Benito Juarez—who dedicated themselves to formulating a new direction for Mexico. Overthrowing Santa Anna in one of the most popular movements since Independence, they instituted a constitutional democracy, promulgated freedom of education, freedom of speech and the press, and passed reform laws aimed at separating church and state.

The Church opposed all these changes. Freedom of education, it said, interfered with its God-given right to instruct; freedom of speech allowed blasphemy; and reform laws depriving the Church of its properties and income destroyed its dignity and splendor. When the new government insisted that the Church sell all properties not used in its daily operations, the Church responded by threatening excommunication to anyone purchasing those properties. When the government insisted that all civil servants take an oath in support of the new constitution, the Church promised excommunication to anyone who did so. The conflicts between church and state escalated to the point of rebellion, then to civil war.

WAR OF THE REFORMS

The civil war, called the **War of the Reforms**, lasted three terrible years and bitterly involved everyone in Mexico. Conservatives shot doctors who administered to liberal, reformist soldiers; liberals shot priests who refused them the sacraments, and churches were sacked and stripped of gilded ornaments. With each conservative victory, the liberals promulgated more severe reform laws. In 1861, the Reformers had won the final battles. Reentering Mexico City with their president Benito Juarez, the liberal reformers nationalized all church properties, closed monasteries and convents, authorized civil marriages and burials, and established reasonable fees for the sacraments. As a priest later explained to the American writer John Reed, "God is good. But He is better in Spain than He is in Mexico."

At least temporarily, Mexico had successfully established a constitutional government, separating the powers of church and state. But the Church, with its military and conservative supporters, had one more move to make. It encouraged France to invade Mexico and establish a monarchy that would recognize the autonomy of the Church. Benito Juarez was to spend four years in exile before he was able to return and serve as Mexico's president from 1867 to 1872. From that time, the Reform Laws of Mexico became a permanent part of Mexican government. Even today, priests or nuns can't be seen in their habits in the streets of Mexico, for such display by the Church is forbidden. Yet, Mexico remains a most Catholic country.

EMPEROR MAXIMILIAN (1862-1867)

Ravaged by war, its treasury more bankrupt than ever, its bridges and roads in a state of disrepair, its countryside plagued by hordes of bandits, Mexico was exhausted. Perhaps a few years of peace would have enabled Juarez to restore the country, but peace was not to be had. To bring order to the economy, Juarez had suspended payment on foreign debts for two years. England and Spain, outraged by the destruction of their citizens' property during the wars, decided to exact payment. France, courted by conservative Mexican clerics and exiles, had more grandiose dreams. **Napoleon III** had been led to believe that French forces would be embraced by the Mexican people, and Mexican exiles had assured him Mexico had plenty of money to pay its debts and to pay for the cost of a French expedition. Dreaming of Cortes' conquest, Napoleon III thought he might enrich himself by such an endeavor. Joining **Queen Isabela II** and **Queen Victoria**, he sent ships to occupy Veracruz.

In January of 1862, naval vessels from all three countries seized Veracruz. England and Spain soon realized that France was after more than repayment of its debt when French ships continued to arrive at the port. Not wishing to be involved in an aggression so clearly illegal, these two nations withdrew in April. Mexican conservatives encouraged the French to occupy the city of **Puebla**, where, they said, a joyful reception would be given by the devout population. Instead, on May 5th, the Mexicans defeated the French at Puebla, forcing their retreat and killing over 1,000 of their troops. This was the last victory for the Mexicans until 1867. Napoleon III, realizing he had been duped as to his Mexican reception, sent 300,000 more troops to Mexico in order to save face. A huge French army was hardly necessary because the Mexicans were too exhausted to fight, and Juarez fled with his cabinet to the north of Mexico and the American border. Mexico now belonged to France.

Conservative Mexicans returned from Europe to reclaim their properties, clerics looked forward to the repeal of the Reform Laws and the return of their land, and Napoleon III continued to dream of the golden opportunities Mexico afforded. All that was needed to satisfy everyone's greed was an emperor of royal blood. Napoleon III asked Archduke Maximilian of Austria to become emperor of Mexico. He accepted.

Maximilian and his wife **Carlota**, princess of Belgium, have inspired a number of romantic novels, but they created only disappointment for those who sought their arrival in Mexico. Maximilian, despite his Catholicism and royal blood, dreamed of creating a just Mexican society in which the noble savages would no longer be oppressed. He actually toyed with the idea of democracy, and one of his first acts was to refuse to repeal the Reform Laws, even after receiving a papal order to do so. As agreeable as his ideas were—to Juaristas if not the conservatives—Maximilian had no practical or leadership experience to enable him to implement them, particularly in turbulent Mexico. Maximilian prepared for his rule by writing a 600-page volume on court etiquette during his voyage to Mexico. But he spent his first night in Mexico City sleeping on a billiard table to avoid vermin in the palace.

As ill-prepared as Maximilian was for the reality of governing Mexico, still he came to love its spectacular scenery and flowers and was fascinated by its Indian peasants. He and Carlota dressed in Mexican clothes, walked among the people and ate Mexican food—all to prove their commitment to this strange country, now their empire. The Mexicans were too exhaused to resist the new sovereigns, and Juarez was too broke to develop an army to overthrow them—until 1865, when everything changed.

Napoleon III had chosen a good moment for intervention in Mexico because the United States was preoccupied with its own civil war. In 1865, however, the American Civil War was over, and the United States informed France that it would not accept a French presence on Mexican soil. Juarez suddenly became well supplied and prepared an army near the American border. Napoleon III, under pressure from his own people and facing a growing Prussian menace, decided to withdraw, but not before 1867. At the same time, Maximilian, following the advice of some conservative advisors, allowed the execution of some Mexican patriots and found himself despised by his beloved subjects.

The conclusion of the **French Intervention** was decided in 1865, but the tragedy of Maximilian and Carlota continued to evolve. Carlota, encouraging Maximilian not to abdicate the throne, determined to persuade Napoleon III and the pope to support him. She set off for Europe, was beset by robbers on the road to Veracruz, was resisted by an ailing Napoleon III, and was informed by the pope that Maximilian had only himself to blame. After so much rejection, this frail princess went insane and never returned to Mexico. Maximilian decided not to abdicate and joined his army at **Queretaro** to fight Juarez' troops. Although he was given a number of opportunities to escape safely by the Juaristas, he refused them. He was executed in 1867.

DICTATORSHIP OF PORFIRIO DIAZ (1876-1910)

As painful as Mexico's progress had been during the 19th century, at least the country found itself with a constitutional and democratic government when Benito Juarez died in 1872. Progress had been achieved in the separation of religious and civil authority; a little improvement occurred in education; and, after the French Intervention, Mexico became a more unified nation. But masses of people remained destitute and illiterate; bandits continued to plague the abominable roads of the Republic; and the economy had not been modernized. True, the first railroad had been completed between Veracruz and Mexico City, but most commerce was carried on the backs of mules or humans. Technology in mining and agriculture remained practically the same as during the 16th century, with even metal nails a luxury. And, of course, the government still was bankrupt. Under the next 34 years of Diaz' dictatorship, social problems worsened and democracy became a charade, yet the economy developed enormously.

By the time Mexico celebrated its 100 years of Independence in 1910, the country had been transformed. Cities boasted broad avenues, trolley cars, and opera houses. Twelve thousand miles of railroad track crisscrossed the country; telegraph lines and telephones connected cities; and 24 modernized ports supported a lively international trade. Mining boomed and oil rigs were erected with foreign technology; and new factories—textile, paper, and steel mills, sugar refineries, and cement and beer plants—doubled the amount of manufactured goods produced in Mexico. Foreign debt was serviced, and the government treasury consistently showed a surplus.

Delegations from all over the world joined Porfirio Diaz in celebrating Mexico's centennial and the dictator's eightieth birthday. They remarked on the stability of the country, its absence of crime and banditry, and its natural beauty. Wealthy Mexicans, dressed in the latest Parisian fashions, showed off their new sophistication by presenting plays in French and exhibiting Spanish art. Over 20 million pesos were spent by the government on entertainment (20 carloads of champagne were consumed at a single ball). All believed that Mexico had found its place in the upper echelons of international society and that the future would bring only further prosperity and glory to the young country. Having failed to look beyond the glitter of this new society, few could imagine that Diaz would be exiled seven months later.

STRONG CONTROL

The key to so much progress had been stability. **Porfirio Diaz**, born in the same state of Oaxaca as was Benito Juarez, made his way in politics through the military rather than the law. By the time he assumed power, he was famous for his heroism in the War of the Reforms, in the defeat of the French at Puebla, and for his successful guerrilla activity during Maximilian's regime. No stranger to the use of force, Diaz spent one-fourth of the annual budget on the armed forces—forces used for domestic pacification. His strong control not only ended banditry, but also terrorized peasants throughout Mexico and silenced any voices of dissent.

There are no drunken riots… little thieving…The least disorderly action, even loud talking in the streets, causes prompt arrest …

J. Hendrickson McCarty, 1888

The modernization of Mexico's economy was accomplished through foreign investments and ownership. Diaz' regime gave such favorable terms to foreigners that wealthy investors flocked to Mexico. Believing its own Indians inherently lazy and worthless, Mexico created an immigration policy encouraging foreigners to settle in Mexico. Land was offered at cheap prices, citizenship was easily obtained, and taxes on investments were reduced. While few immigrants arrived to labor in the factories or fields (Mexican wages were too low), many came to seek their fortunes. The **Guggenheim** family from the United States invested $12 million in Mexico and owned gold and silver mines all over the country as well as their own smelting plant. Yet the preferential treatment afforded foreigners rankled many Mexicans, and the racist attitude of the Diaz dictatorship toward the majority of Mexicans resulted in policies that were to destroy it. Regis Planchet wrote in 1906: "The North American, the foreigner, has prospered in Mexico, but not its own sons." (Quoted by Charles Cumberland.)

Some Mexicans, however, did prosper during this time. Diaz ordered a survey of Mexican lands and the sale of all vacant properties to provide income to the government. Villagers found their traditional communal lands declared vacant. No complaining to the courts corrected these abuses—in some instances, peasants were actually fined for their audacity. While peasant farmers were deprived of their livelihood, large landholders grew richer, as did government dignitaries. One minister appropriated 5,000 acres for himself in Yucatán, and the governor of Veracruz helped his friends take over the lands of numerous villages. The Terrazas family in Chihuahua came to own approximately 7 million acres. By the end of Diaz' term, over 134 million acres had been expropriated from peasants and less than 2% of the total population owned all the land. Those peasants who were able to hold on to their land found themselves surrounded by large haciendas that cut off their water supplies in order to force them out. The owners of so much land seldom worked it. When they did, they cultivated export crops–sugar, coffee, sisal for rope, and beef—which brought them great personal profits. The few grew unbelievably wealthy; the mass of Mexicans faced starvation.

PEASANT WAGES

In order to survive, peasants were forced to work on haciendas. Their plight differed little from the growing labor force of factory workers. All worked 7 days a week for 11 to 12 hours each day. Peasant wages were the same as they had been at the beginning of the 19th century; laborers' wages had declined since the turn of the century, although their expenses for staples like corn had doubled. To make matters worse, peasants and laborers alike were often paid in chits that could be used only in the company or hacienda store where controlled prices were inflated. Being illiterate, peasants couldn't check their bills and often found themselves in debt. Under debt peonage, the peasant became enslaved to the hacienda owners and was unable to leave legally; and his children inherited the debt to ensure their enslavement, too. By forcing employees to spend their salaries in company stores, hacienda and factory owners made profits and, in effect, had free labor.

After 50 years of war and devastation, it is hard to believe that any Mexican would want war again. Yet as Emiliano Zapata would say, "It is better to die on your feet than to live on your knees." A hundred years after Independence and Morelos' call for social equality in Mexico, the majority of Mexicans had less than half the amount of corn and beans to eat that they had in 1810. Malnourished, living in unsanitary shacks without water, they suffered disease upon disease. At a time when the average life span in the United States was 50 years, it was 30 in Mexico. Nearly half of all children died before the age of one. Simply to clothe themselves, it took Mexican laborers and peasants 12 times as many work hours to afford cloth as their counterparts in the United States.

The official response of Diaz to these problems was that the poor themselves were to blame. They were dirty (a bar of soap would cost 25% of their income), lazy (after working 12 hours each day, peasants would try to work a plot of land for themselves in the night), and ignorant (almost all schools were in the cities and accessible only to the upper classes). The following description of social contrasts between the super rich and the super poor in Mexico was written by Francisco Pimental in 1865 (as quoted in Meyer and Sherman).

> *The white dresses like a Parisian fashion plate and uses the richest of fabrics; the Indian runs almost naked. The white lives in cities in magnificent houses; the Indian is isolated in the country, his house a miserable hut. They are two different peoples in the same land; but worse, to a degree they are enemies.*

By 1910, the contrasts had worsened, and the poor had lost their only means of survival—their land.

REVOLUTION (1910-1920)

The Revolution...was an explosion of reality.

Octavio Paz

Marlon Brando immortalized the revolutionary hero **Emiliano Zapata** in *Viva Zapata!*, and other movies captured the bandit spirit of **Pancho Villa**. But these leaders of the peasant rebellion didn't precipitate the Revolution of 1910. Much like the Independence Movement, the Revolution started with demands from the middle class for governmental reforms. It was **Francisco Madero**, a latter-day Father Hidalgo, who called for political reforms in 1910, thereby galvanizing the poor to fight.

FRANCISCO MADERO

Young lawyers and intellectuals argued that Diaz, then 80 years old, should allow the free election of a vice-president so that a smooth transition could occur upon the dictator's death. Incapable of yielding his control, Diaz instead appointed a corrupt governor from the north who had made his fortune selling Indians into slavery. No one dared contest his decision—no one except the relatively unknown Francisco Madero who decided to run against Diaz for the presidency in 1910. Campaigning for political freedom and no reelection for Diaz, Madero soon had an enthusiastic following. During the centennial celebrations, Diaz imprisoned him, but later Madero was able to escape to Texas where he proclaimed himself provisional president. The time for challenging Diaz was ripe, and revolutionary armies blossomed overnight. By May 1910, the rebellion was so successful that Porfirio Diaz fled to Paris.

Madero marched into Mexico City bringing with him the new epoch that the majority of Mexicans wanted. He was elected president under the most open conditions Mexico had ever experienced, and he fulfilled his promises for freedom of the press and assembly, even allowing workers to organize into unions. But Madero, like Hidalgo, did not fully understand the forces that had brought him to power. Though democracy and freedom were fine, they didn't satisfy peasant demands for land reform. As Madero gradually realized that economic change was necessary, he faced a new problem—one that was to be fatal. His own **General Huerta** plotted a coup with the cooperation of the American Ambassador (who was concerned to protect business investments in Mexico). In 1913, Madero was tortured and shot, and with his death, Mexico's relative peace again vanished.

Ambition will ruin itself,
And justice will be the winner
For Villa has reached Torreon
To punish the avaricious

"Soldiers' Song," as reported by John Reed

Two armies of the north and south that had brought Madero to power emerged again to defeat Madero's assassin and Mexico's new president, General Huerta. **Emiliano Zapata**, as general of the south, was less concerned as to who ruled from Mexico City—Madero's presidency had shown him the futility of politics—then he was to reclaim peasants' land. Calling for the immediate redistribution of property and fighting under the banner of "*Tierra y Libertad*" (Land and Liberty), Zapata led his soldiers, all dressed in sandals, sombreros, and the traditional white clothes of peasants, to the haciendas—where they expropriated their former properties and set about tilling the land. Once they had reacquired their land, they fought only when invaded. **Pancho Villa**, the most famous general of the north, represented the arid regions where huge cattle ranches, rather than farms, predominated. His army was composed of cowboys and former cattle rustlers like himself. Villa's gratuitous violence and rapid mood changes frightened most leaders and citizens, but as an escapee from debt peonage he understood the underlying issues of the revolution. When he occupied towns, he set his soldiers to distributing land to the poor. Flamboyant in war and love (once he attempted to abduct a hotel cashier, and almost precipitated an international incident because she was a French citizen), Villa was not destined to become president of Mexico. Nor was the more thoughtful and clear-sighted Zapata. But these two men forced the basic issues of land reform and social change that led to the most important accomplishments of the Revolution of 1910.

With Carranza's whiskers
I'm going to weave a hat band
To put on the sombrero
Of his better Pancho Villa

"La Cucaracha," revolutionary song

REVOLUTIONARY GENERALS

But Villa and Zapata were far from being the only revolutionary generals. Others like **Obregon** and **Carranza**, both of whom later became president, and hundreds of small-town chiefs joined in the anarchy of the times. Petty chiefs sided with the important generals, and eventually nearly everyone fought everyone. Different money was used in different regions and issued by different armies. Men and boys were conscripted by any passing army. Women, finding themselves alone and fearful of assault, joined the armies as spies or arms smugglers. Others became *soldaderas* ("women soldiers"), slinging a rifle on one shoulder, a child on the other, but most often foraging for food and nursing the wounded. So essential were the women to marching armies—making them look like mass migrations—that federal soldiers threatened not to fight when the government banished women from their troops.

Popular among the troops was Adelita
The woman the sergeant adored
Because she was as brave as she was pretty
So even the colonel respected her.

"Adelita," revolutionary song

Cities burned and their residents faced starvation. By 1920, between 1–1/2 to 2 million people had been killed, one Mexican out of every eight. No one survived unscathed.

While Villa and Zapata found they shared certain ideals—as Villa described it, the other leaders had "always slept on soft pillows"—they found themselves separated from the eventual victors. Obregon first marched into Mexico City; then, in 1916, Carranza became president. The Revolution was still far from over, and violence still ravaged the country until 1920. Carranza became a counterrevolutionary, leading Zapata to write to him (as quoted by Meyer and Sherman):

In the agrarian matter you have given or rented our haciendas to your favorites. The old landholdings...have been taken over by new landlords...and the people mocked in their hopes.

When Obregon defeated Villa in the north, Villa retired to the safety of his home state Chihuahua until the United States agreed to supply Carranza with arms. Outraged that the United States should supply his enemy, Villa turned to attacking Americans. War broke out between Mexicans and Americans along the border, and the United States even sent **General Pershing** into Mexico in search of Villa. American forces finally retreated to the border, having spent $130 million in a futile search for the notorious Villa. Finally, Villa was assassinated in 1923, but by Mexicans, and Zapata was murdered by one of Carranza's generals in 1919. According to an eyewitness account, reported by John Womack, Zapata was shot "at point blank, without giving him time even to draw his pistols, the soldiers who were presenting arms fired two volleys, and our unforgettable General Zapata fell never to rise again."

AFTERMATH OF THE REVOLUTION
(1920-1940)

In 1920, Carranza was ousted from the presidency and the cataclysmic violence of the Revolution subsided. The immediate positive effects of the Revolution were only too few, yet they laid the groundwork for accomplishments that were to be realized in the following decades.

Spiritually, the Revolution resulted in a new Mexican nation. Gone were the days when only Spanish and French cultures were admired, and gone were the years when Mexican history began with the arrival of Spanish civilization. The new Mexico recognized the dignity not only of whites, but of mestizos and Indians, too. Historians searched for ancient roots in pre-Hispanic times, novelists wrote of the harsh realities of Indian life in vernacular Spanish, not French, and musicians were inspired by the revolutionary and folk songs of the people. Intellectuals volunteered to visit factories and villages to teach reading, nutrition, the fundamentals of citizenship, and Mexican history to the poor who had never before been incorporated into the nation. New heroes were idealized in place of European ones—**Madero** symbolized democracy; **Zapata**, the rights of the humble peasant. Nowhere was this new nationalism better expressed then in the vast numbers of murals painted onto the walls of public buildings by the great artists **Diego Rivera**, **David Siqueiros**, and **Jose Clemente Orozco**. And no one better extolled the new Mexican culture than the artist **Frida Kahlo**. Mexico rejoiced in its newfound identity. Today, Mexico still is pervaded by this sense of cultural identity and takes enormous pride in its ancient ruins, traditional crafts, and folk songs from every region. Among all the monuments to Mexican heroes, there is not one of Porfirio Diaz.

Politically, the Revolution resulted in the Constitution of 1917, which guaranteed not only democratic freedoms, but also the return of communal lands to Indian peasants and protections for factory workers. The company store was eliminated, as was peonage. In one respect, the Constitution looked back to Spanish law by recognizing that the nation should control water and subsoil wealth like silver and oil. This law had been lifted during Diaz' dictatorship, which had encouraged foreign investment as well as exploitation. (Oil extracted in Mexico cost more there than it did abroad.) While the new Constitution allowed private interests to lease lands and extract riches from them, it permitted the state to regulate their interests for the public welfare. The subsoil would remain part of the nation's patrimony. As completely as the laws of the Constitution embodied the ideals of the new Mexico, their implementation required many years to achieve.

> *The history of Mexico for the next generation was to be the history of a long struggle to make them a reality; and though progress was to be painfully slow, at times imperceptible, it was to be genuine.*

Henry Bamford Parkes

SUCCESS OF THE REVOLUTION

The two decades after the Revolution were marked by serious efforts to achieve progress—efforts that culminated in the remarkable presidency of **Lazaro Cardenas** (1934-1940). For the first time since 1910, a president was elected without violence, lived throughout his term, and resigned peacefully after six years, in accordance with the Constitution. Not only did Cardenas' presidency mark the end of an era of turbulence, it also symbolized the success of the Revolution.

On all fronts, Cardenas fulfilled the ideals of the Revolution: he distributed more than twice as much land as all his predecessors combined, so that by 1940 one-third of the population owned land in contrast to 2% in 1910; he supported the strengthening of unions, which led to wages that supported the basic needs of workers; and he spent massive amounts of funds for schools and health projects in rural areas. One of his most dramatic actions was to expropriate (with financial compensation) oil fields from foreign investors who had defied an order of Mexico's Supreme Court. While this action created enormous diplomatic difficulties, it enabled Mexico to receive international recognition for its right to insist that all companies operating in Mexico abide by Mexican laws—a simple point, yet hard to achieve because of foreign favoritism of the Diaz epoch.

Cardenas' presidency marked the end of the revolutionary period and provided the basis for the stability of contemporary Mexico. By realizing the goals of the social revolution, he convinced Mexicans that change could be accomplished without bloodshed. By expropriating the oil fields, he laid the framework for more rational foreign investment in Mexico during the next period of economic growth. His personal integrity enhanced respect for the office of the presidency and the Constitution. And last but not least, his profound commitment to improving the lot of the poor led to lasting policies in Mexico that were to result in enormous improvements in the literacy and health of its people. By mid-century, the foundation for modern Mexico had been constructed:

*Within two generations, Mexico produced a sturdy peasantry, which
was a part of the national economy...to take the places of a horde of
peons who knew naught of the nation and cared less.... Peons grown
to maturity within the shackles of a Diaz hacienda saw their sons become national and economic leaders.*

Charles C. Cumberland

MEXICO TODAY

Since the time of Cardenas, Mexico has continued to experience
political stability. Functioning under the Constitution of 1917, presidents have been peacefully (Mexico has one of the lowest ratios of
soldiers to population in Latin America) elected every six years, with
a new president each time since no reelection is permitted. While numerous political parties participate in elections, one party—**PRI, or
Party of the Institutionalized Revolution**—dominates the legislature
and has produced every president since the Revolution. Part of PRI's
control of politics results from its ability to absorb most important
factions within the society, from unions and business interests to
peasant organizations. Evidence of PRI's continuing ability to respond rapidly to new factions was seen in its support of an Equal
Rights Amendment for women, which became law in 1974. The
other part of PRI's near-monopoly on government has resulted from
its access to the mass media. Yet throughout the 1980s there have
been growing pressures for greater openness and diversity in government. At times PRI has responded positively, permitting opposition
candidates to receive considerable TV exposure; at other times it has
resisted change—with subsequent allegations of fraudulent elections. In 1988 the opposition parties were allowed their greatest political gains. The PRI candidate Carlos Salinas de Gotari barely
received 50% of the vote, the first time since 1929 that a Mexican
president has been elected with less than 85%. In the Chamber of
Deputies, the opposition parties gained almost half of the 500 seats.
In the Senate, they were represented for the first time. Whether
Mexico now will move toward greater political diversity, the
one-party system has served the nation well during its transition to a
modern state. Martin C. Needler (1971) has written that "the
one-party system in Mexico has assured peaceful succession to power
while allowing for a large measure of civil freedoms. In itself, this is a
dual system worthy of note in Latin America."

POLITICAL STABILITY AND ECONOMIC PROGRESS

Although Mexico severely suffered from the world recession of
1982, particularly from the drop in the price of oil and the burden of

its foreign debt, its economic growth in prior decades had been tremendous. In 1910, Mexico was basically a rural nation with over 70% of its population living off the land. In 1980, only one-third of the workforce was in agriculture, while the same percentage worked in industry. Mexico's agriculture and mining continue to be an important part of the economy, just as they were during colonial times. But unlike the colonial period, commerce and manufacturing now are the two largest contributors to Mexico's gross national product. Mexico's industrial transformation has resulted not only from oil, but from the manufacture of processed food, automobiles (Volkswagen, Nissan, etc.), chemicals, paper, and tires. The change in the complexity of Mexico's economy can be seen in its major exports, which, a few decades ago, were sugar, coffee, lead, copper, and zinc but now include oil, frozen shrimp, chemical products, automobiles, and electrical machinery. From a country that was practically untouched by the industrial age in 1910, Mexico has grown into a nation crisscrossed by roads—including some superhighways—and dotted with dams for irrigation and electrical power. Even remote rural areas are served by buses and electricity.

The people have greatly benefited from Mexico's political stability and economic progress. The improvements can be seen in the enormous increase in the average life expectancy, which is now 65 rather than the 30 years of 1910. The infant mortality rate has declined from 32 per 100 in 1910 to 5 per 100 in 1986. (These remarkable achievements have led to a population explosion—in 1910 the population was about 15 million, in 1990, nearly 85 million—which the government is now trying to control, with some success, through voluntary birth-control programs.) Education has had its impact, too, with 83% of the population now able to read and write, compared to 25% in 1910. Also, the numbers of Mexicans continuing their education beyond secondary school has increased with the opening of public universities; Mexico now graduates as many doctors per capita as the United States.

INDIAN PEASANTS

While Mexico's middle class has grown (25% of the population in 1991) and the majority of the population enjoys an improved standard of living, millions of Indian peasants still have not been assimilated by the new Mexico. Remaining outside the mainstream of the economy, many speak only their Indian language (less than 4% of the population), own no shoes, and live on the edge of survival. Their situation worsened during the 1980s with Mexico's severe economic problems—debt payments constituting 53% of the government's budget and with a 6% annual contraction in the economy. Fortunately the 1990s already show more encouraging signs. With the promise of a free-trade agreement with the U.S. and Canada, the economy is experiencing a bit of a boom: 1991 not only brought the first economic growth in a decade, it came at a rate (4%) higher than any of the Group of Seven industrial nations. Mexico once again is investing in the education and health of its citizens.

ARTISTS

Mexico has matured into a modern nation and participates in the international culture encouraged by television, radio, and movies. Yet it retains a profound pride in its own culture. Only a nation with a strong identity can so consistently produce artists of international reputation like writers **Carlos Fuentes** and Nobel prize-winning **Octavio Paz**, painters **Francisco Toledo** and the late **Rufino Tamayo,** and architects **Ricardo Legorreta** and the late **Luis Barragan**. Mexican popular music competes with the latest rock hits and is exported throughout Latin America. Its popular arts—colorful bark paintings of village scenes and ceramic planters shaped into smiling goats—are sold along with T-shirts emblazoned with the face of the latest movie idol. Distinctive Mexican culture exists side by side with the latest international innovation, but at least it is there to proclaim that Mexico continues to create its unique niche in the modern world.

MEXICAN WAYS

Maya children in the Merida market

He was, like all peons, incredibly poor and lavishly hospitable.

John Reed, 1914

While Mexico is known for its macho men, the warmth and generosity of the people are traits more likely to be encountered by the traveler. Affection is displayed publicly. Men as well as women lock arms while walking down the street and greet one another with warm *abrazos*, or embraces. The **abrazos** often seem to be a formality much like our shaking of hands, but the locking arms is a genuine expression of affection, although—at least for men—foreign to North American customs. Mexican warmth is bestowed upon the foreign visitor, too. On second-class buses, Indian peasants will offer

95

to share their food; in cities and villages, the slightest interest in the country will reap unforeseen rewards—an invitation to a wedding or a serenade in a restaurant.

Alongside the *abrazo* appears the celebrated **machismo**, a complicated phenomenon not always easy to understand or accept. Men constantly try to prove what they perceive to be their manhood. Having a mistress or two in addition to a wife is one sign; dominating and being overly protective of your wife and women friends is another; producing lots of children is still another. Yet side by side with machismo are found non–macho characteristics. Fathers will be extremely tender with children and affectionate with friends. And even the most macho of men may cry in public.

Although women generally play a subservient role, there are notable exceptions. Grandmothers, especially those without husbands, are revered as matriarchs and allowed to do "unladylike" things in public such as drink and smoke. Younger women are now attending universities and pursuing careers in banking, medicine, and government. In the countryside, women peasants dominate the trading in the markets, and when bargaining with them, you'll recognize their strength and stature.

FAMILIES

Families are prized, usually the larger the better, and they form the center of social life for most Mexicans. Young children are smothered with affection by older brothers and sisters as well as by parents and friends. Older children remain at home until marriage, helping to support the family. At parties, whether it be a celebration of some one's saint's day or a baptism, family members of all ages mingle and dance. Members of the family are often introduced by relationship rather than name—*primo* ("cousin"), not Roberto; or *cunada* ("sister-in-law"), not Francisca. Families grow in size through the godparent system, a way of strengthening ties with those who otherwise are mere "friends."

Mexico is a land of color amid great poverty. Traditional Indian costumes are woven in vibrant reds and rich purples; homes painted in shocking pinks; second- and, more often, third-class buses decorated gaily with altars and animals; and balloons colored in orange, yellow, and fuchsia. Colors that are supposed to clash here combine in brilliant harmony. Bougainvillea vie with orange flame trees for your attention, and the most impoverished home will have flowers growing in a tin can to add a touch of color to an otherwise desolate scene.

Mexicans have an incredible attachment to their country. For them, the country is not their government but the land, the mountains, the flowers, the food, the music, the history, the sights and smells. Everyone seems to know the name of every plant, every flower, every bird, the words to every traditional song. Regional attachments are powerful, too, and rivalries common. Although living in Mexico City, a person will identify himself as a Oaxaqueno or Veracruzano or Yucateco and will long for his home, its food, its music, and people. Not surprisingly, people bear nicknames, like Jalisco and Azteca, to record their roots.

NICKNAMES

Nicknames are part of Mexican life. Almost every other Mexican seems to be called "*Gordo*" ("fatty"), a term used without meanness since they happen to find hefty people attractive. The rare thin person is "*Flaca*," and the fair-skinned Mexican beauty "*Huera*" or "*Blanca*." The thousands of Jesuses in the country are nicknamed "*Chu-Chu*," while the rare blue-eyed person becomes "*Gato*" ("cat"). Diminutives are used frequently and affectionately, like Manuelito for Manuel, Juanita for Juana.

Neither our avoidance of contradiction nor our sharp division between fantasy and reality is shared by Mexicans. Stories will be told that contradict what was said a day before without anyone raising an eyebrow. Fantasy mixes with reality so that the two become inseparable in a way that only the Nobel Prize-winning author Gabriel Garcia Marquez can capture. Mexico's strong background in witchcraft and shamanism gives credence to explanations we would accept as fanciful: people will dream of forthcoming deaths or tell of divining past disasters. Miracles such as the appearance of the Virgin of Guadalupe play a large role among Mexicans' beliefs, and supernaturalistic explanations are more readily accepted here than at home. Sometimes our North American skepticism about these explanations leads to interesting results. Once we were told by a friend who lives on a small lake in Mexico that the ducks and geese were disappearing from the water at an alarming rate. Since there had been some recent thefts in the area, we assumed the animals were stolen. But, no, the explanation in the lakeside village was that a gigantic crocodile was living in the lake and devouring the birds. For weeks on end, the villagers stood watch, waiting for this monster to appear. Since crocodiles live in rivers, we put this story down to another imaginative reconstruction of reality until, lo and behold, we received photographs from our friend. Recorded by Kodak were the villagers triumphantly standing over a 9-foot crocodile they had caught in the lake.

WORK

Mexicans work extremely hard, often spending long hours at physical labor. Yet the notorious **mañana** mentality does exist. The dictionary tells you that *mañana* means "tomorrow," but the dictionary is wrong. That is not what it means, at least not in Mexico. If a shoe repairman tells you that your shoes will be ready mañana, he means they will be ready soon, in due time, perhaps in a few days or a week or so. Why does it matter, you have other shoes, don't you? Besides he has lots of shoes to repair, family obligations, friendships that are important, and perhaps a baptism or birthday to attend. The same considerations apply to *ahora*, which a dictionary will tell you means "now." There is no word for "now" in Mexico, although *ahorita* gets a little closer, and *ahoritita* gets closer still.

Be prepared for similar problems even when precise times are given. A Mexican may make a date to pick you up at 7 p.m. She may come at 9 o'clock or never. The bus could have broken down; a friend with a problem may have come over. Since most Mexicans have no phones, she may have been unable to call. We once were invited to a friend's home for a baptism. The baptism was to begin at 4 p.m. *en punto*—"on the dot." Being old hands in Mexico, we arrived promptly at 5:30 only to find ourselves the first guests and our friend in a soccer uniform washing his car. Other guests began to arrive by 6, and by 7 we were ready to go to church. Unfortunately, the father was nowhere to be found. Soon, he was located a few blocks away where he was refereeing a soccer game. The game ended, and by 8 p.m. we set off merrily to the church.

Fortunately for the traveler, Mexico's promotion of tourism has led it to adopt North American attitudes toward time for many tourist concerns. Planes and buses leave as much on time as they do at home, taxi drivers usually pick you up at the agreed-upon time, your hotel wake-up call will come as requested, and your dinner reservation will be honored. Since part of Mexico works on North American time and other parts on Mexican time, you may find yourself in a situation where you are uncertain which framework is being used. When in doubt, simply ask: Mexican time or North American time?

MUSIC

Music and song are an integral part of celebrations, of which there are many. Birthdays, saint's days, holidays, baptisms, farewells—all are occasions for music. Restaurants, bars, and plazas where mariachi musicians perform are popular gathering spots. The **mariachis** dress in the Mexican cowboy, or *charro*, outfits with boots, sombreros, and breeches, and short jackets decorated with silver studs. A group consists of several violinists, guitarists, trumpet players, and a lead singer. The songs tell of unrequited and lost loves, of the heart's yearnings and of life's longings. They are the Mexican equivalent of soulful blues. Mexicans not only know the words to every song, but they all love to perform, too. Often a member of the celebrating party will rise from the table to become the soloist with the mariachi band. Mariachis are also hired for private parties or for courting purposes. And sometimes mariachis appear under a woman's window at dawn to serenade her with the lovely birthday song, "Las Mananitas." Songs you will frequently hear include "Ay! Amigo," "El Rey," "La Paloma Negra," "El Borracho," and "Me Cai de la Nube."

Live mariachis are not always needed for courting. One night about 3 a.m., we were awakened by very loud music and singing. Looking out our window, we discovered an enterprising young man standing next to his car with a portable microphone in hand singing traditional love songs to a recording of mariachi music. He was courting a young woman who lived next door to us. Although the singing went on for at least two hours, no neighbors complained and, as etiquette dictated, the object of this attention remained hidden in her home.

Along with mariachi music, which originated in the state of Jalisco and spread throughout the country, other regional music has considerable popularity. In **Veracruz**, musicians wearing immaculate white outfits with striking red neckerchiefs sing in high-pitched voices the lively and gay *jarocho* songs with many improvised lyrics while accompanying themselves on string instruments. Among the more popular songs are "La Bamba", "El Agualulco," "El Cascabel," and "Canto a Veracruz." In Oaxaca, lyrical and melancholy songs are played on the **marimba**, while in Yucatán guitar trios entertain with melodious and romantic **serenades**.

FIESTAS

On almost any given day, a fiesta will be celebrated in Mexico with villages and cities exploding with color and costumes, music and masks, processions and dance. While frequently gay, many **fiestas** are also solemn affairs, a time to pay homage to a saint, a hero, a tradition.

Fireworks enliven many a fiesta. Often handmade and shaped into towers or attached like pinwheels to frames shaped like bulls (*toritos*), they are ingenious creations that depict burning towers for battles or mock bullfights for fun. While many of the most interesting and traditional fiestas occur only locally, others like the *posadas*, the **Day of the Three Kings**, the **Day of the Dead**, and the **Fiesta of the Virgin of Guadalupe** are national in scope.

Beginning on December 16 and continuing every night through Christmas Eve, **posadas** reenact Mary and Joseph's search for lodging in Bethlehem. These processions move through the streets carrying lighted candles, and at the door of a designated house, the group stops and in melodic song, asks for lodging. After repeated rejections, the door swings open wide, and with shouts of glee the group enters and the party begins. Highlighting the posada is the traditional breaking of the pinata filled with candies and toys.

January 6th, rather than Christmas, is the traditional gift-giving day in Mexico. Boys representing the **Three Kings** wear fake beards, crowns, and long robes, and sit in the plazas of towns where children visit them to have their pictures taken. For parties, a special cake is baked with a small doll inside. By tradition, the guest who receives the slice of cake with the doll must give the next party.

Mexico's fascination with, or sophisticated acceptance of, death has made it into a national holiday, the **Day of the Dead**, celebrated on November 2. For weeks before, markets and bakeries are filled with toys, sweets, and breads all with symbols of death. Special breads are baked in human forms; sweets are shaped into skulls; and toy coffins and papier-mache skeletons appear everywhere. Flower markets overflow with marigolds, the flower that in Aztec times was sacred to the dead. On November 1 and 2, the favorite food of the dead is put out, often in cemeteries, as in the state of Michoacan. The dead return to visit their families, eating the spirit of the food. The next day the survivors celebrate by eating the food's substance and washing it down with good drink.

As the Queen is the symbol of England and the Constitution the symbol of the United States, so the **Virgin of Guadalupe** is the symbol of Mexico. As its patron saint, she is honored on December 12, the day she made her miraculous appearance to a humble peasant in Mexico City. Millions of pilgrims make the journey to Mexico City to pay their respects, many bloodied by the long crawl on their knees to her Basilica, located atop a hill. Beginning in the evening of December 11, the square in front of the Basilica becomes the stage for traditional songs and dances that continue through the night. While the largest celebration occurs in Mexico City, small ones take place in churches throughout Mexico.

FOOD AND DRINK

First-time travelers to Mexico confident of their knowledge of Mexican food are in for quite a surprise. Mexican restaurants at home do not prepare you for the distinctive, subtle Mexican cuisine that is often ranked next to French and Chinese for complexity and variety. After experiencing the varied Mexican cooking with its numerous regional specialties, surprise number two sets in. Most Mexican food is neither hot nor buried under a ton of heavy tomato sauce and melted cheese. Traditional dishes, although flavorful, are normally mild. For those who like food hot, as many Mexicans do, a spicy sauce is served on the side. (Mexicans, by the way, have two different words for "hot." Hot, as in spicy, is **picante**, hot as in heat is **caliente**. If you want to ask whether a dish is spicy, use the expression "es picante?" or simply "pica?")

Mexico is an eating country where people take their food seriously and in quantity. Visitors never need go hungry, even on buses or trains. At scheduled or nonscheduled stops, vendors appear selling sweets, tortas, tamales, nuts, and ice pops through the windows. Some may come aboard to sell their snacks, riding until sold-out, and then jump off, usually in the middle of nowhere. Streets in Mexican cities are filled with *taquerias*, where fresh tortillas are stuffed with various meats and enormous bowls of hot chile sauce are supplied on the side. Evenings, women appear on the streets with braziers for frying filled tortillas, or **quesadillas**.

The pre-Hispanic ingredients of corn, chiles, tomatoes, and beans still play a major role in Mexican cooking even though the native cuisine has evolved with influences from the Spanish and French. Probably the best known of the traditional foods are **tortillas**—Mexico's staple of life—thin pancakes of corn flour (or wheat in the north) prepared in infinite number of ways, whose shape, filling, and method of cooking make them into different dishes. Wrap soft tortillas around beef, chicken, or pork, pour on some hot sauce, and you have **tacos**; fry them crisp and flat, and pile them high with beans, cheese, lettuce, tomatoes, meats and you have **tostadas**; roll and stuff them with meat or cheese, cover with a sauce and bake, and you have **enchiladas**; pinch their sides to form a rim and top with beans, cheese, onions, and whatever else is in the kitchen and you have **sopes**. Stuff them with cheese, potatoes, or squash blossoms, shape them into turnovers, and fry, and you have yourself quesadillas; tear them into strips and bake them with cheese and a chile sauce, and you will be eating **chilaquiles**. The list is endless. Most often, tortillas are used as bread to accompany a meal, and when utensils are unavailable, a properly rolled tortilla makes a handy spoon. Sold by the kilo, tortillas used to be handmade, but the familiar slapping sound of tortillas being made is almost gone now. Hand presses have been introduced, and tiny tortilla "factories" (*tortillerias*) producing fresh, machine-made tortillas are found throughout the country. Corn also serves as the basis for **tamales**, the pre-Hispanic dish made from cornmeal wrapped in a corn husk or banana leaves, filled with chicken or sauce, and steamed.

CHILES

Chiles are essential to Mexican cooking. Once you have seen a market with stall after stall of chiles, you will not be surprised to learn that the country has over 100 varieties—long and short, fat and thin, smooth and wrinkled, in green, black, yellow, and red, sold fresh or dried—sweet, tart, or fiery hot. The chiles, individually or in intriguing combinations, are ingredients in sauces and soups. One type, the dark-green *chile poblano*, when stuffed with ground meat and covered with a savory white walnut sauce topped by red pomegranate seeds, becomes the famous dish, *chiles en nogada*, that is found on menus in late summer and early fall when the walnuts are at their freshest.

SOUPS

Almost any main meal includes a delicious soup. Chicken broth made freshly forms the base for a variety of savory concoctions including *caldo de pollo*, which comes with slices of chicken and fresh avocado and *caldo tlalpeno*, a hearty and spicy vegetable soup enriched by the flavor of the smoky chipotle chile. The abundance of fresh vegetables in the country makes for many excellent vegetable, cream of vegetable (*cremas*), and beef vegetable (*puchero*) soups, while fresh seafood is an ingredient in a variety of soups including the wonderful crab soup, jaibas en chilpachole. The tasty tomato-based noodle soup (sopa de pasta or fideo) is economical and a standard item on most menus, while black-bean soup makes for hearty fare. The regional soup, pozole, from Michoacan, Jalisco, and Guerrero is often difficult to find, but well worth seeking out. Its rich broth is filled with hominy and pork to which are added lettuce, onions, tortilla chips, oregano, and hot sauce to taste. It is addictive. Although soups are called caldos or sopas, beware of sopa de arroz. This is what Mexicans call a dry soup, or what we call rice. Fine and tasty rice it is, and eaten in huge quantities by Mexicans, but soup it isn't.

SEAFOOD

Unbeknownst to most of the world, wonderfully fresh seafood from the Pacific, Gulf, Caribbean, and rivers and lakes is a mainstay of the Mexican kitchen. The most popular and one of the best appetizers is **ceviche**, raw fish "cooked" in a marinade of fresh lime juice, onions, tomatoes, avocados, chiles, and spices. The ceviche came to Mexico in post-Conquest times as the result of the country's trade with the Orient. Oysters, crab, and conch are frequently available also. Red snapper (*huachinango*) and sea bass (*robalo*) are abundant and popular. Fish will often be grilled with butter or covered with a special sauce such as the savory Veracruzano sauce of tomatoes, onions, olives, capers, and chiles. Sweet and succulent shrimps (*camarones*), consumed locally and exported in great quantities, are served cold in cocktails, broiled with butter, or, most scrumptious of all, broiled with garlic (*al mojo de ajo*). Lobster receives similar treatment.

POLLO

Chicken (**pollo**), another mainstay, is quite good and of a higher quality than chicken at home. Turkey (*guajolote or pavo*), one of pre-Hispanic Mexico's contributions to the world, is normally reserved for special occasions. On the most special of these special occasions, the dish will be *mole poblano de guajolote* (turkey with mole Poblano-style), the most famous and complex of Mexico's many mole dishes, made with a variety of chiles and spices as well as a touch of chocolate. Although the thought of even a touch of chocolate over turkey sends shivers down the spine of most non-Mexicans, **mole poblano** should be tried. In the hands of an experienced cook it is truly delicious, a rich blend of flavors, ranking with the finest of Mexican creations. Kitchens throughout the country turn out other intricate moles, all involving a chile sauce, many without chocolate, but all overshadowed by the mole from Puebla.

BEEF, PORK & EGGS

In recent years, especially in the better restaurants, the quality of beef has improved considerably. Probably the most typical beef dish is **carne asada** *a la Tampiquena*, marinated beef, grilled and served with enchiladas, guacamole, baked cheese, and strips of chiles. Fine tournedos and chateaubriand are served in the more elegant restaurants. Complex pork dishes come *pipian*, that is, with a red or green sesame-seed and chile sauce, and *adobado*, in a paste of chiles, sour orange, cumin, and other spices. In inexpensive restaurants, chicken and pork are much preferable to beef, which has a tendency to be tough and dry.

Eggs are popular for breakfast, with **huevos** *a la Mexicana* (eggs scrambled with onions, tomatoes, and hot chiles) and *huevos rancheros* (fried eggs, sunny-side up on tortillas covered with either a green or red hot chile sauce) two of the traditional dishes. No Mexican would consider an egg dish complete without refried beans on the side.

BREADS, DESSERTS & FRUITS

Mexico produces a delicious French type of bread, shaped like elongated rolls, and called **bolillos**. Desserts are another matter. **Flan** (caramel pudding) is most popular, generally soothing yet unexciting. It is tastiest made with coconut when it is called *napolitano*. **Fresh fruits** abound, with delicious mangoes, pineapples (*piña*), cantaloupes (*melon*), watermelons (*sandia*), strawberries (*fresas*), and papayas widely available, but you will want to try some you may not have seen before like mamey and zapote.

You will notice limes (**limones**), but not lemons, just about everywhere. Why Mexicans call limes by the Spanish name for lemon is a mystery. Limes frequently appear on the table along with the salt shaker and a hot chile sauce. Mexicans squeeze lime into and onto most anything—soups, beer, fruit, and fish. Lime is best known to many travelers as the perfect accompaniment to a shot of tequila.

REGIONAL SPECIALTIES

Of all Mexican cooking, regional specialties stand out. Different areas of Mexico are known throughout the country for particular dishes or methods of cooking, and Mexicans away from home will speak with great relish about their local specialties. From the north, for example, there is *cabrito* ("kid"); from Yucatán, suckling pig and *pibil* dishes; from Oaxaca, *mole*; from Veracruz, seafood; from Jalisco, *pozole*; from Michoacan, *sopa Tarasca*, and so on. In the beginning of the "Eating Out" section for each city we describe the regional specialities so you can experience the local cuisine at its best.

BEER

Mexican beers rank with the best in the world, rivaling those from Germany and Holland. **Bohemia**, **XXX** (Tres Equis), and **Tecate** are three of the best-known premier beers; the latter, served in a can, is always drunk after first rubbing the rim with lime and salt. Less expensive, but still quite good, beers include **Superior** and **Carta Blanca**. Fine dark beers are available: **Negra Modelo**, and the somewhat lighter **XX** (Dos Equis). Around Christmas time, but only for a short period, the rich dark beer **Noche Buena** appears.

WINE

Mexican wines have improved considerably over recent years. Although not memorable they are surely drinkable. Among the many producers of whites and reds, Los Reyes and Hidalgo are old standbys but Calafia makes a more reliable wine. For some of the finest of Mexican wines, try those from the vineyards of **L. A. Cetto**, **Don Angel**, and **Clos San Jose**.

THE HARD STUFF

Among the national alcoholic beverages, those produced from different species of the maguey or century plant—pulque, mezcal, and tequila—are the most popular. During pre-Hispanic times, Indians drank pulque during rituals, but now it is drunk for less sacred reasons, mainly by the rural poor. Mildly alcoholic, milky, and foamy, **pulque** is more appealing to North American tastes when flavored with fresh fruit. Made from the sap of the maguey plant, it sours fast and should be drunk as fresh as possible, preferably at the ranch where it is made. **Mezcal** is a much stronger drink, very popular in Oaxaca where it is sold in black clay jugs with a small bag of salt attached. Mezcal is normally drunk straight with a lick of salt and bite of lime. (The curious should know that the tasty salt contains the dried worms found on the maguey plant.) **Tequila** is the best known and, to North American tastes the most appealing, of the maguey drinks. Named after one of the principal tequila-producing towns in Jalisco, it is exported throughout the world. Like mezcal, tequila is traditionally drunk straight with a lick of salt (the regular sodium chloride variety) and a bite of lime. **Sangrita**, a tangy juice-and-chile concoction, is drunk as a chaser. Tequila mixed with lime juice, orange liqueur, and salt becomes the popular, potent margarita. In cantinas, men demonstrate their virility by drinking a submarino—a shot glass of tequila dropped like a depth charge into a glass of beer. (It's not bad.) Mexico also makes more familiar liquors of rum, vodka, and gin.

NONALCOHOLIC BEVERAGES

Among nonalcoholic beverages—**hot chocolate**, a favorite of Moctezuma and once drunk only by the Aztec elite—continues to be quite popular. Coffee is both produced and consumed in quantity. *Con leche* ("with milk"), *solo* or *negro* ("black"), and *de olla* (with cinnamon and sugar) are traditional Mexican **coffee** offerings, but new Italian machines have brought cappucino and expresso to Mexico as well. Refreshing fruit drinks (**licuados**) of cantaloupe, pineapple, and watermelon as well as the sweetest, freshly squeezed orange juice you can imagine can be found at stands and restaurants in most areas. Particularly in demand are **aguas** made from tamarind pods (*tamarindos*) or Jamaica flowers (*jamaicas*). *Horchata*, a drink made from rice or melon seeds, is also favored. The pre-Hispanic **atole**, although not to non-Mexican tastes, is still drunk regularly. Made from corn or rice and flavored with fresh fruits, it is most often served with tamales. Along with these more exotic items, Mexicans consume vast quantities of Coca-Cola and Orange Crush. It is not unusual, although a bit jolting, to see an infant sucking a baby bottle filled with Orange Crush. Of Mexico's own soft drinks, particularly good are Tehuacan and Penafiel drinks of grapefruit (*toronja*) and apple (*manzana*). Mineral water by either of these firms and Sidral (another apple soft drink) are among Mexico's most frequently encountered bottled products.

CRAFTS

What could there be more astonishing than that a barbarous monarch such as he [Moctezuma] should have reproductions made in gold, silver, precious stones and feathers of all things to be found in his land, and so perfectly reproduced that there is no goldsmith or silversmith in the world who could better them…

Hernan Cortes, 1520

The crafts shopper in Mexico today is brought into contact with the spirit of the country—its brilliant sense of color and design, its warmth and humor, its imagination and fantasies, its religious and even its ghoulish and macabre sides. The shopper will find exquisitely embroidered **huipils** from Oaxaca, delicately designed **lacquerware** from Olinala and Patzcuaro, subtle **ceramics** from Tonala and Guanajuato, and the lovely Spanish **Talavera ware** from Puebla with its gorgeous **tiles**—in whites, blues, and yellows—that decorate Puebla church facades and Mexican homes and restaurants. Mexico's humor and fantasy come through in wildly imaginative **candelabra** filled with angels, animals, and even mermaids and the delightful, incongruous **animal groupings** from Acatlan. Mexico's religious devotion is encountered through the numerous portrayals of saints, **Nativity scenes**, and the like in clay, wood, and straw, while the power of pagan religions presents itself through the haunting **Huichol Indian prayer bowls**, **yarn paintings**, and **god's eyes.** And Mexico's macabre side comes through in bizarre **skeleton ceramic musicians** produced for the Day of the Dead and in the ghoulish **ceramic devils and serpents** from Ocumicho.

The variety of Mexican crafts is staggering. You find woven belts, blouses, capes, shawls, serapes, handbags, belts, and hats. Ceramic productions result in pots, dinnerware, vases, and a seemingly infinite number of animal and human figures. Painting finds expression in lacquerware and on ceramics and bark. A wide variety of metals as well as wood, leather, and stones are worked, straw is not neglected, and glass is still handblown.

Through their crafts the Mexican people have traditionally expressed their artistic creativity. Despite increased modernization of Mexican society, the popular arts are still alive and constitute a vital part of the nation's life and economy. Crafts demonstrate how for Mexicans art is inseparable from life. When Mexicans eat, dress, play, or pray, crafts are utilized. Pottery for cooking, a dress for a fiesta, a painting for a prayer, a mask for a ritual dance, or simply a toy for play will be an artistic creation with a long history, backed by a strong tradition.

Crafts are prized and occupy a central place in Mexican culture. In recognition of their importance and artistic merit, the internationally renowned **National Museum of Anthropology** in Mexico City devotes its entire second floor to an exhibition of national crafts. In recognition of the centrality of crafts to Mexican culture, the government supports craft production through its **National Fund for the Promotion of Crafts** (FONART), which sponsors many of the shops where you probably will buy crafts.

ANCIENT INDIAN TRADITIONS

Many of today's crafts carry on ancient Indian traditions. As in pre-Hispanic Mexico, **pottery** production is a major activity, and much of it still is made by hand without the use of a wheel. **Weaving**, then as now, is still frequently done on a backstrap loom. *Huipils* (WEE-peels), long blouses, and *quexquemetls* (kesh-KAY-meh-tahls), capes, worn by Indian women in pre-Hispanic times and depicted on ancient bowls and monuments are still woven today, and the finest, most exquisite ones are worn on special occasions— weddings or fiestas. Spanish influence has been significant. Even on crafts of ancient origin, the design may show Spanish motifs. And some materials and crafts are of Hispanic origin. For example, wool was unknown in ancient Mexico, but with the introduction of sheep into the Americas weaving was done in wool as well as in cotton and fiber. **Serapes** and probably **rebozos** (shawls) resulted from Spanish influence, and many techniques such as glazing **ceramics** were derived from Spain.

CONTEMPORARY CRAFTS

Contemporary crafts, like contemporary food, not only reflect their Indian and Spanish heritage but also regional specializations. Craft production dominates the life of many Mexican villages. Some, for example, are known for a particular type of ceramic, others for a certain lacquerware, and still others for distinctive weaving and embroidery. Throughout this guide, we will mention village specialties so that you will be informed about the special quality crafts available in the area.

Although crafts still thrive in modern Mexico, and some are of an extremely high quality, important changes have taken place. Animal and vegetable dyes—purple from *caracol* (snail), scarlet from the insect *cochineal*, and blue from the indigo plant—have been replaced by less subtle, less rich chemical dyes. And in some areas, ancient techniques have been abandoned. Hand-woven huipils and rebozos have lost popularity to their machine-made counterparts in several villages, and the time-consuming method of lacquerware by incrustation is not frequently used. Yet despite these changes, contemporary artisans have come forth and, drawing on ancient traditions, they are producing museum-quality crafts. Few countries today can rival Mexico for the quality and astounding variety of its native crafts. Both the interested shopper and curious sightseer will be rewarded by a visit to Mexico's many markets and crafts shops. For there you see ancient traditions carried on and the contemporary soul of Mexico on display.

CENTRAL VALLEY:
MEXICO CITY

Cathedral, Mexico City

> *The city floats in emerald circles,*
> *Radiating splendor like quetzal plumes.*
> *Around it warrior chiefs are carried in canoes,*
> *Veiled by a flowery mist.*

Aztec poem, recorded by Angel M. Garibay

HISTORY AND CULTURE

Across the great central plain of Mexico have marched most of the major events of Mexican prehistory and history. This valley spawned the two largest cities in all the Americas in pre-Conquest times—

Tenochtitlan and **Teotihuacan**—and currently sustains one of the largest cities in the world. Human endeavors have deprived the valley of its great **Lake Texcoco**, grazing animals have eroded its once rich soil, and rivers have cut ravines deep into its crust, but nothing has deprived this highland region of its enormous expanse, which covers 3,000 square miles. Elevated over 7,000 feet above sea level, this temperate valley is enclosed by the **Sierra Nevada** mountains on the east, the **Sierra Las Cruces** on the west, and the **Sierra Ajusco** on the south. The majestic snow-covered peaks of the volcanoes **Popocatepetl** (17,761 feet high) and **Iztaccihuatl** (17,343 feet), two of the highest in North America, dominate the valley. Passes through these mountains form the great communication and trade routes of both ancient and modern Mexico—to Veracruz on the Gulf Coast, Acapulco on the Pacific Coast, and Oaxaca to the south.

TENOCHTITLAN

As the Spanish conquistadors approached the Aztec capital of Tenochtitlan (teh-noch-tee-TLAN), they were overawed by this island city with its many towers and stone buildings rising from shimmering Lake Texcoco. This city of 300,000 people amazed them because few European cities approached populations of 100,000. Commerce kept the lake lively with canoes; the city's canal streets reminded them of Venice. As they crossed one of the three causeways to Tenochtitlan, they halted to await their first glimpse of **Moctezuma**, the Aztec king.

> *The Great Moctezuma got down from his litter, and those great Caciques [chiefs] supported him with their arms beneath a marvelously rich canopy of green-colored feathers with much gold and silver embroidery and with pearls and chalchihuites [jade] suspended from a sort of bordering, which was wonderful to look at. The Great Moctezuma was richly attired...shod with sandals, the soles [of which] were of gold and the upper part adorned with precious stones.... Many other Lords...walked before the Great Moctezuma, sweeping the ground where he would tread and spreading cloths on it, so that he should not tread on the earth.*

Bernal Diaz del Castillo, 16th century

At this historic moment, the Aztecs, too, recorded their impressions of the Europeans:

> *They came in battle array, as conquerors, and the dust rose in the whirlwinds on the roads, their spears glinted in the sun, and their pennons fluttered like bats. They made a loud clamor as they marched, for their coats of mail and their weapons clashed and rattled. Some of them were dressed in glistening iron from head to foot; they terrified everyone who saw them.*

The Broken Spears

AZTECS

This encounter between the Old and the New worlds has captured the imagination of many people, making the **Aztecs** the best known of all early Mexicans. Accounts by conquistadors such as **Bernal Diaz del Castillo** have only too dramatically taught us of the Aztecs' gory practice of **human sacrifice**, leaving us with nightmare images of priests with bloody, matted hair, holding human hearts in their hands. But these accounts, and those of the Aztecs themselves, also have provided us with insights into the far more fascinating human, and less sensational, aspects of their society and daily lives, information difficult to glean from the silent monuments of earlier civilizations.

The Aztecs, or Mexica as they called themselves, created an empire that stretched from their city of Tenochtitlan to the Pacific and the Gulf coasts and south through Oaxaca to the coast of Guatemala. These areas often maintained their own rulers, language, and customs but were forced to pay tribute to the Aztecs. Records indicate Tenochtitlan received astounding quantities of goods each year through this tribute system—for example, 2 million cotton cloaks and 7,000 tons of maize. Failure to pay tribute meant war and most likely defeat at the hands of brave Aztec warriors. At the time the Spanish arrived, they found many groups eager to overthrow the Aztecs' economic domination. They also found allies in the **Tlaxcalans**, who had never submitted to their powerful Aztec neighbors. Other peoples, the **Maya** of Yucatán and the **Tarascans** of Michoacan, had remained independent of the Aztecs but carried on trade with them in copper bells, gold and other metals, colorful feathers, jaguar hides, and other exotic items from the tropics.

Trade and tribute flooded the great Aztec market, which according to Bernal Diaz del Castillo had separate sections for gold, silver, and precious stones, for feathers, embroidered goods, hides of jaguar and deer, for rope and sandals, for vegetables, and for fowl, rabbits, and young dogs:

> *I could wish that I had finished telling of all the things which are sold there, but they are so numerous and of such different quality and the great market place with its surrounding arcades was so crowded with people that one would not have been able to see and inquire about it all in two days.... Some of the soldiers among us who had been in many parts of the world, in Constantinople, and all over Italy, and in Rome, said that so large a market place...so well regulated and arranged...they had never beheld before.*

The island city of Tenochtitlan covered an area of five square miles, most of it on landfill that had been created by *chinampas*—mud placed on reeds that were then planted and rooted to the lake bed. The city was planned on a grid, crisscrossed by canals, and lined with houses, many two stories high and arranged around flower-filled gardens. An aqueduct from Chapultepec on the mainland supplied the city with fresh water, and a dyke sealed off a freshwater lagoon next to the city from the salty, and often flooding, waters of Lake Texcoco. The **Sacred Precinct** occupied the center, dominated by the **Templo Mayor**, or Great Temple, dedicated to **Huitzilpochtli**, the war god, and **Tlaloc**, the rain god. Surrounding the Templo Mayor was a wall carved with serpents. In dedicating this towering pyramid temple, the Aztecs allegedly sacrificed 20,000 people. Huitzilpochtli, their tribal god, required human blood to keep the sun moving across the sky, for without such sacrifice the world would end. The Aztecs even engaged in ritual warfare with neighbors simply to supply this bloodthirsty god with captured victims.

AZTEC RULERS

Situated around the Sacred Precinct were homes of nobles, including the palace of Moctezuma. Like all Aztec rulers, Moctezuma was a noble selected "by the gods" to rule. Although the ruler was considered semidivine, he had enormous responsibilities to perform. Before becoming king, he had to prove himself brave in war. As king, he administered the state and military, functioned as chief priest, and was expected to demonstrate his goodwill to the people, caring for them during difficult times. One story relates the good work of a king who would send his aides into the market to buy wares from the poor so they would earn enough to survive. Despite his wealth and revered status, the ruler's duties involved "great labor, sorrow, and penance."

In fact, great labor as well as decorum were expected of everyone in this orderly society. Nobles sat in judgment at court sessions lasting from dawn to night, and artisans as well as farmers started work before dawn. Priests were expected to be celibate, never to lie, and to live in awe of the gods. The manner in which responsiblities were performed was of great importance, too. The Aztecs' even had etiquette books about proper deportment, emphasizing self-restraint and dignity. Each social class was restricted in dress, because as the society grew wealthy the nobles found individuals from other classes, particularly merchants, competing with them in finery. Death was the punishment for a person wearing clothing above his station. But if this seems too severe an attitude toward commoners, it is worth noting that the higher one's status, the more serious the punishment inflicted for a breach of law. A commoner appearing drunk in public had his head shaved, but the same crime committed by a noble was punished by death.

As warlike as the Aztecs were, and as brutal and demanding as their gods were, they created a state of incredible order and refinement. Yet, Aztec civilization appears austere and impersonal. Not until we see their delicate sculptures of squashes, monkeys, and shells do we detect the more poetic aspects of their lives. Fortunately for our understanding of the Aztecs, their songs also reveal this pensive side of their personalities:

> *Will my heart die*
> *As flowers that wither?*
> *On this earth some day*
> *Will my name be nothing? My fame nothing?*
> *Let us at least have flowers!*
> *Let us have singing!*
> *For how shall my heart prevail*
> *When we live on earth in vain?*

Aztec song, recorded by
Angel M. Garibay

BEFORE THE AZTECS

One of the most remarkable aspects of Aztec civilization is the brief period in which it was accomplished. Two hundred years before the arrival of the Spanish, the Aztecs were no more than Chichimeca, or barbarians, from the north, a wandering tribe that had entered the civilized Central Valley. There they worked as serfs and raided cities for wives. Expelled from one place after another, these despised people "whose face nobody knows" finally settled on two swampy islands in Lake Texcoco that no one else wanted. These islands eventually grew together through the establishment of *chinampas* to become the great city of Tenochtitlan, although at first the fierce, formerly nomadic Aztecs did what they knew best—they acted as mercenaries for the mightiest power in the valley, **Azcapotzalco**. By the time the Aztecs destroyed Azcapotzalco in 1428 and became the strongest power in the valley, they had learned Nahuatl, the language of the civilized valley, as well as its technology, writing, astronomy, religion, and arts. Fewer than 100 years remained before Cortes would arrive, yet the Aztecs had time enough to build the mighty empire already described. While bringing their own Chichimec brutality, and perhaps vitality, to ancient Mesoamerica, their customs were borrowed from the civilizations that had been evolving in the Central Valley for more than a thousand years before their intrusion.

As intruders, the Aztecs knew of only one predecessor, the **Toltecs** at Tula. Styling themselves after the warlike Toltecs, the Aztecs fashioned for themselves jaguar and eagle warrior cults and founded a royal lineage on the Toltec god **Quetzalcoatl**. They believed the Toltecs had created the arts, learning, and writing when actually Tula also was an upstart in the valley, founded by another group of Chichimeca as late as A.D. 900.

SIXTH LARGEST CITY IN THE WORLD

The true predecessor of the Aztec nation was **Teotihuacan**. Teotihuacan (150 B.C.-A.D. 700) had a population of more than 200,000 and was the sixth largest city in the world during the height of its power. (In A.D. 622, Teotihuacan may have tied with Alexandria as the fifth largest city in the world. At this time, Constantinople was largest with a population of 500,000, and no European city even qualified for the top seven cities. Not until the 17th century did London grow enough to become one of the seven largest cities in the world.) Teotihuacan monopolized distribution of **obsidian**—the precious volcanic glass used instead of metal—from the Central Valley and received trade items from areas as far away as the American Southwest (**turquoise**) and Central America (**cacao**, or chocolate beans). It may have controlled cities outside the central highlands such as Alta Vista to the north in Zacatecas and Kaminaljuyu to the south in modern Guatemala City. Its elite intermarried with Maya elite at Tikal in Guatemala, and its influence is found throughout ancient Mexico. The centralization of its power and extent of its trade was unequaled by the later Aztecs.

Many traces of the culture and religion of the later Aztecs can be found at Teotihuacan. Here, the gods Tlaloc and Quetzalcoatl were worshiped; here warriors sacrificed their lives to keep the sun rising each morning. Probably even the Aztec language, Nahuatl, was spoken by Teotihuacanos. Yet in developing these traditions, Teotihuacan borrowed from earlier cultures, such as **Cuicuilco** (now on the edge of Mexico City), which built the first stone pyramid in ancient Mexico (500-100 B.C.), and still earlier Central Valley cultures, such as Tlatilco (1000-550 B.C.), which is known to have traded with the first great civilization of Mexico, the **Olmecs** (see Central Gulf Coast chapter).

The Aztecs represented the last manifestation of Indian civilization in the Central Valley, yet, ironically, less remains of their great city

Tenochtitlan than of the cities that preceded them. While you can visit the ruined cities of **Cuicuilco**, **Teotihuacan**, **Tula**, and others that still stand, few Aztec monuments can be seen. Today, much of the Sacred Precinct lies beneath the zócalo of Mexico City, with Moctezuma's palace appropriately under the National Palace. Construction of the metro in Mexico City has unveiled Aztec temples buried beneath this modern city, and excavations have exposed the Great Temple, buried under centuries-old Spanish buildings. Despite such glimpses of the Aztec past, the Spanish victory over the Aztecs speaks most eloquently through the hundreds of Spanish buildings located atop ancient Tenochtitlan.

THE CONQUEST OF TENOCHTITLAN

The Spanish entered Tenochtitlan as guests of Moctezuma on November 8, 1519. Nearly two years later, on August 13, 1521, Tenochtitlan was a smoldering ruin. The intervening years had brought disasters for both Spaniards and Aztecs, yet the determination and brilliance of Cortes decided the final outcome.

After entering Tenochtitlan with his 400 Spanish soldiers and thousands of Tlaxcalan allies, **Cortes** plotted to control the Aztec empire through Moctezuma. Moctezuma was kidnapped and held in the Spanish quarters. Seeking to calm his people, **Moctezuma** told them he was remaining there of his own free will. Other Aztec nobles, who were suspected of rebelling, were also held in the Spanish quarters. For six months, the Spanish were able to remain safely in Tenochtitlan, directing affairs through Moctezuma. Under their orders, gold and precious gems were brought to them from all over the empire. The Spaniards amassed much wealth that, as will be seen, later led to many of their deaths.

As time went on, the Aztecs became increasingly suspicious of the wisdom of Moctezuma's orders, particularly when he allowed the Spaniards to install an image of the Virgin in the temple of their god Huizilpochtli. At last, powerful priests and nobles began to agitate the populace against Moctezuma, yet no overt rebellion occurred until the Spaniards made their first major mistake. Cortes had gone to Veracruz to negotiate with a new contingent of 900 Spaniards who had arrived from Cuba. Those Spaniards who remained alone in the capital panicked, and after giving the Aztecs permission to celebrate a fiesta, the Spaniards attacked them, killing 200 unarmed nobles assembled in the Sacred Precinct. Returning from Veracruz with

Spanish and Tlaxcalan reinforcements, Cortes was allowed to rejoin his troops, but once inside his palace he found himself under seige.

MOCTEZUMA KILLED

Surrounded by a hostile populace and deprived of food and water, Cortes ordered Moctezuma to soothe his people. Moctezuma protested, but finally he was forced to the roof of the palace to make a plea for peace.

The Spaniards claimed Moctezuma was killed by rocks hurled by his outraged people; the Aztecs that he was killed by the Spaniards. However he died, rulership was passed to his brother **Cuitlahuac**, who, having no intention of cooperating with the invaders, set out to destroy them. Hordes of Aztecs attacked the palace of Cortes, only to be cut down by cannons and guns, yet still more attacked.

> *Although we fought like brave men, we could not...get free from the many squadrons which attacked both by day and night, and the powder was giving out, and the same was happening with the food and water....In fact, we were staring death in the face.*
> **Bernal Diaz del Castillo**

Cortes decided his troops should escape in the night, but the Aztecs had lifted the bridges from the causeways to prevent such a retreat. In preparation for escape, the Spaniards built a portable wooden bridge, muffled their horses' hoofs with cloth, and divided up the vast quantities of gold and gems they had acquired. Like Bernal Diaz, many conquistadors were too concerned with their lives to load themselves down with gold, but most were too greedy to leave their fortunes behind. On the rainy, misty night of June 30, 1520, the Spaniards and their Tlaxcalan allies crept out of the palace and headed for the shortest causeway to the mainland. Soon, Aztec sentinels sounded an alarm on their drums, and the fleeing Spaniards found Aztecs attacking them on the causeway and from canoes on the water. The portable wooden bridge broke under the weight of horses and men laden with gold. Those who were able, swam to safety; those weighted with gold drowned. Fewer than half the Spaniards survived this **Noche Triste** ("Night of Sorrows"), and more than 4,000 Tlaxcalan allies died.

Attacked fiercely along the way, Cortes retreated to Tlaxcala. With his forces depleted, his guns and cannons lost, he further feared the Tlaxcalans would turn against him. But the Tlaxcalans' hatred of the Aztecs kept them loyal, and they even provided refuge for the Spaniards. Thus, during the next year, Cortes carefully planned his final attack on Tenochtitlan. Additional soldiers and guns were received from newly arriving Spanish ships, and Cortes was able to conquer or "negotiate" with all the towns surrounding Lake Texcoco until Tenochtitlan was isolated. Cortes, a thousand Spanish soldiers, and 50,000 Indian troops began a seige of Tenochtitlan in the spring of 1521. They attacked the island city from the causeways and from the lake (13 frigates, complete with sails and oars, had been built at Tlaxcala and carried to the lake). What force could not accomplish, starvation did. Still the Aztecs, under their new ruler **Cuauhtemoc** (Cuitlahuac had died of smallpox), held out. They hid dead bodies so their attackers would not know how weakened they had become, and they ate roots, bark, and worms to survive. Cortes described them as "plainly determined to die without surrender..." But defeated they were.

These misfortunes all happened to us.
We witnessed them in anguish.
We lived through them with suffering.
Broken spears and torn hair lie on the road.
Houses are roofless, their walls now stained with blood.

Nahuatl poem, 1528, recorded by
Angel M. Garibay

POST-CONQUEST MEXICO CITY

The new city of Mexico shall be built upon the ashes of Tenochtitlan and as it was the principal and ruling city of all these provinces, so it shall be from this time forward.

Hernan Cortes, 1521

THE CAPITAL

As the capital of New Spain and later as the capital of Mexico, Mexico City shares the history of the Mexican nation. No major event occurred without its being a central part of it. Independence couldn't establish itself in this land before installing Maximilian in this ancient city, and the Revolution didn't succeed without major battles having been fought in the area of the Sacred Precinct of the Aztecs, by then transformed into the main plaza of the modern city.

In 1523, **Charles V** granted the title of Most Loyal, Noble, and Imperial City to the capital of New Spain. The canals of Tenochtitlan were filled with rubble and paved into streets; the first hospital and university in the Americas were established here long before the pilgrims landed at Plymouth Rock. Yet however determined Cortes was to construct a city as great as Tenochtitlan, he was bound to be disappointed. With the Aztec dyke destroyed and sanitary practices abandoned, the new capital became an unhealthful place, often flooded by Lake Texcoco. By 1600, only 7,000 Spaniards and 8,000

Indians resided in this most noble city, a far cry from the 300,000 of ancient Tenochtitlan. (Not until 1900 did this city reach the population level of the Aztec capital.) But the palaces, churches, and civic structures constructed by the Spanish during the years after the Conquest left a grand architectural legacy to the city, today forming its central administrative and commercial section.

Until the middle of the 19th century, Mexico City occupied the same area as ancient Tenochtitlan. Once the power of the Church was curtailed by the Reform laws, however, the government could, and did, expropriate land from monasteries (which covered 47% of the city) in order to build new streets, including Madero and 5 de Mayo, which still form the major thoroughfares of the downtown area. When Emperor Maximilian occupied Chapultepec Castle, he ordered the construction of the elegant avenue, now called La Reforma, to connect the castle with downtown. This established a new direction for city expansion. During the Diaz dictatorship, elegant mansions were built along the Reforma, and this landmark avenue was refurbished to compete in grandeur with the Champs-Elysees. The opulence of the Diaz period also left such landmarks as the Palacio de Bellas Artes.

The most remarkable transformation of the city and Central Valley occurred under Diaz when Lake Texcoco was drained. Since the founding of the Spanish city, the lake had continuously flooded the city. To prevent further disasters, a massive project was initiated to create a drain that cut through the valley and circumvented the surrounding mountains. Today, the dry lake bed is dotted with houses, the monastery of Acolman—which was originally on an island—sits astride the valley floor, and the Aztec towns that fronted the lake have become an integral part of an ever-expanding city. Only the floating gardens of **Xochimilco** testify to the lake environment that once existed in the Central Valley. Draining the lake had an unexpected side effect: with the water table lowered, many structures began to sink and tilt and, although these buildings have been stabilized, their odd angles are still noticeable today.

MURALISTS

The Revolution of 1910 gave Mexico City, and the world, an artistic tradition of great vitality. Postrevolutionary Mexico found itself committed to the education of its people but with few resources. In order to share the newfound sense of the nation's history and purpose with as many people as possible, Jose Vasconcelos, the Minister of Education, commissioned young artists such as **Diego Rivera**,

Jose Orozco, and **David Siqueiros** to cover the walls of public buildings with murals depicting historical scenes. Interior after interior, from the **National Palace** to **Chapultepec Castle** and the **Palacio de Bellas Artes**, were treated to the brushes of the muralist. Today, the vivid realisn. of Diego Rivera, the tragic expressionism of Orozco, the turbulent virtuosity of Siqueiros, as well as the styles of many other artists, reveal the history and aspirations of the Mexican people in buildings throughout the city.

CONTEMPORARY MEXICO CITY

Finally, contemporary Mexico has asserted itself in the capital, tunneling by Aztec remains to create a subway; refurbishing colonial buildings, restoring Aztec ruins by means of the most modern technology; and constructing modern glass towers next to old mansions along the Reforma. Although Mexico City's population barely edged over 300,000 in 1910, today some estimates make it one of the largest cities in the world, with a population in the metropolitan area of 15 million. While the capital city continues to be the administrative and cultural center of the nation, textile mills, automobile assembly and airplane plants, and iron and steel factories have been added to its bustle. As Mexico City grows and vibrates as the great modern center of the nation, the surrounding valley still speaks in the quiet voice of its mountains, pine forests, and vast plain.

MEXICO CITY

And some of our soldiers even asked whether the things that we saw were not a dream....There is so much to think over that I do not know how to describe it, seeing things as we did that had never before been heard of or seen before, not even dreamed about....Gazing on such wonderful sights, we did not know what to say, or whether what appeared before us was real, for on one side, on the land, there were great cities, and in the lake ever so many more, and the lake itself was crowded with canoes, and in the causeway were many bridges...and in front of us stood the great City of Mexico.

Bernal Diaz del Castillo, 16th century

In the heart of modern Mexico City stand Aztec ruins surrounded by colonial mansions with facades of richly carved, deep-red volcanic stone. The palm-tree-lined and flower-filled **Paseo de la Reforma**, rivaling the Champs-Elysees for grandeur, leads to Chapultepec Park, home of one of the great archaeological museums of the world. Between the colonial downtown area and museum-filled **Chapultepec Park**, 20th-century Mexico City announces itself in the **Zona Rosa** whose streets are lined with boutiques, elegant restaurants, sidewalk cafes, tacky souvenir and clothing shops, and discos featuring the latest fashions in music and dance. Within a short distance from the city lie fabulous ancient ruins with towering pyramids as well as charming colonial towns, glorious churches, fascinating marketplaces, traditional Indian villages, and lovely spas and elegant resorts where you can rest your weary tourist bones. And an hour away by plane, the Pacific resorts of Acapulco, Puerto Vallarta, and Zihuatanejo await you. Few cities in the world rival bustling, cosmopolitan Mexico City for the diversity and depth of its attractions and the fascination of its history and cultural heritage.

Amid all these riches, the problem you face in a stay of only a few days is deciding which sights can be eliminated least painfully. Eating and shopping present the same enviable choices. Excellent restaurants abound, serving Mexican as well as French, Italian, American, Japanese, and Chinese food. And tourists have been known to bypass the more famous sights in favor of shopping in the vast array of boutiques, markets, and stores that sell distinctive fashions and handmade crafts. Evenings offer no relief, with theaters, nightclubs, bars, and restaurants presenting traditional Mexican music and shows as well as more international fare.

While preserving its Indian and Spanish heritage, Mexico City has entered the mainstream of the 20th century. Its cosmopolitan atmo-

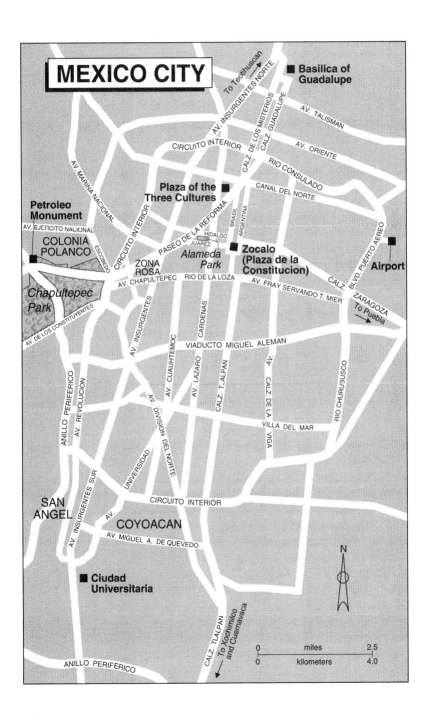

MEXICO CITY

Basilica of Guadalupe

To Teotihuacan

AV. INSURGENTES NORTE

CALZ. DE LOS MISTERIOS

CALZ. GUADALUPE

AV. TALISMAN

AV. ORIENTE

CIRCUITO INTERIOR

RIO CONSULADO

AV. MARINA NACIONAL

Plaza of the Three Cultures

CANAL DEL NORTE

Petroleo Monument

PASEO DE LA REFORMA

BRASIL

ARGENTINA

CIRCUITO INTERIOR

ESCOBEDO

AV. EJERCITO NACIONAL

HIDALGO

COLONIA POLANCO

JUAREZ

Zocalo (Plaza de la Constitucion)

PUERTO AEREO

Airport

ZONA ROSA

Alameda Park

AV. CHAPULTEPEC

RIO DE LA LOZA

AV. FRAY SERVANDO T. MIER

CALZ.

BLVD.

Chapultepec Park

ZARAGOZA

To Puebla

AV. DE LOS CONSTITUYENTES

AV. INSURGENTES

CARDENAS

VIADUCTO MIGUEL ALEMAN

ANILLO PERIFERICO

AV. REVOLUCION

AV. CUAUHTEMOC

AV. LAZARO

CALZ. T. ALPAN

AV.

CALZ. DE LA

RIO CHURUBUSCO

VILLA DEL MAR

VIGA

AV. DIVISION DEL NORTE

UNIVERSIDAD

SAN ANGEL

AV. INSURGENTES SUR

AV.

CIRCUITO INTERIOR

COYOACAN

AV. MIGUEL A. DE QUEVEDO

Ciudad Universitaria

N

CALZ. TLALPAN

To Xochimilco and Cuernavaca

| 0 | miles | 2.5 |
| 0 | kilometers | 4.0 |

ANILLO PERIFERICO

sphere is reflected at the newsstands where papers in English, German, and Japanese are sold. Bookstores, art galleries, and museums fill the city. Mexico City also has 20th-century problems, for as one of the largest cities in the world, its downtown streets are crowded, and massive traffic jams are common. Situated in a valley surrounded by mountains, it suffers seriously from pollution from old cars and buses. Yet if it resembles Los Angeles in its air, it is like New York in its vitality and street life. And when balmy evenings come, calm also appears as people sit in the city's lovely parks and stroll along the romantic **Reforma** lined with monuments to the city's rich past. While joining other strollers, even in late evening, you may suddenly realize that this is a people's city—the streets and parks are used by residents of all ages and at all hours. And you will surely know that you are in a foreign but friendly and fascinating land.

Below, we describe many of the major attractions in the city and surrounding area. Visiting them all and absorbing their atmosphere could occupy you for weeks or months—or years, as they have us—and you need to be selective. We have organized the sightseeing around tours to manageable areas of the city. If you are going to be in Mexico City for only three days, we recommend that you visit the **Zócalo and Historical Center** (Trip 1), **Chapultepec Park** (Trip 3), and take the excursion to the **ancient pyramids of Teotihuacan.** In a stay of any length, you will also want to visit the boutiques, shops, and restaurants in the Zona Rosa. And no trip to Mexico City is complete without at least a brief visit to the **Plaza Garibaldi** for its mariachi music, or to **Xochimilco** for its floating gardens and boat rides. For any trip of less than three days, you are on your own to make further cuts. But you will be sorry.

KEY TO MEXICO CITY

Sights • A culturally rich, dynamic city offering Aztec ruins, colonial buildings, lovely parks, excellent museums, and works of the great 20th-century Mexican muralists.

Shopping • A shopper's paradise with a superb selection of traditional crafts and jewelry as well as modern boutiques featuring the latest in contemporary fashions. Nearby crafts markets provide additional shopping opportunities.

Fiestas • Among the many celebrations, the most festive are Independence Eve, September 15; Fiesta of the Virgin of Guadalupe, December 12; and the Christmas season, December 16 through January 6, the Day of the Three Kings.

Sports • A few hotels have tennis courts and several have pools.

Where to Stay • Excellent selection of hotels, ranging from luxurious contemporary to moderate colonial to centrally located inexpensive hotels.

Where to Eat • A gastronomical heaven—from the best of traditional Mexican and seafood restaurants to fine French restaurants and others serving American, Japanese, Chinese, and Italian food.

Entertainment • Impressive variety from traditional mariachi music to the Ballet Folklorico to bullfights and jai alai to disco. Many bars and nightclubs.

Excursions • Because you can make so many fascinating one-day excursions, including the pyramids of Teotihuacan, a separate chapter is devoted to them—see chapter on Mexico City Excursions.

Getting around Mexico City • Very large, congested city, but many sights within walking distance or a short ride from major hotel zones. Lots of public transportation. Many excursions can be made by bus; but if a car is preferred, numerous car rentals are available. See special section on "Getting to and from Mexico City."

HOW TO GET AROUND

Despite its size, Mexico City need not overwhelm you. *The major tourist sections are laid out in grids so that sights and shops are easily found. Public transportation is exceptionally inexpensive,* and subways, buses, *peseros* (collective taxis), and taxis can take you just about anywhere.

Of the main tourist areas, the zócalo lies farthest east. Moving west from the zócalo, Av. Madero intersects with the main avenue, Lazaro Cardenas, and then changes its name to Av. Juarez as it runs along Alameda Park. The Reforma is one of the main bus, taxi, pesero, and walking routes. It is easy to orient yourself on this boulevard by becoming familiar with the monuments at several of the traffic circles. At the intersection of the Reforma and Insurgentes stands the **Monument to Cuauhtemoc,** the last Aztec emperor. Farther west, the towering **Monument to Independence,** known as "El Angel" because of the gilded angel on its summit, commands the circle at Reforma and Rio Tiber and Florencia. At the next traffic circle to the west you find a modern fountain where the Reforma intersects with Rio Mississippi, just a few blocks from Chapultepec Park. The northern extension of the Reforma (near Juarez) leads to the **Plaza of the Three Cultures** and the **Basilica of Guadalupe.** The **National University** and the residential areas of San Angel and Coyoacan are located in the southern section of the city.

The distance from the zócalo to the beginning of Chapultepec Park is a little more than 2-1/2 miles. Since many of the hotels and tourist sights lie around this route, you can frequently walk to many of your destinations. *All of our recommended hotels and most of the restaurants are located in these major sightseeing areas: zócalo, Alameda Park, Zona Rosa, and Chapultepec Park.*

METRO

Mexico City has an exceptionally modern, clean, and inexpensive subway system consisting of eight subway lines with well-marked stations, stops, and routes. Unfortunately, the subway is always mobbed, especially during rush hours—early morning and early evening; fortunately, though, the people traffic is well managed during those times by subway guards. There are even special cars for women and children to protect them from the crowds (although women and children may ride with the men if it suits them). Luggage is not permitted on the subway. After buying your ticket, place it in the slot of the turnstile. Look at the map of the subway line in the terminal to get your bearings. If you need to change lines, look for "Correspondencias," where more than one line shares a station. To leave the station, follow signs marked "Salida." *Lines 1-3 operate Monday-Friday, between 5 a.m. and 12:30 a.m.; Lines 4-7 and 9, Monday-Friday, between 6 a.m. and 12:30 a.m. Saturday, all lines operate between 6 a.m. and 1:30 a.m. Sunday and holidays, all lines operate between 7 a.m. and 12:30 a.m.*

BUSES

Local buses run along the major thoroughfares including the Reforma, Juarez, and Insurgentes. Selected buses, costing slightly more than regular ones, take on passengers only as long as seats are available. For the most popular route along the Reforma to Alameda Park, take the bus marked "Bellas Artes" or "Alameda." In the reverse direction, the bus takes you to or through Chapultepec Park and is marked "Chapultepec Metro," "Auditorio," "Palmas," or "Lomas." For other bus routes, see the sightseeing section of this chapter.

PESEROS

Peseros, the collective taxis, run fixed routes like buses and charge a set price per person. You see these VW vans and green and white cars along the Reforma and other major routes. Prices are low but not as cheap as the subway or bus. You will find the "Bellas Artes" *peseros* convenient. They run along the Reforma to Alameda Park and Bellas Artes at the intersection of Juarez and Lazaro Cardenas and return on Av. Juarez. They also return from the Hidalgo metro stop (Lines 2 and 3) at the corner of the Reforma and Basillo. Other routes are described under the sightseeing sections.

TAXIS

Taxis flood the streets yet are in great demand. *Their meters are almost never used for either locals or tourists, and since prices are often negotiable, you need to settle the tariff in advance.* By U.S. standards, the fares are low, and tipping is not expected. The small VW taxis are usually the cheapest, the taxis stationed in front of hotels generally cost at least twice as much as those found on the street, although they have the advantage of being available when you need them. Zone rates from train and bus stations have been instituted.

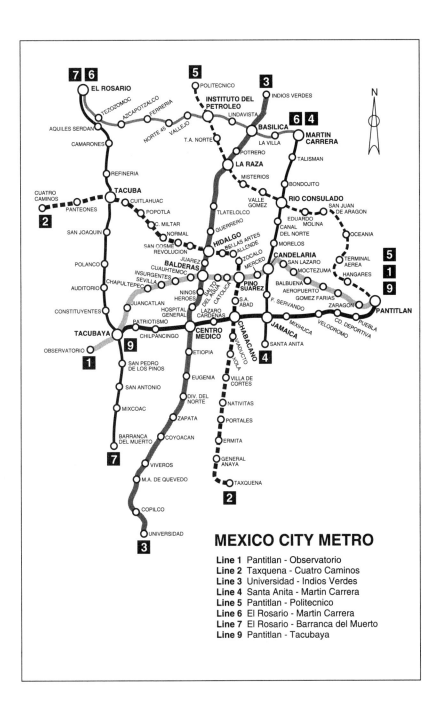

MEXICO CITY METRO

Line 1 Pantitlan - Observatorio
Line 2 Taxquena - Cuatro Caminos
Line 3 Universidad - Indios Verdes
Line 4 Santa Anita - Martin Carrera
Line 5 Pantitlan - Politecnico
Line 6 El Rosario - Martin Carrera
Line 7 El Rosario - Barranca del Muerto
Line 9 Pantitlan - Tacubaya

CAR

It's wise not to drive a car in the zócalo-Alameda-Zona Rosa areas. Traffic is heavy and parking scarce, and traffic patterns can be difficult to understand. Also, traffic police are notorious for their numerous "fines," deserved or not. Avoid the hassle and take taxis or public transportation. *Due to pollution, driving anywhere in Mexico City is prohibited on certain days, depending on the last number of your license plate.* On Monday cars with plates ending in 5 or 6 are prohibited; Tuesday, 7 or 8; Wednesday, 3 or 4; Thursday, 1 or 2; Friday, 9 or 0.

ZÓCALO AND HISTORICAL CENTER (TRIP 1)

This tour takes you to the heart of the historical downtown area with its Aztec ruins, Cathedral, colonial churches and mansions, and 20th-century Diego Rivera murals. The area, designated as the city's Historical Center, since 1978 has undergone extensive excavation and restoration. You need at least a full day to complete the tour. Hotel lobbies and bars along the way provide convenient resting spots. You can get to the zócalo starting point by subway. Take the Metro Line 2 to the zócalo stop or Line 1 to Pino Suarez (with an Aztec pyramid in the station) and walk about seven blocks north.

Zócalo

The zócalo (officially, the Plaza de la Constitucion) carries on ancient traditions. *Formerly the center of the great Aztec capital of Tenochtitlan, it is now the political and religious center of modern Mexico City.* With major Aztec ruins at its edge and surrounded by the Cathedral and National Palace, this huge square, 800 feet on a side, evokes the major eras of Mexican history. Once filled with trees, the now-barren plaza is *most dramatic at night* and especially during holidays when the illuminated buildings and festive decorations vie with images of Aztec rulers and Spanish conquistadors for your attention. Closed to traffic.

Cathedral

On Zócalo; Mon.-Sat., 11 a.m.-5 p.m. • The Cathedral, flanked by its parish church El Sagrario, dominates the north side of the zócalo. Begun in 1562, it replaced an earlier cathedral that Cortes had ordered constructed from stones obtained from Aztec temples. The imposing Cathedral, the largest church in Mexico, *took almost 250 years to complete*, and its various parts reflect a hodgepodge of architectural style—renaissance, baroque, and neoclassical, which combined with the Churrigueresque El Sagrario, provide you with a virtual history of colonial art in one location.

Perhaps as striking as the size of the Cathedral is its tilt, not uncommon for massive colonial buildings in Mexico City. Since the city is built on a lake bed, the loose subsoil is often unable to support heavy structures. Pilings—stakes sunk into the subsoil—were often used to

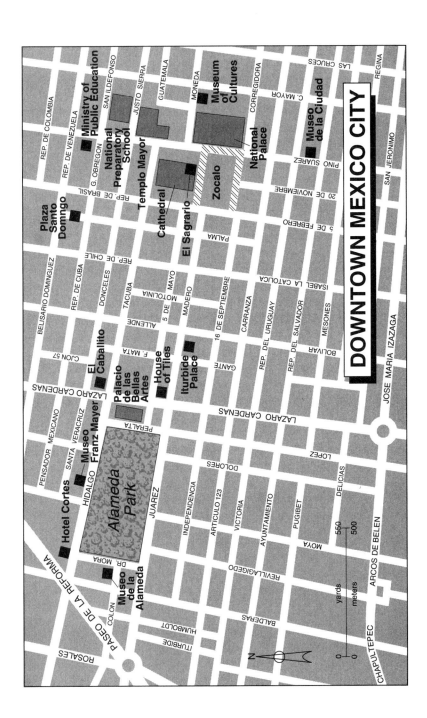

DOWNTOWN MEXICO CITY

help secure the landfill. To prevent further sinkage, frequent reinforcements have been made to the Cathedral's foundation.

The Cathedral's enormous interior takes the form of the cross with a
central nave and side aisles housing 16 chapels, the most favored
devoted to the **Black Christ.** A visit to the interior can be soothing as
well as interesting if you just sit and listen to the occasional **organ
music**. Several chapels are well worth visiting. The second chapel on
the right, the **Capilla de San Isidro Labrador**, contains the famous
Black Christ accompanied by a striking wall of milagros, the silver
ex-voto offerings. Legend tells of a poisoned worshiper who, upon
kissing the Christ figure, had the poison pass from his body to the figure. **The Chapel of the Kings,** located at the end of the nave behind the
main altar, features handsome gilded wood carvings, a stately organ,
and an extraordinary **Churrigueresque** (ultrabaroque) altarpiece that
introduced into Mexico estipites, inverted obelisks shaped into pilasters. The entrance to the **Crypt of the Archbishops**, containing the
remains of Mexico's archbishops, is located in the west transept (on
the left side of the Cathedral as you face the altar) near the side
door.The crypt is open to the public from 10 a.m.-1 p.m.

Continue on the left side to the second chapel from the front. The
Capilla de San Felipe de Jesus contains *an exceptional 17th-century
gilded, polychromed wood sculpture* depicting the martyrdom of San
Felipe de Jesus, who was executed in Nagasaki along with 25 others
after their ship-wrecked galleon landed on the coast of Japan. With
arms extended and lances piercing his body, San Felipe's suffering is
compellingly portrayed. The chapel also contains an exquisite, *delicate
17th-century ebony and ivory crucifix.* Look for the Christ figure known
as "**Lord of Cacao**," which can be found in the 17th-century **Chapel of
St. Joseph** (Capilla de San Jose), the third chapel on the left after you
enter the Cathedral. Shortly after the conquest this statue was especially popular with the local merchants, who continued the Aztec
practice of using cacao beans for currency. The statue was placed at
the door of the first cathedral in order to attract donations of cacao to
support the new cathedral's construction. *The Lord of Cacao now
resides in the glass case on the right side of the chapel.* Finally, the last
chapel on the left (near the Cathedral's entrance), the 18th-century
Capilla de los Santos Angeles, gilded from floor to ceiling, is never so
lovely as when its gold glistens from the natural light. The chapel contains paintings by Juan Correa, a black Mexican who was one of the
most celebrated painters in the Colonial era.

After you leave the Cathedral, turn right and then right again for the
Cathedral Museum (free admission) with displays of the history of the
Cathedral. Here you'll find some handsome old chests, polychromed
wood sculptures, attractive robes, and a lovely 18th-century painting
portraying Juan Diego with the apparition of the Virgin of Guadalupe.

El Sagrario

This parish church adjoins the Cathedral and offers an exuberant contrast. Designed by **Lorenzo Rodriguez**, the most famous Spanish architect of the 18th century, El Sagrario's wine-colored, *tezontle* Churrigueresque facades are showpieces. (*Tezontle*, the deep-red volcanic stone called "stone of blood" by the Aztecs, was a popular construction material in Tenochtitlan. During the colonial period, the Spanish continued to use this light and plentiful stone in their churches and palace facades.) The ultrabaroque ornamental decorations feature richly carved pilasters, inverted obelisks crowned with Corinthian capitals. The effervescent yet graceful sculptural details found throughout the facades make El Sagrario *one of the architectural highlights of colonial Mexico City.*

Underground at the *Peatones* (pedestrian walk) between the Cathedral and National Palace is a subway art gallery with changing exhibits. You may be lucky to find in this unlikely place paintings by Rivera and Orozco.

Templo Mayor

On Seminario; Open Tues.-Sun., 9 a.m.-6 p.m., but you can overlook the ruins from the surrounding streets at any time. Admission fee • The ceremonial precinct of the Aztecs, dominated by the **Templo Mayor** (Great Temple), lies just northeast of the Cathedral. Here, in the heart of modern Mexico City, are the remains of the *most sacred site of the ancient Aztec empire.* Three causeways and a main street met here marking the spot as the center of the Aztec universe. At the time of the Conquest, this area measured some 500 yards on each side and contained more than 70 temples, schools, and related buildings. In the midst of this hallowed site, the Templo Mayor, housing the shrines of the Aztec patron deity and war god, **Huitzilopochtli**, as well as the rain god, **Tlaloc**, was enclosed by a wall of stone serpents and stood out as the most sacred and monumental.

Destroyed by the conquistadors, the ceremonial center remained buried for centuries under colonial-era buildings. For a long time the Templo Mayor was thought to lie beneath the Cathedral. Although its precise location, slightly to the northeast, became known in the early 1900s, it was a chance discovery in 1978 that led to its resurrection. Workers digging underground for the light and power company hit upon a huge, oval stone sculpture measuring 10 feet across and depicting **Coyolxauhqui**, the moon-goddess sister of Huitzilopochtli. The discovery created the momentum for the extensive excavation of this center of the Aztec empire. Just as the Spanish built their new kingdom from Aztec stones and souls, modern Mexico has torn down blocks of colonial buildings and eliminated potentially priceless real estate to expose its deeper Indian heritage.

Hidden for centuries, these great Aztec ruins rise again, but in their new colonial setting, bordered by the **Cathedral**, the **National Prepa-**

ratory School, and the **National Palace**. *To get the best overall view of the site, stay on the outside and walk up Calle Seminario (which becomes Argentina) to the corner of Calle Justo Sierra.* From this vantage point you look outward over awesome piles of stones revealing the different periods of the Temple's construction. The Templo Mayor, in fact, went through at least seven major stages of construction, with each Aztec ruler building a new and more monumental temple over the one of his predecessor, as if to demonstrate by the size of the temple the increased power and extent of the Aztec empire.

Upon entering the site you pass a late stage (stage 6) of the Temple's construction and an *undulating serpent*. As you continue the walk you view open trenches revealing the various stages of construction. In one trench, you may be startled by *several full-length stone sculptures* (reproductions) known as *gatekeepers. You will then come upon the best-preserved Templo Mayor*, which comes from an early stage (stage 2) and was dedicated in 1390. It consists of a stepped pyramid base with stairways leading to two shrines at the top—the one on the right dedicated to **Huitzilopochtli**, and the other, on the left, to **Tlaloc**. Note the *piedra de sacrificios* (**sacrificial stone**) at the Huitzilopochtli temple and, in front of the Tlaloc shrine, *the reclining, painted chacmool sculpture*, resting calmly with its receptacle for human hearts, probably pulled from those victims sacrificed at the top of the temple. At the time of the Conquest this early stage of the Templo Mayor lay safely buried under several layers of later temples, protected for centuries against the onslaught of the Spaniards. When the conquistadors saw the temple in its final stage, it rose to a height of perhaps 150 feet and the shrines at the top, the scene of sacred rituals and human sacrifices, were reached by a steep and most dramatic climb of more than 100 steps. Coming upon the temple with its brightly painted facade adorned with sculptures of feathered-serpent heads, Cortes was so struck that he wrote that its "size and magnificence no human tongue could describe."

Continuing the tour, you will pass the **Temple of the Eagles** with its two eagle heads in front. Perhaps the piece de resistance is nearby in the **Basement of the Eagles** where, beneath the stone benches, polychromed carvings depicting marching warriors and undulating serpents can be found. *(Best seen with binoculars or a telephoto lens.)* As you come out of this area you will see a rather macabre structure, the **Tzompantli Altar**, decorated with more than **200 stone skulls**.

The Museum of the Templo Mayor

This museum houses the enormous finds of the Templo Mayor excavations. More than *100 offering caches* were found, filled with locally made Aztec pieces as well as numerous non-Aztec items from states as far away as Guerrero and Veracruz, providing evidence of the extent of the Aztec empire. And the find of an Olmec mask dating from well before the birth of Christ shows that the Aztecs, like collectors today, valued works of art from the earlier Mesoamerican cultures.

The impressive collection of Aztec art includes a *bar of gold* dropped by a fleeing conquistador on the *Noche Triste* (see Church of San Hipolito below), striking life-size ceramic warriors in eagle dress and a delightful stone carving of a conch shell. The piece that dominates the collection, however, is the magnificent **sculpture of Coyolxauhqui** *(best seen from the floor above)* whose discovery led to the 1978 excavations. It was found at the bottom of the outer staircase (stage 4) leading to the Huitzilopochtli shrine. This location, as well as the portrayal of Coyolxauhqui in a dismembered state, accords with Aztec legends telling of Coyolxauhqui's life on the sacred Serpent Mountain with her mother, the earth goddess, and her 400 brothers. One day while sweeping, her mother was touched by a down feather that miraculously made her pregnant. Upon learning of her mother's condition, Coyolxauhqui became enraged and vowed to avenge this dishonor to the family. She alarmed her 400 brothers, who joined with her in an attack on their mother. Just as the earth goddess was about to be slain, however, Huitzilopochtli, the sun and war god, was born, emerging from the womb armed with shields and darts. He chopped off the head of his sister Coyolxauhqui and threw her body down the mountain, her arms and legs tearing apart in the fall. Huitzilopochtli then proceeded to wipe out her 400 brothers as well. The placement of the Coyolxauhqui sculpture at the base of the temple represented her final resting place after her battle with Huitzilopochtli.

Aztec sacrificial practices had a dual symbolism and were related also to the Coyolxauhqui legend. The sacrifice of victims at the shrine of Huitzilopochtli and the throwing of the victims down the steep steps was a reenactment of the Coyolxauhqui-Huitzilopochtli battle. But Huitzilopochtli was also the sun god, and as people of the sun, the Aztecs were called upon to aid him in his daily struggle against darkness. Since human blood was Huitzilopochtli's nourishment, sacrifices at his shrine were necessary to insure that the sun would win the battle against night and rise again each morning.

National Palace and Diego Rivera Mural

On Zócalo; Open daily, 7 a.m.-7 p.m. Enter through central doorway. Guides are available • The National Palace extends for almost the entire east side of the zócalo. Built on the site where Moctezuma's palace, gardens, and aviary once stood, *the palace dates from 1693 and houses the office of the President of Mexico as well as numerous government departments.* During the colonial period, the building served as the palace of the Spanish viceroys. *Later, it was occupied by the emperors Iturbide and Maximilian and Mexican presidents.* At the north end of the palace is a *museum* and statue in honor of **President Benito Juarez**, who died in this building in 1872. The presidential balcony is located over the central doorway. Here you also find the *liberty bell* rung on September 15, 1810, by the Independence leader Father Hidalgo.

Wonderful *arcaded courtyards* are found in the interior of the National Palace. In the central one, the first *bullfight* in the Americas was held to celebrate Cortes' return from Honduras. In the rear stood Moctezuma's famed *aviary*, described by Cortes as containing "ten pools of water in which were kept every kind of waterfowl known in these parts, freshwater being provided for the river birds, salt for those of the sea. . . . It was the whole task of three hundred men to look after these birds. Each pool was overhung by balconies cunningly arranged from which Moctezuma would delight to watch the birds."

The Second Floor

The elegantly restored Old Chamber of Deputies can be found on the second floor. But the main attraction is the powerful set of **Diego Rivera murals** depicting Mexico's history from its Indian heritage through the Revolution of 1910. Rivera's use of architectural space is masterful; his ability to provide coherence to a wealth of detail, ingenious; and his imagery, haunting. If nothing else, *you should view the set of murals over the main stairway* that present, in often brutal terms, Mexico's history of oppression and struggle and its failures and aspirations.

To find these murals, pass through the central doorway of the National Palace and go left up the stairway to the second-floor balcony. *The painting on the right wall (as you face the array of murals from this vantage point) portrays the early life of highland Toltec, Teotihuacan, and Aztec civilizations, with the god Quetzalcoatl (here shown as white-faced and blond) seated in the center.* Behind his crown of green quetzal feathers is the Pyramid of the Sun and, to the left, the Pyramid of the Moon. Straight ahead on the main wall, the panel farthest to the right represents the United States invasion of Mexico in 1847. Below, Aztecs are shown being forced to destroy the Templo Mayor in order to construct a cathedral in its place. On the top of the next panel to the left Benito Juarez is portrayed holding the Constitution of 1857 and the Reform Laws calling for separation of church and state. In the middle on the right, Fray Bartolome de las Casas, the kindly protector of Indians, is depicted holding out a crucifix as a symbol of justice to the bearded Cortes.

The next panel to the left deals with the Revolution (on top), the War of Independence (in the middle), and the Conquest (below). Holding the "Tierra y Libertad" ("Land and Liberty") sign is the legendary Emiliano Zapata, shown with moustache and sombrero. About one-third of the way down, Hidalgo, balding with white hair, holds the green banner with the image (hidden) of the Virgin of Guadalupe that was carried into battle. Below, bearded Cortes, in a suit of armor and spear in hand, fights a battle while mounted on a white horse.

Moving left again, the panel portrays the Revolution with the white-moustached dictator Porfirio Diaz prominently featured, top left, with sword in hand. Three rows down at the far right, smiling Pancho Villa wears a wide sombrero. Two figures over from Villa is the moustached Madero, shown with white tie, wearing the green, white, and red presidential sash. A dramatic portrayal of the Inquisition dominates the center of the panel. Two victims are chained to the stake, one being strangled, the other burned to death. Below, conquistadors and Indians engage in a fierce, ugly battle.

The final panel at the extreme left of the main wall shows the execution of Emperor Maximilian. Below the brutal conquistador, red-haired Pedro de Alvarado stands guard with whip in hand over a group of Indians engaged in forced labor. To the right, the flame symbolizes the burning of the Aztec manuscripts carried out under orders from the Church. At the bottom, an enslaved Indian is being branded with a hot iron, a practice instituted by the conquistadors to provide the Spanish master with a permanent sign of ownership.

Finally, *the mural next to the staircase on the left wall represents Rivera's vision of the class struggle.* In the top center, whitebearded Karl Marx points to the future. Below are several images of bourgeois society, including a stock market ticker tape. To the right, workers are uniting. And at the bottom, Rivera's sister-in-law, Cristina Kahlo, wearing a red blouse, holds an open book, and artist Frida Kahlo, Rivera's wife, is behind her. These women represent the belief that education will abolish ignorance, illness, and poverty.

Along the second floor are several additional **Diego Rivera murals** portraying various Indian scenes, such as the Aztec market and a Gauguin-like painting of the harvesting of cacao. *The final mural depicts the arrival of a demented-looking Cortes at Veracruz* surrounded by scenes of Indians being branded and hanged.

Supreme Court

Corner of Corregidora and Pino Suarez; Open Mon.- Fri., 8 a.m.-6 p.m. • Next to the National Palace, on the former site of the major colonial market in Mexico City, you find the **Supreme Court.** Inside on the second floor, **Jose Clemente Orozco's** violent **murals** representing injustice among the people and in the courts seem rather incongruous for a court of justice. Not surprisingly, *these murals proved unpopular with government officials, and Orozco was not allowed to complete the series.*

Museo de la Ciudad

Pino Suarez 30; Open Tues.-Sun., 9:30 a.m.-7 p.m. Closed Mon. No admission charge • A few blocks from the Supreme Court at Calle El Salvador is the small, unpretentious colonial square called **Primo Verdad,** marred only by a parking lot on one corner. Fronting the square stands *one of our favorite colonial palaces,* now the **Museo de la Ciudad** (Museum of Mexico City). Built in the 16th century for a cousin of Cortes and renovated in the 18th century for the counts of Santiago de Calimaya, the palace has a deep-red facade of volcanic stone that is surmounted by a frieze of cannons. The richly carved **wooden doors** are especially noteworthy. The foundation stone found on the corner near Calle El Salvador and taken from an Aztec ruin is a sculptured feathered serpent like those seen at the Templo Mayor. Surrounding the handsome, well-proportioned **interior courtyard** are rooms with informative **exhibits** about the evolution of the city from Tenochtitlan through colonial times.

Templo de Jesus Nazaro

Entrance on El Salvador at corner of Pino Suarez. • Cross Pino Suarez to the **Templo de Jesus Nazaro,** which houses the remains of Cortes. A plaque outside the church on the Pino Suarez side *marks the place of the historic first encounter between Moctezuma and Cortes* on November 8, 1519. Cortes reported that they exchanged necklaces here. While Cortes gave Moctezuma one made from glass beads and some pearls, he received in return two necklaces made with precious shells and eight gold prawns, each 6 inches in length. **Orozco murals** decorate the ceiling and upper walls of the rear of the church. Swirling and severe, they take on the violent theme of the Apocalypse. *Because of Orozco's death in 1949, the murals planned for the rest of the church were never completed.* Search the left side of the altar for the **plaque** that marks the location of Cortes' remains.

Hospital de Jesus

El Salvador between Pino Suarez and 20 de Noviembre • If you walk along El Salvador past the church you will come to the **Hospital de Jesus,** founded by Cortes, *the first hospital in the Americas.* To see the hidden, **arcaded courtyard** of this 16th-century building, turn left off El Salvador into the modern hospital, walk to the end of the corridor, and make a left into the hospital proper. *Look like you are on business as you stare straight ahead and walk past the guard and reception desk.*

Calle Corregidora

Continue the tour by reversing your direction and walking back up Pino Suarez to the corner where the Supreme Court is, and make a right onto Calle Corregidora, now a pedestrian mall. Named in honor of La Corregidora, the Mexican heroine in the War of Independence, it was formerly known as the Street of Canoes. During the Aztec and colonial periods, the "street" was a canal forming part of the waterway used for the transportation of goods from lakeside villages to the island city of Tenochtitlan. The restoration of the street to expose the ancient canal may give you some sense of the wonder expressed by the conquistador Bernal Diaz del Castillo from his view on top of the Templo Mayor:

We saw the three causeways which led into Mexico...and we saw the bridges on the three causeways which were built at certain distances apart through which the water of the lake flowed in and out from one side to the other, and we beheld on the great lake a great multitude of canoes some coming with supplies of food and others returning loaded with cargoes of merchandise...and we saw in those cities Cues [temples] and oratories like towers and fortresses all gleaming white, and it was a wonderful thing to behold....

Continue on busy, stall-filled Corregidora until Alhondiga and the **Plaza de la Alhondiga**, now a *lively square reminiscent of old Mexico*, filled with fruit and rope vendors. During the colonial period this was the site of the **public granary**. Go left up Alhondiga. The dock and canal, on the right, stand in front of the **Casa del Diezmo** (Tithe House) where the Church collected its revenue in kind. The Casa del Diezmo is marked by a cross on top.

Church of La Santisima

Santisima and E. Zapata • Head north to the **Church of La Santisima**, completed in 1783 with a wonderful **Churrigueresque facade** attributed to **Lorenzo Rodriguez**, the architect of El Sagrario. Now exposed is the original lower level of the church, which had sunk 6 feet below the street. *Note the top of the tower in the shape of a tiara, the symbol of the papacy.*

Calle Moneda

Walk on E. Zapata back toward the zócalo. The street becomes **Calle Moneda**, named after one of its buildings, the **Casa de Moneda** (Mint), which produced the coins of the New Spain during the colonial period. Closed to traffic, Calle Moneda affords *a pleasant walk past pastel-colored 18th-century buildings with wrought-iron balconies.* The 18th-century **Church of Santa Ines** (corner of Academia), founded by Conceptionist nuns, *displays gracious towers and attractive carved wooden doors.* If you have time, stroll through the peaceful **convent patio**. Across the street you find the **Academy of San Carlos** (National Academy of Fine Arts), which opened in 1785, though its present facade dates from the mid-19th century. Founded as a school for the study of fine arts, it served as an early training ground for many of the great **20th-century muralists**, including Diego Rivera who served as its first Director of Plastic Arts.

At the corner of **Correo Mayor**, originally called the "Street of the Sad Indian," stand two 18th-century mansions. The building on the east side has a **facade** of *tezontle* stone decorated with carvings of the sun and moon and surmounted by a religious statue of La Purisima. Farther along *Moneda at #13* you come upon the **National Museum of Cultures**, housed in the 18th-century former mint. The handsome colonial building served as the showplace for the archaeological treasures of Mexico until 1964, when they were moved to the new National Museum of Anthropology in Chapultepec Park. The **National Museum of Cultures** displays the prehistory and arts and crafts of the peoples from Africa, Asia, Europe, and the Americas.

Open Tues.- Sat., 9:30 a.m.-6 p.m. Sun., 9:30 a.m.-4 p.m. Closed Mon. Admission fee.

Templo de Santa Teresa La Antigua

Lic. Verdad • After leaving the National Museum of Cultures, cross to the other side of Moneda and go up Lic. Verdad, a wonderfully restored street. On the right side you will find the majestic **church of Santa Teresa La Antigua**. Founded by the Carmelites and consecrated in 1684, its various parts date from the 17th to the 19th centuries. Note the interesting **facade** of two stories with its handsome carved **wooden double doors** framed by stately stone columns. The **interior** is worth visiting if only to view the beautiful stained glass windows.

National Pawnshop

Zócalo at 5 de Mayo Open Mon.-Sat., 9 a.m.-6 p.m. • If you return to Moneda for one-half block, you will be back at the zócalo. Cross the zócalo to the corner of 5 de Mayo and the **National Pawnshop** (Nacional Monte de Piedad) located on the site of the Aztec palace of **Axayacatl** where Cortes and his fellow conquistadors were first housed and entertained by Moctezuma and where this Aztec ruler was later held hostage and killed. Today, the rooms of the National Pawnshop overflow with an incredible variety of goods. *You may find antique books, watches, jewelry, enormous stone markings for graves, cut-glass decanters, chandeliers, and bentwood furniture,* suggesting that some wealthy people as well as the poor are in hock.

Detour

The main tour continues a block south along Calle Madero. If you have time, *we recommend a short detour:* another block south and then right on to 16 de Septiembre. Enter the extraordinary art *nouveau* lobby of the **Gran Hotel** (16 de Septiembre #82), originally one of Mexico City's first department stores. (See "Where to Stay," below.) If you walk back to the corner and continue south on 5 de Febrero, you will find the department store, **El Palacio de Hierro** along with some fine **colonial buildings** ending with the Hotel Ontario, corner of Uruguay. Calle V. Carranza, which intersects with 5 de Febrero, is lined in both directions with a number of colonial buildings well worth viewing. Of particular interest is the very attractive *18th-century mansion located at the corner of V. Carranza and Isabel la Catolica (#44).* Owned by the Banco Nacional de Mexico, it was formerly the **Palace of the Count of San Mateo de Valparaiso**. Still farther along, but worth the detour, is **Las Vizcainas** (Colegio de San Ignacio), located just before Lazaro Cardenas on Mesones and Vizcainas. This elegant block-long 18th-century building with a tezontle **facade** and a lovely central **portal** with a handsome wooden door still functions as a school. It is here that **La Corregidora**, the heroine of Independence, studied. Open for visitors only when school is in session.

Calle Madero

The colonial splendor of Mexico City is displayed along Calle Madero, one of the city's original streets and *lined with churches and mansions*, the latter frequently with facades of the rich red *tezontle* stone. This busy street has become more manageable and pleasant in recent years with the creation of pedestrian malls on its intersecting streets of Palma, Motolinia, and Gante. Below are several of the highlights along Calle Madero.

La Profesa Church

Madero at Isabel la Catolica • The 18th-century baroque La Profesa is noted as the place where supporters of the viceregal government conspired to keep the Spanish in power. Despite their plot, independence was ultimately achieved.

Hotel Ritz

Madero 30 • It's well worth dropping into the Ritz to view the wonderful **Miguel Covarrubias mural**, "Afternoon in Xochimilco," located in the piano bar, just off the lobby.

Palace of Jose de la Borda

Madero at Bolivar • Across the street stands the now rundown palace of Jose de la Borda, the enormously rich owner of silver mines in Taxco. Presented as a gift to his wife, the mansion's fame derives from the **second-floor balcony** running the length of the building. The palace was originally planned to occupy an entire block, with an encircling balcony to provide Senora de la Borda with a panoramic view of her city.

Iturbide Palace

Madero 17; Open 10 a.m.-6 p.m. • Extravagant family presents were the order of the day for wealthy Spaniards in the 18th century. The owner of this extraordinary palace built it to serve as the dowry for his daughter who was about to be married to the Marques de Villafont. The building was later renovated and used as Emperor Iturbide's palace during his abortive attempt to establish a Mexican monarchy. The delicately carved wooden **doorway** opens to an exquisite three-story **courtyard** enclosed by elegantly proportioned columns, arches, and carved-stone window casings. This courtyard is often the setting for temporary art exhibits.

San Francisco Church

Madero between Gante and Lazaro Cardenas • The 17th-century San Francisco Church and its **cloister** (the latter entered from Calle Gante #5) are the *only remaining buildings of a monastery that once covered several city blocks*, served as headquarters for the Franciscan order in Mexico, and was a site for the missionaries' training of Aztec youths to preach Christianity in their communities. Most of the monastery was destroyed after the passage of the Reform Laws. Of interest is the stone-arch **entrance** and the Churrigueresque **facade** of the church and the arched courtyard of the former **cloisters** (now a Methodist church).

House of Tiles

Madero 4 • Across from San Francisco Church is one of the more intriguing buildings in Mexico City. Formerly the Palace of the Count of El Valle de Orizaba, the building gets its name from the **facade** covered top to bottom in blue-and-white Puebla tiles. The enormous **glass-covered courtyard**, now a Sanborn's restaurant, is ringed by columns rising two stories and an upper-level balcony whose walls are decorated with tiles and stone carvings. An **Orozco mural** entitled "Omniscience" commands the stairwell to the second floor. You may wonder, why the unusual tiled facade? According to popular legend, the son of one of the later resident counts loved the good life but did not relish work. His angry father, believing that the son would never make anything of his life, one day bellowed, "You will never have a house of tiles!" The rebellious son met the challenge. He married a wealthy woman and subsequently covered the entire facade with tiles. The father's reaction is not known.

Latin American Tower

Madero at Lazaro Cardenas; Open daily, 10 a.m.-midnight. Admission fee. • An engineering marvel, the 44-story modern **Latin American Tower** has been able to remain upright despite resting on the squishy lake bed. Its floating foundation construction has enabled it to withstand numerous earthquakes when shorter buildings crumbled to the ground. On the top is the **Observatory**, which, on a clear day, affords a *magnificent view of the city, valley, and surrounding mountains.*

ALAMEDA PARK AND HISTORICAL CENTER (TRIP 2)

This full-day tour takes you to historic Alameda Park, through the old sections of Mexico City to colonial churches and plazas, and to the beginning of the Mexican mural revolution and some of the finest frescoes by Diego Rivera and Jose Clemente Orozco. Plenty of walking is involved, so wear comfortable shoes. You can get to the Alameda Park starting point by bus (marked "Bellas Artes" or "Alameda") or pesero (marked "Bellas Artes") running along the Reforma or Line 2 of the Metro to Hidalgo. Returning buses and *peseros* are marked "Chapultepec Metro."

Alameda Park

Corner of Av. Juarez and Dr. Mora • Filled with **fountains** and 19th-century French **sculpture**, the park adds calm and beauty to the busy downtown area. Built in the late 16th century, the park's western section, known as **Plaza del Quemadero**, was used for the burning of heretics during the Inquisition. Later, in the 19th century, the park became the fashionable spot for Sunday promenades. Sundays are still popular, if less elegant, with families and couples enjoying the free concerts. Even in late evening people stroll through the park and relax on its benches. Balloon vendors often ply their trade selling fanciful creations. During the Christmas season and especially around the Day of the Three Kings, the park throbs with color, life, lights, and food.

Museo de la Alameda

Balderas at Colon Open Tues.-Sun., 10 a.m.-6 p.m. Closed Mon. • Having survived the 1985 earthquake that destroyed its former home, the Hotel Del Prado, Diego Rivera's spectacular **mural**, *A Dream of a Sunday Afternoon in Alameda Park*, now can be seen in the Alameda Museum. Here it is even more impressive than in its former setting. While the mural contains historical references from Cortes to the Revolution, its vivid color and captivating setting in Alameda Park make it one of Rivera's most engaging and successful works. The center depicts an elegant Sunday promenade in the park, dominated by superbly colored balloons soaring upward to the sky. *The little boy in the center, who holds hands with a fashionably dressed skeleton, is Rivera himself. Behind Rivera, with a hand on his shoulder, is his artist wife, Frida Kahlo.* Rich in color, historical narrative, and social commentary, the mural sustains close examination. Elsewhere in the museum are **photographs** recording the monumental effort required to transport this gigantic mural from the Hotel Del Prado to its present setting just across the street. There are also interesting **exhibits** concerning the painting of the mural and the scandal Rivera caused when he initially painted "Dios no existe" ("God doesn't exist") on the sheet of paper held by the liberal thinker, Ignacio Ramierez ("El Nigromante").

Pinacoteca Virreinal de San Diego

Dr. Mora 7; Open Tues.-Sun., 10 a.m.-5 p.m. Admission fee • A plaque notes that during the years 1596-1771 the burning place of the Inquisition was located in front of this handsome 17th-century building. Inside, on the grounds of the former San Diego Monastery, is the **Gallery of Colonial Paintings**, *displaying the works of some of the most outstanding painters in Mexico in the 16th-18th centuries.* Although religious themes predominate, the wonderful 18th-century still-life, *The Painter's Cupboard*, by Antonio Perez de Aguilar, should not be overlooked. *The Gallery is never so lovely as in the evening when it is occasionally open for concerts.*

Church of San Hipolito and the Causeway of Tlacopan

Hidalgo at Zarco • When you leave the Pinacoteca Virreinal walk up to Calle Hidalgo, cross to the north side of the street, and walk a short distance to the left until you come to the Church of San Hipolito. *Standing in front of this church on Hidalgo, you are on one of the most famous routes in Mexican history.* Formerly the Tlacopan Causeway, it linked Tenochtitlan to the mainland. It was along this route that the Spanish made their ill-fated retreat on June 30, 1520, during the famous *Noche Triste* (Night of Sorrows) when greed overcame wisdom. Loaded down with melted gold and jewelry, many conquistadors drowned in the deep waters of the lake, their treasures lost forever, or so it was thought until recently. In 1981, while digging a foundation for a new building a short distance away, *a bulldozer uncovered a 4-pound gold bar "three fingers in width,"* the size of the bars melted down by the Spaniards. This gold piece was but a small part of the booty dropped by the fleeing conquistadors. It is now prominently displayed in the Museum of the Templo Mayor.

Despite this defeat, the Spaniards displayed their usual resiliency. A year later, on August 13, 1521, the feast day of San Hipolito, Tenochtitlan once again succumbed to Cortes. The **sculpture** in front of the church on the street corner of Hidalgo and Zarco commemorates this event. It depicts an Aztec warrior amid an array of weapons of war, grimacing in pain as he is carried off by an eagle.

Hotel Cortes

Hidalgo 85 at the corner of Dr. Mora • The Hotel Cortes (see "Accommodations," below), is a former hospice for friars. The 18th-century baroque *tezontle* **facade** does not prepare you for the exceptionally handsome and intimate **patio**.

Churches of San Juan de Dios and Santa Veracruz

Proceed east on Hidalgo to the Plaza of Santa Veracruz, flanked on the west by the **Church of San Juan de Dios** and on the east by the **Church of Santa Veracruz**. San Juan de Dios is notable for its 18th-century concave **facade** and Moorish-style designs. Founded by the charitable Juanino order, the church continues to attract the needy. Across the plaza, the sinking 18th-century Church of Santa Veracruz was founded by a brotherhood dedicated to befriending and consoling prisoners. Beginning in the 1920s and until recently, a funeral-wreath market operated in the plaza.

Museo Franz Mayer

Plaza de Santa Veracruz; Open Tues.-Sun., 10 a.m.-5 p.m. Closed Mon. Admission fee • Located in a renovated convent next to the Church of San Juan de Dios, this marvelous museum houses the collection of Franz Mayer, born in Germany but a nationalized Mexican. Well exhibited in a handsome setting are *some of the finest examples of the applied arts of the New World*, including a striking collection of **religious art**—much of it in wood, some gorgeous works in silver, many fine examples of 18th- and 19th-century Spanish pewter, some stunning 17th-19th-century Mexican chests and an extraordinary collection of **Puebla Talavera** ware with many pieces from the 18th and 19th centuries. Some of the other exhibits are of **Chinese porcelain** and **European paintings,** including works by the 17th-century Spanish painter, **Jose Rivera** ("Lo Spagnoletto").

Museo Nacional de la Estampa

Plaza de Santa Veracruz; Open Tues.- Sun., 10 a.m.-6 p.m. Entrance free • Located just to the right of the Museo Franz Mayer, *this museum is devoted exclusively to prints.* Special international **exhibitions** are often featured on the first floor, while the second floor's **permanent collection** includes prints by **Carlos Mérida**, **Jose Guadalupe Posada**, and other major Latin American artists.

Palacio de las Bellas Artes

Lazaro Cardenas between Juarez and Hidalgo; Open Tues.-Sun., 10:30 a.m.-6:30 p.m. • Stroll across the Alameda toward Av. Juarez until you come to the gleaming-white Palacio de las Bellas Artes (Palace of Fine Arts). Built in Italianate style, its stunning **art-deco interior** utilizes some pre-Columbian motifs. The building's scheduled completion date of 1910 was delayed for 24 years because of the Revolution. On the third floor, the marbled interior contains paintings by the four great Mexican **muralists**, **Rivera**, **Orozco**, **Siqueiros**, and **Tamayo**. Rivera's very stylized and stiff *Man at the Crossroads* deals with the themes of oppression, protest and the use of science and technology for social progress, while at the opposite end of the floor, Orozco's powerful *Catharsis*, painted in expressive reds, grays, and blacks, portrays the dehumanization of people by the new technology. The Siqueiros paintings, especially *Democracy Freeing Herself* (depicting a nude woman in chains), rival the Orozco mural for expressive power. Tamayo's more abstract *Birth of Nationality* and *Mexico Today* contrast with the work of his three predecessors by his creation of ethereal and poetic moods.

Bellas Artes serves as Mexico's foremost cultural center. It is home for the **National Symphony** and the **Ballet Folklorico** as well as for international **art exhibitions**, visiting symphony orchestras, and renowned soloists. The theater is famed for its enormous **Tiffany stained-glass curtain** designed by Dr. Atl with a painting of the Valley of Mexico and the volcanoes Popocatepetl and Iztaccihuatl. *The curtain is dramatically illuminated before the Sunday morning performance of the Ballet Folklorico.*

Correo Mayor

Lazaro Cardenas and Tacuba • Across from Bellas Artes stands the Correo Mayor (Central Post Office) looking quite Moorish, but actually built in the early 20th century. The **interior** is worth visiting for its carved wood and bronze work.

"El Caballito"

Tacuba between Lazaro Cardenas and F. Mata • On the north side of Tacuba just past the Correo Mayor is the **Plaza Manuel Tolsa** displaying in its center Tolsa's most famous **sculpture**, *El Caballito* (The Little Horse) portraying Charles IV of Spain on horseback. Cast in bronze, *El Caballito* has been acclaimed as one of the finest equestrian statues ever produced. Cast in 1802, *El Caballito* was originally located in the zócalo but had to be hidden during the years of the Independence Movement because of strong anti-Spanish sentiment. Despite the unpopularity of Charles IV, Mexicans have a strong affection for this statue, which stood for many years on the Reforma at the intersection of Av. Juarez.

National Museum of Art

Overlooking the plaza at Tacuba 8 (Communications Palace) *Admission fee. Open Tues.-Sun., 10 a.m.-6 p.m.* • Opened in 1983 as the **National Museum of Art,** this museum is the only one in the city to exhibit *works that are representative of all periods of Mexico's artistic development from pre-Columbian times to the present.* In addition, it specializes in works from the 19th century. *Particularly striking are the evocative* **landscapes** *of the Valley of Mexico and Oaxaca by Jose Maria Velasco, and Jose Maria Estrada's haunting portrait of Don Francisco Torres (The Dead Poet)* who is depicted with a glorious floral crown that is reminiscent of the painted gourds from Chiapa de Corzo. From the 20th century, Francisco Goitia's powerfully expressive and painful painting, *Tata Jesucristo*, is not easily forgotten, and Miguel Covarrubias' satirical portrait, *The Bone*, is memorable. On the top floor are prints depicting daily life before and during the Revolution by Mexico's foremost engraver and satirist, **Jose Guadalupe Posada**.

Teatro de la Ciudad

Donceles between Allende and Isabel la Catolica • Turn left at Calle Bolivar and then right on Donceles. Next to the Chamber of Deputies is the Teatro de la Ciudad (Municipal Theater). Inaugurated in 1912, this elegant neoclassical building with Corinthian columns presents concerts, plays, and shows of traditional music and dance.

Santo Domingo Plaza and Church

Brasil at G. Obregon • Continue east on Donceles to Av. Brasil, then go left on Brasil for a block to the **Plaza of Santo Domingo**, a charming old plaza exuding authenticity. Only an occasional brand-new car parked on the plaza (to be raffled off) mars the colonial atmosphere. While sitting on a bench or next to the fountain, watch the activity under the arcades that line the western edge of the plaza. Since the mid-18th century *evangelistas* ("public scribes") have worked here writing letters for those unable to write. Today, they continue to perform this service using ancient typewriters to pound out love letters, to complete applications, and to help people communicate with family and friends. Their work has expanded in recent years. The "scribes" now type papers for university students, and the arcades have become a Mexican version of our copy centers with hand-operated printing presses grinding out business cards and public announcements.

The Church of Santo Domingo dominates the north side of the plaza. Completed in 1736, it replaced a 16th-century church that was damaged in a flood. On the lower left of the **facade**, ornate Corinthian columns with foliation and fruit designs frame a niche containing a saint holding a miniature church. Inside, the chapel on the right contains a wall of *milagros,* or ex-voto offerings, many in the shape of legs, giving thanks for miraculous recoveries.

The arches to the left of the church lead to **Calle Leandro Valle**, an interesting street framed on one side by the bulwarks of the church, and the other side by aging colonial homes. This street, which replaced parts of the former monastery of Santo Domingo, gave rise to comments that *it was the stupidest street ever made because it neither came from nor led anywhere.* Students from the nearby medical school noted, however, that the street did have an important function: it connected two very popular bars.

Reminders of the Inquisition can be found at the northeast corner of the plaza (Brasil and Venezuela), where the former home of the **Tribunal of the Holy Office** stands. Used for the Inquisition as a court and prison, today it houses a museum of the history of medicine around its handsome courtyard. On the east side of the plaza, the block-long **Customs House** now occupies the site of the former home of the conquistador **Cristobal de Onate.**

Ministry of Public Education

Argentina 28; Open Mon.-Fri., 7 a.m.-7 p.m. • The Ministry of Public Education (La Secretaria de Educacion Publica) is located just a block away on Argentina between Venezuela and G. Obregon. An impressive display of considerably more than **100 murals painted by Diego Rivera** between 1923 and 1928 surrounds the patios and three floors. After the Mexican Revolution, Jose Vasconcelos, the poet-philosopher and Minister of Public Education, supported muralists by commissioning artists to produce paintings that would promote the development of Mexican cultural values and its historical pride. Rivera's frescoes in the ministry resulted from Vasconcelos' commission. Here again, Rivera ingeniously uses architectural details to heighten the effect of the murals. *Those on the first floor celebrate Mexico with scenes of its daily life, industries, and festivals. There is little on this floor that smacks of the biting political statements so often found in Rivera's works.* Rather, the vitality and dignity of the nation are portrayed. Note especially the glorious painting, *Dia de Muertos* (Day of the Dead) depicting the holy day's festival, with three guitar-playing figures dominating the upper portion while below are throngs of people with vendors selling many of the macabre toys and candies associated with this very Mexican celebration. *Other striking murals on the first floor include the lovely El Canal de Santa Anita,* showing festive, flower-bedecked barges of the canal in a scene reminiscent of present-day Xochimilco; and *La Danza de los Listones,* a gay portrayal of the dance performed with ribbon streamers. For Rivera's clever use of architectural details, see *La Dotacion de Ejidos,* where workers dressed in white attending a meeting are shown, some sitting on top of an actual doorway as another peeks around an obstruction. The murals on the third

floor are more overtly political and satirical. Capitalist greed is carica-
tured in ways you are unlikely to forget in *Banquete de Wall Street* and
La Cena de Capitalista, while Mexican workers, families, and the Revolution are celebrated in a number of other paintings.

National Preparatory School

Justo Sierra 16; Open Tues.-Sun. 11 a.m. to 6 p.m. • As you leave the
Ministry of Education make a right back to the corner of G. Obregon,
then left on to San Ildefonso, the continuation of G. Obregon. Now
closed to traffic, the street is part of the old university area. It is dominated by the gorgeous block-long 18th-century **Jesuit Seminary of
San Ildefonso**, which once housed the National Preparatory School
(La Escuela Nacional Preparatoria). Restored in 1982 and converted
into a museum in 1993, the building features an elegant *tezontle*
facade with a handsome **interior** filled with **murals by Jean Charlot**,
Fernando Leal, **David Alfaro Siqueiros**, and, most notably, **Jose Clemente Orozco,** all commissioned by Vasconcelos. Before turning the
corner at Carmen for the entrance to the Preparatoria, continue east
just past Calle Carmen to the building at San Ildefonso 60. Formerly
the **Church of San Pedro and San Pablo** and later part of the old university, it is now a secondary school. Most striking is the refined,
baroque **doorway** surmounted by the carved coat of arms of the university. Congress met here in the early 19th century, and in 1824 it
issued the first constitution of the newly independent Mexico.

To enter the National Preparatory School, go south on Carmen one
block, then right on Justo Sierra to #16. **Orozco's expressive murals,**
begun in 1923, surround the three floors of the main patio. Here you
can see the beginnings of Orozco's fresco work, including his incorporation of the existing architecture to lend force to his paintings, a
technique later perfected in his series of murals in Guadalajara. On the
first floor, *The Trench* (or "Man's Struggle against Man"), depicting
two men in battle while a third lowers his head as if in shame, is particularly effective in its composition and emotional power. Notice
Orozco's use of architectural structure in the murals on the stairwell
between the first and second floors. On the upper floors, some of
Orozco's murals became sardonic. *In one painting on the second floor
he uses a window arch of the building to hide a hand catching coins that fall
through a hole in a collection box.* In another, a wealthy capitalist dances
with a blindfolded figure of Justice. Still another mural shows the
blind leading those who don't want to see as they trample the poor.
The theme of human suffering shows through in a series of paintings
on the third floor dealing with the tragedy of war. Look especially for
Return to the Battlefield, showing the bent backs of peasants as they
trudge off to war followed by grieving women. *Without showing a single face, Orozco captures the pain of war and the depth of the peasants'
emotions.* On the ground floor, the Bolivar Amphitheater contains a
very early Diego Rivera mural that demonstrates his European training
but not his later, uniquely Mexican, style.

TOUR OPTIONS

At this point you have three choices. You can walk one-half block to Argentina and two blocks south and be in the zócalo. Or, if it is lunchtime, you can walk a few blocks to *one of the city's most historic restaurants*, the **Cafe Tacuba** (see "Eating Out"). Or you can end the tour with a visit to the relaxing **Loreto Plaza** (intersection of San Ildefonso and Loreto). The tilting 19th-century neoclassical **Church of Loreto,** occupying the north end of the plaza, is noted for its large cupola and its connection with the Virgin Mary. As the story goes, the house of birth of the Virgin Mary was flown by angels from its location in Nazareth to Loreto, Italy. The cult of Loreto came to Mexico in the early 17th century and later built the present church. On the east side of the plaza, you find the **Church of Santa Teresa.** This unimposing early 18th-century building, sometimes said to be the most unpretentious church in colonial Mexico, mirrors its origins—it was built for women without dowries.

CHAPULTEPEC PARK (TRIP 3)

This trip takes you to **Chapultepec Park,** which has museums, lakes, restaurants, zoos, and an amusement park. *It highlights one of the world's great museums, the* **National Museum of Anthropology,** *as well as* **Chapultepec Castle,** *former home of Maximilian and now the* **National Museum of History.** Although several days would be needed for the entire tour, in a full day you get an overview of several museums as well as a feel for this vibrant historical park.

Buses ("Auditorio," "Palmas," or "Lomas") run along the Reforma through the park, with a stop at the National Museum of Anthropology. The Chapultepec stop on Line 1 of the Metro is within walking distance of the museum. Some Reforma *peseros* also go through the park past the museum. **Taxis** park next to the National Museum of Anthropology; although convenient, they usually cost substantially more than the taxis that run along the Reforma. *Late in the afternoon when museums are closing, buses are mobbed and peseros and taxis are sometimes impossible to find.* Make your plans accordingly. If desperate, walk up the Reforma to the Hotel Stouffer Presidente or Hotel Nikko Mexico, or over to Mariano Escobedo to the Hotel Camino Real (See "Accommodations," below) for a taxi or a drink.

Rich in history and *home of many of the artistic and historical treasures of the nation,* lovely, wooded Chapultepec Park bursts with humanity on Sunday, when Mexicans celebrate their day of leisure with picnics, boating, soccer, and visits to museums. Vendors appear with colorful balloons soaring to the sky; some families spread out elaborate feasts, while others in hammocks strung between trees sway to the sounds of guitars. Any visitor familiar with France will be struck by the contrast. No "Keep off the Grass" signs are found here. This is a people's park, to be used and enjoyed.

Despite heavy use, the park retains its beauty. About a mile long, and in places a mile wide, it contains many varieties of plants and trees, including the ancient **ahuehuete trees.** The park's name comes from the Aztec, meaning "Hill of the Grasshopper," a reference to the shape of the hill where Chapultepec Castle sits. Beginning in the 15th century, Aztec rulers came here for relaxation and recreation, a tradition continued during the colonial period by the Spanish viceroys.

The park is divided into three sections: the original **Bosque de Chapultepec** (Chapultepec Woods), home of most of the cultural institutions; **Nuevo** ("new") **Bosque de Chapultepec**, dominated by one of the world's largest roller coasters; and a new third section for strolls, picnics, and horseback riding. *Although most colorful on Sunday, the park is a joy to visit any day.* Few parks in the world match its combination of beauty, museums, and recreational facilities.

The National Museum Of Anthropology (Museo Nacional De Antropologia)

Open Tues.-Sat., 9 a.m.-7 p.m.; Sun., 10 a.m.-6 p.m. Closed Mon. Admission fee, admission free on Sunday. Tours in English available for a fee. Cameras, but no flash or tripods permitted • This glorious museum is world renowned for the excellence and depth of its collection of **pre-Columbian art,** the magnificence of its displays, the fascination of its **architecture,** and the comfort of its **surroundings.** Here *Mexico proudly displays masterpieces of its ancient civilizations, making this as much a museum of history as a museum of art.*

Opened in 1964, the museum is laid out around a rectangular patio with rooms devoted to archaeology on the first floor and ethnography on the second. The visitor's comfort is constantly kept in mind: rooms open to the patio and an artificial reed-filled pond allowing you to rest frequently in the fresh air. At the entrance a huge "umbrella" protects the patio from the rain and doubles as a dramatic, cascading fountain. *A walk through the entire museum takes you past three miles of exhibits.* You probably will want to take shortcuts and view the highlights on your first visit. There is one drawback for non-Spanish-reading tourists—*all display labels are in Spanish only.*

In front of the museum stands a massive **stone sculpture of Tlaloc,** the rain god, 23 feet high and weighing 167 tons. To move the statue to the museum from its home in the eastern section of the Valley of Mexico, a special trailer was built and the electrical and telephone wires in Mexico City were raised. Although the move took place during the dry season, lightning, thunder, and rain appropriately accompanied the rain god as he traveled triumphantly through the city to his present place of honor.

On the right as you enter the museum's **Reception Hall** you find a dramatic Rufino Tamayo mural of a serpent and jaguar in battle. The room next to the mural is devoted to special temporary exhibits. **The Sala de Orientacion** (Orientation Hall), also in the main Reception Hall, has regular audiovisual presentations of the major pre-Hispanic cultures. Entering the courtyard, you find on your right introductory exhibit rooms. Next come rooms devoted to the highland cultures of the Central Valley, proceeding chronologically with Pre-Classic,

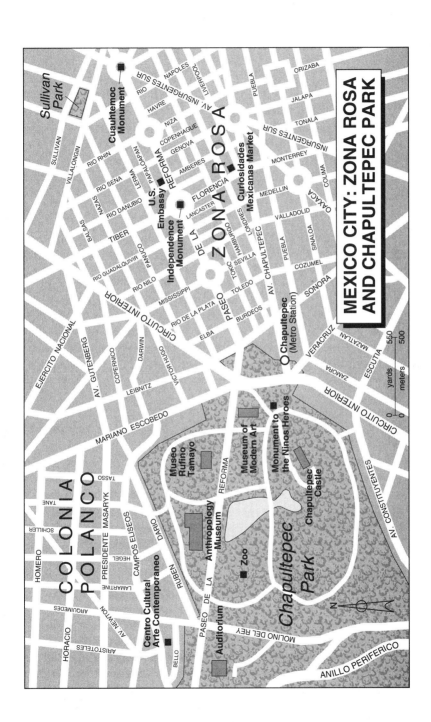

MEXICO CITY: ZONA ROSA AND CHAPULTEPEC PARK

Teotihuacan, Toltec, and culminating with Mexica (Aztec). Finally, on the left, you find Oaxaca, Olmec and Gulf of Mexico, Maya, and north and west Mexico. *If you want to be selective, we recommend you visit the Teotihuacan, Mexica (Aztec), Maya, and Gulf of Mexico (Olmec) rooms.*

Introduction to Anthropology; Mesoamerica; and Origins

These three rooms give you an overview of the field of anthropology, the major Mesoamerican cultures, and the populating of Mexico.

Pre-Classic

This room focuses on the **Pre-Classic cultures** in the central highlands and includes some charming ceramic pieces. Look for the **Olmec-influenced figures from Tlatilco**, including a wonderful acrobat. Some of the delightful tiny two-faced figurines from Tlatilco, although more than 2,000 years old, look like they could have come from the hands of Picasso.

Teotihuacan

A visit to this room is rewarding before or after your excursion to the pyramids of Teotihuacan • You find dramatic **reproductions of the Temple of Quetzalcoatl** and the famous **mural,** *Paradise of Tlaloc.* Some fine examples of Teotihuacan's delicate, thin **orangeware** as well as frescodecorated pottery are on display. Don't miss the ceramic vessel in the form of a bird decorated with conch shells.

Toltec

This room features the art from the archaeological site of **Tula**. Most striking are the 14-foot-tall **Atlantean column** representing a warrior and the reclining chacmool sculpture with a receptacle on his stomach that may have held the hearts of sacrificial victims.

Mexica

This huge, dramatic room houses the **art of the Aztecs**. Many of the temples in the Sacred Precinct of Tenochtitlan (see Trip 1 above) were adorned with frescoes and enormous stone carvings of gods, awesome in their features and fiercely expressive of their power to destroy life, to refuse rain and sunlight unless fed human life. The powerful gods can be found throughout this room. Dominating the room is the **24-ton Sun Stone** (Aztec Calendar) symbolizing the Aztec cosmos. In the center of the Sun Stone is the face of the sun god. Two striking and important pieces are found on the left side (as you face the Sun Stone) of the middle of the room. While the large and brutal **statue of Coatlicue**, the earth goddess, may startle you with its skirt of serpents, the exquisitely carved, colossal green **stone head of Coyolxauhqui**, the moon goddess, combines serenity with monumentality. Near the entrance to the room (on the right as you enter) can be found the **Piedra de Tizoc, a commanding, cylindrical stone**, 8-1/2 feet in diameter, with a relief of warriors and captives carved in a cosmic setting.

Although the many massive stone sculptures are the best known of Aztec art, the room also displays sculptures of animals, humans, and even vegetables showing a more delicate side of Aztec life. Look also for the replica of **Moctezuma's quetzal-feathered headdress** and the interesting **model of the sacred precinct with the Templo Mayor**, which will give you a good idea of why the Spaniards were so overwhelmed upon entering the ancient city of Tenochtitlan.

Oaxaca

Here you find the **art of the Zapotecs and Mixtecs** and objects from the sites of **Monte Alban** and **Mitla**. *There are some wonderful urns, a startling jade bat mask, and an enormous, leathery clay sculpture of a snarling jaguar.* Several tombs for rulers and priests were found at Monte Alban. This room has a **replica of Tomb 104**, complete with mural paintings and an urn of the rain god Cocijo. Some of the finest examples of the delicate and intricate **Mixtec goldwork** and **polychrome pottery** are on display, including a delightful bowl with a hummingbird perched on the rim.

Gulf Of Mexico

In this room is the extraordinary art of the Olmecs, considered by many to be the mother culture of Mesoamerica. As you walk into the room, you encounter one of the colossal stone heads, a portrait of an Olmec ruler. If you make the first right after entering, you'll see some of the most outstanding jade and stone work produced in the Americas. Many of the exquisite jade pieces show the were-jaguar mouth characteristic of Olmec art. The stone sculpture of a serpent with a priest holding an incense bag is remarkable for its incorporation of design into the irregular shape of the stone. *Not to be missed is the case with a baffling scene of some 16 figurines, all in precious jade or serpentine—except for one poor soul in a basalt stone who may represent a sacrificial victim.* This scene was found intact at the Olmec site of La Venta. The basalt sculpture, called *El Luchador* (The Wrestler), combines expressive power with delicacy, making this piece one of the gems of world art.

Maya

Maya art from the Classic period embodies the height of Mesoamerican achievements and ranks with some of the finest art produced in the ancient world. Shortly after you enter the room, on the right, you come upon several **carved limestone stelae** (freestanding carvings) from Yaxchilan. These superb carvings depict important historical events. The stelae generally contain lovely Maya hieroglyphs and show rulers in extraordinary attire with jade bracelets, earplugs, and elaborate headdresses. *Don't miss the magnificent jade mosaic death mask made for the legendary Maya ruler, Lord Pacal.* The room also features an excellent collection of **ceramic figurines** from the burial site on the island of Jaina. Rulers and royalty as well as common folk are depicted in a variety of postures, activities, and pre-Hispanic garments. On display also are some **fine bowls** and delicate **jade and bone carvings**. In the outdoor garden, a temple on the right has three rooms containing reproductions of the famous **battle murals found at Bonampak**. *Discovery of these powerful scenes put to rest the theory that the Maya were not warlike.*

North and West Mexico

The charming **clay figurines** from the states of Colima, Jalisco, and Nayarit are on display. *The art is devoted more to secular scenes of everyday life than to the ritualistic, religious, and ruler-oriented figurines found in other cultures.* Look for the intriguing Oriental-looking **Chinesco figurines** as well as the delightful **Colima dogs and warriors**.

Ethnography

The second floor of the museum is well worth visiting for its striking exhibitions of the crafts and daily life of the contemporary Indian groups whose ancestors are celebrated on the first floor. *For the serious collector of crafts, the exhibits provide an overview of some of the finest works of these indigenous people.* Rooms are devoted to the **Coras** and **Huichols**, **Tarascans**, **Otomis**, **Nahuas**, and Indian groups from the **Sierra de Puebla**. The various Indian peoples from the state of **Oaxaca** are represented, as are several contemporary **Maya** groups and indigenous peoples from the **Gulf Coast**. Representing northwestern Mexico are the **Seris**, **Tarahumaras**, and **Yaquis**.

Chapultepec Castle (Castillo Chapultepec)

Open Tues.-Sun., 9 a.m.-5 p.m. Admission fee • Imposing and elegant, this castle perches on Grasshopper Hill overlooking Mexico City. Here in pre-Hispanic times the Aztecs located their temple in honor of Tlaloc, the rain god. In the 18th century, a palace for viceroys was constructed on this historic site. Later occupied by a military college, the building was defended to the death by heroic young cadets against the U.S. invasion of 1847. The nearby **Monument to the Ninos Heroes** ("Boy Heroes") commemorates that event. Of all its occupants, the castle is best remembered as the home of the romantic and ill-fated couple, Emperor Maximilian and his wife Carlota. They renovated the Castle, added the garden, and built the imperial living quarters known as the **Alcazar.** From her balcony, Carlota could watch **Maximilian's** royal carriage as it traveled down the Reforma to the zócalo. After the fall of the French empire, the castle was abandoned. Although Juarez refused to live here, the castle became the residence of Mexican presidents beginning in the late 19th century. It was said to be a special favorite of **Porfirio Diaz,** whose taste for French elegance rivaled his lust for power. Under orders from President Lazaro Cardenas, the castle was turned into the **National Museum of History** (Museo Nacional de Historia), which opened in 1944.

The rooms of the museum present the history of Mexico from the Conquest to the Revolution of 1910. **Relics** and **mementos, religious and secular paintings,** and **furniture** occupy much of the museum, while the **murals** of several important 20th-century artists, including **Orozco, O'Gorman,** and **Siqueiros,** dominate other areas. *Particularly powerful and engrossing is the Siqueiros mural enveloping the room devoted to the Mexican Revolution.* Although many of Maximilian and Carlota's possessions, especially their furniture and china, are of interest, be sure not to miss their **royal carriage,** crafted in Italy, no doubt inspired by a vision of storybook royalty. For an added treat, you can look at Carlota's bedroom and her bathroom, complete with a marble tub.

Before or after you tour the museum, stroll through the gardens and take in some of the city and park views.

To get to the museum, take the elevator at the end of a tunnel near the entry gate at the foot of the hill (for which there usually is a line on Sunday), or walk along *the lovely, but uphill, path that winds around the hill.*

Monument of the Niños Heroes
Located at the bottom of the hill, the towering **marble pillars** commemorate the heroic defense of Chapultepec Castle by young cadets who died in battle during the U.S. invasion of 1847.

Museum of Modern Art
Open Tues.-Sun., 10 a.m.-6 p.m. Closed Mon. Admission fee • Located on the left side of the Reforma before the National Museum of Anthropology, this museum can be entered from the Reforma or from the Monument to the Ninos Heroes. Composed of modern, circular, twin buildings, *the museum contains a permanent exhibition of some 19th-century, but mostly* **20th-century, Mexican art**, including works by **Frida Kahlo** and **Orozco.** The museum also occasionally houses some of the **major traveling exhibitions** from museums around the world.

Museo Rufino Tamayo Arte Contemporaneo Internaciona
Open Tues.-Sun., 10 a.m.-6 p.m. Admission fee • Located before the National Museum of Anthropology between the Reforma and Melchor Ocampo, this major museum dedicated to **contemporary art** opened in 1981. Its first-rate collection of international art was a gift to the Mexican people from the artist, Rufino Tamayo, whose paintings join those of Picasso, Leger, and Miro to form part of the permanent collection. The museum also presents special exhibitions of such major 20th-century artists as Matisse, Picasso, and Rivera.

OTHER NEARBY SIGHTS
On the Reforma near the Museum of Modern Art is the delightful **Children's Zoo,** filled with animals and amusements. Farther along the Reforma, directly across from the National Museum of Anthropology, is a

popular **lake** with rowboats for rent and swans and ducks nervously dodging the efforts of novice oarsmen. A *torta* ("sandwich") stand is on one side of the lake; on another side is the **Casa del Lago**, an old mansion with a modern wing, where plays, poetry readings, music and dance, and crafts courses are offered to the public. On the left side of the Reforma past the National Museum of Anthropology is the **Zoo** and then the **Botanical Gardens.** If you continue past the Botanical Gardens to Molino del Rey (the street dividing New Chapultepec from Old Chapultepec) and turn south, you come upon **Los Pinos**, the official residence of the president of Mexico.

New Chapultepec Park

The new section of the park contains an amusement park complete with roller coaster as well as a few museums not likely to be of particular interest to the tourist. Also in this section of the park is the **Lerma Water Terminal** with its Diego Rivera mosaic of the ancient rain god Tlaloc covering the bottom of an outdoor fountain. Inside the terminal are some damaged Rivera murals dealing with the importance of water. Rivera's sympathetic treatment of the workers in these murals commemorates the 35 people who lost their lives constructing the tunnel that brings water into Mexico City from the faraway Lerma River. Just off the Periferico is the Amusement Park with its huge roller coaster called "la montana rusa," the Russian mountain. As the Reforma cuts through this section of the park, it passes the **National Auditorium,** where various music and dance performances take place. At the end of the park, the Reforma circles the **Petroleum Monument,** dedicated to Lazaro Cardenas' nationalization of the oil companies. The **Centro Cultural Arte Contemporaneo** (Campos Eliseos at J. Eliot, next to the Hotel Stouffer Presidente and across from the National Auditorium) is housed in an imposing contemporary building and presents changing contemporary art as well as crafts exhibits, almost always of considerable interest. The shop on the first floor sells some quality crafts. *Open Tues.-Sun., 10 a.m.-6 p.m.; Wed., 10 a.m.-9 p.m. Admission fee.*

Lomas de Chapultepec

If you continue on the Reforma past the Petroleum Monument, you enter Lomas de Chapultepec, one of the loveliest and wealthiest of Mexico's residential areas. If you have a car or can afford a taxi, a drive through this part of the city will provide you with scenes of luxurious living. Hidden behind many of the private walls are gardens, pools, and private tennis courts.

COYOACAN-SAN ANGEL-UNIVERSITY CITY (TRIP 4)

This tour combines the old and new, taking you to the **historic residential area of Coyoacan** and two **museums** associated with the artists **Diego Rivera** and **Frida Kahlo.** You go on to visit the **cobblestone streets of old**

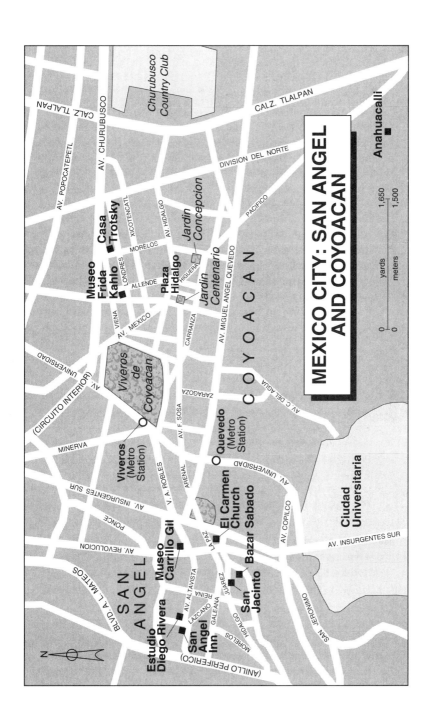

MEXICO CITY: SAN ANGEL AND COYOACAN

San Angel and **Rivera's home-museum,** the dramatic campus of the **National University of Mexico,** the **most ancient stone pyramid in Mexico,** and one of **Mexico's most futuristic buildings.**

Saturdays are best for this trip because you can combine sightseeing with shopping at the popular **Bazaar Sabado** *in San Angel (see "Where to Shop," below).* But even without the shopping addition, the tour is full and will require a minimum of an entire day. If you have only a day for this section of Mexico City, you will want to be selective.

Although the trip really calls for a taxi now and then, most of it can be done by public transportation. The main areas—Coyoacan, San Angel, and University City—lie in the southern part of the city, about a 30-minute taxi ride or a one-hour trip by public transportation from downtown. Each is about 15 minutes from the others.

COYOACAN

After the bustle of downtown, the tranquillity of **Coyoacan** soothes the soul. Coyoacan, lying strategically near one of the principal causeways, was used as a base for the conquistadors' garrison during Cortes' final assault on Tenochtitlan. In the town's main square, under Cortes' orders, the last Aztec ruler, Cuauhtemoc, and other nobles were tortured to reveal the location of Aztec gold. After the Conquest, Cortes established the seat of his government in Coyoacan while the new Mexico City was being built upon the ashes of Tenochtitlan. Today, Coyoacan is an attractive residential community with ancient trees shading streets lined by colonial-era buildings.

To get to the starting point—the Frida Kahlo Museum in Coyoacan—by public transportation, take the Metro Line 3 to the Viveros stop. Leave the station by the Viveros sign, turn right, and then make your first right on to a small street with no name. At Av. Mexico make a right and then at Londres go left until you reach the corner of Allende. It's a pleasant 15-minute walk from the Viveros stop. For Coyoacan center take Line 3 to the M.A. Quevedo stop, walk right to Av. Francisco Sosa and right on Sosa to the center. From the center, it's a 5-minute walk to the museum (5 blocks north on Allende).

Frida Kahlo Museum

Corner of Allende and Londres; Open Tues.-Sun., 10 a.m.-6 p.m. Admission fee • This fascinating yet infrequently visited **museum** was the home of **Frida Kahlo** and her husband **Diego Rivera**. Their deep commitment to the preservation of Mexico's rich Indian heritage is reflected everywhere in this house, a vivid example of the Mexican pride engendered by the Revolution of 1910.

While overshadowed by her more famous husband, *Frida Kahlo was a world-famous artist, too, and considered by some to be a superior painter.* A victim of polio and severely injured in a trolley car accident, she suffered from terrible physical pain—pain that is captured in the haunting, sometimes macabre, paintings on display in the museum. Also displayed is her collection of **Rivera's early paintings**, **Mexican folk art**, and **primitive retablos** (miracle paintings). *The very Mexican kitchen, gaily decorated with tiles and ceramics, is delightful, as is the tranquil garden containing pre-Columbian sculptures.* Kahlo's personal mementos, especially those in her bedroom and studio, provide insight into the lives of socially committed Mexican artists and intellectuals during the first half of this century. The museum is a must for anyone interested in this period so rich in art and so full of social commitment and political fervor.

Trotsky's Home

Viena 45, corner of Morelos, 5 blocks northeast of the Frida Kahlo Museum; Open Tues.-Fri., 10:00 a.m.-5 p.m. • **Leon Trotsky** fled to Mexico in 1938 after losing his battle for power with Stalin. *At first he lived in Frida Kahlo's house, but after a political disagreement with Rivera he moved here.* Despite strong security measures, Trotsky was assassinated here in 1940. Now a museum, it contains an interesting collection of **Trotsky's personal belongings** along with revealing books and newspapers of this period.

Coyoacan Center

The attractive center of Coyoacan is formed by the Jardin Centenario and the Plaza Hidalgo with its relaxing **sidewalk cafes**. Overlooking the plaza, the 16th-century **Church of San Juan Bautista** is filled with gilded gold. On the left side of the plaza as you face the church you will find the **Casa de Cortes**, now a government building, and formerly Cortes' administrative headquarters.

You can take a number of very pleasant walks around the center of Coyoacan. **Calle Francisco Sosa**, running west of the Jardin Centenario is lined with **colonial homes**. This street eventually intersects with Av. Universidad, where you will find the M.A. Quevedo metro stop to the left. Another soothing stroll is in the opposite direction, along Calle de la Higuera, which runs off the Plaza Hidalgo. Continue on Higuera until Vallarta, which borders the lovely **Jardin Conception**. The **house at Higuera 57** has an intriguing story attached to it. Supposedly, Cortes' wife was murdered here shortly after her arrival from Spain, so that Cortes could remain with his female companion, his translator Malinche. In the Jardin Conception, the 18th-century baroque **Chapel of the Conception**, unfortunately, is *open only for special occasions.* If you're hungry, the popular **El Parnaso** (Plaza Hidalgo; inexpensive), with its bookstore for browsing, is the place to enjoy local ambience with your enchiladas.

Anahuacalli-Diego Rivera Museum

Calle del Museo 150; about a half mile from the intersection of Av. Division del Norte. Open Tues.-Sat., 10 a.m.-6 p.m.; Sun. 10 a.m.-2 p.m. No admission fee. To reach Anahuacalli from Coyoacan center, it is easiest to take a taxi, or you can take the bus marked "Iztacala-Coyoacan" that runs on *Calle Centenario. Ask the driver to let you off at Calle del Museo where it is a short walk to the museum. From downtown Mexico City, take Metro Line 2 to Taxquena and then the bus marked "Tasquena Pena Pobre." By car, follow Av. Division del Norte off Insurgentes and follow signs to Museo Anahuacalli* • This **museum** gets its name from the Aztec word for the Valley of Mexico. The building of volcanic stone was designed by the artist **Diego Rivera** and contains his extraordinary collection of **pre-Columbian art**. Over the door of this austere, imposing pyramid-shaped structure is Rivera's statement that with this museum he is returning "to the people the artistic inheritance I was able to redeem from their ancestors."

The **first floor** displays **artifacts from throughout the Valley of Mexico**, principally from Teotihuacan and Aztec times, *but it is on the* **second floor** *that the quality of the collection becomes most apparent.* Here are exhibited an unrivaled **collection of works from the cultures of Western Mexico**—ball players from Jalisco, even a ball- game scene from Nayarit, charming animal figures from Colima, and delightful ceramic couples and musicians from all three areas. The **top floor** is devoted to the cultures of Oaxaca, the Gulf Coast, and the Aztecs.

SAN ANGEL

From the Anahuacalli-Diego Rivera Museum, you must take a taxi to San Angel. From downtown Mexico City, you can reach San Angel by public transportation. Peseros and mini-buses to San Angel run along Insurgentes Sur. They can also be found at the Chapultepec metro stop (Line 1), corner of Av. Chapultepec and Veracruz next to the Pemex station; and on Izazaga outside of the Pino Suarez metro stop. For the return trip, you can pick up the peseros and mini-buses on Av. Revolucion. From Av. Hidalgo or Calle Cuauhtemoc in Coyoacan to Altavista in San Angel, take bus #56 • One of the loveliest areas of the city, with **cobblestone streets** and **gracious homes** that are partially hidden by gates and high walls, **San Angel** (now officially known as Villa Obregon) is *delightful for* **shopping** *on Saturday at the Bazaar Sabado* (see "Shopping"), walking through its narrow streets, and eating at or visiting the exceptionally handsome, colonial **San Angel Inn** (see "Where to Eat"). **Plaza San Jacinto**, a lovely spot to visit any day, is surrounded by colonial mansions and open-air restaurants. The mansion housing the Bazaar Sabado is here, as is the intriguing **Casa del Risco** (San Jacinto 15), an 18th-century mansion housing a collection of 18th- and 19th-century European paintings and furniture. The patio of the Risco holds a truly wonderful **fountain** made of colorful colonial ceramic plates, cups, and saucers from Puebla. *Erratic visiting hours.* To get a taste of the old section of San Angel take the delightful walk along **Calle Benito Juarez** off the Plaza San Jacinto past the 16th century ex-convento **Dominico de San Jacinto** with its lovely **gardens**. Just down the street from the Plaza San Jacinto, at Av. Revolution, corner of Monasterio, is the 17th-century **El Carmen Church and Monastery,** noted for its museum containing remnants of **murals**, handsome **wood furnishings**, and stunning

tiles, especially those in the basement next to the celebrated room housing several **mummified nuns and priests**. *Open Tues.-Sun., 10 a.m.-5 p.m. Admission fee.*

Carrillo Gil Museum

Av. Revolucion 1608, corner of Desierto de los Leones; open Tues.-Sun., 9:30 a.m.-6 p.m. Admission fee • Three blocks north of El Carmen Church, this museum contains a fine collection of works by **Orozco**, **Rivera**, **Siqueiros**, and others. The Orozco charcoals and paintings are particularly compelling; the Rivera collection features some of his lesser-known but wonderful cubistic paintings.

Museo Estudio Diego Rivera

Palmas at Altavista, across from the San Angel Inn; open Tues.-Sun., 10 a.m.-6 p.m. Opened as a museum in 1986 in celebration of the 100th anniversary of Rivera's birth, this building, designed by the noted architect and artist **Juan O'Gorman**, originally served as Rivera's home and studio. Now it houses changing exhibits on the lower floors, and on the top floor—worth a visit for itself alone—Diego's studio filled with his extraordinary collection of **papier-mache judas and calavera figures** which he prized for their powerful expressions of the devil and death. This studio also served as Rivera's salon where he entertained such celebrated visitors as **Leon Trotsky**, Nelson **Rockefeller**, and **Henry Moore**. If you go outside and walk to the rear of the house, you will notice a second house connected by a walkway. This served, for a time, as the home of **Frida Kahlo**, Rivera's artist-wife. The buildings' design amply demonstrates the independence each maintained throughout their loving yet unconventional marriage.

Just across the street from this museum is the **San Angel Inn** (Palmas 50), a lovely spot for a drink or fine meal.

UNIVERSITY CITY (CIUDAD UNIVERSITARIA)

Insurgentes Sur, about 19 km (12 m) from downtown. The quickest way to the university is by metro. Take Line 3 to the last stop, Universidad, where you can then board the bus that makes a circuit around the university with stops at a number of buildings. From San Angel, buses #17, #17A, and #17B along Insurgentes Sur will also get you to the more interesting buildings around the library. From Coyoacan take the metro, Line 3, from M.A. Quevedo to the Universidad stop • Since 1955, University City has been the home of the National University of Mexico (better known as UNAM). Granted a charter in 1551 by Philip II of Spain, the university is the oldest institution of higher learning in the Americas. Today, its 80 modern buildings sprawl over hundreds of acres and serve more than 300,000 students, making it one of the largest universities in the world. Since most students commute to campus, you may better understand the reason for traffic jams along Insurgentes Sur. The most striking features of the campus are the dramatic murals covering several of the external walls of its buildings.

Central Library

The Central Library stands alone, dominating the campus physically and spiritually. Located just off Insurgentes Sur, the facade of the 12-story building is covered on all sides by a colorful and dramatic mosaic of stone, tile, and colored cement. Designed by Juan O'Gorman, the mural portrays the history of Mexican cultures from pre-Columbian times to the present. The huge south and north walls are devoted to the Indian and colonial periods, respectively; the west wall, with its shield of the National University, to the present; and the east wall with the atom, to the future.

Rectory

Administration Building • Southwest of the library stands the Rectory with one wall covered by a three-dimensional mural by Siqueiros. Entitled "People for the University and University for the People," the mural is boldly executed. Because the building can be seen from the road, Siqueiros designed it to be seen and understood by passing motorists as well as pedestrians. The mural's three-dimensionality and multiangularity were the artist's solution to the problem of the moving viewer.

School of Science Auditorium

Jose Chavez Morado designed two murals for this building connected to the 15-story School of Science located in the lower plaza. One deals with the theme of the conquest of energy, while a second symbolizes the oneness of humanity.

School of Medicine

Across the way, on the east side of the lower campus, stands the **School of Medicine**. On its west facade is a **stone mosaic by Francisco Eppens Helguera**, with a large three-faced mask in the center symbolizing the Indian, Spanish, and mestizo peoples that compose Mexico. If you walk south toward the sports fields, crossing the main drive encircling the campus, you will find a side road leading to the **tropical greenhouse**. Overflowing with all the wonderful tropical plants found in Mexico, *the greenhouse can be visited from Mon.-Sat., 9 a.m.-4:30 p.m.* Walk back to the main road and proceed west past the impressive Olympic swimming-pool area. Farther south are a series of strange, silent, dark pyramid structures used as fronton courts. Continue on the main road, cross Insurgentes Sur, and you come to the monumental, oval-shaped **Olympic Stadium,** decorated with stone mosaic figures by Diego Rivera that symbolize sports in Mexico from pre-Hispanic times to the present. As you cross Insurgentes, you will see the Central Library, the starting point for the tour.

OTHER NEARBY SIGHTS

Cuicuilco

About a mile south of University City, off the Periferico and next to the intersection with Insurgentes Sur To get to Cuicuilco by car, take Insurgentes Sur south and follow signs for Tlalpan-Cuernavaca-Mex 95. Exit on the lateral at Villa Olimpica, reverse your direction and head back north on

Insurgentes Sur. A few hundred yards after you reverse direction, you will come upon Cuicuilco on your right • Located in an attractive ecological park the **archaeological site of Cuicuilco** is more of historical than visual interest. The site contains the **first stone pyramid** in Mexico, dating from around 500 B.C. The round platform, about 400 feet in diameter, contains a ramp that once led to altars at the summit that towered 90 feet above the ground. By following this route to the top you sense the massiveness of the pyramid.

Although not a lot is known about Cuicuilco, it did predate Teotihuacan, and its abandonment in the first century B.C. may have set the stage for the growth of the latter city. After Cuicuilco's abandonment, the volcano Xitli erupted, burying the entire site under a lava bed. Excavations have uncovered many antecedents of Teotihuacan culture as well as early examples of irrigation canals. *A* **small museum** *on the site is open from 10 a.m.-4 p.m. Site is open 10 a.m.-5 p.m. Closed Monday. Small fee for museum.*

Siqueiros Polyforum

Av. Insurgentes Sur and Filadelfia; Open daily, 10 a.m.-9 p.m • If, on your way to University City or San Angel, you are heading down Insurgentes Sur, you will be startled by the multisided Siqueiros Polyforum covered with harsh, explosive murals by Siqueiros. Inside, a three-dimensional **mural** depicting the march of humanity was completed by the artist with the assistance of 50 artists and workers.

FLOATING GARDENS OF XOCHIMILCO (TRIP 5)

Festive **Xochimilco** (soh-chee-MEEL-koh) with its canals, carnival air, and flower-bedecked barges may strike you as the ultimate tourist trap until you sort out the scene and notice all the Mexican families. The atmosphere is very Mexican indeed, with vendors, flowers, and music everywhere. On Sunday, the docks come to life as Mexicans pour into the area to enjoy their day of leisure with lots of music, food, drink, and song in a lovely natural setting.

You come to Xochimilco to relax in a **rented barge** and partake of the merrymaking as your boatman glides you through the **canals**. A barge with **mariachi musicians** will pull over to ask if you would like a song. If you agree, their barge will be attached to yours and you will glide together during the serenade. Since musicians and barges are everywhere, you can enjoy the scene without ever renting your own music. The **music** and songs, colorfully **decorated barges**, **canoes filled with vendors**, and **garden surroundings** make this a most unusual and special place to spend a few hours.

You may want to bring a picnic lunch and beverages for your ride. For the adventurous, the Sunday market in town sells some very good *carnitas* ("roasted meat"). Just buy a kilo of tortillas and make your own tacos on board. But, if you don't feel like planning ahead, don't fear. As your boat winds its way through the canals, you will be approached by canoe vendors of soft drinks, beer, sandwiches, tamales, and various other items. The scene may convince you, as it has us, that as long as you have some money, you need never fear going hungry or thirsty anywhere in Mexico.

RENTING A BOAT

When renting a boat, bargaining is expected. Midweek when Xochimilco is rather quiet, bargaining is easier. On Sunday, when there is heavy demand and Xochimilco is most festive, bargaining is much tougher. Although the boats come in various sizes, even the smallest accommodates at least 10-15 people. Going in groups is usually most fun and cheaper (you pay per boat, not per person), although a boat for just two is not unheard of.

HISTORY

During the pre-Hispanic period, Xochimilco was a popular residence for Aztec nobles. The city was a major supplier of vegetables and flowers, which were transported by canoe through canals to the market in the Aztec capital of Tenochtitlan. The canals you see today give you some idea of the intricate system of waterways that once made up this area and by which trade was conducted. The name "floating gardens" or *chinampas* comes from the method of farming used along the lake before the Conquest. The gardens actually were a form of landfill created by mud and reeds and rooted by plants into the lake bed.

Today, Xochimilco is still known for its flowers and produce. After your boat ride, you can go to the market just off the zócalo. There you will find a very large and lovely flower section. While you are in the zócalo, you can visit the 16th-century Franciscan **Church of San Bernardino**. The decorations in the north portal door are very European, with such Gothic details as square rosettes and flowers. Most striking is the west portal, with delicate carved Corinthian columns and angels. The church is well known for its immense main altar, a noble Renaissance work with a fine sculpture of the Virgin Mary. About a block away, on Av. Morelos next to the market, stands the lively Capilla (Chapel) del Rosario decorated in Moorish style with blue and yellow Puebla tiles.

Xochimilco is about 25 km (15-1/2 m) southeast of the center of Mexico City. It is reached by **car** via the Periferico Sur, or take the Calz. Tlalpan from the center of town to the Viaducto Tlalpan to the Periferico Ote. By either route, exit at Jardines del Sur, which will lead you into Xochimilco. Once in Xochimilco follow signs to "Embarcadero" ("pier"). There are two routes for securing public transportation to Xochimilco. You can take **Metro Line 2** from Pino Suarez to Taxqueña, where there are **buses, trolleys**, and **peseros** to Xochimilco. Or you can catch a pesero for Xochimilco outside the metro stop Pino Suarez (Lines 1 and 2) on Calle Izazaga.

PLAZA OF THE THREE CULTURES
AND BASILICA OF GUADALUPE (TRIP 6)

This trip takes you to the former site of the great **Aztec marketplace** (where now you can see Indian, colonial, and modern Mexico side by side) and then to the holiest **shrine** in Mexico (where pilgrimages are made to visit the patron saint of the nation). The trip will take about a half day.

The sites are reached by **metro** *(Line 3 to Tlatelolco for the Plaza of the Three Cultures or Line 6 to La Villa for the Basilica of Guadalupe)*, **bus** or **mini-bus** ("La Villa") or *pesero* ("La Villa"). By **car**, follow Reforma Norte to the third traffic circle north of Alameda Park for the Plaza of the Three Cultures. Continue north to the Calz. Guadalupe for the Basilica. The main entrance to the Plaza of the Three Cultures is on Calle Maria la Redonda. To reach the site from the Reforma Norte, you need to walk west for a few blocks through an apartment complex.

Plaza of the Three Cultures

Located in **Tlatelolco** (tlah-tayLOHL-koh), this plaza lives up to its name by presenting **Aztec ruins**, a colonial church, and modern high-rise apartments and office buildings—all coexisting and symbolic of contemporary Mexico and its Indian and Spanish heritage.

The plaza is built on the **site of Tlatelolco**, which in Aztec times rivaled its southern neighbor Tenochtitlan for power. In 1473, the rivalry ended in a vicious battle. Although Tlatelolco was defeated and incorporated into Tenochtitlan, it retained its great ceremonial center and even greater marketplace, reportedly the largest in pre-Hispanic Mexico. The market astounded the conquistadors for its orderliness, cleanliness, and incredible variety of exotic goods, not to mention its size. Cortes reported that it "is twice as big as that of Salamanca and completely surrounded by arcades where there are daily more than sixty thousand folk buying and selling."

Today, you can see the remains of the **Aztec ceremonial center**. The site was dominated by a soaring pyramid, which, like its neighbor in Tenochtitlan, was surmounted by twin temples. Here several captured conquistadors were sacrificed, their hearts torn out and offered to the gods as their fellow Spaniards, waiting safely nearby, watched in horror. At Tlatelolco, the Aztecs made their final, futile stand against the onslaught of the Conquistadors.

Church of Santiago

Dates from 1609. Note the plaque in front of the church with its moving message commemorating the fall of the Aztecs and the birth of the mestizo nation. The subdued yet sturdy quality of the church seems appropriate for this historic spot. Inside, the striking simplicity of the lovely stone altar blends with the austere environment. Note on the left, the baptismal font said to be the one used for Juan Diego (see below). To the right of the church you can visit the **Franciscan monastery** that housed Holy Cross College, a school for the education of children of Aztec nobles. Here, in the 16th century, **Fray Bernardino de Sahagun** taught and wrote his important **Historia de las Cosas de Nueva España**. After entering the courtyard go to the farthest doorway on the lefthand side to see the remains of **paintings of angels** done by Aztec Indians in the 16th century. These murals are reportedly the only remaining 16th-century Indian paintings in Mexico City. From the second floor of the monastery there is a good view of the attractive **courtyard**. Surrounding the church and Aztec ruins are a group of modern high-rise buildings.

Basilica of the Virgin of Guadalupe

One of the most important shrines of Christendom in the Western Hemisphere, the Basilica of the Virgin of Guadalupe is the most sacred Christian site of the nation and draws visitors from all over the country and the world on regular pilgrimages, many crawling the last mile on their knees. On December 12, the anniversary of her miraculous appearance, hundreds of thousands of people gather here to celebrate the **fiesta of the Virgin of Guadalupe**. As Mexico's first saint, the Virgin has played a role in history: Father Hidalgo's proclamation of Mexican Independence began with the waving of her banner, and the revolutionaries of 1910 fought under her banner as well.

In pre-Conquest times, the hill of the shrine belonged to the earth goddess Tonantzin. Then, the great lake of Texcoco lapped the base of the hill and a causeway connected it to Tlatelolco and Tenochtitlan. Soon after the Conquest, however, the Aztec shrine was destroyed by Spaniards. Shortly thereafter, in 1531, **Juan Diego**, an Indian convert to Catholicism, was walking across the hill on his way to the Franciscan monastery at Tlatelolco when the dark skinned Virgin of Guadalupe appeared before him. In Nahuatl, she asked Juan to go to the bishop to request that a church be built in her honor on the hill. Several visits to the suspicious bishop were unsuccessful. Then on December 12, the Virgin appeared to Juan again and asked that as a present for the bishop he pick roses on the hill where only cactus could grow. And indeed lovely roses were found blooming in the rocky soil; so following instructions, Juan placed the roses inside his cape as he went to plead once more with the bishop for a shrine. This time he met with success. When he opened his cloak to present his gift, the roses were gone. In their place appeared the image of the Virgin of Guadalupe. The bishop needed no further proof. He ordered a chapel built, and had Juan Diego's miraculous cloak displayed prominently inside. **The Virgin of Guadalupe**, identified with the Aztec earth goddess and mother of humankind, became the patron saint of Mexico.

The Basilica

In 1976, the huge modern Basilica was consecrated. Prior to its construction, the Basilica was located in the large 18th-century building that now serves as a museum. The sweeping, modernistic construction of the new structure provides large open vistas for the enormous crowds, but the building lacks the warmth of its predecessor. **Juan Diego's cloak** hangs dramatically inside.

La Capilla del Pocito

(Temporarily closed.) • The 18th-century **Chapel of the Little Well** is located east of the Basilica. Its delicate features and yellow-tiled dome show Moorish influences. The well inside, which supposedly opened under the feet of the Virgin, is renowned for its healing powers. The sick and lame frequent the well to seek benefit from its curative powers.

At the top of the hill, another chapel is built on the spot where Juan Diego gathered his roses.

San Carlos Museum

Puente de Alvarado 50, the western extension of Av. Hidalgo. Open Wed.-Mon., 10 a.m.-6 p.m. Admission fee • On your return to the center of the city, you can make a slight detour for this museum, which has mounted major **international exhibitions**. Its permanent collection of European paintings include works of **Rembrandt**, **Rubens**, **Tintoretto**, **Pissarro**, **Zubaran** and other masters. The imposing, **neoclassic mansion** housing the collection was designed by Manuel Tolsa and originally built for the Count of Buenavista. Its later residents included **Agustin de Iturbide**, who briefly became emperor of Mexico, and **Madame Calderon de la Barca**, author of the early-19th-century book, *Life in Mexico*.

ESSENTIAL MEXICO CITY

SHOPPING

A shopper's nirvana, Mexico City tantalizes and tempts the traveler with an endless variety of shops selling high-quality traditional crafts, contemporary designs, and striking fashions. Unless you are strong-willed, you may find yourself spending more time shopping than sightseeing, and colonial architecture will take a backseat to contemporary crafts. More than likely, you will become part of that familiar departure scene at the Mexico City airport: happy travelers, loaded down with boxes and bags filled with Mexican treasures, wondering how they will fit all their purchases on the plane and where they will put them once back home.

While pre-Columbian art occupies the main floor of the National Museum of Anthropology, the finest examples of the **traditional crafts of the nation** are displayed over the entire second floor, demonstrating their importance to Mexican culture. Before shopping, you might want to visit the museum to view these artistic creations and get a sense of their variety and quality.

Excellent stores specializing in traditional crafts cluster around the **Alameda Park** area, while in the **Zona Rosa** elegant boutiques and shops feature the finest in contemporary leather goods, Taxco silver jewelry, and women's fashions. Souvenir hunters will not be disappointed either. Wherever you turn you will find mementos of Mexico, whether your tastes run to gigantic sombreros or onyx reproductions of the Aztec calendar stone. Additional temptations are not far away. Excursions outside of Mexico City will take you to a number of craft villages still producing quality ceramics and handwoven huipils, rebozos, and serapes.

CRAFTS

Mexico City's crafts stores house the handcrafts of the nation. Since regional specialities pour into the national capital, you can sample from the widest, and often overwhelming, collection of crafts of the country without venturing outside the city. You pay a bit for this luxury, for prices in Mexico City are higher than prices in the producing villages. But the selection is unbeatable, the quality high, and the convenience great. Particularly well represented are the crafts from **Chiapas, Guerrero, Jalisco, Michoacan, Oaxaca,** and **Puebla.** For some items, such as **Huichol yarn paintings** and **beadwork, ceramics** from Tonala, Acatlan, Puebla, and Michoacan, **bark paintings** from Guerrero, and **lacquerware** from Olinala, the selection in Mexico City is often of a higher quality and more extensive than in cities closer to the producing villages.

For crafts from the surrounding state of Mexico, the city is unsurpassed. The gay, effervescent **ceramics** from the village of Metepec, just outside of Toluca, fill local stores. Be on the lookout, in particular, for the huge **"Tree of Life" candelabras**, often polychromed and bursting with a profusion of angels, animals, and flowers. The state's many **serape**-producing villages are well represented in the several stores. With some effort you can also find the fine, delicate cotton **rebozos** from Tenancingo, as well as the **capelike** quexquemetls made by the Mazahua Indians in the state of Mexico and other especially lovely ones from the Sierra de Puebla. From Toluca come **chess and domino sets** carved from bone, horn, and wood, and from Mexico City itself, **hand-blown glass** as well as the wonderfully imaginative **papier mache figures** created by the Linares family.

ZONA ROSA

For many shoppers the Zona Rosa will be the main attraction. The principal streets of Hamburgo, Londres, and Liverpool—as well as the cross streets, especially Amberes and Genova—are lined with boutiques and shops (and more and more frequently a Burger King or T-shirt shop) featuring some of the finest examples of Mexico's work in leather handbags, clothing and luggage, silver platters and pitchers, contemporary jewelry designs, women's resort clothing, and city fashions. **Amberes** is particularly attractive and offers some of the finest shopping in the Zona Rosa. As the popular Zona Rosa gets overly commercialized, many shops and restaurants are opening up branches in the attractive, well-to-do **Colonia Polanco**, an area between the Hotels Camino Real and the Presidente Chapultepec.

Outlets for shopping in the city include markets as well as private and government-sponsored stores. In general, bargaining is expected in the markets, while in the stores prices are normally fixed.

Mexico City awakens slowly. *Stores usually begin to open about 10 or 10:30 a.m. and close around 7 p.m.*, with many of those in the Zona Rosa staying open later. In this highland city, stores do not close during midday for a siesta break, but most close on Sunday year-round, and many close Saturday during the summer.

WHERE TO SHOP

For the serious collector of crafts, **Victor's** (*Madero 8 and 10, Room 305;* ☎ *512-1263; open Mon.-Fri., 12:30-7 p.m.*) is unsurpassed. Established by Victor Fosado, the store continues to reflect his passion for crafts as well as his impeccable taste. Many of the exquisite objects displayed on the second floor of the National Museum of Anthropology are donations from his personal collection. Although selection in the small shop varies, and occasionally we visit and strike out, Victor's has had some of the older, rare lacquerware gourds and trays from Chiapa del Corzo and Uruapan, superb, old chests from Olinala, fascinating masks, fine ceramics, huipils, serapes, and belts. Also for sale is an exquisite selection of traditional Indian jewelry designed by, and made to the specifications of, Sr. Fosado's daughter, who manages the store and operates her own jewelry workshop. Victor's is conveniently located a few doors from Sanborn's House of Tiles on the third floor (the elevator's floor #2). No credit cards are accepted.

Next to Victor's, the highest quality crafts can be found in the government-sponsored stores, located within a few blocks of each other near Alameda Park. Their extensive collections represent some of the finest crafts of the nation and display the incredible diversity and vitality of contemporary artisans. In its attractive colonial building, the **Museo Nacional de Artes e Industrias Populares** (Juarez 44), across from the Juarez statue, houses an enormous collection of ceramics from complete dinner sets made in Puebla, Michoacan, and Guanajuato to delightful, comical Oaxaca figurines. Here also you will normally find some intricately woven fabrics from Chiapas, the sometimes hard-to-find Huichol yarn paintings, delicately lacquered Olinala chests, and the joyful animal ceramics from the studio of Heron Martinez of Acatlan. On exhibit (but not for sale) on the second floor is a superb collection of older crafts including masks, lacquerware, weavings, and musical instruments. A **FONART** (National Fund for the Promotion of Crafts) store is nearby at Juarez 89, and another one is in the Zona Rosa at Londres 136A. The Juarez 89 FONART (also known as **Exposicion Nacional de Arte Popular**) features some of the huge, exuberant Metepec fantasy candelabras. Some are on exhibit, others for sale. Ceramics from several states fill the shelves.

Well worth seeking out is **La Casa de las Artesanias de Michoacan**, located a bit out of the way *behind the Hotel Stouffer Presidente on Campos Eliseos*, at the corner of Temistocles. This store offers some of the finest examples of copperware, lacquerware, ceramics, and jewelry from the craft villages of the state of Michoacan. Many of the **Sanborn's** around the city sell native crafts. The fullest selection can be found on the second floor of Sanborn's House of Tiles (Madero 4).

Located in the heart of the Zona Rosa, the earthy **Mercado Insurgentes** *(small entrances on Londres and Liverpool between Amberes and Florencia)* is an indoor food, crafts, and curios market, colorfully contrasting with its fashionable surroundings. Stalls offer a variety of curios—the popular Mexican *charro* sombreros, pinatas, 101 versions of the Aztec calendar stone, and countless Mexican knickknacks. This is a good place for last-minute shopping for souvenirs for friends back home and to practice the art of haggling.

At the large outdoor **Ciudadela Curio Market** *(Balderas between Donde and Ayuntamiento; Balderas metro stop, then walk north to Burger Boy and turn left)* you have a more open, less congested environment for choosing from an extensive collection of curios and some quality crafts. Indian women from Oaxaca are often here weaving on backstrap looms. In addition to some *fine weavings,* you can sometimes find high-quality lacquered chests and gourds from Olinala, wonderfully elaborate *bark paintings* from the state of Guerrero, and *guitars* from Michoacan. It is here also that you can go native by buying a plastic duck dressed as a mariachi musician to hang from your car's rearview mirror.

At all times of the year, but especially during holiday seasons, Mexicans shop at the **Sonora Market** *(Av. Fray Servando de Mier just east of La Viga),* a few blocks south of the Merced market and metro station. Filled with pottery and medicinal herbs, the market also contains a wide selection of Mexican toys and crafts for the special seasons, and during the Christmas holidays in particular, one of the largest, most joyful collections of *piñatas* you will ever see.

La Lagunilla Market *(Around Rayon, Allende, and Comonfort)* is housed in several huge buildings and sells clothing, food, and household items. Of interest to the traveler is the very large selection of **huaraches** (sandals). And of greater interest should be the Sunday morning outdoor flea market on the streets around Rayon, Liberdad, Allende, and Comonfort. Very popular with Mexicans, the market sells a lot of glassware, pottery, old books, locks, furniture— you name it. You can even find some of the old miracle paintings (retablos), stereoscopic photos of old Mexico, and a few pieces of *fine pottery.* It's a lively, interesting scene, well worth a visit. *To get to the market take the "Villa" bus on the Reforma or a "Villa" pesero to the second glorieta (traffic circle) north of Alameda Park and walk a block or two to the right.*

LEATHER

For exquisite leather goods, you need go no farther than **Aries** *(several locations: Florencia 14; Stouffer Presidente hotel; and the San Angel Inn).* You can choose from jackets, women's suits, luggage, wallets, handbags, and other items.

JEWELRY

Mexico's famous jewelry and Taxco silverwork is widely available throughout the city. Before buying, check the silver to make sure it is stamped "sterling" or ".925" (925 grams for every 1000 grams of alloy). The designs of William Spratling can be found at the museum shop in the **Centro Cultural Arte Contemporaneo** (Campus Eliseos at J. Eliot. See above, Chapultepec Park, Trip 3). **Los Castillo** *(Amberes 41; Londres 132;* and next to the San Angel Inn)* offers a wide selection of handsome designs in silver and other metals. Their Amberes 41 location is especially attractive, with several rooms and a garden. **Tane** *(Amberes 70; Maria Isabel Sheraton, Nikko Mexico and Stouffer Presidente hotels; and San Angel Inn)* sells very high-quality and distinguished silverwork and jewelry.

WOMEN'S WEAR

Several shops feature lovely Mexican designer clothes. **Girasol** *(Genova 39A)* has been producing remarkably fine luxury Mexican fashions for years—ribbon and applique vests and dresses, tasteful, attractive resort clothing, and dyed leather fashions. **Marigen** *(Copenhague 2c)*, like Girasol, sells modern Mexican fashions of colorful fine appliqued and beribboned cotton. The very Mexican, distinctive, and attractive silk-screened fabrics, dresses, skirts, and blouses by Escalera can be found at a variety of shops including **Neus** *(Genova 65F)*, **Telas Escalera** *(Genova 65B)*, and **Palenque** *(Londres 119)*. For less expensive embroidered blouses and dresses, check the Zona Rosa market. For tasteful unisex sports clothing visit the popular **Aca Joe** *(Amberes 19)* and, nearby, **Ruben Torres**. And on the same street, **Polo by Ralph Lauren** *(Amberes 24)* sells men's and women's casual clothing.

GLASS

Handsome hand-blown bubble glasses and pitchers are made and sold at the factory of Francisco and Camilo **Avalos** *(Carretones 5)*, a short walk from the Merced metro stop (Line 1). The popular glasses are very reasonably priced—they sell for about four or five times the price at fashionable boutiques in the United States. For an extra charge the glasses will be well packed for carrying home.

FLOWERS, CANDLES, ONYX, AND OTHER ITEMS

Looking for flowers? Visit the lovely **Flower Market**, *just south of Chapultepec Park on Av. Chapultepec at Av. Constituyentes.* You may be surprised to discover the low prices in this land with seemingly endless vistas of flowers.

For creations in candles—owls, frogs, and floating water lilies—visit **Flamma** *(corner of Hamburgo and Florencia)*. Mexico's famous onyx products are displayed in the huge collection at **Mullers** *(corner of Londres and Florencia)*. The fine selection ranges from onyx tables to chess sets to bookends. Mullers is open Sunday and will ship.

The popular, bulky Toluca sweaters are sold at **Detalles Mexicanas** *(Londres 168)*. For the even more popular Mexican charro sombreros, those huge Mexican hats that travelers love to bring home as souvenirs, try **Tardan** in the arcade near the Hotel Majestic on the zócalo. Handsome, but not inexpensive, contemporary-designed wool rugs are sold by **Tamacani** (*Varsovia 51*, between Londres and Liverpool).

While **Artesanos de Mexico** (*Londres 117, second floor*) fits into no neat category, it has an interesting selection of quality items—colonial furniture reproductions, contemporary Indian masks, chests, weavings, paintings, and a variety of crafts. And at **Sergio Bustamente** (*Hotel Nikko Mexico*) you find large metal and papier-mache animals and figures, and surrealistic ceramic creations of this internationally renowned artist.

BAZAAR SABADO

A number of shops from the Zona Rosa are represented at the very popular Bazaar Sabado, the Saturday-only shopping bazaar held in an 18th-century mansion at *Plaza San Jacinto 11 in San Angel*. More than 100 artisans and shops sell their wares from about 10:30 a.m. to 8 p.m. Two floors are devoted to traditional and contemporary crafts, jewelry, and clothing. There is a restaurant in the patio. Out in the square, artists exhibit their paintings, and on nearby streets, outdoor stands entice you with traditional crafts and curios.

ART GALLERIES

Several art galleries sell the works of contemporary Mexican artists. **Galeria Misrachi** (*Genova 20*) and **Galeria del Circulo** (*Hamburgo 112*) feature some of the most prominent painters, including Tamayo, Carlos Mérida, and Siqueiros. **Galeria Arvil** (*Cerrada Hamburgo 9, between Amberes and Florencia*), normally shows some wonderful Tamayos and stocks a strong selection of art books. **Galeria Pecanins** (*Durango 186*) features the works of such lesser-known but quality artists as Philip Bragar, whose woodblock prints and oil paintings are powerfully expressive of Mexican life and landscape. The Pecanins' location, about 6 blocks south of the Zona Rosa, is an increasingly popular area for art galleries unable to afford the high Zona Rosa rents. In this area, **Galeria OMR** (*Plaza Rio de Janeiro 54, corner of Durango*) is well worth visiting for the work of some outstanding young artists such as Rocio Maldonado. **Florencia Riestra** (*Genova 2J*), also features some of the best young artists. Surely not of the same quality, but nevertheless very popular, is the outdoor art show held every Sunday in **Sullivan Park** (*just north of the intersection of the Reforma and Insurgentes*). For fascinating photographs of old Mexico, including some gems from the Mexican Revolution, head for **Casasola** in the Zona Rosa (*Tokio, corner of Praga, a few blocks past Florencia*). Prices are very reasonable and Casasola will mount the photographs for an extra charge.

FIESTAS

Independence Eve, September 15

On the eve before Independence Day, the president of Mexico gives the cry of Independence. Throngs of people, many in costume, fill the zócalo and surrounding streets, which are lined with vendors selling every kind of taco, fruit, and beverage. The most interesting items for sale, however, are eggshells stuffed with flour and bags of confetti. As people walk to the zócalo they bombard each other with these eggs and confetti in a huge good-willed, free-for-all. Light falls into the zócalo from the surrounding decorated buildings, and even the Cathedral spires are lighted with the red, green, and white colors of the Mexican flag. The square itself is wall-to-wall people, all waiting for the president's reenactment of Father Hidalgo's call for independence. At precisely 11 p.m., as the president appears on the balcony and tolls the liberty bell once rung by Hidalgo, the crowd erupts in a deafening roar that concludes with a thunderous "Viva Mexico!" The Cathedral bells chime in with the general cacophony of the zócalo, and spectacular fireworks both light up the sky and tumble off the roofs of surrounding buildings, making waterfalls of light. Independence Eve is an exhilarating occasion that you can best participate in by wearing old clothes, including a hat to keep flour from encrusting your hair. (Since traffic is prohibited in most of the area surrounding the zócalo, don't try to drive to these celebrations.) September 16 is a more sober holiday, being celebrated with a military parade down the Reforma.

Fiesta of the Virgin of Guadalupe, December 12

Celebrations in honor of the Virgin of Guadalupe begin on the evening of December 11 when hundreds of thousands of pilgrims from all over Mexico arrive in the square of the Basilica of Guadalupe, many crawling on their knees in penitence. Gifts to the Virgin include performances of traditional dances and haunting, prayerful songs. The chanting, singing, and dancing last throughout the night. In the nearby market, stalls are filled with food—the specialty being *las gorditas de la Virgen*—tiny corn cakes in the shape of the Virgin. Throughout the market stalls overflow with curios devoted to Mexico's patron saint. On the streets, photographers ply their trade with props, delightful scenic backdrops that transport the celebrants by way of a photograph into the world of their dreams.

Christmas Season Celebrations, December 16-January 6

While only the smaller neighborhoods perform the traditional posadas and string their piñatas across the streets, the center of the city is so festive that it is worthy of special mention. Lights are strung in the parks and along the Reforma, where piped-in music allows you to stroll in the evening while listening to Handel's *"Messiah."* Restaurants, nightclubs, and the Plaza Garibaldi are never gayer, never more filled with music than at this time of year. On January 6, the Day of the Three Kings, this jubilant season officially ends with festivities in Alameda Park. Alight with decorations, and filled with vendors of colorful balloons twisted into animal shapes, the park is busy with children who have come to visit and be photographed with the representatives of the gift-bearing Magi in the park.

WHERE TO STAY

Mexico City offers a wide array of hotels ranging from luxurious contemporary to intimate colonial to comfortable inexpensive. Since you have more choices than you could possibly want, we have narrowed them down by including only those centrally located near the historical **Zócalo-Alameda Park area**, the tree-lined **Reforma**, the modern **Zona Rosa** shopping-restaurant district, or the handsome and cultural **Chapultepec Park**. While the better, more expensive hotels most often are found in the heart of these areas, some fine moderate and inexpensive hotels are just a few short blocks away.

You may want to splurge in Mexico City and treat yourself to the kind of luxury you could not afford at home. Hotel prices are often below those for comparable hotels in major U.S. cities, and well below prices of Mexican resort hotels. And the quality is high with some gorgeous luxury hotels and several special hotels in other price categories. Although Mexico City has a rich colonial history and a few colonial hotels, the vast majority of hotels are of recent construction.

Most hotels in the moderate to resort expensive categories are air-conditioned, although except for a few days in the warmer months from April to June, air conditioning is not really needed in this highland city. Only a few hotels have pools. Travelers on a tight budget should be pleased to learn that all the hotels listed have private baths. Hotels sometimes fill during Mexico City's peak seasons, December-March, especially around Christmas, and June-August. Here as elsewhere, try to reserve in advance. For reservations, include in the address Mexico D.F., Mexico. Mexico City, as the nation's capital, is known as D.F., "Distrito Federal" (Federal District), or call, using Mexico City's area code, 5.

RESORT EXPENSIVE

Camino Real   ★★★★★

Mariano Escobedo 700; ☎ *203-2121; $209* • Across from Chapultepec Park, this exciting contemporary hotel includes huge, open lobbies flowing into one another with their pinks, purples, and yellows enriched by parquet floors and providing wonderful settings for displays of modern art—a mural by Mexico's foremost contemporary artist, Rufino Tamayo, and a Calder stabile. The effect is extraordinary, making this hotel represent the best in modern architecture. Its 700 rooms are large, tastefully decorated and have marble baths. Luxurious hotel with numerous restaurants, bars, discos, shops, and pool. Tennis courts on roof. Convenient to the museums in Chapultepec Park, and within walking distance of the Zona Rosa. Garage. Very good staff with attentive service. In our view, still the finest hotel in Mexico City despite the new competition. For reservations, call, in the U.S., ☎ 800-722-6466.

Nikko Mexico   ★★★★

Campos Eliseos 204; ☎ *280-1111; $231* • Opened in 1987 and located in Chapultepec Park, this bustling luxury high-rise hotel features 750 large, comfortable, and attractively decorated rooms and suites in subdued colors and fabrics. Rooms on upper floors have dramatic views of the city and surrounding mountains. Several bars and a Japanese as well as a French restaurant. Swimming pool, tennis courts, sauna, steambath, and weight room. The main drawback may be its location. Although it is close to the museums in Chapultepec Park, and the restaurants and shops in Polanco, you need to ride to the Zona Rosa and downtown areas.Garage. For reservations, call, in the U.S., ☎ 800-645-5687.

Stouffer Presidente

Campos Eliseos 218; ☎ *327-7700; $253* • In Chapultepec Park past the National Museum of Anthropology, the Presidente houses more than 750 well-appointed rooms in a modern deluxe high-rise building featuring a striking open lobby with garden and skylight ceiling. Several restaurants, bars, shops, and disco. Same location considerations as its neighbor, the Hotel Nikko Mexico (see above). Garage. For reservations, call, in the U.S., ☎ 800-468-3571.

Maria Isabel Sheraton

Reforma 325; ☎ *207-3933; $256* • This very popular and conveniently located high-rise bustles with tourists, many of whom are returning from shopping sprees across the street in the Zona Rosa. Its 850 large rooms are well appointed and many have excellent views of the Reforma and Independence Monument. Several restaurants and bars, including a very comfortable lobby bar. Shops, small rooftop pool, and tennis courts. Health club facilities are available. Garage. For reservations, call, in the U.S., ☎ 800-325-3535.

Fiesta Americana Reforma

Reforma 80; ☎ *705-1515; $183* • Big and bustling, with 630 recently refurbished, well-maintained rooms, several restaurants, five bars, nightclub with entertainment, and a disco. Located on the Reforma about midway between Zona Rosa and Alameda Park, this sleek hotel is popular with tour groups and conventions and always seems to be in a frenzied state. For reservations, call, in the U.S., ☎ 800-223-2332.

Fiesta Americana Aeropuerto

Benito Juarez Airport ☎ *571-6753; $165* • Opened in 1985, this deluxe hotel of 272 rooms is located just a short walk over a footbridge from the domestic airlines terminal. Convenient for those who arrive late and have an early-morning flight. But you pay for the convenience. Several restaurants and bars. Garage. For reservations, call, in the U.S., ☎ 800-223-2332.

VERY EXPENSIVE

Galeria Plaza

Hamburgo 195; ☎ *211-0014; $171* • With a Zona Rosa location and a lobby dominated by a fountain and attractive garden, the modern

Galeria Plaza offers 450 spacious, well-furnished rooms. Several restaurants, bars, and a 24-hour cafe. Penthouse disco. Pool. Garage. For reservations, call, in the U.S., ☎ 800-228-3000.

Krystal Zona Rosa

Liverpool 155; ☎ *211-0092; $171* • This modern high-rise Krystal in the heart of the Zona Rosa features a handsome lobby with mirrored surfaces, chrome and velvet chairs, and a comfortable bar; 330 well-maintained, good-size rooms. Several bars, restaurant, and pool. Garage. For reservations, call, in the U.S., ☎ 800-231-9860.

Imperial

Reforma 64; ☎ *566-3118; $155* • This small (65 rooms), elegant hotel is conveniently located between Alameda Park and the Zona Rosa in a restored stately mansion. Opened in 1989, the Imperial features a large atrium lobby with plush furnishings and decor. Rooms are attractive and the suites quite large. Attentive service. Bar and restaurant.

Marco Polo ★★★

Amberes 27; ☎ *511-1839; $168* • Opened in 1986 in the heart of the Zona Rosa, the Marco Polo offers modern conveniences and attractive furnishings in a relatively intimate setting of 60 well-designed rooms. All rooms feature sleek facilities for breakfast making and snacks as well as sitting/dining areas. The slightly higher priced deluxe rooms (habitacion de lujo), are well worth the minimal extra cost. Restaurant, bar, and parking.

EXPENSIVE

Aristos

Reforma 276 at Copenhague; ☎ *211-0112; $119* • Modern first-class hotel with good location in the Zona Rosa; 360 large, well-appointed rooms, some with sitting areas and fine views of Reforma. Restaurant, bars, discos. Sauna and shops. Garage. A good buy.

Gran Hotel Howard Johnson

16 de Septiembre 82; ☎ *510- 4040; $88* • On the zócalo, this turn-of-the-century hotel has an extraordinary lobby—a 4-story atrium crowned with an exquisite Tiffany glass dome and surrounded with Art Nouveau gilded balustrades and elevator cages. These elevators, with Tiffany glass and filigree, beat even their dramatic modern counterparts in Hyatt hotels. The 120 rooms, however, do not rival the lobby. We find the size and decor of exterior rooms adequate, but interior rooms very small and not recommended. Suites have views of the zócalo and are well worth the extra cost. Very hospitable staff. Restaurant; bar with entertainment. Garage. For reservations, call in the U.S., ☎ 800-654-2000.

Century

Liverpool 152; ☎ *584-7111; $119* • A hotel of rather garish, modern architecture with a small lobby with chandeliers. Its 143 smallish, modern rooms have private balconies and bathrooms with marble tubs. Several restaurants and bars, including a piano bar with dramatic view on an upper floor. Disco. Pool. Garage.

Ramada Airport

Blvd. Puerto Aereo 502; ☎ *785-8522; $119* • If you arrive in Mexico City late and are departing early the next day on a flight, you may want to stay near the airport rather than going all the way into town. This hotel sometimes is a Holiday Inn and sometimes not, but it always has 333 comfortable rooms, restaurant, bar, and swimming pool. Free transportation from the airport. For reservations, call in the U.S., ☎ 800-228-2828.

MODERATE

Majestic

Av. Madero 73; ☎ *521-8600; $77* • On the zócalo, this handsome colonial hotel is decorated in warm colors of orange stucco and Puebla-blue tiles with a gentle fountain in its comfortable lobby. Only 85 modestly furnished, ample rooms; the exterior ones with views of zócalo are especially recommended, yet they can be noisy. Old-fashioned bathrooms. Popular rooftop bar with views of Cathedral; restaurant with zócalo view. Garage. For reservations, call, in the U.S., ☎ 800-528-1234.

Hotel de Cortes   ★★★

Av. Hidalgo 85; ☎ *218-2181; $89* • The Cortes is not for everyone's taste, yet it's very special for some. Located behind Alameda Park and occupying an 18th-century building that once served as a shelter and hospice for passing friars, the Cortes has only 27 rooms on its two arcaded floors surrounding a lovely, intimate courtyard. Walls are burnt orange; trees, bougainvillea, and a fountain share the courtyard with a quiet restaurant and bar, and all combine to make this a most romantic setting. Rooms do not rival the courtyard. For some reason, the furnishings are modern and not particularly attractive. Doubles are on the small side; but the more expensive suites, especially the corner ones overlooking Alameda Park, are large and recommended. Try for the lighter rooms on the upper floor: their balconies offer soothing views of the sky and the gorgeous courtyard. Indoor restaurant as well as patio restaurant and bar. Garage. For reservations, call, in the U.S., ☎ 800-528-1234.

Casa Blanca

La Fragua 7; ☎ *566-3211; $85* • This modern high-rise is conveniently located one-half block from the Reforma and midway between Zona Rosa and Alameda Park. Its 270 rooms are of good size, comfortably furnished, and immaculate. Very well managed hotel, popular with Mexican businessmen. Courteous service. Large modern lobby and restaurant. Bar and pool on roof. Garage.

Suites Amberes

Amberes 64; ☎ *533-1306; $90* • In the heart of the Zona Rosa, this establishment is more like a small apartment building for travelers than a full-service hotel. Its 28 comfortable and well-maintained suites vary in size from living room-bedroom combinations to 2-bedroom suites. All have kitchenettes. A good value. Parking.

Ritz

Av. Madero 30; ☎ *518-1340; $66* • Decent lobby and 140 rooms; some have sitting areas. Front rooms facing Madero are largest yet same price as others. Interior rooms are small, yet acceptable, with view of plant-filled "courtyard." Restaurant and piano bar. Parking. For reservations, call, in the U.S., ☎ 800-528-1234.

Bristol

Plaza Necaxa 17 at Sena and Panuco; ☎ *208-1717; $75* • A modern, clean, and well-run commercial-type hotel about a 10-minute walk from the Reforma and Zona Rosa; 134 perfectly acceptable, fresh rooms. Popular lobby bar; restaurant. Rooftop pool. Exterior rooms have good views, but they can be noisy. Parking. Good price for the amenities.

INEXPENSIVE

Maria Cristina

Lerma 31; ☎ *566-9688; $65* • Close to the Reforma and Zona Rosa, this hotel with its gardens and neo-colonial lobby is a good buy. 110 comfortable, adequately furnished rooms. We think the service needs improvement, as it is too often indifferent. But the Maria Cristina is still a good deal for the price, and it is the hotel many Mexicans recommend to visiting friends who seek a modestly priced hotel with some Mexican ambience. Breakfast and lunch sometimes served in garden; restaurant and bar. Parking.

Bamer

Juarez 52; ☎ *521-9060; $60* • With a very good location across from Alameda Park, the high-rise Hotel Bamer is one of Mexico City's old standbys and one of the few hotels in the area that survived the ravages of the September 1985 earthquake. Rooms vary, but many are quite large with thick carpeting and full windows that flood the space with light. Oldish but well-maintained bathrooms. Varnished wood paneling in hallways. Restaurant and bar.

Vasco de Quiroga

Londres 15; ☎ *546-2614; $50* • Decently located just a few blocks from the Zona Rosa and close to the Reforma, the Vasco de Quiroga provides a warm environment in a rather cozy hotel of 50 small but attractively furnished rooms. Bathrooms are aging. The Mexican feel to the hotel is enhanced by the handsome, very well-furnished lobby. Restaurant and bar.

Gillow

Isabel la Catolica 17; ☎ *518-1440; $38-$42* • Sheathed in granite with an art deco exterior and basic but modernized rooms and baths, the Gillow provides comfortable, economical accommodations in a downtown location just a few blocks from the zócalo and a short walk to the Alameda. Rooms vary in size and noise. On the whole, the one-bedrooms are quite small but the slightly more expensive rooms with two beds are ample. Some rooms have balconies. Restaurant and bar.

Fleming ★

Revillagigedo 35; ☎ *510-4530; $40* • A block from Alameda Park on a busy street, this modern hotel has an attractive lobby and 75 clean, pleasant rooms with old-fashioned bathrooms. Restaurant. Fine for the price. Parking.

Doral ★

Sullivan 9; ☎ *592-2866; $51* • This high-rise, commercial-style hotel, located next to Sullivan Park near the Reforma, has 104 clean, decently appointed rooms, some with views of the Reforma. Bathrooms are acceptable. Restaurant and bar. Small pool on roof. Garage.

BUDGET

Casa Gonzalez √★

Rio Sena 69; ☎ *514-3302; $22-$26* • A long-time favorite of budget travelers for its homey atmosphere, the Casa Gonzalez is conveniently located across the Reforma from the Zona Rosa. The simple rooms, spread over two houses, vary considerably in the quality of furnishings and amenities, but are comfortable and welcoming as are the several patios. A few parking spaces are available. Optional meals in family dining room.

Hotel Sevilla ★

Serapio Rendon 126; ☎ *566-1866; $30* • Located several blocks off tourist areas near Sullivan Park. Plain lobby. Clean, carpeted rooms with modern bathrooms. Size of doubles varies considerably and is reflected in price range. Small restaurant.

Hotel Antillas

Belisario Dominguez 34; ☎ *526-5674; $29* • On a bustling street in an old section of the city near Santo Domingo Plaza and about a 10-minute walk to the zócalo and Alameda Park, the Antillas has a pleasant carpeted lobby with a comfortable restaurant and bar. The 100 rooms are small, but well maintained. Interior rooms are quietest.

WHERE TO EAT

For the complexity and quality of its cuisines, and the variety and prices of its restaurants, Mexico City is unsurpassed in the country and rivals some of the finest cities in the world, making a trip to this cosmopolitan city amply rewarding just for its food. Restaurants specializing in French, Italian, Spanish,

Chinese, Japanese, and American cooking can be found throughout the city, and the many distinctive regional cuisines of the country are well represented in this national capital. Perhaps most surprising to many visitors is the quality and variety of the fresh seafood served in Mexican as well as Japanese, French, and Spanish restaurants. *Ceviche* (raw fish marinated in lime juice, tomatoes, and chiles), and fresh, delicious *huachinango* (red snapper), *pompano*, *robalo* (sea bass), *camarones* (shrimp), and *langostino* (crayfish) are widely available and receive the special preparations of the various cuisines.

In Mexico City you can dine elegantly and extremely well at a fraction of the cost of comparable restaurants (where they can be found) in the United States. You may be tempted by sophisticated Mexican cooking in gorgeous, restored 17th- and 18th-century haciendas or extremely fine French food in opulent surroundings—all at prices that may well be affordable here, even if not at home.

Travelers on a tight budget will find the food situation to their liking also. Mexico City abounds in restaurants serving a very inexpensive fixed-priced full-course meal (*comida corrida*). And several Italian restaurants serve fine pasta dishes at surprisingly low prices. For those who love to eat—as many Mexicans do—continuously throughout the day, the streets of Mexico City bustle with stalls and small restaurants serving a variety of such inexpensive snacks as tacos and tortas (sandwiches). If your tastes run more to American food, you can find steaks, fried chicken, hamburgers, and sandwiches at a number of restaurants.

Most restaurants are liveliest and most crowded in the afternoons when Mexicans have their main meal. In Mexico City, the better restaurants begin to attract customers about 2 p.m. and fill between 3 and 4 p.m. Inexpensive restaurants, especially those serving a *comida corrida*, will often be jammed by 2 p.m. Normally, men wear ties and jackets in the more expensive restaurants, and in some restaurants this attire is required. Reservations are often essential for the finer, more popular restaurants, so try to plan ahead. If you do not have a reservation, try to get to the better restaurants by 2 p.m. Some restaurants close on Sunday, or, if open, close early, so call ahead. To keep the cost of your meal down, stay away from imported wines and beers. While French and California wines are more expensive than they are in the States, Mexican wines are often reasonably priced and drinkable, even if not exciting. You will discover that some Mexicans will order Cokes with their meals in the most elegant restaurants. You can order one of Mexico's excellent beers without embarrassment.

We have listed the restaurants according to the major areas of the city so that you can coordinate your restaurant selection with sightseeing. Within areas we have arranged the restaurants according to price categories. Since Mexico City overflows with fine restaurants and taco and torta places, any listing—even our selective one—may be too overwhelming. *To help you choose, we have highlighted some of our personal favorites. They are listed first under* **"Special Places."**

SPECIAL PLACES

San Angel Inn

Palmas 50 at Altavista, San Angel; ☎ *548-6746 Reservations needed, espe-cially Saturday and Sunday. About a 30-minute taxi ride from the Zona Rosa* • This former hacienda once served as a meeting place for the revolutionary leaders Pancho Villa and Emiliano Zapata. Today, it is one of the most handsome restaurants in Mexico and serves some of the finest food. While waiting for your table, you can have cocktails in the lovely, tranquil colonial patio complete with macaws, or you can stroll through the 18th-century building and attractive grounds. The menu offers a mixture of French, continental, and Mexican cuisines. You can begin your meal with their superb *ostiones* (oysters) San Angel Inn, the delightful *ceviche,* or one of their several excellent soups. For the main course, you choose from a number of Mexican dishes including *pollo* (chicken) in *mole poblano* or the exotic *huitlaco-che* (a grayish fungus found on corn) in crepes. Several fine seafood dishes are available, including a delicious bass (*robalo*) in *papillote* and the sweet whitefish from Patzcuaro. Their Chateaubriand is excellent. Save room for dessert. The Bavarian cream with strawberries or rasp-berries (depending on season) is celestial. Service is gracious and attentive.　　　　　　　　　　　　　　　　　　　　　*Expensive.*

La Hacienda de los Morales

Av. Vazquez de Mella 525; ☎ *540-3225 Northwest of Chapultepec Park off Av. Ejercito Nacional, about a 20-minute ride from the Zona Rosa* • Dining in this huge, elegant, restored 17th-century hacienda with its extensive gardens and courtyard rivals the experience in the San Angel Inn. The windows in the attractive main dining rooms provide views of ducks and swans frolicking in a pool. The menu, continental and Mexican, offers a number of appetizers and soups including a tasty shrimp Marinera in a tomato and onion vinaigrette. The main dishes include a very good tournedos Enrique IV with a bernaise sauce, duck in a pipian sauce, chicken with *mole poblano,* and a number of other fine fish and beef dishes. Some wonderful desserts are offered. If avail-able, don't pass up the delicious mango mousse.　　*Expensive.*

Isadora

Moliere 50, Colonia Polanco; ☎ *280-55-86 Open 1:30-5 p.m. and 8:30 p.m.-midnight. Closed Sun.* • The Isadora offers a wonderfully innova-tive cuisine utilizing traditional Mexican ingredients in many of its intriguing creations. Located in an attractive townhouse with three dining rooms each with a distinctive decor and ambience, the setting is a bit upscale yet casual and comfortable. For starters there's a deli-cious clam soup flavored with coriander as well as several pasta offer-ings including an interesting offering of ravioli filled with cuitlacoche and covered with a chile poblano sauce. The mixed salad of chicory, watercress, avocado and tomato is highly recommended. Some of the main dishes are sublime. We've particularly liked the filet of esmedregal fish served with a lovely chipotle chile hollandaise sauce along with stuffed eggplant. An offering of savory duck (*pato*) comes with crisp skin, moist meat and a flavorful, but not overly sweet, cherry sauce (*salsa de griottines*). For dessert the fresh fruit sorbets, especially mango, are superb.   *Expensive.*

Champs-Elysees

Amberes 1, corner of Reforma; ☎ *514-0450 Closed Sat. and Sun. and part of the summer* • The first thing to do is to reserve a table in one of the front dining rooms overlooking the Reforma. The rear rooms are much less desirable. The food is French with a Mexican touch, a combination that comes off extremely well and ranks with the best in the city. For appetizers, try their delicious ceviche or the interesting clam soup (*sopa de almejas*). A number of fish and beef dishes are highly recommended. You can choose from tender and flavorful tournedos with bernaise sauce, a delectable trout with hollandaise sauce (*trucha con holandesa*), a fish coquille (*coquile de pescados gratinados*), and the popular bouillabaisse. Daily specials, such as a wonderful fresh tuna in escabeche, are often available. For dessert, do not pass up the strawberries and cream (*fresas chantilly*).   *Expensive.*

Restaurant Lincoln

Revillagigedo 24; ☎ *510-1468 Closed Sun.* • We go to the Lincoln when we have a craving for the freshest and finest seafood. The handsome leather-lined booths and wood-paneled dining room fill with Mexican businessmen who spend hours over lunch consuming vast quantities of the Lincoln's varied seafood. The meal begins with a large bowl of fresh cucumbers, carrots, radishes, and scallions. On the side will be a bowl of pickled heads of garlic (try it, it's interesting) and the smoky *chiles chipotles*. Although the menu includes a number of traditional Mexican meat dishes, the fish is the attraction here. The *jaibas en chilpachole*, a spicy tomato-base crab soup, is unsurpassed. The *huachinango* (red snapper) *a la Veracruzana* (a sauce made from tomatoes, capers, olives, onions, and strips of chile peppers) is especially good. Although not always on the menu, the sweet and succulent *camarones gigantes* (giant shrimp) are normally available—just ask for them *al mojo de ajo* (in garlic). The tuxedoed waiters provide very attentive service. If you do not have a reservation, try to get to the Lincoln by 2 p.m. to get one of the booths   *Moderately expensive.*

Loredo

Hamburgo 29; ☎ *703-2311 Closed Sunday for dinner* • The Loredo offers some of the finest refined Mexican cooking in the city in attractive dining rooms on two levels. The meal begins with a plate of fresh vegetables and tasty *sopes*. The soups are wonderful. We can especially recommend the superb *sopa Mixteca* (a hearty vegetable soup with bone marrow) and the savory *sopa de cuitlacoche*. For the main dish, you can choose the *carne asada a la Tampiquena*, the popular Mexican dish that was created by the restaurant's owner, Jose Loredo. It consists of grilled beef surrounded by spicy strips of chiles, enchiladas, and baked cheese. Many other flavorful Mexican dishes are served, including terrific *albondigas* (Mexican meatballs) in a spicy *chipotle chile sauce* and beef and fish prepared in a variety of interesting ways. In season, Loredo serves delicious *chiles en nogados*. Not on the menu, but normally available, is the very popular *Fuente de Mariscos*, a huge cold platter of fresh shellfish. For dessert, try the *flan napolitano*. During lunch there is often live music provided by a trio. The service is fine, if a bit rushed. **Moderately expensive.**

El Caminero

Lerma 138, one block behind the Maria Isabel Sheraton; also at Ignacio Ramirez 17, near Monument to the Revolution • A Mexican friend once led us here and since then, whenever we return to Mexico City, it is one of our first stops. The fare is tacos, a staple of Mexican life—comparable to hot dogs and hamburgers in the United States—and they are the tastiest tacos we have ever eaten. They come with beef (*biftec*) or pork (*chuleta*) and in several varieties, with melted cheese (*con queso*) or with bacon (*tocino*) and onions, all placed on top of soft tortillas. As a side order try the perfect accompaniment, grilled scallions (*cebolla*). Bowls of fresh Mexican sauces, some fiery hot, line the counters to be added to your tacos. El Caminero is usually crowded; you may have to stand while eating; but if you are lucky you will get a stool at a counter. Ordering can be tricky, and it helps if you speak some Spanish. At the I. Ramirez location there are tables and waiter service on the small mezzanine. This makes life a lot easier, yet somehow it seems like cheating. **Inexpensive.**

Tortas La Perla

Rio Rhin 51, between Lerma and Panuco, across from the Zona Rosa Closed by 8 p.m. and all day Sun. • Tortas are Mexican sandwiches made on an oval-shaped roll, and at their best they make a wonderful snack or light lunch. La Perla is easy to miss; often it lacks a sign. It occupies a hole in a wall and is big enough to accommodate perhaps 10 thin people standing up. Nevertheless, it turns out delicious *tortas* made with layers of sour cream, refried beans, avocados, tomatoes, onions, chiles, and your choice of cheese, chicken, ham, or roasted pork (*pierna*)—the latter is our favorite. To some, La Perla may seem like the ultimate greasy spoon, to others it is a real find. There are no seats: either eat standing up or bring the *tortas* back to your hotel room; or do as Mexicans do—eat your *torta* while strolling along the street.

ZÓCALO AREA

Bar Alfonso

Motolinia 18 at 5 de Mayo, 2nd floor; ☎ *512-0589* • The very attractive wood-paneled dining room bustles with businessmen during lunchtime. We return often to eat one thing, camarones a la vinagrete, jumbo shrimp marinated in a vinaigrette dressing with chopped onions and tomatoes, and served at room temperature. The shrimp come in half or full orders, are sweet and delectable but expensive. You can also get red snapper, chicken, roast kid, and steak, but they do not rival the shrimp, which are outstanding.

Moderate expensive to expensive.

Cafe Tacuba

Tacuba 28; ☎ *512-8482* • The venerable Cafe Tacuba gives you the feel of old Mexico with its walls of lovely Puebla-tile murals and paintings. Its Mexican menu features special enchiladas (*enchiladas especiales Tacuba*), which are more often than not delicate and delicious. The consomme and *tostadas* are also quite good. The rest of the cooking is acceptable, although not exciting. The ambience, however, is an attraction. Open for breakfast, and popular at lunch as well as later in the evening for its variety of *antojitos* (snacks).   *Moderate.*

Hotel Majestic Restaurant

Av. Madero 73; ☎ *521-8600* • The setting is special, on the roof of the Hotel Majestic overlooking the zócalo and the National Cathedral. The restaurant serves Mexican as well as American food and, during lunchtime, a very reasonably priced comida corrida that allows even those on a tight budget to enjoy some luxury. The à la carte menu is more expensive. The food is fine, and the surroundings even better. Popular Sunday brunch often with live mariachi music.

Moderate to moderately expensive.

Prendes

Av. 16 de Septiembre 10, near Lazaro Cardenas; ☎ *585-4199* • Old, established Prendes, with courteous waiters who appear to have aged with the restaurant, specializes in seafood and is extremely popular with Mexican businessmen during lunchtime. Remodeled in 1989, Prendes is now looking fairly elegant, rather than venerable, to the dismay of some of its long-time patrons. Fine for red snapper, pompano, and shrimp.   *Moderately expensive.*

El Cardenal

Palma 23 • Just one block from the zócalo, El Cardenal serves flavorful Mexican dishes in an attractive setting. Many seafood dishes are featured, including oysters with huitlacoche and a variety of shrimp dishes.   *Moderate to moderately expensive.*

Sanborn's

House of Tiles, Av. Madero 4 near Lazaro Cardenas • Part of the Sanborn's chain, this is by far the loveliest of their restaurants. Located in the sun-drenched glass-roofed courtyard of a 17th-century mansion, the restaurant serves traditional Mexican dishes as well as hamburgers and club sandwiches. Food is fine and popular with Mexicans as well as tourists who find the English menus and cleanliness of Sanborn's comforting. On your way to the rest rooms on the second floor, take a look at the Orozco mural at the top of the stairway. Open for breakfast.   *Moderate.*

VIPS

Madero 53 • Part of a chain, open 24 hours, clean and plastic-modern, it serves American as well as Mexican food. ***Moderate.***

Casa de la Malinche

Rep. de Cuba 79, near Santo Domingo Church • Located in an interesting 19th-century building, this restaurant offers, at lunch, a fixed-price buffet of traditional Mexican dishes, mainly stews, as well as à la carte dishes, that are uneven, but include a wonderfully spicy and thick vegetable soup (*sopa de Azteca*). Live traditional music is often featured at lunch. Frequently closed in the evening.
Moderate to moderately expensive.

Hosteria de Santo Domingo

Belisario Dominguez 72, near Santo Domingo Church • Claims to be, and surely looks like, one of the oldest restaurants in Mexico City. In the handsome dining room, it serves traditional Mexican food that we have found to be pleasant but unmemorable. ***Moderate.***

El Cardenal

Moneda 2, second floor, overlooking the zócalo • The trick is to find the entrance, after which you will be treated to a simple restaurant in a great location, serving some interesting Mexican dishes. El Cardenal has no sign, but from the street you can see the restaurant's tables on the second floor. Enter through the doorway numbered 2, walk to the rear, and climb the stairway leading to the dining rooms. There are two pleasant rooms, one with a zócalo view. During lunch, the restaurant fills with government workers from the National Palace. In season, El Cardenal serves very tasty *chiles rellenos nogados* (stuffed chiles covered with a walnut sauce and red pomegranate seeds) as well as chicken, fish, shrimp, and enchiladas. Same ownership as El Cardenal above. ***Inexpensive.***

SNACKS

The tacos and delicious chicken soup at the **Taqueria Beatriz** (Motolinia 32) are described under Zona Rosa Snacks, below. This branch of Beatriz serves tasty seafood as well as recommendable *mole poblano* and *albondigas* (Mexican meatballs). Closed evenings and Sunday. Longing for *churros*, those popular Spanish-style donuts? Head for **El Moro** (Lazaro Cardenas 42, corner of Uruguay), where the freshly cooked churros are served with a variety of hot chocolate drinks. For sweets, try the **Ideal Bakery** (16 de Septiembre 14, off Lazaro Cardenas), which is worth visiting just to view the elaborate cakes, which are artistic creations. **The Dulceria Celaya** *(5 de Mayo 39, near Motolinia)* is another spot to see even if you don't want to indulge. Founded in 1874, the Dulceria is the oldest sweet shop in Mexico. Housed in a charming old building, the shop has a wonderful selection of indescribable, traditional Mexican candies.

ALAMEDA AREA

Restaurant Lincoln

Revillagigedo 24 • One of the best. See "Special Places".

Nuevo Acapulco

Lopez 9; ☎ *521-5950* • A good seafood restaurant, nothing very fancy, but with pleasant surroundings. It serves excellent *ceviche* and good red snapper, pompano, and shrimp. ***Moderately expensive.***

Hotel de Cortes Restaurant

Av. Hidalgo 85; ☎ *585-0322* • Dine in the enchanting, romantic courtyard of this 18th-century colonial hotel. Wonderful setting for lunch, dinner, or just a drink (see "Hotels"). Fine Mexican and continental cuisine. ***Moderately expensive.***

Meson del Cid

Humboldt 61; ☎ *521-1940 Closed Sunday* • A short walk from Alameda Park, the Meson del Cid serves tasty Spanish specialties such as gazpacho, charcoal-broiled quail, paella, and suckling pig in an intimate and very attractive environment with a real Spanish feel. Its small cocktail lounge overlooking a tiny courtyard is a delightful place to stop for a snack of *jamon serrano* (thinly sliced Spanish ham) or **chistorra** (sausage) to accompany your drink. ***Moderately expensive.***

Boca del Rio

Rivera de San Cosme 42; ☎*546-1614* • A bit out of the way in a nontouristy neighborhood, the Boca del Rio serves the freshest of oysters, shrimp cocktails, and *ceviche* in a large, noisy, joyously Mexican atmosphere. Always crowded and bustling, the restaurant often has a marimba band stationed outside, adding to the general merriment. Nothing fancy, and no hot seafood dishes, but first-rate cold shellfish. ***Moderate.***

Sanborn's

Reforma at La Fraqua • Modern edition of the Sanborn chain. See "Zócalo Area."

Denny's

Juarez at Humboldt • Similar to Sanborn's and part of a chain, Denny's serves American as well as Mexican food in modern restaurants. ***Moderate.***

La Parrilla

Lopez 8 • A popular restaurant serving traditional Mexican dishes at reasonable prices and offering a comida corrida at lunchtime. ***Inexpensive to moderate.***

Shirley's

Reforma 108; also in Zona Rosa at Londres 102 • An informal American-style restaurant popular with tourists, Shirley's serves breakfast through dinner. Some Mexican dishes are available, but Shirley's emphasizes food and atmosphere to remind you of home—hamburgers and french fries, fried chicken, club sandwiches, banana splits, hot cakes, and banana cream pie.   *Moderate.*

SNACKS

One of the best taco places in Mexico, **El Caminero** is nearby at Ignacio Ramirez 17. See "Special Places".

ZONA ROSA

Champs-Elysees

Amberes 1, corner of the Reforma • One of the best. See "Special Places."

Loredo

Hamburgo 29 • One of the best. See "Special Places."

Estoril

Genova 75; ☎ *208-64-18* • The setting is appealing—an intimate series of dining rooms enclosed by white stucco walls covered with contemporary art. The food is continental with a smattering of Mexican dishes (all quite good), which accounts for the Estoril's popularity, especially with Mexico City's upper crust—all of whom seem to know the owner and one another. The inventive menu features preparations of the exotic Mexican mushroom, *huitlacoche,* in crepes or in flavorful soups, as well as cream soups of watercress or avocado. Salad preparations are equally appealing with an offering of spinach with chicken livers, and a tangy watercress salad. Main dishes include a variety of beef, shrimp, and fish dishes; among the latter are a number of different preparations of very flavorful sea bass (*robalo*). Despite its emphasis on continental cooking, the Estoril's more Mexican dishes come off surprisingly well. We've been pleased by the *albondigas al chipotle,* Mexican meatballs in a spicy sauce punctuated by the *smoky chipotle chile.*   *Expensive.*

Delmonico's

Londres 87; ☎ *207-49-49* • Popular Delmonico's serves American and continental food in fairly posh, brightly lit surroundings. Famous for its beef dishes, Delmonico's serves—at lunch only—roast beef with Yorkshire pudding. At all times of the day you can order a very tasty cold avocado soup, spareribs, primeribs, as well as a tender and flavorful Chateaubriand, and a few fish and shrimp dishes. Food is quite good, service is attentive, and tourists always seem comfortable and happy here. The dark, wood-paneled bar is attractive for a drink. On weekends, Delmonico's serves an elaborate fixed-price brunch.
                                                          Expensive.

Fonda el Refugio

Liverpool 166; ☎ *528-5823 Closed Sun* • For a long time, el Refugio had the reputation for serving the finest traditional Mexican food in the city. However, we have found the kitchen interesting but not special. The first- floor colonial dining room is the showpiece, with white walls, copperware, and Mexican crafts; the upstairs dining rooms, unfortunately, are plain and without much charm. The menu is purely Mexican with a daily special. If in season try their *chiles en nogados*. Their Wednesday special of *mole verde de pepita*, chicken with a green sauce of pumpkin seeds and chiles, is also quite good. Everyday they serve tasty *chiles rellenos* and a pleasing *mole poblano*. We find that the service is uneven and could use more warmth.   ***Moderate.***

Anderson's

Reforma 382; ☎ *525-1006* • Part of the chain that includes the numerous Carlos N' Charlie's found all over Mexico, Anderson's has the same informal, lively, "fun" atmosphere and the same extensive menu featuring a variety of beef, fish, and shrimp dishes. Wisecracking waiters, decent food, and lots of noise—people do seem to have a good time here; and it's always crowded.   ***Moderately expensive.***

Meson del Perro Andaluz

Copenhague 26; ☎ *533-5306* • Copenhague is closed to traffic, lined with restaurants with outdoor tables, and attracts a young "beautiful people" crowd. Meson del Perro Andaluz is the most popular restaurant on the street, always crowded, and unless you come at an off hour, it is almost impossible to get one of their prime outdoor tables. The interior rooms on several floors are informal, intimate, and attractive. The food is good, with a variety of shrimp and beef dishes leaning toward Spanish. Try their small shrimp in garlic (*gambas en ajillo*).

Moderately expensive.

El Parador

Niza 17; ☎ *533-1840. Closed Sun.* • An attractive Spanish restaurant with such authentic dishes as baby eel and squid complementing the usual gazpacho soup and paella. On our last visit, we found the food disappointing.   ***Expensive.***

Passy

Amberes 10; ☎ *511-0257* • Passy is an intimate and warm French restaurant with a lovely interior garden enhancing the atmosphere. Recommendable offerings include fine chicken liver pate, a very flavorful smoked Sierra fish, tender rack of lamb, and an interesting preparation of quail (*cordoniz*).   ***Moderately expensive.***

Bellinghausen

Londres 95; ☎ *511-9035* • Lively and popular, the Bellinghausen offers an extensive selection of continental and Mexican dishes, and a few German specialties all in comfortable surroundings, whether it be the large, indoor dining room or the more appealing outdoor setting enhanced by chirping birds. The food is fine, and the friendly feel of the restaurant makes for a pleasant dining experience. Red snapper, tournedos and several chicken dishes are featured and the smoked trout is one of the most popular plates.   ***Moderately expensive.***

Circulo del Sureste

Lucerna 12; ☎ *546-2972* • A bit out of the way, about a 10-minute walk from the heart of the Zona Rosa, the Circulo del Sureste specializes in the distinctive and interesting cuisine of Yucatán (see "Eating Out," in the Mérida section). Their *tacos de cochinita* (roast suckling pig) are superb. Other fine Yucatecan specialties include *papadzules*, soft tortillas filled with chopped hard-boiled eggs and covered with a pumpkin seed sauce; *cochinita pibil*, roast pork wrapped in banana leaves and served in a spicy sauce; and *pollo* (chicken) or *camarones* (shrimp) *en escabeche*, a mild pickling marinade. With your meal try one of the Yucatecan beers—Montejo, Carta Clara, or the dark Leon Negra. ***Moderate to moderately expensive.***

La Marinera

Liverpool 183; ☎ *511-3568* • La Marinera serves fresh, basic seafood to throngs of people in a large unassuming dining room. Their *ceviche de jaiba* (crabmeat) is excellent, and their *huachinango* (red snapper) and *robalo* (sea bass) are moist and flavorful. Extensive menu with fresh oysters and a variety of fish dishes. The outdoor tables are pleasant, but you need to arrive before 2 p.m. to get one. While waiting for your meal outdoors, you'll be able to get your shoes shined. ***Moderate.***

Parri

Hamburgo 154 • In the heart of the Zona Rosa, Parri Pollo serves tasty barbecued chicken, tacos, and beer in an informal, lively setting. ***Inexpensive.***

Restaurante Vegetariano

Varsovia 3, one block west of Florencia • The Vegetariano serves tasty salads and vegetarian main dishes at very reasonable prices. ***Inexpensive to moderate.***

A La Maison de Bon Fromage

Hamburgo 241A • This is an intimate French-type bistro serving fondue, quiche, and onion soup at surprisingly low prices. *Closed Sat. and Sun.* ***Inexpensive to moderate.***

INEXPENSIVE COMIDAS CORRIDAS

In addition to those listed above, you can visit **Restaurant Latino** (Reforma 296, near Genova), or try **Restaurant Hamburgo** (Hamburgo 232, corner of Praga). *Closed Sat. and Sun.*

CONVENIENT CHAIN RESTAURANTS

Branches of three chain restaurants all serve American as well as Mexican food and are especially good for breakfast. All are clean and modern with North American decor and moderate prices. You can get anything from hamburgers and french fries to enchiladas. Popular with Mexicans as well as tourists are: **Denny's** (Londres at Amberes; and Reforma 509); **Sanborn's** (Hamburgo at Niza; Reforma at Tiber); and **VIPS** (Niza between Reforma and Hamburgo; Hamburgo 126; and Florencia and Reforma).

SNACKS

In addition to two of our special recommendations mentioned above—
El Caminero (Lerma 138, near Tiber) and Tortas La Perla (Rio Rhin 51)—you can try **Taqueria Beatriz** (Londres 179 between Florencia and Varsovia). **Beatriz** serves very good tacos and tostadas, and the best chicken soup (*caldo de pollo preparado*—containing rice, avocado, onions, and chiles) we have ever eaten. Very flavorful, freshly made tortillas accompany the *caldo* and are used to make the tacos. The small restaurant in the courtyard at **Reforma 408** (*inexpensive*) features a variety of salads, enchiladas, and quiche.

SWEETS AND JUICES

Try the charming tearoom **Auseba** (Hamburgo 159) for some of the best pastries in the city. For ice cream, head for **Santa Clara** (Londres, near Genova), with its large variety of tropical fruit flavors including coconut, mango, and pineapple. All through the city, between the hours of 8 a.m. and 10 a.m., **orange juice** stands appear on the streets selling the freshest, sweetest, hand-squeezed juice you can imagine. The price is about half what you pay in a hotel restaurant. The stands are not normally allowed on the main streets, so you will have to check out some side streets to find them. Once found, just return to the same place each morning. A number of juice parlors can be found throughout the city, offering a variety of fresh juices and fruit salads. In the Zona Rosa try **Jugos Miami** (Hamburgo 105, corner of Genova) or **Makai** (Genova, between Londres and Liverpool).

CHAPULTEPEC PARK AREA

Hacienda de los Morales

Av. Vazquez de Mella 525 • One of the best. See "Special Places."

Las Mercedes

Leibnitz 67, corner of Darwin; ☎ 525-2099 • Just a couple of blocks from the Hotel Camino Real, Las Mercedes serves very good traditional Mexican dishes in a modern, pleasant, suburban atmosphere. Popular with Mexicans, this is a good place to try some of Mexico's distinctive dishes. Las Mercedes offers a number of stews and meats (but very few fish dishes) including *carnitas, mole* chicken, and a very flavorful pork loin in a *huitlacoche* sauce, as well as several tasty soups. Try the savory and spicy *sopa de medula*, a bone marrow soup. Not all dishes are available every day. Wonderfully fresh tortillas are served. During morning hours, Las Mercedes tempts you with a first-rate selection of Mexican breakfasts. If you are up for it, try their *ahogados a la Veracruzana*, poached eggs covered with a spicy tomato sauce of chiles, olives, and capers. *Open daily, 8 a.m.-1 a.m.*

Moderately expensive.

Azulejos

Hotel Camino Real, Mariano Escobedo 700; ☎ *545- 6960* • On Sunday from 1-4 p.m., Azulejos serves a buffet brunch that is truly an extravaganza. At one station you choose from fresh oysters, shrimps, ceviche, seafood salads, and mounds of fresh fruit. At another you select from Mexican specialties, traditional stews and dishes such as mole poblano. And yet another location has a carving block for roast beef and other meats. Live music accompanies your feast. *Expensive*.

Benkay

Hotel Nikko Mexico, Campos Eliseos 204; ☎ *203-4020* • The Benkay is one of the most recent and most expensive Japanese restaurants in the city. *A fixed-price meal for two of high quality will cost about $100.*

Expensive.

Meson del Caballo Bayo

Av. del Conscripto 360; ☎ *589-3000* • Located about a 20-minute taxi ride from the Zona Rosa, and near the Hipodromo racetrack, Meson del Caballo Bayo serves Mexican specialties in five festive dining rooms. On Sunday, the restaurant is mobbed with the beautiful young people of Mexico City, music fills the air, and there are long waits for tables. Same ownership as the wonderful in-town restaurant, Loredo with similar specialties, *carne asada a la Tampiquena* and *sabana*. Their *carnitas* are especially good. Lots of atmosphere and quite attractive.

Moderately expensive.

National Museum of Anthropology Restaurant

National Museum of Anthropology, Chapultepec Park • If you want to eat at the museum, you have one choice. This restaurant often has long lines, but the food is edible with fairly moderate prices for both the à la carte items and the buffet. The fruit salad is fine. Other items include enchiladas, tacos, hamburgers, sandwiches, chef's salad, and ice cream sodas.　　　　*Moderate.*

SNACKS

Happy's Pizza (*Tolstoi 17, near the Hotel Camino Real*) serves good pizza. North American residents flock here, and Mexicans are getting converted, too. Moderate. Next door is **Los Panchos** (*Tolstoi 9*), where tortillas are made in the entrance and used to make tasty tacos. During lunch hours, Los Panchos serves a moderately priced comida corrida. Across from the National Museum of Anthropology, on the lake, is a small stand selling *tortas* (sandwiches) and sodas. If you want to relax and have a snack, buy a *torta* and sit at the stand enjoying the lake scene. **La Baguette** (*Campos Eliseos and Lord Byron, near the Hotel Nikko Mexico*) is a bakery with good bread and pastries.

Several restaurants described in other sections above have branches in the **Colonia Polanco**, just north of Chapultepec Park. They include: **Estoril** (*A. Dumas 24*), **Cafe Tacuba** (*Newton 88*), and **El Parador** (*Campos Eliseos 198, next to the Hotel Nikko Mexico*).

ENTERTAINMENT

The choices are endless. Although you can dance to the latest music in the sleekest environments, you can also immerse yourself in Mexico's distinctive traditional music from the mariachis of Jalisco, to the *jarocho* songs of Veracruz, to the gentle serenades of the tropics. The very popular Ballet Folklorico presents biweekly shows, and in sport you can choose among bullfights, horse racing, and soccer.

BALLET FOLKLORICO

The **Ballet Folklorico** presents its extravaganza of regional dances and music in the elegant auditorium of the Palacio de Bellas Artes on Sunday at 9:30 a.m. and 9 p.m. and on Wednesday at 9 p.m. Extra performances are sometimes scheduled to meet the demand. This colorful, very popular, commercial show sells out fast. Tickets can be obtained at Bellas Artes. If you can't find tickets there or if you want to save time, your hotel or a tour agency usually will be able to make arrangements for you at an added cost. A popular package tour takes you to the Sunday morning Ballet Folklorico, then to the floating gardens at Xochimilco, and ends with the afternoon bullfights. A newer, less famous troupe, the **Ballet Folklorico Nacional Aztlan**, presents a similar show at the lovely Teatro de la Ciudad (*Donceles 36*) on Sunday at 9 p.m. Tickets for this show are cheaper and easier to obtain than for the more famous Bellas Artes' performances.

TRADITIONAL MUSIC: HOTSPOTS

About 5 blocks north of Alameda Park, you come to the **Plaza Garibaldi** at the corner of Lazaro Cardenas and Honduras. We are tempted to describe this plaza as unreal, or even surreal, but neither adjective is right; it is simply Mexican. What you get is a Mexican fiesta every night and even during the day. Mariachi musicians, dressed in their wide-brimmed *charro* hats, tight trousers and jackets decorated with silver, congregate here waiting to be hired for a party or song. Mexicans flock here to celebrate, to mourn a lost love, or just to hear their favorite songs. You may find five to ten different groups performing at once, their music filling the air and mingling with the gaiety of families or young lovers out for the night. You can hire a group or simply wander through the crowded square and listen to the plaintive music paid for by others. Or you can enter one of the surrounding restaurants (**El Tenampa**, very basic with no frills, and **Tlaquepaque** are two of the most popular ones) where you will find more mariachis performing while you sip your drink or eat a snack. Just off the Plaza Garibaldi, the nightclub, **Plaza Santa Cecilia** offers a nightly show of ranchero music. The Plaza Garibaldi functions every day, starts to get very crowded around 9 or 10 p.m., and by midnight (when some people have had too much to drink) can get a little rowdy. Normally, it is most crowded on the 15th of the month, when many Mexicans get paid. But on any evening there is a celebration to behold. Warning: Some tourists find that the earthiness of the Plaza Garibaldi scene makes them feel uncomfortable.

To hear the joyful, lively *jarocho* music of Veracruz, go to **La Fonda del Recuerdo** (*Bahia de las Palmas 39A*; ☎ 545-7260), a restaurant gaily decorated with paper cutouts and pottery. Several Veracruz musical groups—with their harps and guitars—are normally in residence waiting to be hired. Although we have had a few quiet times here, often there are sufficient celebrants willing to foot the bill of the musicians to make your evening here memorable. Recently, a group playing Nortena music has been alternating with the Veracruz musicians to the dismay of both regular patrons and staff. Hopefully, by the time you arrive the all Veracruz format will be in place again. Since this is a restaurant specializing in seafood, you are expected to order some food, although it need not be a full meal. Their shrimp dishes are fine and they serve a very good, very spicy crab soup (*chilpachole en jaiba*). Get here before 9 p.m. to get a seat. By 11 p.m. the place should be jumping. The restaurant is located a bit out of the way, off the extension of Rio Tiber, about a 10-minute taxi ride from the Zona Rosa.

CONCERTS

Free Sunday concerts frequently take place in Alameda Park in the late morning and in Chapultepec Park (*near the Casa del Lago or the National Museum of Anthropology*). The entertainment is varied but usually of interest. Often there are presentations of traditional dances and music. The **Teatro Blanquito** (*Mina and Lazaro Cardenas*) features some of the finest popular singers in Mexico. You won't find too many tourists at the first-rate shows that are regularly offered in the evening, usually beginning at 7:30 p.m.

BARS, CAFES, AND COCKTAIL LOUNGES

Among the many comfortable spots to relax, quite a number provide live entertainment.

Hotel Cortes

The romantic courtyard here is a special setting for a drink. On weekday late afternoons, a trio playing traditional serenades usually is in residence. During the day, the courtyard is an oasis in the busy Alameda area and perfect for relaxing between sightseeing. Try their tasty sangrias (fresh limeade and red wine, with or without vodka).

Hotel Majestic Bar

The rooftop bar of the Majestic often has live music in its dramatic setting overlooking the Cathedral.

Hotel Maria Isabel Sheraton

The open mezzanine "Lobby Bar" provides a comfortable setting for a drink and conversation. Occasionally, there is piano music. Its Jorongo Bar is well known for mariachi music.

Hotel Nikko Mexico

Down a few steps from the lobby is a very popular and bustling cocktail lounge often populated with the dating crowd.

Hotel Camino Real

The bar, La Cantina, features Mexican music in an informal atmosphere. Live entertainment for the price of a drink.

Bar L'Opera

Corner of 5 de Mayo and F. Mata. One of the most handsome bars in

Mexico City, with dark paneling and booths. It's worth peeking in even if you are not in the mood for a drink.

Calle Copenhague

Evenings, Mexicans congregate in outdoor restaurants and cafes on the intimate Calle Copenhague in the Zona Rosa. While music sometimes accompanies the lively street scene, strutting and parading "beautiful people" may provide ample entertainment. You need to come early to get a seat at one of the prized outdoor tables, especially at the popular Meson del Perro Andaluz (see "Where to Eat," above). At any time you can relax at one of the sidewalk tables by ordering a drink.

NIGHTCLUBS, DINNER DANCING, AND DISCOS

If you want to try out your dance technique or see a floor show, here are a few clubs to visit.

Caballo Negro

Fiesta Americana Reforma; ☎ *566-7777* • This club often features big-name Mexican entertainers.

Marrakesh

Florencia 36; ☎ *525-2020* • Very popular, with four clubs under one roof—Gipsy's, a disco; El Morocco, a bar; Casablanca for floor shows; and Valentino's for disco dancing. Open 9:30 p.m.- 3:30 a.m.

Senorial

Hamburgo 188; ☎ *511-9770* • Across from the Hotel Galeria Plaza; you enter this disco club through what looks like a wind tunnel.

Cero Cero

Hotel Camino Real; ☎ *545-6960* • A very popular disco with psychedelic lighting; live and taped music.

Le Chic

Hotel Galeria Plaza; ☎ *211-0014* • Popular, very up-to-date disco with backgammon room attached.

SPORTS

BULLFIGHTS

The popular bullfights are held Sunday at 4 p.m. in the **Plaza Mexico** *(Insurgentes Sur between Holbein and San Antonio)*, the largest bullring in the world, holding more than 50,000 spectators. Seats in the shade *(sombra)* are more expensive than those in the sun *(sol)*, which tend to draw a more unruly crowd. *The main bullfighting season runs from December through March.* During other months of the year, there are bullfights with novice matadors and smaller bulls. Tickets can be bought at the gate or through hotels or tour agencies. Buses marked "Plaza Mexico" run along Insurgentes Sur on Sunday, or you can take a *pesero.*

HORSE RACING

The races are held in the beautiful **Hipodromo de las Americas,** located northwest of Chapultepec Park, off Calz. Conscripto. There are races Tuesday and Thursday at 3 p.m., Friday at 5 p.m., Saturday and Sunday at 2:30 p.m. The season runs for 48 weeks, with no races held from mid-September to mid-October. *Peseros* run along the Reforma to the racetrack. Look for the driver with his hand out the window moving two fingers in a galloping motion. "Hipodromo" buses also run along the Reforma.

SOCCER (FUTBOL)

Soccer is the most popular sport in Mexico, and the rivalries in the professional league are intense. Games are held Sundays and some weekday evenings in the huge 105,000-seat **Estadio Azteca** *located near the intersection of Calz. Tlalpan and the Periferico Sur.* Take metro Line 2 to Taxquena, then the pesero or shuttle train to the stadium. Check with your hotel for times and dates of games.

GETTING TO AND FROM MEXICO CITY

Mexico City is the hub of the nation, with excellent air and bus service to all parts of the country and with numerous major highways radiating from it.

AIR

Mexico City is easily reached by direct flights from most major U.S. and Canadian cities. Internally, Mexico City has flights to all major and many minor cities throughout the country. The two major Mexican airlines, Aeromexico and Mexicana, as well as several regional Mexican airlines, fly the domestic routes.

The **Benito Juarez International Airport** is located in the eastern section of the city. Without traffic, the trip from the airport to the zócalo area can be made in 15 minutes. With traffic, however, the trip can take up to an hour, so give yourself plenty of time to get to the airport. Most airlines require that you arrive at least an hour before flight time. To protect yourself against overbooking, check in well ahead of the flight.

When you enter the airport lobby after going through customs, you will be greeted by a confusing mob scene with lots of people wanting to help you with your luggage or inviting you to take an illegal cab. Simply walk outside the terminal. Transportation from the airport to town is provided by official airport taxis, which operate on fixed rates based on your destination. Buy your ticket at the booth in the baggage area or outside the terminal. During rush hours, the lines for tickets can be quite long. For your return trip to the airport, just ask your hotel to call a regular taxi. The metro (subway) also runs to the airport. Unfortunately, this convenience is of little use to most travelers because no luggage is allowed on the subway. *Peseros* to the airport leave from outside the Chapultepec metro stop on Av. Chapultepec, corner of Tampico.

Several banks have branches in the airport terminal for changing your money. When leaving Mexico you may have to pass through customs before you can convert your pesos into dollars. Remember, there is a departure tax on international flights and some domestic flights. Near Sala A on the main floor you can place your baggage temporarily in coin lockers or, for larger pieces, in a guarded storage area. Nearby, there is a packing service for those many purchases that won't fit into your luggage.

BUS

First- and second-class buses travel from Mexico City to all parts of the country. There are four main terminals, each located on a subway line. But since luggage is not allowed on the subway, you will probably have to reach the terminal by bus or taxi.

Terminal del Norte (**North Terminal**, *Av. de los 100 Metros 4907.* ☎ *587-5967.*) Buses leave here for the pyramids of Teotihuacan, Tula, Guadalajara, Morelia, Queretaro, San Miguel de Allende, Puerto Vallarta, and other cities. There is a tourism booth, too. To get to the terminal, take the local bus #7, which runs north along Insurgentes from the Insurgentes metro station or take metro Line 5 to the stop for T.A. del Norte. Fixed-price taxis leave from the terminal. Buy your ticket inside where you'll also find a Tourism Information booth and a Hotel Reservation booth.

Terminal del Sur (**South Terminal,** *Av. Taxquena 1320.* ☎ *544-2101.*) Buses for Acapulco, Cuernavaca, Taxco, Zihuatanejo, and other cities to the south depart from here. Bus #7D travels from downtown along Bucareli and Guerrero to the terminal. You can also take metro Line 2 to Taxquena and the terminal stop. Again, buy your ticket inside the terminal for the fixed-price taxis stationed outside.

Terminal del Oriente (**East Terminal**, *known as TAPO, Av. Ignacio Zaragoza 200.* ☎ *702-5977.*) Buses for Cancún, Chetumal, Cholula, Puebla, Palenque, Mérida, Veracruz, Villahermosa, and Oaxaca can be caught here. There is a tourism information booth, too. Local bus #100 "San Lazaro" runs along the Reforma to TAPO. Metro Line 1 at the San Lazaro stop is near the terminal.

Terminal del Poniente (**West Terminal**, *Sur 122 at Tacubaya.* ☎ *516-4857.*) The terminal provides service to Toluca, Morelia, and Patzcuaro. Take metro Line 1 to the Observatorio stop or a bus from metro stop Chapultepec.

Bus tickets should be bought several days in advance. If you are traveling on a first-class bus, rather than trudging out to the terminal for tickets, you can try getting them in town at the **Greyhound Office** (*Reforma 27;* ☎ *535-2618*). The office serves as an agent for some of the major Mexican bus lines. Prices here are the same as at the terminals. Open Monday-Friday, 9 a.m.-2 p.m. and 3 p.m.-6 p.m. **Mexicorama**, *located in the Plaza del Angel, Loc. #48, on Londres between Amberes and Florencia also sells tickets for some first-class buses. Open Mon.-Fri., 9 a.m.-6 p.m., and Sat., 9 a.m.-2 p.m.*

TRAIN

The **Buenavista railroad station** is located *just east of Av. Insurgentes Norte, about a mile north of the intersection of Reforma and Insurgentes.* Trains leave here for many of the major cities in the country. Although travel often is slow, the improved special first-class service (*servicio estrella*) on trains such as **El Constitutionalista** to San Miguel de Allende, as well as the central location of the terminal make this form of travel increasingly appealing. Tickets must be bought at the station or through designated travel agents. You should reserve in advance, especially if you want a sleeping compartment. For information on schedules and ticket prices, call the Buenavista station, ☎ 547-3190 or ☎ 547-1084. For reservations, call ☎ 547-8972 or ☎ 597-6177.

CAR

From Mexico City major roads lead north to the U.S. border, south to Acapulco, east to Veracruz and the Yucatán Peninsula, and southeast to Oaxaca and Guatemala. For specific routes, see **"Getting to and from Mexico City"** under your destination.

PRACTICAL TIPS

Mexico City has a year-round temperate climate with brisk morning temperatures from November to February and its warmest weather from April through June. The official rainy season (June-October) really doesn't get under way until July, and even then the showers are usually brief.

Mexico City's altitude of 7400 feet can make you feel light-headed and tired when you first arrive. A late-afternoon nap may be necessary for adjusting. The high altitude combined with severe pollution (especially December-May) may pose problems for those with heart or respiratory ailments. Consult your doctor for advice.

Due to pollution, driving in Mexico City is prohibited on certain days. See **"How to Get Around."** A sweater and raincoat normally will be sufficient to keep you warm any time of the year. Bring comfortable walking shoes for this walking city. Dress is more formal here than elsewhere: the better restaurants expect men to wear jackets and, often, ties, while women's dress should be appropriate for a cosmopolitan city.

Pickpockets can be a problem in crowded subways, buses, and markets. Be sure to guard your valuables.

If possible, plan your trip to include days when special events occur in the city. Sunday holds special charm, for it is the day when Chapultepec Park and Xochimilco are liveliest and when the bullfights take place. On Saturday, there is the Bazaar Sabado in San Angel.

Shops are normally open every day but Sunday, usually between 10:00 a.m.-7 p.m.

The city is simply called "Mexico" (MAY-hee-koh); the country is referred to as "La Republica."

DIRECTORY

Airlines • *Aeromexico* (☎ 228-9910)
  Mexicana (☎ 325-0990)
  Aero California (Reforma ☎ 332; 207-1392)
  Aerocaribe (☎ 559-5748)
  Aeromar (Sevilla at Reforma; ☎ 207-6666)
  American (☎ 399-9222)
  Continental (☎ 203-1148)
  Delta (☎ 207-4013)

American Express • Reforma 234, between Niza and Havre (☎ 533-0380), Fiesta Americana Reforma (Reforma 80), and Hotel Nikko Mexico (Campos Eliseos 204).

Books in English • *American Book Store* (Madero 25) has a superb selection on Mexican archaeology, history, and culture. *Libreria Misrachi* (Juarez 4) for guides and other books on Mexico. *Sanborn's* (throughout city) for popular fiction.

British Embassy • Rio Lerma 71 (☎ 207-2089).

Buses • For local buses, see "Getting Around." For intercity buses, see "Getting to and from Mexico City."

Camera Equipment • American Photo Supply Co., Madero 20.

Canadian Embassy • Schiller 529 (☎ 254-3288).

Car Rentals • Many major as well as minor car-rental agencies at the airport and all over the city. *Avis* (☎ 588-8888); *Budget* (☎ 566-6800); *Hertz* (☎ 592-8303); *National* (☎ 533-0375).

Emergencies • The U.S. Embassy (☎ 211-0042) has an officer on duty 24 hours to handle emergency calls and the Mexican Ministry of Tourism (☎ 250-0123) has an emergency hotline 24 hours a day. You can also dial ☎ 07, the Mexico City emergency number. For the American British Cowdray Hospital (Observatorio and Sur 136) call ☎ 277-5000.

Essentials • *Woolworth* (Reforma 99). *Sanborn's* (at various locations) has clean bathrooms and a check-cashing service, even after banking hours.

Film Developing • Lots of camera stores around town, including FOTO G'Nova (Genova 39) and Foto Regis (Juarez 80). Kodak developing available.

Groceries • Superama (Sena and Balsas).

Newspaper • The English-language paper, *The News*, is sold throughout the city.

Peseros • See "Getting Around."

Post Office • Central Post Office is at Av. Lazaro Cardenas and Tacuba, near Bellas Artes.

Subway (Metro) • See "Getting Around."

Taxis • See "Getting Around."

Telegraph • International telegrams can be sent from offices at Av. Balderas 14, Tacuba 8, the International Airport (open 24 hours) and from many hotels.

Tourist Information • Ministry of Tourism, Av. Presidente Masaryk 172; Tourism office, Amberes, corner of Londres, and at the airport across form Sala A. For tourist information in English by telephone, call ☎ 250-0123 for the latest on museums, festivals, and other attractions throughout the city and country. Unfortunately, we have sometimes found the information provided by the latter sources to be inaccurate. Infotur, ☎ 525-9380, also provides tourist information.

Tours • Most hotels can make arrangements through the many tour agencies for a Sunday tour to the Ballet Folklorico, bullfights, etc. Other agencies offer a wide variety of excursions, including trips to the Silver Cities, and your hotel will be best informed as to which to use. If you prefer a private car with driver for city tours and brief excursions, first-class hotels can make arrangements for you.

Trains • See "Getting to and from Mexico City." For information, call the Buenavista train station, ☎ 547-3190 or ☎ 547-1084. For reservations, call ☎ 547-8972 or ☎ 597-6177.

U.S. Embassy • Reforma 305, ☎ 211-0042.

MEXICO CITY EXCURSIONS

Cortez Palace, Cuernavaca

Every road from Mexico's capital passes through areas with reminders of the ancient and colonial past. Roads wind up mountains
to pine forests and snow-capped peaks, then descend to warmer,
subtropical valleys brilliant with flowers and greenery. Fertile fields
are plowed by oxen; farmers ride their land on burros and horses as
cars and buses pass by on modern highways. *The contrasts in scenery,
people, and monuments are so diversified that entire books have been de-*

voted just to the excursions within a day of Mexico City. We have organized some of these sights around trips to the most popular tourist destinations: the pyramids at Teotihuacan, the colonial cities of Taxco and Puebla, the ruins at Tula, and the 18th-century architectural masterpiece at Tepotzotlan. In addition, we describe resorts and spas near Mexico City where you can relax for a few days before continuing your sightseeing. Each route offers at least some pre-Hispanic ruins and colonial monuments, and all give you a sense of the scenic diversity and enormous expanse of Mexico's Central Valley.

Few travelers are able to visit all the sights listed in this chapter on their first trip. While the **ruins at Teotihuacan** are a must, your selection of other excursions will depend partially on the rest of your itinerary in Mexico. **Taxco** can be saved for another time if you are going to the Silver Cities (on your way to the Silver Cities you might stop at Tula or Tepotzotlan). On the other hand, your choice of excursion depends on your tastes and interests. A traveler seeking a bit of home in a foreign land will take the Taxco route, whereas anyone interested in traditional villages and less traveled spots will head for the sidetrips around **Puebla**.

KEY TO MEXICO CITY EXCURSIONS

Sights • Famous ruins such as Teotihuacan, 16th-century monasteries such as Acolman, colonial towns such as Taxco and Puebla, luxurious resorts and spas, craft markets, and magnificent scenery abound in the region of Mexico City.

Shopping • Taxco is famous for its silver and Puebla for its hand-painted Talavera tiles and pottery; every town has crafts shops, and most villages have special crafts.

Markets • *Chinconcuac:* Sunday and Tuesday.

Fiestas • *Chalma:* Numerous dates (see "Chalma"). *Cholula:* Fiesta of Virgin of los Remedios, September 8. Cuernavaca: Flower Festival, May 2-8. *Taxco:* Fiesta of Santa Prisca, January 10; Holy Week; Silver Festival, around the 1st of December. *Tepotzotlan*: Christmas pageants, December 16-23. *Tlaxcala:* Carnival; Fiesta of Virgin of Ocotlan, 3rd Monday in May. *Tepotzlan:* Fiesta del Rey, September 8.

Where to Stay • Along every excursion route are at least a few decent hotels—in some instances, numerous hotels—in case you plan a leisurely trip extending beyond a day.

Where to Eat • Decent, often excellent, restaurants can be found along each route.

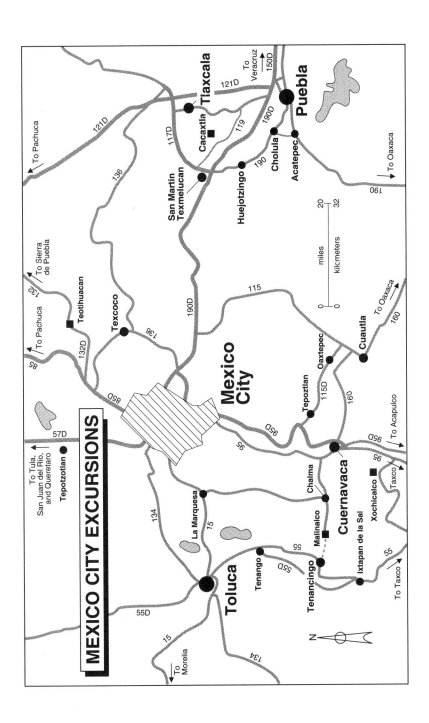

MEXICO CITY EXCURSIONS

How to get around • Buses from Mexico City run frequently to the major destinations of each excursion, but a car allows you to explore other sights along the way.

PRACTICAL TIP

Traffic in Mexico City can make entering and leaving tiresome. Rather than traveling back and forth to the city, plan an overnight outside if you intend to spend two days exploring one area. Also, consider which sights you can visit along the way to the other parts of Mexico on your itinerary

PYRAMIDS OF TEOTIHUACAN AND OTHER SIGHTS

This monumental ruined city with its world-famous pyramids provides a favorite excursion from Mexico City. For visitors unfamiliar with the accomplishments of ancient civilizations in the Americas, Teotihuacan (tay-oh-tee-whah-KAHN) is overwhelming. One of the largest cities in the world in A.D. 600, today even the skeletal remains impress with their numerous temples, nobles' houses, wall paintings, and apartment complexes. More than **75 temples** have been identified along the Street of the Dead; **several hundred murals**, more than **2,000 residential complexes**, and more than **600 workshops** for obsidian, ceramics, and other crafts have been discovered by archaeologists—in addition to the **two massive pyramids**. Although most of these buildings have not been restored, enough can be seen to give you a sense of the grandeur and power of this city. (Also, see earlier history of Central Valley.) Even if you spend most of your day exploring these ruins, you can include a stopover at the 16th-century **monastery of Acolman** if you are traveling by car. However, "Off the Beaten Track," the other side trip described below, might be difficult to fit in. Save it for another visit.

> When all was night,
> When there was no day,
> When there was no light,
> They gathered,
> The gods convened
> There in Teotihuacan.

Aztec myth

The Aztecs called this once great city "Teotihuacan," or "Place Where Gods Were Made." In their view of the world, the Aztecs lived during the period of the fifth sun, which started when the gods sacrificed themselves at Teotihuacan so the sun and moon could be born. While Teotihuacan (150 B.C. - A.D. 700) had been long abandoned by the time of the Aztecs, archaeologists have found some support for the Aztec interpretation of the religious importance of Teotihuacan. *Without doubt, Teotihuacan functioned as a religious mecca—all its architecture is covered with a talud-tablero design that signifies "temple," and its wall paintings repeatedly show priestly processions.* Its religious importance probably reinforced its political and commercial power, because Teotihuacan was not merely a holy place.

While no portraits remain of Teotihuacan's rulers, their presence is noticeable everywhere at this abandoned city, which is an incredible example of urban planning. *Organized according to a grid plan and divided into quadrants by two main thoroughfares, Teotihuacan's orderly development covered eight square miles.* No natural feature was allowed to interfere with the layout of this city; even the San Juan River was canalized to conform to the grid in its passage through town. Each building shows some imprint of the overall plan—from the uniform architecture of the central area to the farthest fringes of the city. No doubt, today's urban sprawl would have appalled Teotihuacan's rulers.

The religious themes in the mural art of Teotihuacan, most of them emphasizing agricultural gods and priestly ceremonies, changed only toward the end of the city's heyday. Most likely, Teotihuacan was a theocracy throughout its history, with ruler-priests using their religious authority to develop commercial monopolies (particularly in obsidian) that provided this city with its wealth. Because warriors from Teotihuacan are represented quite early in other parts of ancient Mesoamerica, especially in the Maya area, force was clearly also a part of its power. Only in the century prior to its collapse, however, were these warriors represented in the art at Teotihuacan itself. The reasons for its collapse are not quite decided. Definitely, other cities on the outskirts of the Central Valley—such as Cholula in Puebla and Xochicalco in Morelia—were growing larger and perhaps blocking Teotihuacan's trade. In the end, buildings along the sacred avenue of this city were burned, but whether there was an invasion or an internal rebellion is not known. The city was abandoned, its power destroyed forever, yet its monuments continued to be places of worship until the Spanish Conquest.

TEOTIHUACAN RUINS

Admissions between 8 a.m.-5 p.m.; site closes at 6 p.m. Admission fee.

PRACTICAL TIP

Keep your admission tickets for visiting different parts of the site.
If you are driving, conserve energy by driving to the north and south ends of the site and to the apartment complexes rather than making the 3-mile round-trip walk along the Street of the Dead. The most interesting sights are at either end of this avenue.
Wear a hat (if you are sun-sensitive) and good walking shoes.

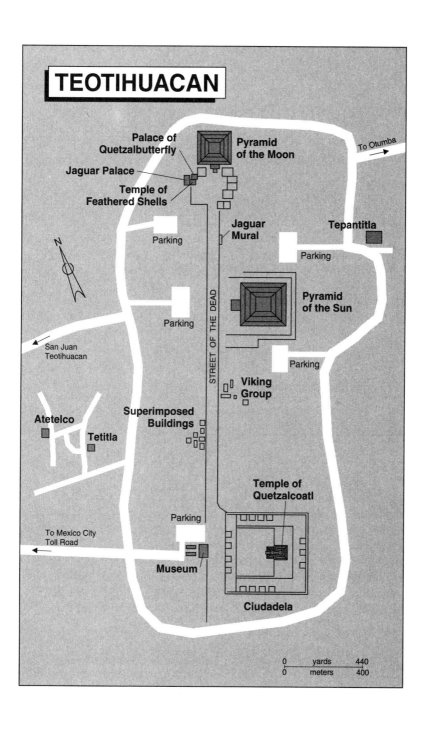

To orient yourself to the ruins, you might immediately climb to the summit of either the Pyramid of the Sun or of the Moon to overlook the remains of Teotihuacan. At this northern end of the city, mountains crowd close to the site, and the Pyramid of the Moon has a backdrop of the sacred Cerro Gordo, which provided Teotihuacan with most of its water. Leading south from the Pyramid of the Moon is the main avenue of Teotihuacan, called the Street of the Dead by the Aztecs because in their time the buildings flanking each side of the street were covered with earth and looked like burial mounds.

The Street of the Dead continues for a mile and a half until it reaches the only standing structure at its end, the **Ciudadela**. Across from the Ciudadela is a modern complex with a museum, restaurant, and shops where Teotihuacan's **Great Compound**, including the principal market, once stood. Though today the Ciudadela seems to mark the end of Teotihuacan, *it was the center of the city from the 5th to 7th centuries,* and the street continued two miles past it. At the Ciudadela, another major avenue ran two miles west and two miles east.

The old center of the city functioned as its administrative and commercial nucleus, and the area of the two pyramids was the heart of all that was sacred and religious. **Palaces** of the upper classes are found throughout these central areas, and the remaining population lived in outlying neighborhoods of apartment complexes. Because only a few of these **apartment complexes** have been restored, looking over Teotihuacan you see farmlands rather than the miles of buildings that once covered this area. *Most of the buildings you do see have been restored by the Mexican government in an archaeological project that was exceeded in cost only by the one to save Abu Simbel in Egypt.* Small stones embedded in the mortar of buildings signify their restoration. Originally, these buildings were plastered and painted, usually red.

Street of the Dead

The architectural harmony of the continuous structures lining this avenue still can be seen. Each **facade** is a variation of the hallmark of Teotihuacan architecture, the talud and tablero-sloping support (talud) for a framed and projecting rectangular panel (tablero). *This talud-tablero shape is found on ceramics and in paintings and signified something sacred.* With its entire length marked by sacred talud-tablero symbolism, the Street of the Dead has been described as an open-air cathedral. On top of these talud-tablero platforms once stood temples and, sometimes, palaces. Often the tablero was decorated with paintings, but few of these have survived. Midway between the Plaza of the Moon and the Pyramid of the Sun, you can see one of these murals under a protective metal roof.

The 130-foot-wide Street of the Dead gives an awesome impression of the numbers of individuals who once trafficked this street. Teotihuacan's own population of 200,000 was supplemented by peoples from all over ancient Mesoamerica on religious pilgrimages and/or business visits to this great state. Since Teotihuacan's market monopolized commerce in the entire valley, between 100,000 and 300,000 other residents of this region needed to enter this city to exhange crops for other essential items at the market across from the Ciudadela. Undoubtedly, they took time to pay religious homage at the pyramids.

Pyramid and Plaza of the Moon

While not as massive as the Pyramid of the Sun, the Pyramid of the Moon and its symmetrically arranged plaza combine to make one of the best-proportioned complexes in the city. Erected around A.D. 300, the Pyramid of the Moon reaches 116 feet in four stages; its summit is actually at the same level as the taller Pyramid of the Sun because it is built on higher terrain. Unlike Egyptian pyramids, Mexican pyramids don't always contain tombs: their purpose was to support temples. Raised above the surrounding area, these temples were reached by staircases during the performance of rituals. The Plaza of the Moon is formal-its temple-topped pyramid was once surrounded by temples on 12 platforms around it. The large altar in the center of this plaza had carvings on its sides and four staircases that, in the Maya area at least, indicate a calendrical or astronomical importance for the structure. This altar is so large that it might have been used for the performance of religious dances during ceremonies. Closer to the base of the pyramid is the unique Structure A, enclosing 10 altars around its walls with one in the center. Its numerous altars and proximity to the pyramid tell us this was an important religious building but, unfortunately, not the kinds of ceremonies performed.

Palace of Quetzalpapalotl

West of the Plaza of the Moon are a number of intriguing buildings with carvings and murals. The first one you encounter is the **Palace of Quetzalpapalotl** (Quetzal Butterfly), discovered in 1962 and reconstructed so completely that it gives an excellent sense of how the elite lived in Teotihuacan more than 1,200 years ago. After you climb the staircase decorated with a serpent's head, you will be in a portico with remnants of a mural on its base. At the northwest corner of this portico is the entrance to the **Patio of Columns**.

Surrounded by carved square pillars, the patio typifies residential architecture at this ancient city. While exterior walls were windowless to provide privacy, sunlight and air reached the rooms of residences through open patios in their centers. Rainwater was controlled by drainage systems in the patios. On the back of the pillars are perforations through which rope might have been threaded or tied for hanging curtains or partitions.

Religious rituals often were performed in these patios. The **carvings** on the square pillars here probably related to the religious practices of the family (families?) living in this palace. On the west side of the patio, the pillars are carved with frontal birds, thought to be owls, which often had warlike associations at Teotihuacan. All the other pillars are carved with profiles of quetzals, tropical birds valued for their green plumage in ancient times. The quetzals contain butterfly symbols, which were images for the soul. Above and below these figures are carvings of flames, symbols for splendor. Art historian George Kubler believes the quetzal carvings may represent the name or lineage of those who lived in this palace, while the owls, with some skeletal features, may represent a warrior cult worshiped by these people. *These carvings once were covered with paint and inset with obsidian discs, some of which are still in place.* Above the columns, you can see remnants of paintings with some symbols for water. The crenelated design projecting from the roof symbolizes "year." These water and year symbols may be associated with the cult practiced in the patio below, because *all rituals in ancient Mexico had the purpose, at least in part, of continuing the agricultural cycle* (or year) on which all life was based. Eight hundred years later, during Aztec times, such cycles were intimately related to warrior cults.

Palace of the Jaguar

Behind the Palace of Quetzal Butterfly and past the Temple of the Feathered Shells, the **Palace of the Jaguar** contains well-preserved **murals**. On the north side of the patio is a series of rooms with remnants of jaguar paintings. These jaguars certainly are not likely to be found in the wild. They wear feathered headdresses and blow conch shells (which also have feathered headdresses). Water drops and curlicues (called "speech scrolls") emerging from the shells may represent prayers for water and fertility. In keeping with this theme, a border above the jaguars contains images of the rain god Tlaloc alternating with a headdress symbol.

Other murals *can be found down a passage at the northwest corner of the patio.* Against a white background are blue and red jaguars in nets held by faded yellow hands. Some people have seen these figures as representing jaguars captured (netted) in a hunt, with the accompanying speech scrolls standing for their protesting roars. Since you might already have the idea that the Teotihuacanos were hardly playful in their art, that conclusion should probably be replaced by art historian Esther Pasztory's interpretation. She believes these scenes represent a myth about the reemergence of the sun from its nightly trip through the Underworld. At Teotihuacan, the netted jaguar symbolizes the night sun. According to ancient myths, the night sun reemerges in the sky after marrying the earth goddess (represented at Teotihuacan as having yellow hands). These murals symbolize the critical moment when the sun is reborn and daylight reappears.

Temple of the Feathered Shells

Returning toward the Palace of Quetzal Butterfly, you pass the entrance to this temple on your left. *The* **Temple of the Feathered Shells** *actually sits underneath the Palace of Quetzal Butterfly because it* *was an earlier structure built between A.D. 200 and 300.* When it was in use, parts would have been open to the sky, and it would not have the subterranean atmosphere created now by the palace above it. Since most temples have disappeared from their platforms and pyramids, the preservation of this lovely structure is quite fortunate. The square **pillars** of the temple facade have low-relief carvings of plumed conch shells—except for the two end ones, which are carved with four-petaled flowers. To ancient Mexicans, conch shells had religious associations with the sea and water, and they were also used as musical instruments. A **mural** along the base of the temple, well preserved due to having been buried under the later palace, still retains some of its color; you can easily make out the birds (parrots?) with streams of water flowing from their yellow beaks.

Temples on the Way to Pyramid of the Sun

As you leave the Plaza of the Moon on the Street of the Dead you see on your right two restored temples named after murals they once contained. The **Temple of Agriculture** murals have completely disappeared through decay, though fortunately drawings of them still exist. Next door is the **Temple of Mythological Animals**, whose murals have been removed to preserve them. On the left is the **Temple of the Jaguar**, named for the mural painted on one of its tableros. In front of the Pyramid of the Sun is the **Patio of Four Temples**. If you climb up this low platform, you will notice four small temples on each corner of an open patio.

Pyramid of the Sun

Covering the same area as the Great Pyramid in Egypt (yet about half as high), the **Pyramid of the Sun** *(700 feet long and 215 feet tall) represents an enormous human accomplishment.* Without beasts of burden, metal tools, or the wheel, the ancient people of this valley assembled 3-1/2 million tons of material, completing this pyramid around the year A.D. 100. It is estimated that the work force must have been about 15,000. The original pyramid did not look exactly like the one we see today. Unfortunately, *in 1905 the stone facing was stripped and rains partially destroyed the exterior surface, making the pyramid shorter and less bulky today than it was originally.* Its reconstructed facade holds many errors—for example, five terraces rather than four—and its thatched-roof twin temples disappeared long ago.

The Pyramid of the Sun is the earliest building still standing at Teotihuacan. Possibly the dense concentration of people involved in its construction led to the creation of this centralized state. Until recently, no one knew why it was built here or whether the Aztec belief that it was dedicated to the sun god was true (although during the equinoxes the setting sun perfectly illuminates this pyramid). Then, in 1971, a cave was discovered underneath the center of the pyramid, along with evidence of religious rituals. Interestingly, ancient Mexican myths state that the sun and moon were born in a cave, and that the center of the universe, the place of origins, is a cave. Over this cave a shrine was constructed around 300 B.C. Thus, centuries before the construction of the Pyramid of the Sun, this spot had been sacred and had attracted pilgrims from throughout the valley. We can well imagine the sanctity of the Pyramid of the Sun, given its location over this cave, and the power Teotihuacan may have exercised in controlling such a religious monument. *Long after the abandonment of Teotihuacan, at the time of the Spanish Conquest, Moctezuma worshiped here every 20 days.*

On the north end of the Plaza of the Sun is the **Palace of the Sun,** a large, complex palace in which elaborate murals were found but removed for preservation. Solar discs featured rather prominently in these murals. Given its size and its proximity to the pyramid, it may have been the palace of the high priest for the Pyramid of the Sun.

Note: *If you are planning to walk to the apartment compound of Tepantitla described below, turn east off the Street of the Dead by following one of the paths leading behind the Pyramid of the Sun.*

Viking Complex
Approximately midway between the Pyramid of the Sun and the Ciudadela on the Street of the Dead is a complex excavated with funds provided by the Viking Foundation. Here two layers of sheet mica, covering an area of 90 square feet, were discovered. While small amounts of mica are found sprinkled on ritual objects, the Viking quantity is unequaled anywhere else. Its significance and purpose still are not understood, but the sheets of mica were "buried" under a concrete floor, perhaps recalling ritual offerings practiced by the earlier Olmec civilization.

Superimposed Buildings
A few patios farther along the Street of the Dead is the complex of **superimposed buildings**. The Street of the Dead in this part of the city is organized into patios at different levels, a way of grading the descent to the Ciudadela (which lies 90 feet below the level of the Pyramid of the Moon).

Ancient Mexicans often built by using earlier structures as fill to make new buildings larger and more grandiose. The series of such buildings here is interesting because the various stages have all been restored. The **older buildings** now lie underground. To reach them you must go down a metal staircase and cross the floor of a patio that today is roofed by the later structure. In the northwest corner is a well preserved **temple** with paintings of green circles representing precious jade discs and a hook motif that might represent a serpent. Also in these underground chambers is a 40-foot **well** that still contains water.

As you continue toward the Ciudadela, you will cross over the **San Juan River**, which formerly was spanned by a bridge the width of the Street of the Dead.

Ciudadela

Climbing stairs facing the Street of the Dead, you enter the enormous **Ciudadela** complex—shaped as a rectangle and covering approximately 1,200 square feet. Surrounded by 12 structures on three sides and a pyramid on the fourth, *the Ciudadela's architecture is believed to have calendrical significance because, including the pyramid, the number of structures add up to the 13 days of the ritual calendar.* The plaza within these structures could have held 100,000 persons. In addition to their ritual significance, the platforms around the Ciudadela once held public and private houses for high-ranking administrators. Two **palaces** have been discovered behind the pyramid. Based on the artifacts found there, archaeologists believe the highest nobles of Teotihuacan society lived in them.

Inside the pyramid is the **Temple of Quetzalcoatl** (or "feathered serpent"), built between A.D. 150-200 and later covered by a larger pyramid (since removed). The **carvings** on its facade are unlike anything found elsewhere at Teotihuacan and provide *a rare instance of architectural sculpture in the round.* Along the bottom of the facade is an inundating feathered serpent amid shells and other water symbols. In the tableros of the various stages are repeated projecting heads of what may be the goggle-eyed rain god Tlaloc and the feathered serpent. Joining these sculptures is the body of the feathered serpent and, occasionally, the rattles on his tail. The staircase balustrades are adorned with heads of the plumed serpent. *These carvings once were colorfully painted*—blue for water, red and yellow on the shells, and green for the precious quetzal feathers of the serpent's yoke. However impersonal and foreign these sculptures seem to us, they still express some of the power that must have awed Teotihuacanos. Just as awesome are the finds of recent excavations inside the pyramid. It seems that 272 warriors, whether native or foreign is unknown, were sacrificed, then interred—symmetrically, of course—around a central burial.

Museum

The small **museum** has been renovated and just reopened in 1993. It is designed primarily to provide background information of Teotihuacan, although special works of art, such as a **fresco** of mythological animals, are on display. (The National Museum of Anthropology in Mexico City has an excellent room on Teotihuacan art, with reproductions of some of its murals, such as those at Tepantitla.) At the entrance to this museum is a reproduction of a colossal **statue** of the water goddess (the original is in Mexico City). Among the many new exhibits is one recreating some of the recent finds from inside the Pyramid of Quetzalcoatl, including a **tomb** of nine warriors wearing jawbone necklaces.

Apartment Complexes

Across the road encircling the ruins, you can visit some apartment compounds that have been partially restored. Numerous families, perhaps related by kinship and work, lived in these complexes and shared a patio for religious rituals. Each of these complexes belonged to larger neighborhoods with which they shared a more elaborate temple complex. Rene Millon, who has directed a mapping project of Teotihuacan, reported that people of different status lived together in the apartment buildings and neighborhoods. While most of the people were farmers, who also supplied labor for massive building projects, others were potters, shell workers, and, most importantly, obsidian workers. Even a compound where foreigners from Oaxaca once lived has been discovered (not yet restored). The three apartment complexes described below have interesting **murals**.

Tepantitla

Near the parking lot behind the Pyramid of the Sun, this **apartment complex** has been restored mostly around the common worship area rather than the living units. Bark beaters that could have been used for making paper or bark cloth, and molds for making figurines, have been excavated here, perhaps indicating the occupations of the former residents. *Modern farmers digging up maguey plants discovered the Tepantitla murals.* Before you enter the main room you can see a procession of elaborately dressed priests, identifiable by the "purses" (incense bags) they carry, who are performing a ritual relating to the sowing of seeds. Inside the main room, **murals** to the right and left of the door depict frolicking individuals totally out of keeping with the rigorous religious format seen elsewhere.

The **mural of the Paradise of Tlaloc** is to the right of the door. The upper panel is a typical Teotihuacan mural with a frontal god, often identified as the rain god Tlaloc but more likely the fertility earth goddess, from whose outstretched hands pour water and precious items. Behind her grows a tree with butterflies and birds. Approaching this goddess are priests. Fragments of the "Paradise" are below this mural.

A lake is formed at the foot of a mountain and two rivers flow out to the sides. Everywhere, small, near-naked figures are swimming and dunking each other in the rivers, playing games. Four individuals swinging a fifth have speech scrolls emerging from their mouths, perhaps indicating singing. Despite all this play, on the extreme lower right is a sacrificial figure, naked, from whose chest flow a red stream of blood and a blue stream of the river. *This is the most explicit evidence of human sacrifice found at Teotihuacan.* It reminds us that even such a playful "paradise" is gained only through the deadly rituals that keep the agricultural cycle continuing, the rains falling, and the sun rising each day.

The mural to the left of the door is even more fragmented, but the parts that remain on the lower section show a stickball game in progress. Dressed in sandals, kilts, and hats, their faces elaborately painted, these little figures hold bats. *They provide the only evidence that the ball game was actually played at Teotihuacan, because no ball court has been found here.* Perhaps the stickball version of the game, rather than the more common hipball, did not require a permanent stone court. Or, as some archaeologists conjecture, perhaps the Street of the Dead, with all its sloping talud surfaces like ball courts found elsewhere, occasionally functioned as the ball court to surpass all other ball courts in size and majesty.

Tetitla

From the museum parking lot turn right onto the circuit road and turn left at trailer park (the second dirt road). Make your first right on another dirt road and you will come to this **apartment complex**—which still has its windowless exterior walls and indications of numerous apartments, each decorated with different types of murals. Although Teotihuacanos usually practiced cremation, several rich burials have been discovered under the floors of this complex. While you make your way through the confusing maze of rooms here, look for fragments of the varied murals on its remaining walls. In the front section you can see human faces painted in a style different from the rest of Teotihuacan and believed to be Mayan. In fact, some of the dress of these figures follow Mayan customs. Farther inside are paintings of grotesque birds with outstretched wings and drops of red blood dripping from their beaks. (These owls probably represented a warrior cult.) Once past these birds you come to the main patio with a center altar looking like a miniature version of the pyramid and temple complexes found at the center of the city.

Around this main patio are a number of murals. In the east room, curious jaguars with feather headdresses and blue eyes sprawl over benches. It is known that the jaguar represents fertility, yet the meaning of this disarming pose remains to be discovered. *Opposite the jaguars, on the west, is the most famous mural of Tetitla.* Called the **Mural of the Jade Tlalocs**, these frontal, nearly geometric representations of a deity may actually be the earth goddess with her yellow hands and painted fingernails. Water and symbols for precious items flow from her fingertips. Her face, partially covered with a jade mask and enormous earplugs, can be discovered just above the level of her hands. A large rectangular headdress adorned with a bird's face and feathers tower above her head.

Atetelco

To reach Atetelco, continue past Tetitla and take your first left onto a dirt road that leads to another road and this apartment complex. Atetelco contains some of the most elaborate **mural reconstructions** at Teotihuacan. They can be found in what is called the Patio Blanco, at the rear.

In this courtyard, for the first time, you can see upper wall decorations. *(Usually, only the baseline paintings have survived because they were buried and protected by falling debris.)* The reconstructions at Atetelco may surprise you with their wallpaper-style repeat designs in the upper level. The walls of all three temples are divided into lozenge shapes by a net design. In each lozenge is painted the same figure over and over again, although each room has a different motif. The three murals on the porticos and those on a small fragment of the west wall represent cosmological themes of a warrior cult.

WHERE TO STAY AND EAT

Several restaurants lie in the vicinity of the ruins, most within walking distance (for those who have not yet exhausted themselves at the ruins). If you can walk no more and are near the Ciudadela, try **El Pyramide Restaurant,** on the second floor of the museum building, with views over the ruins, international and Mexican food, and moderate prices. If you get hunger pangs in the vicinity of the Pyramid of the Sun, walk to the access road behind it and look for the sign of **La Gruta Restaurant**. No description can prepare you for this restaurant in an enormous underground natural cavern. Traditional Mexican music may accompany your meal of either Mexican food or a simple club sandwich (moderate). Near the road to Tetitla is **Pyramid Charlie's**, part of the Carlos 'N Charlie's chain, but with more Mexican accents than usual. There's a pleasant outdoor terrace in addition to the dining rooms and often mariachis accompany your very international meal (moderately expensive). Off the south end of the ruins is the **Villa Arquelogica**, with that we believe to be overpriced food (expensive). But since it's part of a hotel, you'll find it open even if the others aren't. Your cheapest option, of course, is to bring a picnic lunch and enjoy it outside the ruins under a tree (soft drinks available). Or, if you dare, eat at one of the tiny tent restaurants serving antojitos on the perimeter of the ruins.

Hotel Villa Arqueologica   ★★★

☎ (595) 602-44; $54 • Just a 10-minute walk from the museum (left on access road), this hotel provides excellent accommodations at moderate prices. Its 40 rooms are air conditioned. Restaurant, bar, a pool, and tennis court. For reservations, call, in the U.S., ☎ 800-258-2633.

GETTING TO AND FROM TEOTIHUACAN

BUS

You can pick up the buses to "Piramides-Teotihuacan" either at the Terminal Autobuses del Norte or across from the metro stop Indios Verdes, Line 3. To get to the bus terminal, take the metro, Line 5 to T.A. del Norte or a bus on Insurgentes Norte marked for the terminal. At the terminal purchase your tickets at *Sala 8* to the left and rear. On your return, the buses stop outside the main entrance to the ruins near the museum and are marked "Mexico-Metro." These buses run approximately every half-hour.

TOUR

Nearly every hotel and every tour agency can make arrangements for your visit to the ruins. Many of the tours take you to the monastery of Acolman along the way and include lunch.

CAR

Follow Insurgentes Norte out of the city to MEX 85D, the cuota ("toll") road. After paying your toll, follow signs to the right for "Piramides" and MEX 132D. If you take MEX 132 Libre, the free road, you may pass through some small villages, but you will pick up a lot of bus and truck traffic. The total distance is about 48 km (30m) and takes approximately one hour depending on the traffic around Mexico City.

ACOLMAN MONASTERY

This monastery-museum is located about 13 km (8 m) before Teotihuacan. After paying your toll and bearing right onto MEX 132, you see Acolman's massive walls. Turn off at this point to reach Acolman. If you are arriving from the pyramids, exit from MEX 132D at sign for Acolman. There is a small admission fee to this monument, which is open every day but Monday, 10 a.m.-5 p.m.

This **Augustinian church and monastery** is an outstanding example of early 16th-century architecture—*one of Mexico's purest examples of the European Plateresque style.* The church **facade** is exquisitely and soberly carved. The monastery contains remnants of fine **frescoes**, particularly on the walls of the upper story of its main cloister. Rooms along the second floors of the two cloisters contain museum exhibits of **religious paintings** and **pre-Columbian artifacts** found here during 20th-century renovations.

OFF THE BEATEN TRACK

If you're traveling by car, consider following the Texcoco road south off the superhighway near Acolman. Texcoco lies only 8 km (5 m) away. Along the way to Texcoco, you can turn off at the sweater-making village of **Chinconcuac** (cheen-kon-kwac). Chinconcuac's market days are Tuesday and Sunday, but the quality of these sweaters has declined in recent years with the switch from wool to synthetics. On the far side of Texcoco, turn right to the federal agricultural school of **Chapingo**. The grounds of this school are lovely, but not the sole reason to visit. The **chapel** here contains some of **Diego Rivera's finest murals** (*open weekdays, 9 a.m.-2 p.m., 5-7 p.m.*).

TAXCO, CUERNAVACA, AND OTHER SIGHTS

During the first half of this century so many North Americans traveled from Cuernavaca to Taxco and then on to Acapulco that it is not surprising to find that many remained along the way, becoming permanent residents. Their enthusiasm is warranted by the good climate and sights along this route. Special one-day tours will speed you through the center of Cuernavaca and take you on a silver-buying spree to colonial Taxco, but won't provide you with the time to savor Taxco's charm, to stop at the village of **Tepoztlan**, the ruins of **Xochicalco** and **Malinalco**, or the impressive caverns of **Cacahuamilpa**. *If you have only a day, we recommend you spend all of it in either Cuernavaca or Taxco, bypassing the other sights on this route.* Tours and buses take you to both, but a car is best to visit Xochicalco and the **caverns** along the way. Off the beaten track, Malinalco and **Chalma** are too time-consuming to reach by bus. Accommodations in both Cuernavaca and Taxco are excellent.

TAXCO

Picturesque **Taxco** *(TAHS-koh) is the most famous of the historically preserved colonial towns in Mexico.* Built on a hill where silver has been mined since pre-Hispanic times, Taxco's orange-tile roofs, narrow cobblestone lanes, small plazas, and fountains engulf you in their **18th-century atmosphere**. Founded in 1522 by Cortes for the mining of silver, the town truly struck it rich in the 18th century—so rich that silver baron Jose de la Borda offered to pave the road from Veracruz to Mexico City in silver coins if the pope would only agree to visit. Architecturally, Taxco appears much as it did in Borda's time, only the source of wealth has changed from silver mining to silver craftsmanship and tourism.

For many tourists, Taxco is a quick shopping stop for **silver**. For others, its perfect climate and charm make it the ideal weekend resort. Others simply never leave. Whatever your initial plans, consider an overnight. The town's beauty will enchant you more with a longer stay.

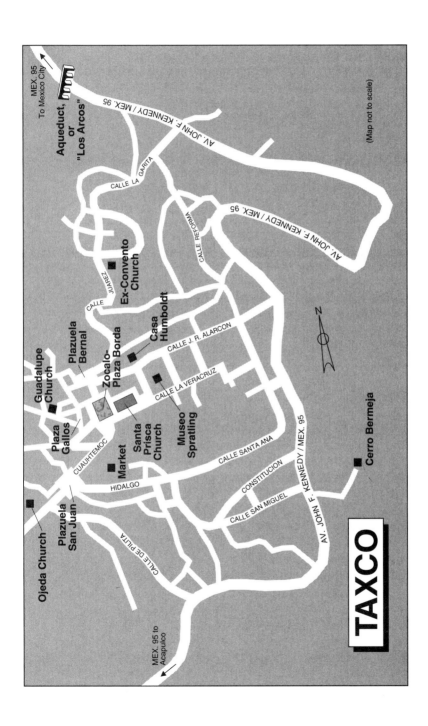

PRACTICAL TIP

Collective vans provide service up the hills to the main plazas of town (7 a.m.-8 p.m.) by following a set route from the aqueduct (El Chorrillo), then up Benito Juarez through the zócalo, down Cuauhtemoc to San Juan Plaza, then down Hidalgo to San Miguel before continuing back on Avenida JFK. Stops along JFK are marked "paradas."

Street names are seldom marked and often change after a few blocks. Use accompanying map for finding addresses as given in this book.

Sturdy walking shoes make walking on steep, cobblestone streets easier, and leaving the driving through the congested and confusing streets to a taxi or combi driver is strongly advised.

Tourism offices *are located on Av. JFK at each entrance to Taxco.*

WHAT TO SEE AND DO

Shopping in Taxco takes you into some fine 18th-century buildings, but you will want to wander through the narrow lanes when the shops are closed, the town is tranquil, and the bells of **Santa Prisca Church** toll authoritatively through the mountain-clear air. From the Plazuela San Juan, you might take the stairs and path up to the 19th-century **Ojeda Church** and from Zócalo, Calle Guadalupe leads up to the **Guadalupe Church**; either route provides fine **views** overlooking Taxco. Wandering can be as aimless as you like because the twin towers of Santa Prisca Church can usually be sighted to guide you back to the zócalo.

Zócalo and Santa Prisca Church

On the peaceful and shaded zócalo is Borda's residence as well as "his" church. Although **Santa Prisca Church** was founded in the 16th century, its present baroque appearance is due to its nearly total renovation in the mid-18th century at the behest of Borda. After becoming wealthy from his silver mine, he gave about 8 million pesos for the refurbishment of Santa Prisca, saying, "God has given to Borda, now Borda gives to God." His money was well invested, for *the church is among the finest in Mexico*. Its massive rose-colored exterior is crowned with a brilliant tiled dome and two ornately carved **towers** that dominate all of Taxco. A finely carved medallion of the baptism of Christ centers the facade while everywhere columns twist or drip with ornament, cherubs frolic amid flowers and vines. While the cohesive exterior designs are merely baroque, the interior is more effusive and imaginative in the Mexican Churrigueresque style. Gilded altarpieces cover the walls, none more magnificent than the high **altar** with its swirling polychrome wooden sculptures. A fabulously ornate organ fills the air with its music, and baroque paintings by the Mexican artist Miguel Cabrera adorn the right transept (look for the portrait of Borda's son, Manuel) and handsome sacristy (right and rear of high altar) where his Nativity and Assumption are considered among his best work.

Plaza de Los Gallos

Just behind the zócalo, off Calle Guadalupe. • Just before this tiny plaza and fountain is the **Casa Figueroa** (Guadalupe 2). *Known as the House of Tears, in colonial times, for the forced labor that the magistrate Count Cadena imposed on debtors* to build his home. If reopened to the public, the **interior** is worth seeing—especially the lavishly **Talavera-tiled bathrooms.**

Museo Guillermo Spratling

Just behind Santa Prisca; Open Tues.-Sat. 10 a.m.-5 p.m., Sun. 9 a.m.-3 p.m.; Fee. • This fine **museum** is dedicated to William Spratling, *the American responsible for reviving Taxco's silver industry through craftsmanship.* Spratling adapted Indian and art deco designs to create the hollow silver and rosewood pieces that made Taxco famous. He trained the first apprentices in his workshop, many of whom have become the noted silversmiths of today. The museum contains Spratling's pre-Columbian collection (with some exceptional Olmec pieces) as well as, in the basement, historical exhibits of the colonial silver mining business.

Casa Humboldt

Calle Juan Ruiz de Alarcon near Calle Pineda. • Easily identified by the rich Moorish designs on its **facade**, this building was originally an inn for caravans traveling between Acapulco and Mexico City. Acapulco was the sole port for infrequent ships bringing goods from the Orient via Spanish Manila, and one can well understand the value placed on the Chinese silks and porcelains that once passed through here. By your visit, the building may house the new **Museo del Virreinato**, devoted to this colonial period. The current name is in honor of Baron Alexander von Humboldt, the German naturalist, who briefly resided here in 1803.

Teleferico

Open 8 a.m. till dusk; Fee. • You can enjoy the most panoramic of all Taxco views by taking the **cable car** lift up to the Montetaxco Hotel. The lift begins its journey near the aqueduct (combis available on Av. JFK).

SHOPPING

Before absorbing yourself in silver shopping, visit the **market** area reached by steps leading down from Cuauhtemoc or by a ramp off Veracruz. You'll find **bark paintings**, **wooden masks**, and colorful **baskets** on the streets along the edge of the market, but mostly produce farther in. The market meanders and sprawls (especially on Sundays) down narrow alleys crowded with goods and people. Whether you're shopping or not, you may enjoy finding your way through this maze, which continues all the way to Hidalgo Street.

SILVER

Since more than 100 silver workshops operate in Taxco, you cannot miss finding silver and seeing craftsmen at work. Taxco silver, internationally famous, is shipped to other parts of Mexico and the world. *Although you have come to the source, the prices are not cheaper, unless you are buying wholesale, than elsewhere in Mexico—and may be even more expensive if you visit the shops with a guide.* Guides receive a sizable percentage of the sale, so it is best to shop by yourself, remembering that in Mexico every item in sterling silver must carry a stamp of "sterling" or ".925." Prices vary according to craftsmanship as well as silver content, so check for a smooth polish and well-finished details, such as hinges. You may want to visit some of the most renowned silver shops, even if you cannot afford to buy. Among the best known are: **Los Castillo** (Plazuela de Bernal 10), which gives a tour of their workshop in town, although you can also visit their larger workshop at Rancho La Cascada (km 100.5 on MEX 95 south); **Pineda de Taxco**, in the Patio de las Artesanias on the zócalo; **Elena Ballesteros** (Celso Munez 4), just around the corner; and **Andres** (across from Posada Mision on Av. JFK) with remarkable pieces from the designs of the greats, such as Spratling and Tapia—both of whose work, along with Antonio Pineda's, can be seen in the small **Museo de la Plateria** (*downstairs in El Patio de las Artesanias on the zócalo; open Tues. Sun. 10:15 a.m.-5:30 p.m.; small fee*)

FIESTAS

As Taxco has become more international, its fiestas have become less traditional. But fiesta time anywhere in Mexico is an opportunity for gaiety and entertainment. The most popular fiesta includes the entire week preceding **Easter**, with Holy Thursday and Friday the most important days. **January 18th**, fiesta of the patron saint, Santa Prisca, is accompanied by processions and dances. The **Silver Festival** has occurred one week each year since 1929 around the 1st of December and attracts major silversmiths as well as many tourists to enjoy the fireworks, mariachi music, and other special entertainment in the zócalo. Reserve your hotel room well in advance for these events.

WHERE TO STAY

Many of the finer hotels are on hills overlooking town, and a few are resort hotels with extensive sports facilities appropriate for a vacation. Most hotels require or prefer meal plans, especially on weekends and holidays, when advance reservations are recommended. For reservations, address letters to Taxco, Guerrero, Mexico, or call, area code 762.

Hacienda del Solar   ★★★★

Calle del Solar; ☎ *2-03-23; $170* • This modern resort occupies an 85-acre ranch 3 km (2m) south of town (turn left off Av. JFK across from tourism kiosk). Here you are in a country retreat dominated by magnificent mountain vistas. The tasteful accommodations reflect this setting, some with cantera stone walls, fireplaces, and hand-paint-ed-tiled baths, and all with views—though some only from the terrace. The 30 units are either junior suites with comfortable sitting areas or deluxe rooms, and they are divided between the restaurant inn, with its relaxed hotel ambience and compelling views of Taxco, and the more countrified settings of the casitas (shared by more than one unit). MAP required on weekends and holidays, but at one of Taxco's best restaurants. Piano bar. Heated pool, putting green, 1 tennis court. Car recommended for getting to town. Write Apartado 96.

Montetaxco

Frac. Lomas de Taxco; ☎ *2-13-00; $95* • This modern resort sits atop a mountain about 3 m north of Taxco (at the end of a steep road off highway) and can be reached by hotel bus or cable car (see "telefe-rico" above). The 160 rooms reflect their Holiday Inn ancestry and are a bit pedestrian, but most have views as compensation. In fact, the spectacular setting and many activities are the attractions here. Sleek restaurant and disco, a piano bar with panoramic views, special enter-tainments such as a folkloric "Fiesta Mexicana." Large heated pool, horseback riding, tennis courts, steam baths and gym, nine-hole golf course, and children's activities. Car recommended. Write Londres 251 in Mexico City.

Posada de la Mission ★★★

Avenida JFK 32; ☎ *2-00-63; $70-85* • This hotel, designed in 18th-century hacienda style, is at the foot of town with nice views of Taxco. The 150 rooms vary in age and price, many with views; the three-star rating and price are for the modern ones, large with two double beds and balcony. The most striking aspect is the heated pool surrounded by a Juan O'Gorman mural. Gardens. Restaurant and two bars, one with views. Parking. Write Apartado 88.

Rancho Taxco-Victoria

Carlos J. Nibbi 5; ☎ *2-02-10; $55-75* • A three-minute walk from the zócalo, this in-town hotel has the atmosphere of the country with lush gardens. The Victoria and nearby Rancho Taxco have combined into one hotel sharing facilities for their more than 100 rooms, some of them small, while others are quite a bargain for their size, modern baths, and terraces with view. The Victoria is one of Taxco's oldest establishments, picturesque and clean, though faded. Glass-enclosed dining room with view. Large pool. Parking. Write Apartado 83.

Santa Prisca ★

Cena Obscuras 1; ☎ *2-00-80; $46* • Only a block from the zócalo and near Plazuela San Juan, this pensione- style hotel is a bit pricey for its 38 plain rooms (some with views), but for a relaxing stay there's a sunny garden, a library, and a lovely restaurant with bar service. Park-ing. Write Aparado 42.

Los Arcos

Juan Ruiz de Alarcon 2; ☎ *2-18-36; $29* • A former monastery converted into a pleasant in-town hotel (one block from the zócalo) with friendly management; 26 rooms sparely but colorfully furnished; some baths a bit worn. Attractive courtyard and bar. A good buy.

Posada de los Castillo

Juan Ruiz de Alarcon 3; ☎ *2-13-96; $30* • A restored colonial mansion offers a pleasant lobby surrounded by 15 small rooms with tiled bathrooms.

WHERE TO EAT

Taxco has so many tourists that it is not hard to find "Americanisms" in the prices and on menus, although Mexican food and other cuisines are also available. Price categories are explained in the Introduction.

La Ventana de Taxco

In the Hacienda del Solar (☎ *2-05-87)* • This is the most gracious restaurant, serving pleasant enough Italian specialties, including penne arrabiate, an interesting salad Sorrentino, and continental dishes such as Chateaubriand. Named for its picture windows overlooking Taxco, this is an elegant place to dine. No credit cards accepted. *Expensive.*

La Pagaduria

On the Cerro de Bermeja • where the Spanish Crown's silver mine once operated (turn left up the street by the Seguro Social complex on Av. JFK; (☎ 2-34-67). Given the few people who make the brief trip here, the food is surprisingly good, from the tortilla soup to the garlic shrimp and beef brochette and on to the mango pie. Fabulous views.
Moderately expensive.

La Taberna

Juarez 12, next to Post Office; (☎ *2-52-26)* • Behind the nicely renovated rooms of this adobe is a garden patio for a pleasant evening of dining on the many pasta (including an unusual and hearty Azteca), continental (pollo Kiev and pork loin ciruela), and shrimp dishes. The most romantic restaurant in town. *Moderate.*

La Hacienda

Hotel Agua Escondido, Calle Spratling, just off zócalo • Good, mostly Mexican food—tasty chicken Hacienda in chipotle chile, tortilla soup and queso fundido—but there are plenty of vegetables served with the entrees and the ensalada Hacienda is one of the best salads in town. Breakfast here is recommended, too. *Inexpensive.*

Bora Bora Pizza

Just off zócalo at Paco's and up the tiny Callejon Delicias • The crust is thick and the cheese plentiful.

Cielito Lindo

A good place for snacking on sandwiches, salads or sweets is this very international restaurant, conveniently located by the zócalo.

Moderate.

ENTERTAINMENT

Late afternoons in Taxco begin with a visit to **Paco's Bar** overlooking the zócalo, where you can drink in the details of the Santa Prisca facade while sipping a good margarita. The panoramic views from the terrace bar of the **Montetaxco Hotel** are spectacular while there's still daylight, but worth the trip only if you have a car or plan to take the even more scenic teleferico (see above). For evening entertainment check out the offerings at the **Montetaxco** (there's a piano bar, disco, and Mexican Fiesta) and the comfortable piano bar at **La Ventana de Taxco**.

GETTING TO AND FROM TAXCO

Tour agencies in Mexico City and Acapulco provide guided trips to Taxco, though this town is just as easily reached on your own by either car or bus. In Taxco, the first-class Estrella de Oro terminal is on Av. JFK near Calle Pilita; second-class Flecha Roja is on Av. JFK near Calle Veracruz.

FROM MEXICO CITY

By **car**, leave Mexico City on the Periferico Sur and hook up with the multilane MEX 95D, the toll ("cuota") road to Cuernavaca, by following signs to Viaducto Tlalpan (not Calzada Tlalpan). After Cuernavaca, continue on MEX 95D toward "Iguala/Acapulco" until the access road for Taxco. When returning to Mexico City, signs for Periferico Pte. take you around the city to Chapultepec Park and the Reforma. The 168km (104m) trip should take 2 1/2 hours. By **bus**, depart from the Central de Autobuses del Sur on Calzada Tlalpan 2205 (Metro Tasquena). Numerous lines ply this route, including the first-class Estrello de Oro. Count on at least a three hour trip.

FROM ACAPULCO

MEX 95 descends from Taxco to Iguala then links up with MEX 95D to Acapulco for a 270 km (167 m) trip that takes 3 1/2 hours now, less when the new toll road, MEX 95D, is completed.

For buses, add a bit more time. First-class Estrella de Oro buses leave from the terminal on the highway several times daily for Acapulco.

CUERNAVACA

Lying just 1 hour 20 minutes south along MEX 95D from Mexico City, Cuernavaca (Kwhere-nah-VAH-ka) can be included on a trip to Taxco or visited by itself for an afternoon lunch at one of its lovely garden restaurants. Many Taxco and Acapulco buses can drop you here, such as Estrella de Oro (terminal south on Morelos; take combi into center), but only Autobuses Pullman de Sur has a convenient downtown terminal (Netzahualcoytl at Abasolo). The trip includes a scenic descent to the subtropical climate of the Morelos Valley, which is about 2,000 feet lower than Mexico City. Here, bougainvillea bloom year round and lavender jacaranda and brilliant flame trees contrast magnificently with craggy mountains.

The benign climate, many springs and rivers, and colorful flowers of this region have attracted visitors from Mexico City since pre-Hispanic times. After conquering the post-classic Tlahuica who lived here in the area called "Cuahnahuac," the Aztecs wintered in a spot now equivalent to the center of Cuernavaca. Spaniards found the area equally appealing, but misinterpreted the Aztec name into cuerna de vaca or "cow's horn." Cortes built his palace here on top of Tlahuica buildings and, in the 18th century, Taxco's silver magnate, Jose de la Borda, built one, too. During the 19th century, Emperor Maximillian and Empress Carlota vacationed here at Borda's palace and enjoyed Cuernavaca enough for Maximilian to buy his own country home—plus another for his mistress, "la India Bonita."

Despite such a splendid history, you won't find Cuernavaca as beautiful as your predecessors did. An industrial complex has polluted the once-clear air so that it no longer sparkles. And thousands upon thousands of American retirees and Mexican weekenders have built sumptuous homes behind high barrier walls that make the town a disappointment to walk in. Unless you visit one of the resort hotels or plan a long stay at one of Cuernavaca's language institutes, a day visit, including a leisurely meal, is more than ample time if you arrive on a day the Brady Museum is closed.

WHAT TO SEE AND DO

Most of Cuernavaca's sights cluster in the center of town in an area of interconnecting plazas. As you walk between the sights, you can stop at the numerous curio stalls on the main square and craft shops and boutiques near the Borda Gardens on Comonfort just off Hidalgo. If you still have time you might seek out Maximilian's **Casa India Bonita** *(Matamoros 200, south in Colonia Acapatzingo; open 9 a.m.-5 p.m. except Mon.; free)*, now the museum of ethnobotany.

Cortes' Palace

Just off the zócalo stands the fortified palace Cortes started constructing in 1530. In later years, this palace housed the state of Morelos legislature, but today it contains the **Museo de Cuauhnahuac** *(10 a.m.-6 p.m., closed Mon.; fee.)* This museum contains displays on regional archaeology including some Tlahuico ruins exposed from under the foundations of the palace, and from the square facing it. Worth the

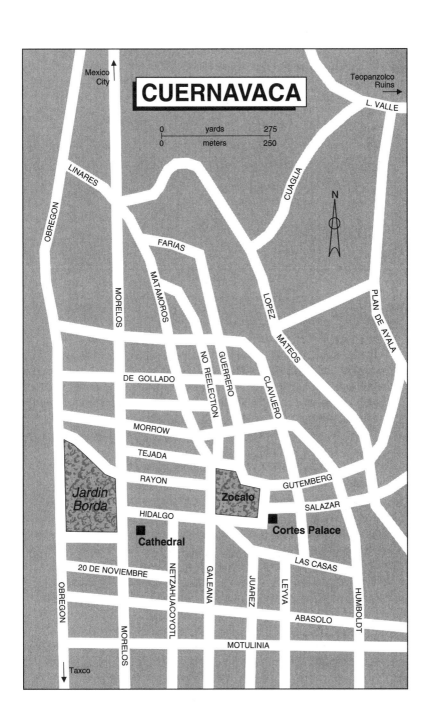

Mexico City

Teopanzolco Ruins

L. VALLE

CUERNAVACA

| 0 | yards | 275 |
| 0 | meters | 250 |

LINARES

OBREGON

CUAGLIA

N

FARIAS

MORELOS

MATAMOROS

LOPEZ

MATEOS

PLAN DE AYALA

DE GOLLADO

NO REELECTION

GUERRERO

CLAVIJERO

MORROW

TEJADA

RAYON

GUTEMBERG

Zocalo

SALAZAR

Jardin Borda

HIDALGO

Cortes Palace

Cathedral

LAS CASAS

20 DE NOVIEMBRE

NETZAHUACOYOTL

GALEANA

JUAREZ

LEYVA

HUMBOLDT

OBREGON

ABASOLO

MORELOS

MOTULINIA

Taxco

trip to Cuernavaca are the **Diego Rivera murals** on the second floor that were commissioned by Dwight Morrow, the former U.S. Ambassador to Mexico. Recounting events in Mexican history, the various panels span from the Spanish Conquest to the Revolution of 1910, where Morelos' revolutionary heir, Emiliano Zapata, is prominently displayed. One vivid panel shows Aztec jaguar and eagle warriors battling the conquistadors.

Museo Robert Brady

Netzahualcoyot 7 • From Cortes' Palace, walk west on Calle Hidalgo before turning left to this wonderful museum, once the home of the American collector and artist, Robert Brady. The 16th-century convent tower converted by Brady into his home (called "Casa de la Torre") remains lavishly decorated with his collection of international folk art and antiquities (primarily Mexican, but Haitian, African and Asian, too) and paintings by 20th-century artists such as Frida Kahlo and Rufino Tamayo, Marsden Hartley and Milton Avery—even the bathrooms must be seen to be believed: one has a Diego Rivera drawing. (*Open Thurs.-Fri. 10 a.m.-2 p.m. and 4-6 p.m., Sat. 10 a.m.-2 p.m., by guided tour only —you can reserve one in English, ☎ 18-85-54 and sometimes for concerts in the courtyard; fee.*)

Cathedral

Back "on Calle Hidalgo" you come to the fortresslike cathedral, one of the oldest in Mexico, where a recent renovation revealed some unusual frescoes dating from the time of Spain's trade and exploration in the Far East. In 1597 San Felipe and 25 missionaries crashed ashore near Nagasaki, Japan, where they were crucified. The news of their martyrdom was announced in Cuernavaca by these murals, painted by an unknown artist returning to Mexico on Spain's Manila galleon. Particularly interesting are the Japanese-style fish painted around the door and the mural showing the Spanish friars approach to Nagasaki.

Jardin Borda

A few steps from the cathedral at Hidalgo and Morelos is the entrance to Jose de la Borda's 18th-century estate. Once suffering from decades of disuse, the house has been attractively refurbished into a cultural center and the formal gardens now include a duck pond and an amphitheater for concerts. (*Open 10 a.m.-6 p.m., closed Monday; small fee.*) In early May, Cuernavaca's Flower Festival takes place here.

WHERE TO STAY

If you want to remain overnight in the area, you might consider one of the resort hotels listed later in this chapter under "Resorts and Spas near Mexico City." Within the town are pleasant first-class hotels and too few inexpensive ones. Reservations on weekends are necessary. *Write Cuernavaca, Morelos, or call area code 73.*

Las Mananitas ★★★

Ricardo Linares 107; ☎ *12-46-46; $90-300* • Only seven blocks from downtown but worlds apart, this former colonial mansion opens to an exquisite garden filled with exotic birds. The inn offers dining in one of Mexico's most respected restaurants (located in the garden) along with 23 handsomely furnished units, the best ones suites and some with garden terraces and fireplaces. Lounge with music. Pool. Arrangements for golf and tennis. Garage. No credit cards. Write Apartado 1202.

Cuernavaca Racquet Club ★★★

Francisco Villa 100, 5 km, 3 m north of zócalo near Zapata statue; ☎ *11-20-67; $130* • On the grounds of the former estate of a Swedish magnate, this Clarion inn includes 501 tastefully decorated suites, all with separate living rooms and some with wood-burning fireplaces and patios. The old mansion houses the indoor restaurant and bar; the gardens enclose nine tennis courts (tennis whites only; no fee) and pool. Sauna for men. Valet parking. For reservations, write Apartado 401 or call, in the U.S., ☎ 800-228-5151.

La Posada de Xochiquetzal ★★★

Calle Leyva 200; ☎ *18-69-84; $70-75* • With the best location for sightseeing, the Posada is just two blocks from Cortes' Palace. The thick walls of this converted colonial mansion render the lovely gardens inside an oasis of tranquility in the city center. The 21 rooms—most very ample junior suites—vary, but their Mexican decor includes warm colors and comfortable furniture, attractive baths and verandas. Good restaurant, lounge with music. Large pool with restaurant. Guarded parking. Write Apartado 203.

Cadis √★

Obregon 329; ☎ *18-92-04; $30* • The only pleasant inexpensive hotel we've found here. Located behind Las Mananitas, the Cadis is a 15-minute walk or five-minute bus ride to the zócalo. The 10 rooms are small but acceptable, the ambience friendly, and there's a pool. Restaurant, bar, parking. Reserve in advance. Apartado 1-400.

WHERE TO EAT

One of the best reasons to visit Cuernavaca is to eat a leisurely afternoon meal in one of its fine garden restaurants. **Las Mañanitas** *(Linares 107)*, in the hotel of that name, offers the best reason of all. Relaxing over a drink in the garden where peacocks stroll among Zuniga sculptures, and dining on international dishes such as cold shrimp bisque, roast duckling, and pork loin adobo (menu changes daily) makes for a splendid afternoon. *The garden opens at noon, and the restaurant serves between 1-4:30 p.m. and 7-11 p.m.; expensive; no credit cards, reserve at* ☎ *18-07-21.*

Pleasantly quiet and only three blocks south of Hidalgo in the center is **Baalbeck** *(Netzahuacoyotl at Motulinia)* with its lawns and continental cuisine complemented by Moorish arcades for dining and some Lebanese specialties such as a tasty kafta kebob, and decent tabouli salad. *(Open 1 p.m.-11:30 p.m.; moderate plus; 18-59-64)*. Also close to the zócalo is **Allegro** on the garden terrace of the Posada Xochiquetzal and with a reputation for good northern Italian as well as Mexican cuisine. *(Open 1:30-5:30, 7:30-11; closed Mon.; no credit cards; moderately expensive.)*

More informal dining is plentiful in the center. Right across from the cathedral is **Marco Polo** *(Hidalgo 26, upstairs)*, a lively Italian restaurant with red and white tablecloths serving good pizza with hand-thrown dough, and freshly prepared pastas such as spinach lasagne and a hearty, if not delicate, cannelloni. *(Open lunch till 11:30 p.m. daily; inexpensive)*. Around the zócalo you can snack or enjoy an inexpensive comida corrida at either the **Universal,** so popular it doesn't need a sign but can be recognized by its awning, or the much quieter hangout of the gringo community, **Los Arcos** *(next to post office)*. For salads or fruit, pastries and croissant sandwiches, head for **Pasteles de Vienes**. *(Tejada 120 near Comonfort; 8 a.m.-10 p.m. daily)*.

TEPOZTLAN

Just off MEX 95D about 20 km (12 m) east of Cuernavaca, Tepoztlan has the same fine climate and convenient location as its more famous neighbor. • Tepoztlan's village atmosphere and striking setting—at the foot of the craggy hills where Emiliano Zapata so successfully eluded capture—have attracted its own resident artists and foreign population. On weekends the village almost bustles with its Saturday market and visitors retreating from Mexico City. The coffee shops cum galleries hum with conversation and classical music, the several crafts shops open longer hours (**Sandia Azul**, on Revolucion near the church, has fine folk art), and the hotel in town offers a vegetarian Sunday brunch. Every day the fortress-style 16th-century **Domenican church and convent** dominates the main square like a mountain of stone; inside its vast atrium, the Indian artisans who carved the church portal seem to speak through its designs. Around the rear of the church, the tiny **Museo Carlos Pellicer** *(Gonzalez 2; weekends 10 a.m.-6 p.m., Tues.-Fri. closed 2-4 p.m.; small fee)* exhibits interesting pre-Columbian artifacts from around Mexico (Olmec masks, Western Mexican figurines, some Maya bowls). On a clear day Tepoztlan can be best enjoyed by the hearty from atop **El Tepozteco**, a hill at the end of Av. Tepozteco where an Aztec-period shrine to the god of pulque can be visited. While there remain some carvings in the inner chamber of the shrine, you may not find them worth the one-hour, exhausting climb. *(Open 9 a.m.-4 p.m. daily; fee.)*

If your visit coincides with the centuries-old pilgrimage to the god of pulque (September 8), or you simply want to relax here, there's the in-town ★★**Hotel Tepoztlan** (Industrias 6; ☎ [739] 5-05-22; $70), modern and well-maintained with 40 rooms, some with the terrific views provided by the hotel's hillside location, a restaurant, pool, and parking. And for good food, try the coffeehouse and restaurant **La Luna Mextli** (*Revolucion, across from church; inexpensive*).

Bus service from Mexico City is provided by Cristobal Colon; from the Cuernavaca market, take a colectivo.

RUINS OF XOCHICALCO

These hilltop ruins are about 45 km (28 m) southwest of Cuernavaca and at the end of a scenic drive through the Morelos Valley. • Xochicalco's (zoh-chee-KAL-koh) **dramatic location** overlooking the **Morelos Valley** reminds you most of Monte Alban in Oaxaca, and the unusual mixture of styles in the **carvings** on its **Temple of Quetzalcoatl** will fascinate those who have visited ruins throughout Mexico. Follow MEX 95 toward Taxco to the exit for Alpuyeca, where you follow signs to Alpuyeca and Las Grutas, then right at sign for Xochicalco after 12 km, 7.5 m. No bus service to ruins.

Seldom visited and relatively unknown compared with Teotihuacan and Tula, Xochicalco may hold one of the keys to understanding Mexico's ancient past. It poses important puzzles for archaeologists and challenges some of the basic cultural distinctions made between the central highlands and southern lowlands.

Archaeologists don't know who built Xochicalco. They do know it was inhabited from about 200 B.C. until about the 11th century A.D. During its period of greatest occupation and monument building (A.D. 500-900), it covered 600 acres of mountaintops and slopes and was the center of a population of 10,000 to 20,000 people. This peak period spans from the last phase of Teotihuacan to the development of Tula. Teotihuacan and Tula—urban, expansionist, and with rigid and repetitive art styles—are considered paradigms of central highland civilizations that gradually evolved into the Aztec Empire. Because two centuries separate these cities, archaeologists have been concerned to explain how central highland culture was transmitted from Teotihuacan to Tula. Xochicalco, bridging the time gap between the two, provides part of the answer. Indeed, Tula's ball court is quite definitely copied from the one at Xochicalco.

Despite Xochicalco's potential role as keeper of this highland culture, it introduced cultural elements from the far away lowland civilizations such as the Maya. *Xochicalco has the earliest ball court found in the Central Valley,* yet its shape is similar to Mayan ball courts. Unlike Teotihuacan, Xochicalco's monuments are carved with hieroglyphic writings and symbols with both Oaxacan and Mayan elements. More surprising, ceramics found at this site are mostly derived from the Mayan area; very few are from Teotihuacan. So many respects of its architecture and art show Mayan influence, some archaeologists propose that Xochicalco was a Mayan outpost in the central highlands.

Ruins

Open 9 a.m.-5 p.m. Admission charge. • Xochicalco's most interesting structure, the **Pyramid of Quetzalcoatl**, sits on the highest courtyard of the site to the north, and was dedicated to the god Quetzalcoatl, or the plumed serpent. The rattles of carved serpents still decorate balus-trades by the staircase, and the large sloping panels (taluds) are carved with undulating feathered serpents. Also within these panels are hiero-glyphs and seated cross-legged figures. In other sections of the plat-form are carvings of more seated figures with headdresses, necklaces, earplugs, and other attire that are typically Mayan. Even the cross-legged posture is Mayan. *Since most of the hieroglyphs surround-ing these figures have not been deciphered, it is not known who they rep-resent,* but the double outline of their bodies may signify that they are mythological or deified individuals. Such double outlining is charac-teristic of sculpture from El Tajin in Veracruz. Although these carv-ings are distinctive and easy to make out, time has erased their colors. On top of the platform, parts of the original temple walls remain standing, but the wooden-beam roof has completely disappeared. The temple is carved with warriors of the coyote and eagle cults holding rectangular shields.

Some of the **carvings** of the Pyramid of Quetzalcoatl have astronomi-cal and calendrical significance. Anthony Aveni identifies serpents swallowing the sun disk as representing eclipses, and archaeologists have deciphered some hieroglyphs of calendrical importance. Other aspects of Xochicalco support the importance of astronomy here. **Caves** found down the hillside north of this pyramid had been partially hollowed by humans. Two verticle shafts through the roofs of the caves (one can be seen by following signs to "observatorio") allow the sun to penetrate during the equinoxes. These caves also may hold the key to the name of this ancient city, which means "Places of the House of Flowers." The meaning is associated with birth, and caves are asso-ciated with ancient Mexican creation myths.

Just to the right of the Quetzalcoatl pyramid (when you're facing it) stands the **Pyramid of the Stelae**, where three carved, free-standing slabs with hieroglyphics were discovered and now are displayed in the National Museum of Anthropology in Mexico City. These slabs, or stelae, are characteristic of the Maya. Farther to the south, or right, you can overlook or descend to a **plaza**, where a stela covered with yet undeciphered hieroglyphics still stands.

West of the plaza you descend to an impressive, 200-foot-long I-shaped **ball court**. Its sloping inner surfaces were used in the ball game, and its uncarved rings functioned like baskets for goals. Ter-races around the court might have been occupied by spectators during a game. During the equinoxes, the sun rises and sets along the east-west orientation of this ball court, indicating astronomical and cere-monial significance for this "game." Off the ball court runs a causeway ending at an unrestored pyramid. Along one side of the causeway are 20 circular bases. While it's not certain what these bases were, they may have supported columns that would have formed a roofed colon-nade such as those found at Monte Alban and Chichen Itza. Across

from these bases is the **Palace**, a multichambered complex that may
have served as a residence for nobles. A sweat bath has been identified
inside this structure.

LAS GRUTAS DE CACAHUAMILPA

Cacahuamilpa's (ka-ka-whal-MEAL-pah) extensive **caverns** *contain many
dramatic formations that are made all the more fantastic by lighting techniques
and background music.* While eight miles of passages have been explored,
the end of this underground world still remains to be discovered. A **tour**
through these caverns covers about one-half mile and lasts 1-1/2 hours,
but though you must enter with a guided tour you can leave earlier on your
own; admission fee; tour in Spanish only, but the sights are what count.
The tours leave between 10 a.m. and 3 p.m. daily about every hour on the
hour. Food stands, a restaurant, even a swimming pool are here for your
added pleasure. Walking sticks and dried floral arrangements from the surrounding mountains are sold by vendors. *To reach the caves from Xochicalco,
follow the signs for Cacahuamilpa and continue on MEX 166 until it almost intersects with MEX 55 about 25 km (15-1/2m) later. To reach the cave directly
from Cuernavaca, exit MEX 95D at Puente de Ixtla and continue south on MEX
95 for 25 km; from Taxco follow MEX 95 (not MEX 95D) north to MEX 55
which, after 8 km (5m), intersects with MEX 166 at the caves. If you love caverns and can't afford a car rental, take a Tres Estrellas del Centro Combi bus
from the second-class bus terminal in Taxco or an Autobus de Zacatepec-Mexico
from the Pullman terminal in Cuernavaca.*

OFF THE BEATEN TRACK

*Although the Aztec ruins at Malinalco are among the most interesting in the
Central Valley, they require a special effort to visit.* Located next to the rather
seedy religious pilgrimage center of Chalma, **Malinalco** is most reliably
reached on MEX 95 or 95D from Cuernavaca via the Tres Marias exit
(about 25 km, 16 m). Then you continue around the lagoons and falls of
the **Zempoala National Park** to the west before dropping another 25 km to
Chalma. Malinalco lies 8 km west of Chalma. The greatest virtue of this
route is that it is paved. Others, such as MEX 166 between Xochicalco and
the Cacahuamilpa caves, are temptingly direct, but should not be taken
without inquiring locally about road conditions. From Chalma, you can return to Mexico City (100 km, 62 m) on paved roads through the beautiful
wooded region of the Desierto de Leones, then, at La Marquesa, on the
multilane Toluca highway. From Malinalco, the hotels and spa at Ixtapan
de la Sal (see below) are not far, but part of the 14-km road to nearby Tenancingo is only hard-packed, not paved.

MALINALCO

*Of all the Aztec ruins still visible, the Temple of the Jaguars and Eagles in the
town of Malinalco fascinates the most.* Its powerful yet refined sculptures,
and its darkly mysterious cave-temple, transport you back to Aztec times

when warrior initiation rites were performed inside its walls. As worthwhile as a visit to these ruins is, **you should know that a 30-minute walk up a steep hillside is required to reach them**. In the town itself, the 16th-century **monastery** on the zócalo has wonderful **murals** painted around its cloister.

Ruins

Open 10 a.m.-4:30 p.m. Admission fee. • In 1476, the Aztecs conquered Malinalco and established a military outpost on the sides of this hill. Their ceremonial center was still under construction at the time of the Spanish Conquest. The warriors who lived here were no ordinary soldiers, but jaguar and eagle knights belonging to the prestigious Order of the Sun. All were of noble birth and renowned for their bravery. Death in war, or capture and subsequent sacrifice, guaranteed them immortality as stars in the night sky. *While many of the ruined buildings at this site relate to religious ceremonies performed for the sun god or for a warrior's death and deification, only one—the Temple of Jaguars and Eagles—remains in complete enough condition to provide you an awesome sense of Aztec ritual and art.*

You can easily recognize the **Temple of Jaguars and Eagles** by its reconstructed thatched roof. After Spanish conquistadors burned and destroyed this site, Augustinian monks appropriated its building stones for their monastery in the town below. *This remarkable temple survived such assaults because it is carved in one piece out of the mountainside itself.* As you climb the stairs, you see remains of two jaguar **sculptures** on each side; and a damaged figure in the center of the stairs once held a banner. Flanking each side of the door are pedestals—a war drum with a jaguar pelt on the left and a coiled serpent on the right—that once held jaguar and eagle knights. The doorway itself is the huge gaping mouth of the Earth Monster—its fangs still visible and its flattened tongue functioning as a door mat. Once inside the dark and circular cave-chamber, you notice the skillful **carvings**—stretched pelts of a jaguar; and eagles encircling the wall; an eagle carved into the center of the floor. Hewn out of one piece of bedrock, this unique chamber reminds you most of a kiva in the American Southwest, but the exceptional sculpting is purely Aztec. Inside this chamber, sons of nobles were initiated into the Order of the Sun by having their noses pierced and ornamented with either the claw of an eagle or the fang of a jaguar.

CHALMA

This dingy one-street village, nestled in a gorge near the tumbling, turbulent Chalma River, is one of the great **religious pilgrimage centers** in Mexico. The object of this devotion is the miraculous figure of the Lord of Chalma, now housed in a 17th-century church. El Senor de Chalma first appeared in a cave sacred to Indians. After his statue was discovered in 1533, he rid the remote region of wild animals and rescued natives from danger. So popular is El Senor de Chalma that pilgrimages in his honor have to be staggered throughout the year, with each region assigned an annual date. The largest pilgrimage occurs on Pentecost, when up to 15,000 people from the Mexico City area camp in the open, performing religious ceremonies and dances. Other important dates are January 6, the first Friday in Lent, Holy Week, and Christmas.

TULA AND TEPOTZOTLAN

A visit to the famous Toltec ruins of Tula can easily be expanded to include Tepotzotlan with its fabulous church and monastery containing treasures from Mexico's colonial period. These sights can be seen in one day if you are traveling by car. Though buses do not connect the different sights, they can take you to either Tula or Tepotzotlan. The best place for lunch is Tepotzotlan.

TULA

In legend, ancient Tollan (Tula) was the seat of the powerful Toltecs, the civilizing people who created writing and science. So fabulous was this legendary city that its temples were supposedly faced in gold and turquoise. In reality, the first Toltecs, led by their chief Mixcoatl, were Chichimeca ("barbarians") from the north who invaded central Mexico and settled at Tula in the 9th century. Borrowing from the culture of the local inhabitants, the Toltecs built their city and established their empire (A.D. 950-1200), the first of the warrior states that rose in Mexico during the Post-Classic period.

Whatever the Toltec's greatness might have been and whatever wealth they achieved, archaeologists have found few precious items at Tula and no temples covered with gold. In fact, this site was stripped and sacked by later invading Chichimeca, who found much to admire and so took it. (Tula at that time was already greatly reduced in population and had previously been burned by other northern groups.) These Chichimeca, later called the Aztecs, modeled themselves after the Toltecs and intermarried with their elite to enhance their prestige. Such marriages continued throughout Aztec history, and even today descendants from a marriage of Moctezuma's son reside in the modern town of Tula and use the title of Duque de Moctezuma de Tultengo.

What does remain of the crumbling city still expresses the fierce military spirit of the Toltecs. Frieze after frieze shows processions of warriors with spears; even temple columns are carved with warriors. Yet from this seemingly brutal civilization comes one of the most benign hero-god sagas, that of Ce Acatl Quetzalcoatl ("One Reed Feathered Serpent"). Ce Acatl Quetzalcoatl was pure, chaste, and peace-loving. Some early Spanish historians related that he opposed human sacrifice, although most archaeologists doubt this. He became embroiled in a struggle with his brother, Tezcatlipoca ("Smoking Mirror"), and was banished from Tula. One story says he immolated himself and rose as the morning star, but other versions claim he traveled east, where some archaeologists believe he established his cult at Chichen Itza (see "Yucatán and Campeche"). Carvings of the ruler Ce Acatl can be seen at Tula and on a rock carving outside of the site. The god Quetzalcoatl is represented in many carvings as the feathered serpent and the morning star.

Ruins

Open 9 a.m.-5 p.m. Admission fee. Museum opens at 10 a.m.; closed Mon.
• The little that remains of this once-large urban center is focused on the area of the **Pyramid of Quetzalcoatl** with its gigantic **Atlantid figures**. The pyramid dominates the north side of a great plaza flanked by a **ball court** on the west and **Pyramid C** on the east. Pyramid C was so stripped of its facing that it cannot be reconstructed. And the adoratorio in the center of the plaza was destroyed in the 19th century by the French explorer Charnay, who mistook it for a tomb. Fortunately, enough is left of the Pyramid of Quetzalcoatl and its flanking colonnaded buildings for you to imagine how this site once looked.

The temple that stood on top of the pyramid has totally disappeared, but the 15-foot-high **Atlantean columns** that once supported its roof were found safely buried in the pyramid and placed in their original positions (with the exception of the lighter-colored one that is a reproduction of an original on display in the National Museum of Anthropology in Mexico City). The colossal Atlantean warriors wear diaperlike loincloths, pillbox headdresses with feathers, the symbol of the warrior on their chests, and round sun shields on their backs. Originally, their eyes may have been inlaid with obsidian and shell. They clutch spears in their left hands, a spear-thrower in the right. A second row of columns with low-relief carvings of warriors supported the roof of the inner chamber of the temple. The incomplete column represents the ruler Ce Acatl Quetzalcoatl.

The **colonnade** in front of the Pyramid of Quetzalcoatl may have served as a reviewing stand or place where the elite could observe ceremonies in the great court while being shielded from the sun by its former roof. A bench, originally running the length of the colonnade, is still partially carved with processions of warriors surmounted by a serpent and cloud design on top that has been interpreted to stand for the Toltec leader Mixcoatl ("Cloud Serpent"). Two **chacmool sculptures**—reclining life-size figures holding a receptacle (for human hearts?) on their bellies—are found in this area. Behind the colonnade and to the west of the pyramid, the **Burnt Palace** has three chambers, each with a central patio and with more benches. The square depressions in the floors were for fires. This palace may have functioned as both a residence and an administrative center. *The middle room contains the best-preserved bench carvings.*

On the rear of the pyramid are **friezes** of prowling jaguars and coyotes and eagles devouring human hearts. In Aztec times, jaguars and eagles symbolized the most honored military orders, perhaps deriving their prestige from this Toltec origin. The monster with a face emerging from its mouth is a symbol of Quetzalcoatl as the morning star. *Such friezes may have once covered the entire pyramid, but only the tenons that* *held the facing in place remain.* Behind the pyramid is the Coatepantli, or **Serpent Wall**, depicting rattlesnakes devouring skeletons. Since geometric meander designs were often used by the Mixtecs to indicate town names, the meander of the Coatepantli may have such a significance.

Another **ball court** is located behind the Pyramid of Quetzalcoatl, and numerous other complexes are in the outlying areas, but most of the interesting sculptures found there have been removed to the **museum** near the entrance, which also contains other carvings found at the site. *Based on the paucity of jewels and exotic objects displayed, the Aztecs must have done a thorough job of looting.*

GETTING TO AND FROM TULA

Tula lies about 80 km (50 m) north of Mexico City and can be reached easily by bus or car. By **car**, take the Reforma through Chapultecpec Park to the Petroleo Glorieta in Polanco, where you turn onto the Periferico Norte. The Periferico via Satelite runs into the toll ("cuota") road to Queretaro (MEX 57D). Exit from the toll road at the second exit for Tula and go straight until you pick up the Tula signs (20 km, 12.5 m). The ruins are a little over a mile from the modern town of Tula. Autobuses del Valle de Mezquital runs **buses** every quarter of an hour to Tula from the Terminal Central de Autobuses del Norte. After the 80-minute ride, you can take a taxi or colectivo from the zócalo.

TEPOTZOTLAN

Tepotzotlan ("Place of the Hunchback" in Nahuatl), with its remarkable museum and ultrabaroque church, can be reached off the same toll road as Tula (MEX 57D), but it lies closer to Mexico City (35 km, or 22 m, to turnoff; then 1 m off the highway). To reach Tepotzotlan by **bus**, go to the Terminal Central de Autobuses del Norte and ask to be dropped off the Tula bus at the MEX 57D exit. Or take a **colectivo** from the Tacuba metro stop (1-1/2 hours).

From every part of Tepotzotlan's zócalo **views** of majestic mountains can be seen, but not even they should detract your attention from the exquisitely carved profusion of reliefs on the 18th-century **facade** of Tepotzotlan's church. *The* **interior** *of this national monument offers one of the best-preserved examples of Mexico's fantastic Churrigueresque style gold-encrusted altars,* altars carved upon altars, mirrors and saints everywhere, and

all receding and framing yet another gold-encrusted figure. Once, while attending a concert in this **Church of San Francisco Javier**, it took us the entire length of the performance to comprehend the pattern of decorations. Also not to be missed here is the octagonal **Camarin de la Virgen**, hidden behind the Capilla de la Virgen de Loreto.

Both the church and its monastery, founded by Jesuits in the 16th century, now are operated as a museum (open Tues.-Sun. 11 a.m.-6 p.m. Admission fee).

The monastery has been restored to show the chapels, kitchen, refectory, and even the gardens as they were during the colonial period. In addition, many of its rooms house the **National Museum of the Viceregal Period** (the colonial period when Mexico was ruled by Spanish viceroys). Colonial treasures on display include religious paintings and sculptures, gold and silver chalices, imports from trade with the Orient, and folk art. It is an exhibit of fascinating contrasts, from a formal European-style Altar of the Virgin of Sorrows to a colorful peasant altar made of corn, black and red beans, and sunflower seeds.

Folk plays, called *pastorelas*, are performed in one courtyard of the monastery every evening between December 16 and 23. These performances are very popular, so reserve through one of the tour agencies in Mexico City and dress warmly.

Surrounding the zócalo are a number of cafes and souvenir shops. Here you can buy wooden chocolate stirrers or have your name painted on a coffee mug. The attractive **Virreyes Restaurant** serves a tasty, inexpensively priced comida corrida. The **Hosteria de Tepozotlan** served some exceptional Mexican dishes—light quesadillas and rich chiles en nogadas—on our last visit to its handsome courtyard located in the monastery. *(Moderately expensive; closed Mon.)*

PUEBLA, CHOLULA, AND OTHER EXCURSIONS

Overwhelmed by its proximity to Mexico City, this region has always been treated inadequately as a day-excursion from the capital. Perhaps the new airport will someday provide flight connections to enhance its attractiveness as a destination worthy of a leisurely visit. The region is especially rich in sights and scenery. *The colorful, tiled buildings of colonial Puebla have long attracted tourists.* While this fourth largest Mexican city has grown industrialized, its handsome center still holds many museums and religious buildings pleasing for a day tour. Near the city are the **ruins of Cholula** as well as **Acatepec** and **Tonantzintla**, towns with two of our favorite provincial churches. Just a bit farther away is **Huejotzingo** with its exceptional 16th-century monastery and museum. A loop off the Mexico City-Veracruz toll highway to Puebla takes you to the **ruins of Cacaxtla** with its spectacular Mayan-style murals and the picturesque **colonial town of Tlaxcala**. And the highway itself provides dramatic **scenery** as it climbs to Rio Frio, deep in verdant pine forests at 11,000 feet, and descends to plains dominated by the snow-covered peaks of the volcanos, **Popocatepetl** ("Smoking Mountain") and **Iztaccihuatl** ("White Lady"). Popocatepetl still smokes but last erupted in 1802; White Lady is completely extinct. According to Aztec legend, these volcanoes immortalize the love between the princess Izta, as she is affectionately known, and the brave warrior Popo, who met a tragic fate reminiscent of Romeo and Juliet.

PRACTICAL TIP

You can visit both Cholula and Puebla by bus in one very full day, if you must. With more time you can add on the provincial churches and Huejotzingo, overnighting in either Puebla or Cholula. The further addition of the Tlaxcala loop could be squeezed into a two-day visit if you have a car, but you'll enjoy yourself more by spending a night in Tlaxcala or back in Puebla/Cholula. A visit to the faraway mountain village of Cuetzalan adds even more nights. • Good accommodations are available. All these sights are connected by bus or colectivo, with the exception of the ruins of Cacaxtla. • You can rent a car in Puebla (Budget, Zaragoza ☎ [53], 36-20-28) or Mexico City, or take a tour (check with the Puebla and Tlaxcala tourism offices).

PUEBLA

Like Cholula, its neighbor in ancient times, Puebla straddles the important trade corridor between the port of Veracruz and Mexico City. Located on a large, fertile plain dominated by four of Mexico's greatest mountain peaks, this city was founded by the Spanish in the 16th century to replace Cholula. Its strategic location caused some of Mexico's major battles to be fought here: first against the United States in 1847; later against the forces of Napoleon III in 1862, when 2,000 Mexican soldiers defeated 6,000 Frenchmen. Although the French later defeated the Mexicans, this historic event is still commemorated by a national holiday on May 5th, which is most vigorously celebrated in Puebla.

Rich clay deposits made ancient Cholula a major pottery center of the Aztec empire and brought Puebla world fame with its Spanish-style Talavera tiles and dishes. Often called the city of tiles, Puebla's colonial center is notable for its **tile-covered residences** and shimmering **tiled church domes**. Not only an important commercial center, Puebla has been a religious center as well, with 100 churches and convents that secretly functioned through the worst of Mexico's religious reform period. Its colorful architecture and museums of religious and Talavera art make Puebla unlike any other city in Mexico.

WHAT TO SEE AND DO

Puebla has successfully refurbished its historic center, rescuing it from asphyxiating fumes by limiting traffic and banishing the bus terminal to the outskirts. The central market has been relocated, too, creating more ample sidewalks for viewing the colonial architecture. At night the domes of many churches are illuminated and the brick and tile facade of **San Francisco Church** is beautifully highlighted (*Heroes at Av. 10 Oriente*). At any time, the sidewalk cafes around the tree-shaded zócalo are good spots for enjoying the delightful new ambience of old Puebla.

The zócalo, anchored on its south side by the Cathedral, is a good spot to get your bearings. Most important sights lie nearby or are spread out among the seven blocks to the north so that you probably won't need the buses that run north and south on Avenida Heroes, east on Avenida 10 Oriente, and west on Avenida 12 Oriente. By walking you can pause at interesting colonial residences along the way to the sights below, such as **Casa de las Munecas** (*2 Norte, near zócalo*) and **Casa del Dean** (*16 de Septiembre 505 at 7 Poniente; Tues.- Sun. 10 a.m.-5 p.m.; fee*), the oldest house in Puebla (1580), its 16th-century interior murals open to the public. The helpful **tourist office** near the Cathedral (*at Av. 5 Oriente 3; 10 a.m.- 8 p.m., Sun. till 2 p.m. only;* ☎ *46-12-85*), should be checked for walking tours of the city as well as tours of the region. *But whatever you do, don't miss the Museo Amparo and the Chapel of the Rosary.*

Cathedral

Although baroque, this 17th-century gray-stone **cathedral** is rather austere. *The second-largest cathedral in Mexico after the one in the capital, its interior spaces are both impressive and well-proportioned.* Over the high altar is Manuel Tolsa's fine baroque, called "Mexican neoclassical" baldachin (c. 1816). *Tourist hours: 10:30 a.m.-12:30 p.m., 4-6 p.m.*

Palafox Library

Just behind the cathedral, on Av. 5 Oriente and upstairs in the Casa de la Cultura; Open Tues.-Sun., 10 a.m.-5 p.m., this library is well worth a visit; fee., you will find what was the finest **library** in the New World during the 18th century. Donated to the city by the Bishop Juan de Palafox y Mendoza in 1646 and housed in his handsome residence, the library grew to contain 43,000 books and maps from that period, all of which are now rare. *Open Tues.-Sun., 10 a.m.-5 p.m., this library is well worth a visit; fee.*

Museo Amparo

Turning right down Calle 2 Sur to 9 Oriente, you come to this exceptional **museum** of **pre-Columbian and colonial art** that opened in 1991. Housed in a restored colonial mansion, the marble floors and amber windows provide an appropriately exquisite setting for this formerly private collection. Organized around various themes of Mesoamerican civilizaton, the ground floor exhibits unusual pieces—a Teotihuacan figurine of a ballplayer (no ball court has ever been found at that site), fine Maya bowls, and a nearly 3-foot-high Nayarit terra cotta of a tattooed woman. Upstairs, the works are arranged chronologically and include a pensive Olmec figure called "The Thinker," terrific terra cottas from Nayarit, fine classic-period Maya bowls and Jaina figurines, and a black vase surmounted by a monkey from El Tajin. Unbelievably, the best is yet to come: *The true masterpieces— none more impressive than the carved Maya throne from the area of Palenque—are found in the last room.* Emerging from the pre-Columbian section, you come to the heart of the old mansion with its **ornate ceilings** and courtyard. Here are rooms of stunning **colonial art**—an 18th-century Chinese screen, a roomful of polychrome wooden saints. Signs are in both Spanish and English; rental headsets available; bookstore. *(Open 10 a.m.-5 p.m. (exit at 6 p.m.), closed Tues.; free on Mon. only.)*

Bello Museum

Walking back toward the zócalo, you might turn to Av. 3 Poniente 302 for this 19th-century **Italianate residence**, now a **museum** but still ornately furnished and with special collections of Talavera tile, ironwork, painted bateas and fabulous chests, Chinese ivory, and more.

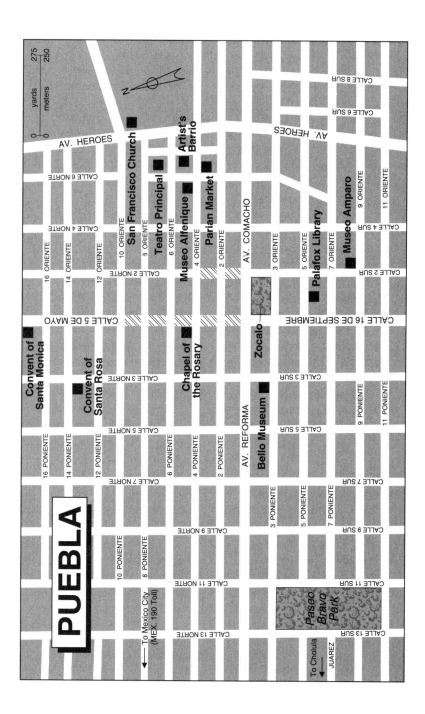

(Open 10 a.m.-5 p.m.; closed Mon.; small fee. Visit by guided tour only (in Spanish), so expect some delays.)

Chapel of the Rosary

Back at the zócalo, follow Calle 5 de Mayo north just beyond Av. 4 Poniente, where you will find the Church of Santo Domingo—which, according to Poblanos, contains the **eighth wonder of the world**. Contrasting with the austere lines of the cathedral, the 17th-century Capilla del Rosario (left transept) is lavish, from its stucco musicians and gilded mermaids and cherubs down to its 18th-century tiles. Miraculously harmonious despite the wealth of detail, the gilded stuccowork covering every inch of the chapel walls represents the finest in Mexican craftsmanship. In the soft morning light this chapel simply gleams. (*Open 7 a.m.-1 p.m. and 3-8:30 p.m.*)

Santa Rosa Artesanias

Continue up 5 de Mayo until you come to Av. 12 Poniente. Turn left for a block to Calle 3 Norte and you will arrive at this converted **Convent of Santa Rosa** that houses numerous displays of crafts from the state of Puebla, including some fabulous ceramic fantasies and candelabras from Acatlan and Izucar de Matamoros. Puebla is known for its cuisine, and its most famous dish, mole poblano, is said to have been created in the fabulous kitchen here, which is decorated in many designs of Talavera tiles. Various folktales explain the creation of this sauce of 24 ingredients—from an angel whispering its recipe into the ear of one of the nuns to a wind blowing everything in the kitchen into a disarray that was swept up and dumped into a pot. Whether or not you like mole poblano, you'll admire this kitchen. There is also a crafts shop. (*Open 10 a.m.-5 p.m.; closed Mon. By guided tour only; small fee.*)

Convent of Santa Monica

Walk up Calle 3 Norte to Av. 18 Poniente 103 and you will be at this **17th-century convent**, which responded to Mexico's Reform Laws of 1857 by going underground. The Reform Laws made educational institutions such as convents and monasteries illegal, and gave the government the right to confiscate Church properties. Property listings must have been poorly maintained in those days because three convents in Puebla were able to survive clandestinely for nearly 80 years until they were discovered by authorities in 1934. *Entering the Convent of Santa Monica gives you a sense of the years of secrecy, because you first pass into an ordinary residence and then through a door disguised as a cupboard.* (The original entrance to this convent was through the church, but with the Reform Laws this entrance was covered over by a choir stall.) The convent is now a **museum** displaying all the religious and personal objects found in the three secret convents. While most of these pieces are of academic interest, you will enjoy visiting the large cloister with its dashing **Puebla tiles** and tranquil **fountain**. (*Open 10 a.m.-5 p.m., except Mon; fee.*)

Museo Alfenique

Return toward the zócalo on Calle 5 de Mayo and turn left onto Av. 4 Oriente. Continue three blocks to the corner of Calle 6 Norte to reach this **18th-century "gingerbread" house**, *the best example of Poblano-style architecture.* The **facade** of this three-story residence is stately, with red bricks and blue and white tiles, but outlining the windows, roof, and each story is a frothy white **ornamentation**, which led writer Erico Verissimo to say it was "more the work of a confectioner than of an architect." The history **museum** inside exhibits intriguing 16th-century documents and 19th-century photos, as well as period furnishings from the 18th century. *Open 10 a.m.-5 p.m., except Mon.; small fee.*

Teatro Principal

A block east of the Alfenique you come to the tranquil area of the Parian Market and Artist's Barrio (see "Shopping" below). Turn left up Calle 8 Norte to 8 Oriente and you come to this **theater** and its attractive **plaza**. Completed in 1759, the theater still functions with weekly performances.

Museo Regional de Puebla

A few miles to the north from the center is a large park with a **colonial fort** overlooking the city. In this Los Fuertes area are several **museums**, including the **Regional Museum** with its well-displayed collection of Poblano art and artifacts from pre-Hispanic times *(including one of the largest carved jades yet discovered)* through the Spanish conquest and the Mexican revolution. Take the "Fuertes" bus from Av. 10 Oriente and 5 de Mayo. *Open Tues.-Sun., 10 a.m.-5 p.m.; fee.*

SHOPPING

Talavera tiles and ceramics are still produced in Puebla at "factories" called **azulejerias**. The ceramics are most often painted with blue and white designs, and sometimes you can find a complete dinner set. *Since the quality of this work is good, the prices are not cheap, but cheaper than what you would pay in the United States.* Two are not far from the Convent of Santa Monica: **Casa Rugerio** *(Av. 18 Poniente 111)* usually has artisans displaying their techniques, but the high prices make it essential to bargain here; **La Trinidad** *(Av. 20 Poniente 305—knock to gain entrance)* has more delicate designs and lower prices. Less centrally located is **Uriarte** *(Av. 4 Poniente 911)*, but **Artesanias DIF** *(north portal of zócalo)* often sells some fine examples of their work along with pottery from around the state of Puebla.

A second **DIF** branch, with a greater variety of regional crafts, is located in the tourist office *(Av. 5 Oriente 3)*. Antiques and contemporary galleries, talavera pieces and replicas of colonial furnishings can be found in the shops on the **Plaza de los Sapos** *(Av. 7 Oriente and 6 Sur)* and surrounding streets. At the **Parian Market** *(between 2 and 4 Oriente on 6 Norte)*, you can find other locally made items, most notably onyx bowls, fruits, and other knickknacks that are sold throughout Mexico. Next to the Parian Market on Calle 8 Norte is the **Barrio del Artista** displaying the paintings and sculptures of Poblano artists. And the turn-of-the-century iron splendor that once housed the **Victoria Market** *(5 de Mayo, just past Santo Domingo)* may be reopened on your visit as a cultural center and crafts market.

WHERE TO STAY

Hotel prices have climbed quite a bit in Puebla. If you are on a budget, check the facilities in Cholula and Tlaxcala. For reservations, call area code 22.

Aristos

Reforma and Calle 7 Sur; ☎ *32-05-99; $90* • Within walking distance of all the sights and with the best in-town comforts, this hotel occupies two fully modernized turn-of-the-century buildings. The 160 units include some suites; all are air-conditioned and comfortable. Numerous lounges with entertainment, one on the rooftop; several restaurants and shops. Pool, gym, and Jacuzzi. Garage.

Posada San Pedro

Av. 2 Oriente 202; ☎ *46-50-77; $74* • This modernized hotel in the town center offers a bustling lobby and a tranquil courtyard with pool over which look most of the 80 carpeted rooms. Restaurant and bar with nightly entertainment. Garage. Seems overpriced.

Lastra

Calzada de los Fuertes 2633; ☎ *35-97-55; $81* • In a quiet wooded section near the fort and museums above the city, this modern hotel is walkable downhill to the center, but requires a taxi or "Fuerte" bus back. If the construction materials were a bit sturdier, this hotel would actually feel luxurious. The lobby has a chandelier, the common areas are well-appointed, and the 60 rooms are carpeted, and with quite good baths. Restaurant, bar with entertainment. Pool, parking.

Palacio San Leonardo

Av. 2 Oriente 211; ☎ *46-05-55; $78* • This hotel has a small 18th-century lobby roofed with stained glass and an attractive rooftop area; its 75 rooms are plain—try to get one on the top floor. Pool (often under repair). Restaurant, bar.

Colonial

Calle 4 Sur 105; ☎ *46-41-99; $44* • In a pleasant cul de sac without much traffic, yet just off the zócalo, this 70-room hotel occupies a large, colonial building. The common areas are attractive; the sunny double rooms, many with floor-to-ceiling windows, are as vast as the baths—with hand-painted tiles—are tiny. Restaurant. Bar. Reserve in advance.

WHERE TO EAT

You may have tried nachos and tostadas, ceviche and enchiladas, but until you try *mole poblano* you haven't been initiated into the intricacies of

Mexican cuisine. Created in Puebla, this sauce is served on enchiladas, chicken, and most traditionally, turkey. Best known for its ingredient of chocolate, *mole* is far from sweet or chocolate-flavored. Its rich, deep color comes from a variety of chiles ground together, and its flavor is enhanced by ground nuts, seeds, and spices. The little chocolate added is in the form of ground cacao beans. So many ingredients compose this sauce that every cook's version differs. Even if you don't like mole the first time, the second or third version might enthrall you.

Several *fondas* specialize in serving regional cuisine in small, quaint establishments, but in our opinion one far surpasses all the others. The **Fonda de Santa Clara** *(Av. 3 Poniente 307)* not only serves a large portion of one of the tastiest *mole poblanos* we've ever eaten, it offers an exotic array of dishes such as *tinga poblana* (shredded pork with tomatoes, cheese, and avocado) and seasonal delicacies such as *chiles en nogada* and *huitlacoche* (a mushroomy black fungus from the maize plant). In the evening you can enjoy *antojitos* such as tamales or tortillas twisted and filled to make *gorditas, molotes*, and *empanadas*. The moderate prices here might be higher than other spots, but the portions and quality make them worth it. If your budget is just too tight for the Santa Clara, then head straight for the **Restaurant La Princesa**, on the west side of the zócalo. This locally popular restaurant is not pretty, but it's clean and offers tasty food served in ample portions at low prices. The *comida corrida* often includes *mole poblana* and the restaurant is open day and night, so you can breakfast here, sip a *cappuccino*, or enjoy a good *torta de pollo*. For regional candies—jellied fruits, sweet potato *camotes*, and coconut concoctions—check the *dulcerias* on Av. 6 Oriente between Calles 4 and 5 de Mayo.

If all this regional cuisine is not to your liking, then check out the branch of **Sanborn's** *(Av. 2 Oriente 6)* with an attractive restaurant tucked away in a back colonial courtyard complete with fountain. As usual the food is both international and Mexican as well as decent. Moderate. For some greens, try a salad or some nopalitos (cactus) with cheese at **El Vegetariano** *(Av. 3 Poniente 525; inexpensive)*. And for a complete change, splurge at the **Bodegas de Molina** *(San Jose del Puente, off of MEX 190 libre 3 km from center; open 1 p.m.-midnight; ☎ 49-06-51; expensive)* where the beautiful people dine in country-style elegance. In a 16th-century hacienda and mill surrounded by shady grounds with waterfalls, the restaurant is decorated with antique doors, old beams, and thick carpets. The food ranges from Caesar salad and stuffed trout to roast beef and a few Mexican specialties—including mole poblano, of course. A bit difficult to find, though reachable by colectivo. Call for directions, or take a cab.

ENTERTAINMENT

Starting around 9 p.m., a few squares fill with *mariachis* who hope to be hired for a party or even just a song. One such spot is Plaza do los Sapos *(Av. 5 Oriente and 6 Sur)*, another Calle 3 Sur at *9 Poniente*. **Teorama** *(Reforia and 7 Norte)* is a bookstore cafe (salads, desserts) with music at night.

GETTING TO AND FROM PUEBLA

AIR

Although there is an airport (22 km, 13-1/2 m on MEX 190 toward Huejotzingo), there isn't always service. Sometimes the small jets of Aeromorelos (☎ 46-62-22) connect with Oaxaca, Huatulco, Acapulco, and Cuernavaca.

BUS

ADO and Estrella de Oro provide nearly continuous first-class bus service to Puebla. The trip takes about two hours and starts at the Terminal Oriente (TAPO) near the metro stop San Lazaro. The Puebla station (Central Camionera) is 20 minutes from the center. To reach it take "CAPU" or "China Poblana" buses (along all the major streets) or combis (going north on Av. Heroes at 7 Oriente).

CAR

Puebla lies 130 km (81 m) east of Mexico City. The exit route via Fray Servando de Mier, then the Calzada Zaragoza highway, can take you through some of the most congested traffic and worst pollution in Mexico City. Leave early or during the lunch siesta to avoid delays. Calzada Zaragoza takes you to the toll highway, MEX 190D, which has an exit for Puebla. MEX 190 libre (without the "D") is a much slower and older free road. (Cuota means toll.) If you are taking the leisurely trip to or from Puebla, consider adding the loop to Cacaxtla and Tlaxcala described at the end of this chapter.

On your return, you will notice an unusual highway arrangement as you start the descent from Rio Frio. To avoid casualties on this curvy section of the highway, an emergency lane is marked for cars with bad brakes. It cuts across other lanes before ending in a sand pit. This section of the highway is subject to hail storms and fog. If you plan to travel after dark, we advise that you leave the driving to someone familiar with this section of the road (such as a bus driver).

CHOLULA

Only 14 km (9 m) west of Puebla, these pre-Conquest ruins can be reached by driving west on Av. Juarez in Puebla, then following "MEXICO libre" signs to San Juan Cholula, where you exit and look for the pyramid. Colectivos (Puebla center at 6 Poniente and 13 Norte) and buses (from Puebla's CAPU camionera) run every 15 minutes and can drop you at the pyramid.

Looking much like one of the hills surrounding Cholula, even to the church on its summit, *the grass-covered* **pyramid of Cholula** *is the largest building ever erected on earth*. With a volume of 3 million meters, its base covers 46 acres and its height rises to 198 feet. Unlike the Great Pyramid of Egypt or the Pyramid of the Sun at Teotihuacan, Cholula's pyramid grew to its extraordinary size through centuries of superimposing building upon building. Actually, this pyramid contains a smaller, earlier one that is larger than the Pyramid of the Moon at Teotihuacan. Even the model in the museum here fails to capture what this mammoth structure would look like cleared of its vegetation and restored.

Apart from the pyramid, little remains of the city the Spaniards described as having 400 temples and more than 40,000 houses. The size of the population can only be guessed—on one afternoon alone the conquistadors massacred 30,000 people here (and then, in thanksgiving, founded the Remedios church atop the pyramid, dedicated to their patron saint). Excavations have shown, however, that Cholula was very important throughout most of Mesoamerican history. As a center for the worship of the god **Quetzalcoatl** who, according to the Aztecs, created the arts, agriculture, and science, Cholula attracted pilgrims from all over Mesoamerica; as a center located on the trade routes from the central highlands to Oaxaca and the Gulf Coast, it attracted merchants as well. *Occupied from at least 300 B.C. until the present time, Cholula may very well have the longest continuous history of any central Mexican site.* Yet few details of its history are known. Teotihuacan influences can be found supporting the view that Cholula cooperated with its great neighbor in facilitating trade to other areas. Around A.D. 700, Cholula was conquered by peoples from the Gulf Coast who also disrupted Teotihuacan's trade and contributed to that city's collapse—and perhaps gave rise to Cacaxtla nearby. During later centuries, other foreign groups settled here, but little is known of that period except that Cholula had no contact with its Toltec neighbor at Tula. *The Cholulans were famous for their fine Mixteca Puebla-style ceramics* (Moctezuma insisted his food be served only on these dishes) and a mural style that can be found as far away as the Yucatán Peninsula. After the Conquest, Cholula continued to be an important city, sustaining, according to folklore, a church for every day of the year. A plague during the 16th century contributed to Cholula's decline, and power shifted to Puebla. Today, its status is no more than that of a provincial town.

SIGHTS

Just seeing the **pyramid** is worth a brief visit to the town. Covered with scrub and wildflowers, its crevices cavelike, its trees filled with birds, the pyramid is like a park and offers pleasant walks, one up the steep stairs (*west side of pyramid*) to the church of **La Virgin de los Remedios** (*no charge; on Sept. 8, dances and ceremonies are performed* *at the church in honor of the Virgin*). A more countrified walk begins just before the stairs—look for a dirt path leading off to the right. After a brief walk, you'll look over the restored plazas, one an acre in size, on the south side of ancient Cholula. However, you must pay if you want a more thorough visit to the **ruins** (*10 a.m.-5 p.m.; ticket office north side of pyramid*) with their small **museum** (*when facing ticket booth, to the left and behind you*) and a walk through the **tunnels** (*entrance just to right of ticket booth*) that have been excavated inside the pyramid and provide access to the restored plazas. A visit to the town zócalo (*two blocks west of pyramid*) and the **Capilla Real** (*left side of the cathedral*), fronted by a vast atrium used as an open-air chapel to accommodate all the Indian converts in the 16th century, and you've seen the best of Cholula.

WHERE TO STAY AND EAT

Villa Arqueologica
2 Poniente 601; ☎ *[22] 47-19-66; $70* • On the south side of the pyramid, a branch of this chain of handsome, functional inns with 40 rooms (a/c), restaurant, bar, tennis, and pool. For reservations in the U.S., call ☎ 800-258-2633;

Calli Quetzalcoatl
Portal Guerrero 11; ☎ *[22] 47-15-33; $50* • Right on the arcaded side of the zócalo and more tranquil than most Puebla hotels, this modern, colonial-style hotel is a good buy for its 15 carpeted if smallish rooms, restaurant, and pool. Both of these hotels offer pleasant dining, the Calli being more moderate in price.

SNACKS

For an inexpensive comida corrida, try **Los Portales**—a cafe next to the Calli.

SANTA MARIA TONANTZINTLA

To reach this village church characterized by local exuberance and folk charm, take the Chipilo mini-bus (marked CAPU-Cholula-Chipilo) from either the terminal in Puebla or from Cholula (1-1/2 blocks from zócalo in direction of Atlixco). By car, follow the Atlixco sign south off the Cholula zócalo until (3 km, 1 m) you can no longer go straight. A few steps away is the church.

While the facade of this **church** is not ornate, its glazed Pueblan tiles glimmer in the sunlight. The restrained lines of this exterior poorly prepare you for the riot of color inside. Every millimeter of surface shimmers with gilded foliation and colorfully painted cherubs astonishing you with their gaiety and splendor. Completed by 1830, the church is dedicated to the Virgin Mary, who seems to have replaced the Aztec mother goddess known as "Tonantzin," patroness of this town in pre-Conquest times. (*Open 9 a.m.-6 p.m.*)

SAN FRANCISCO ACATEPEC

Using the directions for Tonantzintla, but continuing left at the dead end, you come to this village **church** *with its famous* **Puebla-style facade** *after 2 km (1 m).* Because Puebla was the colonial center for tile production, many of the churches in this region, like the buildings in Puebla itself, are ornamented with this local material. *No other church competes with the one in Acatepec for its extravagant use of tiles.* Arranged in geometric patterns, tiles of blue, yellow, and orange dazzle you with their delirious placement everywhere on this facade. Walking through the beautiful **paneled doors** of this church, you enter an **interior** that was not to be outdone by its exterior. A fire in 1939 destroyed most of the interior, but fortunately it has been restored to its former exuberance. Some of the original wall paintings and folklike designs remained undamaged under the choir stall and above the sacristy door. A few neon altar enhancements continue the folk tradition. (*Open daily 9 a.m. -6 p.m.*)

Any CAPU bus or colectivo running on the church side of the road takes you to Puebla. By car, to return to Puebla or MEX 190D (toll road) to Mexico City, turn left at Acatepec and continue for 10 km (6 m) to the outskirts of Puebla. Turn left onto Av. Hermanos Serdan to reach the toll road. You can also link up with Mex 119 for the Tlaxcala loop at this juncture.

HUEJOTZINGO

Colectivos and buses leaving from the Puebla CAPU terminal (30 km, 18 m) and from Cholula center (11 km) carry you along MEX 190 (Mexico Libre) to the main square of Huejotzingo. By car, you can also stop here on your way to Puebla from Mexico City by exiting the toll road at San Martin Texmelucan for the "libre." At the square, you can refresh yourself with a sip of the town's specialty *sidras*, or ciders, before visiting this magnificent *Franciscan monastery* across the street.

Once inside the fortified walls of the Franciscan monastery, you're encompassed by the 16th century when Spain had just conquered the native population. The massive monastery was most likely built from the stone of the pre-Columbian town it replaced. The immense **atrium**, or open-air chapel, retains its four corner shrines carved with angels and framed with outsized Franciscan-cord motifs in a sharp, flat style that betrays the hands of Indian stonecutters—a style seen again on the Aztec-like column of the double archway to the side of the church portal. However, the Indian presence was soon lost— plagues in the 1570s and after depleted the population that once filled the atrium; the only art style to survive would be European—as can be seen inside the **church**. Behind the high altar is a noble Renaissance retablo (1586) painted and gilded by the Flemish artist Simon Pereyns—one of only three early retablos still in its original setting.

The monastery itself is now an attractive **museum** (*Tues.- Sun. 10 a.m.-5 p.m.; fee*); its refectory, chapels, and friars cells have been restored. An upstairs cafe overlooks the tranquil countryside dominated by the snow-capped Malinche volcano.

CACAXTLA-TLAXCALA LOOP

This loop off MEX 190D can be approached from either Mexico City and Huejotzingo or, in reverse, from Puebla. It takes you through a wonderful part of the state of Tlaxcala, where the conquering Spaniards encountered their most important Indian allies. The route allows you to visit the fascinating **archaeological site of Cacaxtla** and the **colonial town of Tlaxcala**. *To start this trip from Mexico City, exit from MEX 190D at San Martin Texmelucan and follow signs to the right for Tlaxcala (MEX 119).*

CACAXTLA

Cacaxtla is near the village of Nativitas just off MEX 119, about 17 km (10-1/2 m) from Texmelucan. Once you turn onto MEX 119 at Texmelucan you'll soon pick up signs for Nativitas and Cacaxtla. At the ruinas sign turn left and continue 2 km up the hill to the entrance. The drive from Mexico City takes 2-1/2 hours. Be careful—the small roads along this route often have *topes* with no forewarning. The ruins are a 10-minute walk from the parking area. There is no public transportation to the ruins, so you need to rent a car in Puebla or try to arrange a tour through the Puebla or Tlaxcala tourism offices.

These **ruins** hold a rare treat for travelers interested in Mexico's ancient past. In 1975, vividly colored murals in excellent condition were uncovered at Cacaxtla. These **murals** startled the archaeological world, for they were painted in the realistic art tradition found in the Mayan area far to the south near Palenque. *No other work of art from ancient Mexico approximates these murals in their realism and their display of details of clothing and customs except the famous Maya murals found at Bonampak.* While the ghastly realism of Cacaxtla's battle mural may make you yearn for the abstract symbolism of the warrior cults at Teotihuacan, the recognizable, expressive human faces on the mural make the people of this lost culture seem much more immediate and understandable.

Cacaxtla grew to importance during turbulent times in the central highlands (A.D. 650-900). In the 7th century, Teotihuacan had weakened greatly and collapsed soon thereafter. Its ally Cholula had been conquered, perhaps by peoples from the Gulf Coast and southern area of Mexico who settled at Cacaxtla. These foreigners blockaded Teotihuacan's profitable trade route down to the coast and the southern part of Mexico, thereby contributing to that great city's collapse. Chaos must have followed Teotihuacan's collapse, with various groups struggling for power in the resultant political vacuum. The archaeological evidence from Cacaxtla dramatizes this period. The city is defensively located on a mountain and surrounded by a moat; its battle mural depicts two groups of warriors fighting to the death. Even the art style of Cacaxtla's murals, with their combination of

Teotihuacan motifs and Maya realism, indicates a mix of peoples. Rather than the highly symbolic religious paintings with their priestly processions at Teotihuacan, Cacaxtla's show a concern for the secular struggles of a later epoch. Whether these paintings were made by Maya from the Palenque area, by the coastal Putun Maya, or even by Teotihuacanos who were Mayanized, remains unknown.

Note: The signs at the ruins identify these people as the Olmeca- Xicalanca (not to be confused with the Olmecs). These are the people at the time of the Spanish conquest, at least seven centuries after the murals were painted.

Ruins

Open 10 a.m.-5 p.m. Admission fee; restaurant, small museum. Binoculars useful. • As you come to the end of the donkey path, you'll see the massive hill-like platform covered with a protective roof. After you climb the steps up this hill, just to the right are Buildings A and B with the most famous **murals**. However, the designated path through the site leads off in the opposite direction, saving the best for last. Along the way, you'll see some other murals—two Maya-like dancers (rear of platform) and maize plants sprouting human heads (in a stairwell, center of site)—*some discovered as recently as 1990.* Then, as you finally approach Buildings A and B, there's a broken **pillar** carved with a figure like a Mayan stela.

The platform base of **Building B** is painted on both sides of its staircase with Cacaxtla's famous **battle scene.** *Though originally this mural included 48 warriors, only 17 remain completely intact.* Two groups of warriors engage in intense and brutal battle. Defeated, and sometimes mutilated, warriors sprawl on the ground while victorious warriors, holding spears and round shields, stride above them. The dramatic and realistic action depicts one victorious warrior grabbing the neck of a defeated one while a slumped and wounded warrior is about to be speared from behind. The energy and expressiveness of the individual scenes are unified by a Maya-blue background and a surface pattern created by the contrasting white of the warriors' sashes.

We cannot pretend to know who these warriors are, but two different ethnic groups may be represented. The victors wear jaguar pelts while the defeated wear bird helmets. As you will see at Building A, these jaguar and bird themes become quite important. The fluid style of the mural, the body outlining and eye shapes, and even the blue color are most typical of the Maya area. Some art historians see the defeated group as Mayan. Yet, although it is true that many of these poor souls have the slanted foreheads characteristic of the Maya (who practiced cranial deformation), so do some of the victors.

A little above and to the right of Building B is **Building A**. Not only are the **murals** in the same Mayan style as the battle scene but the building itself also shares its floor plan with temples at the Mayan site of Palenque. *The best-preserved murals are on the north and south panels* *of the portico and on the two door jambs adjacent to them.* Though the meaning of these murals is debated, it is significant that they carry the jaguar and bird symbolism of thc warring factions from Building B. The key to these murals may lie in the stucco carving you can see on the north, or left, panel. This carving probably framed the entire doorway, but most of it was destroyed by looters in 1975. A remaining figure sits with one leg crossed over his knee in a position reminiscent of ruler portraits found in the Maya and Veracruz areas. Some archaeologists think that this ruler's power may have resulted from his resolving the differences between the jaguar and bird people. If so, these murals could represent something like a peace treaty between the warring factions.

TLAXCALA

To reach Tlaxcala from Cacaxtla, you need not return to Texmelucan. After descending the hill from the ruins, turn left onto MEX 119 at stop sign and continue all the way through Nativitas until the road splits left to Tlaxcala, right to Puebla. Wander along the country road past the striking Texoloc church into Tlaxcala (17 km, 10-1/2 m).

Tlaxcala is so small today that it is hard to appreciate this region's importance during the Conquest. Without the Tlaxcalans, who composed most of Cortes' forces, the Spaniards would not have defeated the Aztecs. When Cortes was first defeated by the Aztecs during the Noche Triste, he retreated to Tlaxcala. From here he built his fleet of ships for the final attack on the island capital of the Aztecs. As a reward for their loyalty, the Tlaxcalans were granted a noble city and were exempted from paying taxes. Though this royal city was one of the largest in the 16th century, the population was decimated by a plague in the middle of that century and never recovered.

The entire colonial section of Tlaxcala, with its sienna-orange and rose-colored buildings, has been tastefully restored. Along one side of the zócalo is the **Palacio del Gobierno**, the blunt Aztec-style carvings around its 16th-century portal a testament to the fact that this is *the oldest civic building in Mexico.* Inside, the main stairwell was painted with murals on Tlaxcalan history in the 1960s by D. H. Xochitiotzin. Across the square is **La Casa de Piedra**, which may have opened by your visit as the **Instituto Tlaxcalteca di Cultura** (*entrance may be around block at Guerrero 15*), with art ranging from colonial polychrome statues to a Frida Kahlo painting. Just at the end of the zócalo sits the striking **parish church**, with a red-brick and blue-tile facade. A block or so to the south of the zócalo, you come to the **Church and Monastery of San Francisco**. Founded in 1526 and rebuilt during the 17th and 18th centuries, *the church has one of the finest geometrically carved wooden ceilings in Mexico.* The chapel to the right of the high altar contains some fine polychrome niche figures as well as the simple font where Cortes witnessed the baptism of four Tlaxcalan nobles. An inscription reads: "Here the Holy Gospel had its beginning in this new world." The plaza outside the church was the outdoor chapel for the multitudes of

Indians, and the charming "Calle de la Capilla Abierta" leads back down to the main street of Juarez.

On the hillside above the town is the famous **Sanctuary of the Virgin of Ocotlan**, built in the 18th century by the Indian architect Francisco Miguel. Its white **facade** framed by red tiles dazzles you with its Churrigueresque sculpture. The Virgin of Ocotlan miraculously answered prayers for water during a drought in the 16th century. The fabulously **ornate interior** of her sanctuary (especially the camarin) appropriately expresses the gratitude of her worshipers. On the third Monday in May, processions accompany her statue as it is taken from its sanctuary for visits to neighboring churches. Open daily, this basilica is worth a detour. You can climb up to it by following the steep Calle Zitlapopocatl (*off the main street of Juarez*), taking a colectivo across from the bus terminal, or, upon driving into Tlaxcala from Cacaxtla, turning right just after the Pemex, then 1 km later turning left after the **panoramic viewpoint** of the city.

PRACTICAL TIP

For a map and perhaps even a city tour, check with the tourist office (Juarez, rear of Palacio del Gobierno; ☎ *2-00-27; 9 a.m.-1 p.m., 4-7 p.m., Sat. 9 a.m.-3 p.m.).*

WHERE TO STAY AND EAT

Mision Park Plaza ★★★

Km. 10 Carretera Apizaco-Tlaxcala; ☎ *[246] 2-01-78; $80* • This hotel, on the grounds of Atlihuetzia, has a waterfall with a 96-foot drop, and is dominated by the snow-capped volcano, La Malinche. This modern mountain resort provides an enjoyable retreat yet lies only 15 minutes from downtown Tlaxcala. There are 50 more-than-ample and comfortable rooms, a large heated indoor pool, gym with sauna and steam bath, and a restaurant overlooking the waterfall. To reach by car, leave Tlaxcala on Juarez north, then follow signs to Pachuca/Apizaco and exit at Atlihuetzia.

Albergue de la Loma ★

Guerrero 58; ☎ *[246] 2-04-24; $32* • Although on a busy street, most of this hotel is set back and atop a hill overlooking the city. Those of the 20 rooms with views are a great buy, but if you have heavy luggage you'll want to stay below. Restaurant with view. Parking. The Albuergue Loma restaurant might entice you with its view (inexpensive; limited menu).

Meson Taurino

Independencia 15 at Guerrero; ☎ *2-43-66; moderate* • Dine in the garden or by windows overlooking it while enjoying a sopa Tizatlan (squash flower soup), a fish filet cantora (with mushrooms and nopalito cactus), and salad. There's steak and the like, too.

HOW TO GET AROUND

Colectivos shuttle back and forth from the second-class **bus** terminal southwest of town. It's easy to catch them along the main drag of Independencia/Juarez or on Lardizabal, one block past the zócalo. At the terminal you can catch **colectivos** running every 10 minutes or so to Puebla's CAPU terminal; second-class buses run to Puebla and Mexico City. By **car**, it's best to leave Tlaxcala from the north where highway MEX 117D links you to MEX 190D at Texmelucan (23 km, 14 m) for Mexico City (2-1/2 hours), or takes you in the opposite direction (to the right) for Santa Ana Chiautempan where highway MEX 121 south takes you quickly to Puebla (35 km, 22 m). **Note:** *From Puebla, follow signs to Tlaxcala but once across MEX 190D—unless you're heading for Cacaxtla—follow the Santa Ana Chiautempan signs to avoid congested MEX 119.*

OFF THE BEATEN TRACK
CUETZALAN

Although it is part of the Sierra de Puebla described elsewhere (see Central Gulf Coast map), the magnificent **village of Cuetzalan** (kway-SAL-en) and its equally magnificent **Sunday market** can be most easily reached on an excursion from Puebla. Second-class buses provide transportation from Puebla, but traveling by car is easy enough during daylight once you get out of Puebla (follow Oriente 14 toward Amozoc). The route is along MEX 129/125 to Oriental, then MEX 129 in the direction of Teziutlan until you turn left at the signal for Zacapoaxtla. Upon entering Zacapoaxtla, turn right just before the Pemex, continue through town, and then descend to the river valley floor before climbing up to Cuetzalan, where the pavement ends (170 km, 105 m).

Cuetzalan is three hours from Puebla across a wide and fertile valley surrounded by snow-covered peaks, then up into the pine-covered Sierra de Puebla, where log cabins bedecked with flowers, mist-filled barrancas, and traditionally dressed Nahua women dominate the landscape. *Once the narrow winding road brings you to the subtropical valley of Cuetzalan, you will feel you have stumbled upon a legendary lost city.* Here, amid the wild and tangled verdure of the Sierra, emerge the stark white buildings of Cuetzalan. In this isolated spot you will find a substantial Spanish colonial town, lovingly terraced into the steep mountainside and built of impressive stone, with a massive church and cobblestone streets. Once in Cuetzalan and once you find a place to park (the zigzagging streets are initially confusing, so you might want to hire one of the boys you'll most certainly meet at the town entrance), you can stroll the streets, shadowy and romantic at night, visit the tiny **Museo Regional** (just off zócalo next to Posada Jackelin), or walk to the edge of town to view the cemetery and small **Sanctuario de Guadalupe**, with its spire made of ceramic pots. But the real reason to visit is the **Sunday market**. *Starting on Saturday evening, Nahua Indians from the surrounding valleys start arriving and setting up their stands in the splendid zócalo. By midmorning on Sunday tropical flowers fill half the market and in*

the other half women barter over embroidered blouses, woven wool fajas (or sashes), and lacy quexquemetls. You can also buy these crafts at the few town "boutiques," along with huacals, woven rope carryalls. *Another time to visit is around October 4, when Cuetzalan celebrates its famous feast of San Francisco de Asis for several days, including the weekend, with many traditional dances such as that of the Voladores.* Also, you might make the trip to the **ruins of Yohualichan**, really an excuse to make a journey through lushly tropical and rural Mexico. The ruins consist of a plaza with buildings in the style of the Pyramid of the Niches at El Tajin and are located next to the Yohualichan town plaza, where Nahua women sit Sunday afternoons weaving lacy shawls. *(Ruins closed Mon., Tues.; Fee).* Bus leaves from the Banamex; *in rainy season 4-wheel drive is necessary*—some truck drivers will take you on this two-hour round-trip excursion for a fee).

Though you can fit in the round trip from Puebla and back in one day, you should start very early. If you want more time or if you plan to return to Mexico City, which is a good five hours away, then you need to overnight in Cuetzalan. The only hotel that has all private baths with its rooms as well as hot water is the **Posada Cuetzalan** *(Zaragoza 8;* ☎ *(233)102-95; $30),* which also has an acceptable restaurant, a bar, patio, pool, and garage. Although this small hotel is expanding, it can't meet weekend demand. Reserve in advance and arrive early Saturday afternoon. You'll find eating pretty much confined to the Posada.

RESORTS AND SPAS NEAR MEXICO CITY

Many of the fine resort hotels outside the city occupy colonial haciendas whose orchards, gardens, aqueducts, and arches provide marvelous settings for swimming, golfing, horseback riding, and tennis. *All have a warmer climate than Mexico City because they are located in valleys of slightly lower altitude.* Mexicans enjoy spending their holidays and weekends at these resorts, so reserve in advance. (Also, see Taxco, above).

If instead of staying at a resort you prefer to spend a few hours testing thermal springs, plan a visit to Tequisquiapan (see Index) or Ixtapan de la Sal (see below). Both have public areas with extensive grounds, dressing rooms, pools, and inexpensive hotels. Buses run to these small towns, but not as frequently as you might like.

SAN JUAN DEL RIO

North of Mexico City sit the twin resort areas of San Juan del Rio and Tequisquiapan. By following the toll road to Queretaro (MEX 57D) for 172 km (107 m) and taking a right after the San Juan del Rio exit at "Querenda-Galindo," you arrive at a resort development with two hotels and the San Gil condominium development golf club:

Antigua Hacienda Galindo   √★★★★

☎ *(467) 2-00-50; $100* • After exiting MEX 57D, turn left, then left again across a bridge and go 6 km in order to reach this elegant resort that sits on an hacienda once owned by Cortes and later used as a monastery. The exceptionally handsome common areas, furnished with antiques, are in the restored manor house, which has 30-foot ceilings. Its 160 rooms and suites are in modern wings that blend with the original architecture. Some slightly higher priced rooms have private Jacuzzis and large, furnished balconies overlooking the garden. Beautiful clay tennis courts, horseback riding, huge pool, and extensive grounds. Access to golf at San Gil. Restaurant and bar. For reservations write Apartado 16, San Juan del Rio, Qto.

La Mansion de Andrea   ★★★

☎ *(467) 2-01-20; $138* • Just to the right of the highway exit, this hotel is on a beautiful estate with lush gardens filled with birds; 100 rooms and suites overlook these grounds (preferred) or courtyards covered by bougainvillea. In a rustic colonial style, these accommodations contrast with the more formal elegance of the Galindo. Pool, putting green, and tennis. Access to golf at nearby San Gil. Restaurant and bar.

NEAR CUERNAVACA

Cuernavaca's wonderful weather and location near Mexico City have made it a favorite weekend spot. Even Aztec nobles and conquistadors had retreats in this region. Only 61 km (38 m) from Mexico City, Cuernavaca can be reached quite rapidly on the toll highway MEX 95D (unless you hit a weekend traffic jam).

Hacienda de Cortes

10 km (6 m) south of Cuernavaca (convenient combi service), and a few miles from MEX 190, in the village of Atlacomulco; ☎ *(73) 15-88-44; $194* • The pools, fountains, and gardens of this sugar plantation formerly provided Hernan Cortes with his favorite retreat. This modernized yet romantic hotel is a wonderland of gardens filled with the sounds of water and birds in a setting from the colonial past. The dining room exists amid the walls of a 16th-century sugar mill and the pool floats you past centuries-old columns. The 22 suites are luxuriously, and sometimes flamboyantly, furnished. The junior suites are an exceptional buy. Pool, Jacuzzi, horseback riding; access to golf in Cuernavaca.

Hacienda Cocoyoc

32 km (20 m) east of Cuernavaca on MEX 138; 95 km (59 m) from Mexico City and 2 1/2 km south of MEX 115D at the Oaxtepec exit, at Cocoyoc; ☎ *(735) 6-22-11; $86* • Once a Dominican monastery, the 16th-century cloisters and chapel still stand on the 22 acres of this resort development. The modern hotel, villas, and condominiums are built around colonial walls, arches, and an aqueduct. Ancient trees, dating from the time Cocoyoc was an Aztec spa, grace the lovely gardens. As marvelous as the grounds are, we found the rooms at this 325-unit hotel surprisingly small. Five restaurants and bars, disco. Three large pools, 3 tennis courts, 9-hole golf course, in addition to organized activities and playground for children.

IXTAPAN DE LA SAL

This charming and immaculate town attracts tourists with its thermal springs and pleasant Sunday market. Public pools are fed by the **mineral springs** that are said to be good for arthritis, rheumatism, and blood pressure. For a fee, you can have a dressing room and linger all you want in the warm (not hot) waters on the landscaped grounds. For a slightly higher fee, you can indulge in a Roman bath lined with onyx and adorned with statuary. Massages are available for very nominal fees. The town is located on MEX 55, the road running between Toluca and Taxco, and lies approximately 80 km (50 m) south of Toluca and 60 km (36 m) north of Taxco, from which there is bus service. The fastest route from Mexico City is in the direction of Toluca, with a turnoff before that city at La Marquesa, and then connecting with MEX 55D at Tenango for this 133-km, (80-m) or 2-hour trip.

Hotel Kiss   √★

Blvd. San Roman and Av. Juarez; ☎ *(724) 3-09-01; $95 AP* • A modest clean, motel-like establishment located right across from the spa and offering 65 rooms and a pool, along with three meals a day at inexpensive prices.

Hotel Ixtapan   ★★★★

Blvd. Las Jacarandas and Diana Circle; ☎ *(5) 566-2855; $149 AP* • This is the hotel that made the spa famous. On acres of wooded land, this bathing spa offers fine gardens landscaped into terraces with fountains, pools, arches, and neoclassical statuary—some of which give it a sumptuous atmosphere akin to a Busby Berkeley stage set. Its 250 rooms are comfortable and ample and furnished in 50s moderne; many have private balconies. Dining room, bar, nightly entertainment that might include a choice of movies, a performance in the theater, or the Saturday nightclub with dancing fountains. In addition to access to the public spa facilities next door, there are 2 large pools, 1 thermal; a health and beauty center (fee) offering facials and massages as well as individualized exercise and diet plans; tennis, 9-hole golf course, horseback riding, children's playground, bowling, horse-drawn carriages for sightseeing, shops, and much more. For reservations, call, in the U.S., ☎ 800-223-9832. Expensive, but price includes three meals daily of very American cuisine. Fee for transportation from Mexico City airport.

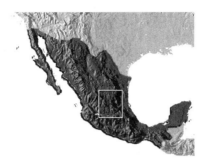

SILVER CITIES

The Colonial City of Guanajuato

> *Without the Indies or its trade, Spain would fall from its greatness, because there would be no silver for your majesty, for the ministers, for private individuals, for those holding...inheritances, which all comes from the Indies...Were the Indies lost, gone would be the income of those kingdoms, and your Majesty must seek a remedy....*

Marques de Varina, 1687
(as translated by Stein and Stein)

Silver. No other word so embodies the history of this region in the north Central Valley of Mexico. Silver not only made Spain wealthy, but it also created Guanajuato, San Miguel de Allende, and other cities in this region. Before silver, this area was an arid region disdained by the Aztecs. With silver, the area became rich with towns so sumptuous that they currently attract thousands of tourists each year. The king of Spain may have been delighted that his colony in Mexico produced as much silver as all other areas of the world combined in the 18th century, but the same silver that made Spain great also created wealthy Mexican-born Spaniards who grew resentful of their second-class status. Their resentment fueled the revolution against Spain and made this region the Mexican "Cradle of Independence" in 1810.

PREHISTORY

The enormous Central Valley of Mexico continues northwest past Queretaro to San Luis Potosi, past Guanajuato to Zacatecas. Driving through the undramatic scenery of this area with horse and cattle ranches and farms irrigated by modern hydraulic systems, you see no geographical barriers, no natural boundaries to divide the north central plain from the area to the south. *Prior to the Conquest, however, the aridity of this northern plain acted as a buffer between the great civilizations of ancient Mexico to the south and the bands of people to the north whom the Aztecs called "Chichimeca" ("Sons of Dogs") and who lacked pottery and architecture.*

At the time of Cortes' arrival, the Aztecs had forsaken the impoverished north as unworthy of their interest. While the Aztecs did negotiate with some of their northern neighbors in order to gain their cooperation in defending the Aztec territory, this system of defense extended only as far north as modern Queretaro. Spaniards encountered some of these bands of **Chichimeca** and described them as eating prickly pears from cactus, roots, rodents, even spider eggs and black beetles. They had no clothing or permanent houses. Sometimes the Chichimeca would dress up by decorating their bodies with red ocher or black and yellow paint.

Understandably, few ruined cities have been discovered in this region, and many of the Indians living today in this area, such as the Otomi, arrived from the south after allying with the Spaniards. Nonetheless, archaeologists have been discovering architectural remains of earlier civilizations in this border area, cultures that probably flourished during more humid times when the frontier area could be cultivated. But even these earlier cultures did not have true centers or dense concentrations of peoples. A distinctive, early pottery called Chupicuaro (dating from about 300 B.C.) could be found throughout most of the buffer region of Guanajuato and Queretaro, but architecture dates mostly from A.D. 600-1200, when a pre-Tula culture settled in this area and from which Tula itself may have evolved. For-tified areas are found even farther to the north at places like **La Que-mada**, near Zacatecas, which may have been constructed to defend Mesoamerica from Chichimeca invasions. During this period of more benign weather, the Chichimeca were concentrated much far-ther north than in Aztec times. But the better weather was not to sustain these cultures. As drought hit the extreme north, Chichime-ca were driven south, displacing and destroying the fragile cultures in the border regions. Even Tula probably fell because of pressure brought by the massive migrations of people fleeing from drought. Later Chichimeca, like the Aztecs themselves, wandered through this border area and eventually upset the balance of power in Me-soamerica.

COLONIAL PERIOD

By 1535, most of Mexico had been conquered, but not the north. Though adventurous and gold-crazed Spaniards had explored the New World all the way to Florida in their search for riches, the testy nomadic tribes and arid climate of the north central plateau held off the Spaniards until 1548. In that year a group of friars, sent to pacify and convert Chichimeca in Zacatecas, discovered **silver mines.** The first silver rush of the Americas had started. Soon mines were discov-ered at **Guanajuato**, **San Luis Potosi**, and other spots.

While the Spaniards found precious little of their cherished gold, they had discovered more than enough silver. *Even today Mexico is the largest silver producer in the world.* During the colonial period, **Zacatecas** produced one-third of all of Mexico's silver, and in Gua-najuato the Valenciana mine alone produced one-fourth. These min-ing camps attracted entrepreneurs to supply them and farmers to raise food and cattle. Since a safe trail for transporting the silver had to be established through this rough region, military posts were es-tablished at strategic points. Although Chichimeca raids against these growing settlements continued for some time, the friars effec-tively pacified most of the area and caused other Chichimeca to re-treat farther north.

Mining camps, military posts, and trading stations grew into cities supported by silver. Some miners, and many suppliers and farmers, became lavishly wealthy. *By the beginning of the 17th century, Zacate-cas had become the third largest city in Mexico.* During the 18th cen-tury, Guanajuato's size and opulence rivaled that of Mexico City. Other towns like **Queretaro** and **San Miguel de Allende** were not to be left behind, and used their wealth to build baronial mansions and ornate churches.

While the wealth of the colonial period remains in the historically preserved architecture of these cities and the still successful farms and cattle ranches of the area, no monuments stand to the terrible labor spent in drawing ore from these mines. Initially, the Chichimeca were enslaved and forced to work the mines, but their inadequate numbers led to other Indian groups being uprooted from their traditional communities to work in the mines. When Spain outlawed these practices, wages were offered that attracted enough laborers, but the conditions in which they worked often led to their death. Some drowned in mine floods, many died from explosions, and others from disease. All were required to haul 150 to 300 pounds of ore on their backs out of deep, damp mineshafts often filled with noxious gases. Historian Charles C. Cumberland says:

> *They performed prodigious feats: a third of a mile descent into the bowels of the earth and a return trip carrying 200 pounds of ore every hour during a twelve-hour work day took enormous stamina and will to work. These expenditures did not placate the concessionares, who constantly complained of their workmen's inefficiency and malingering.*

These abuses were to be remembered by laborers when they joined the Independence Movement.

INDEPENDENCE MOVEMENT

By the end of the 18th century, there had emerged a wealthy class of creoles, those born in Mexico but of Spanish blood. As rich and comfortable as these creoles were, they resented their inability to participate in the highest levels of government and church. Only the peninsulars, who were born in Spain, were chosen for such high offices. Unable to compete with the peninsulars, the creoles had devoted themselves to areas disdained by their Spanish superiors—ranching, agriculture, mining, and commerce, particularly in the provincial areas outside Mexico City. Although for creoles in the Silver Cities such occupations had led to considerable wealth, they still were unable to persuade Spain that they deserved to be appointed to positions of influence and governance. Increasingly alienated, creoles throughout provincial Mexico began to consider the benefits of independence.

No provincial area had wealthier, more demanding creoles than that of the Silver Cities. Not too surprisingly, it is in this region that members of the creole aristocracy began seriously to plot the overthrow of Spain. Social gatherings and cultural events in towns like Queretaro and San Miguel de Allende became disguised opportunities for these wealthy revolutionaries to discuss strategies. Leaders like **Ignacio Allende** organized a clandestine army and gathered weapons; priests like **Father Hidalgo** tried to convert other clerics to the cause. They planned to proclaim independence on December 8, 1810, and expected most creoles to support their cause. Spain would soon withdraw from their country, they thought, allowing them to take the positions formerly held by the peninsulars. Instead, they set Mexico on quite a different course.

FATHER HIDALGO

Royalists learned of this plot and started arresting conspirators in Queretaro on September 13, 1810. Instead of preventing the revolution, they prematurely precipitated it. One arrested conspirator, a woman known as **La Corregidora**, was able to send a message to the town of San Miguel de Allende warning that their plot had been discovered. Upon receiving this message, Allende and others gathered in the parish of Father Hidalgo to decide what to do. They agreed they could only go ahead with their plans, but immediately rather than months later. At dawn on Sunday, September 16, Father Hidalgo called his Indian and mestizo parishioners to mass. *Invoking the blessing of every poor Mexican's favorite saint, the Virgin of Guadalupe, he proclaimed independence from Spain. His impassioned speech was received so enthusiastically that Hidalgo found himself leader of an unexpected army of Indians and mestizos.* He had unleashed their anger from years of oppression. The colonial period in Mexico had not only discriminated against the creoles, it had impoverished and nearly enslaved the Indians and most of the mestizos through debt peonage. As with the laborers in the silver mines, it took little to unleash their anger and frustration. Seeing scant difference between the creoles and peninsulars, however, they cared nothing for the objectives of creole independence. They did care for a new order that they hoped would give them some land and dignity. Joining Hidalgo and the fight for independence, they totally redirected the movement.

If the December plot had not been discovered by the Royalists, perhaps Mexico would have gained its independence as easily as the creoles had hoped. Allende would have led a disciplined army into the field rather than the inexperienced Hidalgo with his unruly masses armed with miner's picks, machetes, and slings. What did happen was so brutal and frightening to most creoles that they withdrew their support for independence. As Hidalgo entered his first battle in Guanajuato, even he lost control of his army. Breaking into the town's granary where all the peninsulars were hiding, the army mutilated and killed everyone—men, women, and children. The town was rampaged and sacked. These atrocities by the revolutionaries were met by equal atrocities on the part of the Royalists. The way for independence had grown into a bloodbath that raged through Guadalajara and other cities. *When creole leaders like Hidalgo and Allende were captured and shot, the civil war turned into a social revolution that was a good century ahead of its time* (see chapter on "Mexican History"). For not until 1822 did Mexico receive its independence, and then it was the independence originally sought by the creoles, with none of the reforms to satisfy the Indians and mestizos.

MODERN HISTORY

Though ten years of war may have gained independence, it left the Silver Cities ravaged. Many mines had been so damaged or flooded that they could no longer produce. A scorched-earth policy had destroyed farms; food was scarce, and transport difficult due to banditry. Public buildings were abandoned; people were destitute. A U.S. diplomat traveling in Mexico just after 1822 described a town near Guanajuato:

> *San Felipe presented another melancholy example of the horrors of civil war. Scarcely a house was entire; and, except for one church lately rebuilt, the town appeared to be in ruins.*

Mexico was so vulnerable that it seemed to attract foreign aggression. Invaded by both the United States and France, Mexico struggled through the 19th century devastated and bankrupted by war. Not until the regime of **Porfirio Diaz** at the turn of the century did Mexico become stable enough to reinvest in its silver mines and rejuvenate its economy.

Today, Mexico's Silver Cities are economically successful again. Mexico produces twice as much silver now as it did during the colonial period. But the wealth of this region is even more closely tied to commercial metals that never interested Spain—lead, zinc, and copper. Modern industry, such as an oil refinery in Salamanca and a Ralston Purina factory in Queretaro, also plays an important role in the area's economy. Modern irrigation techniques have made this once-arid, rejected land a major agricultural center in Mexico.

SAN MIGUEL DE ALLENDE

San Miguel de Allende's excellent climate and small-town intimacy have attracted American artists and retirees for decades. Its colonial heritage, protected by law, may not attain the architectural splendor of nearby Guanajuato, but its **spas**, **art galleries**, and **art institutes** combine to attract many American students and tourists for prolonged stays. Fine inns and international cuisine bring even jet-setters weary of the flashiness of the usual winter resorts. San Miguel's appeal is mostly atmospheric—its soft pink **facades** turning softer and shadowy at sunset, its **narrow streets** winding past **18th-century mansions**. Many tourists pass through San Miguel, stopping only to buy at its many shops or to see the magnificent views of the town from El Mirador or Instituto Allende. A more leisurely stay of a night or two enables you to enjoy fine walks through town and a most relaxing swim in the warm **thermal waters** of nearby spas and a visit to the **shrine at Atotonilco**.

San Miguel's name has undergone several transformations reflecting its history. As San Miguel de los Chichimecas, the first settlement was no more than an Indian mission established by Franciscan friars in the 16th century. As San Miguel El Grande ("the great"), the town had grown wealthy supplying nearby silver towns with leather, candles, harnesses, and stirrups in the 17th century. *San Miguel El Grande is preserved as one of Mexico's designated historical colonial cities,* but its new name pays homage to the town's native son, **Ignacio de Allende** (ah-YEN-day), leader of Mexico's Independence Movement.

KEY TO SAN MIGUEL DE ALLENDE

Sights • One of the historically preserved colonial towns of Mexico, San Miguel is small but cosmopolitan and a delight to walk in

Excursions • Thermal springs feed nearby popular spas; and the Shrine of Atotonilco is a must for students of Mexican mural art.

Sports • Horseback riding, golf, swimming, and some tennis.

Shopping • Galleries make for excellent browsing and buying, with works of the many local artists and shops with local tin-, aluminum-, and brasswork, weavings and Talavera ceramics, as well as crafts from all of Mexico and even other parts of Latin America.

Famous Fiestas • Last Friday of Lent and Palm Sunday; Winter Chamber Music Festival; Independence Day, September 15-16; Feast day of Saint Michael on September 29 and nearest weekend.

Where to Stay • Fine small inns ranging through all price categories and outlying resort hotels provide good accommodations. Camping, too. Reservations recommended, particularly in the winter.

Eating Out • Quite international. Many hotels require meal plans

Entertainment • Lots to choose from for so small a town, including classical music concerts and plays in English.

Getting Around • The town's atmosphere is best absorbed on foot, but there are plenty of taxis and buses. Some car rentals. There's a garage on Calle San Francisco #10, just off zócalo.

PRACTICAL TIP

Bring thick-soled shoes for walking cobblestone streets.
Good, better-than-springlike weather, all year.
Most shops close between 2-5 p.m., but reopen until 7 p.m.

WHAT TO SEE AND DO

The individual buildings of San Miguel don't warrant any special effort, but the combined impact of their well-proportioned and carefully finished facades make the town a delight to stroll through. Any stroll, whether down **Calle Canal** for shopping or through the market and its nearby profusion of **churches**, presents opportunities to see baronial **mansions** adorned with coats of arms and patron saints as well as colonial churches, or the homes of patriots of the Independence Movement.

As you plan your visit in San Miguel, you might want to include some of the following sights on your tour. To see the well-tended gardens and homes behind the walls on many streets, take the **house-and-garden tour** (fee) that leaves from the Biblioteca on most Sundays (the proceeds go to the town library fund).

PRACTICAL TIP

Our favorite walk in the late afternoon doesn't pass any particularly famous building, yet it is full of architectural details and narrow romantic streets. Walk down Cuna de Allende to Calle Hospicio on the way to El Chorro (Calle Barranca). Once the site of the mission of San Miguel de los Chichimecas, El Chorro still provides the town's water supply from its springs and affords pleasant views. Return down Subida del Chorro to the picturesque public laundry place and continue past the tranquil Benito Juarez Park before turning onto Aldama, a handsome street of well-maintained 18th-century residences that ends just behind La Parroquia.

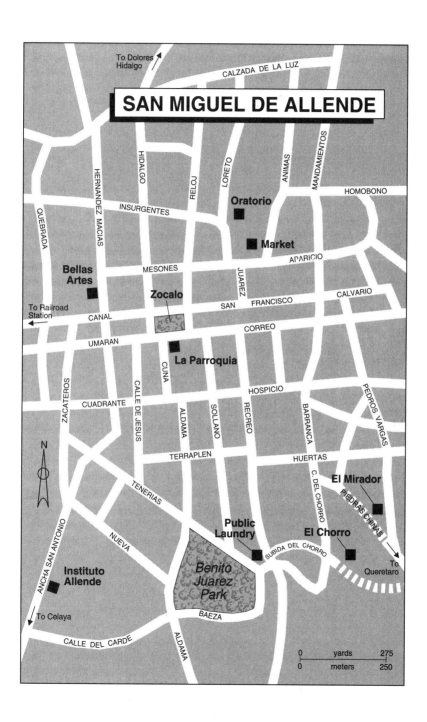

Plaza Allende

Canal and Hidalgo • The zócalo in the heart of town, its trimmed trees and *popular park surrounded by 18th-century mansions*, is dominated by the parish church, **La Parroquia**. In the late 19th century, the self-trained Indian architect Zeferino Gutierrez designed this Gothic-style facade. Given its frothy, pink appearance, he might have spun it of cotton candy. The **interior** still reflects the styles of the 17th- and 18th-century portions of the church, including the left side chapel containing the revered **Senor de la Conquista**, made of corn paste, in a technique developed by Tarascan Indians. In a nearby side chapel are the striking modern **murals** painted by A. Tommi.

As you tour the zócalo, looking into **shops** and **art galleries** occupying what used to be 18th-century residences of San Miguel's elite, *you pass some of the most important historical buildings in this town.* The number of buildings facing the zócalo that were **homes to patriots** of Independence demonstrates that San Miguel was a hotbed of revolutionary activity against Spain. The **birthplace of Ignacio de Allende** with its corner statue of this leader of Independence, is marked by a plaque stating "Here was born he who was to be famous everywhere." Now the **Museo de la Casa de Allende** (Cuna de Allende), you can visit the refurbished house and its historical exhibits (open Tuesday-Saturday 10 a.m.-4 p.m.; Sunday 10 a.m.-2 p.m.; free). Diagonally across the plaza on the particularly attractive street of Reloj is the **Casa de los Conspiradores**, home of Allende's brother and the location of meetings to plot the course of Independence. The **Casa Quemada** with its arcade on the corner of Correo is yet another home of an Independence patriot, Marshal Francisco de Lanzagorta.

Other homes are excellent examples of the architecture of the first half of the 18th century. On the corner of the zócalo and Calle Canal stands the palace of the **Mayorazgo de la Canal**, whose home, with its elaborate wooden door and facade sculpture (Calle Canal), is *one of the most impressive in town.* (Restored **interior** open during special exhibits.) The **Casa de los Perros** (House of the Dogs), a few steps off the zócalo at Umaron 3, is the home of another Independence hero, **Juan de Umaron**, and named for its delightful balcony supported by stone dogs.

Instituto Allende

Calle Ancha de San Antonio 20 • Located at the end of a vigorous, partially uphill walk from town, the Instituto occupies yet another former residence of the prominent 18th-century Canal family. You can still see an image of the family patron saint, the Virgin of Loreto, on the facade. For a while this estate served as a convent, but in 1952 it became part of the state University of Guanajuato, specializing in fine arts. *Today, it is a popular place of study for American students.* Wandering through its lovely **patios**, you come upon a student exhibit room and a small **museum** of 18th-century religious art. Through the institute to the left, you will come upon an excellent **view** of La Parroquia and the town below.

El Mirador
Pedro Vargas in front of Posada La Ermita • Here is a fabulous **view** of the town and distant mountains. You can reach El Mirador by climbing the many steps behind El Chorro (see walk to El Chorro) or by an uphill walk along Correo to Pedro Vargas (also called Real de Queretaro). Or you can, of course, simply drive there or take a taxi.

Market and Churches
The colorful vegetable market spills beyond its location near Calles Juarez and Mesones, *especially on Sunday*, and occupies Insurgentes as it descends past a profusion of churches and convents. The most interesting church is the **Oratorio**, its cypress-tree-shaded atrium set a few steps above the market and its 1714 facade decorated with foliated columns. In 1734, the wealthy Canal family paid for the addition to the Oratorio of a chapel dedicated to their patron saint, the Virgin of Loreto. The main entrance to this **Chapel of Santa Casa de Loreto** is in the rear of the church but blocked by a grill. Through the grill you can see sumptuously gilded **altars** and two niches with sculptures of the "Count" and his wife, below which lie their tombs.

Bellas Artes Centro Cultural
Hernandez Macias 75 • After you've finished shopping on Calle Canal, you might turn off it at the Church of the Immaculate Conception to visit this art institute housed in an impressive, **neoclassical cloister** from the 18th century. This cultural center, also known as **El Nigromante** ("the sorcerer," nicknamed for a 19th-century political thinker), has been painted with **murals** by **Pedro Martinez de Monterrey** and students of the school. One room contains a very unfinished mural by Siqueiros.

EXCURSIONS

Shrine of Atotonilco
Located about 15 km (9 m) north on road to Dolores Hidalgo, then left for 2 km at the first major paved road after the spas. • Founded in 1748 by Father Felipe Neri de Alfaro, over the centuries this sanctuary has grown to a large architectural complex with six chapels. Its walls abound with every style of Mexican **mural** art imaginable, from exuberant baroque and restrained academic to folk-art forms of flowers and fruits and Goya-style devils and angels, even poems and Biblical passages. These murals—so profuse they sometimes overlap and spill over to the doors—express the devotion of Mexicans to this sacred shrine. **"Atotonilco" means "place of the hot waters"** in Nahuatl (nearby are **thermal springs**). Buses to Atotonilco (marked "Santuario") leave from the market near Mandamientos.

Spas

On your way to Atotonilco, you will pass turnoffs for public thermal spas. •
The best known is **Taboada** (8 km, or 5 m). These warm thermal
waters, rich in bicarbonate of soda, are so relaxing you won't want to
move for days. There is an admission charge and dressing rooms are
available. Nearby is the **Hacienda Taboada**, on the same access road as
the public Taboada spa, but farther along. Its well-tended gardens and
well-maintained thermal pools open to visitors for a set fee; on weekends, the Hacienda offers admission to its facilities for the price of its
afternoon buffet, often accompanied by music. Transportation to
Taboada leaves from the market near Mandamientos.

SHOPPING

Colonial industries that made San Miguel rich in the 18th century continue today in the form of crafts. **Wrought iron** locks, lamps, and door-
knobs; tin lamps and candelabra; leather saddles and belts; and wool
serapes, or rugs, are among the most traditional items on sale in San
Miguel. Traditional, too, are the regional **Talavera ceramics**, or tiles,
vases, and dinnerware that are at their most alluring when painted in the
refined style of Guanajuato's Capelo or in the colorful fruit designs of Dolores Hidalgo's Alvaro Mora. The presence of resident American artists and
two art institutes in town have given a contemporary feeling to much that
is sold—rug patterns change frequently and tin lamps and sunburst mirror
frames often have brass and copperplate details or have been transformed
into pewter-looking aluminum. *This mixing of Mexican and American arts
and crafts traditions has successfully attracted many tourists to San Miguel for
the sole purpose of shopping.* Other items are sold in the shops, too, from
crafts from all over Latin America, to embroidery work and bubble- knit
cotton sweaters, from neocolonial furniture to indescribable bric-a-brac.
Last, but not least, art galleries display and sell the work of resident artists,
some of it quite good.

Shops cluster conveniently around the zócalo and streets radiating from it.
Here you find numerous **art galleries** as well as the consummate San
Miguel shop, **Casa Cohen** *(Reloj 12)*. Its carved colonial facade encases a
hardware store of very traditional wrought iron and brass light fixtures,
locks, and door knobs that share their space with prints by the local artist
Eugenia Lewis. (For the largest selections of brass and tin mirrors, lamps,
and the like, browse along Ancha San Antonio on the way to the Instituto
Allende). More endearing to the hard-core shopper, however, are the excellent crafts shops found in the surrounding blocks. Right on the zócalo,
La Princesa *(San Francisco 2 at Reloj)* sells exquisite examples of Talavera
vases by Capelo. **La Calaca** *(Mesones 93)* specializes in Mexican folk art;
whether Oaxacan ceramics or Guerrero masks, the collection often includes signed works by the country's best-known artisans as well as the
simply funky. **Veryka** *(Zacateros 6-A)* offers magnificent embroideries and
woven rugs from Mexico and as far away as Peru, along with Huichol yarn
paintings and Guatemalan belts. A few doors away is **Casa Maria Luisa**

(*Canal 40 at Zacateros*), with attractive furnishings and decorators' items that include the gaily painted dishes of Mora. There are many more shops, too many to list, but among them you might look for **El Pegaso** (*across from post office*) with its ethnic jewelry and clothing, its leather goods and crafts; the warehouselike **Zarco** (*Hospicio at Conde*) with Mexican crafts (lots of blown glass and Talavera ceramics on our last visit) at good prices but some imperfections; **El Antico** (*Plaza Colonial at Canal 21; closed Wed.*), with older pieces like ex-voto paintings and antiques; and **Artesanias Vasquez** (*Mesones 85*), for handpainted tiles and planters.

FIESTAS

The intimacy of San Miguel makes it a special place for celebrations, as the festivities more easily overtake the town. While **Christmas** season celebrations are the same as in the rest of Mexico, San Miguel's narrow streets offer a good opportunity to observe **posadas**, the gentle singing of various neighborhood children as they reenact Mary and Joseph's search for lodging each night from December 16-24. **Easter** celebrations include a procession with El Senor del Columno carried from the shrine of Atotonilco and arriving to a joyous reception at dawn on Palm Sunday, but San Miguel's special small-town atmosphere prevails most on the last Friday of Lent when private homes open to visitors for prayers before splendidly decorated family altars. **Independence Day**, September 15-16, is most enthusiastically celebrated with traditional dances and fireworks in this town where the movement was born. The **feast day of Saint Michael**, the town's patron saint, so captures the spirit of traditional Indian dancers that it is celebrated for several days, not just on September 29, but also on a weekend following close to it on the calendar. Dancers from throughout the state of Guanajuato are greeted by local dancers at a spot called Cruz del Cuartos, where they all perform before proceeding to the zócalo in proud processions carrying sculptures of flowers. Dances in the zócalo, fireworks, and music round out the celebrations. In December San Miguel sponsors its annual **Chamber Music Festival**.

WHERE TO STAY

Befitting its attraction to American students of the arts of all ages, San Miguel offers an excellent variety of quality hotels and inns, many atmospheric and full of colonial details. Several resort spas are situated just outside of town for those who wish to visit the area while enjoying a leisurely winter vacation. Reservations are essential during the Christmas and winter season (December 15-April 15) when visitors often come for long-term stays, booking up the posadas and small inns that offer discounts for month-long residencies. With all the students residing in town, competition for the less expensive hotels can be intense all year long, so reservations are recommended. (To address correspondence, write to San Miguel de Allende, Guanajuato, 37700 Mexico.) Some hotels require meals, either two (MAP) or three (AP) each day. To call, use area code 465.

SPAS

Hacienda Taboada ★★★★

km 8 on highway to Dolores Hidalgo; *2-08-50; $208 AP* • Fifteen minutes outside of San Miguel de Allende is this very attractive resort with 60 rooms and bungalows arranged around gardens full of bougainvillea and two thermal spring pools (one large and warm, the other smaller and hot). All very spacious rooms have private balcony or patio facing the gardens and are decorated with colorful rugs and bedspreads. Lovely tiled bathrooms have enormous sunken tubs. Food is plentiful, wholesome, and tasty. Very popular with Mexican families. Tennis. Horseback riding available. Courtesy bus service to San Miguel, and arrangements made for tours of surrounding area. Parking. For reservations, write or call Mexico City: Adolfo Prieto 1219, 03100 Mexico, D.F.; 575-7177.

Rancho El Atascadero ★★★

Prolongacion Santo Domingo; *2-02-06; $95* • A mile from the center of town on Queretaro highway, turn left at sign, and you will find this oasis on the dry hills outside of San Miguel. A converted 17th-century hacienda, this tranquil hotel has 50 simply furnished yet comfortable and ample rooms and suites (all with fireplaces) around small gardens with fountains. Common rooms have rustic charm. Restaurant, bar. Heated pool and Jacuzzi, tennis, handball, and sauna. Courtesy bus into town 8:30 a.m.-3 p.m. Parking. For reservations, write Apartado 103, San Miguel de Allende, Guanajuato.

VERY EXPENSIVE: IN-TOWN

Casa de Sierra Nevada ★★★★

Hospicio 35; *2-04-15; $98-218* • An exquisite, tasteful inn with 22 units, mostly suites distributed among three colonial mansions. Suites are like private homes within the larger mansions, surrounded by patios and gardens; some duplexes, a few with fireplaces and each in a distinctive decor. All this renovation has been accomplished while maintaining colonial authenticity. The common areas, including one of the best restaurants in town and a handsome bar, surround a quaint open-air colonial courtyard. Access to country club facilities. Personal checks, but no credit cards accepted.

Villa Santa Monica ★★★

Baenza 22; ☎ *2-04-51; $145 CP* • Idyllically set across from Juarez Park yet conveniently within town, this lovely inn offers eight junior suites, each more than ample, each distinctively decorated with folkloric touches and warm colors and all with fireplaces and terraces. A number have garden views and all are arranged around the 18th-century courtyard of this mansion. Restaurant. Bar. Tiny tiled pool. Write Apartado 686.

EXPENSIVE: IN-TOWN

Villa Jacaranda Hotel   ★★★
Aldama 53; ☎ *2-10-15; $95-120* • On one of San Miguel's most colonial streets, you'll find this modern and intimate inn, its 18 units a variety of casitas and apartments terraced around a hillside garden. Most of the units are suites with their own terraces and sitting rooms, large bedrooms, and handsome Talavera-tiled baths, and all are handsomely furnished like a private home. Restaurant (one of the finest in town), lounge, Jacuzzi, and small pool. Parking.

Hacienda de las Flores   ★★★
Hospicio 16; ☎ *2-18-08; $115-136 MAP* • This intimate inn offers 12 junior suites arranged around a lovely garden. Each unit varies, some have fireplaces, others have bathrooms and tubs lavishly decorated with Talavera tiles, and all are charmingly furnished with Mexican arts and crafts. Good restaurant. Lounge with wood burning fireplace and video movies some nights. Small, well-heated pool. Helpful management. MAP peak season. No credit cards.

MODERATE: IN-TOWN

Mansion del Bosque   √★★
Aldama 65; ☎ *2-02-77; $65-70 MAP* • The very pleasant inn offers 23 varying units situated on different levels and around small courtyards and sitting areas. The units vary in size, some have fireplaces or Jacuzzi (expensive), others have window seats, all are nicely appointed. Long-term stays preferred January through March. Comfortable lounge with library. Restaurant. Write Apartado 206.

Aristos San Miguel   ★★
Ancha San Antonio 30; ☎ *2-26-99; $41 CP* • Formerly part of Instituto Allende, this rustic hacienda-style hotel with extensive and secluded gardens lies on the edge of town, 1 km south of zócalo. The large lobby and rooms are open, light, and airy, and many of the 70 rooms share a balcony overlooking gardens. Restaurant and cocktails. Pool. Parking. A bit out of center, but next to Instituto Allende. For reservations, write Apartado 588.

INEXPENSIVE: IN-TOWN

Posada de la Aldea   ★★
Ancha San Antonio; ☎ *2-12-96; $55* • Opposite Instituto Allende and Hotel Aristos, this hotel is designed as a modern facsimile of a colonial plaza, complete with chapel on one side. Comfortable, if simple, rooms with tiled baths; some have view of San Miguel (better from second-floor rooms). Dining room, bar. Pool. Parking.

Posada de San Francisco   ★★
Plaza Principal 2; ☎ *2-14-66; $55* • A converted colonial building on zócalo, the Posada's convenient location has attracted tourists for many years. Clean, if a little worn, this hotel has lovely patios with

fountains, especially the one off its handsome colonial lounge. Rooms vary considerably, some have tranquil views of garden, others of zócalo. For reservations, write Apartado 40.

Posada de las Monjas   ★

Canal 37; ☎ *2-01-71; $40* • There are really two sections of this friendly hotel of over 60 rooms: the pink-stone converted convent with its older, cheaper rooms, and the modern, more expensive wing. The new rooms—large, decorated in warm colors, and airy—are recommended. Many small patios dot the winding corridors connecting the wings. The rustic and homey lobby is in the convent section. Restaurant. Lounge. Parking.

BUDGET: IN-TOWN

Quinta Loreto   √★

Callejon Loreto 15; ☎ *2-00-42; $32* • An exceptional buy, but hard to find. Follow Reloj for two blocks, turn right on Insurgentes and then left down Loreto to almost the end of the street. Thirty clean and decent rooms surround a luxuriant tropical garden; the newer ones are recommended. Friendly service and popular restaurant. Pool. Tennis. Parking.

Posada Carmina

Cuna de Allende 7; ☎ *2-04-58; $42* • Right across from La Parroquia is this family run establishment. The 15 rooms are worn, yes, and some have shared baths, but most are large and there's always something cheery about them— large windows, a huge tub, or a sitting area. The kindly service more than makes up for any deficiencies in the rooms. Restaurant. Write Apartado 219.

CAMPING

Trailer Park La Siesta

3-1/2 km south of town on Celaya road • Offers the facilities of the Motel La Siesta: coffee shop, pool, tennis, and playground. Sixty spaces for trailers with all hookups.

WHERE TO EAT

Food in San Miguel reflects the preferences of its resident American population. There is an emphasis on "continental" cuisine, some of it quite good, but even the most Europeanized menu may include some Mexican highlights. Price categories are explained in the "Introduction."

Some of the finest restaurants are in the hotels. **Villa Jacaranda** *(Aldama 53;* ☎ *2-10-15; 7:30 a.m.-11 p.m.; closed Monday)* has one of the most interesting and reliable menus, offering loin of veal as well as the usual beef with bearnaise, pork loin a l'orange, and cashew chicken as well as some Mexican and seafood dishes. Although a few of the dishes, such as the *tournedos al chipotle* covered in melted cheese, seem to need a bit of nouvelle cuisine leavening, all the food is pleasingly prepared and, at times, delightful. Moderately expensive. On the other hand, the **Sierra Nevada** (*Hospicio 35;* ☎ *2-04-15; 1-4:30 p.m. and 8-10:30 p.m., when ties and jackets are recommended; closed Tuesday*) offers nouvelle cuisine, although the preparation can be uneven. Nonetheless, the likes of sashimi, duck breast, and sea bass in tomato and basil are served along with a choice of more continental dishes such as steak with bearnaise. And there are pastas as well as seasonal Mexican delicacies like mushroomy *huitlacoche*. Whether your meal is served in the handsome formal dining room or on the lovely patio, the ambience may make up for some of the unevenness in the food. Expensive. The second floor view of La Parroquia from the restaurant at **Hacienda de las Flores** (*Hospicio 16;* ☎ *2-18-08; 1-4 p.m. and 7-11 p.m.; closed Monday; no credit cards*) makes afternoon dining especially pleasant. The homemade pastas are good, as are such Mexican dishes as chicken with a sauce of red and green tomatoes that share the menu with continental listings. Moderately expensive.

There are pleasant patio restaurants to explore apart from the hotels. One of the loveliest is **Bugambilia** (*Hidalgo 42*), which also happens to serve fine Mexican cuisine, from the more unusual *chiles en nogadas* (meat-stuffed chiles in a walnut sauce with pomegranate seeds) and chicken in coriander to the earthy pozole, or hominy soup with lots of mix-ins, make up the menu. Moderate. **Mexico Lindo** (*Mesones 80; closed Sunday at 8 p.m.*) serves international dishes and seafood on its tranquil patio, but it is the Mexican food that locals order—nopal cactus salad, *sopa de medula* (savory bone marrow soup), pork en adobado, and the like. Moderate. **Pepe's Patio** (*Mesones 99; closed Monday*) attracts the American crowd with its quarter-pounders, fajitas, and Sunday buffet (noon-5 p.m.). Moderate. The original **El Patio** (*Correo 10; closed Tuesday*), a covered courtyard hung with plants, is popular with residents for its stuffed sea bass, ribs, and salads. Moderate and up.

Inexpensive restaurants also offer a variety of cuisines. **Mama Mia** (*Umaran 8; breakfast through late evening desserts*) serves up pasta and a tasty minestrone, pizza, and salads along with a few Mexican dishes in a comfortable garden patio overlooked by a gigantic rubber tree and bougainvillea. A good spot at night when there's entertainment. Inexpensive. **La Terraza**, an outdoor cafe conveniently located on the zócalo, is a good place for snacks, including omelets, nachos, and hamburgers. Open daily, 9:30 a.m.-8 p.m., but **Posada Carmina** (*Cuna de Allende 7*) around the corner, serves a more reasonably priced breakfast in its pleasant colonial courtyard, where you can also enjoy inexpensive comidas corridas. For midmorning hunger pangs head to the **Panaderia La Colmena** (*Reloj 21*) for freshly made empanadas filled with fruits or tangy meats. If you're not counting your pennies, relax over one of the newspapers or magazines from the rack at **La Dolce Vita** (*Canal 21 in Plaza Colonial; 10 a.m.-10 p.m.*) while you sip a fancy coffee or try one of their ice cream concoctions (just plain coconut is good, too). And there is a handsome branch in Bellas Artes.

ENTERTAINMENT

It's hard, particularly on weekends, not to find some live music in bars or restaurants. Throughout most of the week **Mama Mia's** has Peruvian flute music and the like in the restaurant and a variety of performers, mostly jazz or classical guitar, in its bar. (Cover charge; no music Monday and Tuesday.) And **La Fragua** (Cuna de Allende 3), popular with local gringos, has changing attractions in its bar. So large is the American community that cine bars have sprung up around town offering not only reasonably current film hits, but also film restrospectives. On our last visit, the **Villa Jacaranda** and **Mama Mia's** had some of the more interesting offerings. Also, this community cherishes its concerts, plays, and lectures (many are given in English) as well as charitable functions (such as the special Saturday excursions of Centro de Crecimento). To keep up with all the happenings, check the weekly newspaper *Atencion* or the postings at **Colibri** (Sollano 30).

GETTING TO AND FROM SAN MIGUEL

AIR

No service. Van service to and from Mexico City airport (see Directory "Airlines").

BUS

Many bus lines—Tres Estrellas de Oro and Flecha Amarilla (more like second-class buses) among them—provide service from Mexico City's Terminal Norte and from Guanajuato. They take about four hours from Mexico City and about two hours from Guanajuato. Newer, deluxe "Plus" buses make the run to Mexico City as well.

CAR

The toll road, MEX 57D, from **Mexico City** to Queretaro (see "On the Road" at the end of the Silver Cities chapter) is heavily trafficked. Delays will come in reaching this road from Mexico City during rush hour (take the Reforma to Petroleo Monument, then Periferico Norte to highway). If you don't plan to visit Queretaro, exit at the first sign to San Luis Potosi in order to bypass the congested traffic around Queretaro and connect with MEX 57. Turn at the sign to San Miguel on MEX 57 and continue 35 km (22 m) on a quiet two-lane country road. You will enter San Miguel by El Mirador, one of the best views of this town and surrounding countryside (in front of Posada La Ermita). Total distance: 290 km (180 m) or about 3-1/2 hours. See "On the Road," for sights along this route.

To reach **Guanajuato**, follow Hernando Macias south past the Instituto Allende and then follow signs to Celaya. At about 13 km (8 m) out, the road branches to Guanajuato and continues almost to the entrance of that city. Total distance: 90 km (56 m) or under 1-1/2 hours. A more time-consuming route goes via **Dolores Hidalgo**. See "On the Road" for this route.

TRAIN

As usual this is not your most rapid form of transportation, but it is a popular one in the case of the *servicio estrella* cars of El Constitutionalista that make the daily 5-1/2-hour trip to and from Mexico City comfortable.

DIRECTORY

Airlines • No commercial airlines. Viajes Vertis, Hidalgo 1 (☎ 2-18-56), or your hotel, can arrange van service from Mexico City airport.

American Express • Hidalgo 1 (☎ 2-18-56); weekdays 9 a.m.-2 p.m., 4-6:30 p.m.

Books in English • Colibri (Sollano 30) with good selection of books on Mexico; Lagundi (Plaza Colonial, Canal 21) with periodicals and paperbacks; Biblioteca (Insurgentes 25) is the library, which has a bilingual collection and occasionally sells extra books.

Buses • Central de Autobuses, 1 km west of zócalo on Canal.

Car Rentals • Gamma Rent-a-Car, Hidalgo 3 (☎ 2-08-15).

Golf Club • de Golf Malanquin, nine holes, km 5 of Celaya Highway.

Groceries • On zócalo.

Horseback Riding • Valle de Alcocer, 1 mile out on Queretaro road.

Post Office • Calle Correo 18.

Spanish Courses • Academia Hispano Americano, Mesones 4, and Instituto Allende, Calle Ancha de San Antonio 20, are among the many options available.

Telegraph • Calle Correo 18.

Tennis • At Golf Club, see previous page.

Tourist Office • On zócalo, next to La Parroquia. Open 10 a.m.-2:45 p.m., 5-7 p.m. weekdays; 10 a.m.-noon weekends (☎ 2-17-47).

Tours • House-and-garden tour Sundays (except during December and major holidays). Leaves at 11:45 a.m. from the Biblioteca (Insurgentes 25); walking tours and excursions from Travel Institute (Cuna de Allende 11; ☎ 2-00-78) and other agencies.

Train Station • 1 km west of zócalo on Canal (☎ 2-00-07).

U.S. Consul • Av. Hernandez Macias 72 in rear of Plaza Colonial (☎ 2-23-57; 2-00-63 for emergencies only).

QUERETARO

Colonial architecture in Queretaro is sometimes gaily ostentatious, often harmonious, and always pleasing to the eye. If you can force yourself to turn off the highway into the industrial ring that now surrounds this prosperous city, a few hours strolling its historical streets will make you forget there is a 20th century.

Even the briefest visit through the cobblestone streets lined with small parks, fountains, and plazuelas can include Queretaro's most famous sights. Around the zócalo, or Jardin Obregon, there are a number of picturesque streets closed to traffic. To the east, Calle 5 de Mayo connects with the nearby Plaza de la Independencia. Only a few blocks to the west of the zócalo, Calle Madero leads to ultrabaroque, Churrigueresque masterpieces of the Museo del Arte and the Santa Clara Church. A third masterpiece, the Santa Rosa de Viterbo Church, can be seen by adding the time to walk five more blocks.

KEY TO QUERETARO

Sights • The colonial center of this city is filled with fine 18th-century churches and mansions and small squares and parks.

Fiestas • September 14 is the Fiesta de la Cruz, followed by Independence Day celebrations on the 15th and 16th of September. Nativity celebrations begin December 16 and end on Christmas Eve with processions of biblical floats.

Where to Stay • Limited but good in-town accommodations.

Where to Eat • Regional specialties like *carnitas*, as well as international cuisine.

Getting to and from Queretaro • Central sightseeing area has many streets closed to traffic so that walking is the best way to visit most sights. Park your car around the Alameda or, with luck, find a space under the Plaza de la Constitucion. Local buses run along the main streets.

Practical Tips • The sights can be seen in a few hours on your way to San Miguel or Guanajuato, but the loveliness of an evening stroll here makes it a fine place to overnight, too. • Many sights close from 2-4 p.m. and reopen in the evening (except Sunday).

WHAT TO SEE AND DO

Jardin Obregon

Calles Madero and Juarez • There are so many plazas in Queretaro that it is only too easy to confuse them, especially since they often seem to have more than one name. This main plaza or zócalo, dominated by

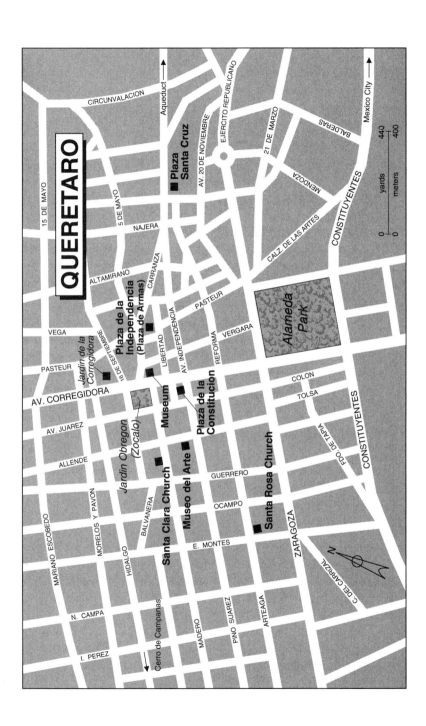

QUERETARO

15 DE MAYO
CIRCUNVALACION
Aqueduct →
EJERCITO REPUBLICANO
AV. 20 DE NOVIEMBRE
21 DE MARZO
BALDERAS
Mexico City →
5 DE MAYO
NAJERA
MENDOZA
CONSTITUYENTES
440
400
yards
meters
0
0
ALTAMIRANO
CARRANZA
CALZ. DE LAS ARTES
VEGA
PASTEUR
Plaza Santa Cruz
Plaza de la Independencia (Plaza de Armas)
16 DE SEPTIEMBRE
LIBERTAD
AV. INDEPENDENCIA
PASTEUR
REFORMA
VERGARA
Alameda Park
Jardin de la Corregidora
AV. CORREGIDORA
AV. JUAREZ
Jardin Obregon (Zocalo)
Museum
Plaza de la Constitucion
COLON
TOLSA
CONSTITUYENTES
ALLENDE
MORELOS Y PAVON
HIDALGO
BALVANERA
Santa Clara Church
Museo del Arte
GUERRERO
OCAMPO
Santa Rosa Church
FDO. DE TAPIA
CONSTITUYENTES
MARIANO ESCOBEDO
E. MONTES
ZARAGOZA
N. CAMPA
Cerro de Campanas
MADERO
PINO SUAREZ
ARTEAGA
C. DEL CARRIZAL
N
I. PEREZ

the Church of San Francisco, is the best place to start your walk in old Queretaro. Just to the northeast of the zócalo is the 0, a nook of a garden with a statue dedicated to this heroine of the Independence movement.

Santa Clara Church and Neptune Fountain

Calles Madero and Allende • Walking west from the zócalo on Madero, you pass the ornate **Casa de la Marquesa** (Madero 41), then cross to a garden graced with a neoclassical **fountain** designed by Mexico's famous architect **Francisco Eduardo Tresguerra**s in 1779. Next to it is the church of the convent of Santa Clara, *the wealthiest nunnery in all of Mexico in the 18th century.* The church facade does little to prepare you for its rich, gold-laden **interior**, rococo altarpieces, and exceptional choir screen.

Museo del Arte

Calle Allende 14 between Madero and Pino Suarez Tuesday- Sunday 11 a.m.-7 p.m., free • Walking nearly a block south on Allende, you come to *one of the finest buildings in Queretaro.* Once the convent of the **Church of San Agustin**, then a governmental complex, and now a beautiful **museum** of colonial paintings and polychrome wooden sculptures, this building is typical of the dashing Queretaro style of the 18th century. Even if you aren't interested in paintings by **Miguel Cabrera** and **Juan Correa**, you might enjoy the **architectural details** revealed by a visit. Caryatids with expressive faces but abstract bodies tapering to a single leg adorn the ground level of the **Churrigueresque courtyard**, while the second level is graced by atlantes known as the "deaf-mutes" for their strong hand gestures. And if you're lucky, the bells of San Agustin will be frantically ringing while you admire the angels standing guard around its tiled dome.

Church of Santa Rosa de Viterbo

Calles Arteaga and Montes • Continuing south on Allende to Arteaga and turning right, you arrive at a fine **plaza** and Santa Clara's rival for richly embellished interiors. The **facade** has rather strange volute buttresses—like monumental commas punctuated with gargoyles. The tower and dome were remodeled by Tresguerras in 1785. But none of the restraint of this famous architect is found in the earlier, **18th-century interior** of this church. Its rococo altarpieces are ornate, though delicate, and its Churrigueresque pulpit and hammered-gold choir screen are spectacular.

Museo Regional

Corregidora 3 Open Wed.-Sat. 10 a.m.-6 p.m., Tues. and Sun. 10 a.m.-3:30 p.m. Fee. • Across from the zócalo, in a **17th-century Franciscan monastery**, is the historical **museum** of Queretaro. Queretaro's involvement in the Independence movement, its fame as the battleground against the French where the forces of Benito Juarez defeated and executed the Emperor Maximilian, and its glory for being the seat of a congress in 1917 when Mexico's constitution was drafted are documented in this museum by photographs and memorabilia. There are a few pre-Columbian pieces exhibited along with colonial paintings—including a Juan Correa altarpiece.

Plaza de la Independencia

Calle 5 de Mayo and Pasteur; also called the Plaza de Armas. • Just to the east of the zócalo, you come to this lovely square along pedestrian streets lined with multicolored homes and shops. Its intimate park is surrounded by particularly harmonious **18th-century mansions.** On one side is the recently renovated **Palacio Municipal**, formerly known as the **Casa de la Corregidora**. La Corregidora (Josefa Ortiz de Dominguez) was the wife of a town alderman in 1810 when she warned Allende, Hidalgo, and other Independence leaders that their conspiracy to gain independence from Spain had been discovered. This news, sent from her home, which is now the Municipal Palace, precipitated Hidalgo's proclamation of independence a few days later on September 16.

Plaza de la Cruz and Aqueduct

East of the Plaza de la Independencia, Calle Carranza merges with Avenida Independencia after four blocks where you arrive at the plaza of the **Templo de la Cruz** ("cross") • This church and its cross mark the spot where the Spaniards, in 1531, conducted their first mass in this area after defeating Chichimeca Indians in hand-to-hand combat. Foreigners seem to have an affinity for this spot, because Emperor Maximilian and his troops located their barracks here during their battles against Juarez. Continuing a few blocks on Independencia, you can get a **view** of the huge 18th-century aqueduct that still supplies Queretaro with most of its drinking water.

Cerro de las Campanas (Hill of the Bells)

Situated on the western outskirts of town • This hill is famous as the location of Emperor Maximilian's execution in 1867. The huge statue of his victorious opponent, Benito Juarez, is balanced politically by the presence of a chapel dedicated to Maximilian and paid for by the Hapsburgs of Austria.

WHERE TO STAY

There are several comfortable hotels in Queretaro, but only El Meson (below) offers first-class accommodations right in the historic center. If your preference is for colonial ambience and the Meson is full, you might want to plan your visit to Queretaro to allow time to get to San Miguel de Allende (an hour away) or Guanajuato (two hours away) for the night.

For reservations, write Queretaro, Qto. 76000, or call ☎ area code 42.

El Meson de Santa Rosa   √★★★

Pasteur Sur 17, Plaza de la Independencia; ☎ *14-57-81; $85-105* •
Located in an 18th-century mansion on one of Queretaro's loveliest plazas, the inn offers 21 handsome suites (some duplexes; some

smaller junior size), each uniquely decorated and many with fireplaces and marble baths. The suites surround sienna orange courtyards decorated with fountains, tiles, and stencil-designed walls. Pool. Bar with music. Restaurant. Valet parking. The only car approach to the hotel is via Calle 5 de Mayo.

Mirabel   √★★

Constituyentes Ote. 2; ☎ *14-35-35; $40-50* • Just across from the Alameda and within easy walking distance of the zócalo, this modern and clean hotel provides more sophisticated lodgings than its price might indicate. Decorated in modish earth colors, its 170 a/c rooms include carpeting, drapes, and separate dressing rooms. Price varies with size of room. Restaurant, bar, and parking.

WHERE TO EAT

There is no lack of tiny spots serving up snacks and regional specialties. **El Chiquilin** (*Corregidora Sur 47)* is bare, even grungy, but its moist carnitas, or roasted pork, and delicious *pozole* (hominy soup) are worth the discomforts and affordable on any budget. Starting at 7 p.m., you can order these specialties along with tacos and tostadas, but in the afternoon only *carnitas* are sold (by the kilo). While evening opens countless *torta*, or Mexican sandwich, joints (try **Loncheria Willy's** *Jardin Obregon at Juarez;* till 9:30 p.m.), there are too few international restaurants in the central area. The restaurant at the **Meson de Santa Rosa** somewhat rectifies this situation with the quiet elegance and stenciled walls of its dining room, or its patio tables next to a fountain. You can choose among some Mexican specialties along with onion soup gratinee and beef stroganoff. (*Open 7:30-11 a.m. and 1-10 p.m.; Sundays till 5 p.m.; reserve at* ☎ *4-57-81; moderate.*) For a bit of both the regional and international, go to the **Fonda del Refugio** (*Jardin Corregidora 26; Open 1-10 p.m.; moderate)* with its great location. On a sunny day, you can sit under its sidewalk awning and enjoy either traditional Mexican dishes (such as *queso fundido*) or international fare (like oysters Rockefeller). Another pleasant choice is an outdoor table on the Plaza de la Independencia at the **Cafe 1810** (*Open 9:30 a.m.-9 p.m.*). Although the continental dishes can be pricey, the comida corrida is inexpensive, and a lighter meal of quiche and soup or even just a nicoise salad or dessert is possible.

SHOPPING

The best area to stroll and browse through shops is in the pedestrian section of the **Plaza de la Independencia**. Right on the south side of the plaza is the government-sponsored regional crafts complex, **Casa Queretana**. Across the way is the best crafts shop in town, **Alexandra** *(next to the Meson de Santa Rosa).* Within a half block are a number of art galleries and a funky no-name shop full of old dolls and memorabilia *(at Pasteur Norte 8).* Near Santa Clara, you sometimes can find special exhibits of crafts at the **Casa de la Marquesa** *(Maderos 41).*

GETTING TO AND FROM QUERETARO

AIR

No commercial flights.

BUS

Tres Estrellas de Oro, Omnibus de Mexico, and the more second-class but more frequent service of Flecha Amarilla leave Mexico City from the Terminal Norte and provide service to the towns of this region, including Queretaro.

CAR

MEX 57D, a rapid toll road from **Mexico City**, connects with Queretaro after 225 km (140 m) in about 2-1/2 hours depending on traffic in Mexico City. To get to MEX 57D, take the Reforma through Chapultepec to the Petroleo circle, then turn onto Periferico Norte.

MEX 57 turns north toward San Luis Potosi at Queretaro and takes you to the turnoff for **San Miguel de Allende** after 29 km (18 m). Another 35 km (22 m) on a country road takes you to San Miguel.

MEX 45D, a toll road, arrives in Celaya after 47 km (29 m) then continues its rapid path to Salamanca and Irapuato before reaching the Guanajuato exit (see below "On the Road" after San Luis Potosi). Total distance to Guanajuato: about 120 km (74 m).

The most pleasant route to Morelia is not via MEX 45D, but rather along the country roads passing through Huimilpan, Amealco, Acambaro, and Zinapecuaro, before entering Morelia. Total distance: 210 km, 130 m, or 3-1/2 hours.

TRAIN

Star Service daily on the renovated El Constitutionalista connects with Mexico City (four hours) and San Miguel de Allende (1-1/2 hours).

DIRECTORY

Buses • Near center, across from Alameda on Constituyentes.

Car Rentals • *National* (☎ 16-52-40) and others.

Post Office • Arteaga between Juarez and Allende.

Railway Station • Northwest of the zócalo on Av. Cuauhtemoc.

Tourist Office • 5 de Mayo #61 near Plaza de la Independencia. Open 9 a.m.-2 p.m. and 5-8 p.m. Monday-Friday; 10 a.m.-1 p.m. weekends (☎ 14-16-30).

Tours • Check status of free city tours at Tourist Office.

GUANAJUATO

Guanajuato (gwah-nah-WAH-toh) captivates you first with baroque theaters and mansions, then by even more baroque Churrigueresque churches, and finally immerses you in fine colonial architecture. It entices you into its labyrinth of alleys meandering up and down hillsides, opening into the most charming plazas, and narrowing to near nonexistence in the Alley of the Kiss. It delights you with its red, yellow, and pastel facades adorned with flower boxes, and with the quiet shade of its pocket parks. Like a Spanish maiden in her black lace mantilla, Guanajuato is compellingly, poetically beautiful, yet somehow aloof.

Guanajuato, unlike its Silver City sister Taxco and its 18th-century neighbor San Miguel, seems distant from its tourism. More famous colonial heritage towns of Taxco and San Miguel focus on their arts and crafts and provide their American communities with the amenities of the good life. Guanajuato is more intellectual, proud of its university, and so conservative as to still perform Cervantes' plays in its public squares. It remains thoroughly and delightfully Mexican, preoccupied with its leadership as the capital of the state of Guanajuato, proud of its history as the wealthiest silver-mining city in colonial times and distinguished battleground of Mexican Independence. Only in the most recent decade has Guanajuato responded to tourism, opening hotels of international caliber and promoting the International Cervantes Festival. Nevertheless, it remains somewhat aloof, a trait that can be frustrating when you seek a satisfying restaurant. Guanajuato repays this slight by offering a real face of Mexico with all its allure.

KEY TO GUANAJUATO

Sights • Romantic, elegant colonial town whose churches, plazas, and narrow streets make it among the most beautiful of Mexico's historically preserved towns.

Excursions • Suburban Valenciana church and silver mine offer panoramic views and one of Mexico's finest ultrabaroque churches.

Fiestas • The International Cervantes Festival takes place for about three weeks in the fall. Numerous religious festivals.

Shopping • Limited but fine Talavera ceramics available.

Where to Stay • Some handsome and reasonably priced hotels.

Where to Eat • Limited, but a few attractive restaurants have opened.

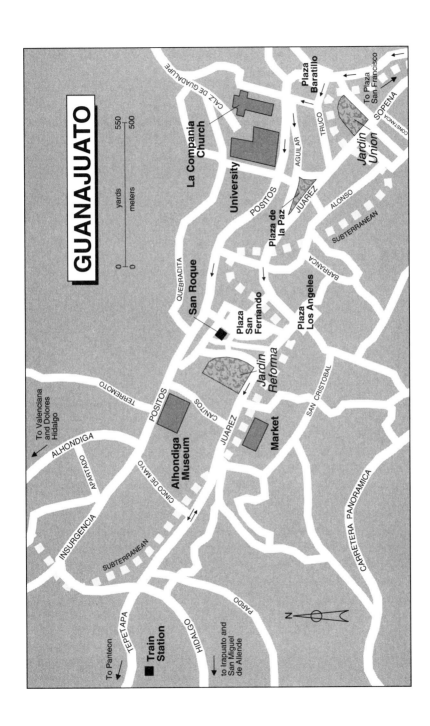

Entertainment • A few bars offer music and dancing; musicians stroll around Jardin Union cafes in season.

Getting to and from Guanajuato • The major thoroughfare going south is the Subterraneo, or underground tunnel; going north is the above ground Av. Juarez. Traffic barred from many areas, including the Jardin Union and Calle Sopena. Walking is the best way to see most of this town, so park your car. Taxis and buses ("Presa-Estacion" runs through town) are available, but remember that to head south you must go into the Subterraneo. No car rentals, but tour agencies operate in town.

Practical Tips • Excellent, warmer than springlike weather year-round. Thick-soled shoes are needed on the cobblestone streets. Shops close 2-4 or 5 p.m. and reopen in the evening.

WHAT TO SEE AND DO

Guanajuato is a walking town, or as its residents say, an alley-walking town. Most streets have no car traffic at all, although congested Juarez and Positos, which run the length of town to the north of Plaza de la Paz, enable you to rest in an occasional taxi or bus. Southbound traffic is diverted under the town through the striking **Subterraneo**, a sight in itself, constructed of monolithic stones and powerful arches where a river once flowed. The following description of Guanajuato's sights walks you through the major plazas and monuments, but if you have time you will enjoy wandering off this route to follow tiny streets with surprising vistas and quaint houses, all more romantic in the soft light of evening. And even more romantic when accompanied with serenades provided by one tour agency's *callejoneada*, or alley walking tour.

Jardin Union and Teatro Juarez

Calle Juarez • There are so many plazas in this town, we find it hard to say which is the zócalo, but the elegant **Jardin Union**, *a shaded and intimate park with handsome turn-of-the-century light posts and several outdoor cafes, is the best candidate.* The 18th-century Churrigueresque **Church of San Diego** and the sumptuous **Teatro Juarez** face this park along Calle Juarez. Teatro Juarez was inaugurated by dictator Porfirio Diaz in 1903 with a performance of the opera Aida. The low price of admission to this theater lets you see the opulence characteristic of this epoch, as every surface vibrates with gilded and brightly painted Moorish panel designs. *Open 9:15 a.m.-1:45 p.m. and 5-7:45 p.m. Tues. to Sun.*

Museo Iconografica del Quijote

Calle Sopena at Plaza San Francisco; Tues.-Sat. 10 a.m.-6 p.m., Sun. till 2:30 p.m.; free • Just two blocks from the Jardin Union is this delightful **museum** filled with *art inspired by Cervantes' masterpiece, Don Quixote.* The paintings and prints include works by some of Mexico's finest

artists (**P. Coronal** and **Posada** among them) as well as more renowned
international ones (like **Salvador Dali**).

Plazuela del Baratillo

*Walking through the Jardin Union away from Juarez, the street narrows
and meanders off to the left to this small plaza, also called Plaza Manuel
Gonzalez* • The center of this pleasant spot is graced by a **fountain**
donated to Guanajuato by the Emperor Maximilian. Continue past
the fountain and bear left to a seeming dead end that is actually the
side of the Church of La Compania.

Church of La Compania

Calle Positos • The soft rose-colored stone **facade** of this **18th-century
church** is carved in the exuberant Mexican ultrabaroque style of Churrigueresque. Even its **wooden doors** are finely detailed with carvings of
heads created from shell and foliage motifs. The interior of this most
monumental church contains two **paintings by Miguel Cabrera**, and
its **neoclassic dome** is a town landmark. Built by the Jesuits before
their expulsion from all of Spain, this church was part of a convent and
college complex next door. The well-proportioned **patio** of the convent, along with its good view of the dome, can be seen in what is now
a preparatory school. The college has evolved into the present state
university.

University of Guanajuato

Calle Positos • The rather fantastic, Moorish **facade** of this state university blends so well with the architecture of Guanajuato that it dis-
appoints you to learn it was constructed as recently as the middle of
this century. *Much like a stage set, little of architectural interest waits
behind its walls.* University art exhibits can be seen in **El Atrio**, under
La Compania on Positos.

Museo del Pueblo

*Calle Positos 7; Tues.-Sat. 10 a.m.-2 p.m.; 4-7 p.m.; Sun. 10 a.m.-2:30
p.m.; fee.* • Just a few steps further along from the University, is this
attractive **museum of art** that includes paintings from the 18th
through 20th century. **Colonial period religious art** is best represented.

Museo de Diego Rivera

*Calle Positos 47; Tues.-Sat. 10 a.m.-1:30 p.m., 4-6:30 p.m.; Sun. 10
a.m.-2:30 p.m.; fee.* • This is more than simply *the house where Mexico's
famous mural artist was born* around the turn of the century. While the
ground floor has been furnished to the period, the next two floors are
hung with some fine Riveras—Cubist works from his years in Paris
(including the exceptional *Sailor at Lunch*, 1914); drawings, and portraits from the thirties. The top-floor exhibits are dedicated to local
artists. *From here you can continue on Positos to the Alhondiga or retrace
your steps a block and turn right for the Plaza de la Paz.*

Plaza de la Paz

Calle Juarez • From the University, turn left down an unmarked street just beyond the Museo del Pueblo. At the end of this street you will see the orange **facade** of the **Basilica of Our Lady of Guanajuato**, on the Plaza de la Paz. Inside this baroque basilica, a venerated and bejewelled **wooden statue** of the town's saint is displayed on a pedestal of solid silver. Surrounded by splendid private residences, *this plaza demonstrates the wealth received by some of Guanajuato's citizens from its silver mines.* The residence at Juarez 73 belonged to the **Count del Rul and Valenciana**, owner of the richest Guanajuato silver mine of Valenciana. This **neoclassic residence**, with its sculpted, overhanging cornice, was built by the famous architect Eduardo Tresguerras around the end of the 18th century. Next door, at Juarez 77, is the former **Palace of the Governor**, rebuilt in French neoclassic style around 1900. Across the street at **Juarez 62** are strong, studded wooden doors with lion's head door knockers belonging to the 18th-century residence of the Counts of Perez Galvez.

Plazuela de los Angeles

Calle Juarez • You can continue down Juarez to this square or, if you have a good sense of direction, turn left down the steps of Calle Estrella and right onto Alonso and alley-walk your way to this broad and spacious **square** surrounded by yellow and orange **facades**. In the middle of the shops in this plaza, a tiny street, Callejon del Patrocinio, leads a few steps later to the picturesque **Callejon del Beso** (Alley of the Kiss) on the left, *a street so narrow two could kiss from buildings on either side.*

Plazuela San Fernando

Walking down Juarez just past the previous square, turn right off the street into the quiet and relaxing square of San Fernando • A few small cafes, shade trees, and benches provide an oasis from the traffic of Juarez.

Plazuela San Roque

Without returning to Juarez, follow one of the small cobblestone streets to the left of San Fernando. • The restrained facade and Moorish doors of the 18th-century **Church of San Roque** faces the plaza made famous over the years by the outdoor performances of Cervantes *Entremeses*—short pieces once performed between the acts of longer plays. The platform in this square is only part of the stage, as the balconies of surrounding buildings are used as well. These *Entremeses* are still performed as part of the grander International Cervantes Festival (see "Fiestas").

Jardin de la Reforma

To the left of San Roque, steps lead down to yet another tranquil and shaded park • You might want to sit here before reentering the bustle of Juarez.

Market

Calle Juarez • Looking much like a turn-of-the-century experiment in **caste-iron architecture**, this large **indoor market** filled with hordes of people and produce is surprisingly clean and quiet. Its balcony offers for sale a variety of regional crafts and curios, but *the most interesting local curio can be found just inside the main entrance.* There you will find nut-flavored candies shaped into mummies gaily playing trumpets and guitars—typical of Guanajuato and its famous mummies, typical of this region famous for **candy**, and so very Mexican in its ghoulish humor.

Alhondiga de Granaditas Museum

Open Tues.-Sat., 10 a.m.-2 p.m. and 4-6 p.m., and Sun., 10 a.m.-3:30 p.m. Fee. • Follow the street perpendicular to Juarez directly in front of the market and you will come to this **museum** on Calle Positos. Once a granary, then a fortress during the Independence Movement, and later a prison, this building now houses an attractive series of **exhibits on local history**, crafts, including 19th-century Talavera ware, and even archaeological artifacts. Before entering, *notice the hooks on the corners of this building from which Spanish Royalists hung the decapitated heads of the great leaders of Independence—Hidalgo, Allende, Aldama, and Jimenez.* So insistent were these Spaniards on conveying the dangers of revolution to the populace, they displayed these heads for ten years until Mexico, despite such threats, won its independence from Spain. These themes repeat in **Jose Chavez Morado's murals** found in the main (1955) and south (1966) stairwells.

NEARBY SIGHTS

Valenciana Church and Mine

4 km (2-1/2 m) along Dolores Hidalgo Road • Buses marked "Valenciana" take you to the center of this former **mining village** or you can make this very **scenic trip** in a cab.

The great silver mine of Valenciana plunged almost 2,000 feet into the earth during its peak years, making it the deepest mine in the 18th-century world. Its riches contributed not only to Mexico's status as the greatest silver producer in the world but also to the personal wealth of its owner, **Don Antonio Obregon y Alconcer**, who became the first Count of Valenciana. In thanks to God for his good fortune, Don Antonio constructed one of the great churches of Mexico, the **Templo de San Cayetano,** dedicated in 1788. In the lovely, rose-colored **plaza** of the former mining village nestled in the massive mountains above Guanajuato, *this great work of Churrigueresque architecture vibrates with profuse sculpture in stone and wood and with exuberant gilded altarpieces.* Its intricate inlaid pulpit is one of the finest in Mexico. No wonder the curate in Guanajuato became jealous of this "chapel" and prevented the completion of its second church tower.

Guanajuato has started to rework some of its silver mines, but the Valenciana mine, once the richest in Mexico, is closed. A visit to that mine, some distance from the church, lets you see its former administrative buildings and peek down its currently inundated shaft called "the mouth of hell."

Ex-Hacienda San Gabriel de la Barrera

3 km (2 m) from market, just off Irapuato Road.; Open 9 a.m.-dusk; fee. • There have been many owners since the founding of this **hacienda** in the 17th century, but it is the most recent one (circa 1940), who transformed the plazas where silver was processed during the 18th century into magnificent **formal gardens**. Today you visit these romantic gardens set amid ancient walls, as well as some elegantly furnished rooms in the main house, including an unbelievably ornate **family chapel**.

El Pipila Monument

To get a bird's-eye **view** of Guanajuato, either walk or take a cab to this enormous **sculpture** above town. To walk, follow Calle Sopena from the Jardin Union and take the first right. *This hefty uphill walk may be unappealing to you after touring town, so you might drive or take a cab* out toward the Irapuato road, turning left at the Pemex station and climbing for 2 km to the monument. El Pipila was the young hero of the Independence Movement who enabled Hidalgo's forces to capture the Spanish Royalists hiding in the Alhondiga when he crawled to the building and set it on fire.

Museo de Panteon

1 km (.6 m) north of tourist office—turn left at sign Presa-Estacion; *Open daily 9 a.m.-6 p.m.; fee.* • Buses along Juarez will take you within walking distance of this **display of mummies** (momias in Spanish). You have to pay a small admission to see this macabre collection of cadavers that have been preserved through some element in the soil. They are lined up for your appreciation in a special chamber near the parking lot of the town's cemetery.

SHOPPING

Although Guanajuato is not a shopper's haven, it has recently witnessed a revival of the majolica ceramic techniques introduced into the region by the Spanish. This high-glazed pottery, also called **Talavera**, emphasizes complex, greenish-hued designs rather than the blue-on-white found in the more famous Puebla ware. A master of this style is **Capelo**, whose elegant work can be bought at **Ceramica Capelo** *(Carcamanes 57)*, his home and workshop found up the hill behind **La Compania** *(follow Calle San Jose from post office; in a block, bear left)*. More affordable are the simpler yet cheerful mugs, creamers, and plates found at **Ceramica de Gorky** *(Calle Pastitas near Parque Embajadores; take taxi or call 2-43-06 for directions)*, the workshop of Gorky Gonzalez. Easier to find is **Artesanias DIF** *(off Jardin*

Union, behind Teatro Juarez), where there is a decent selection of Talavera as well as the tin-and-brass mirrors and other crafts of this region.

FIESTAS

The **International Cervantes Festival** occurs for about three weeks in October and November. The cultural program varies from year to year, but in addition to the Cervantes *Entremeses* acted in Plazuela San Roque, previous years have included performances by Rudolph Nureyev, the Comedie Francaise, National Theatre of England, Ballet of Stuttgart, Chinese Acrobatic Troupe, and symphony orchestras from all over the world. Art exhibits and film retrospectives fill out a schedule already bursting. *Plan your trip at least six months in advance.* For information, write: Festival Internacional Cervantino, Emerson 304, 9th piso, Mexico D.F. 11570, Mexico.

Guanajuato's size and beauty make any fiesta pleasurable. Three are celebrated for the **Virgin of Guanajuato**: on May 31 and the nine preceding days; on August 9; and on the third Sunday of November. All three celebrations are accompanied by dances, processions, and fireworks. The **last Friday in Lent** is the **Fiesta de las Flores** (flowers) in the Jardin Union from 7 a.m. to midday, and Christ's fall from the cross are reenacted on **Good Friday** at La Compania. **Independence Eve** is celebrated joyously at the Alhondiga on September 15.

WHERE TO STAY

Many attractive and recommendable hotels are available, most of them situated in renovated colonial buildings. Many hotels are opening on the outskirts of town where the building restrictions of this historically preserved town don't hinder expansion. Fortunately, the bus to Valenciana runs past many of these hotels, but they are most convenient for those with cars. During the International Cervantes Festival, rooms are completely booked up months in advance. Some people are forced to stay as far away as San Miguel in order to attend the performances. Reservations for this festival not only are essential, but should be made at least six months in advance (address correspondence to Guanajuato, Gto.) To call, use area code 473.

EXPENSIVE

Real de Minas   ★★★
Nejayote 17; ☎ *2-14-60; $80* • At the edge of town before the Irapuato highway begins, this neocolonial-style, modern, comfortable hotel is a more handsome, Mexican version of Howard Johnson's. Its 175 rooms are large and well-appointed with carpeting, dark-wood furnishings, ceiling beams, and tiled baths with shower stalls. Dining room and bar. Small pool and a tennis court that could use some attention. On bus route.

MODERATE

Parador San Javier

Plaza San Javier; ☎ *2-06-26; $82* • On the edge of town, toward the road to Valenciana, spread the grounds and gardens of this converted colonial hacienda. Its 120 units are in modern wings, but antiques decorate the lobby, a former chapel has been integrated into the dining room, and the hacienda reservoir, complete with waterfall, forms part of its handsome bar. Unfortunately, a plastic breakfast room has been recently added to this colonial perfection. Size and charm of rooms vary, but some (particularly the more expensive junior suites and suites) are large, with brick-domed ceilings or even fireplaces. Meandering pool, restaurant, bar, disco. Parking.

Castillo Santa Cecilia

2.3 km toward Valenciana; ☎ *2-04-85; $100* • Although some of its walls may be from the 17th century, this "castle" is more like a turreted Sheraton Tara. Its 100 rooms include some old standard doubles, but what you want are the more deluxe rooms in the newer wings. The hotel is the favorite of many, but not us. We prefer the authenticity of the San Javier. Restaurant, bar, entertainment, even a private chapel with Sunday services. Pool. Access to golf and horseback riding. Parking. For reservations, write Apartado 44.

Ex-Hacienda San Gabriel

km 2.5 on road to Marfil; ☎ *2-39-80; $75* • A contemporary hotel, built next to the grounds of the 18th-century hacienda of the same name that is now a park. The hotel, designed with colonial architecture in mind, but utilizing light woods, is a little stark. The 70 rooms are quite large and sunny with light wood walls in the modern, well-appointed bathrooms. Good service. Restaurant and bar. Tennis and pool. Parking. A good buy, but only for those with cars. The entrance on the Marfil road is difficult to navigate or even to find, but a second entrance lies just 1/2 km off the Irapuato highway.

Posada Santa Fe

Jardin Union; ☎ *2-00-84; $80* • In the main square, on a street closed to traffic, the Posada's location couldn't be better. The flamboyant colonialstyle lobby contains not only a restaurant and bar but also an officially designated museum of the historical murals painted here by local artist Manuel Leal. A terrace restaurant is next to the park. The 40 rooms vary in size and price (the quieter interiors tend to be too small); all are old-fashioned but comfortable. Parking.

San Diego

Jardin Union 1; ☎ *2-14-99; $85* • Attractive colonial hotel with great location on main plaza. Hand-painted tiles decorate the walls; small patios add interest; and second-floor restaurant overlooks the square. Exterior rooms may be a bit noisy, but some have balconies overlooking gardens. The 60 rooms and suites are plain, but with modern baths. Restaurant, bar. Jacuzzi. Pay garage. Write Apartado 8.

INEXPENSIVE

El Carruaje

on road to Valenciana km 1; ☎ *2-21-40; $48* • Across from Hotel Castillo Santa Cecilia, this attractive and pleasant motel has about 40 well-maintained rooms decorated with bark paintings and other warm touches. Restaurant, bar, and small pool. Parking.

Hosteria del Frayle

Sopena 3; ☎ *2-01-88; $48* • Only a few steps from Jardin Union, this former silver mint has been converted into a very pleasant, small, unpretentious hotel, with authentic colonial detailing. The 38 rooms have nicely tiled baths; some interior ones are handsome, but too small; the exterior ones are larger. Helpful service. Restaurant, bar. Pay garage.

BUDGET

El Socavon   √★

Alhondiga 41 A; ☎ *2-48-85; $40* • Located a few blocks from the Alhondiga, the delightful El Socavon ("mineshaft") may not be as central as hotels in the Jardin Union area, but this well-maintained hotel provides recommendable rooms in the budget category. Its enthusiastic owner, Jose Luis Bustamante, designed the lobby, restaurant, and bar to have the heavy stone walls and intimate ambience of a silver mine. The rooms on the upper floors surround open patios and are light, airy, and very pleasant. Baths show Sr. Bustamante's attentiveness to details with handsome copper sinks. An exceptional buy in this category.

Casa Kloster

Calle de Alonso 32; ☎ *2-00-88; $27* • This old but very charming pension won't be quite the same without Sr. Perez, but his widow is trying to maintain the homey ambience that has so long attracted families and student groups on a budget. Seventeen basic, utilitarian rooms without private bath around a courtyard filled with birds and plants. Popular with families and student groups on a tight budget who enjoy the homey atmosphere.

WHERE TO EAT

For years tourists have complained about the small number of restaurant options outside hotel dining rooms. While the situation is still not ideal, an increasing number of attractive independent restaurants open each year. Price categories are explained in the "Introduction."

For ambience, the **sidewalk cafes at the Jardin Union** can't be beat for a relaxing drink or snack. Where else could you sit in such perfect position for people-watching or listening to the Sunday midday band concert?

Among these cafes, the **Posada Santa Fe** is especially recommended for its traditional food. On weekends, women pat out fresh tortillas and casseroles simmer with daily specials—if *tlacoyos*, or tortillas stuffed with *huitlacoche or flor de calabaza*, are available, don't pass them by. Evenings bring tasty antojitos, tamales and the like, and pozole; at breakfast there may even be prickly pear in the fruit salad. Moderate.

Two other restaurants offer interesting menus and good ambience for moderate to moderately expensive prices. **Tasca de los Santos** *(Plaza de las Paz 28)*, a handsome Spanish tavern, has a limited menu but flavorful paella, a hearty *fabada*, or bean stew, and good *entremeses* and *queso fundido* with Spanish chorizo. Open 8 a.m. to midnight every day, this restaurant also offers an inexpensively priced breakfast and a moderately priced comida corrida. The **Venta Vieja de San Javier** *(Plaza San Javier 1, across from the Parador San Javier)*, has its dining room in this handsomely restored hacienda with beamed ceilings and gray stone arches. The menu offers some very traditional Mexican dishes, such as the densely delicious mushroom flavor of their *crepas huitlacoche*, as well as continental dishes like the very good marinated mushroom appetizer (champignones ajillo). This restaurant is also a fine spot for an evening *merienda* of tamales, or desert and hot chocolate. Open 2 p.m.-midnight except Sundays.

Most of Guanajuato's less expensive restaurants are so starkly plain they remind you that eating is a necessity if not always a pleasure. Fortunately, there are some exceptions. **Casa Valadez** *(Jardin Union and Sopena)*, with its spacious paneled rooms, is one of them. Here you can enjoy one of the best breakfast buys in town or try the comida corrida that is more imaginative in its offerings than most. In the evening the middle class gathers here to dine or just to enjoy a coffee or pastry (the dark chocolate cake is good). Throughout the day this is a pleasant spot. The menu is extensive with Mexican (the *caldo Tlalpeno* is full of vegetables and spicy as it should be) and continental specialties (even salads.) Inexpensive to moderate.

For American food, the Plazuela San Fernando is the place to go for the most pleasant branch of **Pizza Piazza**, where you can enjoy a decent pizza at outdoor tables on the square *(noon to 11 p.m.; inexpensive)*. **Bing's**, *down from the Basilica, Plaza de la Paz*, for ice cream. **El Cubilete**, *Juarez 188*, for Mexican candied fruit and nuts, including peanut brittle.

ENTERTAINMENT

There are more cultural events than you can possibly attend during the International Cervantes Festival, yet even during the rest of the year you might check the schedule of the elegant Teatro Juarez for performances—those of the symphony, the **Filaharmonica del Bajio,** are recommended. Midday Sundays usually bring a band concert in the Jardin Union.

Some of the hotel bars with their colonial ambience provide the best way of passing an evening. Try **El Pozo** at the San Javier hotel, with its waterfall and reservoir and entertainment nightly after 9 p.m.; or join locals for the views from the bar at the **Motel Guanajuato** (km 2.5 on road to Valencia).

GETTING TO AND FROM GUANAJUATO

AIR

No flights but the airport at Leon (50 km, 30 m north on MEX 45) is just over one-half hour away by rental car and has both Aeromexico, ☎ (471)6-62-26, and Aeromar—☎ (471)3-63-03—flights to Mexico City.

BUS

Flecha Amarilla runs the most frequent service in this region connecting Guanajuato with Morelia, San Miguel, Dolores Hidalgo, Mexico City, and San Luis Potosi, but check for the most direct bus ("directo"). For first-class service, check Omnibus de Mexico (reservations in town at Juarez 10) and, for the Pacific coast, Tres Estrellas de Oro.

CAR

San Miguel is 1-1/2 to 2 hours away, depending on the route. The faster route starts on the west edge of town (follow "Silao" signs out of center); the longer, more scenic route begins from Valenciana and continues via Dolores Hidalgo (see "On the Road" at end of chapter).

Guanajuato can be reached from **Mexico City** via Queretaro (MEX 57D) and Celaya (MEX 45D), and then a turn at a well-marked exit above Irapuato. Total distance: 345 km (214 m): total time: four hours.

Morelia lies 180 km (112 m) and 3 hours south of Guanajuato on MEX 43. But to get to MEX 43, you will want to be careful to avoid going through the congested cities of Irapuato and Salamanca by taking the desviacion, or bypass road. To do this, take the Irapuato road from Guanajuato, then follow signs for MEX 45 libre (not MEX 45 D cuota) towards Queretaro and Irapuato. Before Irapuato, follow this same road in the direction of Salamanca. Outside Salamanca you'll pick up the first signs for MEX 43 and Morelia. For a description of the rest of the route check "On the Road" in the Morelia chapter.

From nearby Irapuato, MEX 110 and then MEX 90 connect with **Guadalajara** after 257 km (159 m). Total time: four hours.

TRAIN

The rail service to Guanajuato is less practical than usual, even for Mexico, as it is not on the direct rail line from Mexico City but is connected to that line by a subsidiary service from Queretaro (3-1/2 hours). Although there is Star Service on this line, connections to Mexico City could easily be missed.

DIRECTORY

Airlines • No commercial airlines. Nearest airport is in Leon.

Buses • Central Camionera, 7 km, 4 m south with taxi and bus connections to center.

Car Rentals • None.

Groceries • Super (Juarez 51 at Plaza de los Angeles) and the market.

Parking • Pay lots off the Subterraneo, north of Calle Alhondiga, and behind Hotel San Diego.

Post Office • Ayuntamiento 25, near La Compania.

Railroad Station • Calzada del Panteon.

Taxis • Stationed throughout town.

Telegraph • Sopena 1.

Tour Agencies • Transportes Turisticos de Guanajuato, under basilica on Plaza de la Paz offers city tours including Valenciana, El Pipila, and the Panteon. Viajes Viva Mexico, Juarez 210, offers evening walks accompanied by musicians.

Tourist Office • Juarez and 5 de Mayo (☎ 2-15-74). Open Monday-Friday 10 a.m.-2:30 p.m., and 5-8:00 p.m.; and 10 a.m.-2:00 p.m. on Saturday and Sunday.

ZACATECAS

Wedged into a narrow gorge formed by surrounding mountains, the streets and houses of Zacatecas nestle tightly together as they spill over the surrounding slopes. Zacatecas has been undergoing a burst of construction of new homes and commercial buildings, but its **colonial center**, with plazas and sudden dead ends or archways, has been preserved and refurbished, making for fine **strolls** through tiny lanes where the light might draw your eye to a roof line carving of a lion or a handsome pinkish stone pediment. *Such walks are what make Zacatecas special,* and they are made easy by the size of the town (it's only about six blocks from the aqueduct down the main street of Hidalgo to the cathedral, and only a few more blocks to the ruins of San Francisco). You can easily orient yourself by marking the main intersection of Hidalgo and Juarez before wandering through the alleyways above Hidalgo and below it to the other main street of Aldama. Or if you prefer skywalks, take the **teleferico** (cable car) ride between the two hills flanking town.

KEY TO ZACATECAS

Sights • This modern town with a colonial heart offers one of Mexico's most ultrabaroque churches and an unusual skyride in cable cars over the city.

Excursion • The ancient fortified site of La Quemada is worth a stop if you are in the area.

Shopping • Semiprecious stones from nearby mines, wood carvings, and leather charro goods.

Where to Stay • Good selection.

Where to Eat • Limited.

Entertainment • Limited.

Getting to and from Zacatecas • A few of the sights are actually outside the center of town, so you will have to rely on buses, tours, and cabs if you don't bring your own car. In town, it's best to park your car and walk.

Practical Tips • Plan a stop if you are driving to Mexico from the States, otherwise Zacatecas is too much out of the way. More north than Mexico City and higher in altitude, Zacatecas can be much cooler in the winter. Snow is rare, but not unheard of.

WHAT TO SEE AND DO

Plaza Civil

Avenida Hidalgo • The town's zócalo is flanked by a number of interesting **18th-century colonial buildings** like the **Palacio Municipal**, but its most famous structure is the **cathedral**, constructed between 1718-1752. No other church in Mexico can match the intricacy and exuberance of its **facade**. Rich and elaborate foliate designs cover every speck of space not covered by life-size sculptures. Its ocher stone seems to ripple in the sun, creating an even richer, pinkish texture in the late afternoon. Art historians, overwhelmed by its sophisticated technique as much as its profusion of design, have struggled to name its style. Others have created legends to explain it, saying that a sculptor sentenced to death was given a reprieve to finish this church. He was clever enough to make so much work for himself, he lived to a natural death. Elizabeth Wilder Weismann made the best and simplest statement: "If anything can be called Mexican—it is the cathedral of Zacatecas."

Museo Pedro Coronol

Calle del Correo. Open 10 a.m. - 2 p.m. and 4-7 p.m.; closed Thurs.; Small admission fee. • Leaving the cathedral behind you , you come to Calle del Correo and, just to the right the **Santo Domingo Church** and plaza. Here in the former Jesuit college and convento of Santo Domingo is Zacatecas' impressive **museum of fine arts** with rooms devoted to pre-Columbian as well as African masks, Chinese bronzes and Japanese woodblock prints as well as Goya prints, and excellent 20th-century European and American prints. Even more amazing than the sophistication of the museum for so small a town is the fact that it was all part of the private collection of the artist **Pedro Coronel**.

San Francisco Ruins

Plaza San Francisco. 10 a.m.-8 p.m. • A pleasant walk north of the Plaza Civil on Hidalgo takes you to the Conquistador Fountain and then (following Abasalo) to the garden and ruins of this majestic colonial church. The ex-convent has been renovated for the **Museo Rafael Coronel** (10 a.m.-2 p.m., 4-7 p.m., Sun. till 5 p.m., closed Tues.; small fee) with its outstanding exhibit of **Mexican masks** from the collection of Pedro's brother.

Cerro La Bufa

Tues.-Sun., noon-7:30 p.m.; admission fee; reached from teleferico by elevator. • La Bufa is the highest peak around Zacatecas so it really is not too near the sights around the plaza civil, but is from this part of town that you can decide to climb up to either **La Bufa** or the **Cerro do Grillo** for the **teleferico** over town. (Driving to either is possible, too: the road to La bufa is out Calle guerrero, the one to Grillo is reached of MEX 54 near the Aristos Hotel. Minibuses run to La Bufa from the stop on Tacuba near the cathedral; service is especially frequent on

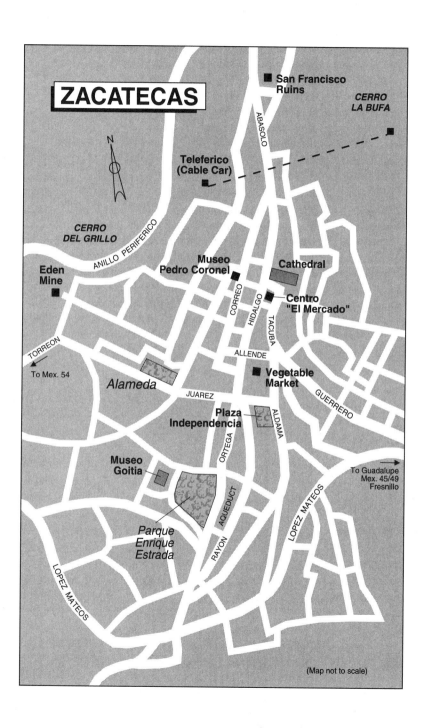

ZACATECAS

San Francisco Ruins

CERRO LA BUFA

ABASOLO

Teleferico (Cable Car)

CERRO DEL GRILLO

ANILLO PERIFERICO

Eden Mine

Museo Pedro Coronel

Cathedral

CORREO

HIDALGO

TACUBA

Centro "El Mercado"

TORREON

To Mex. 54

ALLENDE

Alameda

JUAREZ

Vegetable Market

GUERRERO

Plaza Independencia

ALDAMA

ORTEGA

Museo Goitia

To Guadalupe
Mex. 45/49
Fresnillo

AQUEDUCT

LOPEZ MATEOS

Parque Enrique Estrada

RAYON

LOPEZ MATEOS

(Map not to scale)

Sundays). Before the cable cars carried you 300 yards above the city, people still visited the summit of La Bufa for the spectacular **views** it provided, and to pay homage to the Virgin with the miraculous healing powers in the 18th-century **Chapel of the Virgin of Los Remedios**. In addition, there is now a small history **museum** *(closed Mon.; small fee)* with *some interesting photographs of the Mexican revolution.* The **Cerro del Grillo** boasts its won attraction with the **Eden Mine**, one of the 1,000 silver mines surrounding Zacatecas and also among the two-thirds that are no longer worked for ore. Instead it is set up to show tourists the inside of a mine and the difficulties of those who once worked there. A small train takes you through tunnels for a brief distance and guides walk you to other parts.

Museo de Francisco Goitia

Av. Gen. Enrique Estrada 102, Open Tues.-Sun., 9 a.m.-2p.m. and 4-6 p.m.; small fee • Following hidalgo south of the Plaza Civil (perhaps taking a detour down the street with Casa Jaquez, then turning right through the byways of the **vegetable market**) and continuing on Av. Ortega, you arrive at the **Parque Enrique Estrada** and the aqueduct. Through the park is the **mansion** of a former governor that now houses this museum. Here you can see works of Zacatecas-born artists who have achieved international fame—the intense charcoals of **Francisco Goitia**, the fine paintings of **Pedro Coronel** and his brother, **Rafael**, and the sculptures of **Jose Kuri Brena**. The museum also houses temporary exhibits.

Church and Convent of Guadalupe

On MEX 45/49 6 km (4 m) east Open Tues.,-Sun. 10 a.m.-4:30 p.m. by tour; fee • In the small town of Guadalupe is this elaborate **church** and convent, founded in 1707 for the training of missionaries sent to the Spanish colonies in what is now the U. S. Southwest. Its museum has an abundance of **religious paintings** depicting suffering and martyrdoms. Its gilded neoclassical **Capilla de Napoles** testifies to the wealth silver brought, and still brings, to this area. Minibuses run from fountain on Aldama to neighboring Gualalupe.

BRIEF EXCURSION

La Quemada

55 km (34 m) south on MEX 54 then left at pyramid sign for 2 km Open daily, 10 a.m.-4:30 p.m. Small admission fee. • For those used to the more elaborate sites of ancient Mexico, La Quemada (A.D. 400-1300), also called **Chicomoztoc**, may be disappointing. It represents an extremely northern and peripheral expression of Mesoamerican civilization. North of La Quemada, there were only the less developed cultures of Chichimeca. As a frontier site, La Quemada and smaller surrounding sites were probably organized to defend the northern border of ancient Mexico. Its fortified situation along the top of cliffs forming the pass to the Malpaso-Jerez Valley would have enabled La Quemada to block Chichimeca from entering this open valley, which led only too easily to ancient Mexico's major population centers. However, during its greatest period (A.D. 600-800) this site may have been a way station on the trade route known to exist between central Mexico and the U.S. Southwest. This site was burned in the distant past, and so few artifacts have been unearthed here by archaeologists that the question remains: Who were La Quemada's collaborators to the south? The Teotihuacanos? No one knows. Nor is there any evidence for the imaginative claim that La Quemada is the legendary ancestral site of the Aztecs, the Chicomoztoc (place of the seven caves).

The fortress did not support much of a residential population, but it was connected to smaller sites by raised and paved causeways like those found in Yucatán. Thirteen such causeways have been discovered, although few can be seen today. What can be seen are the towering walls of layered stones, highly reminiscent of Chaco Canyon and other sites in the U.S. Southwest, a partially reconstructed pyramid in the Mesoamerican style, colonnades, and part of a ball court, all found at the various levels of this dramatically situated site.

SHOPPING

As you walk about town, you inevitably will enter the **Centro "El Mercado"** (between Hidalgo and Tacuba near the cathedral), originally the town market in the 19th century but now refurbished into a classy shopping mall. Here you can shop for the best of what Zacatecas has to offer. Fancy leather charro, or cowboy goods including tooled saddles and belts, can be purchased at **La Espuela de Oro** for a price; semiprecious gems and mineral stones, onyx wares, and even the local wines (Carrera and Los Pioneros) can be purchased in other mall shops.

WHERE TO STAY

For reservations, write the following hotels at Zacatecas, Zac., Mexico, or call ☎ area code 492.

RESORT EXPENSIVE

Quinta Real ★★★★
Rayon 434, near the aqueduct; ☎ *2-91-04; $180-205* • Built into the former town bull ring, this modern hotel provides not only the best accommodations, but also the most intriguing ones. All 49 units are suites, some with Jacuzzi. Attractive common areas, gardens, shops, restaurant, and bar. Parking.

MODERATE

Paraiso Radisson Zacatecas ★★★
Hidalgo 703; ☎ *2-61-83; $156* • Located across from the cathedral, this handsomely renovated colonial building couldn't be more conve-

nient. There are 116 rooms and junior suites, most opening onto quiet courtyards or a patio with fountain. Restaurant and bar. Parking. For reservations, call in the U.S., ☎ 800-333-3333.

Gallery   ★★★
Lopez Mateos and Callejon del Barro; ☎ *2-33-11, $72* • Only a few blocks from the Plaza de la Independencia, this Best Western hotel offers 130 carpeted, ample and well-maintained rooms in conjunction with restaurant, bar with entertainment, and a rooftop pool with view of town. Garage.

Aristos Zacatecas   ★★
Loma de la Soledad; ☎ *2-17-88; $80* • Overlooking the city from MEX 56, and about a 15-minute downhill walk into town, this modern hotel has 120 comfortable, if a little worn, rooms with private balconies or patios. Restaurant, bar, and decent pool. Parking.

INEXPENSIVE

Posada de la Moneda
Hidalgo 413; ☎ *2-08-81; $40* • The best of the in-town budgets, this older establishment had experienced some recent renovations so that its wooden detailings are varnished and the tiny bathrooms of its 30 rooms are tiled. Exterior rooms recommended. Restaurant, bar.

WHERE TO EAT

El Pastor
Plaza de la Independencia • This simple, but locally popular little restaurant is our favorite. It becomes jam packed at peak hours so that you often have to share a table. There are no utensils, only tortillas. There is just one item to order: chicken roasted over a wood fire until the skin is crispy, the meat juicy. You can vary your order by asking for *un cuarto* (a quarter), *un medio* (a half), or *uno entero* (a whole), and you can avoid some of the crowds by coming at off hours like 6 p.m. But whenever you visit, it probably will be for some of the best chicken you've tasted in a while. *Open lunch till 9 p.m.; budget prices.*

La Cuija
Tacuba 5 in the Centro "El Mercado" • This is an elegant restaurant, with its striking arches and alcoves, its table-prepared continental specialties, and its occasional serenata music. Although we found the food quite pricey for its quality, the sopa Tlapena was fiery and good even if the enchiladas were heavy, the steaks were tender, and the service was attentive. *Open 1:30-midnight daily; moderately expensive.*

Acropolis
Hidalgo in Center "El Mercado" • Conveniently located across from the cathedral, this is a place you find yourself returning to often for a capuccino and a moist cake of *tres leches,* or an ice-cream sundae or

grilled cheese sandwich. It's a good place to rest and snack. *Open 10:30 a.m.-10 p.m.*

PRACTICAL TIP

You might try the disco inside the Eden Mine but make sure you dress warmly. (Thursday to Sunday 10 p.m.-2 a.m.)

GETTING TO AND FROM ZACATECAS

AIR

Mexicana connects Zacatecas with Los Angeles, Tijuana, and Mexico City. The airport lies 23 km, 16 m north of town on the Fresnillo road. Taxis and combis (from the Mexicana office at Hidalgo 406) are available for the trip to and from town.

BUS

The most rapid bus route to Mexico City is via San Luis Potosi. The trip takes about 8 hours. There is also frequent service to Guadalajara and Ciudad Juarez at the U.S. border with El Paso. Local minibuses marked "C. Camionera" leave from Calle Tacuba near the cathedral and provide ample transport between the center and terminal (10 minute trip; service till 9 p.m.).

CAR

Like the ruins of La Quemada, Zacatecas is on the edge of Mexico's most interesting sights and takes a special effort to visit unless you are entering Mexico from El Paso or going to Guadalajara from Laredo. Otherwise, it is 390 km (234 m) from Queretaro via San Luis Potosi, 312 km (193 m) from Guadalajara on MEX 54, and 325 km (202 m) from Guanajuato on MEX 45.

TRAIN

Servicio estrella is available on the Division del Norte, the Mexico City (14 hours) overnight train to the border at Ciudad Juarez (22 hours from Zacatecas). Most "C. Camionera" buses stop at the station.

DIRECTORY

Airlines • Mexicana, Centro "El Mercado" at Hidalgo ☎ 406 (2-74-29).

Buses • Central Camionera, southern edge of town.

Car Rentals • At airport and first class hotels: AMMSA (☎ 2-35-76) and Budget (☎ 2-94-58).

Groceries • Casa Jaquez, Hidalgo 202.

Post Office • Allende, between Aldama and Hidalgo.

Railway Station • South end of Av. Ortega.

Taxis • Plaza de la Independencia (Juarez near Aldama) and next to cathedral.

Teleferico • Cable car service from Cerro La Bufa to Cerro del Grillo above the Eden Mine; 12:30-7:30 p.m.

Telegrafos • Hidalgo at Juarez.

Tours • Cantera Tours in Centro "El Mercado," Hidalgo near the cathedral.

Tourist Office • Hidalgo, across from cathedral. Open 9 a.m.-2 p.m., 4-8 p.m., closed Sun. (☎ 2-66-83).

SAN LUIS POTOSI

Once silver and gold mines were discovered here, San Luis Potosi quickly grew to become one of the three richest towns in 17th-century New Spain. San Luis continued to prosper during the 18th century when most of its fine churches were built, and in the 20th century the discovery of petroleum nearby assured its importance for the decades to come. *Today San Luis is a modern city encompassing a colonial center that, in contrast to the rose-hued softness of other silver cities, seems stern rather than captivating.* But this is a substantial old city to visit, its cold stone walls often melting into the brilliance of an **18th-century church** and just as often enclosing small, yet interesting **museums**. *Since the sights cluster around three main plazas that are within easy walking distance of each other, you can see historic San Luis in a matter of a few hours.*

KEY TO SAN LUIS POTOSI

Sights • Within a few hours you can enjoy the brief walks between the city's three major colonial plazas and visit the fine churches and museums surrounding them.

Shopping • Limited.

Where to Stay • Decent, low-priced hotels.

Where to Eat • A good selection of international and Mexican cuisines.

Entertainment • Limited.

Getting to and from San Luis Potosi • Walking is the easiest way to visit the major sights. Buses, taxis (not so plentiful), and car rentals available.

Practical Tips • A good place to stop-over on a road trip; otherwise too isolated to make the long trip here worthwhile. Most shops close 2-4 p.m. then reopen in the evening.

WHAT TO SEE AND DO

Plaza de Armas
Carranza and Hidalgo • This zócalo, also known as the Jardin Hidalgo, can be quickly recognized by its **19th-century kiosk** and the **Cathedral** (Othon and Zaragoza) standing on the east side. Although the cathedral is impressive for the formality of its **interior**, *this plaza is less important for the sights it offers than as a place of orientation.*

Plaza del Carmen

Othon and Escobedo • Just two blocks east of the zócalo on Othon, you come to this famous plaza with its bronze Italianate fish **fountain**. Standing on its east side is the 18th-century Churrigueresque fantasy called the **Templo del Carmen** *(Othon and Villerias)*. Although the original central altarpiece has been replaced by a neoclassical one designed by Tresguerras, time has not diminished the robustness of the side chapel. As art historian Joseph Baird said:

If the facade of el Carmen chatters in many languages of ornament, with a distinctly local accent, this incredible triumph of the retable [altarpiece] design shutters with almost hysterical brilliance.

Next to the church is the 19th-century **Teatro de la Paz** that was unfortunately remodeled in this century to look like a mausoleum. Across from the theater is the **Palacio Federal** *(Calle Villerias)*, which contains the excellent **Museo de la Mascara** with its permanent, as well as changing exhibits of traditional masks from all over Mexico. *Open weekdays 10 a.m.-2 p.m., 4-6 p.m.; weekends 10 a.m.-2 p.m.; free.*

Plaza San Francisco

Universidad and Vallejo • By taking Villerias out of the Plaza del Carmen and then turning west—or right on the stately **Calle Universidad**, you arrive at the loveliest of San Luis' plazas in five blocks. Handsome **mansions** surround this tree-shaded and tranquil **plaza** that is dominated by the sienna-orange facade of the **Church of San Francisco**, founded early and renovated repeatedly, particularly in the late 18th century. Next to the church (to the right facing it) is the **Museo Regional de Arte Popular**, housed in a notable 19th-century private home. There are a few exhibit rooms here, particularly on the local rebozos from nearby Santa Maria del Rio, but the rest of the museum is devoted to the sale of crafts from all of Mexico. *You'll definitely want to walk around the Church of San Francisco, following Universidad past another plaza then returning up the side of the church on Galeana so you can visit the* **Museo Regional Potosino** (#450). This museum is in the convent of the Church of San Francisco, and its primary attraction is the **18th-century Capilla de Aranzazu**, the private, yet overwhelmingly ornate chapel of the Franciscans. Just outside the chapel is a very powerful **17th-century crucifix** and a collection of **retablos**, or folk paintings given in thanks for miraculous interventions by a favored saint. On occasion, temporary exhibits are mounted in the downstairs rooms. *Open Tues.-Fri. 10 a.m.-1 p.m., 3-6 p.m.; Sat. 10 a.m.-noon, Sun. till 1 p.m.; free.*

Casa de la Cultura

Carranza 1815 • In addition to the pleasing collection of **colonial antiques**, and religious and ancient **Huastecan art** on display here, there are also changing exhibits of local art. Although located 2 m west of the zócalo, *the trip here gives you a chance to see modern and wealthy San Luis.* (Follow Carranza out of the zócalo, past the Plaza de

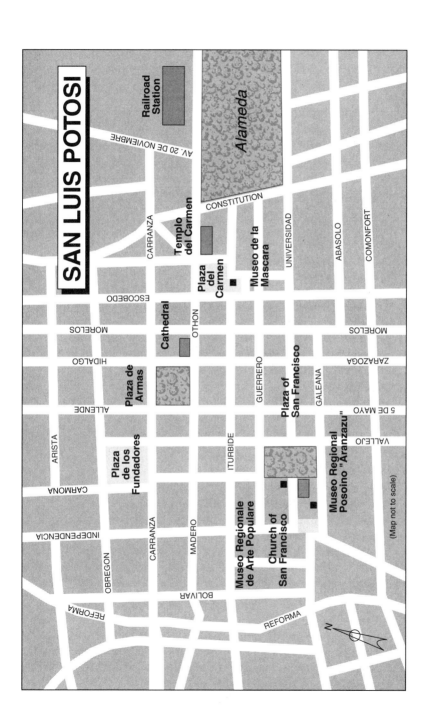

los Fundadores to Calle Reforma where Carranza becomes a two-way boulevard lined with boutiques and fancy restaurants. At the boulevard you can pick up the bus marked "Morales" that passes the Casa de la Cultura). *Open Tues.-Fri. 10 a.m.-2 p.m., 4-6 p.m.; Sat. 10 a.m.-2 p.m., 6-9 p.m.; Sun. 10 a.m.-2 p.m.; small fee.*

SHOPPING

Apart from the few antique shops that cluster on Carranza just before it turns into a boulevard, the place to shop is the Museo Regional de Arte Popular on the Plaza San Francisco.

WHERE TO STAY

San Luis Potosi has a number of motels on its periphery for those who want to stay near the highway, but since the restaurants and sights in town make for a more pleasurable break in any long driving trip, we list more of those. For reservations, write these hotels at San Luis Potosi, SLP, or call, area code 48.

Panorama Hotel ★★★
Carranza 315; ☎ *12-17-77; $70* • A fine, older hotel right in the center and very well-maintained, with a modern lobby and 120 bright and ample, if not stylish, rooms. Good service. Two restaurants, including one on roof, and bar. Pool. Parking. Write Apartado 659.

Hotel Real Plaza ★★★
Carranza 890; ☎ *14-69-69; $70* • On the modern boulevard extension of Carranza and about a 20-minute walk to the zócalo, this modern 14-story hotel has a small lobby and 138 decent-sized and modishly furnished rooms with tiled bathrooms. Restaurant. Parking. Write Apartado 231.

Cactus Motel ★★
MEX 57 near Glorieta Juarez; ☎ *12-18-71; $57* • Renovated in 1992 by its new owner (Howard Johnson), this complex offers 110 well-appointed rooms, with air conditioning. Restaurant. Nightclub. Pool with waterfall; garden. Parking. Write Apartado 393, or call in U. S., 800-654-4656.

Hotel Filher
Universidad 375 at Zaragoza; ☎ *12-15-62;$24* • Conveniently located between the zócalo and Plaza San Francisco, this hotel has a large colonial lobby with plastic furnishings. Its 50 rooms are basic but definitely acceptable and clean, even if the bathrooms are old. Nice restaurant. Parking.

WHERE TO EAT

The food in San Luis Potosi is surprisingly good and reasonably priced. .

Los Vitrales

5 de Mayo 300 at Guerrero; open 1 p.m.-midnight except Sunday till 6 p.m. only; 12-98-82 • For just moderate to moderately expensive prices, one can dine amid chandeliers and mural-painted walls and ceilings in the elegant mansion. Yet the spinach salad here is delicate, the canneloni quite decent, and the Chateaubriand tender and more than ample. (If you can, arrange your meal here in the afternoon, when business people bring it to life.) Valet parking.

La Gran Via

Carranza at Reforma; 1 p.m.-1 a.m.; 12-28-99; moderate to moderately expensive • Another pleasant place to dine, where the food is decent, the service good, the ambience a bit surburban. The handsomely Spanish atrium hints at the specialties here—paella, fabada, gambas ajillo—in addition to steaks and seafood. Piano music most evenings.

Los Cazadores Potosinos

Carranza 700 just beyond Reforma; lunch through dinner, closed Tuesday; 12-93-04; inexpensive to moderate • Mexican specialties such as *lomo adobado* (pork in a slightly bitter chile sauce) and *pollo pibil* (barbe-cued chicken Yucatecan style) predominate here at modest prices but in an attractive setting. Traditional Mexican music many evenings.

La Parroquia

Carranza 303, south side of Plaza de las Fundadores; 7 a.m.midnight daily; inexpensive • Without any ambience whatsoever, La Parroquia is as plastic as a restaurant can be. The food here is just terrific and the crowds prove it, whether for really fresh huevos rancheros in the morning, a budget- priced comida corrida in the afternoon, or just a snack of one of the best pozoles in Mexico, a moist *tres leches* cake with coffee, or simply a refreshing fruit licuado.

La Posada El Virrey

Plaza de Armas, north side; 7 a.m.-11 p.m. daily; inexpensive • For a change from La Parroquia, you can sit here in a colonial indoor patio while enjoying your decent pozole and tostadas, good licuados and enchiladas, and a budget comida corrida as well as banana splits.

ENTERTAINMENT

As already mentioned, a number of the restaurants have evening enter-tainment. In addition you might want to check the schedules of the **Teatro de la Paz,** where there often are ballet and symphony performances or even jazz, and **Casa de la Cultura,** where chamber music concerts and lectures are frequent.

GETTING TO AND FROM SAN LUIS POTOSI

AIR

The regional airline Aeromar connects San Luis Potosi with Mexico City daily except Sun. The airport is located about 20 minutes north of town and 5 km off MEX 57. Taxis, colectivos, and car rentals are available.

BUS

Numerous bus lines, both first and second class, run frequently from the Central Camionera (10 minutes east of zócalo) to Zacatecas (2-1/2 hours), Guanajuato, Monterrey, Mexico City, and Guadalajara.

CAR

San Luis Potosi is on the major route (MEX 57) from Mexico City to Monterrey, and then on to the U.S. border at Laredo (1223 km, 758 m; see "Getting to Mexico"). It lies 200 km, 120 m north of San Miguel de Allende and Queretaro on MEX 57 (see "On the Road") and 190 km, 114 m east of Zacatecas on MEX 49.

TRAIN

San Luis Potosi is a major railroad junction, but the only efficient service for tourists is by *servicio estrella* on the **Regiomontano** from Nuevo Laredo and Monterrey to Mexico City (dreadful schedule in the wee hours) and **El Constitutionalista** to San Miguel de Allende and Mexico City (9 hours).

DIRECTORY

Airlines • Aeromar, Carranza 1055, Suite 304 (☎ 17-79-36).

American Express • Carranza 1077.

Buses • Central Camionera, 10 minutes east of Plaza de Armas near Universidad.

Car Rentals • At airport and in town, Kar (☎ 12-32-29) and National (☎ 12-55-44).

Post Office • Morelos 235, 4 blocks north of zócalo, then right one block.

Railroad Station • On Othon, next to Alameda Park, east of Plaza del Carmen.

Telegrams • Escobedo 200, just south of Plaza del Carmen.

Tourist Office • Othon 130, near cathedral, and on second floor (☎ 12-31-43). Open 8 a.m.-8 p.m. weekdays; 8 a.m.-1 p.m. Saturday.

U.S. Consul • Carranza 1430 (☎ 12-15-28); 9 a.m.-1 p.m.

ON THE ROAD

The **scenery** along these routes does little to complement the beauty and diversity of the **towns** to be visited. The northern Valley of Mexico lacks the splendor of the Sierra Madres, but this monotonous plateau is rich in agriculture and minerals, and numerous towns along its roads are worthy of a stop.

ROUTE I: MEX 57D MEXICO CITY TO QUERETARO

Tepotzotlan

> *Turnoff at 40 km (25 m) to this* **village** *5 km away. See chapter on Mexico City Excursions.*

Tula

> *Turnoff at 54 km (33 m) marked "Petroleo-Tula" to ruins 21 km away. See chapter on Mexico City Excursions.*

San Juan del Rio and Tequisquiapan

Turnoff at 159 km (99 m) marked "San Juan del Rio." This lively **weekend resort area** is situated among mineral springs and farms producing wine and cheese. Both small towns cater to the tourist, with shops and vendors selling fine locally woven baskets, and San Juan specializes in **local cheeses and sweets**, while Tequisquiapan produces **wicker furniture**.

San Juan del Rio,

> *just off MEX 57D 52 km (32 m) from Queretaro*, has an elegant **resort development** on its outskirts with golf, tennis, and horseback riding. Unless you've planned a leisurely stay at one of these resort hotels *(see "Mexico City Excursions")*, San Juan's convenient location near the highway makes it ideal for a quick meal and shopping binge. You can find everything you need by driving down the main street of Juarez, which eventually reconnects with MEX 57D. *At Juarez 28 Oriente* is **Los Corceles Restaurant,** an attractive spot serving seafood, steak, and salads at very moderate prices. Continuing through town, look for **La Venta** *(Juarez 131 Poniente)*, a tiny, immaculate restaurant fronted by a garden and serving Mexican dishes and a comida corrida at inexpensive prices.

Although **Tequisquiapan** lies farther from the highway *(20 km, 12.5 m north of San Juan on MEX 120)*, this picturesque village, known for its thermal springs and Sunday market, actually may lure you into a longer stay. Many of its cobblestone streets are closed to traffic, and numerous boutiques offer their wares from under lovely, restored colonial arcades. Also a dip in one of the public thermal springs can be enjoyed for a small fee at spots like the **Balneario El Relox**. Or you can take the full thermal treatment by staying at the adjacent ★★**Hotel Balneario**

El Relox *(Morelos Norte 8 near zócalo; 467-300-06; $47 AP)*, a reliable and typical hotel with 50 simple rooms on pleasant grounds with 2 open-air pools and 17 covered "family" ones. If you aren't staying at a hotel and forced to eat your/meals there, then you'll be happy to know about **Las Brasas Restaurant,** just off the zócalo on Morelos Sur and specializing in Argentine-style grilled meats. The cuts may be too thin for northern tastes but the meat is nonetheless flavorful and moderately priced.

San Luis Potosi
Turnoff at km 221 (137 m). This bypass of Queretaro takes you to MEX 57 north and passes the turnoff for San Miguel de Allende (see above) before continuing to San Luis Potosi (200 km or 120 m).

Queretaro
Turnoff at 225 km (140 m). See "Queretaro," above.

Slow route to San Miguel de Allende and San Luis Potosi
Turnoff to MEX 57 at 226 km (140 m).

ROUTE II: QUERETARO TO IRAPUATO ON MEX 45D

Celaya
At 45 km, 28 m, Celaya is the turnoff to Guanajuato 73 km or 45 m away.
• This candy-making town produces *cajetas* of milk and sugar tasting much like our caramels. As the birthplace of Mexico's great architect, Francisco Eduardo Tresguerras, this town appropriately contains what is considered to be his masterpiece, the **Church of Nuestra Senora del Carmen**. Finished in 1807, El Carmen not only is an excellent example of neoclassical monumentality, but it shows unusual artistic unity. The versatile Tresguerras also created most of the sculptures and paintings within the building.

Irapuato
Near Irapuato (97 km, 60 m), are the turnoffs to Guanajuato (north 55 km or 34 m) and Morelia (south on MEX 43, 111 km or 69 m). • Irapuato is a busy commercial town based on agriculture, particularly strawberries. As you drive past you should see stand after stand selling lovely baskets of berries as well as bowls of strawberries and cream.

ROUTE III: SAN MIGUEL TO GUANAJUATO VIA DOLORES HIDALGO

The old road connecting San Miguel and Guanajuato twists and climbs up the scenic Sierras to the small historic town of Dolores Hidalgo, which is at the apex of a triangle formed by Guanajuato 58 km (36 m) to the southwest and San Miguel de Allende 40 km (25 m) to the southeast. Second-class bus service operates along this Hidalgo road, and some drivers take the mountain curves as if they were on a joy ride (about a 2-hour trip).

The part of the road from San Miguel is easy to negotiate and passes *fabricas* ("factories") of Talavera-style ceramic vases, planters, and wall tiles.

Dolores Hidalgo is of interest only for having hosted a major event in Mexican history. From the steps of the 18th-century church, Father Hidalgo made his famous *grito* or proclamation of independence on September 16, 1810, launching Mexicans into war with the Spanish Royalists. **Hidalgo's home**, now a museum with period furnishings, can be visited (two blocks from the church at Morelos). **Museo de la Independencia** (one-half block to the left on Zacatecas facing the church). In truth, these small museums are recommended only for devotees of local history. *Open weekdays 9 a.m.-2 p.m., 4-7 p.m.; weekends 9 a.m.-3 p.m.; small fee.*

MICHOACAN AND GUADALAJARA

Countryside near Guadalajara

> At length we came to the end of this extraordinary mountain-forest,
> and after resting the tired horses for a little while in a grove of pines
> and yellow acacias, entered the most lovely little wood, a succession of
> flowers and shrubs, and bright green grass, with vistas of fertile corn-
> fields bordered by fruit trees—a peaceful scene, on which the eye rests
> with pleasure, after passing through these wild volcanic regions.
>
> Madame Calderon de la Barca, 1840

HISTORY AND CULTURE

The youthful chain of the western Sierra Madre mountains spreads
wide at the state of Jalisco near its capital of Guadalajara before con-

tinuing south through Michoacan to create magnificent plateaus surrounded by rugged, forested mountains as it approaches Mexico City. These highland plateaus are endowed with fertile lands and lakes rich in fish ("Michoacan" means "place of fishermen"). But like the similarly endowed west coast of the U.S., these are regions of seismic activity. The most recent volcanic eruption was in 1943, when the peak of El Paricutin fascinated the world by emerging from a tranquil Michoacan cornfield, transforming Don Dionisio's ranch into a volcano one mile in diameter at its base. The mountains drop precipitously to the Pacific Coast, creating a strip of land that has become a tropical paradise for many, its most famous resort being Puerto Vallarta.

PREHISTORY

As rich and tempting as this western region must have been to civilizations that flourished in Mexico's Central Valley, it remained outside their domain. While the western peoples lived in permanent settlements based on agriculture and traded with such Central American civilizations as Teotihuacan and the Toltecs, they neither copied the accomplishments of their neighbors nor created a strong political state of their own until the 12th century—when a group called the Tarascans established themselves in Michoacan. Little is known about these western cultures, but they developed quite distinctively from the rest of ancient Mexico.

One of the most tantalizing aspects of these west coast cultures lies in the increasing evidence that they periodically had contact with other cultures from Central and South America. The most compelling evidence for this contact comes from the **shaft-tomb cultures** in Jalisco and the nearby states of Colima and Nayarit. *Deep shaft tombs, used to bury perhaps a generation or even several generations of a single family, are found nowhere else in Mexico, but they are quite prevalent from Panama all the way south to Peru.* Archaeologists believe sea contact between Mexico's west coast and either Panama or Ecuador would have been quite feasible by canoe. They don't know which peoples might have visited Mexico's shores or how often they may have come, but the discovery of South American-style adobe huts on the west coast and the distinctive shaft-tomb culture have convinced archaeologists that such contact did occur. **Metallurgy**, known so long in South and Central America, may have been introduced into Mexico by such contacts. Metal objects, which were quite precious

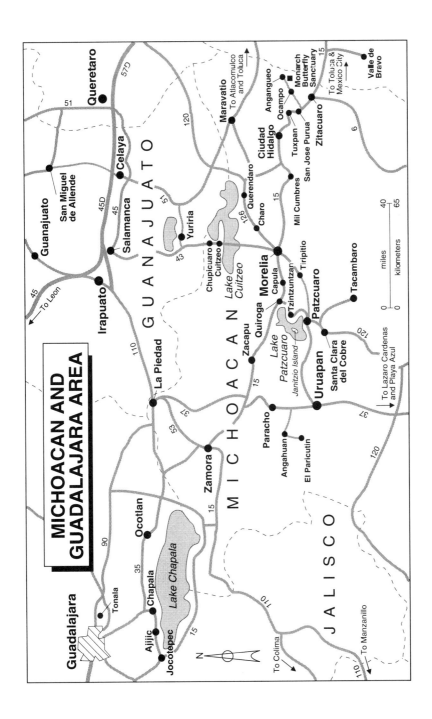

in the rest of Mexico, are found in profusion in the west, even being used for ordinary tools like fish hooks.

Dating from approximately 250 B.C. - A.D. 600, the shaft-tomb cultures left some of the earliest, most charming, pre-Conquest artifacts in this western area. **Ceramic figurines** show the dress of both women and men complete with nose plugs, earrings, body-paint designs, and tattooing. Statues portray daily activities, with women holding their children, and men and women embracing. Other ceramics show battles and religious ceremonies; some show people sitting on porches and steps of steep-roofed houses. *The most famous ceramics include delightful dogs from Colima.* Yet however much can be gathered about the lives of these people from their art, archaeologists have enormous difficulty filling out their story. Most of these ceramics have been stolen from tombs to be sold in art galleries around the world; few undisturbed tombs remain for legitimate excavations, and many have been totally destroyed. While the shaft tombs were not constructed after the Late Classic period, this western area remained populated through the Post-Classic period and until the Conquest. *Spaniards have left us the interesting information that quite a few chiefdoms in this area were ruled by women.*

No one is certain where the later Tarascans came from before settling near **Lake Patzcuaro** in Michoacan during the 12th century, but they told the Spaniards they came from the north or Chichimeca area. Around A.D. 1370, the Tarascan king **Tariacuri** started consolidating his territory by forming a Triple Alliance of his city, **Patzcuaro**, with **Ihuitzio** and **Tzintzuntzan**. *By the 15th century, the Tarascans controlled all the territory encompassed by modern Michoacan and influenced regions as far away as Guadalajara and San Luis Potosi.* Their power was certainly due to a disciplined militia and the use of **copper weapons** against the stone and wooden weapons of their opponents. Even the mighty Aztecs were unable to conquer them. *In 1478, the Aztecs advanced into Tarascan territory with 24,000 troops and were forced to retreat after losing 20,000 men to the Tarascan army.* The Aztecs never again risked such humiliation, refocusing their attentions to the south of Mexico toward Guatemala. If Cortes' arrival had been delayed by a few decades, the Spaniards might have encountered Tarascans rather than Aztecs in the Central Valley.

Spanish conquerors described the Tarascans as superior to other Mexicans in intelligence, industry, and beauty of their Purepecha language. Tarascan metallurgy was quite advanced and used for practical items like axes and chisels as well as decorative items such as bronze bells molded into the shape of turtles and fish with gold bodies and silver fins. They were equally expert in feather and lapidary work and built ceremonial centers like the one at their last capital, Tzintzuntzan, in *an architectural style distinctive from all other sites in Mexico.* Their power ended in 1522 when they submitted peacefully to the Spaniards.

COLONIAL PERIOD

As the Spaniards marched toward the Aztec capital of Tenochtitlan, the Aztecs asked their powerful enemies the Tarascans to unite with them against this foreign invasion. Never trusting the Aztecs, the Tarascans refused—and lost the opportunity to save their own empire. By the time the Spaniards advanced on Michoacan in 1522, the Tarascans had been so awed by the destruction of the Aztecs, they didn't dare fight. Dressed in rags to show his subservience, **Tangaxoan**, the Tarascan ruler, submitted to the Spaniards and converted to Christianity. In 1523, the Spaniards continued their exploration to the north and west of Michoacan. Spurred on by Aztec reports of lands ruled by women, the Spaniards reached Jalisco and Colima searching for the legendary Amazons. While they did find village communities ruled by women, some quite elderly, the Spaniards were disappointed by their lack of gold. Ports were established along the Pacific Coast; ship building was begun to launch explorations to even richer lands.

The peaceful exploration and conquest of the western region was disrupted in 1530 when the notorious **Nuno de Guzman** decided to establish a territory for himself in this region. Guzman had been president of the most powerful ruling body in Mexico. *His reign represented one of the most corrupt and oppressive periods in early Mexican colonial history.* Realizing that Spain was about to remove him from office, he set off to conquer the west with 300 Spaniards, 7000 Indian allies, and 10,000 pigs and sheep—all paid for by funds stolen from the royal treasury. He set the tone of his conquest at the Tarascan capital of Tzintzuntzan. Angered that the Tarascans did not give him enough gold, he tortured and killed their ruler Tangaxoan by dragging him behind a horse and then slowly burning him alive. Throughout the remainder of Guzman's march into Jalisco and other northwest states, his brutality greatly reduced the Indian population and forced the survivors to flee into the mountains. While he established the northwest territory of **New Galicia**, he left a legacy of violence that later would erupt. Eventually his misdeeds caught up with him. He was recalled to Spain where he spent two decades as a prisoner of the Spanish court.

NEW GALICIA

The capital of New Galicia became **Guadalajara**, *named after Guzman's Arabic birthplace in Spain*, "Wad-al-had-jarah." *Many of the Spaniards who originally explored the area abandoned their lands for Peru in search of the more profitable gold being discovered there.* During this period of sparse Spanish settlements, the Indians rebelled. The **Mixton War**, as the rebellion was called, lasted from 1538 to 1542 and resulted in the near capture of Guadalajara. The Indians were remarkably successful, hiding in remote hilltops and raiding Spanish settlements. They defeated the forces of the governor and even an army led by the famous conqueror **Alvarado**, who was himself killed in these battles. *The Indians were defeated only when the Spaniards, for the first time, equipped their Indian allies with horses and guns.* Those rebel Indians who survived retreated even farther to the isolated mountain areas of the Huichol and Cora tribes, where they remained independent of Spain until the 18th century. The Jalisco area found itself with few Indians, and Guadalajara grew into "the most Spanish of Mexican cities."

Michoacan's history followed a completely different direction from that of New Galicia, thanks to the ministrations of its bishop, **Vasco de Quiroga**. After Guzman had destroyed the peace in the Tarascan area, Spain asked the very honorable and successful attorney **Don Vasco** to join the Church in order to redress the wrongs Guzman had inflicted on the Tarascans. Although Quiroga was already in his sixties at the time, he studied for the priesthood and in 1533 was sent to Tzintzuntzan. *Much influenced by Thomas More's book,* Utopia, *he established a "hospital" as an Indian center for teaching not only religion but also trades and self-government.* When he was appointed bishop in 1538, he resisted pressure from the city of Valladolid (now Morelia) to establish the seat of his bishopric in that town, wanting to remain closer to the Tarascan Indians he sought to protect. He established the seat in **Patzcuaro** and set about creating "hospitals" in all Tarascan towns. The Tarascans attained self-sufficiency in agriculture and made extra money through the sale of their crafts, encouraged by the training received in the "hospitals." *Even today, each Tarascan village is known for its craft: Santa Clara for copper; Patzcuaro for lacquerware; Paracho for guitars.* Because of Don Vasco, the Tarascans, unlike the Indians of New Galicia, continue to dominate the culture of Michoacan, where they are locally also known as the Purepechas. As it says on the church in Tzintzuntzan, Vasco de Quiroga was a pious and just man, "loving the Tarascans like Christ himself." After Don Vasco's death, the new bishop moved to the more Spanish city of **Valladolid**, which then became the capital of Michoacan.

MODERN PERIOD

As New Galicia and Michoacan entered the 19th century, they had grown increasingly prosperous. **Guadalajara**, in particular, had expanded commercially with the opening of the nearby port of **San Blas** and a thriving textile industry. Being far away from Mexico City and Spain's greatest seat of authority, the predominately creole population felt little loyalty to the mother country. Instead, they smarted under Spain's restrictions on commerce and its refusal to allow Mexican-born Spaniards to participate in the highest levels of government. Like their neighbors in the silver cities such as Guanajuato, they became increasingly sympathetic to the cause of independence. (See chapter on Mexican History.) When **Father Hidalgo** declared independence in 1810, he was able to march into both Valladolid and Guadalajara without a battle. Hidalgo established himself in Guadalajara, where he proclaimed the end of Indian enslavement. *In 1928, after independence was gained, Guadalajara became the capital of the state of Jalisco*; and Valladolid was renamed Morelia in honor of its native son **Jose Maria Morelos**, leader of the Independence Movement, who stood for racial equality, the abolition of compulsory tithes, and the redistribution of hacienda land to peasants.

Today Morelia and Guadalajara are both great educational centers in Mexico. *Whereas Morelia has maintained its Old World charm and intimacy, Guadalajara has burgeoned into the second largest city in Mexico.* Both capitals are redistributing centers for agricultural products, but Guadalajara also has considerable industry, including tequila and beer factories.

CONTEMPORARY INDIAN LIFE
PUREPECHA

The Tarascans, or **Purepecha**, as their descendants prefer to be called, now live primarily in the west-central section of the state of Michoacan, an area substantially smaller than the one they occupied before the Spanish Conquest. *European influence penetrated quickly and deeply into Tarascan civilization, beginning with the activities of the conquistadors and missionaries who successfully eliminated many* *features of Tarascan life* and continuing through the late 19th century when the development of the **lumber** industry brought railroads and increased mestizo culture into the Tarascan area. *Virtually no traces of pre-Hispanic Tarascan religion remain;* the former gods as well as the ancient rituals have now been forgotten. In their place, the contemporary Purepecha have adopted the Catholicism taught by **Vasco de Quiroga**. Continuing from pre-Hispanic times, however, is the emphasis on crafts, with woodworking, weaving, pottery making, and lacquerwork still important features of their economy. **Fishing**, once a vital part of Indian life, has been on the decline recently. Although the handsome hand-carved canoes still glide through **Lake Patzcuaro**, the picturesque butterfly nets so often seen in tourism promotional photographs have all but disappeared.

The Purepecha continue to live principally by **farming**, *their major crops still the pre-Hispanic ones of maize, beans, and squash.* They continue to trade and exchange goods through the pre-Hispanic market system, often traveling long distances to sell farm goods and handcrafts. Any resulting wealth is rarely exhibited in dramatic changes in home, diet, or dress. Instead, *Purepechas splurge on elaborate weddings and religious festivals,* during which times these normally reserved people fill the streets with parades, music, and dancing.

WEDDING & FESTIVALS

Weddings are often set in motion in a rather unusual way with a prearranged "kidnapping" by a future groom of a reluctant bride. Although the bride has agreed in advance to the kidnapping, she screams and resists when the time comes. The groom takes her to a secret place and seduces her while his relatives and friends head for the home of his future father-in-law to seek his consent for the marriage. Consent is almost always granted, drinking parties inevitably follow, and the wheels are set in motion for the exchange of gifts, civil and religious ceremonies, and several celebrations that will mark this important event.

DANCE OF THE LITTLE OLD MEN

Numerous religious festivals also bring Tarascan villages to life, highlighted with the dance of **Los Viejitos** ("the little old men"). This popular dance dates from pre-Hispanic times, but its original significance is uncertain. Spanish chronicles report that then as now, the dance brought gales of laughter from the audience. *Boys dressed as tottering old men appear in white cotton pants, wide-brimmed hats, serapes, and silk neckerchiefs. Covering their faces are wooden masks carved as caricatures of old men, and in their hands are hand-carved* *wooden canes,* the better to hobble with. The shouting and clowning and music and dance that follow make these some of the most joyous and memorable occasions in village life.

HUICHOLS

You will be struck first by their exquisite dress—men with richly embroidered capes, shirts, and pants, with woven belts and delicately embroidered small pouches, beaded bracelets, a woven bag slung casually over the shoulder, and, on special occasions, a decorated straw hat framing their strong and handsome faces. The image is memorable. We still stop in our tracks and stare whenever Huichol men stride into town on shopping trips to Guadalajara or Mexico City.

Women dress in embroidered materials also, but their outfits lack the flamboyance of the men's. *The Huichols are probably the one indigenous group in Mexico where men's dress is even more elaborate and elegant than women's.*

The approximately 14,000 Huichols live in a mountainous area northwest of Guadalajara that includes parts of the states of Jalisco, Nayarit, and Zacatecas. No one knows their precise origins, but it is to the mountain plateaus where the Huichols now live that Indian survivors of the Mixton War retreated in the 16th century. *The rough terrain has kept the Huichols relatively isolated and protected from foreign influence.* Although the Spanish finally took control of the area in 1722, Spanish, and particularly missionary, influence has been minimal. Today, the Huichols lead a traditional way of life, preserving many rituals, customs, and beliefs inherited from their pre-Conquest ancestors.

RELIGION OF THE HUICHOLS

Huichols live in an all-encompassing religious-magical world controlled by over 100 deities and filled with ritual art through which Huichols communicate with the gods. Perhaps, more than any other indigenous group, their art is inseparable from their religion and their religion essential to their daily life. Through ritual offerings of feathered arrows, beaded gourd bowls, small yarn paintings, votive tablets, yarn god's eyes, polychrome stone disks, as well as food and drink, Huichols pray to the gods who control all natural occurrences, sometimes capriciously, and who must be appeased by frequent ceremonies and festivals. The connection of religion and art extends even to Huichol dress. The embroidered designs on their clothing have religious-magical significance.

Since the relationship with the gods is a personal one, they are classified by kinship terms, and their pre-Conquest roots are obvious. Some, like the sun and fire gods, are grandfathers, while the rain gods are aunts, and the gods of maize, deer, and peyote are elder brothers. Since many of the gods live in sacred caves, pilgrimages to these sites are frequent, and ritual offerings to the idols are necessary to ensure good health and a successful harvest.

Although Huichol religion still is fundamentally pagan, some elements of Catholicism have crept in. Huichols perform baptisms and accept Christ and various saints as minor deities. But these Christian elements have Huichol interpretations. The statues of Christ and the saints speak to the shaman priests in the Huichol language. And according to one popular legend, Joseph gained Mary's hand by winning a Huichol violin-playing contest.

SHAMANS

Myth and magic come to life through the activities of the shaman-priests and the annual peyote pilgrimages. The shamans' supernatural powers, reinforced by the sacred eagle and hawk feathers in their hats, include the divination of the causes of illness and the ability to heal. When necessary, shamans can cloud the sun to bring rain. As the religious leaders with the widest knowledge of Huichol rituals, shamans lead the chants that pass on the ancient Huichol traditions to the young, telling them of the world's creation and the origin and significance of Huichol customs.

One of the most sacred roles of a shaman is that of leader of the annual peyote hunt. Each year, groups of Huichols make a pilgrimage of several hundred miles to **Wirikuta**, a desert plateau in Zacatecas, believed to be their sacred homeland. The trip is highly ritualized and intense, for the route taken follows as closely as possible (though in reverse) the route traveled by the original Huichols from Wirikuta to the present Huichol homeland. At Wirikuta they hunt and take peyote, a sacred hallucinogenic cactus, that transforms the pilgrims into deities and returns them to the celestial world of their gods. The experience is said to be mystical and ineffable, a feeling of oneness with the universe, a return to paradise. They remain in this state until called back by the shaman to normal time and life—a life, nevertheless, with deep ancient roots and filled with magic, religion, and art.

MORELIA

Of all Mexican cities, Morelia best evokes the grandeur of Spain. Massive and austere, and too handsome to frolic in colors, it is built in the earth tones of Madrid. Morelia is an imposing city, with colonial buildings, churches, monasteries, formal plazas, and a great cathedral. You come here to savor colonial Mexico; even your hotel room may be located in a handsomely restored 18th-century building.

Morelia's rich history extends from the days when it was home for brutal conquistadors and for two of the most kindly and revered friars, **Juan de San Miguel** and **Don Vasco de Quiroga**, through the Independence Movement when its native son, the rebel priest, **Jose Maria Morelos**, served as one of the leaders in the war to liberate Mexico from Spain. Morelos' feats became legendary. Starting with an unarmed group of 25 followers, he soon organized and led a well-armed contingent of some 9,000 men that gained control of Mexico from the Valley of Mexico to the Pacific Coast. *In his honor, the town of Valladolid was renamed Morelia in 1828.*

Today, Morelia stands as the capital of the state of **Michoacan**, its atmosphere enriched by the **University of Michoacan** and the **Conservatory of Music.** Its past has been preserved in numerous buildings of historical interest, several of which are architectural gems from the colonial period. *Although the population is now over 800,000, the city is still calm and manageable, with many of the principal sights found within a small area around the center of town.* Here **evening walks** are well rewarded with the many murals in colonial buildings made dramatic by night lighting and with many **museums** open for a visit until 8 p.m. The location of Morelia adds to its attractiveness, with its proximity to some of the finest **craft-producing villages** in Mexico and some of the most magnificent countryside— mountains, forests, and lakes—you will encounter anywhere.

KEY TO MORELIA

Sights • Replete with imposing colonial architecture and places of historical interest. Its Cathedral may be the finest in Mexico.

Shopping • The state of Michoacan is second only to Oaxaca for the variety and high quality of its native crafts. The Casa de las Artesanias has a fine selection of crafts from the entire state.

Where to Stay • You can choose from handsome colonial hotels in town or resorts outside of town. Some acceptable inexpensive and budget hotels can be found.

Where to Eat • The tasty whitefish from nearby Lake Patzcuaro is popular. A fair selection of restaurants.

Entertainment • Cultural events in this university city add diversity to the limited music in the hotel bars.

Fiestas • September 16, Independence Day, with parades and evening festivities in the zócalo, especially celebrated in this birthplace of the great Independence leader, Morelos.

Getting Around • Easy town to do mainly on foot. Many principal sights near center of town (as is the garage at Zaragoza 65). Bus, car tours, combis, or taxi needed for the few out-of-the-way places. Main street in town is Av. Madero (Poniente and Oriente) and combi vans and "Directo" buses run this street, and then on to Av. Acueducto.

Practical Tips

Pick up maps for Patzcuaro and Uruapan at the Tourist Office in Morelia. They are better than the maps you can find for these towns locally. Weather excellent year-round. Morelia's good altitude produces a temperate climate.

WHAT TO SEE AND DO

Plaza de Armas and Cathedral

The Cathedral rises at the center of the city flanked on the west by the Plaza de Armas (zócalo), also known as the **Plaza de los Martires** (Martyrs), and on the east by the smaller **Plaza Melchor Ocampo**. The zócalo forms a focal point for the city—with gardens, treelined walks, and a large silver-roofed kiosk. The zócalo derives its name of "los Martires" from the brutal killing on this site of several rebel priests, including Father Matamoros, a follower of Morelos, who were actively involved in the War of Independence.

Although the first cathedral of Michoacan was located at Patzcuaro, an ancient capital of the Tarascan empire, the episcopal seat was moved to Valladolid (the former name of Morelia) in 1580, where it has remained ever since. *Construction of the present* **Cathedral** *began in 1660 and took some 84 years.* The wait was worthwhile. One of the glories of church architecture in Mexico, this majestic building with powerful well-proportioned towers soaring to the sky is imposing without being overwhelming. The facade's soothing earth tones extend to the **two towers**, which rise to a height of some 200 feet, *the tallest in Mexico.* A tiled dome balances the subtle, subdued hues of the Cathedral's facade. The exquisite **interior** surprises because it lacks the flamboy-

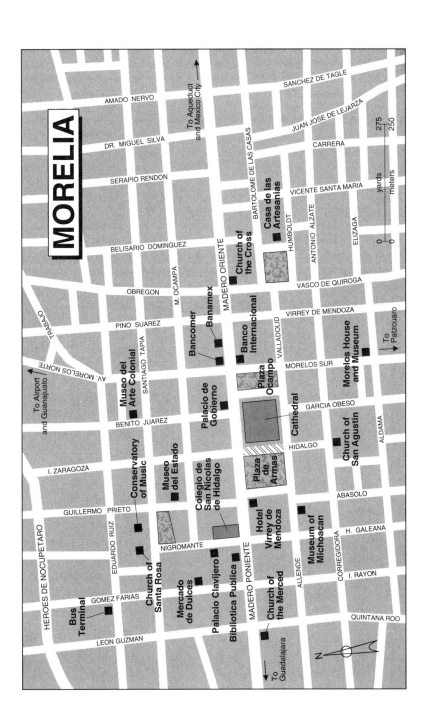

MORELIA

ance often found in Mexican churches. Instead, in each of the three naves you find delicate, muted, and restrained designs, making this *one of the most harmonious interiors in Mexico.* The **dome** is particularly elegant with its coffered paneling. **Paintings** by the noted colonial artist **Miguel Cabrera** decorate the sacristy. The Cathedral boasts that its handsome Churrigueresque **organ** is *one of the finest for tone in all of Latin America.*

Hotel Virrey de Mendoza and Church of the Merced

At the corner of the zócalo, west of the Cathedral, stands the **Hotel Virrey de Mendoza**, formerly an **18th-century mansion**. It's worth a walk inside to view the **lobby** covered by a glass atrium and surrounded by a colonnade. If you continue west on Av. Madero Poniente (Pte.) for three blocks you will come upon the **Church of the Merced** *(Av. Madero Pte. and Quintana Roo).* Completed in the early 18th century, the church has two sets of **Moorish wooden doors** (one along Madero) carved into geometric and foliate designs. Note, too, the **ornate window** above the main door.

Mercado de Dulces

Head back along Madero Pte. toward the Cathedral. After one block, Madero intersects with Gomez Farias where you will find Morelia's famous Mercado de Dulces (**Sweets Market**) extending for one block in an arcade above the street between Madero Pte. and Santiago Tapia. *Known throughout the country by sweets-loving Mexicans,* the market features exotic candies, such as *ates* and *chongos,* made of tropical fruits like mangos, guayabas, and tamarind crystalized into sweet chunks, or ground into soft balls, or shaped like jellied fruits. And stands sell peanut, walnut, pepita, and unidentifiable brittle. For those on diets or with other interests, one area of the market sells a variety of curios and leather belts.

Colegio de San Nicolas

After leaving the market, walk back to Av. Madero Pte. and make a left. At the corner of Nigromante (the street sign still features the old street name, "Calle de la Compania"), you will find the Colegio de San Nicolas de Hidalgo. Founded in 1540 by **Bishop Vasco de Quiroga**, this *second-oldest college in the Americas* was originally located in Patzcuaro but moved to Valladolid (Morelia) 40 years later. Two of the leaders of Independence were associated with the Colegio: **Miguel Hidalgo** was both a student and professor who taught **Jose Morelos** here. Today, the building houses a preparatory school. Its **neoclassical facade** runs in clean lines broken by the pediments over large windows and the attractive grillwork of the balconies. The handsome **interior courtyard** is enclosed by two floors of arcades, the upper one contains a **mural** on Tarascan life.

Biblioteca Publica and Palacio Clavijero

The Biblioteca Publica (Public Library) and Palacio Clavijero can be found across the street on Nigromante. Housed in the **17th-century**

Church of La Compania, the Biblioteca's paneled interior contains an important collection of **Jesuit manuscripts**. Its neighbor, the **Palacio Clavijero**, today is the home of the **Tourist Office** as well as various government offices. However, this 17thcentury building, named after the brilliant teacher Francisco Javier Clavijero, was formerly a Jesuit college. In the 18th century, Clavijero gained fame for his wide-ranging scientific knowledge and for his mastery of numerous languages, including Latin, Greek, and Hebrew as well as the Indian languages Nahuatl and Otomi. *The building itself is of some interest for its carved wooden doors with foliate designs and the interior courtyard with an arcade and fountain.*

Jardin de las Rosas

Farther down Nigromante at the intersection of Santiago Tapia you will come upon the tranquil, tree-lined Jardin de las Rosas (**"Garden of the Roses"**) with bronze **statues** of Vasco de Quiroga and Cervantes, surrounded by **18th- and 19th-century buildings**. The 18th-century **Church of Santa Rosa** facing the Jardin was originally a convent for Dominican nuns. Above the Moorish wooden portals of its **twin facades** are carved friezes and crocodile rainspouts. Inside there are remnants of floral frescoes and Churrigueresque **altar screens**.

The plain facade of the **Conservatory of Music** overlooking the Jardin is lined with columns and arches. One of the oldest music schools in the Americas, *the conservatory has gained international fame as the home of the well-traveled and acclaimed Children's Choir of Morelia.* You may want to drop in to chance hearing a rehearsal or learning about an upcoming concert.

At the end of the plaza is the **Museo del Estado** *(Guillermo Prieto 178)* with a number of exhibition rooms, including one on the daily life of the Tarascans, or Purepechas as they also are known. *The* **archaeology room** *is the most interesting with well-displayed bowls and figurines from the earliest culture in the region, the Chupicuaro,* as well as all kinds of ancient jewelry including Tarascan gold and copper bells. *(Open weekdays 9 a.m.-2 p.m., 4-7 p.m.; closed Sunday; Free.)*

Museo del Arte Colonial

If you continue east on Santiago Tapia, then turn left at Juarez, you come to this small museum *(Juarez 240)* containing **religious art** from the 16th through 18th centuries, including some exceptional wooden crucifixes. In one room there are paintings by **Miguel Cabrera**; his Josef with Christ Child is very affecting. *(Open 9 a.m.-2 p.m., 5-8 p.m.; closed Monday; Free)* A few steps away from the museum is th**e Casa de la Cultura** *(Morelos Nte. and Zapata)* where there often are exhibits of contemporary art.

Palacio de Gobierno

The Palacio de Gobierno (State Capitol) is a few blocks away on Madero Oriente (Ote.) just past Benito Juarez and diagonally across from the Cathedral. The plaque on the building announces that this is the "Palacio de los Poderes," letting you know in no uncertain terms that these offices are to be taken seriously; it is the **Palace of the Authorities**. Formerly a seminary, it lists among its graduates such historic notables as **Morelos**; the revered intellectual, social reformer, and member of Benito Juarez' cabinet, **Melchor Ocampo**; as well as the infamous and cruel briefly reigning emperor of Mexico, **Augustin de Iturbide**. **Murals** decorate the second-floor and the stairwell, the latter ones are by far the most powerful. Painted in the 1950s by the noted Michoacan artist **Alfredo Zalce**, they portray the Liberators of Mexico. In one scene, Hidalgo and Morelos are depicted with swords in hand leading a group of armed workers. Other scenes represent the unpopular rule of Maximilian, Santa Anna, and Porfirio Diaz, and the struggle of the oppressed. *Open daily 8 a.m.-10 p.m., free.*

Colonial Restoration

To see *some of the finest examples of Mexico's emphasis on historical preservation and restoration for modern use*, proceed a half block east of Madero Ote. to the corner of Morelos Norte. Here you will find three of the most handsome banks you will ever visit, a far cry from those at home. The **Bancomer building** is a former 18th-century mansion with a well-preserved interior of colonnades, courtyard, and wrought-iron staircase. Next door, the **Banamex building**, originally built in 1750, served as the administrative center for the collecting of tithes given to the parishes. Note the **courtyard with portico**, the intriguing *fountain* made from large ceramic jars. Across the street at Madero Ote. 24 stands the equally well-restored **Banco Internacional.**

Church of the Cross

Farther east at the corner of Madero Ote. and Vasco de Quiroga you will find the little-visited but impressive Church of the Cross. Behind the neoclassical facade, the single nave with unadorned, massive Romanesque stone arches leads to a starkly lighted **altar**. A few stained-glass windows add one of the few touches of color to this simple yet powerful **interior**.

Museum of Michoacan and Church of San Agustin

The Museum of Michoacan is nearby *(Allende and Abasolo; southwest corner of the zócalo)*. Built in 1758, this baroque building served as the residence of Emperor Maximilian during his visits to Michoacan. Now it houses a **museum of history**, one that is well worth a visit. The history is told through art, be it a chac mool sculpture from the ancient Tarascan kingdom at Tzintzuntzan or a remarkable 17th-century crucifix made from a tree limb ("Cristo de una pieza"). *(Open Tues.-Sat. 9 a.m.-7 p.m.; Sun. 9 a.m.-2 p.m.; Hefty fee)*

Church of San Agustin

(about a block south of the Museum on Hidalgo) was built during the 16th century. San Agustin's austere exterior is complemented by a tranquil park found in one of the patios of the ex-convent.

Morelos' Birthplace and Home

A handsome library on Corregidora, and next to the San Agustin park, is the house where **Jose Maria Morelos** was born on September 30, 1765. The house that Morelos later bought can be found just two blocks away at the corner of Morelos Sur and Aldama. Now a **museum**, this colonial building contains a collection of mementos, paintings, and furniture from the life of this national hero who was martyred in the Independence Movement. *Perhaps the most unusual of Morelos' belongings, for those with maudlin interests, is the blindfold Morelos wore when executed by a firing squad.* "To die is nothing when it is for my country that I die." *Open daily, 9 a.m.-7 p.m.; small admission fee.*

Aqueduct

Walking, or taking the combi or "directo" bus for about 1 km east on Madero, you come to the impressive **Tarascan fountain**, and then turn right on to the even more impressive Avenida Acueducto where the **18th-century stone aqueduct** with 253 arches begins its one-mile span. Built in 1785 to alleviate the drought that for a two-year period had parched the surrounding valley, *the aqueduct now is never more beautiful than at night when its arches are spotlighted.* Just east of the aqueduct you come upon **Calzada Fray Antonio de San Miguel,** *a romantic street for a stroll with a wide tree-lined walk running down the center and surrounded by attractive but modest 18th-century houses.* This street leads into **Plaza Morelos** where the University of Michoacan has some of its buildings. On the west side of Av. Acueducto is the **Bosque Cuauhtemoc,** a large park where you find the **Museo de Arte Contemporaneo** (Acueducto 18) with its changing exhibits of works by Mexican artists and its permanent collection of Morelian artist Alfredo Zalce. *(Open 10a.m.-2p.m., 4-8 p.m. except Mon.; Free.)*

SHOPPING

The state of Michoacan is second only to Oaxaca—and even this could be contested—for the quality and variety of its native crafts (see Patzcuaro "Shopping" for a description of regional crafts). In Morelia, the **Casa de las Artesanias** (also called **Palacio del Artesano**), located in the ex-convent of San Francisco next to San Francisco Church *(1/2 block east of Vasco de Quiroga, between Bartolome de las Casas and Humboldt),* has an excellent, large selection of crafts for sale from all over the state. Rooms on two floors overflow with crafts, including **lacquerware** from Uruapan, **copperware** from Santa Clara de Cobre, **guitars** from Paracho, **green pottery** from Patamban and San Jose de la Gracia, wonderful **ceramics** from Capula, delicate brown **pottery** from Tzintzuntzan, fine **serapes** from several villages, and the delightfully weird, grotesque **ceramic figures** from Ocumicho. Don't miss the upper floor, not only for the small rooms, each devoted to the crafts from a particular village, but also for the fine exhibition of crafts (not for sale). *Open Mon.-Sat. 10 a.m.-8 p.m. Sun. 9 a.m.-3 p.m.* An enormous Tarascan style building houses **a branch of the Casa de las Artesanias** at the Convention Center on Ventura Puente, 2 m from center. *Open 10 a.m.-2 p.m., 4-8 p.m.; closed Sun. afternoon and Tues.* For specialty items stop by **Casa Cerda** *(Zaragoza 163)* where works by the Cerda family can be purchased, not cheaply however. Here you can find the wooden dishes lacquered and painted in gold by Esperanza Cerda who has received considerable recognition for her Patzcuaro-style work. Another family member produces the wooden plates in the complicated, and now rare, technique of lacquer encrustado (used by her ancestors as early as the 17th century), and yet others produce intricately embroidered blouses. *Open 9 a.m.- 9 p.m.; ring the doorbell.*

If you plan to go on to **Patzcuaro** and the craft villages around the lake, you will there have the opportunity to buy many of the crafts offered in Morelia. However, no one place in Patzcuaro or any of the surrounding villages has the comprehensive selection of crafts offered for sale at the Casa de las Artesanias.

WHERE TO STAY

It's hard not to be captivated by some of the 18th-century colonial hotels in Morelia—not so much by their amenities, which are equaled elsewhere, but by their architectural details and ambience. Morelia also offers a very fine resort hotel in the hills outside of town. You don't have a wide choice of hotels in Morelia, yet you do have some good choices. No air conditioning, but it's not needed. *For reservations write Morelia, Michoacan, Mexico or call ☎ area code 451.*

EXPENSIVE

Villa Montana   ★★★★

Santa Maria Hills, 3 km (2m) south of MEX 15 ☎ *4-02-31; $123 CP* • Situated in the hills, with dramatic views of Morelia, this resort inn offers 69 units, mostly suites arranged around beautiful gardens and tranquil patios. Each unit varies, some are multi-leveled, many have fireplaces and private patios, all are handsomely decorated with Mexican antiques, arts, and crafts. Good restaurant, bar with entertainment, and craft shop. Pool, tennis, access to 9-hole golf course, and game room. Write Apartado 233. To reach the resort drive out Morelos Sur cross MEX 15 (by detour to right) and continue up into the Santa Rosa hills.

Calinda Quality Morelia   ★★★

5.5 km (3.5 m) south of town on MEX 15 at Av. Camelinas 3466; ☎ *4-57-05; $92* • This well-maintained, modern Quality Inn has a highway location across from the Plaza America that is most convenient for those with cars, although taxis and combis are available. The 126 rooms are a decent size, carpeted, and well-supplied for comforts. The lobby cocktail area (with entertainment) and restaurant are very popular with the local Mexican middle class. Good service. Pool and

Jacuzzi. Tennis. Parking. To reach, turn right onto Ventura Puente off Av. Acueducto at the end of the park and continue to the Convention Center at MEX 15 where you turn left. For reservations, in U.S., call ☎ 800-228-5151.

MODERATE

Hotel de la Soledad

Zaragoza 90, 1 block north of Cathedral; ☎ *2-18-88; $67* • The antique carriages and thick arches surrounding a tranquil garden remind you that this was the first inn of Morelia; it began as a coach station for Augustinian monks. An exceptionally handsome 18th-century building, its restaurant and lobby are under the arcades, and the bar is off to the side. The 60 rooms vary considerably in size and airiness, but all have high, wood-beam ceilings. To get the best rooms, ask for a room on the main courtyard with two double beds.

Hotel Catedral

Zaragoza 37; ☎ *3-07-83; $57* • A few steps from the zócalo, this intimate colonial hotel has an attractive lobby in a glass-roofed atrium, and 40 comfortable rooms with modern bathrooms. Handsome restaurant (breakfast only) and bar. Entertainment.

Virrey de Mendoza

Portal Matamoros 16 ☎ *2-06-33; $88* • This 18th-century former mansion on the zócalo has been converted into an attractive hotel with a striking glass-covered atrium housing the lobby. The restaurant, with an antique dining set once belonging to Viceroy Mendoza, and the 52 rooms retain their colonial ambience despite a recent renovation. Some rooms in front have spectacular views of the cathedral and city as well as attendant noise.

INEXPENSIVE

Mansion Acueducto

Av. Acueducto 25; ☎ *2-33-01; $37* • Located a bit out of the center of town along the aqueduct, this turn-of-the-century mansion has a wonderful Victorian lobby and dining room with massive pieces of antique mahogany furniture and lacy curtains. The rooms in the main building are large but rather bare, with older bathrooms. The newer motel-like wing has ample and functional rooms around a garden and large pool. Parking. A very good buy.

Casino

Portal Hidalgo 229; ☎ *3-10-03; $46* • Right on the zócalo behind a sidewalk cafe is this hotel with 50 small but carpeted rooms with tiled baths. Quite obviously in the center of everything yet surprisingly tranquil. Bar and restaurant.

WHERE TO EAT

You can find some regional specialties, including the famous mild-flavored Patzcuaro whitefish (*pescado blanco de Patzcuaro*) and the tart Tarascan soup (*sopa Tarasca*). Rabbit, quail, and kid are regionally popular, too. Some local shapes are given to maize here where *huchepos* (also spelled uchepos) are like a sweet corn bread, *corundas* like corn ravioli, a bit heavy for our taste, and tamales are narrow and flavored with chorizo. In addition to regional specialties, you can find international seafood and steaks as well.

Practical Tip

Although many centrally located restaurants remain open late in the evening, few Morelians eat then, preferring their main meal in the late afternoon. Those under the arcades, however, are always lively. Price categories are explained in the Introduction.

In the area of the zócalo you have some very good choices for traditional food. No place can quite match **Los Comensales** (*Zaragoza 148; open 8 a.m.-10 p.m. daily; no credit cards; inexpensive*) for its plant-filled patio and extensive menu. For snacks day and night, the antojitos are good—the tamales are flavorful, the *huchepos* delicate, and the *sopes* (like a soft tostada) piled high. The soups are good, too, whether the *medula* (bone marrow) or *Tarasca*. The main dishes range from quail to seafood, and from *mole* (on Sundays) to the bacon-flavored chicken *Los Comensales*. There's even a salad Los Comensales, full of vegetables. About five blocks from the zócalo, but well worth the walk is **El Pescador** (*Cuautla 77, a half block off Madero Pte.; daily till 6 p.m.; moderate*). If you happen to dine on a Sunday, this plain restaurant will be bustling with local families eating their favorite seafood to the accompaniment of live traditional music. *The* dish to order here is the *sopa marinera*, a rich, spicy broth traced with cumin and brimming over with crab, shrimp, fish, and the like. An order is a meal in itself, but if you also want to try the whole *huachinango dorado*, half-orders are accepted. If you want your seafood closer to the zócalo, try the ceviche and Patzcuaro whitefish or the Sunday *paella* at **Boca del Rio** (*Gomez Farias and Santiago Tapia; 8 a.m.-6 p.m. daily; moderate*). More upscale in ambience is the **Casa d' Enrique** (*Hidalgo 54; open 8 a.m.-8 p.m., closed Sunday; moderate*). It serves *cecina* (dried, salted, and seasoned meat) with melted cheese, *puntas de filete albanil* (filet tips), and *cordoniz al carbon* (quail) cooked to perfection, all of which are very tasty. Right on the zócalo, under the arcades of Av. Madero, is outdoor cafe **Bar Casino Restaurant** (*open all day; inexpensive to moderate*). The Casino is a good place to sample Michoacan specialties, an appetizer of *Patzcuaro* sardines or *cabrito* (roasted kid), a *comida corrida* or simply some decent *taquitos*, stuffed with chicken and served with cream. For a meal in lovely colonial surroundings, you can dine in the handsome restaurants found in the hotels. The **Hotel de la Soledad**

(*inexpensive*) serves a fabulous Mexican buffet accompanied by mariachis in the garden arcade starting at 2 p.m. on Saturday.

If you find yourself having mid-morning hunger pangs, stand in line with the Morelians in front of **Tortas Planchadas** (*Madero Pte. 392*), a hole in the wall near the Tourist Office. It serves warm Mexican sandwiches (we like *pierna*, or pork, the best). If you want your snack while sitting down, **La Copa de Oro** (*Juarez 194-B*) is a clean spot serving juices and tortas. When all this Mexican food is no longer appealing, try **Govinda** (*Morelos Sur 39, found by going through the side entrance of the bank*), a small, pleasant restaurant serving a Hindu vegetarian set meal from 1-5 p.m. (closed Sunday; inexpensive). Or walk toward the aqueduct, to **Tony's Pizza** (*Madero Ote. 688 and Madero Pte. 619*), where the pizza's not bad.

ENTERTAINMENT

Evenings in Morelia are more often than not spent sipping coffee with friends. No place is more popular for this favorite pastime than the outdoor cafes under the arcades along Av. Madero across from the zócalo. Here in the social center of Morelia, you can sit and relax, have a snack at the **Bar Casino,** or an exotic fruit drink and coffee at the **Cafe Catedral,** perhaps get a shoeshine, and savor the life of Morelia. The location bustles all day with lots of police whistles to go along with the traffic and piped-in music. One of the popular songs played during our last visit was none other than "Strangers in the Night." Despite the music, the atmosphere remains very Mexican. If you want a quieter scene, walk down Zaragoza to the tiny **Cafe Versailles** (at corner of Melchor Ocampo) for an espresso and dessert. The **Colibri** (Galeana 36) is a coffee house with music.

Morelia is also full of student plays and concerts, some of them quite good. On any given day a poster will suddenly appear, announcing a classical guitar concert in one of the museum courtyards, or poetry readings at the **Casa de la Cultura.** Symphony orchestras sometimes perform at the **Teatro Morelos** (Convention Center). To keep abreast of these happenings, check at the Tourist Office for its list of weekly events. Otherwise check the **hotel lounges** for entertainment—the Cathedral or Soledad, or the Calinda Morelia for its popular piano lounge.

GETTING TO AND FROM MORELIA

AIR

The regional airline *Aeromar* connects Morelia with Mexico City daily except Sunday. The airport, 25 km, 15-1/2 m from the center, has taxis, colectivos, and car rentals available. Arrange in advance with your hotel for special taxis to airport.

BUS

Buses connect Morelia with Guadalajara, Guanajuato, Mexico City, and Patzcuaro. Buses leave from the *Central Camionera* (V. Gomez Farias and E. Ruiz).

CAR

Greatly facilitating exits from the city is a *libramiento*, or beltway of sorts, that has been created around much of the city, from the north near the Guanajuato/Salamanca road and circling southeast past the various roads to Mexico City, and exiting on the southwest toward Guadalajara and Patzcuaro, where MEX 15 itself completes the loop on the west and south. You can actually avoid entering the historic center if you are traveling from Mexico City, for example, to Patzcuaro.

To Patzcuaro. For this lovely 45-minute drive (50 km, 31 m), you can approach MEX 15 from either Morelos Sur or Madero Pte. Soon the road becomes the four-lane MEX 120D to Tiripetio (about 20 km), where you pick up the old country road to Patzcuaro (turn right at fork just beyond Tiripetio). From here you climb mountains to pine forests and pass rich and hilly farm and grazing land. You can see Lake Patzcuaro and Janitzio Island with its towering statute of Morelos during the last leg of the trip. For an alternate route via Quiroga see "Patzcuaro."

To Mexico City. There are two basic routes to Mexico City, the Via Corta (shortcut), and the exhausting but dramatically scenic one through the Mil Cumbres (MEX 15). If you take the scenic route, the trip takes almost 5-1/2 hours; the less mountainous shortcut, 3-1/2 for its 310 km, 192 m. If you want to avoid the slowest part of the scenic route, but still have the option of visiting those sights after the Mil Cumbres park (see "On the Road" below), you can join MEX 15 on MEX 51 at Querendaro (40 km, 25 m) from Morelia.

You need to make the basic route choice when leaving Morelia, exiting on Madreo Ote. to Av. Acueducto, then picking up either the Mil Cumbres exit or the shortcut MEX 126 Maravatio exit to the north, both off the *libramiento*. The **shortcut** passes through villages like Charo, but after Querendaro it picks up speed as it passes through scenic valleys of orchards and farms. Outside Maravatio (80 km) you pick up some toll roads by following signs to MEX 15D at Atlacolmulco, from where you reach Toluca. The MEX 15 **scenic route** (see "On the Road," below) winds through the pine-forested Sierra Madre Occidental along a spiraling road that offers magnificent views. After passing through the national park of Mil Cumbres, the road becomes less difficult, yet remains scenic. Near San Jose Purua there's rolling farmland while steep mountains mark the butterfly sanctuary around Angangueo and nearby Zitacuaro. Near Valle de Bravo you hit the huge, flat valley of Toluca, dominated by the Nevado de Toluca, an extinct, snow-capped volcano. Here the shortcut joins the scenic route for the final 65 km into Mexico City, a distance facilitated by many lanes of highway (including those of MEX 15D, the new toll that cost over U. S. $6.00 for a 14-mile stretch when it first opened in '93; maybe truck boycotts have lowered the fee) but clogged with traffic and plagued by accidents. Caution is advised, and during the sudden hailstorms and torrential rains of summer, brief stops are advisable.

To Guadalajara. (See Guadalajara and "On the Road," below to Irapuato.)

To Guanajuato. (See Guanajuato and "On the Road," below to Irapua-to.)

TRAIN

The El Purepecha train that is complete with an observation car and connects Morelia with Uruapan, Patzcuaro, and overnights to Mexico City.

DIRECTORY

Airlines • Aeromar, 20 de Noviembre 110 ☎ (2-85-45).

Buses • Main terminal is located about 4 blocks from the zócalo at Valentin Gomez Farias and Eduardo Ruiz.

Car Rentals • Budget, at airport and Convention Center ☎ (5-00-23 ext. 51).

Combis • Madero Poniete between Quintana Roo and Rayon marks the beginning of the route east on Madero and then down Av. Acueducto. Service till 9 p.m.

Essentials • Woolworth Mexicana (Madero Oriente between #38 and #58).

Post Office and Telegrams • Located in Palacio Federal (Madero Oriente 369 at Serapio Rendon).

Spanish Courses • Centro Cultural de Lenguas, Av. Madero Ote. 560 ☎ (2-27-23).

Taxis • Available on street.

Tourist Office • Located in Palacio Clavijero, Nigromante 79 ☎ (3-26-54). Open 9 a.m.-8 p.m. weekdays, till 7 p.m. weekends.

Tours • For city walks or regional excursions contact your hotel or Tours Lindo Michoacan ☎ (4-99-43) and Transporte Turistico Valladolid ☎ (4-73-84). Of all Mexican cities, Morelia best evokes the grandeur of Spain. Massive and austere, and too handsome to frolic in colors, it is built in the earth tones of Madrid. Morelia is an imposing city, with colonial buildings, churches, monasteries, formal plazas, and a great cathedral. You come here to savor colonial Mexico; even your hotel room may be located in a handsomely restored 18th-century building.

ON THE ROAD

MEX 43—IRAPUATO TO MORELIA

Salamanca

At 20 km, or 12 m. • An **industrial town** based on oil-refineries, which is best to avoid by taking MEX 45 libre from Irapuato (see details in Guanajuato chapter). Once you get around Salamanca and go through the smaller town of Valle del Santiago, MEX 43 climbs through rich farming and cattle-grazing country, in an area increasingly populated by Purepecha Indians as you approach Morelia.

Yuriria

Turnoff at 45 km (30 m) and then go 3 km to town. • This small, seldomly visited town has been designated a national historical monument for its exceptional **16th-century Augustinian church** and **monastery**. Situated near the vast shores of the artificial, crater-filled lake you've been passing for some time, Yurira was a major Tarascan settlement before the Conquest. The church, with its Plateresque facade transforming into the folkloric, and its elegant **interior** with a *trompe l'oeil* **coffered ceiling,** is worth the brief detour. (Open daily.)

Cuitzeo

At 100 km, 60 m. • The small **fishing village** of Cuitzeo with the harmoniously carved portal of its **16th-century church**, is beside the enormous but extremely shallow **lake of Cuitzeo**. So shallow is this lake that during a particularly long dry season it seems to evaporate, leaving a surreal lake-bottom landscape. When full of water, you seem to skim across its surface as the road passes over a dike about 4 kilometers in length.

Morelia

At 130 km, 81 m.

MEX 15—MORELIA TO MEXICO CITY

The long, scenic route between these two cities follows MEX 15 all the way. No buses or trucks travel the first 50 miles of this route; for the faster bus route see "Getting to and from Morelia." From Morelia to Ciudad Hidalgo, there are no gas stations or restaurants.

Mil Cumbres (Thousand Peaks)

At 70 km, 44 m. • The official **viewing point** over the *magnificent forests and mountains of this national park* is located in the Sierra Madre Occidental. Nearly two hours of driving the 40 miles of twisting roads up and down these mountains covered with stately, silent **pine forests** will already have convinced you of its thousand peaks before you actually arrive at this official point. *On our last visit, the small restaurant here had nothing to eat but bags of crushed potato chips.*

Turnoff for MEX 51

At 79 km, 49 m. • This is the intersection of the faster route between Morelia and Mexico City.

Ciudad Hidalgo

At 103 km, 64 m. • Gasoline and roadside restaurants.

San Jose Purua

At 134 km, 83 m.

★**Spa San Jose Purua** • *6 km, 4 m south of MEX 15;* ☎ *(5)510-4949;* *$150 AP* • Surrounded by mountains, orange groves, and other tropical vegetation, this spa couldn't have a more spectacular **setting** in which to relax over a meal. If you stay a few days you can test the **thermal waters**, but note that *the rooms we saw of the 240 units were worn and spartanly furnished, graced only by the views; the bathrooms were more than worn.* Dining room, bar, and disco. Pool and individual, enclosed thermal baths, plus massages, jogging tracks, game room, and access to horseback riding.

Turnoff for Angangueo

At 142 km, 88 m • You'll see some fruit and curio stands on the highway marking the turn to this mining village (21 km, 13 m on a paved road through Ocampo where you turn right at zócalo, then left at end of pavement, before continuing on to Angangueo). The purpose of any visit to Angangueo is to make connections to the **Monarch Butterfly Sanctuary** *(November through March; 8 a.m.-6 p.m., no entry after 5 p.m.; fee).* Although there are weekend tours here that can be arranged through Mexico City (one tour agency is Grey Line; ☎ 533-1663), you can drive to Angangueo yourself and negotiate for a ride to the sanctuary in a four-wheel drive truck. The price is the same whether there is one or 20 using the truck (about $25 U.S.). *The drive is rough, taking nearly an hour to negotiate 6 km up to the mountain sanctuary where the butterflies migrate each year from as far away as Canada.* The cost is worth it if you've never seen the monarchs during their winter hibernation, eerily and unrecognizably clustered into massive cocoon shapes that hang from the fir trees. Their number is so great that the boughs creak from their weight and they litter the ground like autumn leaves. They are more active when the sun warms their wings. The best place to make arrangements is at the **Albergue Don Bruno** *(Morelos 92;* ☎ *[725] 8-00-26; $35)* on the main street. Since you'll need at least half a day to make this detour from MEX 15, you might want to consider making overnight arrangements at San Jose Purua, or here at the Don Bruno, which offers decent food during set meal hours *(moderate)* and 10 small, pleasant rooms around a garden *(budget).* We've heard that an alternate, if rugged, route avoids the village of Angangueo as well as the need for a truck but involves a 1-hour walk. If you want to try this, continue straight where the pavement ends in Ocampo—and get clear directions first.

Zitacuaro

At 150 km, 93 m. • This agricultural and lumbering center is surrounded by another beautiful, wooded **national park**, along mountainous roads not as sinewy as those around Mil Cumbres. Serapes and wood carvings made locally are sold along the road.

Villa Victoria

At 191 km, 118 m. • The road passes a river, where you can see people bathing, and the lake of the **Victoria Dam**. Women from Villa Victoria are known for their embroidered blouses and the tablecloths they sell along the road.

The **turnoff for Valle de Bravo** is marked. *This access road (35 km, 22 m) is the faster route to Valle de Bravo when you're approaching from Morelia.*

Valle de Bravo
Turnoff at 238 km (148 m) • A winding road leads to this village *(68 km, 42 m)*

Practical Tips

Off this triptik is an alternative route between Valle de Bravo and Toluca/Mexico City that is preferred by many: from Valle de Bravo follow the Nevado de Toluca road to MEX 134, then turn north to Toluca.

A favorite weekend resort of many Mexico City residents, especially foreigners. This immaculate **town** nestled in **pine forests** has the picturesque qualities of a Swiss village. An **artificial lake** created by a dam, Presa Miguel Aleman, provides boating, fishing, and swimming for the weekenders. A **Sunday market** provides local color, pottery for sale, and some very good Mexican food. **Views** over the dam, innumerable **waterfalls**, and **mountains** in this area can be gained by driving outside of Valle de Bravo in the direction of **Colorines** or **Avandaro**. Or just drive straight through town to the *costera*, or waterfront, and enjoy your surroundings while eating at one of the floating restaurants that are only too happy to serve you some of the local **trout**. Accommodations range from pleasant enough in-town hotels such as **Los Arcos** *(Bocanegra 310,* ☎ *[726] 2-00-42)*, and rustic cabins in the woods to the elegant ★★★**Avandaro Golf Club & Spa** *(in Avandaro 7 m south of Valle de Bravo;* ☎ *[726] 2-00-03; $120)*. This 300-acre resort has private homes and weekend villas in a country club setting. The 130 rooms and suites of the hotel share the facilities of the complex. Restaurant and bar. Pool. Fees for 18-hole golf course, tennis, health and fitness center; access to horseback riding and sailing. There are package rates for golf and spa vacations. Limo from Mexico City airport. Located near lake, 7 m south of Valle de Bravo. Contact in Mexico City at ☎ 536-7388.

Toluca
At 246 km, 153 m. • At the foot of the often snow-covered Nevado de Toluca, the city of Toluca commands Mexico's highest plateau (minimum altitude, 8,600 feet). As capital of the state of Mexico, Toluca has become a modern industrial center with a symphony orchestra, a university, numerous museums, and many government buildings. Quite wealthy, it has built a wide, tree-lined boulevard, called Paseo de Tollocan, that meanders through the city, linking it with MEX 15. In the center, the old portales still line the streets and the Zócalo has been refurbished. If you visit, look for the **Cosmovitral botanical gardens** here *(Lerdo and Juarez, south of Paseo; parking beneath square;*

open Tues.-Sun., 9 a.m.-5 p.m.; free), created in the old market building now covered with stained-glass murals. If you have extra time, visit the ultra-modern **Centro Cultural Mexiquense** (*6 km, 4 m from center; Tues.-Sun., 10 a.m.-6 p.m.; free*). This complex of museums is located toward the foot of the Nevado de Toluca (*take Paseo to Carranza, turn left, and follow signs*) and exhibits an immense tree-of-life ceramic sculpture from Metepec as well as other fine examples of regional crafts in its **Museo de Culturas Populares**; an unusual carved wooden drum from Aztec Malinalco is in its **Museo de Antropologia**.

Despite its museums, this busy city is mostly visited for its location at the crossroads of the Morelia and Mexico City highways (regardless of the route) as well as for MEX 55 and MEX 55D leading to Taxco and Acapulco. Many restaurants are available, including a cafeteria at the Centro Cultural and the very tradiitonal **Hosteria de las Ramblas**, two blocks from the central plaza (*Poral 20 de Noviembre 107; open breakfast through early dinner; inexpensive*)—try the appetizers of chalupas and sopes. Just 8 km on MEX 15 toward Mexico City is the convenient ★ ★ ★ **Castel Plaza Las Fuentes** (*Paseo Tollocan km 57.5; Apartado 813; [72] 16-28-56; $90*), a modern business hotel with 100 rooms, restaurant, bar with entertainment, an indoor heated pool, and even tennis.

Mexico City

At 310 km, 192 m on MEX 15, you arrive in Mexico City through Chapultepec Park and continue on the Paseo de la Reforma to reach the city center. The 65-km, 40-m drive from Toluca is mostly on a multilane highway, but it is heavily trafficked and often winding. Plan on an hour's drive.

PATZCUARO

The **pine-forested mountains** of the high **Sierra Madres** and the tranquillity of **Lake Patzcuaro** (POTS-kwah-row) infuse this **rustic town** with a melancholy atmosphere unique in Mexico. Visiting its **Indian market** filled with hammered copper pitchers and wool serapes, or watching the Purepecha, descendants of the Tarascans, paddle across the lake in their dugout canoes, *you can observe traditions that date back to before the conquest,* when Patzcuaro ("place of temples") was the capital of the Tarascan kingdom. Walking its **cobblestone streets** lined with one-story homes topped with sloping, orange-tiled roofs, *you are transported back to the 16th century, when Patzcuaro was the capital of Michoacan* under Bishop Vasco de Quiroga. When this kindly ecclesiastic died, the capital was moved to Morelia, and Patzcuaro became a backwater during the later centuries of elaborate architectural styles. Having skipped centuries of fashion, Patzcuaro today is worn and wonderful, rooted in the 16th century, and as traditional as the Purepecha themselves.

Although some travelers merely stop in Patzcuaro for the Friday market or for a shopping spree in this great crafts center, they miss its special atmosphere and beauty, which require a few nights' stay to appreciate. Spectacular scenery can be seen during a boat ride across the lake or on the roads through the pine forests to craft villages and the ruins at Tzintzuntzan. Its atmosphere is never absorbed better than in leisurely walks through town and quiet evenings before a fireplace.

KEY TO PATZCUARO

Sights • In this very traditional, atmospheric town you will find early colonial architecture, Purepecha Indians, and the relaxing country ambience of a highland lake and pine forests.

Excursions • Small craft-producing villages, pine forests, and lake views provide short, worthwhile side trips from town, as do the small ruins of Tzintzuntzan.

Shopping • Excellent crafts, from quality lacquer plates and copperware to weaving and the most delightful straw creations, can be bought in shops and markets. Market days: *Patzcuaro*, Friday, and smaller ones Tuesday and Sunday; *Erongaricuaro*, Sunday.

Famous Fiestas • Holy Week in Tzintzuntzan and Patzcuaro; annual Copper Fair around mid-August in Santa Clara del Cobre; Day of the Dead on November 1-2 at Janitzio and Tzintzuntzan; Fiesta of the Virgin of La Salud on December 7-8 in Patzcuaro.

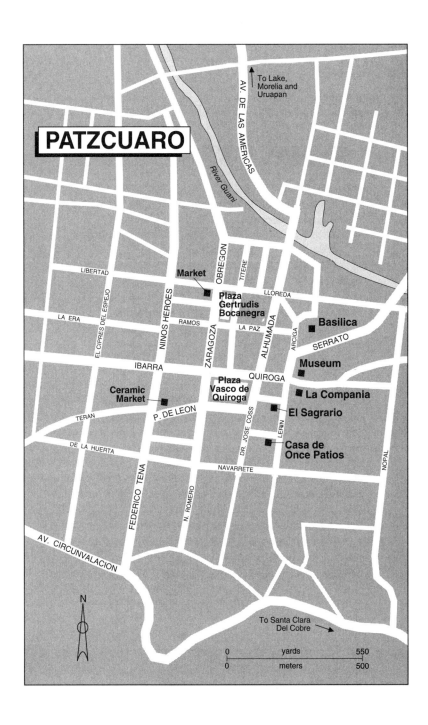

PATZCUARO

To Lake,
Morelia and
Uruapan

AV. DE LAS AMERICAS

River Guani

LIBERTAD

LA ERA

EL CIPRES DEL ESPEJO

NINOS HEROES

RAMOS

ZARAGOZA

OBREGON

TITTERE

Market

**Plaza
Gertrudis
Bocanegra**

LLOREDA

LA PAZ

ALHUMADA

ARCIGA

Basilica

SERRATO

IBARRA

QUIROGA

Museum

TERAN

**Ceramic
Market**

P. DE LEON

**Plaza
Vasco de
Quiroga**

DR. JOSE COSS

LERIN

La Compania

El Sagrario

DE LA HUERTA

**Casa de
Once Patios**

FEDERICO TENA

N. ROMERO

NAVARRETE

NOPAL

AV. CIRCUNVALACION

N

To Santa Clara
Del Cobre

| 0 | yards | 550 |
| 0 | meters | 500 |

Where to Stay • Comfortable hotels at bargain rates in all but deluxe categories. Camping, too.

Where to Eat • Patzcuaro whitefish and other lake specialties at reasonable prices.

Entertainment • Limited.

Getting Around • On foot in town and by second-class buses, combis, or taxis for excursions. No car rentals.

Practical Tips

Patzcuaro is over 7,000 feet in altitude, and its lake breezes make it cooler than most highland areas, particularly in the evenings. Summer rains turn to drizzles here, making it much like New England in the fall. Bring a warm sweater.

Street names in the center of town change each block, so rely more on your sense of direction than on addresses.

Most stores close between 2-4 p.m. and many restaurants, especially those not in hotels, close by 9 p.m.

WHAT TO SEE AND DO

Plaza Gertrudis Bocanegra

This plaza is usually the first place one stumbles upon in Patzcuaro. It is not the main plaza, which is discussed next, but rather the hub of commercial life, including the famous **market** that starts on the west side of the plaza and spills back into neighboring streets on its most important day, Friday. Once called the Plaza San Agustin for the 16th-century church on its north side, it has been renamed for the town's heroine and martyr of the Independence Movement. Not only has the name of the plaza changed, but also the church now is **La Biblioteca.** Inside this library is an impressive, richly colored **mural by Juan O'Gorman** that provides an excellent introduction to the history of this area. The upper half shows Tarascan customs and beliefs, such as the creation of the lakes by volcanic eruptions. The center is devoted to the Tarascan victory over invading Aztecs (seen here as captives). The lower part depicts the tortures of the Tarascans by the sadistic conquerer Nuno de Guzman. The Indian woman on a horse is Erindira, niece of the Tarascan ruler, who is said to be the first Indian woman ever to mount a horse when she rode off to find other Tarascans to fight the Spaniards. The very bottom presents the town's famous bishop and protector of the Indians, Don Vasco de Quiroga. To the side is the plaza's new namesake, Gertrudis Bocanegra. *Open Mon.-Sat., 9 a.m.-7 p.m.; in summer, closed Sat.*

Plaza Vasco de Quiroga

One block south of Plaza Bocanegra • This quiet and elegant **zócalo**, surrounded by the predominantly **16th-century mansions** of Patzcuaro's nobility, is dedicated to Bishop Quiroga, affectionately known as *Tata* ("father") Vasco. His statue stands in the center of the square's ancient shaded park. The nobles have disappeared now, but their houses are used as hotels and shops—that of a marquis is now the **Municipal Palace**. The crafts shop at number 48, with fine carved wooden doors on the second floor, belonged to Prince Huitzimengari, son of the last Tarascan ruler (who abdicated to the Spaniards).

Casa de los Once Patios

House of Eleven Patios • If you walk just a bit up Calle Dr. Coss from the Plaza Vasco and turn left up a small street with steps, you will come to the entrance (on your right) of this **18th-century ex-convent** den and seeing artisans embroidering blouses or delicately painting gold onto black lacquer. Across from this ex-convent is one of Don Vasco's 16th-century "hospitals."

Calle Lerin

Just past the Casa de los Once Patios, turn left onto a small street whose name seems to change constantly but whose curving path passes through the religious heart of colonial Patzcuaro. • On the left near Calle Portugal stand the massive, weathered buttresses and wall of **El Sagrario**. Dedicated in 1717, this **church** contained the statue of the town's venerated Virgin de la Salud until it was transferred to the Basilica during this century. A bit farther on the right is Patzcuaro's first cathedral, **La Compania**, built by Don Vasco de Quiroga in the 16th century. When the capital was moved to Morelia in 1566, Jesuits took over this church, whose years now weigh heavily on its crumbling walls. Though its floorboards creak under your footstep, a visit **inside** its walls is quite moving (closed during lunch). In front of the Museo de Artes Populares (which was the College of San Nicolas, also founded by Don Vasco), is a **16th-century well**. A local legend relates that, upon hearing the town lacked water, the good Tata Vasco set out with his cane "of neither gold nor silver, but of wood"; when he tapped the ground with his cane at this spot, water sprang forth. It is said his cane is preserved in La Compania Church, but we couldn't find it.

Museo de Artes Populares

Quiroga and Lerin; Open Tues.-Sat., 9 a.m.-7 p.m., and Sun., 9 a.m. - 3 p.m.; Admission fee • Housed in a building of *one of the earliest colleges in the Americas* (1540), this delightful **museum** has numerous display rooms surrounding a glorious garden **patio**. Some of the workers at the reception desk speak English and are very knowledgeable about the town's history. Guides accompany you in each room, but for the most part they speak only Spanish (their presence is a polite way of protecting the collection). No matter, for these exhibits speak for themselves. The first several rooms display **colonial crafts** and **furnishings**, including an original floor with a design made of cattle bones embedded in cement, apparently a common practice in colonial times.

One room has **16th-century frescos**, recently exposed from under centuries of paint. Most of the rooms display the crafts for which this region is famous, including some styles that no longer can be found. One of the rooms uses the wooden spoons, copper plates, and ceramics of Michoacan to create a marvelous **traditional kitchen**. Exquisite **lacquerware** from the 18th and 19th centuries, primitive *retablos* (paintings recounting miracles), and a **16th-century crucifix**, "*Cristo del Pareo,*" made in the Purepecha *pasta de cana* technique round out these fine exhibits. (Pasta de cana was a pre-Hispanic Tarascan technique of making idols that became quite popular with the Catholic Church. An easy-to-model paste of cornstalks and orchid glue created hollow figures, which were easily carried in religious processions.) Behind this colonial building is a traditional **Purepecha wooden house** sitting on top of a 12th-century stone platform of their ancestors. The platform dates from before the time of the unification of the Tarascan empire at Tzintzuntzan (entrance from within museum).

Basilica of Nuestra Senora de la Salud

Arciga and Buenavista. Lerin turns into Arciga as you walk past the museum and continues for a few short blocks until you come to an enormous church plaza. • This church was started by the busy Don Vasco as a cathedral, but his plans were never completed. Most of the present basilica results from building projects in more recent centuries, and it is a surprisingly sumptuous church that has been built for the Virgin de la Salud (health), venerated by the populace for her miraculous healing powers. But judging by the offerings surrounding El Senor de la Cana near the entrance, he too responds to the people's prayers.

EXCURSIONS

Within 20 minutes of town lie villages with distinctive offerings of crafts, convents, or ruins. The routes to these villages provide spectacular scenery with either closeup views of Indian life on the shores of the lake or panoramic views of the whole area from high in the mountains. Another excursion, certainly the most popular, is on the lake itself. *All the road trips can be made by car or second-class bus from the Central Camionera.*

Lake Patzcuaro

4 km, or 2-1/2 m, from town • Even if you don't have time to take a **boat ride on the lake**, you will want to visit its shores and see its enormous expanse (about 30 miles in circumference). The dock area is especially lively on the morning of the **Friday market**, with families and fishermen arriving in dugout canoes and cooks selling fried fish to passersby. The scene is lovely even without the famous butterfly nets of the fishermen, now used only on special occcasions. Apparently, these nets, brought out on some fiesta days, belong more to traditions of the past than to the present.

Once boats plied back and forth across the lake, taking you to distant villages like Erongaricuaro. While much of this service has been discontinued with the opening of a road, it is still quite easy to take a boat to the largest island in the lake, **Janitzio** (ha-NEAT-see-oh). A huge statue of Morelos, hero of Independence, dominates the lake from its location atop Janitzio. When you visit this small island with its **fishing village**, you can climb to the top of the island for a fabulous lake view. Collective boats with wooden benches for passengers gather at the dock between 7 a.m. and 6 p.m. Fares are controlled by the Tourist Department, and tickets (inexpensive) must be purchased at an office on the dock. The trip to Janitzio takes one-half hour each way and gives you an hour to explore the island.

To drive to the lake, follow Avenida de las Americas to just before the Pemex station. Turn left at sign for Uruapan and then follow the muelle sign for the dock. There is a small parking fee at the lot behind the dock. Buses and combis marked "Lago-Centro" run to the dock, and those marked "Santa Ana" pass within walking distance. Ask for the *muelle* (MOY-yeah).

Tzintzuntzan

17 km (10-1/2 m) along the old Morelia road • It takes only 20 minutes to drive to this village whose name means "Place of the Hummingbird" in Purepecha. Originally the capital of the Tarascan empire, it was also the first capital of this Spanish province and is presently the center of a **crafts industry** producing **ceramics** and **strawwork**. The road leads you through cattle and horse country along the edge of the lake. If you are taking the bus from Patzcuaro, take one marked "Quiroga," which passes through Tzintzuntzan.

The Ruins of Tzintzuntzan (sin-SOON-sahn)

To the right of the road just before you enter town (turn right at sign marked "Las Yacatas." Open 10 a.m.-5 p.m.; small admission charge. • Capital of the Tarascan empire during the last years before the arrival of the Spaniards, Tzintzuntzan was the seat of an empire covering the entire state of Michoacan. *On their arrival in this region, the Spaniards estimated that 40,000 Tarascans lived in this pre-Hispanic city* and described these ruins as holding temples in which burned perpetual fires to their primary god, **Curicaueri** (god of fire). Palaces of nobles and homes of artisans lay below the religious center. Only the *ruins* of these religious buildings, called *yacatas*, remain today. They are built on a massive artificial platform that is the hill you must climb before paying your admission fee. The ancient Tarascans ascended more majestically by a broad staircase, now rubble. Five *yacatas*, perhaps dedicated to the five principal gods of the Tarascans, dominate the area from the height of this artificial hill. The unique shape of the *yacatas* distinguished Tarascan culture from the more famous of Mexico's ancient civilizations. Rectangular platforms are attached to circular ones to form a kind of T-shape. Circular temples with conical roofs once crowned each of these strangely shaped pyramids. Although no carvings embellish what is left of this ceremonial center, it provides a wonderful **view** of the lake and modern village below. The museum exhibits include a scale model of how the ancient city once appeared.

Main Street

The **main street** of the town is lined by innumerable shops selling local **ceramic plates** painted with fishing scenes, and **straw weavings** of crucifixes, lampshades, delightful mobiles, and other charming bric-a-brac. The only way to resist all the bargains before you is to retreat to the town's **16th-century church and monastery.** In 1526, four years after the Spanish subjugation of the Tarascan empire, Franciscan friars arrived in Tzintzuntzan to begin converting the Tarascans to Christianity. The enormity of their responsibility can best be judged by the size of the **courtyard** alone, which is said to equal three football fields. An outdoor chapel faces onto this courtyard, which was the only space large enough to accommodate the thousands of Indians in need of conversion. A plaque relates a *miracle* that occurred here in 1540, greatly facilitating the conversion process. During the catechism, a holy saint flew in the air above the crowd and swooped down to kiss a devout Tarascan woman, who was so delighted that she was christened Feliz ("happy"), a name which then became popular in Mexico. Remnants of **frescos** cover walls of the monastery (open 10 a.m.-5 p.m. daily). The town was deprived of its importance in 1540 when Don Vasco de Quiroga moved the seat of his diocese to Patzcuaro, where there was more ample water and land for founding a Spanish city.

Ihuitzio

Along the road between Patzcuaro and Tzintzuntzan you will pass a sign for Ihuitzio, a small village with ruins of another pre-Hispanic Tarascan site. These unrestored ruins are not very interesting, although they once included five yacatas. A chacmool sculpture, similar to those found at more famous and faraway ruins such as Tula and Chichen Itza, was discovered here.

Santa Clara del Cobre

18 km (11 m) south of town • If you are traveling by car, leave town on Ninos Heroes and then follow the initial signs to Ario de Rosales. The short drive to this town climbs to pine forests that present breathtaking panoramic **views** of the lake area.

This **picturesque town** of Santa Clara del Cobre ("copper"), was founded by Vasco de Quiroga to promote the Tarascan's skills in working **copper**. This craft industry continues today, and the town provides most of Mexico with its worked copper. Even the kiosk in its zócalo and the lamps and candelabra in its churches are made of copper. As you walk through town gazing into the shops selling copper frying pans, plates, pitchers, bells, and copper everything, you can hear the soft sound of hammering that becomes all pervasive during the annual **copper fair** (mid-August). If you follow your ears, you will see these fine products being made in local workshops—one of the finest is the **Galeria Tiamuri** *(Obregon 141, one block behind you as you face the kiosk from Morelos, the main street; closed Tuesday)*, a cooperative that produces the unusual silver and copper jewelry and plates of artist Ana Pellicier. Following the main street from the kiosk, you pass a copper store with beautifully shaped vases *(Morelos 252)* before reaching the **useo del Cobre** *(across from Morelos 295; 9 a.m.-2 p.m., 3-6:30 p.m. daily; free)*. This small museum displays and sells some prize-winning copper creations.

> **AUTHOR'S OBSERVATION**
>
> *If you've driven out this way, you might consider adding a lunch in Tacambaro (35 km, 21 m)—see restaurants below.*

Erongaricuaro

21 km (13 m) around lake • To reach this **Tarascan village**, *drive Avenida de las Americas and turn left at the Pemex, then follow the lake road past the* muelle. The paved road ends at this village. Second- class buses leave from the terminal at Ahumada 68 in Patzcuaro.

This beautiful ride around the lake replaces what used to be a beautiful boat ride across it. The drive enables you to observe the **daily life of the Purepecha** as well as the quiet lake dotted with solitary fishermen patiently waiting in their boats among the reeds. Unless you make this trip during Erongaricuaro's **Sunday market** (mostly vegetables and firewood, but very traditional), you won't find much to see and do in town. There are some good **views** over the lake, a **16th-century Franciscan church** and a **decaying zócalo**. In fact, *it seems so far from the rest of the world we find it hard to believe that Andre Breton and other French surrealists managed to discover this town, much less live in it, during World War II.* Whatever is or isn't happening in Erongaricuaro, the short, **scenic drive** is most gratifying. Along the way you can drive over the causeway to **Jaracuaro,** which was an island until recently, or see if you can find any masks being made in the village of **Tocuaro** (the town on the left coming from Patzcuaro, just before the causeway).

SHOPPING

Shopping is one of the main pastimes in Patzcuaro, and with good reason, for the state of Michoacan is one of the major craft-producing centers in Mexico, and Patzcuaro has one of the country's most famous Indian markets, offering for sale many of the crafts of the region. The main market day is Friday, but Tuesday and Sunday are also market days. On any day you will find yourself constantly in and out of the numerous small shops around town inspecting, and most likely buying, some of the many examples of the regional popular arts. *Patzcuaro is a particularly good place to shop for lacquerware, rebozos, serapes, sweaters, straw items, huaraches, copperware, and handwoven fabric.*

Many of the crafts produced today trace their origins to pre-Hispanic times and their continued strength to the support of Bishop Vasco de Quiroga, who did much to encourage native artists and artisans. The area is still noted for its ceramics, weaving and embroidery, wood carving, copperwork, and lacquerware. On the whole, crafts from Michoacan are reserved, lacking the spontaneity and gaiety of the crafts from Oaxaca, but the reserve does not detract from their appeal. Rather it seems more in keeping with the tranquillity of the area and its people.

CERAMICS

While shopping for the better crafts, you will want to look out for the specialities from certain villages. *Ceramic production dominates the life of several towns.* Some of the best ceramics come from **Capula**, where the rich chocolate-color **pottery** is made in molds, hand- painted with polychrome decorations, often of stylized fish, and takes the form of bowls, casseroles, and dishes. **Tzintzuntzan** also produces some attractive molded brown pottery, although more recently it has been turning out handsome cream-colored ceramics—platters, cups, and saucers—with simple, often delightfully painted fishing scenes. From **San Jose de la Gracia** come handmolded, deep- green **ceramics**, the color resulting from the glaze containing copper oxide. Probably most unusual and striking are the *pinas* (*"pineapples"*), which are actually **ceramic water jars** shaped like pineapples and displaying the grooves and bumps peculiar to the fruit, and even bearing a lid on top molded in the form of a spiky crown. Not to be missed are the bizarre **ceramic figures** from **Ocumicho**. Surrealistic, sometimes frightening, sometimes amusing, they portray devils, serpents, and animals—often all three together—devouring one another.

The finest examples of these ceramics are not always available in Patzcuaro. On our last visit, the largest and best selection was available in Morelia. And, as is often the case in Mexico, some of the best examples are sent to Mexico City, where they are sold in government-sponsored craft stores (see "Mexico City: Shopping").

WEAVING

In weaving, **Patzcuaro** produces an abundance of handloomed fabrics (*mantas*), often in the form of tablecloths and napkins (the best ones are cotton, *puro algodon*). The region also produces some fine serapes, many in alternating grays, whites, and blacks, but some rare ones in jet black or deep fuchsia. The richly colored indigo cotton rebozos worn by the Purepecha women are particularly interesting, and knitted thick (and rough) wool sweaters have become a regional specialty.

WOODWORKING

Woodworking continues its popularity in **Patzcuaro**. The forests surrounding Patzcuaro provide the red pine for the hand-carved tables, chests, chairs, and children's furniture and toys. Wooden masks are carved for special festivals and for such traditional dances as "Los Viejitos." From wood also come the guitars from Paracho, **the guitar capital of Mexico.**

Famous throughout Mexico, these instruments are said to rival the finest produced in Spain. As nonmusicians, we leave it to you to judge.

COPPERWARE

Santa Clara del Cobre is *the* copperware-producing village in Mexico. The hand-hammered and polished copperware takes a variety of forms, ranging from huge containers capable of holding a small horse to frying pans, vases, and even jewelry.

STRAW WEAVING

From **Tzintzuntzan** come some delightful straw creations—mobiles, fish, helicopters, and planes as well as interesting representations of angels, crucifixes, and the Virgin Mary. Attractive sisal rugs, difficult to find elsewhere in Mexico, can be found in Patzcuaro.

LACQUERWARE

Of all its crafts, however, the area is probably best known for its lacquerware. Some archaeologists have speculated that in pre-Hispanic times this part of Western Mexico may have been the center of diffusion for lacquer techniques from Arizona to Argentina. During the colonial period, lacquerwork expanded to include such household items as chests and sewing boxes. Yet the pre-Hispanic tradition continued with work on gourds and wooden platters. Some of the exquisite lacquerware from Uruapan and Quiroga made during the colonial period are now museum pieces. Although much contemporary lacquerware is crude and garish, **Patzcuaro** still produces some lovely work, including that by the Cerdas, a family whose work was as respected in the 17th century as it is now.

Uruapan made a unique type of lacquerware by a method known as incrustation. Designs, usually of flowers, were incised on a lacquered background, carved out, filled with a different colored lacquer, rubbed with the palm of the hand, and polished. The procedure was tedious and difficult, but the results, extraordinary. Unfortunately, today the designs usually are simply painted directly over the background.

Patzcuaro is famous for its delicate, intricate designs, the best with gold inlays and some with the less expensive bronze. The lacquerwork is done on chests, trays, boxes, and pendants. The Oriental as well as Spanish flavor of the designs from Patzcuaro and Uruapan has raised speculation of early direct contact with the Orient. A more likely, but less exotic, explanation is that the influence resulted from the importation of Oriental lacquerware into Mexico during the colonial period. Nevertheless, the influence is there, and the lucky traveler to this area is the beneficiary.

WHERE TO SHOP

If you have planned your trip wisely, you will be in Patzcuaro on a Friday and begin your day with a trip to the **market**. Located next to Plaza Gertrudis Bocanegra and extending west and south for several blocks, on Fridays the market overflows with Purepecha from the surrounding area buying and selling food, household necessities, clothing, and crafts. This is one of the major Indian markets in Mexico, crowded but calm, and subdued with a melancholy air about it as befits this lakeside village surrounded by mountains and forests. Stands sprawl over several blocks offering for sale fruits and vegetables, straw items, wooden spoons, tablecloths, serapes, heavy woolen sweaters, copperware, and lacquerware. Wander at your leisure through the narrow streets and narrower paths between the stands. Nowhere will you suffer the hard sell typical of the more tourist-oriented markets. If you stroll over to the corner of Ponce de Leon and Ninos Heroes, three blocks southwest of the Plaza Gertrudis Bocanegra, you will find the colorful **ceramic market** dominated by Purepecha women and offering some cheaper, utilitarian pottery.

The market area is a good place to buy serapes, woolen sweaters, and rebozos. For ceramics, lacquerware, fabrics, copper, and straw creations, however, hold off until you see the normally better quality items in the town shops and the Casa de los Once Patios.

For an interesting selection of quality crafts with some of the best prices in Patzcuaro, walk over to the **Casa de los Once Patios** (see "What to See and Do"), a quiet "shopping center" where a number of small shops, many devoted to a single craft, are housed in a former convent. Here you will find some of the best Patzcuaro lacquerware: delicately painted plates, boxes, earrings, and pins—many with black backgrounds and brilliant gilded colors, either with gold inlay (advertised as 23.5 kts) or less expensive bronze. Some of the best examples are in the first patio. Here and elsewhere throughout the 11 patios you can see artisans engaged in their intricate craft. At other shops in the patios you can find copper and some silverwork, including silver cups and silver reproductions of Purepecha wedding and ceremonial jewelry, embroidered dresses and blouses, creations in straw, and hand-loomed fabrics (tablecloths and napkins; check to see if they're all cotton, or *algodon*), Paracho guitars as well as sisal rugs.

Elsewhere, there is plenty to choose from. Our favorite shop is **Tzintzuni** (Calle Quiroga, between the museum and P. Vasco; no credit cards), with fine crafts from all of Mexico as well as exceptional works from this region. Here you can find Ana Pellicer silver and copper jewelry, Francisca Rodriquez's folk paintings and chests, and unusually fanciful pieces from Ocumicho and Tzintzuntzan. Across from the basilica, **La Galeria Dos** (Arciga 20) has some unusual crafts and decorator items, including quality Oaxacan serapes and Talavera ware—with prices to match. You can find huaraches, regional serapes, and charro leather goods at **La Montura Regional** (Plaza Vasco 56, north portal) and the now rarely made laquerware encrustado at the venerable **Casa Cerda** (Calle Dr. Coss, on left at end of first block south of P. Vasco). You might want to check out the *fabricas* on the entrance road into town (Av. de las Americas). Along with numerous neocolonial furniture shops, there are: **El Arte de las Mantas** (at #123), which makes some of the best cotton tablecloths and placemats, and will even make them to order for you—remember to bargain; **El Gobelino** (at #119), with wool and cotton rugs; and, closer to town, **Mex-Ubeda Tapetes** (at #25), specializing in hemp rugs.

FIESTAS

The **Day of the Dead** ceremonies on the island of Janitzio have become so internationally famous that the thousands of tourists attending the nightlong vigil on November 1 have just about destroyed the beauty they come to observe. At midnight the ceremony begins and villagers proceed to the cemetery carrying candles, traditional flowers (marigolds), and food and drink to sustain the souls of the deceased. Once the dead eat the spirit of the food, the living eat its substance. The entire night is spent in candlelight at the cemetery and nearby church with prayers, singing, and drinking for the souls of dead ancestors. Near sunrise, so many candles have been lit for the dead that photographs can be taken by their light. Although the Janitzio celebration is the most famous, the one at the cemetery of the nearby village of Tzintzuntzan has grown popular, too. Local tourism officials have responded to the demand for these events by arranging special boats to Janitzio but there are still delays.

During **Holy Week**, other moving ceremonies occur in both Tzintzuntzan and Patzcuaro. Residents of Tzintzuntzan perform passion plays starting on Holy Thursday with the Last Supper and ending on Good Friday with the Fall from the Cross. There is also a straw-crafts fair in the village at this time. On Good Friday, Patzcuaro is famous for its Procession of the Crosses.

The night of **December 7** begins the fiesta of the miraculous *Virgin de La Salud,* when thousands of pilgrims, many of them Purepecha dressed in traditional costumes, fill the streets. The following day and night include masses at the Basilica, processions, and fireworks. The famous regional "Dance of Los Viejitos" is performed with usual good humor as young men act the role of "old men" who try to get their rickety joints to dance a lively jig. A crafts fair accompanies the celebrations.

For a week around the Fiesta of the Assumption (August 15), Santa Clara del Cobre celebrates its annual **Copper Fair.** Floats and religious processions accompany competitions for prizes for the best copper craftsmanship.

WHERE TO STAY

For so provincial a town, Patzcuaro has surprisingly attractive and decent hotels at low prices—so low in fact, that we should put a √ for good buy next to each hotel. Most of the year it is quite easy to find accommodations in these hotels, especially during the week. On weekends, when Mexicans arrive for a relaxing time away from the cities and tourists arrive for the Friday market, hotels are fuller. During the Day of the Dead festival, reservations are necessary six months in advance. If you are without a car, you will probably prefer the in-town hotels, but buses and combis marked "Lago-Centro" and "Santa Ana" run regularly along the Av. de las Americas, making the hotels there accessible to you as well. Although some hotels have pools, you will probably find a fireplace more useful from June through February.

To address correspondence, write to Patzcuaro, Mich., Mexico. To reserve by phone, call area code 454.

MODERATE

Posada Don Vasco   ★★★

Av. de las Americas 450, 2 km from town; ☎ *2-02-27; $63* • On the road between the town and lake spreads this comfortable, colonial-style hotel built around courtyards and gardens. A new wing has increased the Posada's capacity to about 100 rooms. The new rooms are large and pleasant, with carpeting and balconies or patios. Some of the older, and less expensive, rooms can be small, but occasionally they have fine views of the lake. A separate trailer park is next to the hotel. The atmosphere here is never better than in early evening when fires are lit in the main cocktail patio to rid the night of its chill. While the Posada is not in the town's center, it provides much of the local evening entertainment, with its ancient, unautomated bowling alleys, billiard tables, and movies. Heated pool and tennis court, too. Restaurant has evening entertainment. Parking.

INEXPENSIVE

Mision San Manuel   ★★

Plaza Vasco de Quiroga at Portal Aldama 12; ☎ *2-13-13; $35* • In a converted 16th-century mansion, this hotel with fine colonial arcades and rich wood detailing is a good addition to Patzcuaro's hotels. Its 19 rooms are cozy; those with high woodbeam ceilings and working fireplaces preferred. All have modern tiled bathrooms. A good buy and location in the center of town. Restaurant, bar. Parking.

Mansion Iturbe   ★

Plaza Vasco de Quiroga at Portal Morelos 59; ☎ *2-03-68 $37* • This former 17th-century mansion still has an abundant, overgrown garden courtyard and 10 large rooms with high ceilings and lots of sunlight. Some rooms have view of plaza. Restaurant.

Los Escudos   ★

Plaza Vasco de Quiroga at Portal Hidalgo 73; ☎ *2-01-38; $34* • A rustic hotel with rooms around colonial courtyards; its 30 rooms with fireplaces can be small; those on the second floor are best. Pleasant service. Restaurant.

BUDGET

Meson del Gallo   ★

Dr. Coss 20; ☎ *2-14-74; $28* • Close to the Plaza Vasco de Quiroga, this modern hotel has 20 small yet bright rooms and 5 suites around small gardens and a pool. Restaurant and bar. Parking.

Posada de la Basilica   ★

Arciga 6; ☎ *2-11-08; $30* • An intimate and attractive inn housed in a 17th-century building. Better rooms can be found than the 11 here, though some of these, despite their old baths, can be pleasant and have working fireplaces. Unique for such a centrally located hotel, however, is the view of the mountains and lake from the patio and restaurant/lounge.

Hosteria de San Felipe ★

Lazaro Cardenas 321; ☎ *2-12-98; $49* • On the same road as Posada Don Vasco (despite the different street name), but a bit closer to town, this small, quiet motel has its 13 rooms arranged around a garden cum parking lot. Rooms are large for the price and furnished in contemporary colonial style. Restaurant and bar. Parking.

CAMPING

El Pozo Trailer Park

About 3.3 km from town on the road to Morelia, right next to the lake; 20 sites with all hookups, laundry, boat, fishing.

WHERE TO EAT

While Patzcuaro has not yet reached the stage of tourism where tournedos bearnaise is served, Italian coffee machines and cappuccino have become the rage. Its local cuisine is distinctive, if a bit bland. Lake Patzcuaro gives to this mountainous region a variety of fish. Subtle *pescado blanco de Patzcuaro* (whitefish), considered a delicacy in Mexico City's restaurants, is plentiful here. The *trucha* ("trout") is less famous but more flavorful. These fish are prepared in a variety of styles, *al mojo de ajo* ("grilled with garlic"), *natural* or *a la plancha* ("plain" and "grilled"). But usually they will be prepared with a light egg batter and then sauted *(rebozada)*, a style that best enhances their delicate flavor. Two other fish specialties are seen on menus as *botanas*, or appetizers, and are sold along the wharf—*charales*, which we think are sardines, and *boquerones*, which we believe are smelts. Both these tiny and flavorful fish are simply fried or fried and then tossed with tomatoes, onion, and chiles a la Mexicana.

Another dish found in most restaurants is the very traditional *sopa Tarasca*, a tomato-base soup with the slightly bitter taste of *pasilla chile* plus cheese, cream, and tortilla pieces. It's addictive to those who like its rich flavor, and you could find yourself dreaming about it during cool fall evenings at home.

There is not a great deal of variety in local restaurants, and the offerings tend to be dull, yet adequate. All are pretty quiet at night, with those clustering near the dock often closed by 6 p.m. and those in town by 9 p.m. The best prices on lake fish are down near the dock, where the afternoon scene can be quite lively with strolling musicians and day trippers, especially on market day. Right on the dock are numerous little restaurants frying up the lake fish and serving them at bargain prices. We particularly like **Las Truchas** (*toward the end of the dock*), not only because it is one of the few with a view of the lake, but also because it prepares its charales and trucha to order, not in advance. For greater refinement in service and ambience, you need to head a block inland from the lake, where **La Carreta** serves *sopa de pescado* and red snapper as well as the lake fish at moderate prices. The priciest fish is at the attractive **Posada Don Vasco** *(open breakfast; 1-4 p.m.; 7-10 p.m.)* one of the busier restaurants, especially those nights (Wednesday and Saturday) when it offers traditional music. Here you might choose the *sopa de Tarasca*, the empanadas, or even a green salad. Most town restaurants cluster around the Plaza Vasco de Quiroga, where **Los Escudos** is an intimate and good spot for stopping throughout the day, for a breakfast of *huevos Michoacanos,* for an inexpensive comida corrida, or simply a torta at lunch, or for just a nighttime cappuccino (beware—it's often served with karo syrup). Elsewhere on this square, such as at **El Patio** which sometimes has traditional music, or **Dona Paca** *(Hotel Mansion Iturbe)* with its thick *Tarasca* soup, you'll find the same modest price range and similarly acceptable food. The more adventurous, however, might just join the locals at one of the chicken stands that open up in the late afternoon around the arcades of the Plaza Gertrudis Bocanegra.

If you have an afternoon to spend driving through the magnificent Michoacan sierra, perhaps after having explored Santa Clara del Cobre, you might enjoy the tasty and abundant comida corrida at **El Tejaban** *(in Tacambaro, 50 km or 31 m; call ☎ (454) 6-04-32 to reserve and check hours; inexpensive.)* Set on a hillside next to a waterfall and with a panoramic view over the countryside found just before you enter Tacambaro, this snappy restaurant offers a number of daily entrees (mostly grilled meat dishes) that determine the price of the set-price meal. You'll be served garlic bread, enchiladas, and spicy soups, as well as dessert. The food is traditional; the drive memorable.

ENTERTAINMENT

Patzcuaro goes to sleep quite early. As you wander about the market square in the evening and check on what the women are cooking up on the street corners, you will discover that the town is very quiet. Apart from the synthesizers pumping away at too many restaurants, including **Los Escudos** and the **Posada Don Vasco** most nights, there is little happening. The famous regional dance "Los Viejitos," can be enjoyed Wednesdays and Saturdays at the **Posada Don Vasco.**

GETTING TO AND FROM PATZCUARO

AIR

No direct flights, but the Morelia and Uruapan airports are less than an hour away by rental car.

BUS

First-class **ADO** and almost first-class **Flecha Amarilla** connect Patzcuaro to the rest of Mexico with daily service to Morelia, Uruapan, and direct service to Mexico City.

TRAIN

Trains, which first opened this region to tourists, still connect the town to Morelia and Uruapan and include daily service on the overnight *servicio estrella* El Purepecha to Mexico City with reclining seats.

CAR

Two roads connect Patzcuaro to **Morelia**. Both roads start at the end of the Av. de las Americas, but the faster one is marked "Tirepetio." This is the road to take, followed by signs on the Morelia libramiento for Maravatio, if you are going to Mexico City (see "Morelia" for details). The older Quiroga road takes you through Tzintzuntzan and adds about 15 minutes to the Morelia trip. Both routes are scenic, paved, and less than 60 km (37 m) long. Take the Quiroga route if you're going to **Guadalajara** (turn north onto MEX 15 at Quiroga) or if you want to dawdle in craft villages —in Tzintzuntzan; in **Patambicho** with its stone carvings sold along the highway; in **Quiroga** center with its shops and market selling guitars from Paracho, varnished baskets, and whatnots from the region; and in Capula (18 km, 11 m south of Quiroga on MEX 15 in the direction of Morelia, then 2 km east on a dirt road) where you can buy some fine examples of the local pottery at the community shop Alfareria de **Capula** (hours uncertain; be willing to ask around and wait for the keeper of the keys).

The road to **Uruapan** starts to the left near the Pemex station on the Av. de las Americas and takes about one hour to traverse its distance of 69 km (43 m). The drive is through rolling mountains until you descend to the subtropical vegetation of Uruapan. At an intersection marked Playa Azul-Carapan, either direction will give you access to the *centro*.

DIRECTORY

Airlines • No commercial airlines.

Buses • Central Camionera, on southern outskirts of town; P. Gertrudis Bocanegra, for buses to station and lake.

Car Rentals • None.

Groceries • Super Centro, Plaza Vasco 20.

Post Office • Calle Obregon 40, off Plaza Gertrudis Bocanegra.

Railway Station • Past the Pemex station on way to lake.

Taxi Stand • Plaza Gertrudis Bocanegra.

Telegraph • Calle Titere 14, off Plaza G. Bocanegra.

Tourist Office • In the Municipal Palace (Plaza Vasco de Quiroga, west side; ☎ 2-18-88); *open 9 a.m.-2 p.m. and 4-7 p.m., Sunday 9 a.m.-4 p.m.*

URUAPAN

If you are arriving from quiet Patzcuaro, the tropical bustle of this prosperous commercial city takes some getting used to. As a major agricultural center producing tropical fruits, particularly avocados, Uruapan is surrounded by fabulous, fertile land justifying the Purepecha meaning of Uruapan as "place where the flowers bloom." The city itself, however, is becoming increasingly modern, congested, and less attractive to the tourist. Although the animated **Plaza Morelos**, the town zócalo, gradually ingratiates itself into your heart, and the fine regional **museum** of Huatapera is worth a visit, the true sights lie outside the town center and include the magnificent Parque Nacional Eduardo Ruiz and La Tzararacua waterfall.

KEY TO URUAPAN

Sights • The area, famous for its luxuriant subtropical climate and forests, attracts weekend hikers and horseback riders. For the tourist with limited time, Uruapan has nothing worthy of a detour. If you are in the vicinity, the Parque Nacional and regional museum are enjoyable to visit.

Excursions • The pine forests and impressive La Tzararacua waterfall are near the city and tours to the Paricutin volcano can be arranged.

Shopping • As the area has prospered from its farms, the traditional crafts have deteriorated, but embroidered blouses, wooden chess sets and guitars can still be found.

Festivals • The state fair during Holy Week is an excellent time for people watching and shopping for regional crafts.

Where to Stay • Modern hotels provide decent accommodations.

Where to Eat • Good traditional Mexican food, and one new restaurant catering to more international tastes.

Entertainment • Hotel bars offer music, and one hotel has a nightclub.

Getting Around • The most spectacular sights are the parks outside the city, for which bus transportation and car rentals are available.

Practical Tips • Uruapan is tropical and warmer than nearby Patzcuaro.

WHAT TO SEE AND DO

Plaza Morelos

This large, busy square full of sidewalk vendors selling fruits and empanadas is truly the heart of the city, with hotels, restaurants, churches, the market, and shops all within close proximity. Of the greatest tourist interest is **La Huatapera,** an exceptionally handsome 16th-century hospital and church founded for the education and care of Tarascan Indians. Now converted into the **Museo Regional de Arte Popular,** this small museum displays pottery and crafts from all over Michoacan, but its piece de resistance is its excellent collection of Uruapan laquerware. *Open Tues.-Sun., 9:30 a.m.-1:30 p.m. and 3:30-6 p.m.; No admission fee.*

Parque Nacional Eduardo Ruiz

On the border between town and its outskirts, about a half mile from the zócalo on Independencia, is one of Mexico's most magnificent parks, with lush, verdant scenery and flowers. As the River Cupatitzio flows through the park, bringing the soothing sound of water to every nook and cranny, it forms fountains, waterfalls, and lovely pools. *Open daily 6 a.m.-6 p.m.; No admission fee.*

EXCURSIONS

La Tzararacua Waterfall

11-1/2 km (7 m) on road to Playa Azul • To reach the wild grandeur of this majestic **waterfall**, just turn right off the Playa Azul road at the sign and continue briefly on dirt road to the parking area. (Buses leave from the zócalo.) From the parking lot, you have the choice of walking for about a mile or riding a horse through fine pine forests to the point where the placid **River Cupatitzio** begins its 100-foot drop, hissing and foaming, into the valley below.

El Paricutin

40 km (25 m) west on rough road toward Los Reyes at village of Angahuan • The sudden eruption of this volcano in 1943 left behind a massive, dormant mountain and a surrounding **moonscape of black lava** that buried numerous villages. At Angahuan you can arrange for horses and a guide to ascend the volcano or you can take a tour out of Uruapan. Buses from the zócalo to Los Reyes can drop you at Angahuan.

SHOPPING

Uruapan now only rarely produces the exquisite encrusted lacquerware on display in the museum, but nearby villages still produce crafts—embroidered blouses, guitars, carved-wood chess sets—and you can sometimes find these items in shops or by meandering through the picturesque daily **market** filling the streets behind La Huatapera. For odds and ends, follow Corregidora (the market street running parallel with the zócalo) to Independencia, where these streets form Plazuela Izazaga. Visit the stores here before continuing up Independencia almost to Parque Nacional, where a few shops specialize in musical instruments from the village of Paracho. In front of the park, there is a curio market. The best shop we found was a little farther past this curio market in the Hotel Mansion de Cupatitzio; it was open daily, 10 a.m.-6 p.m.

WHERE TO STAY

Two kinds of hotels, serving different clientele, exist in Uruapan. In the zócalo area, the hotels exemplify the progressive, commercial spirit of this town. Outside the center, the hotels cater to weekend vacationers looking for a picturesque resort to relax in. (Address correspondence to Uruapan, Mich., Mexico.) To reserve by phone, call area code 452.

MODERATE

Mansion del Cupatitzio

Parque Nacional; ☎ *3-21-00; $63* • While definitely catering to the resort-seeking crowd, this attractive colonial-style hotel is within walking distance of the zócalo. Surrounded on two sides by the beautiful national park and its waterfalls, the 44 large, comfortable rooms with balconies have views either of the park or of the pleasant garden and swimming-pool area. Restaurant, bar. Parking. Write Apartado 63.

Plaza Uruapan

Ocampo 64; ☎ *3-34-88; $54* • The Plaza is located on a corner of the zócalo. This modern, commercial hotel houses a shopping mall in addition to the usual hotel amenities. Its 124 units are quite large and carpeted. Front rooms with balconies on top floors are best; some of the junior suites have views of the orange-tiled roofs of the town and of the surrounding mountains. Restaurant, popular bar and weekend disco, coffee shop. Garage.

BUDGET

Motel Pie de la Sierra

Km 4, Carretara de Uruapan; 2-1⁄2 km (1-1⁄2 m) from zócalo on Carapan road; ☎ *4-25-10; $38* • This hotel's best asset is its setting by a large pool framed by verdant mountains, gardens, and wooded grounds. A popular weekend spot with Mexicans, it has 43 ordinary rooms with fireplaces and plain baths. Pool, restaurant, bar, gameroom. Parking. Write Apartado 153.

Villa de las Flores

E. Carranza 15; ☎ *4-28-00; $27* • This intimate town hotel consists of 29 old, yet pleasant rooms around courtyards with a profusion of potted plants. Rooms in rear courtyard are quiet. Quite a bargain. Small restaurant.

WHERE TO EAT

There are two very pleasant restaurants with tranquil settings and decent, if not fantastic, food. The restaurant at the **Motel Pie de la Sierra** offers both Mexican and continental specialties, as well as substantial comida corrida at a very inexpensive price. We found the appetizers placed on the table very good, the consomme excellent and the beef brocheta quite good even if we were somewhat disappointed in other items. For its beautiful setting with panoramic views of mountains, it's worth dining here despite the unevenness in the food. *Open daily during set meal hours; reserve a window seat for Sunday comidas at ☎ 2-15-10; moderate to inexpensive.* Slightly less expensive is the restaurant at the **Mansion del Cupatitizio.** Overlooking the gardens, the restaurant serves both Mexican and continental specialties, both chicken with mole and shrimp dishes. *Open lunch and dinner during set hours; moderate to inexpensive.*

In town, **La Pergola** (south side of the zócalo) serves everything from breakfast to filet mignon, from cappuccino to enchiladas suizas. Pleasantly furnished and very popular, this is a good place for sitting or dining at any time. *Open 8 a.m. till 11 p.m. daily; inexpensive comida corrida and other items, otherwise moderate.*

For snacks or budget meals, we recommend the market. This **Mercado de Antojitos** (behind the museum) must be the only market planted with a rose garden. Mexican dishes like *cecina* and *chile relleno* are served at prices to warm the heart of any bargain hunter (and clean enough to recommend). Just one-half block off zócalo is the **Cafe Tradicional de Uruapan** (E. Carranza) where you can enjoy dessert with a hot chocolate or cafe. *Open 8 a.m.-2 p.m.; 4-9 p.m.; Sun. 8 a.m.-2 p.m.*

ENTERTAINMENT

Hotel bars offer most of the entertainment in town. During our last visit, the **Hotel Plaza Uruapan** lounge on the second floor was packed with locals enjoying the music of a trio. The Plaza also has a weekend disco.

GETTING TO AND FROM URUAPAN

AIR

Aeromar flies small planes to and from Mexico City daily except Sun. In Mexico City ☎ 207-6666.

BUS

First- and second-class buses connect Uruapan with Guadalajara; Patzcuaro, then on to Morelia and Mexico City and to the Pacific beach town of Playa Azul. The terminal, 1 km from zócalo, can be reached on the buses marked "C. Camionera."

TRAIN

Trains run a few times a day between Uruapan and Mexico City, with stops in Patzcuaro and Morelia, but the most comfortable train is the overnight *servicio estrella* El Purepecha (12 hours to Mexico City) with reclining seats.

CAR

MEX 120 to Playa Azul is deceptively short (260 km, 161 m) in distance—maneuvering the curves on this road as it descends the mountains to the coast can easily take you 5 hours.

To reach Guadalajara, follow MEX 37 to Carapan for 76 km (47 m), then link up with MEX 15 going west to Guadalajara for the remaining 245 km (152 m).

Morelia via Patzcuaro is less than two hours away, but if you have already traveled this route (see "Patzcuaro"), you might want to return to Morelia via Carapan on MEX 37 and continue east into Morelia on MEX 15. This route totals 189 km (117 m) and is about 60 km (37 m) longer than the Patzcuaro road, but takes you through the Tarascan guitar-making village of **Paracho** and the larger town of **Zacapu,** once a pre-Hispanic Tarascan center and now dominated by a 17th-century Plateresque church and monastery.

DIRECTORY

Airlines • Aeromar ☎ (3-50-50).

Buses • Local buses leave from the zócalo area. For the **Parque Nacional**, take those marked "Quinta" or "Parque Nacional." For **La Tzararacua**, take those so marked. The **long-distance bus** terminal, called **Central de Autobuses**, is on the north edge of town near the Patzcuaro road.

Car Rentals • Budget Rent Auto ☎ (3-59-07) at the Plaza Purepecha 204, on the edge of town.

Post Office • On Cupatitzio, a block south of the zócalo.

Railway Station • Edge of town on Paseo Lazaro Cardenas.

Taxi Stand • Along zócalo.

Telegraph • Ocampo 8, just off the zócalo.

Tourist Office • In Hotel Progreso, on 5 de Febrero 17 off the zócalo. Open Monday-Friday, 9 a.m.-2 p.m., 4-7 p.m.; Saturday 9 a.m.- 2 p.m. ☎ (2-06-33).

Tours • Tours Cupatitzio in the Hotel Tarasca offers regional excursions ☎ (3-56-35).

GUADALAJARA

Guadalajara reminds you of the United States accented with Mexican charm and color. Many of its over 3-1/2 million residents live in attractive suburban areas with large shopping malls and even stores called Sears and Gigante (Giant). Capital of the state of Jalisco and the second largest city in Mexico, Guadalajara's old downtown area shows some of the same wear and tear of our own cities. Fortunately, the part containing the most important sights—Orozco murals, the regional museum, and the Teatro Degollado—has been refurbished into what must be one of the world's largest malls, the Plaza Metropolitana. Plaza after plaza artfully lead you past gardens, fountains, and historic sights. The neighboring town of San Pedro Tlaquepaque has numerous boutiques and art galleries, excellent restaurants in attractive settings, and like no other place in the world—mariachi music at almost any time of the day. And there's the favorite weekend getaway, Lake Chapala, only an hour away.

Given Guadalajara's size, it can be difficult to cover all its sights in a limited time. If you have only one day, we recommend you spend the morning visiting Orozco's murals and the Metropolitana area and the afternoon enjoying yourself in Tlaquepaque. Jose Clemente Orozco (1883-1949) was one of Mexico's great 20th-century artists working in the muralist tradition following the Revolution of 1910. His powerfully expressive murals depicting Mexico's history and its peoples have received international acclaim. Orozco created some of his finest work in Guadalajara, and a visit to this city wouldn't be complete without seeing his murals in the Hospicio Cabanas, the University of Guadalajara, and the Palacio de Gobierno.

KEY TO GUADALAJARA

Sights • Large, pleasant city with interesting colonial center and spectacular murals by Orozco. A good base for visiting nearby crafts villages and resorts.

Shopping • An enormous daily market makes for good shopping as do nearby Tlaquepaque and Tonala. Excellent ceramics.

Fiestas • October is a busy month, with Guadalajara's Autumn Festival and the Fiesta of the Virgin of Zapopan. On June 29, Tlaquepaque celebrates the Fiesta de San Pedro.

Sports • Swimming; tennis at hotels and golf at country clubs; boating at Chapala.

Where to Stay • While limited in the budget category and centrally located hotels, this city offers an excellent variety of quality hotels and camping.

Where to Eat • Lots of variety, from sophisticated international restaurants to regional ones specializing in such local items as *birria, pozole,* and Chapala whitefish.

Entertainment • Varied and extensive from ballet to bullfights.

Excursions • Gay Tlaquepaque with its fine boutiques and mariachi musicians, pottery-making Tonala, and Lake Chapala are all nearby. Famous Pacific resorts like Puerto Vallarta and Manzanillo are short flights away.

Getting Around • This large city is spread out, requiring more bus and taxi travel than most Mexican towns, but the service is efficient. Car rentals and buses available for excursions.

Practical Tips • Wonderful, slightly warmer than springlike climate all year round. • Although Mexico's second largest city, Guadalajara's prices are quite reasonable. • Many shops and agencies close between 2-4 p.m. • Establish price of taxi fare in advance.

HOW TO GET AROUND

Guadalajara is at least three separate areas, with the colonial center of town being the most important for sightseeing, its extensive residential districts providing some of the more elegant hotels and restaurants, and Tlaquepaque providing shopping, mariachi music, and Mexican food. You will be forced to move about considerably to do all the things that will interest you-walking simply won't work here. So that you won't waste your time finding the central sightseeing area in this large city, we think a few tips on getting around are in order. If you are staying in a hotel out of the center in the area of the **Minerva Circle** or beyond (or even if you are visiting museums in this area), you can catch the Par Vial bus into town on Hidalgo and return to the Minerva Circle on this bus anywhere along Juarez-Vallarta. This bus route is also the best way to drive back and forth into town. With the total remodeling of the center, many streets suddenly end at a pedestrian area, and some become one way. Hidalgo takes you all the way into the Cathedral before continuing underground to Calzada Independencia. Most parking is underneath the plazas, so the only indication that a garage is near are the signs marked "E." The most convenient garages are off the Hidalgo tunnel. To return to the Minerva Circle area, follow Juarez to Vallarta past Los Arcos. Buses also run to other areas you will want to visit, such as #275, running south on Av. 16 de Septiembre to Tlaquepaque and north to Zapopan; combis also run fixed routes. Taxis are convenient, but you need to negotiate the price in advance. The drivers don't pay any attention to the price on the meters. For further information, see "Getting to and from Guadalajara".

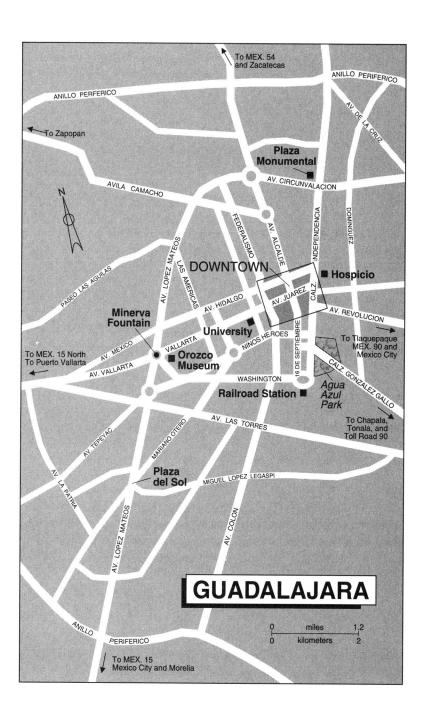

To MEX. 54
and Zacatecas

ANILLO PERIFERICO

ANILLO PERFERICO

AV. DE LA CRUZ

To Zapopan

Plaza
Monumental

AV. CIRCUNVALACION

AVILA CAMACHO

N

FEDERALISMO

AV. ALCALDE

INDEPENDENCIA

DOMINGUEZ

DOWNTOWN

Hospicio

AV. LOPEZ MATEOS

LAS AMERICAS

AV. HIDALGO

PASEO LAS AGUILAS

AV. JUAREZ

CALZ

AV. REVOLUCION

Minerva
Fountain

University

NINOS HEROES

16 DE SEPTIEMBRE

To Tlaquepaque
MEX. 90 and
Mexico City

VALLARTA

AV. MEXICO

To MEX. 15 North
To Puerto Vallarta

AV. VALLARTA

Orozco
Museum

CALZ. GONZALEZ GALLO

WASHINGTON

Railroad Station

Agua
Azul
Park

To Chapala,
Tonala, and
Toll Road 90

AV. LAS TORRES

AV. TEPEYAC

MARIANO OTERO

AV. LA PATRIA

Plaza
del Sol

MIGUEL LOPEZ LEGASPI

AV. LOPEZ MATEOS

AV. COLON

GUADALAJARA

| 0 | miles | 1.2 |
| 0 | kilometers | 2 |

ANILLO

PERIFERICO

To MEX. 15
Mexico City and Morelia

WHAT TO SEE AND DO

Most sights, be they colonial palaces, Orozco murals, museums, or the market, are within a series of continuous plazas sectioned off from most traffic and, fortunately, most of the congestion of the old downtown. Starting either at the Plaza Laureles or at the Hospicio, you can walk along pedestrian plazas lined with fountains and gardens—because the traffic is shunted underground in a most ingenious manner, preserving the historical center of this rapidly developing modern city. This section is called the Metropolitan Plaza. If you get tired, take horse-drawn carriages from the stands in front of the market and the Museo Regional. While not all of Guadalajara's sights are within this area, we will start with those that are.

METROPOLITAN PLAZA AREA

Cathedral

Guadalajara's Cathedral (Alcalde and Hidalgo) sits amid four of the city's most important colonial plazas. The main entrance faces west on **Plaza Laureles,** with its massive fountain and arcades of shops; the side entrance faces the Rotunda on the north; the south side borders the zócalo, or Plaza de Armas while the remaining side borders the Plaza de la Liberacion. The facade of the Cathedral, and actually the entire church, is strangely harmonious given its potpourri of styles from Renaissance, Gothic, baroque, and even Byzantine. Its interior *(closed Thursday and Sunday at noon for confirmations)* was originally planned with three naves to create separate seating space for the different social classes: Spanish officials, landowners, and Indians. Over the door of the sacristy is a painting, *The Assumption of the Virgin*, by the Spanish artist Murillo.

Plaza de Armas

The Plaza de Armas has a magnificent kiosk in the center, with a profusion of curlicues and columns carved like maidens. These maidens reappear on the doors of the 18th-century **Palacio de Gobierno** on the east side of this plaza (Corona and Morelos) and easily recognized by its cornice of cannons. In 1810, Father Hidalgo and his troops for Independence settled themselves in Guadalajara, and from this palace Hidalgo proclaimed the end of slavery in Mexico. Commemorating the events of Independence, **Orozco** painted his powerful mural of Hidalgo inside this palace. *Open 8 a.m.-8 p.m.; no admission fee.* Orozco used the confined architectural space so well that as you look up the first staircase on your right you are completely encompassed by the looming figure of Hidalgo. As you climb the stairs, other sections of the mural emerge, revealing the devastation that results from war, despotism, and dogma. Another Orozco mural can be found on the second floor if you go through the doorway marked "Congreso." Hidalgo is portrayed on the ceiling, and Juarez on the wall.

Rotunda

The park around the Rotunda (north side of the Cathedral) provides

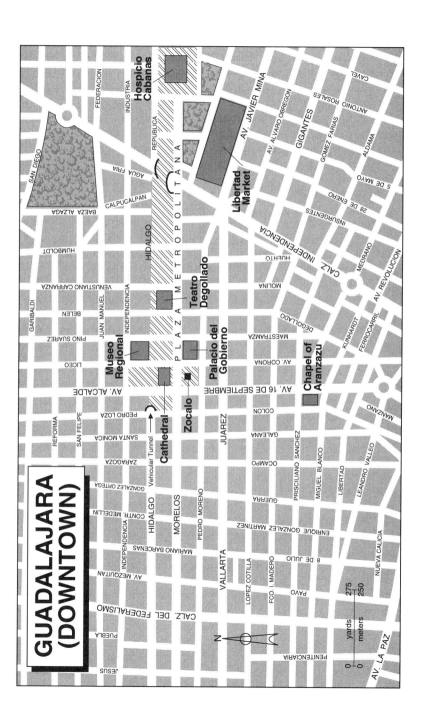

GUADALAJARA (DOWNTOWN)

shady relief after the openness of the other parks. In its center is a neo-classic rotunda formed by Doric columns honoring illustrious persons in the region's history. On its east side is a handsome, late-17th-century seminary converted into the **Museo Regional de Guadalajara** (Corona and Hidalgo). In the rooms around the arcaded courtyard are a variety of exhibits extending from the region's prehistory to modern times. On the first floor, you can see delightful preconquest ceramics from Colima, Nayarit, and Jalisco. The second floor contains a well-known collection of colonial paintings by Jose de Ibarro, called the Murillo of Mexico, as well as historic and ethnographic exhibits. *Open Tuesday-Sunday, 9 a.m.-3:45 p.m.; Small admission fee.*

Plaza de la Liberacion

The enormous Plaza de la Liberacion has only some rose gardens and two fountains to break its rather severe and formal proportions, yet it provides a spectacular approach to the **Teatro Degollado** at its eastern end. Inaugurated in 1866, this theater is built at the location of the original Indian village that preceded Guadalajara. Today it is hard to imagine such a history for this spot, adorned as it is with this well-proportioned, neoclassic theater. The theater's foyer is ornately decorated with chandeliers and gilded doors, and its ceiling vault is covered with an extraordinary painting depicting canto 4 of Dante's *Divine Comedy.* Since performances still take place here, the entrance is sometimes restricted.

Plaza Tapatia

As you walk farther east past the Teatro Degollado, you come upon the pedestrian mall completed in 1982 that connects the main plazas with the previously isolated Hospicio Cabanas and the Mercado Libertad. Tree-lined and adorned with impressive modern fountains and sculptures, this Plaza Tapatia enables you to stroll peacefully above the congestion of the Calzada Independencia.

Hospicio Cabanas

Crossing over the Calzada Independencia, the mall leads to the handsome, neoclassical Hospicio Cabanas, founded in 1801 as an orphanage and now converted to the Instituto Cultural Cabanas. While the building's innumerable patios and courtyards no longer ring with the laughter of children, its former chapel reverberates still with Orozco's most famous murals on every wall and vault. Primarily in cold grays and blacks, Orozco passionately expresses the timeless forces of military might and despotism, of human suffering and even charity that were embodied in the Spanish Conquest of Mexico and that still exist in modern society. Orozco's genius is never clearer than in his spatial manipulations of ceiling vaults, using their strange shape to create elongated, manneristic bodies and their location to create awesome perspectives. The best example of this technique is his mural *Man of Fire* in the central dome. To help avoid getting a kink in your neck looking at the ceiling murals, the museum provides table-size benches to lie on, or mirrors for those who prefer their feet on the floor. The mirror-reflected image of the *Man of Fire* is particularly effective, making you feel yourself falling into the fires of hell. *Open Tues.-Sat., 10:15 a.m.-6 p.m., and Sun., 10:15 a.m.-3 p.m.; Small admission charge. Photographs without flash allowed.* In nearby galleries you can admire Orozco prints and drawings.

Mercado Libertad

As you leave the Hospicio Cabanas, turn left, and you will come to the Mercado Libertad (see "Shopping"). Just before you enter the market, notice the animated modern sculpture of a horse stampede to your left. From the market you can cross Javier Mina on an overpass and arrive at the **Plaza Mariachi** (see "Entertainment").

AROUND TOWN

More Mural Art

When Orozco returned home to Guadalajara in his fifties, he started painting murals that were more distinctive and mature than his previous work. The first of these masterpieces was painted at the **University of Guadalajara,** to be followed by the work you've already seen at the Palacio de Gobierno and the Hospicio. All of this work was completed between the years 1935-1939. Inside the auditorium of the university's French Renaissance building (Vallarta 975) are two murals. The one behind the stage rivals, if not excels, the work of Goya in its unforgettable expression of human suffering and terror. Orozco had witnessed some of the worst violence of the Revolution of 1910, and this powerful mural is testament to the truth of his statement that "Art is knowledge at the service of emotion." The second mural, in the dome of the auditorium, demonstrates Orozco's dramatic use of architectural space while providing an allegory of the progress of science. *Open Mon.-Fri. when university is in session.; no admission fee.*

When you are in the center of town, you might look for the pedestrian mall along Calle Colon, just off Juarez and one block west of the Plaza de Armas. To one side is the **Oficina de Telegrafos,** a 19th-century neoclassic building that contains a minor mural by Siqueiros, one of the three great 20th-century muralists along with Orozco and Diego Rivera.

Buses marked "Par Vial" run up Juarez and Vallarta Los Arcos and return via Hidalgo.

Parque Agua Azul

Calzada Independencia Sur and Constituyentes • Guadalajara's largest park contains a bird sanctuary, and a special section for children has a train that takes them, and anyone else, around the park. Along its edge bordered by a mall formed by Calzada Independencia Sur and 16 de Septiembre are two places you might like to visit: **Museo Arqueologia de Occidente,** a small undistinguished building in the mall just in front of the entrance to the park that is easy to overlook but contains a collection of charming pre-Hispanic ceramic art from Jalisco, Colima, and Nayarit. A visit is worth the small admission charged. *Open Mon.-Fri., 10 a.m.-1 p.m. and 4-7 p.m. Sat. and Sun., noon-7 p.m. but hours change frequently.* The **Casa de las Artesanias de Jalisco,** near Constituyentes, is discussed under "Shopping."

As you are coming or going from this park to the zócalo area, you might want to stop to see the **Chapel of Our Lady of Aranzazu**. While part of the neighboring Church of San Francisco, this 18th-century chapel (on the west side of 16 de Septiembre) is far more sumptuous, with three Churrigueresque and gilded altarpieces.

Buses marked "Camionera" run down 16 de Septiembre and Insurgentes Sur to the Parque Azul.

Basilica Zapopan

Calzada Avila Camacho, 7-1/2 km (5 m) • Considerably outside the center of the city, Zapopan forms a village within the larger metropolis. Its 17th-century church is dedicated to the patron saint of the state of Jalisco, the little Virgin of Zapopan. From this church, the early friars set out to convert and pacify the Chichimeca ("barbarian") Indians who had fled into the mountains. In 1542, one friar dedicated the 13-inch statue of the Virgin to the Indians, and since then she has been revered. The baroque church is decorated with niches in her colors of blue and white. Numerous retablos (small paintings depicting the miracles she has performed) can be found in a room to the left of the craft store, **Artesania Huichola** (see below). Given the traditions of this church, it is not surprising that it alone has been able to convert many of the independent Huichol Indians to Catholicism. While you aren't guaranteed to see one of the colorfully dressed Huichols on your visit, the church does maintain a small exhibit and salesroom of Huichol crafts to the side of the Basilica. Artesania Huichola is open daily from 10 a.m.-1:30 p.m. and 4-7 p.m. and sells some Huichol beadwork, yarn paintings that have become adequately admired to be sold in New York City galleries, and exquisite embroidery work.

Bus #275 runs along 16 de Septiembre, Alcade, and Calz. Avila Camacho to Zapopan. Bus #24 runs between Plaza del Sol and Zapopan on Lopez Mateos.

SHOPPING

The state of Jalisco produces some high-quality crafts that are sold in a few stores in Guadalajara and many shops in nearby Tlaquepaque and Tonala. Ceramics from Tonala and, particularly, those from the studio of Jorge Wilmot are some of the finest in all of Mexico. The many varieties of Huichol ritual art and clothing are highly prized, often difficult to find, but well worth the effort to seek out.

Tonala ware comes in a variety of styles and forms, including water pitchers, vases, plates, birds, and animals. Although much of it is of high quality, the delicate and intricately designed ceramics of Jorge Wilmot are unsurpassed and internationally famous. Wilmot's high-temperature fired ceramics are subtly colored, often have an Islamic or Oriental feel about them, and are decorated with traditional animal, flower, and sun motifs. If in doubt about whether you are getting one of Wilmot's creations, check the piece for his "W" trademark. Surprisingly, quality Tonala ware is sometimes difficult to find in Guadalajara, but is available in Tlaquepaque, Tonala, and Ajijic (see "Excursions").

The fascinating religious art of the Huichols, through which they communicate with their gods, extends to their clothing. Shirts, capes, trousers, and skirts in wonderfully multicolored cross-stitch embroidery come with designs of the sacred deer and eagle. Woven and delicately embroidered shoulder bags, sashes, and small pouch belts feature sacred as well as geometric designs. Formerly done in wool, they are now more often found in cotton due to the scarcity of sheep in the region. Huichols also produce interesting and inventive beadwork that takes the form of earrings, bracelets, necklaces, and belts in geometric, animal, or flower patterns. Votive gourd bowls, used as offerings to the gods so that they will listen to the Huichols' prayers, are decorated with beadwork or yarn. A coating of beeswax is applied first to the gourd, then the design is formed by pressing glass beads or yarn into the wax. The intriguing multicolored sacred yarn paintings are produced similarly, but this time the beeswax is applied to plywood upon which the yarn is pressed. These very stylized paintings often express Huichol religious beliefs or portray Huichol traditions and rituals. Shamans, deer, and peyote appear prominently in many of these lively and highly imaginative paintings, which have been exhibited in major museums in San Francisco, Chicago, and New York. Probably the most popular objects of Huichol art are the god's eyes that are found throughout Mexico and the United States. Made by winding colored yarn on sticks to form a cross, the god's eyes appear individually or as several crosses bound together. Despite their popularity, god's eyes do have religious significance. They are said to be symbols of the power of seeing and understanding unknown things. Through the god's eyes, the Huichols address prayers to the gods so that the eyes of the gods will rest with favor on the supplicants.

Other interesting crafts from this region include very attractive blown red glass, fine huaraches, *charro* (Mexican cowboy) paraphernalia, multicolored serapes worn by *charros* and mariachi musicians, tin candelabra and mirror frames, and additional ceramics, especially the exuberant polychrome creations from Santa Cruz de las Huertas and the popular Tlaquepaque-molded miniatures of market vendors, musicians, and wedding parties.

WHERE TO SHOP

You will want to visit the huge, sprawling **Mercado Libertad,** located just off Calzada Independencia around Javier Mina and Rodriguez. This market houses hundreds of stalls and features what we imagine is the largest collection of huaraches (sandals) in the universe. Guadalajara is noted for the quality of its footwear, and the huaraches are no exception. They come in a dazzling array of styles; you can even find the green and white huaraches sometimes worn by the Huichols. Serapes, blouses, baskets, guitars, straw items, ceramics (not of the highest quality), and a vast quantity of curios fill the stalls. The upper floor contains countless typical market restaurants, cleaner than most, and, as usual, offering the cheapest meals in town. Although we have eaten there and not gotten sick, you may want to be more cautious. The adventurous, however, can choose from shrimp, *pozole* (delicious), chicken, *birria,* and a variety of soups. The traveler on a tight budget can eat a full-course meal (*comida corrida*) for a little over a dollar at a number of restaurants. If your watch isn't working, you'll be happy to know that several watch repairmen ply their trade in between the restaurants. You can have a bowl of *pozole* and get your watch fixed at the same time. What more could you want from life?

For crafts shopping in Guadalajara, the two government-sponsored stores are sometimes worth visiting. The **Casa de las Artesanias de Jalisco** (Jalisco Museum of Popular Arts), located in Parque Agua Azul (for directions, see "Parque Agua Azul," above), has a selection of crafts from the state of Jalisco as well as other parts of Mexico, and permanent exhibits of Huichol art, handblown glass, pottery, and textiles from Jalisco. *Open Mon.-Fri., 10 a.m.-7 p.m., Sat., 10 a.m.-4 p.m., and Sun., 10 a.m.-2 p.m.* **El Instituto de la Artesania Jalisciense** (Alcade 1221, which is about a 10-minute drive north from the Cathedral) has a selection of regional crafts, often of mediocre quality. *Open Mon.-Fri., 10 a.m.-8 p.m., and Sat., 10 a.m.-7 p.m. Closed Sun.* For a shop devoted solely to Huichol art, try **Artesania Huichola,** next to the Basilica Zapopan (see "Basilica Zapopan," above). The silver-studded costumes and broad hats of the charro originated in Guadalajara. If you are interested in belts, spurs, horsewhips, or even saddles, you might visit **El Charro** (Juarez 148), or for boots, their shop at Juarez 132. For some of the best shopping for traditional and contemporary crafts as well as for women's fashions, head for Tlaquepaque, just a short ride from downtown Guadalajara, or visit Tonala for its ceramics (see "Excursions"). If for some reason you miss out on shopping for crafts in this area, don't fret: the crafts of Jalisco can be found all over Mexico. If you are traveling on to Puerto Vallarta or Mexico City, you will find that these cities have particularly good selections of crafts from this region.

FIESTAS

Every October, for most of the month, Guadalajara sponsors an **Autumn Fiesta**, with international companies performing symphony concerts, opera, and ballets. There are rodeos, bullfights, and even golf and tennis tournaments. Every day brings a parade or an exhibition by *charros.* Around the Parque Agua Azul, musicians play nonstop amid craft exhibits. For details write the Mexican National Tourist Council at 405 Park Ave., New York, NY 10022.

The best week of the Autumn Fiesta may well start on **October 12,** when it coincides with the celebration for the **Virgin of Zapopan**. As patron of

Jalisco, the Virgin's statue is taken from its home at the Basilica of Zapopan on tour of all the churches in this diocese. On October 12, she returns to Zapopan along the festively decorated Calzada Avila Camacho, accompanied by thousands of her followers. Throughout the following week, traditional dances are performed in the courtyard of the Basilica.

Tlaquepaque gaily celebrates the **Dia de San Pedro** on June 29 with hordes of mariachis, dancers, and parades.

WHERE TO STAY

Guadalajara's most modern hotels often are not close to the major sights. Many are located in the city's modern shopping center, Plaza del Sol, over 20 minutes by car from the center but reachable by #258 bus from Calle San Felipe downtown. Unless you have come to Guadalajara to see one of the largest shopping malls in Latin America (we thought we saw Macy's in the distance), there is no particular reason to be attracted to the Plaza del Sol-except for its hotels, discos, and restaurants that have aggregated there in a disorderly fashion. Other modern hotels are slightly more convenient in their location near the Minerva Circle. Less expensive central hotels are not plentiful but quite acceptable. Only a few are in restored colonial buildings offering exceptional atmosphere. If you are looking for first-class accommodations, you most likely will be staying outside the center where many hotels have added executive service sections for business travelers.

Address correspondence to Guadalajara, Jal., Mexico. To reserve by phone, call area code 36.

RESORT EXPENSIVE

Quinta Real   ★★★★
Av. Mexico 2727 at Lopez Mateos; ☎ *(15-00-00); $209* • Located a few blocks from the Minerva Circle, the Quinta Real opened in 1986, but it looks like it could be centuries old. Although the construction is new, the Quinta Real utilized lots of stone and old wooden doors and beams to create a most tasteful, handsome and intimate colonial environment. Throughout the hotel you come across traditional Mexican furniture and furnishings, walk through earth-colored tiled hallways, and listen to recorded classical music. The hotel is small, consisting of 45 suites and 8 standard rooms. Each suite is distinctive and on 2 levels. The decor is eclectic, and sometimes overdone with "gold" wall lamps and French touches vying with traditional Mexican decorations. Some suites have Jacuzzis. The hotel is located at a busy intersection, and parts of it can be noisy. The most desirable accommodations are those with views of the inner grounds and pool area. Unfortunately, some overlook the rear parking lot. Bar and handsome French restaurant. Attentive service.

VERY EXPENSIVE

Camino Real   ★★★★
Av. Vallarta 5005; *(47-80-00); $189* • A modern and extensive
motel-style complex with lawns, gardens, and fountains located about
15 minutes from the center, its 225 attractively furnished and carpeted rooms are very large, with small furnished terraces or balconies.
All air-conditioned. Just beyond the Minerva Circle, this hotel is
quiet, with a sedate, suburban atmosphere and efficient service; four
pools, one tennis court, putting green, and numerous restaurants, bars
with entertainment, and a nightclub. Parking with watchman. For reservations, call, in the U.S., ☎ 800-722-6466.

Fiesta Americana   ★★★★
Aurelio Aceves 255; *(25-34-34); $209* • This modern high-rise is on
the Minerva Circle. It has a Hyatt Regency- style atrium and glass elevators that reveal fabulous views of Guadalajara from the upper stories. Four hundred air-conditioned, large, attractive rooms,
distinguished by molded seating and desk area, all have views on one
side of the city and large marble bathrooms. Restaurants, nightclub,
bar with music, pool, and tennis courts. Good service. If you can
afford it and wish to avoid the 17-km drive from the airport, a helicop-
ter will deposit you on the roof. Garage. For reservations, call, in the
U.S., ☎ 800-223-2332.

Hyatt Regency   ★★★★
Av. Lopez Mateos s/n; *(22-77-78); $154* • This pyramid- shaped
hotel is part of an enclosed shopping mall at the Plaza del Sol. Its 350
rooms are very large and tastefully decorated even if few of their windows afford views. Several restaurants and Mariachi bar. A health spa,
pool, and—though it's hard to believe—a skating rink surrounded by
two stories of shops. Parking. Helioport. For reservations, call, in the
U.S., ☎ 800-228-9000.

Crowne Plaza Holiday Inn   ★★★
Av. Lopez Mateos 2500; *(34-10-34); $190* • This hotel in the Plaza
del Sol may not be as sumptuous as the Hyatt but we find it airier,
brighter, and warmer. There are 300 large rooms with ample baths in
either the tower or garden section. 3 restaurants (one rooftop), bar
with entertainment, disco, and secured parking. Pool in attractive garden setting, a tennis court, and putting green. For reservations, call,
in the U.S., ☎ 800-465-4329.

MODERATE

Calinda Roma   ★★★
Av. Juarez 170; *(14-86-50); $77* • Located in the center of a busy
street, this commercial-style hotel is fairly modern and well maintained, with 177 clean, ample, carpeted rooms and suites (all air-conditioned). Restaurants and bar with entertainment at lobby level, as

well as rooftop terrace with restaurant and small pool. Garage. For reservations, call, in the U.S., ☎ 800-228-5151.

Fenix ★★

Av. Corona 160; ☎ *(14-57-14); $85* • Centrally located. The lobby area bustles with its shops and lively lobby bar. Its 250 air-conditioned rooms are fresh and decent if old-fashioned. Restaurant, bar with entertainment, rooftop bar, and disco. Sauna. Parking. For reservations, call, in the U.S. ☎ 800-528-1234.

Hotel de Mendoza ★★

Venustiano Carranza 16; ☎ *(13-46-46); $81* • Great location on a quiet street just around the corner from Teatro Degollado and Plaza de la Liberacion, this modernized colonial-style hotel has dark wood detailing. The 104 air-conditioned rooms are very large and carpeted. Superb view of the cathedral from rooftop bar. Restaurant, coffee shop, bar with entertainment. Pool. Garage. Write Apartado 1-2453.

Vista Aranzazu ★★

Av. Revolucion 110; ☎ *(13-32-32); $81* • Located between Corona and Degollado near the San Francisco church, and only a 10-minute walk from the zócalo, this modern hotel has two buildings across the street from each other. Restaurant, coffee shop, bar with entertainment, and nightclub. The 500 air-conditioned rooms are on the small side but decently furnished, fresh, and clean. Pleasant service. Parking.

Vista Plaza del Sol ★★

Mariano Otero and Lopez Mateos; ☎ *(47-88-90); $96* • In the Plaza del Sol, this modern hotel offers 350 somewhat small but clean, pleasant, air-conditioned rooms. Restaurants, bar, and nightclub; swimming pool and Jacuzzi. Parking. Like the other hotels in the Plaza del Sol, this one is recommended for those who want to be out of town in a shopping center.

INEXPENSIVE

Frances ★★

Maestranza 35; ☎ *(13-11-90); $55* • Just off Plaza de la Liberacion, this pleasant hotel in the center of town has a colonial atmosphere and colonnaded lobby that more than offset its lack of air-conditioning; 60 decent rooms vary in size, some with small balconies and all with small tiled bathrooms. Lobby-level bar and restaurant. Parking available under nearby Plaza de la Liberacion. Friendly service.

BUDGET

Universo ★

Lopez Cotilla 161; ☎ *13-28-15; $33-40* • A modern, centrally located hotel with decent-sized rooms (some exceptionally large for a bit more money), all carpeted and with small bathrooms. Restaurant. Parking.

Posada Regis

Av. Corona 171, across from Hotel Fenix; $34 • The tiny entrance on a busy commercial street leads to the second floor, where you find an enclosed courtyard surrounded by 22 rooms in this charming, old-fashioned, budget hotel. Rooms are unrenovated but comfortable and clean. Many have large windows overlooking Av. Corona, and can be noisy. Friendly, family atmosphere. Inexpensive restaurant in the courtyard.

WHERE TO EAT

Guadalajara's sophistication is reflected in its variety of restaurants ranging from Mexican to Japanese; its size is reflected in the geographical spread of the location of its restaurants. While we have tried to emphasize restaurants with a central location, we have included some in other areas of the city as well so you can have a broader choice.

Many of the most typical Mexican restaurants are in Tlaquepaque and Chapala and listed under those excursions, but the city and its market also offer opportunities to eat not only Mexican food but some regional specialities. Like many northern ranching areas, Guadalajara's most typical dishes involve specially prepared meats, some of them quite unusual, like *criadillas* (bull's testicles), *pancita* (stomach), or tripe that is often served at brunch time. *Birria* is most famous in this region and consists of steamed or barbecued lamb, goat, or pork. The word *birria* is used in Mexico's northwest to mean "mess," so this dish is considered a savory mess flavored with oregano, cumin, mild chiles, and other spices, often served as a soup or in tacos. The state of Jalisco is famous for its *pozole,* or pork and hominy soup topped with lettuce, onion, radishes, and often oregano, although this spice is more typical of Michoacan's *pozole.* You add lime juice and hot chile sauce to suit your taste. This extraordinarily inexpensive but delicious dish is hard to find in restaurants but is plentiful in the market and small street stands that open in the evening in the neighborhoods behind the market and at the Plaza Mariachi. Other Mexican meat dishes are extremely popular here, such as tasty *carnitas,* or pork chunks, and *barbacoa,* steamed or barbecued mutton.

As in most Mexican cities, restaurants tend to get busy after 3 p.m. for lunch and after 9 p.m. for dinner. If you arrive earlier you probably won't need reservations, but you may find the restaurant very quiet. Less expensive restaurants, particularly those with comidas corridas, can get busy much earlier in the afternoons. On Sunday, all restaurants are busy in the late afternoon and early evening and tend to close by 9:30 p.m. Price categories are explained in the Introduction.

INTERNATIONAL CUISINE

In addition to the more regional restaurants that follow, Guadalajara has many international spots, particularly in the Plaza del Sol and Minerva Circle area. You might try the sauerbraten and fondue at the **Chalet Suizo** (Hidalgo 1983; ☎ 15-71-22) or the tempura at the elegant and expensive

Suehiro (La Paz 1701; ☎ 26-00-94), but our favorite is **Recco** (Libertad 1981), found by following Chapultepec a few blocks off Vallarta. This comfortable restaurant, located in a former residence, prepares its food with the freshest ingredients. The emphasis is Italian (the attentive owner is from a village near Genoa). Recco serves a number of pleasing pasta dishes including spaghetti with pesto, as well as a variety of fish and meat preparations. Try the shrimps potpourri-shrimps with scallions, mushrooms and chiles in a delicate parsley-flavored white wine sauce. Good salads. Fine service. *Open daily for lunch and dinner;* ☎ *25-07-24.* Moderately expensive.

MODERATE PRICES

For more moderate prices and traditional food, try **Los Otates** (Av. Americas 28 on the corner of Morelos). Its decor is simple but clean and its food, including *tostadas, enchiladas,* and even *pozole,* is tasty and popular. *Open daily, 1:30-midnight;* ☎ *15-00-81; inexpensive.* For greater variety, try **Copa de Leche** (Juarez 414), a Guadalajara institution with a central location. It takes up two floors, each offering something different. On the second floor, El Balcon offers terrace dining. Mexican dishes like its tasty *carne asada Copa de Leche* and seafood like *camarones Copa de Leche* (shrimp wrapped in bacon and cheese) are quite good. Also, a modestly priced comida corrida is available in the afternoon. Moderate. On the first floor is a sidewalk bar and behind it an elegant restaurant serving seafood and continental dishes like Chateaubriand against a background of piano music. *Open daily lunch and dinner;* ☎ *14-53-47; moderate.* In a tranquil colonial courtyard on the Plaza Tapatia, **La Rinconada** (Morelos 86) serves some steaks and salads along with its decent Mexican offerings like *tasajo en adobo* (a bit like jerked meat). *Open lunch and dinner. Moderate.* For food with a Spanish accent, just a short walk from the downtown area, try **El Meson de Sancho Panza,** (*Marcos Castellanos 114;* ☎ *25-28-98*) a popular, comfortable restaurant serving garlic soup (*sopa de ajo*), Spanish sausages (*chorizo*), and shrimps with garlic (*camarones al ajillo*). There are plenty of other fish and meat dishes to choose from. The food is tasty and the service warm. Moderate. For moderately priced American food try **Brazz** (16 de Septiembre 724) for its steaks and prime ribs, or **Denny's** (Juarez and 16 de Septiembre) for pancakes at breakfast and hamburgers throughout the day. *Open 24 hours.*

Scattered throughout the downtown sections are numerous inexpensive restaurants. **El Molino Rojo** (in the Hotel Frances) provides the most attractive environment for the midday comida corrida. Good service. **El Farol** (Pedro Moreno 466 on the second floor) is quite pleasant and very popular with its wide choice of Mexican dishes at very low prices—*chiles rellenos,* tacos, chicken, and much more. Open till 1 a.m. daily. Along Calle Colon at Juarez runs a pedestrian mall containing the outdoor cafe **Los Vitrales.** Its location and low prices make it a popular and pleasant stopping place for a drink, snack, or *comida corrida.* For inexpensive vegetarian food, try the first block of Calle E. Gonzalez Martinez as it runs off Juarez. Here is **El Aguacate Loco** (#126), with a comida corrida. For real budget prices, you might try the market with its seemingly hundreds of counters offering Mexican food, especially *pozole*, under reasonably clean conditions.

ENTERTAINMENT

If you have only one night, you might spend it in Tlaquepaque (see below) to make sure you absorb the mariachi music for which Guadalajara is famous. If you can't get to Tlaquepaque, then consider the **Plaza Mariachi** (next to the market on Calz. Independencia). Here you can sit at one of the cafes on the small square, order your drink and hire your own musicians to play for you. *Closes at 11:30 p.m.* Less traditional in ambience, but with good traditional mariachi and serenata music is **El Pueblito Cantina** in the Hyatt Regency. *Opens at 7 p.m. Closed Sun.* Also, you can try one of the Fiesta Mexicana offerings of music, traditional dances, and buffet at most first-class hotels, where you will surely get a chance to see the *jarabe tapatio*, or Mexican Hat dance, which originated in Guadalajara. The **Holiday Inn** offers a variation on the theme with its Parrillada Nortena, and the **Fiesta Americana** features live mariachi music along with its Sunday buffet.

For the culture of the city, you might try a dance performance of the **Ballet Folklorico** at the Teatro Degollado most Sundays at 10 a.m. and at the Cine Teatro Cabanas at Hospicio Cabanas, Wednesday at 8:30 p.m., or even check the schedule of the Teatro Degollado ☎ 14-47-73 to see when this city's symphony orchestra will be giving a performance. The **Instituto Cultural Cabanas** has two branches, one at the Hospicio Cabanas with musical performances and art exhibits, and another at Angora Ex-Convento Carmen (Juarez 612) with films and other cultural events. Right in the **Plaza de Armas** you can enjoy free band concerts on Thursdays and Sundays starting at 6 p.m.

Sunday offers hearty entertainment. During the winter, there are **bullfights** at the Plaza Monumental on the very northern end of Calzada Independencia. You will have a choice of tickets in sunny (cheaper) or shady sections of the stadium. During the summer, you can go to Jalisco's famous rodeos, or **charreadas,** and see Jalisco cowboys dressed in their silver-studded and leather-tooled costumes (mariachi costumes are borrowed from these *charros*). The charreadas normally take place on Sunday at 2 p.m. Check with your hotel for one of the several locations most convenient for you.

Most hotel bars offer live music during cocktail hours, and quite a few even have "happy hours" with two drinks for the price of one between either 5-7 or 6-7 p.m. The large, lobby bar at the **Fiesta Americana** bustles and is alive with music at all hours. One of our favorites, for its excellent view of colonial Guadalajara, is **Bar El Campanario,** on the rooftop of the Hotel de Mendoza. *Open evenings. Entertainment begins at 9 p.m.*

The hotels seem to control the nightclub and disco scene, from the Fenix's **Discomics** in the center to the Holiday Inn's da Vinci at the Plaza del Sol and the Fiesta Americana's **Stelaris,** offering name performers in the Minerva Circle area (advance ticket purchase sometimes necessary: ☎ 25-34-34).

GETTING TO AND FROM GUADALAJARA

AIR

There are both international and national flights into Guadalajara. Direct international flights are available from numerous North American cities; flights to Puerto Vallarta also often stop in this city. Within Mexico, numerous flights connect with Mexico City and beyond; Mexicana offers direct flights to many Pacific Coast beaches and Aero California to Los Mochis.

The airport lies 17 km (10-1/2 m) from town along the highway to Chapala. Taxis and combis (#625 runs on Juarez every hour for return) are available.

BUS

Guadalajara is extremely well connected with the rest of Mexico by bus. First-class buses even run to the U.S. border. Omnibus de Mexico and Tres Estrellas de Oro are among the first-class bus lines available, and in addition to their trips to the border, they run to Mexico City, Guanajuato, Patzcuaro, and Morelia, as well as to the Pacific beach resorts of Manzanillo and Puerto Vallarta. All leave from the Nueva Central Camionera, located outside of Tlaquepaque on the highway to Tonala and Mexico City, and linked to the center by #275 bus running along Av. 16 de Septiembre, combi, and taxi.

TRAIN

There is *servicio estrella* train service to Mexico City (El Tapatio, 12 hours overnight and popular), to Manzanillo (El Colimese, 7-hour daytime service), and to Mazatlan, Nogales, and Mexicali (Del Pacifico, 33 hours). #60 and #62 buses run to Juarez and Independencia from the station.

CAR

MEX 15 leads to the Pacific Coast. MEX 15 north to Tepic (then south on MEX 200) takes you to Puerto Vallarta after 5 hours and 375 km (235 m); MEX 15 south leads to MEX 80, the road to Barra de Navidad (295 km, 183 m; about 4 hours), as well as to the new toll road, MEX 54D, for Manzanillo via Colima (3-1/2 hours when road is completed). Two routes can be followed between Guadalajara and Mexico City, the faster taking you past, but not into, the Silver Cities. By connecting with Irapuato at MEX 110 after following the toll road of MEX 90 out of Guadalajara then follow 45D to 57D. The total trip should take you a good 7 hours (less when the superhighway to Irapuato is completed), but you can take a more leisurely trip by staying overnight in one of the colonial cities. The slower, more scenic route takes about 9 hours on MEX 15 south to Morelia, and along the way you can turn off to Patzcuaro. Again, there are good accommodations in both these towns to enable you to break up your trip.

DIRECTORY

Airlines • *Aeromexico* ☎ (25-25-59) Av. Corona 196; *Mexicana* ☎ (47-22-22) 16 de Septiembre 495; *Aero California* ☎ (26-19-01) Lopez Cotilla 1423; *American* ☎ (89-03-04).

American Express • Vallarta 2440 ☎ (30-02-00).

British Consulate • Calz. Gonzalez Gallo 1897 ☎ (35-82-95).

Buses • Nueva Central Camionera (also called "Terminal de Autobuses") on the highway to Tonala and Mexico City, just southeast of Tlaquepaque.

Canadian Consul • Hotel Fiesta Americana, local 30 ☎ (25-34-34, ext. 3005). Weekdays 10 a.m.-1 p.m.

Car Rentals • Many agencies at both airport and in town. A few are *Avis* ☎ (15-48-25); *Budget* ☎ (13-00-27); *Hertz* ☎ (14-61-39).

Carriage Stands • Horse-drawn carriages available for rent in front of Libertad Market and Museo Regional.

Golf and Sports • Bosques *San Isidro*, at km 14-1/2 on the Saltillo highway, offers 18-hole golf course, riding trails, and thermal springs. *Club de Golf Atlas*, between Hotel El Tapatio and airport on Chapala road, has 18-hole course designed by Texan Joe Finger. *Santa Anita Club de Golf*, 6 km (4 m) east on MEX 15, has 18 holes of golf. Also, see "Sports Clubs" listing at end of Chapala section, below.

Groceries • Gigante (Juarez and E. Gonzalez Martinez).

Railroad Station • 16 de Septiembre, at its more southern end past Parque Agua Azul.

Telegraph • Calle Colon near Juarez.

Tourist Office • Juarez 638 in Convento del Carmen and Morelos 102 on Plaza Tapatio ☎ (58-22-22). *(Open Mon.-Fri., 9 a.m.-9 p.m.; Sat. and Sun., 9 a.m.-1 p.m.)*

Tours • Panoramex, through most hotels or call ☎ (10-50-05).

Train • Information: ☎ (12-39-25).

U.S. Consulate • Progreso 175 ☎ (25-27-00); emergencies, ☎ (26-55-33); 8 a.m.-2 p.m. weekdays.

EXCURSIONS FROM GUADALAJARA

SAN PEDRO TLAQUEPAQUE

Tlaquepaque (Tlah-kay-pah-kay), *5 km (3 m) east of Guadalajara on Revolucion*, where mariachi music originated and where Guadalajara's popular ceramics and hand-blown red glassware are made, has blossomed into a most attractive town, offering some of the best shopping in all Mexico. It can be reached after only a 20-minute ride by following the Calzada Independencia Sur south and turning left at Av. Revolucion. At a Pemex station and traffic circle, keep left of the gas station to continue on Revolucion. Less than a mile later, the tree-lined median ends and you are in Tlaquepaque. Take the first right to reach the zócalo or "El Parian." #275 buses run along 16 de Septiembre and those marked "San Juan de Dios-San Pedro- Tonala" run along Calzada Independencia before turning toward what is alternately called San Pedro or Tlaquepaque.

Once a separate town and resort area for wealthy Guadalajarans, Tlaquepaque retains its distinctive atmosphere, although it is now officially part of the city. Its zócalo, **El Parian,** has long been *the* place to go for mariachi music, with its sad songs sung in crackling voices to the accompaniment of guitars, violins, and trumpets. So important is the music that the open garden of the zócalo has disappeared inside a building containing numerous cafes where you can sip a drink while ordering songs from the musicians. El Parian is open from 11 a.m. to midnight, but it becomes most lively on Sunday and at night when countless mariachi groups, all dressed in their *charro* costumes, serenade anyone willing to pay for a song. While children play in the garden and waiters rush about with food and drink, adults sing their favorite songs and dance as the mood takes them. (Tip: Prices for drinks are the same throughout El Parian. The food is not terrific, but okay for a snack of *tostadas or queso asado.* Bathrooms are best avoided.) While El Parian has the earthiest "scene," **El Meson del Mariachi** (Chamizal 500) offers name performers in a very comfortable garden setting. The price per song is astronomical, but the superb stage show *(4 and 8:30 p.m.)* guarantees a lively time at this favorite local spot. *(Reservations recommended:* ☎ *43-10-04; open 1-11:30 p.m.)* To reach El Meson, follow directions to Tlaquepaque. Chamizal lies on the opposite of the Pemex station traffic circle.

Competing with the traditional Tlaquepaque ceramics and glassware are exceptionally fashionable boutiques lining the cobblestone streets of Juarez and Independencia, which begin at El Parian. Both these streets have fine shops, but a stroll through the few blocks of Independencia that are closed to traffic is rewarding even for those with no desire to buy. Independencia's handsome colonial buildings afford many views into private gardens and stylish galleries like that of **Sergio Bustamante** (at #236), with its tranquil garden pool nurturing live flamingos. The surreal quality of Bustamante's art displayed in this gallery-from his jewelry to life-size papier-mâché and metal animals-distinguishes it from the many copies sold elsewhere in town. **Antigua de Mexico** (at #255) has a splendid foyer with metal sculptures by the Indian artist Xochitiotzin. Inside this colonial mansion are decorators' exhibits of antiques and furnishings and a sumptuous private garden in the back. Nearby is the **Museo Regional** (#237), with excellent exhibits of the crafts for which this region is so famous. *Open 10 a.m.- 4 p.m. Tuesday-Saturday; 10 a.m.-1 p.m. Sunday.*

WHERE TO SHOP

For *shopping* while you stroll, you have an enormous choice of shops selling all sorts of crafts, especially ceramics from Tlaquepaque and Tonala, as well as leather boots and Mexican designer clothes. **Arte Cristalino** (*Independencia 163*) stocks the largest selection of this town's red glassware. **Tete** (*Juarez 173*) has the most extensive collection of crafts, some high quality, Rincon Huichol (*Independencia 210B, inside a courtyard*) offers a small choice of Huichol crafts, and **Puente Viejo** (*Juarez 159*) has a very nice selection of tin butterflies and fish. **El Aguila Descalza** (*Juarez 120*) is a clothing boutique selling exquisite (and expensive) appliqued and beribboned Mexican designer clothes, and, sometimes, a piece or two of fine Tonala ware. **Irene Poulos** (*Independencia 186*) also features very attractive designer fashions for women. For all sorts of cowboy boots, try **Botas Michel** (*Juarez 160*). Most of these shops close on Sunday; on other days they close at 6 p.m. and between 2-3 p.m.

WHERE TO EAT

Most restaurants in Tlaquepaque offer mariachi music with meals and most serve regional specialities of grilled meats and birria along with international dishes. As a rule, the restaurants are open 11 a.m. to midnight, but don't expect mariachis much before 3 p.m. **El Abajeno** (*Juarez 231*) serves regional specialities in a large courtyard with one enormous tree shading its tables. Service is most pleasant, and the carnitas (roasted pork) with guacamole and queso fundido are quite good. Moderate prices. **Los Corrales** (*near El Parian at Juarez 101A*) is an attractive garden restaurant serving charcoal-grilled meats, seafood, and Mexican specialties at moderate prices. **Los Amigos** (*Independencia 270*) serves an inexpensive menu turistico each afternoon in its garden patio. Catering to the tourist trade is the lovely **Sin Nombre Restaurant** (*Madero 80*). The waiters not only recite the daily menu but they sing, play the guitar, and otherwise entertain you. The limited menu changes often, but we ate a fine salad and an interesting beef dish, but found our fish filet to be without texture or flavor. *Open Mon.-Sat., noon-7 p.m., Sun. 1 p.m.-6 p.m.;* ☎ *35-45-20; moderately expensive.*

TONALA

Located *11 km (7 m) east of Tlaquepaque*, can be reached by #275 buses running on Av. 16 de Septiembre or #103 buses on P. Moreno. Or, if you have a car, you can catch the Carretera Los Altos outside Tlaquepaque for Tonala. From Guadalajara take Gonzalez Gallo to Lazaro Cardenas. Follow signs for Zapotlanejo-Mexico Libre-Tonala. Exit at Tonala and continue until you reach a wide cobblestone street. Make a left on to this street and continue to the center.

In pre-Hispanic times, the village of Tonala ruled surrounding smaller villages including Tlaquepaque. When the Spaniards arrived, they were surprised to find that Tonala's chief was an elderly woman with the unpro-

nounceable name of Chihualpilli Tzapotzingo. The first Guadalajara was
established here before it was moved to its present location. In modern
times, Tonala has grown famous for its soft-blue-glazed ceramics—plates,
birds, and cats—all designed with delicate bird and flower motifs. These
ceramics are some of the finest produced in Mexico. A visit to Tonala is rewarding for its ceramics museum, market and craft stores.

To view an exquisite collection of Tonala ceramics, you should visit the
Museo Nacional de la Ceramica (*Constitucion 100, between Hidalgo and
Morelos. Open Tues.-Fri., 10 a.m.-5 p.m., Sat. and Sun., 10 a.m.-3 p.m.;
Admission free.*), located two blocks north of Av. Juarez and the zócalo.
On display are some superb older examples of Tonala ware, and poly-
chrome ceramics from Santa Cruz. The museum also has a small, but
high-quality collection of ceramics from Puebla, Oaxaca, and Michoacan.

On Thursday and Sunday, which are the **market days,** Tonala bursts
with life as the streets surrounding the zócalo overflow with stalls selling a
variety of goods and ceramics, but not of the highest quality. For the best
ceramics, you need to visit the shops found on several streets near the zócalo. You will probably arrive at the zócalo from the west by the main
street, Av. Juarez. Running north-south off Juarez are Hidalgo and Morelos, both good shopping streets. Although the Sunday market is the liveliest, many of the better craft shops close on that day. **Galeria Bernabe**
(*Hidalgo 83. Open daily and Sunday.*) makes and sells quality ceramics and is
a good place to begin your shopping. Other stores worth seeking out are
Ceramica (*Morelos 100*) and **Los Caporales** (*Morelos 161*).

LAKE CHAPALA

Whether you want to visit villages around Mexico's largest lakes, *50 km
(31 m) south on MEX 23*, for a long weekend of golfing and relaxation or
for a very Mexican Saturday or Sunday of strolling along the waterfront
and eating to the accompaniment of mariachi music, You can reach Lake
Chapala in less than an hour on MEX 23 past the airport or by the frequent
buses and *combis* leaving from the Nueva Central Camionera.

Around the lake are numerous Indian fishing villages, but two attract the
most tourism: Chapala and Ajijic (ah-hee-heek). Chapala and Ajijic have
been transformed from colonial settlements into retirement communities
for Americans and Canadians. Gone are the days when these quiet villages
attracted only artists and writers (including D. H. Lawrence, who wrote
The Plumed Serpent here); instead, today's retirees enjoy the area's beautiful climate aided by golf clubs, symphony and art societies, and garden
and bridge clubs. The lake, with its fine sunsets, remains the primary focus
of life in these towns and, like Guadalajarans, you can enjoy your weekend
eating at waterfront restaurants and taking boats across the lake.

CHAPALA

Chapala is the center of activity on weekends. Malls adorned with flowers and wrought-iron lamps lead to the lakefront and pier where you can
rent launches. Gardens line the Paseo Ramon Carona along the waterfront,

where you can picnic or nap; everywhere, vendors sell snacks and curios. The most popular place to spend the late afternoon is in one of the restaurants with lake views and mariachis. All serve *pescado blanco* and *caldo Mishi* (fish soup), although most of the fish no longer comes from the lake. We recommend **Cazadores** (Paseo Ramon Carona at Madero), located in the former resort home of the Braniff airlines family. Seated on the tranquil, shady veranda of this restaurant you can choose from the authentic regional dishes offered. The *ceviche* is fresh and flavorful, the pescado blanco attractively presented, and the house specialty is *chamorras de cerdo*, pork in mole wrapped and cooked in banana leaves. Your tequila will be served with a tomato-flavored, house-prepared *sangria* and you can finish with a creamy, sweet drink of the very traditional *Rompepe*. (Moderate. Closed Monday.) Across Madero on the "beach" is the **Beer Garden,** a longtime favorite in Chapala. (Moderate.) Or rent a boat and eat at one of the small restaurants on **Isla de los Alacranes.**

AJIJIC

As you continue west of Chapala, you pass the resort developments of Chula Vista and La Floresta before coming to the cobblestone lanes of **Ajijic,** tucked between the mountains and the lake (8 km, 5 m, west of Chapala turn left into the town). This village turned chic with fine boutiques, inns, and foreigners' homes is a good place to shop, especially for clothes. The shops (open 10 a.m.-6 p.m.) near the waterfront and Calle Morelos are worth a visit, particularly **Mi Mexico** (Morelos 15) with its diversified collection. Here you can find quality crafts from all over Mexico, including ceramics and Huichol beaded work, Josefa designer clothes, and Escalera fabrics.

For eating, there are a number of spots to please the most North American tastes, and **La Nueva Posada,** on the shores of the lake at Guerra 9, is the heart of the local American scene. The hamburgers and apple pie are good, the Mexican food quite decent. You can even snack in the piano bar to the accompaniment of "Hello, Dolly." Other pleasant restaurants include: **Senor Pier** (3 blocks from the Posada at Morelos and the waterfront), right on the town pier and with lake views to accompany the fajitas and ribs; **Los Naranjitos** (Hidalgo 122A), near the zócalo, a favorite for its fresh fish in pesto and salad bar-and there's decent pizza, too. All these restaurants have sandwiches and soups as a choice for lunch; all are moderately priced.

As you leave Ajijic toward the west, you pass **San Juan Casala** (7 km, 4 m), with its spa and thermal springs famous for its geyser shooting a jet of boiling water 200 feet into the air every hour or so. Continuing around the lake past Jocotepec (another 10 km, 6 m), you can pick up MEX 15.

SPORTS CLUBS

Chula Vista Country Club, west of Chapala near Ajijic, has a 9-hole course.

Brisas Country Club, 8 km (5 m) east of Chapala on the road to Guadalajara, also has a 9-hole course.

Club Nautico, next to Hotel Real de Chapala, has a marina, tennis courts, and a pool.

WHERE TO STAY

To reserve by phone, call area code 376.

Real de Chapala

Paseo del Prado 20; ☎ *5-24-68; $89* • Overlooking the lake 6-1/2 km, 4 m from Chapala in the community of La Floresta, this hotel offers fine grounds shaded by eucalyptus, views of the lake, and a suburban atmosphere. Its 85 suites (some with private pools) are spacious and well decorated, with views of either the lake or gardens. Restaurant, piano bar. Pool, tennis, access to golf and horseback riding. Parking. Write Av. Lazaro Cardenas 3260 P.B. in Guadalajara, Jal.

Danza del Sol

Zaragoza 165; ☎ *5-25-05; $85* • On the west side of Ajijic, the multiple gardens, rambling colonial style, and modern facilities of this former condo development may make up for its location away from the lake. The 45 units are really apartments with full kitchens, fireplaces, and, often, patios. Restaurant and bar. Pool. Tennis. Parking. Same contact information as the Real de Chapala.

La Nueva Posada

Guerra 9; ☎ *5-33-95; $60 CP* • Formerly La Posada Ajijic, this popular inn has been relocated just 3 blocks to the left of the pier and set back on the "beach." The new inn retains its old charm with pleasant gardens, stenciling on the walls, and warm colors. The 11 rooms are really junior suites; those with lake views are especially recommended. Garden, pool and indoor restaurant; popular bar with entertainment. Write Apartado 30.

Nido √

Madero 202; ☎ *5-21-16; $27* • In the center of Chapala, this hotel with its old chandelier and tiles has more character than your basic budget. Its 30 rooms are adequate, its restaurant and bar quite popular. Pool, too.

OAXACA

Santo Domingo Church, Oaxaca

Before us lies the gleaming, pinkish-ochre of the valley flat, wild and exalted with sunshine.

D. H. Lawrence, 1927

HISTORY & CULTURE

   Two chains of the rugged Sierra Madres converge at Oaxaca, forming one of the most spectacular valleys in the world. Oaxaca, capital of the state of the same name, is located there in the same central valley as the ancient city of Monte Alban. Three other valleys branch to Etla, Zaachila, and Tlacolula, completing the great valley complex of ancient and modern Oaxaca. With an altitude of 5,000 feet, Oaxaca enjoys a springlike climate year-round. The dry season lays bare mountains eroded into startling shapes, while the summer rains render the landscape more gentle and green.

ANCIENT OAXACA

Reminders of the prehistoric past of Oaxaca are present everywhere in the valley. On your way to visit the many restored ancient cities, you pass suspicious mounds that once were a village or town. Thousands of descendants of the residents of these former cities populate modern towns founded by the Spaniards. Only recently has the history of these ancient cultures revealed itself through the patient work of archaeologists.

At one time, it was thought that the central valley of Oaxaca had been covered by a prehistoric lake. What else could explain the lack of evidence for human occupation before the sudden beginning of the impressive city of Monte Alban in 500 B.C.? The lake was believed to have disappeared in an earthquake, allowing peoples from other areas, perhaps Olmecs or mountain Mixtecs, to populate the valley and establish Monte Alban. Recently, however, new evidence of human occupation dating from 9000 B.C. has enabled archaeologists to reconstruct a gradual development of Oaxacan civilization by local peoples—the Zapotecs, who still dominate life in the Oaxaca Valley.

Before the founding of Monte Alban, these Zapotecs formed a complex culture, traded with the Olmecs on the Gulf Coast for exotic items of jade and shell in return for their obsidian tools and magnetite mirrors, and developed perhaps the most advanced hieroglyphic writing and calendrics in Mexico at that early time. The upper class lived in substantial homes, buried themselves in stone tombs, and built ceremonial centers with pyramidal platforms. In fact, evidence shows that these local people, and not outsiders, prepared the way for the great civilization at Monte Alban.

Monte Alban, high on a mountaintop that had to be leveled before the city could be built, was far above the fertile valley floor that had supported the Zapotecs for millennia. Why would these Zapotecs with their increasing comforts and culture want to level a mountaintop? Archaeologist Richard Blanton proposes that better, more central control of interregional affairs was needed as population increased. So the elite from the three valley arms of Etla, Zaachila, and Tlacolula formed a confederacy, and they selected Monte Alban as their capital because of its neutral, yet central, location. Striking evidence exists for this theory. During the first phase of Monte Alban (500-200 B.C.), three discrete residential sections, corresponding with the three valleys of the confederacy, developed alongside the ceremonial center. Further, no new monumental architecture was constructed at other valley sites during this period. By 200 B.C., the population of Monte Alban had reached 16,000, representing half of the entire valley population. Not only had the elite created a new capital, they also centralized power at Monte Alban, rendering their former valley towns mere provinces under their control.

DECLINE OF MONTE ALBAN

Monte Alban exercised control of the valley until its virtual abandonment in A.D. 700. It waged wars and constructed monuments commemorating its victories; it conducted long-distance trading with Teotihuacan near Mexico City (where there was a Monte Alban quarter) and with the Maya to the south. It buried its nobles in elaborate tombs painted with multicolored frescoes, and it constructed temples and residences using the first columns found in ancient Mexico. Near the end of its hegemony, the population of Monte Alban grew to 26,000 people. Although the valley towns also increased in number and in population and constructed public buildings during these later phases (Monte Alban III, A.D. 250-700), Monte Alban remained the seat of this regional civilization of exceptional art, writing, and statecraft.

After the decline of Monte Alban, control of the area's population became decentralized, reverting back to the valley, where there were 10 or 12 politically autonomous communities—some new, such as Lambityeco; some stronger than others, such as Zaachila and Ocotlan. The reasons for this drastic change are not well understood. Since the Classic style of Monte Alban III continues during period IV (A.D. 700-1250), although in a degenerate manner, it is unlikely that the collapse was due to an invasion. Richard Blanton believes the fall of Teotihuacan around the same time, and with it a serious potential military threat to Oaxaca, made the costly administrative functions of Monte Alban less important. Perhaps people could find no reason to continue to supply and support a central authority. Given the simultaneous collapse of both Monte Alban and Teotihuacan, however, it is possible that larger pan-Mesoamerican changes had occurred that are not yet clearly understood.

The last period before the arrival of the Spaniards brought with it a number of invasions. Mixtecs from the surrounding mountains invaded the Oaxaca Valley. Although the Zapotecs remained and continued many of their traditions, the Mixtecs controlled towns and exacted tribute. Monte Alban declined to a mere cemetery as period III tombs were reused and filled with offerings of Mixtec gold jewelry and lapidary work from this period of Monte Alban V (A.D. 1250-1520). In addition to these offerings at Monte Alban, Mixtec influence can still be seen today in the tombs at Zaachila and the exquisite palaces of Mitla.

In period V, we enter an era with written histories, for the Mixtecs recorded their conquests and genealogies with painted pictographs in manuscripts called codices, some of which have survived. We also have Aztec accounts about how their troops were sent to Oaxaca in the latter part of the 15th century to control trade and receive tribute in gold, cotton mantles, and cochineal (a precious red dye that later became popular in Europe). The Spaniards, too, made reports, describing the Aztec soldiers and tribute collectors who had established a fort in the center of the valley. Despite these new sources of information, it is difficult to sift out shifting alliances of Mixtecs, Zapotecs, and Aztecs, with their intermarriages, rebellions, and wars. It is even hard to know who the victors were, for in the end no great power comparable to the state of Monte Alban emerged. It is easier to say who endured, because the only Indian language spoken in the Oaxaca Valley today is Zapotec.

HISTORY

Oaxaca has not been a leader in most major events of Mexican history, but its fertile valleys and strategic location between the Central Valley of Mexico and the south have resulted in its involuntary involvement in those events. Though Oaxaca was occupied by the Spanish as early as 1521, Diego de Ordaz did not find his Mixtec and Zapotec charges submissive. Not until Cortes had completely subjugated the Aztec capital of Tenochtitlan could sufficient troops be sent to subdue the 1-1/2 million inhabitants of Oaxaca.

The Spanish, like the Aztecs, raised their fort in the center of the great valley and founded what now is the capital city of Oaxaca. Cortes had been interested in the area since first hearing that gold could be found there. When relieved of his rule of New Spain by Charles V, he was compensated with large landholdings in Oaxaca and the title of Marquis del Valle de Oaxaca, a grant kept in his family until the Revolution of 1910. Charles V well expressed the values of his epoch when he wrote that the grant was to be given to Cortes for his "good services...in the Conquest, and the great benefits resulting therefrom, both in respect to the increase of the Castilian Empire and the advancement of the Holy Catholic Faith."

DOMINICAN FRIARS

The province of Oaxaca constituted one of the first four dioceses created in New Spain. Dominican friars, having no opportunity to establish their order in the richer Valley of Mexico, which the more powerful Franciscans controlled, invested their energies in Oaxaca. Using the skill and labor of the Mixtecs and Zapotecs, they established 160 churches by 1575. This legacy still impresses visitors, as many Dominican churches, having been built solidly with thick, fortress-like walls to resist earthquakes, remain today.

As symbolic as all the church construction may have been, there were fewer friars than churches, and even fewer who could communicate in Zapotec or Mixtec. The friars soon came to suspect the depth of the Indians' conversion. Fray Francisco de Burgoa expressed his frustration and dismay upon learning that the Zapotecs believed the wine and bread of Holy Communion represented the food accompanying the dead on their journey through the Underworld, a belief from their "former" religion. Such unfortunate misunderstandings between peoples from totally separate worlds led to the Inquisition. But however abusive the Inquisition was, it failed to destroy traditional Indian beliefs, many of which are practiced today, blended with Catholicism.

Whatever the depth of conversion of the Indians, the whites of Oaxaca were devoutly Catholic at the time of the 1810 Independence Movement. The Church was vehemently opposed to Independence, and Oaxaca's bishop called Father Hidalgo "an instrument of the devil." Understandably so, for under Spanish rule the Dominican Order alone had amassed 25 percent of the land in Oaxaca. The province chose to remain Royalist. Oaxaca soon was invaded by Independistas led by the patriot Morelos, and eventually this state became free of the Spanish Crown along with the rest of Mexico.

By an irony of history, devout Oaxaca next produced Benito Juarez, the first Indian president of Mexico. President Juarez led the reforms against the Church, prohibiting the clergy from owning property (with the sole exception of actual church buildings). Porfirio Diaz, another president as famous as Juarez but despised for his dictatorship, was also born in Oaxaca. Diaz, who started his career as a guerrilla leader in the Reform Wars, became a general under Juarez. He was forced to surrender to the French in 1864 but, using a lasso, escaped from jail in a heroic manner and returned to harass his former captors. Although Diaz started his career as a local hero, Oaxaca early joined the Revolution of 1910 against his dictatorship.

MODERN OAXACA

Today the Oaxaca Valley remains populated with Zapotec Indians, the mountains with Mixtecs, and the town with mestizos. The economy is not a rewarding one for most of the people. Mixtecs have encountered devastating erosion of their highland areas, and their young people have migrated to Mexico City. The central valley of the Zapotecs, however, remains fertile, adequate to grow the major crops of maize and beans. Maguey, used to produce the alcoholic beverage mezcal, and peanuts are cultivated as cash crops. But no cash crop has replaced cochineal, a red dye favored by both Moctezuma and later Europeans, which disappeared with the discovery of chemical dyes.

Some villages supplement their farming by continuing to produce craft specialties with a skill passed down since pre-Spanish times. Tourism, Oaxaca's major industry, has reinforced the production of these crafts. Tourism has had its most noticeable impact on the prosperity of the mestizo middle class in the capital city, where more and more cars are added to the streets each year and where an increasing number of students attend the state university. Yet the benefits of tourism are hard to discern in the lives of most Indian peasants. As anthropologist Ralph Beals describes, peasant spending is quite unlike ours:

> *Many pig raisers...recognize that the enterprise is unprofitable but consider it to be a form of forced savings; the pig is really a live piggy bank. Numerous informants...state, in effect: If I had the cash I would spend it on day-to-day luxuries (and luxuries can be defined at a very low level here). If I have to feed the pig I can't get at the money and at the end it returns a sum large enough to make an investment or meet a critical emergency. In other words, if the choice is between buying new clothing or feeding the pig, the clothes can be patched or worn a little longer.*

CONTEMPORARY INDIAN LIFE

The Saturday market in Oaxaca is the most obvious manifestation of Indian life encountered by the traveler. Here, Mixtecs, Mixes, Triques, Zapotecs, and other Indian groups from all over Oaxaca—the coast, interior mountains, and the valley—can be seen. With the increasing use of store-bought clothes, the differences among these groups have become more subtle to the unpracticed eye—among the women, however, one can still note various embroidery styles on blouses, different colors on belts tied around their skirts, and distinctive ways of braiding their hair. Women not only attend the market to buy, they also dominate its commerce by bringing goods from their villages and selling them after rough bargaining sessions. In ancient times, Indians conducted their commerce in similar markets. At the foot of Monte Alban, archaeologists have discovered evidence of a market area, and in the town of Ocotlan, the conquering Spaniards observed a huge market taking place—a tradition that continues to this day. Today, the Oaxaca market is the largest Indian market in Mexico, and one of the most exciting occasions for observing a tradition that has endured for millennia.

While markets bring together many diverse Indian groups, the Oaxaca Valley is populated by the Zapotecs. Unlike Indian groups in remote regions of the state, the valley Zapotecs are most open to the modern world. Nonetheless, they retain a dread of the world that is more characteristic of ancient beliefs than the Catholicism they now practice. Evil is expected from all quarters—from rains that don't come at all to malevolent spirits that bring misfortune—and to avoid such disasters, rituals must be performed constantly. Some rituals are performed in church; others in cornfields with candles, copal (incense used since ancient times), and flowers; and still others are performed daily, such as washing hands before and after meals to prevent insects from destroying plants. Although practitioners of Catholicism, the Zapotecs continue to placate the rain god and other spirits that inhabit their world.

ILLNESS

Religious views also infuse Zapotec medical practices. Doctors are tolerated, but at best they treat the symptoms of an illness, not its cause. When ill, Zapotecs often treat themselves using herbal remedies—wild garlic for high blood pressure, mint for sore eyes, and a special basil for worms. If an illness persists, the causes are diagnosed through divination assisted by hallucinatory mushrooms, the entrails of a fowl, or even playing cards. Hotness felt in the head and the loss of appetite may be due to anger, which, in turn, has made the person vulnerable to night forms or evil air. Sleepless nights or stomach problems may be due to soul loss caused by a frightening encounter with a person or supernatural spirit. Witchcraft or failure to perform satisfactorily one's ritual duties may cause other illnesses. Curing is performed by a native healer (curandero) or shaman. Preventive health care is practiced, too, through diet, the wearing of crosses or rosaries, and even through cigarette smoking, which is believed to ward off witches.

OAXACA CITY

Beautiful Oaxaca (wha-HAH-kah) offers one of the liveliest and most authentic Indian markets and some of the finest colonial architecture in Mexico. As if that's not enough, nearby are many fascinating ruins, particularly world-famous Monte Alban and Mitla. All of these exceptional sights are located in a breathtaking, scenic valley. You will also be captivated by the atmosphere of the town itself, and will find yourself relaxing to savor it better. Those who love Oaxaca return often to linger, enjoying the tranquillity of this provincial capital and the dignity and quiet humor of its native people, the Zapotecs.

The usual first visit to Oaxaca starts with an early Friday morning flight into town and ends with a Monday morning departure. A long weekend trip can encompass the major ruins of Monte Alban and Mitla, touring and shopping in town, the markets in Oaxaca and Tlacolula, and Sunday evening music in the zócalo.

ESSENTIAL OAXACA CITY

KEY TO OAXACA

Sights • The town has fine colonial architecture that becomes exceptional in the case of the Church of Santo Domingo, two excellent archaeology museums, and one of the best Indian markets in Mexico; and it provides a comfortable base for visits to magnificent ruins and craft villages in the surrounding valley.

Excursions • The scenic Oaxaca Valley is full of ruins, including the fabulous ones at Monte Alban and Mitla; Indian villages and markets; and colonial churches. A quick flight lands you at the Pacific beaches of Puerto Escondido and Huatulco for a change of scenery. (See chapter on Pacific Coast Resorts.)

Fiestas • The Guelaguetza in July; Fiesta of the Virgin of Soledad, December 16-18; the Night of the Radishes, December 23; and Christmas Eve.

Shopping • Regional crafts, particularly serapes and pottery, are excellent. The many markets and superior crafts shops make Oaxaca one of the best shopping areas in Mexico. Markets abound, but the Saturday market in Oaxaca is the largest and the Sunday market in Tlacolula the most interesting. Traditional market days are: *Tlacolula*: Sunday. *Etla*: Wednesday. *Zaachila*: Thursday. *Ocotlan*: Friday. *Oaxaca*: Saturday.

Where to Stay • A few first-class hotels; many fine inexpensive and budget hotels are available, in addition to camping. The popularity of the weekend markets and the fiestas make it important to reserve your hotel room in advance for those times, especially for first-class hotels.

Where to Eat • Interesting regional cuisine, but gastronomical delights are still rare.

Entertainment • In the early evening Oaxaca provides concerts in its zócalo and has sidewalk cafes for drinks and conversation.

Getting Around • The town is pleasantly walkable, and taxis, rental cars, and minibuses are plentiful for excursions.

PRACTICAL TIP

The warm mountain sun and temperate climate of Oaxaca make it a good place to visit year-round. The rainy season (June-October) sometimes can bring storms lasting for a few days in September and October.

Bank lines always seem to be long. Bring your Cirrus bank card for use in automatic teller machines ("Caja Permanente").

Many shops close 1:30-4 p.m. and reopen in the evening.

WHAT TO SEE AND DO

Oaxaca takes great pride in its colonial heritage. Building ordinances prevent construction that would mar its architectural integrity, a commitment to historical preservation that is the tourist's gain. Walking through Oaxaca, you encounter charming modern uses of old buildings. A stop at an art exhibit can be an opportunity to see the interior of one of the Cortes family's houses (Alcala 202), while visits to the Regional Museum and the Presidente Hotel take you to beautifully renovated former monasteries. And a small repair shop can occupy what used to be the portal of a massive colonial structure. Early morning and late afternoon wanderings through town, when the light enriches the colors of buildings, are rewarded with the discovery of a lovely small park, a street of arches (upper Garcia Vigil), a colonial pedestrian way (Alcala), or a startling panoramic view. Apart from these informal pleasures of Oaxaca, there are major sights to include in your walks.

Zócalo, Cathedral, and Government Palace

The zócalo, with its lovely bandstand, huge shade trees, and benches and sidewalk cafes for relaxation, is the center of Oaxaca's social life. It is a great social equalizer where you find middle-class merchants, Indians from villages, serape vendors, and university students mingling with international tourists. Closed to traffic, it is an intimate square where you will find yourself returning often to enjoy its atmosphere. The Government Palace borders its south side, portals the remaining three sides, and the Cathedral dominates the north corner.

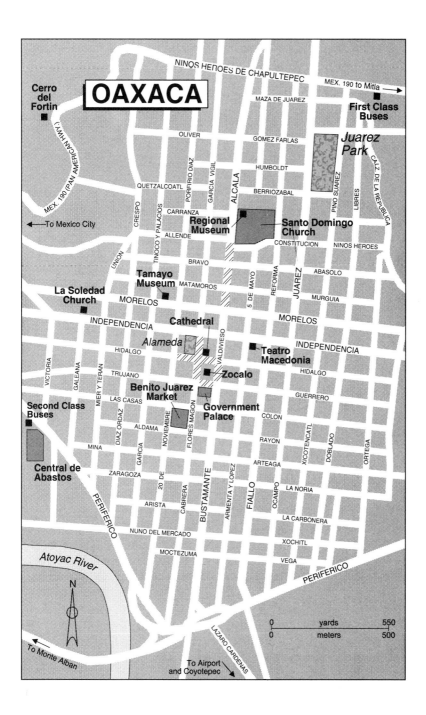

OAXACA

Cerro del Fortin

NINOS HEROES DE CHAPULTEPEC

MEX. 190 to Mitla

MAZA DE JUAREZ

First Class Buses

MEX. 190 (PAN AMERICAN HWY.)

OLIVER

GOMEZ FARLAS

Juarez Park

HUMBOLDT

QUETZALCOATL

BERRIOZABAL

CALZ. DE LA REPUBLICA

PINO SUAREZ

LIBRES

To Mexico City

CRESPO

TINOCO Y PALACIOS

PORFIRIO DIAZ

GARCIA VIGIL

ALCALA

CARRANZA

ALLENDE

Regional Museum

Santo Domingo Church

CONSTITUCION

NINOS HEROES

UNION

BRAVO

ABASOLO

Tamayo Museum

MATAMOROS

5 DE MAYO

REFORMA

JUAREZ

MURGUIA

La Soledad Church

MORELOS

MORELOS

INDEPENDENCIA

Cathedral

INDEPENDENCIA

HIDALGO

Alameda

VALDIVIESO

Teatro Macedonia

HIDALGO

VICTORIA

GALEANA

MIER Y TERAN

TRUJANO

Zocalo

Benito Juarez Market

LAS CASAS

GUERRERO

Second Class Buses

DIAZ ORDAZ

ALDAMA

Government Palace

COLON

XICOTENCATL

DOBLADO

ORTEGA

GARCIA

NOVIEMBRE

FLORES MAGON

RAYON

MINA

ARTEAGA

Central de Abastos

ZARAGOZA

20 DE

CABRERA

BUSTAMANTE

ARMENTA Y LOPEZ

FIALLO

OCAMPO

LA NORIA

PERIFERICO

ARISTA

LA CARBONERA

NUNO DEL MERCADO

XOCHITL

Atoyac River

MOCTEZUMA

VEGA

PERIFERICO

N

0 yards 550
0 meters 500

To Monte Alban

LAZARO CARDENAS

To Airport and Coyotepec

Construction of the Cathedral started in 1544 but was not completed for 200 years—if it can be said to have been completed at any date, given its history of pillage and subsequent restoration. The handsome, lacy facade displays a deep baroque relief of the Assumption over the center portal. The interior is somewhat disappointing, but you might be lucky to see its outdoor plaza enlivened by a performance of the local orchestra. Well worth viewing is the imaginative, evocative mural entitled "Cosmogonia de las Culturas Indigenos de Oaxaca," in the Government Palace. Painted by Garcia Bustas in 1987, this is not the main mural in the Palace, but rather can be found by crossing the courtyard and going up the left stairwell.

Church of Santo Domingo

Alcala and Gurrion Normally closed 1-4 p.m. • The Church and Monastery of Santo Domingo (founded in 1575) suffered during the French Intervention and Reform Period when the monastery was converted into barracks and the church into stables. Fortunately, the refurbished splendor of the church interior remains to astound us all. The massive, earthquake-resistant facade does little to prepare you for the exuberant interior. Stark white walls contrast with gilded and colorfully painted stucco sculpture. A provincial charm pervades, especially above the entrance apse where the famous genealogical tree flourishes with "its leafy tendrils and bunches of grapes, among which solemn busts blossom like male and female flowers" (Elizabeth Wilder Weismann). The tree is said to represent the family of St. Dominic, although a later addition of the Virgin Mary to the treetop has caused some confusion. The **Capilla del Rosario** (Chapel of the Rosary), built from 1690 to 1731, is really a small church equal to the main one in gilded profusion and charm.

The monastery continues to be used as a barracks, but one of its cloisters has been transformed into the Regional Museum of Oaxaca.

Regional Museum of Oaxaca

Alcala and Gurrion Open Tues.-Fri., 10 a.m.-6 p.m.; Sat.-Sun., 10 a.m.-5 p.m. Admission fee. • Attached to Santo Domingo Church, this imposing colonial monastery, now a museum contains—on the second floor in Room 2—a spectacular collection of Mixtec art and jewelry found in Tomb 7 at Monte Alban, representing one of the most extraordinary burials discovered in Mexico. The Mixtecs reused Tomb 7 sometime after A.D. 1400, when Monte Alban had been long abandoned. Not until 1932 were the more than 500 precious objects buried there recovered by archaeologist Alfonso Caso. On display are transluscent alabaster vessels, delicate obsidian ear ornaments, a rock-crystal cup, and a jade quetzal-bird lip plug, all demonstrating the virtuosity of Mixtec lapidary work. Yet if any aspect of the collection can be selected as the most remarkable, it is the goldwork.

Most pre-Conquest gold was lost through the plundering of Spanish conquistadors, and this one burial more than quadrupled the number of known Mexican gold objects. Metal working techniques probably were learned from Costa Rica or Panama, possibly even Peru. Despite the achievements of those areas, many believe that the Mixtec work is the finest in the Americas. The most exquisite gold pieces, particularly some of the pectorals and rings, were made by the lost-wax method. *Cire-perdue*, or lost wax, is a complex method beginning with a clay core on which a design is carved, then covered with a coating of wax. An outer layer of clay is then put over the wax and the entire mold is heated to liquify the wax, which is then poured out. In the resulting empty space, liquid gold is poured into the mold where it hardens. The gold is freed from the mold, then treated and polished repeatedly.

In one display case are three masterpieces of this technique: *Mascara de Dios* (mask of the god Xipe Totec); *Pectoral de Oro* (gold breastplate); and *Pectoral de Oro Varias Secciones* (four-piece gold pectoral). Note the detail of the rope tying a Xipe Totec mask to a warrior's head in the piece on the right. The uneven hair is not an artist's error but an accurate representation of the warrior hairstyle. On the Pectoral de Oro (on the left), the fineness of the headdress and the detail of the three-string necklace with bird pendant are exceptional.

The museum contains many other displays including exhibits of Indian costumes from the region, religious art from this Dominican monastery, and pre-Hispanic art from ruins in the Oaxaca Valley, particularly from Monte Alban. Plans are underway to do the badly needed renovations of this museum.

Instituto de Artes Graficas

Alcala 507, across from Santo Domingo Church Open Mon. and Wed.-Sat., 10 a.m.-2 p.m., 4-7 p.m.; Sun., 11 a.m.-5 p.m.; closed Tues.; donation. • The renowned contemporary artist, Francisco Toledo, has donated this lovely colonial mansion as well as much of this collection of graphic art to his native state of Oaxaca. The impressive permanent collection includes works by world masters, from Goya and Picasso to Mexico's Orozco, Rivera, Siqueiros, and Tamayo. Temporary one-artist exhibits sometimes replace the permanent collection. Recent shows of the works of Jose Guadalupe Pasada and Rufino Tamayo were particularly impressive.

El Museo de Arte Contemporaneo ("MACO")

Alcala 202 Open Wed.-Mon., 10:30 a.m.-8 p.m.; closed Tues. Admission fee. • Opened in 1992 and located in the stunningly refurbished Casa de Cortes, this museum of Oaxacan contemporary art exhibits the works of some of the state's leading artists including Tamayo, Rodolfo Morales and Toledo. The first floor houses a library with an excellent selection of books on art from around the world.

Rufino Tamayo Museum of Pre-hispanic Art

Morelos 503, near Porfirio Diaz Open daily except Tues., 10 a.m.-2 p.m. and 4-7 p.m.; Sun., 10 a.m.-3 p.m. Admission fee. • The museum represents 20 years of selection and collection of pre-Columbian art by the revered artist Rufino Tamayo, who died in 1991 at the age of 91. Tamayo donated his collection to Oaxaca, his native state. The pieces are well displayed to show their special beauty and power. The collection, ranging from the Olmec period to the Aztec, includes exceptional works from Veracruz and the west coast cultures. The tranquil garden of this renovated colonial building is a wonderful spot to relax.

Basilica de la Soledad

Independencia and Galeana (entrance on the plaza) Museum open Mon.-Sat. 10 a.m.-2 p.m. and 12-2 p.m. on Sun.; donation. • This church, with its undulating facade like an enormous altarpiece, was built between 1682-1690 as the sanctuary of the patron saint of Oaxaca, the Virgin of Solitude, and also commemorates the location of the miraculous appearance of her image in 1620. In that year, a muleteer discovered he was traveling with one more mule than he had started with. Upon reaching the site of the present church, the extra mule collapsed and died, and a lovely statue of the Virgin was found in the mule's pack. This statue, clothed in gold-embroidered black velvet, can be seen in its gilded glass enclosure inside the church, along with a startling profusion of chandeliers and lunging angels. Processions in honor of the Virgin begin in the bird-filled adjoining plaza. A museum behind the church has an odd collection of regional costumes and memorabilia as well as a stunning selection of old votive paintings dedicated to the Virgin.

Church of San Felipe Neri

Independencia at Tinoco y Palacios. • The lovely 18th-century Plateresque facade with a statue of St. Felipe Neri over the portal is like an altarpiece, but a very staid one compared with the exuberant, gilded Churrigueresque main altarpiece inside. Colonial paintings fill the numerous side altars.

Church of San Agustin

Guerrero at Armenta y Lopez. • Close to the zócalo, this church is well worth the short walk just to see the facade with its sensitive sculpture of St. Augustine who is portrayed in the manner of the Madonna of Misericordia, with his protective cape extended over kneeling figures.

Teatro Macedonia de Alcala

Armenta y Lopez and Independencia. • This charming example of the Belle Epoque style would be an important part of anyone's tour if only the hours of admission were more predictable. They are not predictable because the building still functions as a theater, open only for rehearsals or performances. The comfort and compactness of the theater might be adequate inducement to your trying to attend an evening performance. If you are passing by, at least check to see if the theater is open.

Benito Juarez Museum and House

Garcia Vigil 609. Open Tues.-Sun., 9 a.m.-7 p.m. Admission fee. • If you especially enjoy visiting former homes of the great, you might want to visit this house where Mexico's equivalent to Abraham Lincoln first resided in town as a servant. The house belonged to Father Salanueva, who taught Juarez Spanish and provided him with his education. The museum contains mementos of the period.

Cerro del Fortin

Hill of the Fort. • Walk along Avenida Crespo until you are almost out of town. A long stairway on your left leads to the statue of Benito Juarez at the top of the Hill of the Fort. The panoramic view of the city from here is worthwhile, especially in the evening. The Cerro can be reached by car from the Pan American Highway near the Hotel Victoria. It's thought that on this hill, the Aztecs established their fortress to guarantee an open trade route to the south and to collect tribute from the valley towns for Moctezuma, but to date no confirming archaeological evidence has been found.

SHOPPING

No area of Mexico rivals Oaxaca for the richness, variety, and quality of its native crafts. For many visitors, exploring the local and surrounding markets and shopping for crafts is the highlight of a trip to Oaxaca—and with good reason. In Oaxaca's popular arts you encounter its rich Indian and Spanish heritage and the continuing pride and creativity of its people.

An abundance of crafts floods the markets and shops. The pre-Hispanic *huipils* (or **blouses**) still are woven on backstrap looms, whether they are the bright red ones from the Mixteca Alta or the delicate cotton brocades from Amusgo. **Ceramics** continue to be made without a potter's wheel—from the finely shaped black, satiny bowls from Coyotepec, to the "embroidered dolls" made in the tradition of the late Teodora Blanco from Atzompa, to the carved pots by the Porra family of Atzompa and the silly bells shaped like mischievously grinning cows from Ocotlan. For some of the finest Ocotlan ceramics, look for the signed works of Josefina Aguilar. Delightful **wood carvings** from Arrazola and San Martin Tilcajete create everything from farm animals to fanciful mermaids, all painted fearlessly in brilliant colors. The works of the master Manuel Jimenez (Arrazola), and Jesus Sosa (Tilcajete) are particularly prized. Spanish influence can be seen in the tin Christmas ornaments, the steel **machetes** and knives engraved with macho slogans, and in the wool so finely woven into the serapes, or **rugs**, from Teotitlan del Valle, the shawls from Mitla, and the colorful **belts** and small delicate purses from Jalieza. Huaraches (sandals), **straw goods**, colorful hammocks and bags, and embroidered blouses can be found in the markets, and the silver crosses from Yalalag as well as the gold **filigree jewelry** based on Mixtec techniques, can be found in the shops. As if there were not enough to choose from, Oaxaca also produces finely woven bolts of cotton cloth that are made into attractive placemats and **ta-**

blecloths. The sheer abundance and variety of crafts can be overwhelming—or an opportunity for joyful indulgence.

PRACTICAL HINTS

In Oaxaca, as elsewhere, bargaining is expected in the markets, but generally not in the shops. Some of the finest crafts can be found in the better stores, particularly the ceramics and jewelry, and often rare huipils or weavings. It is tempting to go to the villages where the crafts are made; however, be warned. Although prices are often lower in villages and the selection sometimes vast, the best village products are often brought to Oaxaca. Still, a visit to the villages can be fascinating for the chance to see the artisans working in their homes and to purchase a very personal creation before it is shipped to Oaxaca or some foreign land. If you are buying clothing, realize that colors might run and fabrics might shrink. No market vendor will be very helpful to you on these matters. If the piece of clothing is too large, señora, it will shrink. If it fits just right, of course, señora, it will not shrink. Care in cleaning is the only answer. Before buying black pottery, check that it's not "burnished" with shoe polish that rubs off with a moist finger. And make sure your wool rug lies flat, with even edges and that it doesn't glisten in the sun from synthetic threads.

WHERE TO SHOP

You have your choice among several markets in and outside Oaxaca and a variety of craft stores in town. We describe here only the ones in Oaxaca—its market, or better, markets, as well as our favorite shops.

The Saturday Market

This market sprawls over a large area on the outskirts of town. To get there take a cab or walk (about 20 minutes) from the zócalo down Flores Magon to Las Casas, and turn right on Las Casas. Across the railroad tracks and to the left you will come upon the market.

The principal market *(Central de Abastos)* of Oaxaca is one of the largest, most colorful, and vibrant in Mexico. Although it sells some tourist items, it still is a market in the pre-Conquest tradition-a place where the people from the city and surrounding villages come to buy and sell. It is open every day, but it explodes with color and people on Saturday. If you are near this area late on Friday or very early Saturday morning you will see Indians pouring into the market on burros or arriving in overcrowded, dilapidated buses that somehow, miraculously, have made it safely through the mountains. By midmorning the market is alive and pulsating, and buying, selling, and trading are in full force. Aisles and stalls are filled with everything from flashlight batteries and plastic combs to fruits, vegetables, herbs, meat, fish, baskets, blouses, and serapes. There is fascination in exploring the stalls and finding so many items mysterious to us but essential to the life of Oaxaquenos— such as cal, looking much like chalk but actually lime used to soak corn before it is ground into flour. You also may encounter the stalls with medicinal herbs for cures passed down over the millennia—herbs to cure everything from liver disease to impotency, from soul loss to hangovers. (But don't photograph these herbs without asking permission. The curers have strong views about the powers of the plants; often they believe photographs rob them of potency.)

The presentation of the food is a matter of pride and salesmanship. Walk through the fruit and vegetables area—where delicate, polished tomatoes and apples are arranged in carefully created architectural mounds. Here you can't fail to be impressed by pile upon pile of fresh and dried chiles (Mexico has 100 or so different kinds). And look for the garlic vendors, ambulatory women wearing garlic as crowns on their heads.

You will find the people in the market talkative, and invariably friendly. And, no doubt, you will be struck by their handsome features and dress. The regal, stately Tehuana women will command your attention as they march through the market in their huipils richly embroidered in dark purples, crimsons, and reds. Their size and stature can't fail to impress. Miguel Covarrubias reports that a slim Tehuana is thought to be in poor health and that the women of Tehuantepec compliment one another with "*Que frondosa!*" (*frondosa* in the sense of a great leafy tree)—that is, "How fat and luxuriant you look!"

As you listen to the market women converse, you will realize that your rudimentary knowledge of Spanish fails you and that what you are hearing sounds very Oriental. In fact, what you probably are hearing is Zapotec or Mixtec (or a close relative), the native languages of many of the market people. These languages are tonal, like Chinese, where the meaning of a word is dependent upon the pitch of the voice, and so the sounds are lyrical. Fortunately, many vendors also speak some Spanish, and a few some English or a universal sign language, so you will be able to make purchases with little difficulty.

At some point you will want to wander over to the serape area, dominated by gregarious, friendly men (Zapotec men are noted for their speechmaking), where you will find a large selection of Teotitlan serapes. This is your time to engage in some tough, but always good-natured, bargaining. After a purchase following a long bargaining session during which each of you expressed outrage at the other's incredible offers, you will no doubt receive a warm handshake and a big smile.

Benito Juarez Market

The market is near the zócalo, in the area bounded by 20 de Noviembre, Flores Magon, Las Casas, and Aldama. Until recently, this indoor market was the main market area for Oaxaca, with the stalls overflowing into many of the surrounding streets. With the relocation of the main market to the edge of town, this market is less lively. But still you can find serapes, huipils, straw goods, leather items, and, in surrounding shops, pottery. The persistent buyer can sometimes find exquisite Amusgo huipils here. They are usually not on display, so ask for them at stalls where other huipils are shown—you may find a gem. Open daily.

La Mano Magica

Alcala 203 • This art gallery and crafts shop features a selective collection of very high-quality crafts—ceramics, wood carvings, serapes, and more —including some exquisite examples not found elsewhere in Oaxaca.

ARIPO

Garcia Vigil 809 • Located several blocks north of the zócalo, ARIPO offers a wide selection of quality crafts including some fine ceramics, weavings, and straw. In the rear of the store you can see artisans weaving.

Artesanias Cocijo

Plazuela del Carmen Alto • Located just north of Santo Domingo Church in a plaza filled with Trique women weaving and selling their goods, Cocijo often has some especially fine wood carvings and masks as well as very good ceramics.

Chimalli

Garcia Vigil 513A • Chimalli has interesting ceramics and wood carvings, as well as other crafts.

Victor

Porfirio Diaz 111 • is operated by Ramon Fosado, who has an extensive knowledge of Oaxacan crafts, and is the son of the owner of the outstanding shop with the same name in Mexico City. Although the stock is often slim and the display disappointing, Victor is usually the only place in town where you can find some of the older, more traditional items, such as indigo dyed skirts from Pinotepa Nacional, and natural wool colored serapes from the Mixteca Alta region of Oaxaca.

Yalalag

Alcala 104 • Located in a former mansion with a pleasant courtyard, Yalalag has a fine and extensive collection of crafts. The rooms surrounding the courtyard feature pottery from Coyotepec and Ocotlan, wood carvings from San Martin Tilcajete and Arrazola, a good selection of masks, huipils, rebozos, and serapes, and crafts from other parts of Mexico. For a better selection of serapes, try **El Cactus** (Alcala 401).

Oro de Monte Alban

On Gurrion, across from Santo Domingo church • The specialty here is in fine reproductions of Mixtec jewelry from Tomb 7.

ART GALLERIES

Along with its crafts, Oaxaca has long been proud of its artists, particularly the renowned Rufino Tamayo (1899-1991) and Francisco Toledo (b.

1940). In recent years several art galleries have been sustained by a new generation of artists, many continuing in the local tradition of magical realism. Since the paintings of the Oaxacan olympians, Tamayo and Toledo, aren't usually sold here (you can find Toledo graphics in the better galleries, however), it's easier to discover the work of those who just now are developing international reputations, such as Maximino Javier and Rodolfo Morales. And there are other fine artists, both Oaxacan and foreign, working in a variety of styles: Look for the "primitive" village scenes of Felipe Morales, the realistic still lifes of Kate Corbett, the magical realism of Eddie Martinez, and the often witty papier-mache sculpture of Adrianna Alaniz. Although most of these artists are represented in **La Mano Magica** (Alcala 203) or **Galeria Quetzalli** (Alcala 307), Morales and Martinez usually exhibit in the **Galeria del Arte de Oaxaca** (Trujano 102, 1/2 block west of zócalo), which specializes in magical realism.

FIESTAS

Fiestas in the region of Oaxaca are famous both for their number and excitement. You should check with the Tourist Office to see if any fiestas will occur during your visit. You might wish to plan your visit around the more famous fiestas described below.

Guelaguetza or Lunes del Cerro ("Monday on the Hill")

This folklore festival is very popular with tourists. Representatives from the seven regions of the state of Oaxaca perform indigenous dances, including the famous *Danza de las Plumas* (Feather Dance) in traditional regional costumes. Small gifts typifying each region—oranges from the Sierra Juarez and palm hats from the Mixtecs—are thrown to the crowd in the tradition of the Guelaguetza, which is Zapotec for "gift." The events take place in the amphitheater at the Cerro del Fortin, but tickets can be bought in advance if you check with the Tourist Office or your hotel. The festival is performed twice, always on a Monday at the end of July or early in August. **Practical tip**: Wear a hat for protection against the sun.

December Festivities

Oaxaca celebrates the Christmas season joyously. Celebrations begin with the Fiesta of the Virgin of La Soledad, continue through the Night of the Radishes, are punctuated with Christmas posadas, and end with Christmas Eve processions through the town and around the zócalo until everyone is called to Midnight Mass by the simultaneous ringing of all the town's church bells. These festivities are accompanied by the eating of *bunuelos,* crisp crepes with syrup in a bowl that you, and everyone else, smash for good luck in the New Year. Posadas commemorate the journey of Mary and Joseph to Bethlehem and their search for lodging *(posada).* Starting with the evening of December 16 and ending December 23, small processions go through neighborhoods knocking on doors and singing for lodging. Finally, at the home designated for the evening's pinata party, the door is open with much fanfare.

Fiesta of the Virgin of La Soledad

The patron of Oaxaca is honored from December 16-18. Oaxaquenos from all over come to join in the religious processions and ceremonies. Fireworks and foodstands are set up in the plaza outside the Basilica de la Soledad, which was built to commemorate the miraculous appearance of the Virgin's statue in the 17th century. Starting at 7:30 p.m. on December 16 at the Basilica, the procession of floats, dancers crowned with flower sculptures, and bands wind their way through the night and return to the Basilica only after the sun rises. During the evening of December 17 and 18, fireworks and music fill the air of the Basilica's plaza.

Night of the Radishes

On December 23, booths are set up around the zócalo for the display and sale of radishes sculpted into extraordinary shapes, including complete Nativity scenes. Vendors offering balloons and lovely birds constructed with tiny dried flowers add to the festivities. The exceptional popularity of these exhibits results in endless lines of people waiting to view the radish creations. To avoid hours of waiting, you should get to the zócalo by 6 p.m. to make your tour of the booths.

Christmas Eve

Starting around 9 p.m. music and fireworks accompany floats through the streets and around the zócalo for a grand finale. Everyone in Oaxaca seems to attend, and the gaiety ends only with the insistent ringing of the church bells for late Mass.

WHERE TO STAY

Oaxaca offers fine accommodations at prices considerably below those of comparable hotels at resorts. Many of the hotels we can recommend most highly are located within a short walking distance of the center of town, the zócalo. A few others lie on the outskirts of town.

Oaxaca tends to attract people for long stays—and with good reason. If you find yourself in for a prolonged stay, check the Oaxaca Lending Library (Alcala 305) for apartment listings, or try the Posada San Pablo, which rents only by the month, or the Hotel Senorial, which offers special long-term rates. Normally, Oaxaca has sufficient hotel space to meet the demand; however, for certain peak times, rooms in the better hotels are very difficult to come by and must be booked far in advance. Rooms in inexpensive hotels sometimes can be found at the last minute. You can expect difficulty finding accommodations during the Christmas season, particularly December 16-25 and during fiestas. Ordinarily, because of the Saturday market, hotel space for weekends is scarcer than weekdays. We have gone to Oaxaca on weekends without reservations, however, and we have always managed to find an acceptable room. We wish you the same luck! Better yet, though, reserve in advance by calling area code 951 or writing to the desired hotel at Oaxaca, Oax., Mexico.

VERY EXPENSIVE

Presidente ★★★

5 de Mayo 300, at corner of Plazoleta Labastida; ☎ *6-25-35; $150* • The Presidente is the most attractive hotel in Oaxaca and one of the colonial gems of Mexico. Conveniently located about 4 blocks from the zócalo; it was formerly El Convento de Santa Catalina de Siena, originally built in 1576 and opened as a hotel in 1975. Remnants of colonial paintings can still be found on its thick stone walls. Many rooms surround intimate flower-filled patios bordered by 16th-century arches; some rooms overlook a swimming pool. As one would expect of a restored convent, the 90 rooms vary in size and quality of light. In general, we have found the rooms on the second floor more attractive than those on the ground floor. All rooms are tastefully decorated with native weavings and crafts. Bathrooms are modern with walls of beautiful Mexican tiles. We think the service should be more attentive and for that reason alone we have reduced this hotel from 4 stars. There is a lovely restaurant and cocktail lounge; and the hotel provides street parking. Although room prices are exorbitant by Oaxacan standards, treat yourself to it if you can. For reservations, call, in the U.S., ☎ 800-468-3571.

EXPENSIVE

Victoria ★★★

Off the Pan American Highway (MEX 190); ☎ *5-26-33; $100-150* • On a hillside on the outskirts of town, this hotel has a wonderful view of Oaxaca and the valley. It offers a variety of very comfortable, modern accommodations, and many of the 151 rooms have views. The pleasant standard rooms, some with mountain views, are located in the main three-story building; the very large junior suites all have stupendous views; and the bungalows (standard rooms with terraces) are set amid the lovely gardens. (For light sleepers, bring your ear plugs against the highway noise that filters up to some of the rooms.) The Victoria is a modern, well-maintained hotel with good service. Restaurant and bar with panoramic view, cocktail lounge with entertainment, and a disco. Tennis court and large pool. Parking. Although you can make the interesting downhill walk into town without difficulty, you need good legs to climb the hills back from the zócalo to the hotel. But the Victoria provides drop-off service to and from the zócalo, 7 a.m.-9 p.m. Write Apartado 248.

Mision de los Angeles ★★★

Calz. Porfirio Diaz 102; ☎ *5-15-00; $98* • Located north of the Pan American Highway, this hotel spreads over extensive grounds and has an atmosphere of suburban calm and comfort. The modern 125 units are decent-sized with good tiled baths, and most are located in low-rise buildings with balconies. Other units can be found in modern bungalows with patios. Restaurant, lounge with entertainment, and disco. Large pool and gardens, tennis courts, and game room. Parking. The zócalo is a 20-minute walk away, but taxis are normally available.

MODERATE

Fortin Plaza

Av. Venus 118; ☎ *5-77-77; $85* • Not far from the Victoria, but set closer to the road, is this modern hotel—a virtual Oaxacan high-rise with six stories. Opened in 1987, this contemporary hotel offers 100 attractive rooms, most with terraces and views of the city or mountains. Restaurant. Bar. Well-landscaped, but smallish pool. Parking.

INEXPENSIVE

Senorial

Zócalo, Portal de Flores 6; ☎ *6-39-33; $50* • The small, undistinguished entrance may be somewhat difficult to find since it is in the midst of stores and restaurants on the zócalo. Inside, however, the Senorial is a well-run commercial hotel. Its 130 rooms vary. Although all are exceptionally clean, many are small and nondescript, others large with some charm. Those in the rear overlook the small swimming pool. The more expensive rooms are air-conditioned. A restaurant, roof garden, bar, and pay parking lot are available. Service is good and the location very convenient—especially for those addicted to the zócalo. Parking one block away on Trujano. No credit cards.

Gala

Bustamante 103; ☎ *4-22-51; $55* • Located just a few steps off the zócalo, the Gala has a contemporary, tasteful decor throughout its lobby and common areas, and houses 36 well-appointed rooms with modern baths. Exterior rooms can be a bit noisy, but they are preferable to the smaller interior ones. Service could be warmer. Restaurant.

Marques del Valle

Portal de Claveria; ☎ *6-32-95; $50* • Located on the zócalo, its onyx-paneled lobby is lively and its plainer upper stories are airy and clean, if somewhat barren. The exterior rooms are decent-sized and some have views of the zócalo; the interiors look out on a plain atrium; all 160 rooms are comfortable and have simple yet acceptable baths. Located next to the Cathedral, the restaurant and outdoor cafe are very popular.

Villa de Leon

Reforma 405; ☎ *6-19-77; $45* • The Villa de Leon has a decent location just around the corner from the Presidente. It provides 30 small, but clean and attractively furnished rooms, some however, with the strange feature of showers not separated from toilets. Bar.

BUDGET

Las Golondrinas √★

Tinoco y Palacios 411; ☎ *6-87-26; $30* • Opened in December 1989, and about a 6-block, uphill walk from the zócalo, Las Golondrinas has quickly become the favorite budget hotel of many travelers to Oaxaca. Its owner, Jorge Augusto Velasco, has created an intimate, homey environment for the 24 simply furnished rooms, spread out around several patios, in both old and new wings, all with private baths, but a few bathrooms located outside of the room. Rooms vary in size, ambience, and light. Some have beamed ceilings; most are without views and with small windows. Breakfast served outdoors in one of the pleasant patios. Very attentive service. You'll be made to feel most welcome. A special buy for those seeking a warm, atmospheric budget hotel.

Principal √★

5 de Mayo 208; ☎ *6-25-35; $30* • Located a half block from the Presidente and 3 1⁄2 blocks from the zócalo, the Principal is another favorite budget hotel in Oaxaca and one of long standing. In an attractive colonial building, 23 rooms surround a whitewashed, sun-filled courtyard, providing a cheery, friendly, and intimate atmosphere. Several rooms have been renovated, but a few are without windows and very small, so check the rooms first. Some of the triples, with cathedral ceilings and exposed brick, are your best choice. Outside the second-floor rooms, on the plant- filled balcony surrounding the courtyard, you can sit, read, and relax. A special buy.

Posada San Pablo ★

Fiallo 102; ☎ *6-49-14; $290/mo.* • Near the corner of Independencia, the small Posada is housed in an attractive colonial building with 10 furnished apartments often available at reduced rates by the month only; occasionally rented by the day. Because some residents stay a long time, these exceptional bargains are often full. They're clean, too.

WHERE TO EAT

Among Mexicans, **Oaxaca's cuisine** ranks among the most popular and sought after in the nation. Although for many foreign travelers, the regional specialties are an acquired taste, they are well worth seeking out. For the nonexperimental visitor, restaurants abound serving more Americanized food—fried chicken, steaks, and even hamburgers. Oaxaca's restaurants certainly do not reach the culinary heights of other cities—especially not Mexico City—yet some restaurants and dishes surely will please. You should, of course, be on the lookout for some of the local specialties: *mole negro Oaxaqueno*, Oaxaca's most famous dish, chicken or turkey covered with a complex, rich, dark sauce made from at least four different kinds of chiles and a variety of spices; *coloradito*, a personal favorite, pork or chicken smothered in a red sauce flavored by chiles, tomatoes, garlic and sesame seeds; *verde con espinazo*, pork in a green sauce of white beans, chiles, parsley and epazote; *almendrado*, chicken in a tomato based chile sauce with cinnamon; and *amarillo*, pork in a chile sauce heavily flavored with cumin.

Tamales Oaxaquenos—soft corn dough filled with mole negro, wrapped in banana leaves, and then steamed—are prized throughout Mexico, as is anything made with the lovely, mild Oaxaca string cheese, quesillo, which is often found melted in quesadillas, but is an ingredient in many other dishes as well. Perhaps, not as well known, but in our minds worthy of mention, are Oaxaca's wonderful *chiles rellenos*, chiles stuffed with picadillo, a flavorful shredded pork concoction. *Clalludas*, Oaxaca's popular, unusually large, hard tortillas are frequently found in markets and on some restaurant menus, as are *chapulines*, a local delicacy, which we have not acquired a taste for, nor in all likelihood will you—fried grasshoppers eaten with a squeeze of lime.

Not to be ignored, but to be eaten with caution, are the fresh and delicious *cacahuates enchilados* sometimes served in cafes as *botanas* ("snacks") —peanuts roasted with chile powder, chiles, and garlic. The wise tourist will have a cold bottle of Mexican beer readily available when eating these peanuts. Finally, there is *mezcal*, a strong drink, somewhat similar to tequila. The fermented juice is obtained from the baked agave plant. In Oaxaca, mezcal is sold most typically in black clay jugs made in the nearby village of Coyotepec. A delicious salt (forget that it is made from dried worms found on the agave plant) is packed in a small bag attached to the jug. Take a lick of the salt, a shot of mezcal, wince, and feel like a real Oaxaqueno.

Numerous dishes from other regions of Mexico can be found in restaurants in Oaxaca. A welcome addition is the green salad now served in several restaurants. Prices are reasonable, and dress is casual. Most restaurants fall into the inexpensive and moderate categories. Price categories are explained in the Introduction.

THE ZÓCALO AREA

Around the zócalo—one of the most pleasant areas in all of Mexico for eating and drinking—can be found a number of restaurants, some with outdoor cafes. Find a table, relax, and watch the rich life of Oaxaca pass in front of you. A morning visit enables you to watch the city gradually wake up in the sparkling Oaxaca sun. And it is a time of calm, for the vendors are not yet out in full force. For a leisurely breakfast, the outdoor cafe of the **El Marquez,** in front of the Hotel Marquez del Valle is a good choice. You might want to begin with fresh orange juice or a fruit plate, followed by *huevos a la Mexicana* (eggs scrambled with tomatoes, onions, and chiles) or *huevos rancheros* (fried eggs covered with either a red or green tomato and chile sauce. For an even more local choice, order the *huevos en salsa con frijoles* (sometimes also called *huevos a la Oaxaquena*), tangy and tasty scrambled eggs floating in a spicy tomato sauce flavored by chiles and the popular herb, epazote, accompanied by a bowl of flavorful beans. El Marquez has an extensive menu that includes Oaxacan specialties and a good chicken consomme. Open throughout the day. Inexpensive to moderate.

If you cross the zócalo to the west side you will find the justly popular **Del Jardin,** which has a friendly, energetic atmosphere. Del Jardin is a very popular gathering place for afternoon and evening drinks. At lunch or any other time of the day, try their *tostadas de tinga.* Tinga is a stew containing pork and sausage with onions, tomatoes, chipotle chiles, and various spices; *tostadas de tinga* make a wonderful snack or meal, depending on how hungry you are. Inexpensive to moderate.

A doorway next to Del Jardin leads to the second-floor restaurant **El Asador Vasco,** which is immensely popular with tourists for its terrific location overlooking the zócalo and its front tables with wonderful views. Specializing in Spanish dishes, El Asador Vasco has Mexican and American food as well. The kitchen is very uneven and the service often inattentive and irksome. Yet on occasion we've had good *sopa de tortilla,* flavorful *camarones al ajillo* (shrimp with garlic), and a pleasing *pollo al chilindron* (Basque- style chicken). Moderately expensive. Very popular, so reservations are recommended ☎ (6-20-92). Request a balcony table with view.

AROUND TOWN

Located in a handsome colonial courtyard the **Hosteria de Alcala** (*Alcala 307*) serves some fine food that includes a good mixed salad, interesting soups (try the *sopa Azteca*), a tasty breaded breast of chicken covered with a *chile poblana* cream sauce *(pollo a la Poblana)*, and flavorful, tiny garlic shrimp in a casserole *(camarones al ajillo)*. Moderate.

Catedral (*Garcia Vigil at Morelos*) is a comfortable restaurant with an attractive setting and attentive service. Located just two blocks from the zócalo, the Catedral offers outdoor dining in an intimate courtyard. Although the food is inconsistent, the *caldo tlapeno* is sometimes rich and savory, the *mole poblano* is good and their more American offerings, such as filet mignon, are fine, and the *pie de nuez* (walnut pie), when available, should not be passed up. Moderate to moderately expensive.

Two hotel restaurants, the one at the **Hotel Victoria** (*off the Pan American Highway*) and **El Refectorio** i*n the Hotel Presidente (5 de Mayo 300)* provide very special settings. The Hotel Victoria, located on a hill above town, offers a most dramatic panoramic view with your meal and is definitely worth a visit, while El Refectorio is a handsome restaurant in a restored 16th-century ex-convent. Although the food in neither place will remain long in your memory, the settings will. Prices at El Refectorio are expensive; at the Victoria, moderate.

REGIONAL SPECIALTIES

For the regional specialties of Oaxaca you have a few good choices. **La Casita** (*Hidalgo 612A*) overlooks the Alameda. Open for lunch only (daily, except Thursday, 1 p.m.-6 p.m.), the pricey La Casita features such authentic Oaxaca dishes as *verde de espinazo, pollo almendrado, mole negro, empanadas de amarillo, coloradito con lomo* (a personal favorite), *clalludas,* and a savory soup made from the nopal cactus *(caldillo de nopalitos).* Very popular with locals, La Casita usually fills by 3 p.m. Recently the kitchen has become uneven and we've had some disappointing meals. Moderately expensive. A more consistent choice is **La Coronita** (*Diaz Ordaz 208, about a 5-minute walk from the zócalo*). Although La Coronita lacks the views and ambience of La Casita, its food is good and the prices better for the regional specialties. Here you can find *mole negro, colorado, amarillo,* a tasty verde with chicken *(pollo)* rather than pork and very good *costillitas* (ribs) and *carnitas.* La Coronita also serves a *comida corrida* at bargain prices. Although not on the menu, *chapulines* (fried grasshoppers) are sometimes available for the adventurous. Popular with locals. Inexpensive.

Some interesting regional food can be found *a bit out of town* at **Yu Ne Nisa,** better known as **Ofelia** (*Amapolas 1425,* ☎ *566-99*). Located in a converted garage of a house in the residential area, Colonia Reforma (north of the Pan American Highway; 15-minute taxi ride from zócalo), this tiny restaurant features the intriguing cuisine of the Isthmus of Tehuantepec. Presided over by its owner, Ofelia, who always wears the traditional dress of the Isthmus, the restaurant specializes in seafood but also offers such exotic items as armadillo and iguana (as platters or in tamales). The large plate of assorted appetizers *(botanas)* is quite good and includes delicious *chiles rellenos.* Seafood specialities include good smoked red snapper *(huachinango).* Moderately expensive.

For decent seafood in-town, try **La Quebrada** (*Armenta y Lopez 410; open 10 a.m.-6 p.m.*). We've particularly enjoyed the fresh appetizers, *tostadas de jaiba* (crab) and *tostadas de cazon* (shark). The spicy crab soup, *chipachole de jaiba,* is recommendable, if not overly complex, and the *camarones en escabeche* (tiny shrimp marinated in garlic and oil), is our personal favorite. Prices are quite reasonable for seafood. Moderate.

El Biche Pobre (*Calz. de la Republica 600, about a 20-minute walk or a short taxi ride from the zócalo*) is one of our favorite restaurants in Oaxaca. Very popular with Oaxaquenos, El Biche Pobre specializes in large, filling, wonderfully flavorful platters of *botanas,* or Mexican snacks, which include *tamales, quesadillas, carnitas, chiles rellenos, tostadas,* and a host of other delights. When ordering, just ask for *botanas,* nothing else need be said. Open daily, 1 p.m.-6 p.m. Sometimes live Mexican music. Inexpensive.

If you have been shopping all morning at the Benito Juarez market, and are in the mood for an authentic *comida corrida* at one of Oaxaca's old standbys, head for the restaurant **Casa Elpidia** (*Miguel Cabrera 413, a 15-minute walk south from the zócalo. Just follow Flores Magon until it changes to Miguel Cabrera, then continue to 413*). As you approach, you will no doubt be mumbling to yourself that there is no restaurant here, that you have been misled by yet another guidebook. Don't fret—413 is the place. Don't be timid. Push the door open; enter the courtyard, an oasis from the afternoon sun, filled with plants and birds; walk across the courtyard, and try to get one of the outdoor tables. You may find yourself sharing your table with a Mexican family. At this point, panic may set in when you realize that no one speaks English. Just relax, listen to the chirping of the birds. Non-Spanish-speaking tourists can survive here easily. Chances are that a waitress will bring you the set meal of the day without asking any questions. If she does approach with a question, just nod your head in the affirmative, smile, and if you would like something to drink just say "*cerveza*" or "*refresco*" and stick up the appropriate number of fingers. Food is served family-style. Normally, you will begin with a plate of appetizers including carnitas and *empanadas*, followed by soup (brought out in a huge tureen), then a meat dish or two, rice and/or beans, and dessert. The food is not memorable, but the atmosphere and dining experience should please. Service is warm and pleasant. Open for lunch only, 1-5 p.m. Inexpensive.

SNACKS

For food more in the line of snacks, **El Meson** (*Hidalgo, just off the northeast corner of the zócalo*) is particularly recommendable for its tasty tacos, especially the *tacos de chuleta* (pork) and the *rajas con queso y crema* (fairly mild chile peppers with cheese and cream). Using freshly made tortillas, El Meson offers a variety of other fillings as well. For a side dish try their grilled scallions (*cebollitas*). The sauces on the table should be added to the tacos in small doses: they are fiery hot. Other good choices include *sopa de campesina*, a kind of Mexican egg drop soup, *caldo de gato*, a hearty beef vegetable soup, and *frijoles charros*, a delicious bowl of beans. Although El Meson is open for lunch, the special taco menu is available only in the evening. For fine French pastries, especially strawberry tarts, walk around the corner of the zócalo to **Tartamiel** (*Trujano 118*). Here you can also get a slice of the deliciously moist Mexican cake, tres leches. Another excellent choice for pastries as well as first-rate baguettes is **Rome** (*Armenta y Lopez 203 A*) just one block from the zócalo.

ENTERTAINMENT

Entertainment in Oaxaca is focused primarily in the **zócalo,** which comes to life most evenings with live music emanating from the bandstand. Band music is featured a few nights of the week, but more to our taste are the **marimba concerts.** A marimba consists of two wooden xylophones, one larger than the other, played by about eight musicians at once. The music is enchanting and much of it is indigenous to the Oaxaca area. Just before the concert begins is the time to rise (reluctantly!) from your precious seat at a sidewalk cafe, walk up to the top of the bandstand, watch the marimba group play, and enjoy the music along with Indian families from the mountains resting after a long day at the market and mestizo Oaxaquenos out for their evening entertainment. The marimba group, Marimbas del Estado de Oaxaca, are justly famous in Mexico. You will surely hear them play two of the loveliest songs from the Oaxaca: "La Zandunga," probably the most popular song in Tehuantepec (the song played by the Tehuantepec delegation at the Guelaguetza), and "La Llorona" ("The Weeper"), the haunting, plaintive song also from the Tehuantepec area. During the intermission and after the concert, the Marimbas del Estado de Oaxaca sell their recordings, which make a wonderful souvenir of Oaxaca. On Sundays, around noon, orchestral concerts normally take place in front of the cathedral.

The cocktail lounge next to the restaurant at the Hotel Presidente, serves some of the best margaritas we have ever tasted (can there ever be a really bad margarita?). While at the Presidente you should take a stroll through the lovely gardens and patios, and ask to see the colonial nuns' laundry (located just past the cocktail lounge). Normally, on Fridays the Presidente presents a Mexican folklorico show with regional dances. Check for specific time. The bar at the **Hotel Victoria** provides a most dramatic view of the Sierra Madres and the surrounding valley. For a more student atmosphere and musical entertainment on weekends, try the very pleasant **Cafe El Sol y La Luna** (Margarita Maza 409, one block off Juarez near the Pan American highway). The **Teatro Macedonia de Alcala**, described earlier, is the place to go for concerts (a schedule of events is usually posted on the front door). Also worth investigating for cultural events is the **Centro Cultural R. Flores Magon** at Alcala 302.

GETTING TO AND FROM OAXACA

AIR

Mexicana and Aeromexico both provide daily service for the lovely 50-minute flight—especially when the plane dips into the Oaxaca valley—from Mexico City. All other connections on the major airlines must be made via Mexico City. However, *Aerocaribe* offers flights to Tuxtla Gutierrez and Acapulco as well as to Villahermosa then on to Mérida and Cancún (from Villahermosa, there also are flights to Mérida, via Aeromexico). *Aviacsa* flies to Tuxtla Gutierrez continuing to Villahermosa, Mérida, and Cancún. *Aeromorelos* flies to Puerto Escondido and Huatulco as well as Puebla and Cuernavaca.

Only collective vans provide regular service for the 15-20 minute ride from the airport. Reservations for the return trip to the airport can be made at the vans' office, Transportes Aeropuerto, on Calle de Leon, just off Alameda Park near the Hotel Monte Alban-note that taxis can be cheaper when shared.

BUS

Frequent and efficient bus service provided by *Cristobal Colon* and *A.D.O.* connects Oaxaca and Mexico City Terminal Oriente (TAPO) at Metro stop San Lazaro. First-class buses also connect Oaxaca with Puebla, Tehuantepec, San Cristobal, Veracruz, and Villahermosa. To reach Puerto Escondido, check with a local travel agent or go to the ticket booth at the Hotel Meson del Angel (Mina 518), for the express bus that leaves from the Hotel Meson del Angel, or take the second-class Flecha Roja bus via Puerto Angel; only the hearty should take the unpaved, direct route to Puerto Escondido (see "Puerto Escondido"). For all bus service reserve in advance.

TRAIN

Even if you have lots of time, think twice before taking the train to Mexico City. The trip is scheduled to take 14-1/2 hours.

DIRECTORY

Airlines • *Aeromexico*, Hidalgo 513 ☎ (6-37-65); *Mexicana*, Independencia and Fiallo 102 ☎ (6-84-14); regional airlines include *Aerocaribe* ☎ (5-93-24), *Aviacsa* ☎ (3-18-09); and *Aeromorelos* ☎ (6-30-10).

American Express • Valdivieso 2, just off zócalo ☎ (6-27-00).

Bakery • *Bamby* (G. Vigil at Morelos)

Banks • *Banamex* (Hidalgo at Armenta y Lopez) and *Banco Confia* (Hidalgo at 20 de Noviembre), for cashing traveler's checks. Banamex has an automatic teller machine that accepts Cirrus cards. The cambio on Valdivieso has short lines but poor exchange rates.

Books in English • *Libreria Universitaria* (Guerrero 104); *Ramona's* (Hidalgo 807), near zócalo; and *Oaxaca Lending Library* (Alcala 305).

British Consul • Hidalgo 817, office #5 ☎ (6-56-00); 10 a.m.-1 p.m. weekdays.

Buses • *First-class Buses:* Ninos Heroes de Chapultepec near Emiliano Carranza. Second-class Buses: next to Central de Abastos market, across railroad tracks at end of Calle Trujano. Buses for most excursions leave from here.

Canadian Consul • See "British Consul."

Car Rentals • Agencies have offices in the airport and town, among them: *Dollar*, Matamoros 100 ☎ (6-63-29) and *Budget* ☎ (6-06-11, Stouffer Presidente Hotel).

Combis • Collective buses to Monte Alban leave from the Hotel Meson del Angel (Mina 518 at Diaz Ordaz). For airport vans, reserve at office on Calle de Leon, just off Alameda Park.

Groceries • *Supermercado La Lonja* on zócalo.

Post Office • Independencia and Alameda Park.

Railroad Station • On Pan American Highway near intersection with Av. Hidalgo.

Spanish Courses • *Instituto Cultural Oaxaca*, Av. Juarez 909 at Pan American Highway, Apartado 340 ☎ (5-34-04); Centro Idiomas, Universidad Autonoma Benito Juarez, Armenta y Lopez near Borgoa, Apartado 523 ☎ (6-59-22).

Taxis • In front of the Cathedral by Alameda Park.

Tourist Office • Located next to the Alameda at Independencia 607; open weekdays, 9 a.m.-3 p.m. and 6-8 p.m.; Sat., 10 a.m.-1 p.m. Another office at 5 de Mayo, corner Morelos.

Tours • Agencies in hotels like the Victoria, Presidente, and the Marquez del Valle can arrange most excursions around Oaxaca.

U.S. Consul • Alcala 201, office #204 (☎ 4-30-54); weekdays 9 a.m.-2p.m.

OAXACA EXCURSIONS

MONTE ALBAN RUINS

Even if you dislike ruins, you should (we are tempted to say "must") visit Monte Alban. The power that belonged to this ancient city is still present in its commanding mountain view of surrounding valleys. The entire life of the region lies before you, isolated and contained by the endless folds of the Sierra Madres. To get to these ruins, 9-1/2 km (5-1/2 m) west of Oaxaca, follow M. Cabrera out of Oaxaca and turn right at dead end, then make a left U-turn over the railroad tracks. Cross the bridge over the Atoyac River. Bear right at the fork after the bridge and continue on a paved road, which nonetheless requires caution once it starts climbing to the ruins. Special buses leave several times a day for the ruins from the Hotel Meson del Angel (Mina 518 between Diaz Ordaz and Meir y Teran). Refreshment stand and bathroom facilities are available at the ruins.

Practical Tip

Check the hours for the tombs, as they often are closed earlier than the site. Open 8 a.m.-5 p.m. Admission fee.

Please Note: The government is in the process of replacing the carvings at the site with plaster cast copies. The originals are being placed in the site museum where they can be better protected. Until this project is completed, you may find that some of the carvings described below are missing from the site. Also, excavations going on through 1994 may reveal new sights.

As a consolation for completing the tortuous road to the ruins, you may appreciate knowing how privileged you are to enter the great ceremonial plaza of Monte Alban. In the last period of its occupation (A.D. 450-700), no path led to this plaza, leading archaeologists to believe it was off-limits to all but the most elite. As you enter the plaza, the Ball Court and some carvings will be on your left and the North Platform on your right. This impressive plaza best illustrates Monte Alban's power and authority over the surrounding valleys. Control over untold numbers of people was necessary to level the mountaintop (500 B.C.), to transport materials up the mountain, and to sustain monumental building projects for 1,200 years— all without pack animals or wheeled transport. And yet, the plaza is only a small part of this ancient city, which covered 15 square miles of terraced mountain. The population reached its highest level in the last phase, when 26,000 people lived on the terraced slopes. The remains of their residences are still seen, not as palaces, but as piles of stone or clay mounds. About 10 to 15 percent of these people were craft specialists, working with obsidian,

stone, shell, and ceramics. But what did everyone else do? It is hard to believe the valley population supported such an enormous class of elite priests
and administrators, yet apparently the people did—at least until A.D. 700,
when Monte Alban was abandoned.

Great Plaza

The Great Plaza was frequently reconstructed, building superimposed
on building. Most buildings seen around the plaza are from the last
and Classic period (A.D. 250-700). Distinctive of Classic period
architecture is the open tablero style, or panels with double borders
on three sides. The pyramid platforms once were crowned with temples and residences, and most were plastered with stucco painted
white. Excavations have exposed some of the earlier, and most interesting, structures at Monte Alban, particularly Mound J and the Danzante Wall.

East Side Of The Great Plaza

On your walk to Mound J, you pass two structures on your left to
explore. The first is a platform fronting an altar. A stairway in this
platform leads down to an underground tunnel, which has been
cleared as far as the altar, although originally it continued to the central platforms. This tunnel must have provided Zapotec priests with
the means of appearing suddenly and mysteriously before their audi-
ences. The second structure is one of the last buildings on the left, a
pyramidal platform of a palace. On top are the remains of the open
patio surrounded by chambers with sleeping benches; a tomb is in the
center. Given the important location of this palace, it must have
belonged to either a high priest or a member of the nobility.

Mound J

Both the arrow shape and orientation of this building are odd.
Archaeologists suspect that such buildings, disruptive of the overall
symmetry of a site, had astronomical functions. Indeed, research at
Monte Alban has discovered Mound J is aligned with the rising of a
star that indicates the zenith passage of the sun—that eerie day of the
year when at noon open spaces are filled with shadowless light and
facades are contrastingly dark and obscured.

Strangely enough, archaeologists do not interpret the many carved
slabs on the facades as having astronomical significance. Instead, the
weathered carvings on the "arrowhead" section are said to represent
conquests. The upside-down heads are dead rulers suspended from
hieroglyphs for the names of defeated towns. Some of the other hieroglyphs may date the successful battles. Supporting this militaristic
interpretation is a 2-mile defensive wall at Monte Alban built at the
same time as Mound J (200 B.C. - A.D. 250). Even more compelling
evidence for the militarism of the Monte Alban civilization has
resulted from research by archaeologist Joyce Marcus, who identified
a few of the towns mentioned on the slabs. Excavations at one town
uncovered a fortified area guarding the main pass to Tehuacan: on one

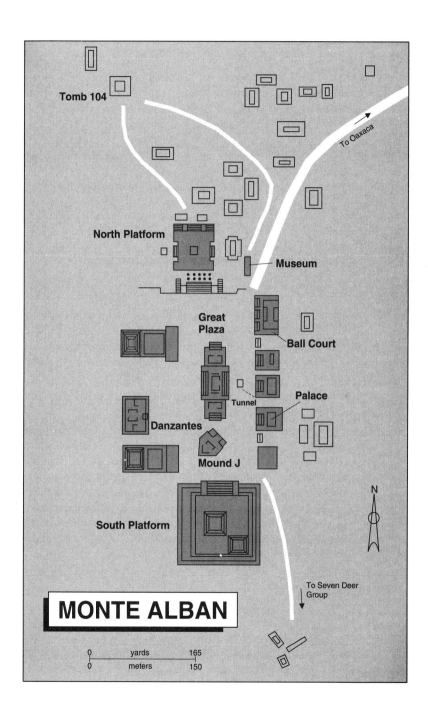

Tomb 104

To Oaxaca

North Platform

Museum

Great
Plaza

Ball Court

Tunnel

Palace

Danzantes

Mound J

South Platform

N

To Seven Deer
Group

MONTE ALBAN

0	yards	165
0	meters	150

side of the pass were Monte Alban ceramics; on the other, Tehuacan ceramics.

In addition to the conquest slabs, there are the so-called *danzante* ("dancer") carvings incorporated into the sides and top of the building. Their upside-down, backward, and sideways placement—and their juxtapositions with later carvings—indicate that they were reused and not designed especially for Mound J. Such "recycling" continued through the history of Monte Alban. Danzantes can be found on the corners and bases of many of the Classic-period structures, particularly the North and South Platforms, where they would have been plastered over with stucco. Perhaps the incorporation of these earliest carvings sanctified the later buildings.

Danzante Wall And Patio

This perplexing gallery of danzantes, with their closed-eyed, floating, and often contorted nude male figures, dates from the earliest period at Monte Alban (500-200 B.C.). The wall was the facade of one of the earliest buildings at the site, very little of which is now visible, it being buried under a Classic-period building. About 138 carvings were found in the areas of the wall and patio, and more than 200 others were found reused throughout the site, particularly at Mound J. Some of these carved slabs include very early yet developed examples of hieroglyphic writing, leading some archaeologists to make the hotly disputed claim that Mesoamerican writing originated in Oaxaca. Very little of the writing has been deciphered.

Fascination with the danzantes has led to a multitude of theories as to what they represent—dancers, acrobats, swimmers, ballplayers, shamans in ecstatic trances, and even a medical pathology lab. Considering the range of theories inspired by these carvings, they may be an ancient version of the Rorschach inkblot test. Yet archaeologists are increasingly convinced the danzantes represent slaughtered captives, lying on their backs and sides. At one valley site, a danzante slab was found embedded in the floor between the doors of two public buildings where it would have been trod upon repeatedly, a sign of contempt not often afforded swimmers or shamans. And nudity, rarely seen in ancient Mexico, is usually a sign of debasement reserved for prisoners. Also, the next period at Monte Alban, seen at Mound J, continues the theme of slaughtered captives but in a more sophisticated style. In other parts of Mesoamerica during this time, there are abundant sculptures of prisoners and signs of conflict.

South Platform Area

Before leaving this end of the Great Plaza, look at the classic-period carvings at the eastern and western corners of the unexcavated South Platform. The elaboration of style and hieroglyphic writing achieved during the classic period is interesting after visiting the earlier buildings. The themes evident in the danzantes and Mound J also continue into this phase, as some of the carvings are of prisoners—individuals often dressed in animal costumes of opossum or jaguar and with their hands tied behind their backs (see "Eastern Corner"). From the top of the South Platform there are fabulous views of the site.

Group of Seven Deer

A path around the eastern corner of the South Platform leads to the area called Seven Deer. There is not much of interest to see in terms of carvings or architecture because the area is in a ruinous state, but the walk is quite beautiful (insect repellant advised). As you round the platform corner, you may be treated to a pantomime of a supposedly recent discovery of a dirt-covered "*autentica*" figurine by someone who has been patiently waiting in the bushes hoping to make a sale. If you want the souvenir, start bargaining by calling it a "*falso*," or fake, which it certainly is.

North Platform

In front of this massive platform stands a stela carved on all four sides but eroded so that it is difficult to distinguish its designs. East of the stairway, you encounter a sanctuary with carved door jambs that enclose a stela showing an important seated individual with feathered headdress and staff. The stairway of this platform led to a great colonnaded hall—the earliest known use of columns in Mexico—that extended to the area of the sunken patio, where the altar originally supported a stela. Many believe this patio area was part of the ruler's palace. Continue through the sunken patio, up the stairs, and to your left, where a screen protects a small carving of a jaguar. Then follow the path on the northwest leading to the Northern Cemetery and Tomb 104.

Tomb 104

Monte Alban produced some of the most elaborate tombs in Mesoamerica. Of the 170 tombs excavated at this site, Tomb 104 contains the finest sculpture and some of the best-preserved wall paintings. The tomb dates from the middle of the Classic period, and its frescoes show stylistic influences from Teotihuacan near Mexico City. Over the door of the facade sits a clay urn of a seated god with the mask of the rain god Cocijo in his headdress. To the side is the original stone-slab door, covered with hieroglyphics. Though at times difficult to see, the burial chamber is embellished with colorful frescoes of persons or gods, a yellow bird (perhaps a parrot) standing on a box, a serpent, and more hieroglyphics. Most of the symbols are not yet understood; some believe the figure standing on the right with a serpent headdress is a maize god and others think such figures represent the royal ancestors of the deceased. When this tomb was opened, only one skeleton, that of a man, was found. The niches once contained bowls of food for his journey through the Underworld. The murals were developed in stages: First an outline in diluted red dye was drawn on the walls, and in the case of this tomb, some of the original outline can still be seen. Then, after the colors were filled in, they were separated by black charcoal lines.

To return to the entrance of the ruins with its **museum**, you can follow the path below the tomb area toward the east.

MITLA AND MUCH MORE

The 40-minute drive to Mitla excels in sightseeing opportunities and magnificent scenery. Since you most likely will be visiting the ruins at Mitla, you might want to schedule a day with a car along this route 44 km (29 m) east on the Pan American Highway (MEX 190), selecting another ruin or two, the fascinating Sunday market in Tlacolula, or the serape-making village of Teotitlan del Valle. By bus, it is quite feasible to combine the Tlacolula market and Mitla ruins in one day. But unless you are practiced in boarding buses through windows, arrange your trip so you do not leave Tlacolula in late afternoon when the market ends. Second-class bus service is frequent, leaving from the terminal near the Central de Abastos market every half hour. Other second-class buses go to Tlacochahuaya. However, on Sundays the service unofficially may end at 2 p.m. even though a 6 p.m. return bus is scheduled. Taxis also are rare during the Sunday afternoon comida hours.

The best place we've found to eat along this excursion route is in Teotitlan. But if that's not convenient, try **Chipi Chape**, on the left side of the Pan American Highway between Oaxaca and Tule (coming from Oaxaca), across from the Posada Los Arcos. Open Tuesday-Sunday, 12-6 p.m. This breezy, thatched-roof restaurant specializes in seafood, but has good chicken and regional specialties as well. We've particularly liked the rich chicken consomme. The whole fish is generally fine. The pastries and cakes are also recommendable. Inexpensive to moderate. Other restaurants are mentioned under Teotitlan del Valle, Tlacolula and Mitla.

El Tule

12 km (7 m) • *On the left side of the road, in a churchyard*, is the great tree of Tule. Based on estimates that it is over 2000 years old, this cypress would have been large enough to provide ample shade to the lords of Monte Alban. It's worth the small entrance fee to inspect its 162-foot girth more closely, along with that of "the son."

Tlacochahuaya

18 km (11 m) • Turn right and continue 2 km. The village and church are off the beaten tourist paths but the church is open from 10 a.m.-2 p.m. and 4-6 p.m. (admission fee). If not, wait while word of your arrival reaches the keeper of the keys and the church interior will be your reward. In the meantime, you can look for the eroded Dainzu slab (see below) built into the health center entrance (there are 11 such carvings said to be incorporated into various buildings of the village) or enjoy the "lion" statues protecting the *ayuntamiento* ("municipal building"). The festive and colorful interior of the church, disguised by the spareness of its facade, is one of the best examples of the expressiveness achieved by Mexican artists, unsophisticated in European tastes and often untrained in techniques. The folk artists' delight in the profusion of painted, brilliantly colored flowers on walls and ceiling—and the chirping of birds in the eaves—diminishes the effect of the fine, "more sophisticated" gilded altars. The flower motifs are repeated even more joyously and profusely on the small organ case in the choir loft. This Dominican church and monastery were built in the 16th century, and the church was rebuilt in the 17th and refurbished in the 18th.

Dainzu

23 km (14 m). Open 8:30 a.m.-5 p.m.; admission and parking fees • Turn right at the Dainzu sign and continue for 1 km on the dirt road to these ruins (small admission and parking fees). Anyone fascinated by the danzantes of Monte Alban will enjoy a visit to Dainzu, which has more than 30 low-relief carved slabs. Only a small part of this site is excavated. A ball court (dated much later than the platform and slabs) and a patio containing a pre-Classic tomb can be seen in addition to the temple carvings. There are carvings on the top of the hill behind the temple platform, but they are inaccessible. The site is tranquil, with a beautiful view of the valleys and mountains. The occasional passing of cows with their gently ringing bells adds to the pleasure of visiting here.

The carvings date to approximately 200 B.C., or the beginning of Monte Alban II. Although similar to the danzantes in their location on the temple platform wall and in their floating postures and low-relief style, the Dainzu figures are on the whole far more energetic and fluid, and carved in deeper relief with more detail. They are also different in that there is no controversy about what the figures are doing. All but four are playing ball. The remaining four are said to be patron gods of the ball game. The players hold a ball in their right hands, wear arm and leg protectors and "knickers." They also wear a distinctive helmet with a face guard. Most helmets have jaguar-ear designs, but some have feathers instead. (At Monte Alban, there is one danzante wearing such a helmet and easily identifiable as in the Dainzu style.) The wall becomes more dramatic upon consideration of the large slab of a very fat figure at the far right. Here, the only standing figure faces in the direction of the players, so all the others face toward him. Although the figure's hands are eroded, archaeologist Ignacio Bernal reports that a similar figure on the hilltop holds a ball in his right hand and with his left attacks a ballplayer with a sword. (*Tip: Although eroded, the carvings become clearer as you spend time looking at them.*) One of the ballplayers most easily discerned is found in a tunnel near the parking area. Near the tunnel is a tomb with a jaguar carving encompassing the door. Perhaps it symbolizes the jaguar sun of the underworld. It is believed that the graceful, curvilinear style, the seated posture, and themes of these carvings show influence from the Izapa area, which is considered the predecessor of the Maya art style.

Teotitlan del Valle

26 km (16 m) • Turn left onto a paved road and continue for 4 km (2-1/2 m). Teotitlan has been famous for its weaving since pre-Hispanic times when it paid tribute to overlords in Zaachila with cotton mantles. This long tradition continues in the patios of practically every home, where you can see Zapotec families weaving the fine woolen serapes, or rugs, of Oaxaca. Numerous shops line the main street of Juarez and a serape market can be found by turning right on to Hidalgo at the end of Juarez. Two stores with good selections of quality serapes are **Casa Santiago** (*Juarez 52*) and next door, **Isaac Vazquez** (*Juarez 44 and also Hidalgo 30*). Bargaining is expected. The small, tranquil village includes a surprisingly large colonial church and a plaza, a testament to its former importance. Incorporated into the church tower and courtyard walls are fragments of pre-Hispanic carved stones. The attractive ambience of the **Restaurant Tlamanalli** (*Juarez 39; lunch only; moderate*) will tell you it's for tourists, not villagers, but the limited menu offers well-prepared traditional food—a memorable chepil soup with freshly gound corn and squash blossoms, a very good mole negro, and tropical sorbets (try the black zapote negro).

Lambityeco

About 28 km (17 m); open 8:30 a.m.-5 p.m.; admission and parking fees • Just before Tlacolula, look for the small pyramidal structure on the right belonging to these ruins. Just a brief stop, when you are on your way elsewhere, will be well rewarded.

The two houses excavated at this site give you a feeling of more immediacy with the past than most ruins. The first house was discovered during the excavation of the pyramid. It reveals the well-preserved stucco heads and names of a couple, "1 Movement" (the man on the left) and "10 Reed," who are buried beneath the courtyard of what was presumably their house. An altar is flanked by two friezes of couples and their accompanying names. The men carry human bones symbolizing bravery in battle. It is speculated that the burial and friezes establish the lineage of this elite family. Such secular themes are typical of the post-Monte Alban period. The tomb of the second house was found under many later constructions and is revealed now only due to the excavations. A stairway is flanked by two carvings of Cocijo, the Zapotec rain god, which are in excellent condition. The facade, originally forming the west wall of a patio, has very early and simple examples of the step-fret design that was later so elaborated at Mitla.

Lambityeco dates from around A.D. 700-900 and was inhabited, like other valley sites, after the abandonment of Monte Alban. After 900, it is believed that the center shifted to Yagul. The exact size of the site cannot be determined because some of it lies beneath the present

town of Tlacolula, but other mounds can be seen as you look toward
the modern town. The excavated area is at the outer edge of the site,
which may say something about how elite "1 Movement" and "10
Reed" really were.

Tlacolula

After 32-1/2 km (20 m) • Turn right into town. The heart of the **Sunday market** takes place in a walled plaza through the church courtyard
and spills over into the streets. It is a congested, fascinating market,
intensely Indian. Your presence will be unacknowledged, but known.
After absorbing the many colorful scenes, such as women selling finely
woven baskets under beautiful shade trees, you might want to relax
under the bougainvillea, fiercely pink when in bloom, in the church
courtyard and watch the families coming in from the mountains for
the important weekly occasion of market day. The 16th-century
church is known for its gilded ultra baroque **Chapel of Santo Cristo**. If
you are fortunate, you will visit during a mass accompanied by local
marimba musicians and much enthusiastic singing. Just to the right of
the tiny square before the church you will find the clean, inexpensive
restaurant of the **Hotel Guish Bac** ("Tlacolula" in Zapotec) where a
cooling drink or huevos a la Mexicana might hit the spot.

Yagul

About 35 km (22 m); open 8:30 a.m.-5 p.m.; admission and parking fees •
Just beyond Tlacolula, turn left at a sign and continue 1-1/2 km on
the paved road to these ruins. Beautifully situated they include a fortress at the top of the hill; a central ceremonial district on the lower
slope with palaces surrounding patios, older pyramidal mounds, the
largest ball court in the Oaxaca Valley, and some 30 tombs; and a surrounding area dotted with unexcavated domestic dwellings.

Excavations of the central district revealed a long history of occupation. Although occupied in the pre-Classic phase (500-150 B.C.),
Yagul flourished during Monte Alban V (A.D. 1250 to the Spanish
Conquest) with a style very similar to, but less sumptuous than, the
palace architecture of Mitla. Apparently, Yagul continued into modern
history, although shifting its location. Spanish chronicles indicate a
town of Tlacolula was locally called "Yagul," and the ruins of Yagul
are known as the "old town" in Tlacolula.

As important as these ruins are to archaeology, for the visitor they
simply add to the beauty and interest of this magnificent spot. While
you enjoy the view and walk among the large candelabra-shaped organ
cactus, you can look for some of the more interesting carvings and
tombs. In the patio closest to the parking lot is Triple Tomb 30. One
of its interior passages has two stone heads flanked by carved, rather
than mosaic, step-fret designs. The original door lies nearby with similar patterns. Also in the patio is a large stone sculpture so eroded it is
hard to determine what it is, although it is believed to be a jaguar.
Since the Mixtec who built this patio are not known to carve animal

sculptures, the "jaguar" could be from an earlier period, perhaps as early as 400 B.C.

On a higher level than the tomb you walk past the restored ball court, which is similar in plan to those at Dainzu and Monte Alban, then come to another patio with a long palace structure on the north side. The back of this structure still has traces of the original 40 yards of step-fret mosaic in patterns identical to those at Mitla. This mosaic faces the mazelike Palace of the Six Patios. On the north side of the area of the Six Patios is a steep path, that may be too arduous for some to climb, leading to the fortress and panoramic views. If you do climb to the fortress, you should look at the top of the path for Tomb 28 dating from classic Monte Alban times and carved with Zapotec hieroglyphs. The fortress is very similar to the one associated with Mitla, providing further proof of the strong cultural relationship between these two sites during Monte Alban V and confirming archaeologists' belief that this period was one of increasing conflicts and militarism.

Mitla

At approximately 40 km (25 m), the road forks; bear left to Mitla • As you drive into Mitla, you will pass a number of mezcal shops (expendios de mezcal) and crafts shops specializing in woven goods, especially rebozos. There is a not-very-good curio market near the ruins.

At the intersection along the main street you find the **Frissell Museum** *(open daily, 9 a.m.-5 p.m.; donation)* to your left. The museum displays pre-Hispanic pieces from the Oaxaca Valley; we particularly like an exhibit demonstrating the stylistic evolution of the rain god Cocijo that makes the complex Zapotec art style more comprehensible. The museum is housed in **Posada La Sorpresa**, an 18th-century hacienda with a restaurant in its shaded patio. La Sorpresa is an informal and restful place to visit before or after the ruins, for such traditional Mexican dishes as mole and cecina at moderate prices. For a Mexican meal at lower prices, but without La Sorpresa's ambience, try **La Zapoteca**, on the right side of the road to the ruins, just past the center of town. Inexpensive.

Mitla Ruins

About 1/2 km from the town center, next to three-domed church. Admission charge. Open 8 a.m.-5 p.m. • These ruins are famous, and justifiably so, for the fineness of the many mosaics of geometric patterns, called step-frets, decorating the palace walls. Variations of the step-fret pattern are repeated, combined, and contrasted like a Bach fugue. The profusion of mosaics, inside and outside the palace walls, masks the exactitude and skill necessary for perfectly cutting and fitting the small stones into their patterns.

The palaces in the two areas you will visit are considered the finest architecture that the Mixtecs produced. Stone monoliths are used as lintels and tomb roofs, but most remarkably as columns. These stones

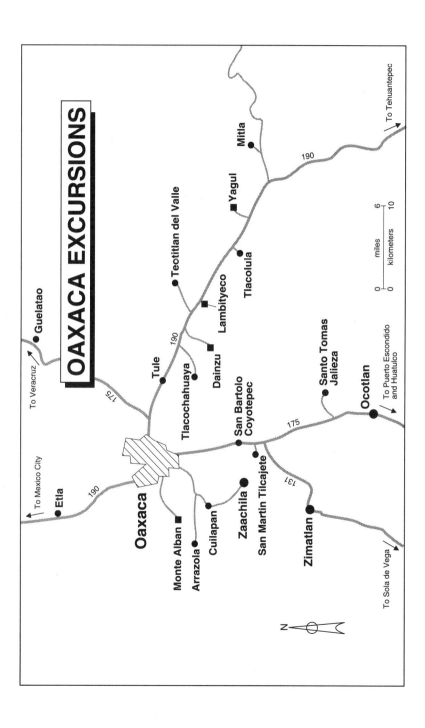

OAXACA EXCURSIONS

were brought from a nearby quarry without draft animals and were shaped and finished without metal tools. In contrast to the pyramid-temple architecture at Monte Alban, these ruins show a secular rather than religious focus. The palace-patio complexes are believed to have been residences and civic buildings. The palaces date from quite late, probably no earlier than A.D. 1400, and are the architectural analogue of the exquisite Mixtec jewelry and lapidary work displayed at the Regional Museum of Oaxaca. Ancient Mitla has a much longer tradition and covers a larger area than the palace complexes indicate. Although five main clusters have been excavated, structures have been found surrounding Mitla as far as 2 km from town. A fortress on a hill just beyond the town confirms the militarism of the late period described in the Mixtec Codices. The actual plan of Mitla is unknown because it is believed that many of its structures have either disintegrated or have been destroyed by the development of the modern town. The Mitla area has been inhabited since preceramic times, perhaps as early as 7000 B.C., based on stone implements and wild seeds found in some caves. Excavations of the ruins of the south side of the river show that Mitla participated in the developing civilization of Monte Alban I (500-150 B.C.) and subsequent Zapotec periods with pyramid and temple structures. The site flourished, however, only in the late, and last, period before the Conquest.

The two main complexes to visit, the Group of the Columns and the Church Group, are separated by a road and a church. The Group of the Columns has two large quadrangles or patios; the first is known for its hall of columns, the second for the Patio of the Tombs. The Church Group should be seen especially for the original paintings in its last patio.

In the first quandrangle of the **Group of the Columns**, the patio is surrounded by buildings on only three sides. The most important building is the north palace, reached by a stairway. After passing through one of its three entrances, you find yourself in the great gallery with its row of six columns. A narrow passage with a very low ceiling, which many believe was constructed for defense, leads to a small inner patio that may have been the inner sanctum of the high priest. More step-fret patterns decorate the rooms surrounding this patio. After the palace, take the path leading south out of this quadrangle to the **Patio of the Tombs**, believed to have been the administrative center of the ancient city. In this courtyard you can visit two cruciform tombs with step-fret designs on their walls. When the original lintel of one of these tombs ("Tumba #1" on the north side) collapsed, it was replaced—still in ancient times—by a column known locally as the "Column of Life." It is said that by embracing the column and measuring the distance between your fingers, you learn the number of years remaining in your life. After discovering such news, it is only appropriate to head toward the church.

The **Church Group** originally was composed of three patios, but the first patio has been mostly replaced by (and recycled into) the church. At the rear of the church, next to some columns, enter one of the remaining ancient patios. Across this patio (to the right), go through a tiny passageway and into the small, third patio of this group. Because of the paint that fortunately was preserved on this building, archaeologists have been able to reconstruct its original appearance. Most of the walls and the patio floor were painted deep red, but the step-fret designs were painted in contrasting white. A painted frieze in red and white added richness. Some of the frieze remains and is in the style of the Mixtec Codices preserved from that time. You can still see some of the figures accompanied by their names in Mixtec hiero- glyphs.

CUILAPAN AND ZAACHILA

When combined with the Thursday livestock market in Zaachila, this short excursion has a little of everything—fine scenery, ancient ruins, and a colonial monastery. If you are driving, take Av. Juarez until the Periferico where you turn right. Follow signs for Parque del Amor, Xoxocotlan and Zaachila. About 10 km (6 m) along the way, consider taking a detour by following the well-marked road to **Arrazola** (5 km), the village known for its brightly painted wood carvings and the home of many artisans, includ-ing master carver Manuel Jimenez, whose work is found in many U.S. mu-seums. Second-class buses can drop you at Cuilapan on the way to Zaachila (18 km, 11 m). There are also second-class buses to Arrazola.

Cuilapan

13 km (8 m); open 10 a.m.-6 p.m.; fee for exconvent • After bypassing Xoxocotlan, follow signs to these impressive and abandoned 16th-century Dominican churches and convent. The roofless first church has a Renaissance facade and a noble columned nave. Its arches frame fine views of the valley and mountains. The low, thick-walled construction, typical of the Oaxaca Valley, was used to make the buildings earthquake-resistant. The quiet countryside makes it diffi-cult to imagine why the Dominicans found it necessary to construct such large churches at this location. Before the Conquest, Cuilapan was a Mixtec center with a population of over 13,000. But in the early years after the Conquest, Cortes ordered that the Mixtecs from other areas be congregated at Cuilapan. The population may have grown to 70,000 before the devastation of the later epidemics. An interesting testament to this early period of Mixtec- Spanish interaction remains on the back of the first church. A stone embedded in the wall com-memorates the founding of the church in 1555 and its completion in 1568. The dates are well carved—in Mixtec hieroglyphs. Perhaps as an afterthought, or upon the complaint of a Dominican friar, the left panel was clumsily inscribed with the equivalent date in the conquistadors' calendar—"1555." The second church is closed, but the convent still has fragments of frescoes on its walls and it can be visited.

Zaachila

18 km (11 m) • There is nothing quaint about Zaachila. Yet its prehistoric past can be seen in the ancient Zapotec urns incorporated into its church clock tower, in the carved monolithic stones in the zócalo, and in the two excavated tombs sometimes open to the public. A visit to these traces of the past is best scheduled on Thursday, Zaachila's market day.

The tombs are located behind the church and down a path to the right. The official, if not always reliable, visiting hours are 10:30 a.m.-5:30 p.m. *(admission fee)*. It is believed that this mound represents a Zapotec stronghold later conquered by the Mixtecs. Although this area had participated in the Classic Monte Alban civilization, the tombs are Mixtec and represent the period before the Conquest. These tombs were found intact at the time of their excavation in 1962 because of the vigilance of the villagers who had protected them. The intensity of their feelings toward their past was only too clear to the archaeology team—which had to work at the site under armed guard. Preserved in Tomb 2 were some of the finest examples of Mixtec polychrome pottery, jewelry, and carved animal bones (similar to those on display at the Regional Museum of Oaxaca). Because these objects are now in Mexico City in the National Museum of Anthropology, Tomb 2 no longer holds much interest. Tomb 1 is worth a visit to see its painted plaster figures representing gods, including the Lord from theLand of the Dead, and two male ancestors of the deceased named"9 Flower" and "5 Flower."

PRACTICAL TIP

In the mood for some traditional Mexican food served in a rustic outdoor setting? On the left side of the road before entering Zaachila, you'll find La Capilla serving wonderful coloradito and savory mole negro accompanied by freshly made tortillas and complimentary mezcel. (Serve yourself a shot from the communal barrel). Moderate.

COYOTEPEC AND OCOTLAN

The 32 km (20 m) drive on MEX 175 toward Puerto Angel to these towns is easy (exit Oaxaca on the south side and follow airport signs until you're on MEX 175) and especially scenic after Coyotepec. You can add a short jaunt (1 km off road) to either **San Martin Tilcajete,** visiting homes of wood carvers (ask directions for "figuras de madera" at shop across from church); or to the zócalo of **Santo Tomas Jalieza** to buy tightly woven and figured cotton belts and bags. Second-class buses leave for them from the new terminal near the market. There are two Coyotepecs and two Jalieza s—keep the saints' names in mind.

San Bartolo Coyotepec

12 km (7 m) • Black clay pottery is made by villagers here, but it was Rosa Real who made it famous by demonstrating her skill to tourists for many years. The blackware is made in the pre-Hispanic tradition, without a potter's wheel, and many of the shapes are the same as those from the Mixtec period just before the Conquest. The satiny black color results from lead oxide in the clay. You will have no trouble finding pottery to buy, but check **Alfareria Dona Rosa** (turn left off MEX 175) where Valente Nieto, the maestra's son, carries on her tradition with demonstrations in this ancient pottery making technique (Fri. 9 a.m.-2 p.m.). Look for handsomely shaped canteras, or water jugs. For more contemporary and artistic pieces, visit Daniel Salas and son, Luis, at **Coyotl** (on left of highway as you enter San Bartolo; more expensive).

Ocotlan

32 km (20 m) • A visit is best on market day, Friday, when the exchange of basics from food to firewood occurs. Ocotlan is known for its comic ceramic bells and humorous figurines. Made by the three Aguilar sisters, these ceramics can often be found filling every room and courtyard of their homes (just to the right of the road as you enter town). The more elaborate village scenes of Josefina Aguilar have become famous. The town has a captivating church, its white-painted lacy carvings contrasting with the greenish hue of its stone facade. The devotion of the villagers to the Christ figure inside can be seen in his hand-sewn white-lace trousers and the colorful ribbons pinned on his cloak.

ON THE ROAD

MEXICO CITY

There are two direct routes to Oaxaca from the capital: (1) via Cuautla and MEX 190 or (2) via Puebla-Tehuacan and MEX 150 and 131. The Cuautla route is more scenic, but difficult and longer. You leave Mexico City on the Periferico Sur by following signs to Viaducto Tlalpan, not Calzada Tlalpan. (You enter Mexico City by following signs for Periferico and Pereferico Pte., and then Pedregal to Chapultepec Park.) The 548-km (340-m) trip takes about 8-1/2 hours. A twisting road takes you through the Sierra Madres and provides some gorgeous vistas. Two important ceramic-producing villages are on this route, Izucar de Matamoras and Acatlan. A stop at either village can be rewarding. In **Acatlan** (about 5 hours from Mexico City) try to track down the ceramic workshop of **Heron Martinez**. If you are lucky, frequent questioning of the locals will lead you there through dusty streets. If you are luckier, the *fabrica* will be open, and you will meet the family carrying on the tradition of the deceased master of Mexican ceramics and a creator of candelabra bursting with gay birds, flowers, and, on occasion, mermaids. Past the zócalo, as you exit town, there are convenient hotel restaurants with parking, like the Monte Alban. Another convenient stopping place is the restaurant in the modern Hotel Casablanca on the highway just beyond Huajuapan de Leon, about 3 hours (180 km) outside of Oaxaca. About 2 hours (110 km) from Oaxaca, you pass the imposing 16th-century church and convent of **Yanhuitlan**, which is best to visit in the morning when the church is open for a mass. The convent is open 10 a.m.-5:30 p.m. Small admission fee.

The Puebla-Tehuacan route cuts out mileage, much of the winding mountain driving, and much of the dramatic scenery, yet it is still scenic. The 505 km (313 m) can be covered in about 8 hours if you leave Mexico City at the crack of dawn and have the good fortune not to run into a massive traffic jam near the airport before you get on to the multi-lane, high-speed Calz. Zaragoza, this route's exit road from Mexico City. Take 150D to the first exit past Puebla (for Tehuacan and Jalapa). A good stopping place is **Tehuacan** (3-1/2 hours from Mexico City), a handsome town noted for its mineral waters. The **Restaurant Penafiel** located on the very attractive zócalo provides good food in a comfortable environment (inexpensive). If the lovely gardens of the zócalo or the subtropical climate of this town appeal to you, you might consider: ★ **Hotel Mexico**, *Independencia Pte. 101 at Reforma;* ☎ *(238) 2-00-19; $45* Just one block west of the zócalo, this colonial-style hotel offers 87 fresh units opening on a central patio. Rooftop garden, dining room, and pool. Garage.

To continue to Oaxaca, take MEX 131 (sometimes also marked 908 or 135). The road takes you past caves where archaeologists have found ancient tiny corn cobs, proving that the staff of Mesoamerican life was first domesticated in the Tehuacan valley. Domestication took millennia, from 7000 B.C. to 2500 B.C.

TEHUANTEPEC

If you are continuing on by car from Oaxaca to Chiapas or Guatemala, you will head toward Tehuantepec, 4 hours and 258 km (160 m) away via MEX 190, a continuously curving, very scenic mountain road. Tehuantepec itself can be avoided unless it is fiesta time or you want to stop for a stroll through the zócalo and the adjacent market where the stately Tehuana women preside dressed in their richly embroidered huipils. If it is fiesta time in Tehuantepec, you will be in for a treat as the Tehuanas parade through the streets in their very best huipils and finest jewelry. On January 22, the Festival of St. Sebastian is celebrated with the most prominent Tehuanas (*Capitanas*) leading a parade of unmarried girls and newlyweds through the street. From June 22 to June 26, Tehuantepec celebrates the Festival of St. John; on June 30 begins the 6-day Festival of St. Peter; on August 15 begins the 10 day Festival of the Assumption of the Virgin Mary; and September 10 is the Festival of the Birth of the Virgin Mary. Just outside of Tehuantepec on the left side of MEX 190 heading toward Tuxtla Gutierrez is the ★**Hotel Calli** ☎ (*971-500-85; $45*), with 100 modernized rooms and a nice garden and pool. Although the restaurant is a bit pricey, its air conditioning provides welcome relief.

SAN CRISTOBAL DE LAS CASAS AND GUATEMALA

If you continue along MEX 190 for another 4 hours you will be in Tuxtla Gutierrez and within striking distance of San Cristobal de las Casas. From San Cristobal you can continue on to Guatemala (see "San Cristobal" in the "Chiapas" chapter).

NOTE: Check "Driving Tips" for U.S. travel advisories on Guatemala.

The alternative road to Guatemala, faster but less scenic, is along the coastal MEX 200, which intersects with MEX 190 about 1 hour past Tehuantepec. Follow signs for **Arriaga** and Tapachula. On the outskirts of Arriaga can be found the ★★**Auto Hotel El Parador** ☎ (*966-201-35; $35*), a modern motel with large, clean, air-conditioned rooms, and a restaurant. Farther on just past Arriaga is **Tonala**, a simple town with brightly colored buildings, a stela in the zócalo, and an archaeology museum (closed Sunday). **Restaurant Nora** (Independencia 10, just east of zócalo) is clean and inexpensive. The trip from Arriaga to Tapachula and the Guatemalan border takes you past sugarcane fields and banana plantations, a total of 258 km (160 m) and 3.2 hours. Total driving time from Oaxaca to Tapachula is about 10 hours. Hot and steamy **Tapachula** has two fine motels but little else to keep you there. The best is the ★★**Lomo Real** ☎ (*962-614-40; $120*) located on a hilltop west of town at Km. 244 of MEX 200 offering large air-conditioned rooms, a pool, and a restaurant. Also recommended is the ★★**Hotel Kamico** ☎ (*962- 626-40; $90*) conveniently located on Prolongacion Central Oriente Carretara á Guatemale, also with air-conditioned rooms, a pool, and restaurant. About a half hour from Tapachula is the beach town of **Puerto Madero**. Although you may be tempted to stay there, don't. We found no acceptable hotels—despite what some locals may tell you. There are, however, some good, inexpensive, but run-down beach restaurants near the center of town serving tasty crabs and shrimp. The water in the center of town is too rough for swimming. You need to go to the south end of town near the Naval Station for a pleasant swimming area. Shortly after leaving Tapachula, on both sides of MEX 200, you will find the important, but rarely visited, archaeological site, **Izapa**. Dating from 100 B.C. - A.D. 250, Izapa is believed to be the transition culture between the early Olmec civilization and the later Maya one. The most interesting section is reached on the right at a sign for "Zona Archaeologica Grupo F."

PACIFIC COAST RESORTS

MEX 175 exits Oaxaca via the airport road and Ocotlan, before climbing through the often misty and beautiful sierra to **San Jose Pacifico** where the **Restaurant Rayito de Sol** (near km 132; budget) offers sustenance, with its hearty, regional food. Try the huevos en salsa, scrabbled eggs smothered in a spicy tomato sauce. From there, the road winds down to the lush tropics of banana plantations and Tarzan-size vines until it arrives, five hours later, at Pochutla and the crossroads of MEX 200 (240 km, 149 m). Puerto Angel lies a few miles straight ahead; Puerto Escondido, 70 km, 43m north; and Huatulco, 40 km, 25 m south.

CENTRAL GULF COAST

Veracruz

> *Veracruz, a little corner where*
> *The sirens go to bathe.*
> *Veracruz, your beaches are*
> *Flooded with stars,*
> *Palm tree and woman.*

Song by Augustin Lara

HISTORY AND CULTURE

Only the tropically verdant Tuxtla mountains disrupt the flat coastal plain along the Gulf of Mexico extending between Tuxpan in Veracruz and Villahermosa in Tabasco. Broad rivers rush through these flat, productive lands where tropical flowers and fruits flourish. Along the shores of the Gulf, coconut palms bent by stormy winds line quiet beaches. The Veracruz coastlands sharply rise to the foothills of the Sierra Madre Oriental, where flowers, vanilla, and coffee are nurtured by the subtropical climate of towns like Jalapa, Fortin de las Flores, and Papantla. Farther inland, the Sierra Madres reach their highest peak at Orizaba to form some of the world's loftiest valleys.

ANCIENT GULF COAST CIVILIZATIONS

The most ancient world civilizations of Egypt and Mesopotamia arose in environments of adversity without abundant plant and animal life. To cultivate the land, these peoples needed irrigation; to irrigate the land, they needed to control the great Indus and Nile rivers; and to control the rivers they needed a central authority, which led to the formation of civilized states. Based on these Old World examples, archaeologists reasoned that all civilizations could arise only under adverse conditions. Yet the first civilization in Mesoamerica arose not in the desert, but in one of its wettest and most bountiful regions. Olmec civilization developed in the south of the Gulf Coast, where the many rivers—including the Papaloapan, Coatzalcoalcos, and Tonala—cut through tropical rain forests and mangrove swamps on their way to the sea. Here jaguars, crocodiles, and deer thrived; here fish abounded in the rivers; and here heavy rains and mists made the dry season practically unknown and allowed crops to grow year-round. Without cultivated crops, the region was rich. With the introduction of corn from the highlands, the area was a land of plenty.

The origins of civilization in Mexico not only confounded Old World archaeologists (leading some to find it "highly suspect") but also eluded New World archaeologists until recent decades. At first, the few works of art known from the Olmec region were dated (without making excavations) to the period of A.D. 600-900. The results of preliminary excavations at the Olmec site of La Venta shocked the archaeological world by showing an antiquity from 600 B.C. Another surprise was in store at the Olmec site of San Lorenzo, where radiocarbon dates (published as recently as 1969) established the beginnings of this civilization at 1200 B.C. The surprises may be far from over. Too few Olmec sites have been excavated, and others may await discovery under the lava flows near Lake Catemaco and under millennia of undisturbed jungle growth.

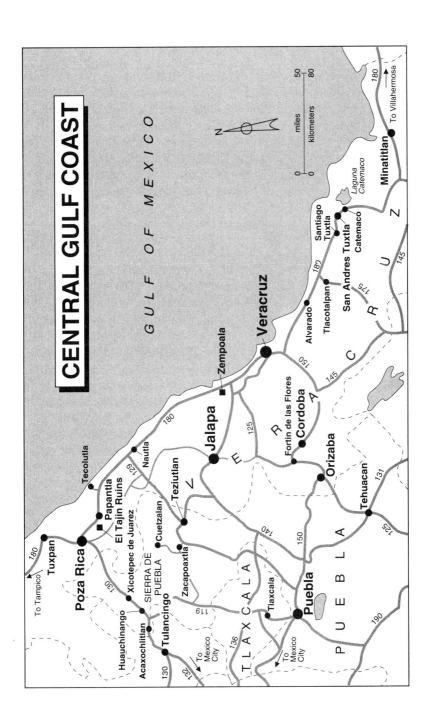

CENTRAL GULF COAST

GULF OF MEXICO

To Villahermosa
180
Minatitlan
Laguna Catemaco
Catemaco
Santiago Tuxtla
San Andres Tuxtla
175
V E R A C R U Z
145
Tlacotalpan
Alvarado
180
Veracruz
150
145
C
Zempoala
Fortin de las Flores
Cordoba
A
125
Orizaba
R
Tehuacan
131
Nautla
180
129
Jalapa
E
Tecolutla
Teziutlan
V
Cuetzalan
Papantla
El Tajin Ruins
Xicotepec de Juarez
140
150
125
Tuxpan
Poza Rica
SIERRA DE PUEBLA
Zacapoaxtla
To Tampico
180
130
Huauchinango
Acaxochitlan
Tulancingo
119
Tlaxcala
Puebla
P U E B L A
190
130
132
T L A X C A L A
136
To Mexico City
To Mexico City

N
miles
kilometers
0 50
0 80

Olmec civilization is best known for its works of art displayed in museums (Villahermosa, Jalapa, and Mexico City have fabulous collections) rather than for its ceremonial centers—constructed mostly of earth rather than stone—which have left little to reward the tourist making the enormous effort required to visit them. Yet the architectural achievements revealed through excavations are impressive. Even before 1200 B.C., and at a time when only minor public buildings existed in Mesoamerican villages, the Olmecs began construction of an enormous artificial plateau at San Lorenzo that grew to over 3000 feet long and almost 2000 feet wide. On the plateau they constructed some 200 earth mounds for residential and ceremonial buildings. An elaborate drainage system connected with artificial ponds was built with 30 tons of imported basalt. Later, at La Venta, the first truly impressive pyramid was built, fluted and shaped like a volcano. While few people lived at these sites, the magnitude of human effort required to accomplish these first Mesoamerican ceremonial centers indicates that their rulers could command the labor of peoples from large regions.

Monumental sculptures carved in basalt—some weighing 50 tons —are the hallmark of Olmec art. Yet no basalt existed at either San Lorenzo or La Venta. About 30 miles from San Lorenzo and 80 miles from La Venta are the basalt deposits of the Tuxtla Mountains where the Olmecs went to cut their enormous slabs of stone, and from where they had to transport them without wheeled vehicles or draft animals. Most likely they dragged the basalt to a river and then transported it on rafts to their centers. The basalt was carved into 20-ton portrait heads of rulers, into massive thrones symbolizing divine descent, and into mythological animals and muscular human bodies. The realism and awesome monumentality of these sculptures in the round were never again to be achieved in Mesoamerica. But their symbols for rulership and gods were to continue throughout the evolution of Mesoamerican civilization.

Smaller, more portable, examples of Olmec art have been discovered throughout most of Mesoamerica, particularly the exquisitely polished jades of the La Venta period (900-400 B.C.), carved with the were-jaguar motif that was practically an emblem of the Olmecs. The were-jaguars, or humans with jaguar facial features like snarling mouths and, occasionally, fangs, are so prevalent that the Olmecs often are called the "Jaguar People." But in their trade for obsidian (for tools), jade, and iron ores (for mirrors), the Olmecs left more than small objects along their routes. Their symbolism was used in pottery to provide prestige to the elite in Oaxaca and the Central

Valley: their carvings and paintings are found in caves from as far as El Salvador and the Pacific Coast state of Guerrero in Mexico. Chalcatzingo in Morelos even has monumental Olmec sculpture, perhaps showing the presence of a permanent Olmec community far afield of its heartland in the Gulf region. So elaborate have been the Olmec influences found over most of Mesoamerica that some archaeologists have wondered whether their trade was accompanied by actual conquest.

OLMEC CIVILIZATION ENDS

Why, or even when, Olmec civilization ended is not known. First, Olmec power shifts from San Lorenzo to La Venta around 900 B.C. Then, La Venta seems to decline, perhaps around 400 B.C., but it could have been earlier or later so scanty is the evidence. In some places, such as Tres Zapotes, Olmec objects continue to be made until 100 B.C., but they are mixed with other cultural influences. Whenever it declined, Olmec civilization left a legacy that evolved into the diverse cultures of the central highlands and southern lowlands—the two areas that later dominated Mesoamerica. Olmec trade routes formed the geographical limits of what would become Mesoamerica. Its impressive ceremonial centers and elaborate works of art set a pattern for later systems of social prestige and authority. Its religion already included the rain god, the feathered serpent god who became Quetzalcoatl, and the earth and fire gods. Its universe included the layers of the sky, the earth, and the Underworld. And its ballplayer figurines from 1200 B.C. show that in this land of rubber, the ball game had already evolved. Even if the Olmec civilization were not the mother culture for later Mesoamerican civilizations, its exquisite art—achieved through superhuman effort—would have singled it out as exceptional.

While the importance of the Gulf Coast during the earliest period of Mesoamerican civilization is undisputed, this region later settled into a second-class status. Instead of generating the symbols of culture and initiating trade throughout Mesoamerica, it became a land bridge for trade between the more powerful central highlands and the southern Maya area. The few excavations in this region indicate an ebb and flow of influence, sometimes from the highlands, sometimes from the southern area, indicating perhaps the relative power of each through time. The most important exception to this secondary role can be found at the ruined city of El Tajín.

TAJIN SCROLL DESIGNS

Occupied by A.D. 250, El Tajin flourished from A.D. 600-1100, when it developed a unique architectural style of flying cornices and recessed niches. The site has numerous wall panels carved with narrative scenes of the ball game and embellished with the most characteristic trait of its style—the interlaced scroll pattern. Tajin scroll designs probably evolved from the earliest Maya style found at Izapa, but their striking similarity to Chinese bronzes has led some people to speculate that their origin lies across the Pacific. Tajin's distinctive scroll style can be found on some monuments at Teotihuacan, but Tajin also traded with southern areas where it may have created renewed interest in the ball game that thrived during the Late Classic period. Tajin was burned and destroyed, perhaps by Chichimeca barbarians invading from the north, and it was abandoned around A.D. 1100, not to be rediscovered under its dense cover of tropical vegetation until the 18th century.

The conquering Spaniards found the Gulf Coast region densely populated and, in the central area, dominated by the Totonacs, whose capital was at Zempoala. Zempoala's state, called Totonacapan, extended into the mountainous region of the Sierra de Puebla. Not long before the arrival of Cortes, the Aztecs had subjugated Totonacapan into a tribute-paying state. Resenting the authority of the Aztecs, the Totonacs allied themselves with Cortes and found themselves, without a struggle, subjects of a new power.

GULF COAST HISTORY

While the length of the Gulf Coast acted as a land bridge between the southern and central parts of Mesoamerica in ancient times, the sea became the port of entry and exile during historical times. At the modern port of Veracruz, Cortes established the first formal European settlement in Mexico, and here the Spanish lowered their last flag before departing from newly independent Mexico. Later, British, U.S., and French ships arrived to seize the port and make claims upon the fledgling nation, while Mexico's turbulent politics led to presidential exiles like Santa Anna and Porfirio Diaz sailing from Veracruz to safer lands.

The most romantic and, perhaps, the most tragic period of Veracruz occurred during colonial times. The wealth of the colony accumulated in Veracruz, waiting for the arrival of the Spanish galleon each spring. The arrival of the galleon attracted merchants who set up tents on the beaches and engaged in a great commercial fair that determined their incomes for the next year. Pirates, too, were attracted to Veracruz. Acting as agents of Britain, France, and Holland, they protested Spain's monopolistic commerce with her colonies by stealing what they could not legitimately buy. Veracruz was one of their favorite ports of call, and call they did—John Hawkins, Francis Drake, and the notorious Nicolas de Agromonte. In 1683, the buccaneer Lorencillo sacked Veracruz for three solid days. For three days, Veracruzanos were denied food and water, women were tortured and raped, and the town was pillaged. So thorough was Lorencillo in seizing everything that even today Veracruzanos explain the loss or misplacement of something by saying "Lorencillo took it."

GULF COAST TODAY

Politically, the region is calm today, but commercially, it is booming. The rich land supports citrus and tropical fruits, vanilla, sugarcane and coffee plantations, and cattle ranches. The rivers and sea are rich, too, and the fishing industry, particularly shrimping, competes on the international market. As if the region did not have enough natural resources, oil and natural gas now dominate its economy.

CONTEMPORARY INDIAN CULTURE

The Totonac and Nahua Indians, and a few Otomi, living in the region today probably are not descendants of the builders of the great Olmec civilization or El Tajin. The area was subject to massive migrations in ancient times, so the original builders of the ruins may have moved on as they were displaced by other groups. In fact, some archaeologists think the ancient Olmecs moved south, where they became the Maya; others think the residents of Tajin moved north and became the Post-classic Huastecs. Whatever the truth may be, the Totonacs did build Zempoala, and the Nahuas (who call themselves *mexicanos*) probably descend from the Aztecs (who called themselves *mexica*).

Although Totonacs still live in the region of Zempoala and Nahuas live near Catemaco, these coastal Indians have been studied little and carry on few obvious traditions. Yet in the less accessible Sierra region, beginning at the foothills near Papantla and climbing to the Sierra de Puebla, the Totonacs, Otomi, and Nahuas still wear clothing reminiscent of ancient times, continue to conduct their trade in markets, and continue to accompany their religious fiestas with the ancient Dance of the Voladores (see "Papantla,").

The most traditional Totonac live in the Sierra de Puebla with their Nahua neighbors. Their world view and religious practices include remarkable similarities to those of ancient Mesoamerica. They believe they live in the world of the fifth sun, which will be cataclysmically destroyed just as were the four worlds preceding it. Their universe is layered with four evil levels under the earth and numerous levels above. In the uppermost level lives the creator sun god who now shares his summit with Catholic saints. (See the chapter on "Ancient Mexico.")

The Nahuas practice their Catholicism mixed with pre-Hispanic practices, too. Even their revered Virgin of Guadalupe is tinged with pagan beliefs. When the dark-skinned Virgin first made her miraculous appearance in the 16th century, she spoke in Nahuatl—the language of the Aztecs and the Nahuas—and was confused with the Aztec mother goddess, Tonantzin. Today, saints as well as rain gods must be appeased to avert disasters, especially during the summer growing season when the threat of drought is greatest. Most Nahua fiestas occur during the critical summer months, but in November, Day of the Dead ceremonies are performed in the Aztec tradition of feeding the souls of the dead with tamales and squash and offering their spirits marigolds, the flower Aztecs held sacred to the dead.

In Aztec times, bark paper was used to make books and to perform religious ceremonies. Today, only the Otomi village of San Pablito continues to pound the bark of wild fig trees to make the amate paper of ancient times. One use for the paper is bark painting, but the most prevalent use in the Sierra de Puebla is witchcraft. White paper invokes protection; brown paper is used in black magic. The paper is cut into dolls that can be found in many craft shops in Mexico City—those dolls with shoes (seldom worn by Indians) are evil, those with bare feet, good. Some dolls are adorned with vegetation and represent fertility gods that are used in agricultural ceremonies.

VERACRUZ

Veracruz is the consummate tropical port city, full of character and gaiety. Its mix of peoples—some with red hair, some with blue eyes, many with mixtures of European, Indian, and African blood—testifies to its history as the point of entry for Cortes, pirates, and slave traders, as well as invading U.S. and French forces. Even today, freighters from around the world bring new peoples to this thriving port. Sea breezes mingle with the exuberant sounds produced by Veracruz musicians on their guitars and marimbas, and the sun brightens the spirit of Veracruzanos as they hawk their goods or sit chatting at sidewalk cafes.

Veracruz' dramatic history failed to leave much of an architectural record for the visitor. In early colonial days, malaria and other tropical diseases prevented long stays in the port. The population remained low, and its buildings, except for the fortresses, were constructed of wood. Not until the 18th century were stone buildings constructed here. Even without the fine colonial heritage of other Mexican cities, Veracruz captivates with its forts built against pirates like Francis Drake, its white buildings shimmering in the sun, and its distinctive atmosphere. A day soaking up its atmosphere, another lounging at its beaches, and one or two for excursions make for an enjoyable and unusual vacation.

KEY TO VERACRUZ

Sights • This port city pulsates with tropical rhythms; its zócalo thrives with musicians and vendors. The engaging atmosphere is not matched by comparable sights, but nearby beaches and excursions compensate for this lack.

Excursions • The flower-filled town of Jalapa with its magnificent museum of ancient art, the ruins of Zempoala, and the tropical river village of Tlacotalpan are within easy striking distance.

Shopping • Limited to seashell knickknacks and a few crafts shops.

Sports • Swimming and tennis at some hotels.

Fiestas • Carnival celebrations in Veracruz begin 5 days before Lent; Tlacotalpan exuberantly celebrates the Fiesta of the Virgin of Candlemas for a week around February 2.

Where to Stay • First-class hotels and a variety of other accommodations.

Where to Eat • Both sea and river fish available, with red snapper, shrimp, crab, octopus, and pompano providing most of the fare. Decent restaurants abound, serving a variety of fish soups and Veracruz-style dishes.

Entertainment • Sultry evenings by the zócalo listening to music while sipping drinks. A few night spots available, too.

Getting Around • Efficient bus service between the zócalo and beaches and between the city and excursion areas. Car rentals available. To orient yourself in this city, consider north to be on your left as you face the water. Note that the Malecón is one-way for a few blocks near center, so that to drive to the beaches Zarogoza is the road to follow out of town initially.

Practical Tips • Gulf Coast weather is not as predictable as the Pacific Coast's, with storms sometimes occurring even during the "winter" season between November and March. During summer, these tropics are hotter, more humid, and subject to torrential rains. Beaches here lack the sparkle of the Caribbean and Pacific coasts, but they are popular with Mexicans during school vacations and they provide pleasant interludes between sightseeing. This area is not heavily trafficked by foreign tourists, so don't expect the tourist facilities and internationalism of Mexico's other coasts. Shops close for the traditional siesta between 1-4 p.m., but stay open later in the evenings.

WHAT TO SEE AND DO

Zócalo

The town zócalo is the place to absorb Veracruz. While the 18th-century church, La Parroquia, and the Municipal Palace will take little of your time, the cafes in the arcades provide a lively scene any time of day. Musicians stroll about, playing as the mood hits them or when someone requests a song. Although they are most active at lunchtime and in the evening, we have been serenaded at breakfast. Around noon, vendors of freshly caught crab (*jaiba*) and shrimp wander among the cafe tables, their shouts of "Jaiba! Jaiba!" punctuating the buzz of conversation. In the evening, the zócalo becomes an opera set with its Municipal Palace, transformed into a white, spotlighted Moorish fantasy, as the backdrop for the action. Band concerts, and sometimes even local talent nights, vie with the *marimbas* at the cafes where the long line of ceiling fans seem to whirl more madly than usual. Vendors of Veracruz cigars, sailors off their anchored freighters, Mexican tourists and foreign ones, make their entrance onto this stage with Veracruz families and merge into a seething scene that only a performance of *Aida* can equal.

Other Town Sights

Just beyond the zócalo, where the Malecón begins, are the docks and port for freighters and fishing boats. From here you can see the **Fortress of San Juan de Ulua,** connected to the mainland by a bridge and reached by buses running from Lerdo and Landero y Coss. Built to

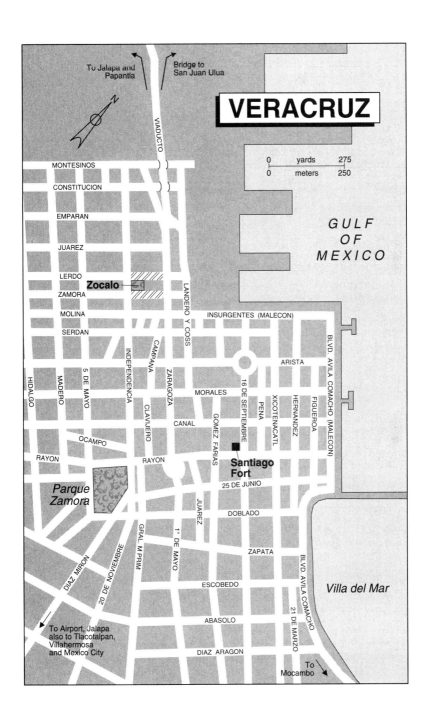

defend colonial Veracruz against pirates, in the 19th century the fort
became a notorious prison whose cells would be under water during
high tide. Today, however, it's a tourist spot. Treasure has been
recovered from a shipwreck just off the island; the jewelry and gold
may have been from one of Cortes' lost shipments to Spain. Open
Tues.-Sun., 9 a.m.-4:30 p.m. Another way to see the fortress (at least
the exterior) is to take a 40-minute **harbor cruise** from the dock across
from the Emporio Hotel (fee).

Following Landero y Coss beyond the cheapie *coctelerias* near the
Malecón, you walk through a park and past some pleasantly restored
buildings until you dead-end at Canal and the frothy 19th-century
facade of the **Instituto Veracruzano de Cultura** (temporary exhibits).
Turn left and you arrive at the massive **Baluarte Santiago** (16 de Septiembre at Canal). Built in 1636 as part of a fortified wall around the
city, this fort is all that remains.

Beaches

Where the Malecón curves away from the city to the south and
becomes Blvd. Avila Camacho is **Villa del Mar,** the most popular
in-town beach. If the water doesn't appeal to you, you can watch a
lively game of beach baseball. Or pay a fee at the Villa del Mar restaurant to use their swimming pool. The beach can be reached by buses
running along Zaragoza at Serdan and marked "1° de Mayo" or "Villa
del Mar." **Mocambo** is close to Veracruz, only 9 km (6 m) from the
center of town, beyond Villa del Mar. Food, drinks, chairs, and anything else the vendors want to sell are available, including some Veracruz music. Restaurants have beach chairs, dressing rooms, and even
pools, and a charge for their use. Buses leave for Mocambo on Serdan
between Landero y Coss and Zaragoza, or you can drive out on the
continuation of the beach road to the Mocambo Hotel where you turn
left for the beach.

SHOPPING

By following Calle Zamora off the zócalo to Landero y Coss, you come
to the **Mercado de Artesanias** with its hundreds of stalls selling curios.
Some of the seashell creations here are in irresistably bad taste. If you want
hand-rolled cigars, postcards, miniature tall ships, gardenias, vanilla extract, or just about anything else, spend your evening in a cafe by the zócalo watching the continuous stream of vendors.

FIESTAS

Starting the Friday before Ash Wednesday and continuing for five days,
Veracruz bursts with color, processions, dances, and even more music and
gaiety than usual. These Mardi Gras celebrations, probably the best in
Mexico, attract tourists from all over. Most of the festivities center around
the zócalo and begin late in the afternoon, continuing into the night.

EXCURSIONS

Jalapa

Located 116 km (72 m) northwest on MEX 140, 1-1/2 hours from airport
First-class ADO bus service (and, from Mexico City, deluxe Uno service.)
• As you wind your way along the road to Jalapa (also Xalapa, pronounced hah-LAH-pah), you climb to over 4000 feet and into a more
benign climate than that of the coast. In the colonial past when
Veracruz' climate was unhealthy, merchants and sailors came to this
safer altitude to conduct their business, thereby establishing the
importance of Jalapa as the capital of the state of Veracruz. Today, Jalapa is a pleasant city and its superb archaeology museum has one of
the finest pre-Hispanic collections in Mexico.

The first place to visit is the magnificent **Museo de Antropologia**
(Tues.-Sun. 9:30 a.m.-5 p.m.; closed Mon.; fee; cameras permitted for
a fee, but no flash). Designed by the renowned architectural firm of
Edward Durrell Stone, the modern museum provides a dramatic setting for the equally stunning art. The collection contains sculptures
and figurines of all of Veracruz' great cultures from the early Olmec
to the Classic period—with its madly grinning burial figurines—to the
Totonac civilization of Conquest times. Some of the monolithic pieces
are from San Lorenzo, the oldest known center of great civilization in
Mexico (1200-900 B.C.). They include colossal heads, which were
portraits of Olmec rulers, and one enormous sculpture of a human
torso without a head. While the heads never had bodies, these torsos
once did have heads, though not one has been found complete. There
also are more finely preserved Olmec sculptures, including an exquisite green-stone carving from Las Limas of a person holding a human
baby with jaguar facial characteristics. And don't miss the unusually
expressive and near-life-size ceramic figures of the serpent-belted
birth goddess, toys with wheels (which found no practical use in
ancient times), and finely carved "palmas" that were part of the ball
game ritual. All of these latter pieces date from the Classic period
(A.D. 600-900) in Veracruz. *Entering Jalapa from Veracruz, follow*
"Mexico" signs to bypass the downtown, then pick up Av. Jalapa and
museum; from the Central de Autobuses (5 km from center), buses and
combis run to centro as well as museum.

After you visit the museum, you might go to the colonial section of
this city (about 5 km from museum and bus terminal; buses, colectivos, and taxis available from each). Although there are no major
sights, you can sit in the Parque Juarez, stroll around the lake (a few
blocks south of Parque Juarez), or walk the colonial Callejon Dia-
mante (off the main street of Enriquez). Or maybe you just want to
dine. **La Casona del Beaterio** (Zaragoza 20, near Parque Juarez
behind State House; 8 a.m.-10 p.m.: inexpensive) is an attractive restaurant around a garden and with decent food. For overnight stays,
the ★★**Xalapa** (*Victoria y Bustamante;* ☎ *[281] 8-2222; $80*), on a

hill above the main street of Enriquez, 5 minutes from center, offers many amenities including a pool and parking, 180 carpeted and modern rooms, and a bar with entertainment as well as a good cafeteria where locals go for their evening enchiladas and snacks. For a tranquil retreat, drive or take a colectivo to picturesque **Coatepec** (10 km, 6 m), with its waterfalls, parks, and ★★★**Posada Coatepec** (*Hildalgo 9, 2 blocks from the shady zócalo;* ☎ *[281] 6-0544; $115*), an 18th-century mansion renovated into a tasteful inn of 27 rooms (mostly suites) furnished with antiques; sauna, Jacuzzi, elegant restaurant, and parking. For those on tight budgets, try overnighting in Veracruz.

Zempoala

The ruins of Zempoala (also Cempoala, meaning "abundance of water") can be reached from Jalapa as well as from Veracruz *40 km (24 m) north of Veracruz, just off MEX 180. Open 8 a.m.-6 p.m. Admission fee and fee for parking.* • You might want to include them in a day trip to Jalapa by following the signs near Rinconada to MEX 180 and Cardel on your return from Jalapa instead of continuing on MEX 140 into Veracruz. First-class buses leave from the main ADO terminal for the town of Zempoala. The ruins are just on the outskirts of the town.

The ruins offer little sculpture but hold plenty of historical interest. It is here that Cortes and his soldiers first came after landing at Veracruz, to meet the "fat cacique" who ruled the 30,000 Totonacs of this city. So hungry for bounty were the Spaniards that they mistook the white stucco finish of the buildings, gleaming in the sun, for silver. The Totonacs became the first Indian allies of the conquistadors.

Although today the central plaza of the ancient city has been restored to show the architecture of Zempoala around the time of the Conquest, the area had been a ceremonial center since about A.D. 900. Around a grassy plaza are a number of pyramids and platforms, which the Spaniards reported were topped with buildings of palm. Time has eroded the stucco and painted surface of these buildings, exposing the smooth, river-polished stones and the cement made of ground shells used in construction. The plaza with a circular altar is in the section of the ancient town where Cortes camped with his troops and their horses. Other ancient buildings can be found in the surrounding corn fields and in the modern village of Zempoala, where nearly every backyard contains some remnant of ancient times. Tiny museum at site entrance.

Tlacotalpan

Located 85 km (53 m) southeast of Veracruz on MEX 180; past Alvarado take a right turn and continue 15 km (9 m) to this town. Second-class buses leave from the Central Camionera on Calle La Fragua. • Once an important port for river traffic and a winter home for wealthy Veracruzanos (and their hideaway during pirate attacks), this picturesque town on the Rio Papaloapan ("River of Butterflies") offers an enchanting opportunity for a road trip past the shrimping village of Alvarado and along the fertile banks of the Papaloapan. Brightly painted houses with gingerbread-white designs line the quiet streets of this town. To the left of the Posada de Lala, you find the zócalo with its flamboyant town hall and the columned houses of the wealthy backing onto the river along Av. Miguel Chazaro. The wonderful interior of the Church of Candalaria becomes the focus of the community during the **Fiesta of the Virgin of Candlemas** (February 2 and several days before and after). The charming **Posada de Lala** (Carranza 11) is a modestly priced, clean hotel, but most likely you will want a place to eat, not sleep. Try its restaurant (inexpensive) for some of the excellent local fish (☎ 4-25-86).

WHERE TO STAY

In recent years, a number of first-class resort hotels have opened in the beach areas just outside the city. Since transportation is easily obtained into town, these hotels provide a pleasant beach environment from which to visit the port city. Most of the in-town hotels are modern as well, if seldom deluxe. In selecting your hotel, it is good to remember that the zócalo and busier commercial streets can be noisy, so in those areas choose a room with air conditioning so you can keep your windows closed. Price categories for a room for two are based on the highest rate at the hotel, but many of these hotels have less expensive rooms, which could place them in a lower category. For reservations write, 91910 Veracruz, Veracruz, Mexico, unless another town is noted, or call area code 29.

EXPENSIVE

Mocambo
8-1/2 km (5 m) south of town, Mocambo Beach; ☎ *37-16-51; $90* • Once the only hotel in this popular beach area, the Mocambo may be older than others and its service might show some tropical languor, but its gardens and pleasantly old-fashioned architecture make it our favorite in Veracruz. The hotel sits above the Gulf and public beach; the walk down to the pools and beach is gracefully terraced. Many of the 90 air-conditioned rooms have been modernized; the best have views and king-size beds. Restaurants, poolside snack bar, veranda bar with sea view. Large pool. Parking. Write Apartado 263.

Hostal de Cortes
Blvd. Avila Camacho at corner of Las Casas; ☎ *32-00-65; $93* • Located across from Villa del Mar beach, this modern hotel has an airy, pleasant lobby, good service, and 103 well-appointed and carpeted rooms and suites with a/c, some with balconies and sea views. Good restaurant, bar with live music. Shops. Pool and access to golf and fishing. Parking.

Veracruz
Independencia at Lerdo; ☎ *31-22-33; $90* • Located just across from the zócalo, this polished and contemporary hotel provides some of the

most comfortable in-town accommodations. The 115 air-conditioned rooms are carpeted and tastefully furnished; those with front balconies have views of the zócalo and rooftops. Restaurant and bar with terrace; sun deck with view of port and small pool. Garage. Write Apartado 451.

Emporio

Paseo de Malecón; ☎ *32-00-20; $106* • On the harbor in the center of city, this modern, commercial-style hotel has a great location. While only those exterior rooms with port views rank 3 stars, many of the 202 rooms are carpeted and with balconies; all are air-conditioned. Restaurants and bars; large pools, one indoor. Pay parking.

INEXPENSIVE

Colonial

Miguel Lerdo 117; ☎ *32-01-93; $37-42* • This modernized colonial-style hotel of 180 rooms sits amid the action of the zócalo with amazing calm. Its newer rooms cost more than the older ones; all have air conditioning. Sidewalk cafe; bar; heated indoor pool. Pay garage.

Villa del Mar

Blvd. Avila Camacho next to the Hostal de Cortes; ☎ *31-33-66; $51* • Outside the center and across from the beach, this older hotel has modernized and air-conditioned rooms as well as simpler bungalows without a/c. Restaurant and bar; good pool. Parking. Write Apartado 145.

BUDGET

Baluarte

Canal 265 at 16 de Septiembre; ☎ *36-08-44; $32* • On the plaza dominated by the Fort of Santiago and only a 10-minute walk from the zócalo, this five-story hotel is designed in plastic modern and has 60 very clean, air-conditioned rooms. Small restaurant and garage.

WHERE TO EAT

Throughout the rest of Mexico you find dishes cooked a la Veracruzana, but there is no better place to try this style than in Veracruz. Not surprisingly, this Veracruzana sauce of tomatoes, capers, olives, and onions is most often served with fish, but it's also popular with chicken. Even stuffed crabs (*jaibas rellenas*) have many of these ingredients included with their bread-crumb topping. Other regional dishes include a variety of soups like *caldo largo de camarones* (shrimp) or crab in *chilpachole*, a spicy—often fiery—tomato broth. In Veracruz, seafood tends to find its way into everything, including the empanadas (most often stuffed with crabmeat). If you like simpler dishes, try grilled red snapper with garlic (*al mojo de ajo*) or without. Price categories are explained in the Introduction.

Although you can find seafood nearly everywhere, the restaurants around the zócalo are the liveliest. Here you will be treated to the passing parade of vendors, shoe shiners, and musicians while you eat your evening dinner. If you tire of the bustle and hustle, pass through the outdoor cafes to the inside of the restaurants. Our favorite restaurant here is the well-known and moderately priced **Prendes,** where the service includes such after-dinner refinements as finger bowls. The stuffed crabs and ceviche are good; the whole grilled pompano (priced per kilo) and *camarones gigantes* are superb. If Prendes is out of your budget, just sit at any table under the arcade around noon and wait for the shrimp vendors to pass by. For a good price you can order a pile of boiled shrimps to peel while enjoying the cafe's beer.

Not all zócalo dining involves seafood. In fact, the mountainous region of Veracruz has long produced coffee, and the port has been involved in its trade for just as long. Sipping coffee at **La Parroquia** (on Independencia across from the zócalo) is part of this coffee tradition. It certainly is the most popular spot for a breakfast of *cafe con leche* sipped to the accompaniment of marimba music. (The outdoor tables are worth the wait.) When you're ready to pay for a refill, join the others in ringing your glass with a spoon and wait for the arrival of the waiter with two steaming pots, one of milk, the other of rich coffee. The food here is good, too, from breakfast specials to Mexican antojitos (inexpensive; 6 a.m.-1 a.m.). There's a branch on the Malecón near the Emporio Hotel, where you catch the evening breeze while eating ice cream (open 5 p.m. on).

There are even traditional spots to eat on weekends and holidays—the very casual restaurants in the fishing villages of **Boca del Rio** and **Mandinga,** two of the few places where the high-pitched voices and harp of Veracruz music can be heard. Boca del Rio restaurants line the avenue where the Jamapa River flows into the Gulf, but *the* place to enjoy both food and music is near the entrance to town at **Pardino's** (Zamora at Revolucion, moderate). However, our favorite seafood restaurant is in the earthy, lakeside village of Mandinga—an unlikely place to find such sumptuous fish. *Sunday afternoons, when Mexican families enliven these basic surroundings*, is the best time to visit **Casa Uscanga** (inexpensive and up; closed at 6 p.m.; parking to rear of restaurant). Enjoy the five-star chipachole, the whole seabass a la Veracruzana, or simply a pile of shrimp ordered by the kilo (try *camarones blancos grandes* when available), listen to Veracruz songs, and maybe even rent a boat for a lake tour. Boca del Rio lies just to the left of MEX 180, 13 km (8 m) toward Villahermosa—turn at the second sign, not the first, for the village. Mandinga can be reached 7 km (4 m) further on, by taking the first left off MEX 180 after the Boca del Rio bridge. Buses on Serdan near Zaragoza run on to Boca del Rio from where you can get a taxi to Mandinga, if you want.

Back in Veracruz, you might want a complete change of pace. Try **La Tana del Lupo** (1 de Mayo 1230, just 4 blocks from the Villa del Mar beach; ☎ 31-63-92; moderate). This Italian restaurant, run by Roman-born Aldo Marchione and his Mexican wife, offers such authentic options as marinated wild mushrooms, delicate homemade ravioli, and, often, rabbit cacciatore. Or maybe you want some bargains on seafood. Try the fish filete served with vegetables at the in-town branch of **Pardino's** (Malecón at Landero y Coss)—the flan neapolitano is good, too. The simple **Restaurant Villa del Mar** (open till 6 p.m.) offers you sea views over the Villa del Mar beach with prices similar to Pardino's. And top it all off with a brief walk from the zócalo for the delicious ice cream and homemade cones ("canastas") at **Santa Clara Helados** (Molina 310).

GETTING TO AND FROM VERACRUZ

AIR

Veracruz is served by Mexicana (Mexico City) and by the small jets of both Aerocaribe (Villahermosa, Mérida, then Cancún) and Aerolitoral (Villahermosa, Monterrey). Car rentals and collective vans at the airport provide transportation to the city, 8 km (5 m) away.

BUS

Buses connect this city to most others in Mexico. Service with Mexico City is excellent. Several buses run each day to Mérida. Oaxaca to the south and cities to the north can also be reached by bus. ADO is the major first-class carrier here and offers it deluxe Uno service to Villahermosa, Puebla, and Mexico City (6 hours), but second-class buses are available to small towns in the vicinity of Veracruz.

CAR

If you are making a round trip between Mexico City and Veracruz, you can choose among several routes, varying your trip each way. On one leg of the journey, you might consider spending an extra night on the road to visit the ruins of El Tajin at Papantla and drive through the beautiful and traditional area of Sierra de Puebla. (See "Papantla.") The more direct routes to Mexico City take between 6 and 7 hours—depending on the amount of traffic you encounter in Mexico City and, in the case of MEX 150D, the amount of traffic along the Orizaba Pass. From Mexico City, follow Calzada Zaragoza out of the city to the toll route (MEX 190D) to Puebla. (See chapter on Mexico City Excursions.) At Puebla you have a choice of routes. The most trafficked is the toll road MEX 150D (follow signs for "cuota," not "libre"), which passes near the resort town of Fortin de las Flores. (See "On the Road.") While Mount Orizaba sits amid both direct routes to Veracruz, its snowcapped peaks towering over 18,800 feet, MEX 150D plunges through the Orizaba Pass, which can be a grueling drive when there is a lot of traffic. The distance to Mexico City is 475 km (295 m). At the intersection with MEX 180, turn left onto 180 for Veracruz. The alternate route avoids the Orizaba Pass: leave MEX 190 at Puebla and continue to Veracruz via Jalapa and MEX 140, following the colonial trade route between the capital and its port. This route is about the same distance, and the road is usually good, sometimes even 4 lanes.

The route south to Villahermosa is along MEX 180. The 6-1/2-hour trip is along mostly flat roads, except in the area of the Tuxtla Mountains and Lake Catemaco (see "On the Road"), a good place to rest or stay overnight. The only serious traffic you encounter on this 485-km (300-m) trip is in the oil-boom areas of Coatzalcoalcas and Villahermosa, but the 4-lane toll road (MEX 180 D) near those cities avoids most of the congestion.

TRAIN

Servicio Estrella (star-service) between Mexico City and Veracruz on the overnight El Jarocho is fairly reliable but still takes 10 hours.

DIRECTORY

Airlines • *Mexicana*, Av. 5 de Mayo at Serdan (☎ 32-22-42); *Aerocaribe* (☎ 35-05-68); *Aerolitoral* (☎ 31-52-32).

American Express • *Viajes Olymar*, Camacho 2221 (☎ 31-31-69).

Bank • *Banamex*, Juarez 190, cashes traveler's checks 9-11 a.m.; 24-hour Cirrus ATM.

Buses • Central Camionera and ADO, Av. Diaz Miron at Orizaba—which is enough out of the center to require a town bus. Take one marked "Diaz Miron" on Av. 5 de Mayo.

Car Rentals • At airport and in town are: *Avis* (☎ 32-25-16); *Budget* (☎ 31-21-39).

Consulates • *U.S. Consul* (☎ 31-58-21), 8:30 a.m.-3 p.m.; *British Consul* (☎ 31-09-55).

Groceries • *El Alba* (Lerdo 280, 1 block from zócalo).

Post Office • Plaza de la Republica near docks.

Train Station • A few blocks to the north of the zócalo, near the waterfront.

Tourist Office • In the Municipal Palace on the zócalo (☎ 32-99-42). Open daily 9 a.m.-9 p.m.

Tours • *Viajes Olymar* (see "American Express") offers city and excursion tours, as do many travel agencies.

ON THE ROAD

TO MEXICO CITY VIA MEX 150

The initial climb to 3000 feet from Veracruz is relatively unscenic, but after approximately 120 km (74 m), MEX 150 becomes the toll road MEX 150D at **Córdoba,** the coffee capital of Mexico. Surrounded by coffee plantations and verdant vegetation, Córdoba has become too commercial to be of much tourist interest, though tours can be arranged to the haciendas.

About 7 km (4 m) farther on, you arrive at the exit for **Fortin de las Flores** ("Fortress of Flowers"), whose name is partially derived from a military outpost established here during the colonial period. This town's perfect climate encourages the cultivation of gardenias, azaleas, and camellias, and its nurseries attract weekend visitors. A flower festival takes place each year around the end of April. This is a convenient place to stop for a meal or even spend the night. On the zócalo is **Restaurant Jardin**, with good Mexican food. Or you can try the dining rooms at the following two hotels.

Hotel Fortin de las Flores   ★★

Av. 2 between calles 5 and 7; (☎ 271) 300-55; $41 • A few blocks from the MEX 150D exit and subject to noise from nearby train tracks, this hacienda-style hotel, formerly a deluxe spa, has 120 rooms, most modernized and air-conditioned; some suites retain balconies and fireplaces. Good restaurant, bar. Pool with floating gardenias (seasonal). Game room. Movies. Parking. Inexpensive.

Posada Loma   ★★

Carretera Nacional 150, km 333; (☎ 271) 3-06-58; $45 • Just past the Hotel Fortin, turn left onto Av. 1 to find this homey inn surrounded by 17 bungalow-style units. The rooms are simply furnished, without air conditioning but with fireplaces and terraces, and set amid the extensive grounds of a nursery. Dining room; set meal hours. Small pool, squash court. Parking.

After Fortin de las Flores the road starts to climb through more dramatic scenery, passing the town of **Orizaba** on the way. This bustling, commercial town is home to the Moctezuma Brewery, manufacturer of Superior beer. Tours of the brewery (cervezeria) are happily provided. Just beyond, the climb begins through the mountain pass and then you arrive on the plateau that leads to Puebla.

MEX 180 SOUTH TO VILLAHERMOSA

About 130 km (81 m) south of Veracruz, the flat coastal road begins its gentle climb into the tropical rain forest of the Tuxtla Mountains. The scenery here is spectacular, and the hush of the countryside seems to hold whispers of the ancient past. Deeper into the jungle are abandoned sites of the Olmec civilization, such as Tres Zapotes. Soon you enter an area of quiet and sometimes, mist and pass the tumbling hill village of Santiago Tuxtla with its immaculate white houses and tiled roofs and San Andres Tuxtla, center for hand- rolled cigars. Then you come to the turnoff for the lake village of **Catemaco** (164 km, or 102 m) surrounded by the verdant, coneshaped peaks of the Tuxtla volcanoes. Olmec sculptures and jade figurines have been found throughout this region. Although the Olmec established their centers along tropical, inland rivers, they came to the Tuxtlas to quarry basalt. Actually, the La Venta pyramid, round and fluted, is an Olmec copy of one of these volcanoes.

Catemaco offers more than a convenient stop. You may even want to make an excursion here by first-class ADO buses from Villahermosa and Veracruz. Lake Catemaco is one of the most beautiful and least developed in Mexico, and rivers create waterfalls and tropical enclaves in the surrounding area, while white egrets and monkeys inhabit its islands. The sleepy town has a Sunday market, and on July 16 its church is the site of a pilgrimage to the miraculous powers of its Virgin of Carmen. You can arrange fishing or a boat tour of the lake and its islands (map and prices posted on waterfront). In the nearby village of **Santiago Tuxtla** (27 km, or 17 m north), a colossal, 9-foot tall Olmec head is displayed in the zócalo; across the street, a museum displays another colossal head—you can glimpse it from the street (left of the entrance) or pay a fee to see the few other Veracruz artifacts (daily till 6 p.m., Sun. till 3 p.m.). For yet another colossal head, but little else, take a 1/2-hour trip by taxi or bus to the **Tres Zapotes Museum**. (From Santiago Tuxtla, turn right onto MEX 180. Soon you cross a small bridge after which you turn right onto a paved road. Continue for 8 km or 5 m before taking the first right onto an unmarked road and continuing 13.5 km or 8 m. When you enter the village of Tres Zapotes, the museum is to the left of the "intersection.") While the late Olmec site of Tres Zapotes is more difficult to reach and provides no rewards for the visitor, the museum exhibits a few of the Olmec sculptures discovered there. (Open daily 9 a.m.-5 p.m. Small fee.)

Accommodations in Catemaco are adequate if not deluxe. While a few hotels are in town around the zócalo, you might prefer those with lake views. (For reservations, write Catemaco, Veracruz, Mexico; to call, the area code is 294.)

La Finca   ★★
2 km (1 m) south of Catemaco on MEX 180; ☎ *3-03-22; $58* • With a fine location on the edge of the lake overlooking the volcanoes and town, this modern, first-class motel offers 36 air-conditioned rooms, each with a well-designed terrace and lake view. Good restaurant and bar. Pool; boat rentals. Parking. Write Apartado 47.

Castellanos   ★
5 de Mayo and Commonfort; ☎ *7-02-00; $33* • Right on the zócalo of Santiago Tuxtla, this surprisingly pleasant and well-maintained 6-floor "tower" offers 49 air-conditioned units, a restaurant, and even a pool. Parking. Write Santiago Tuxtla, Veracruz.

Motel Playa Azul   ★
Carretera Sontecomapan km. 2; ☎ *3-00-01; $24* • Although reachable by local buses and just a mile from town (turn left off lake road by the Koniapan hotel, then right at hotel signs), on a road often made poor by heavy rains, the Playa Azul is probably best for those with cars—especially since the restaurant doesn't always function. This hotel has a beautiful, forested, and somewhat isolated lakeside setting. Yet its 100 very comfortable if plain rooms (a/c) are sadly arranged in motel rows without views (those in garden are a bit better). Restaurant with plastic decor. Lakeside pool; boat rentals. Parking. Write Apartado 26.

Posada Koniapan   √
Malecón and Av. Revolucion; ☎ *3-00-63; $20-24* • Within walking distance of the Catemaco zócalo and wharf area, the Koniapan's 22

rooms are clean, somewhat spare, yet comfortable; most are air-conditioned. The second-floor rooms have balconies with lake views. Restaurant that opens most reliably in the afternoon; small pool. Parking.

Not surprisingly, Catemaco has no gourmet restaurant, but it does offer lake perch (called *mojarra*), snails (*tegogolos*), and sardines (*topotes*) from the lake and, unfortunately, monkey meat (*carne de chongo*). Perhaps it's best to stick with the fish or chicken and *pellizcados* (special tortillas) that are served at the open-air restaurants along the lakefront. Of the two old reliables, both inexpensive, we prefer the food at **La Luna**, but the garden with lake view at **La Ola** is a pleasant place to enjoy decent food (but don't order the greasy *pellicados*). The second-floor open air perch with lake views at **7 Brujos** (closed Mon.) may represent a new, more upscale Catemaco. The choice of food is similar to the others, but a bit more sophisticated—as is the bar. And the prices are only slightly higher. Another new spot is the outdoor terrace of the **Hotel Catemaco** (zócalo; inexpensive), convenient for breakfasts, fruit salads (to eat it without sherbet, say "sin nieve"), and desserts.

After you leave Catemaco for Villahermosa and sights beyond (make sure you glance back to see the spectacular view of the lake and mountains from this perspective), the road gradually descends to the coast again. The rest of the trip is along a flat road that passes the heartland of the oil industry and the Coatzalcoalcos River that once was home to the Olmec at San Lorenzo. This leg of the trip to Villahermosa should take about 4 hours.

PAPANTLA AND EL TAJIN

Nestled amid rolling hills and lush tropical vegetation, the provincial town of Papantla (pah-PAHN-tlah) and the ruins of El Tajin (tah-HEEN) offer some of Mexico's loveliest scenery. While their isolated location in the vanilla-producing country of northern Veracruz makes them less convenient to visit than other sightseeing areas, this isolation provides a haven to travelers seeking spots off the well-worn tourist paths. Here, the Totonac Indians dress in crisp-white, ballooning costumes and still perform the ancient ceremony of the Dance of the Voladores (Dance of the Acrobatic Pole Flyers). Here, too, the magnificent ruins of Tajin might belong only to you, so few are the tourists who visit, yet Tajin's size and importance in ancient times was equal to that of Uxmal in Yucatán. In Papantla the voladores perform in front of the church Sunday evenings and vendors sell vanilla beans twisted into crucifixes or scorpions; otherwise there is little to entertain.

KEY TO PAPANTIA AND EL TAJIN

Sights • The magnificent scenery provides an excellent setting for visiting this traditional Totonac Indian area containing the exquisite ruins of El Tajin.

Fiestas • Corpus Christi, celebrated with the Dance of the Voladores.

Shopping • Limited to vanilla products, especially vanilla-bean sculptures.

Where to Stay • Limited.

Where to Eat • Hotel restaurants serve local seafood and typical Mexican cuisine.

Entertainment • A quiet evening sitting on the zócalo of Papantla will have to suffice.

Getting Around • A car or taxi is best to visit the ruins of Tajin; second-class buses run nearby

Practical Tips • The ruins of El Tajin can be visited in a long one-day excursion from Veracruz, but if you don't mind the limited accommodations in this area, you can better absorb provincial Mexico by staying the night. If you are driving to Veracruz from Mexico City, consider taking a little extra time to follow the route through the seldom-visited Sierra de Puebla described under "On the Road." Take insect repellent to the ruins and, during the hot and humid summer weather especially, try to visit the ruins as early in the day as possible.

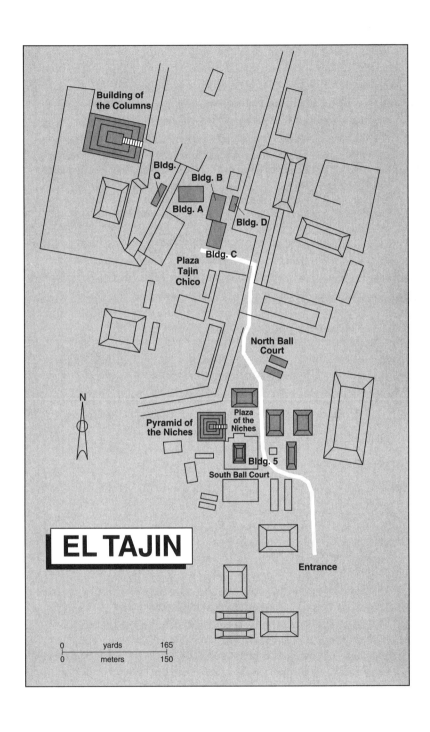

Building of
the Columns

Bldg.
Q

Bldg. B

Bldg. A

Bldg. D

Bldg. C

Plaza
Tajin
Chico

North Ball
Court

N

Pyramid of
the Niches

Plaza
of the
Niches

Bldg. 5

South Ball Court

EL TAJIN

Entrance

| 0 | yards | 165 |
| 0 | meters | 150 |

RUINS OF EL TAJIN

Open 9 a.m.-5:30 p.m. with museum hours more variable. Admission and parking fees. Refreshments and craft shops. On-going excavations.

El Tajin lies about 13 km (8 m) from Papantla. To reach the ruins follow the signs off MEX 180 at the foot of town or drive up past the church from the zócalo and turn right onto 16 de Septiembre. Turn left at the first dead end; bear left again to remain on pavement; then right at the second dead end. At this point follow the Poza Rica road for 5 km (3 m) before turning right to the entrance of El Tajin (1 km or .6 m). You need two buses to get to the access road of the ruins; then you need to walk about a half mile to the entrance. Go to Chote from the second-class bus terminal; then switch to a Poza Rica bus and ask to be dropped near El Tajin.

The great site of Classic Veracruz culture sits in an extremely fertile area of the foothills of the Sierra Madre Oriental. Tajin's central area alone covered 146 acres, but now luxuriant tropical vegetation dominates the center, disguising most of its ruined buildings. Though the hills of the area prevented Tajin from being organized according to the formal composition of most Mesoamerican cities, the individual buildings are gracefully designed to create rhythmic contrasts of light and shadow. El Tajin's prominence began around A.D. 600 when its ruler constructed the Pyramid of the Niches (perhaps as his tomb), and later reached its peak (A.D. 900-1100) in the reign of 13 Rabbit who constructed much of Tajin Chico. The city's prominence during that time may have derived from cacao (chocolate beans) and vanilla, important trade items of the past that grow in this area. Of all ancient cities, Tajin shows the greatest preoccupation with the ritual ball game (eleven courts have been discovered here, more than at any other site) and attendant ceremonies of human sacrifice. Some evidence indicates that the ball game's popularity spread throughout Mesoamerica in the Late Classic period along with trade in cacao. If so, Tajin must have been a leader in Mesoamerica at that time. The collapse of Classic-period cultures around A.D. 900 is little understood, but Tajin survived a bit longer than most, only to be invaded and destroyed around 1100.

Plaza of the Niches

The structures surrounding this plaza best exemplify Tajin's unique architectural style. Square, deeply recessed niches decorate the platforms of buildings, making them more ornate than most buildings in ancient Mexico. Flying cornices add to the play of light and shadow on these structures, contrasts made more vivid in the past when the entire structure was red, the niches black, and frets blue. Various geometric patterns, like the step-fret design, cover the balustrades and various parts of the building, adding to their already rich texture. The most famous building of Tajin, the **Pyramid of the Niches**, borders the west side of the plaza. Rising to a height of 60 feet, it is composed of six tiered platforms plus a mostly destroyed temple on the top. Niches decorate every layer, even the altars located along the staircase. Originally there may have been a total of 365 niches, symbolizing the number of days in the solar year. Whether the niches ever contained anything is unknown. Little remains of the carved panels that once adorned the temple.

Walking around a building to the south of the plaza, you come to the staircase of **Building 5** —where a carved freestanding statue of the God of Death stands on the first platform. As you continue to the southern edge of this building, you come to a ball court on your right.

South Ball Court

The carved panels on this ball court narrate rituals of human sacrifice and display the ornate scroll patterns typical of Tajin. The north wall carvings fascinate the most, with depictions of ballplayers dressed in all their paraphernalia. The panel on the right of this wall shows three ballplayers with kneepads, thick waist belts (or yokes), and "palmas" projecting up from the belts. The central ballplayer is about to be sacrificed by the figure on the right who holds an obsidian knife. On the extreme left of this panel the god of Death witnesses the scene. The central panel is not nearly as well preserved, but a reclining figure—looking much like a chacmool sculpture—appears to have been sacrificed. The panel on the left has two ballplayers as its central characters. The individual with his arms crossed and wearing elaborate ball-game equipment faces another who holds an obsidian knife. Apparently we are seeing yet another scene of sacrifice. Though the panels on the south wall don't seem to depict ballplayers, themes of human sacrifice are continued. Sacrifice is most easily seen in the panel on the right, where a prone man with crossed arms is surmounted by another man dressed in a bird costume (perhaps he represents a member of the cult of eagle warriors known in later Aztec times). Flanking these two figures are individuals providing musical accompaniment to the ceremony—the musician on the right strikes a percussion instrument; the other shakes a rattle. Surrounding all these scenes are elaborately interlaced scrolls that transform into human and grotesque faces (see the south central panel, especially).

North Ball Court

As you return through the Plaza of the Niches and continue north, you come to this ball court at the foot of Tajin Chico. In 1988, this area was reconstructed; the ball court was restored. Like the South Ball Court, it is carved with panels, but they are not in very good condition. The best-preserved panel can be found on the right of the north wall. A seated figure with intertwined serpents is surrounded by the scroll motifs and surmounted by a grotesque mask combined with a human body. Whether these panels showed sacrificial themes like the other ball court can't be determined.

Tajin Chico

Just beyond the ball court you continue up the path that takes you to the administrative area of Tajin, called Tajin Chico (Little Tajin).

Although the area is mostly unrestored, making it hard to tell where one building ends and another begins, it is a fine spot to wander about and discover columns, carvings, and even the pointed, corbel arches framing doorways that usually are found only in the Maya area. **Building C** is the best-preserved structure; **Building A** has a corbel arch entrance to the structure atop its platform; and **Building D**, reached through a subterranean door, has retained much of its wall decoration. Looming above the plaza of Tajin Chico is the **Mound of the Building Columns**. Although this structure is no more than a tree-covered hill today, once the stairs leading up to this complex were flanked by columns and covered with a roof of corbel arches. The columns were made of superimposed drums, entirely carved with narrative scenes depicting the military exploits of King 13 Rabbit. Some remnants of these carvings can still be seen at the site, others are in the museum, and still others have been lost forever, as they were sold in the market in Papantla.

Museum

At the entrance gate for the ruins is a museum that could more properly be called a warehouse shed for many of the sculptures and carvings unearthed during excavations. Here you can see a freestanding carving from the Pyramid of the Niches that is in a style most typical of the Maya site of Tonina in Chiapas. Here, also, are parts of the columns from the Building of the Columns; one section is carved with short, nude captive men and their taller, well-dressed captors.

FIESTAS AND ENTERTAINMENT

The **Dance of the Voladores** is a thrilling acrobatic display that used to be performed by the Totonac Indians of Papantla only on Corpus Christi Day (usually at the end of May or the beginning of June). Now the ceremony takes place every Sunday in the Papantla church courtyard at 8 p.m. (or thereabouts) and allegedly every day at the entrance to El Tajin, usually at 11 a.m. and 3 p.m. (or whenever there are enough people). *The Spanish friars, thinking that the Dance of the Voladores was only a dangerous sport, not a religious ceremony, never prevented it from being performed.* As a result, it is one of the few ancient rituals that has endured to this day. Once it was performed throughout Mesoamerica; today only the Indians in this northern region of Veracruz and the neighboring Sierra de Puebla still preserve its traditions. On the day of the dance, five men dressed in brilliant red costumes climb a towering pole and perform ceremonies to the four directions of the universe. The captain of the dancers stands on a small drum at the summit of the pole and accompanies the performance with flute and drum; he plays the drum by courageously stamping his feet. The captain symbolizes the fifth direction of the ancient universe, its center. The other four, with ropes tied around their ankles, fling themselves into space with their heads pointing to the ground and fly like birds around the pole until they land on the ground, feet first. Indians performing this feat today admit to not fully understanding its significance, yet they know that the four "fly-ers" must make 13 revolutions each around the pole (the last performance we saw was much slower and had many more revolutions). The total num-ber of revolutions adds up to the 52 years of the ancient and sacred Calen-dar Round. Formerly, the dancers dressed like macaws, a bird that symbolized the sun in pre-Conquest times.

WHERE TO STAY

While Papantla is the only town of interest in the area, its facilities are commensurate with the few tourists who visit the region. The accommoda-tions in town are adequate for an overnight stay, but for better ones you need to expand your sights to the nearby oil town of Poza Rica ("rich well") or as far away as Xicotepec de Juarez (see "On the Road"). The Gulf Coast road to Veracruz is sprinkled with small hotels and campsites, none particular improvements, but all boasting the beach and sea. Following are a few hotels for this region; make sure you note the right town when mak-ing reservations in this state of Veracruz.

Hotel Tajin   ★
Jose Nunez 104; (☎ 784) 201-21; $60 • Located just to the side of the Papantla zócalo, most of the Tajin's 60 rooms overlook this hill town. Although the hotel is plain and simple, its front rooms are bright, airy, and the most recommendable in town. Air conditioning available. Restaurant and bar. Parking.

Poza Rica Inn   √★★
km 45 Carretera Poza Rica-Papantla; (☎ 782) 319-22; $47 • This is the best hotel in the area. Just on the edge of Poza Rica, but with none of its ugliness, the hotel sits on a hill to the side of MEX 180, 18 km, 11 m north of Papantla. The 40 rooms are fresh, modern, and air-condi-tioned. Restaurant. Pool. Shops. Parking. Just 1/2 hour from El Tajin.

Hotel Balneario Tecolutla   ★
Matamoros s/n; (☎ 784) 509-01; $38 • A half hour from Papantla in the town of Tecolutla (30 km, 19 m, east on MEX 180, then 11 km, 7 m, from Gutierrez Zamora turnoff) and reached by following Teco-lutla's main street to the end, this hotel provides the best beach. The 72 rooms are clean, plain, and fan-cooled. Handsome, if mediocre, restaurant; bar; pool and garden fronting beach. Parking.

WHERE TO EAT

The most relaxing place to people-watch in Papantla is **La Terraza Res-taurant**, on a second-floor balcony overlooking the zócalo. The licuados, or fruit frappes, are a favorite here; the *queso fundido* is a good choice. The best food probably is served at the **Hotel Tajin**. Try their tasty *sincronizadas*. Both are inexpensive. If you happen to be swimming in Tecolutla, try the open-air, beach restaurant of **Don Rafa**. (Entering Tecolutla, turn left onto

Obregon and continue to beach where the restaurant is just to the right). The shrimp diablo and *manos de Guanaja* (stone crabs) are recommended. Moderate.

GETTING TO AND FROM PAPANTIA

AIR

No service.

BUS

Buses leave from Veracruz and stop at Tecolutla and Papantla, a trip that lasts about 3-1/2 hours. Buses also run to Mexico City from Papantla and Tecolutla. From Papantla the trip through the Sierra de Puebla is 280 km (174 m) to the northern bus terminal of Mexico City.

CAR

The drive north to Papantla from **Veracruz** is along the flat, well-paved MEX 180 lined with beaches (beware of unmarked topes). To break the monotony you might want to stop for a swim or swing 1 km off road south of Vega de Altatorre to the tiny ruin of **Las Higueras,** with its museum (copies of murals from A.D. 500-800; originals in Jalapa museum). After the Tecolutla toll bridge, MEX 180 swings inland and gradually climbs the foothills to Papantla (follow signs to Poza Rica). Total distance: 235 km (146 m). Total time: a little less than 3-1/2 hours. The 174-mile trip to **Mexico City** via MEX 130 and 132 cuts through traditional Indian villages and some of the finest scenery in Mexico. The road is not difficult to handle, except for the tortuous trip through the mountains before Xicotepec de Juarez. The trip takes between 4-1/2 to 5 hours. For more information, see "On the Road."

DIRECTORY

Airlines • None.

Bus Terminals • First-class ADO, on entrance road (MEX 180); second-class and local buses, on 20 de Noviembre near entrance road.

Car Rentals • None.

Groceries • Market, on zócalo.

Post Office • On Azueta, down left side of market from zócalo.

Taxis • On zócalo.

Telephones • Farmacia del Centro, on zócalo.

Tourist Office • Buried in Municipal Palace on zócalo (☎ 2-01-77).

Vanilla • Shops on entrance road (MEX 180).

ON THE ROAD

If the Papantla region is off the beaten tourist path, the drive through the Sierra de Puebla to Mexico City is even more so. As you leave the foothills of Papantla and climb to Huauchinango, you enter a fertile highland area producing coffee, apples, and peaches, and often rising to pine forests over 7500 feet above sea level. The area once was the domain of the Totonacs when their capital was at Zempoala. Over time, the Aztecs conquered them and Nahuatl speaking people settled here, sharing the Sierra with the Totonacs. Today, the traditional Totonacs and Nahuas live in these mountains, mostly in villages inaccessible by car. You can see them at the markets, the women in long skirts tied with thick handwoven belts and wearing pre-Hispanic quexquemetls over their embroidered blouses. The region is beautifully green and rich, dotted with lakes, and often misty and cool. The villages and markets are worth visiting for those who don't mind seeking out the small hotels that can be found in the towns of this area. To drive this route leave Papantla on MEX 180 to Poza Rica, where you follow MEX 130 to Xicotepec de Juarez.

XICOTEPEC DE JUAREZ

About 100 km (62 m) from Papantla, this town is home for a wonderful restaurant and delightful inn, √★★**Hotel Mi Ranchito** (Zaragoza 267; ☎ 776-402-12; $53), with 50 heated and comfortable rooms, pool, tennis next to waterfalls, and gardens. Located just off MEX 130. On June 24, pilgrims bring offerings to celebrate the Fiesta of St. John the Baptist, and traditional dances accompany the events.

HUAUCHINANGO

Only 19 km (12 m) from Xicotepec de Juarez, Huauchinango (oo-whah-chee-NAN-goh) takes about a half hour to reach as you make the gentle climb up the mountains and valley dominated by the lovely river and dam of Necaxa. Huauchinango (the extra "u" in the name distinguishes it from "red snapper") is the main market town for both Totonac and Nahua Indians. On Saturday, stalls brim over with the fruits and flowers of the region, and often one can find decent embroidery work here. The Azalea Festival coincides with the Festival of the Lord of the Holy Burial on the third Friday in Lent. Festivities continue for a week and often include the Dance of the Voladores. If you're ready to eat, try to wait for **La Cabana**, located 24 km (15 m) further on toward Acaxochitlan. This quaint, log- cabin restaurant serves its own chorizo sausage and grilled meats at very moderate prices.

ZACATLAN

About 16 km (10 m) after leaving Huauchinango, turn onto MEX 119 to Apizaco in order to reach the town of Zacatlan (42 km, or 26 m, south). In the center of apple orchards and dramatic pine-covered mountains where Nahua and Totonac villages lie hidden, Zacatlan offers a Sunday market. On May 15, it celebrates the Fiesta of St. Isador, the farmer, with ceremonies for blessing the corn and apples. On the Sunday before August 15, the annual Apple Festival takes place. Sometimes you can find wonderfully heavy wool blankets here in natural colors of white and brown. From Zacatlan, a 100-km unpaved road (MEX 88) makes its way to beautiful Cuetzalan (see Index).

ACAXOCHITLAN

If you have followed MEX 130 without any detours, you have passed through Acaxochitlan, a quiet, pine-forested area dominated by a large artificial lake. Only 30 km (19 m) separates this town from Huauchinango. Acaxochitlan (ah-kah-zoh-chee-TLAHN) has a colorful Sunday market, yet practically any day you can buy from roadside stands the apple cider, fruit wines, and preserved fruits for which this town is famous.

PAHUATLAN

You might consider a journey to Pahuatlan (pah-whah-TLAHN)—a journey, we say, because you seem to descend to another world on the 28 km (17 m) road leading to this most Nahua village. The turnoff to the north is more or less 10 km (6 m) past Acaxochitlan on MEX 130. The road is unpaved and takes one hour in the dry season as it makes its way through pine forests and then snakes its way down a mountain to the village thousands of feet below. During the descent you overlook the breathtaking valley where San Pablito, a traditional village that still produces amate, or bark paper and cutouts used in healing ceremonies (and for casting spells, too, it's said), is located. If you have plenty of time and good, dry weather, this trip is worthwhile on a Sunday when there is a market in Pahuatlan. The village, nestled into a fold of the mountain, has narrow winding cobblestone streets overhung with Swiss-style tiled roofs. Its men dress entirely in white except for their serapes, and the women wear indigo-blue skirts wrapped with thick red wool belts and topped with finely embroidered blouses. A more traditional market in a more picturesque setting would be hard to find. Pahuatlan's fiesta day occurs on January 28 when the Dance of the Voladores is performed. Now there is even a quaint inn, the √★ **Hotel San Carlos** (2 de Abril #26) complete with restaurant, bar, good craft shop, pool, and parking. (Reserve in Mexico City at ☎ 551-3859; $28). Next door to the hotel is **Tlapalcalli Artesanias**, where you can find paintings on San Pablito bark paper as well as other interesting crafts. If you stay the night, you'll have time to visit San Pablito

(1/2 hour in dry season) and look for the Otomi bead work made there as well as observe the papermaking process.

TULANCINGO

About 22 km (14 m) from Acaxochitlan you reenter a more modern world. Although Tulancingo has a Thursday market, we advise you to just stay on MEX 130 because on our last visit the town smelled like the old Secaucus. If you're hungry, wait for the fresh air farther ahead and **La Posta Restaurant** (moderate). From here you leave the Sierra de Puebla. Look for signs to MEX 132 and Mexico City. MEX 132 turns into the toll road MEX 132D near the pyramids of Teotihuacan (63 km, or 39 m, from Tulancingo). If you want to visit the ruins before continuing into Mexico City, consider staying overnight at the hotel near the ruins (see "Teotihuacan").

VILLAHERMOSA

Villahermosa (vee-yah-air-MOH-sah) functions not only as the capital of the state of Tabasco but also as the pulse of Mexico's oil in dustry. Since the 1970s oil boom, Villahermosa has used its wealth to create superb museums and to renovate its downtown into tree-lined pedestrian streets, fronted by brightly painted houses and restored mansions, such as the grandiose **Casa de los Azulejos** (Juarez at 27 de Febrero). A visit is a must just to see the Olmec collection in **Parque La Venta** and the excellent archaeological exhibits at the **Cicom Museum**. However, Villahermosa is hot and, as the transportation hub of the region, often congested. For this reason, many travelers prefer to schedule only a few hours in Villahermosa—landing at the airport and making a quick swing through the two museums before heading for Palenque. But an overnight here gives you a full day of sightseeing at the museums and the ruins of Comalcalco, or of more leisurely enjoying your hotel pool in the heat of the day.

THE ESSENTIAL VILLAHERMOSA

KEY TO VILLAHERMOSA

Sights • Two fine archaeological exhibits—Parque La Venta with its masterpieces of Olmec art in a junglelike setting, and the CICOM Museum with its exceptional collection of both Maya and Olmec art.

Excursions • The famous ruins of Palenque are only two hours away in Chiapas for an easily arranged day excursion, although we recommend staying overnight in Palenque. The less famous ruins of Comalcalco are easily accessible from Villahermosa.

Where to Stay • First-class to moderate hotels recommendable, but demand is high from commercial travelers. Reservations essential. No camping.

Where to Eat • Surprisingly limited.

Getting Around • The two museums are slightly outside of the downtown area, requiring transportation by bus, colectivo, taxi, or car. Most first- class hotels are on the outskirts as well.

Practical Tips • Arrange your car rental for this region in Villahermosa—airport or town.

WHAT TO SEE AND DO

A brief visit would be to drive along the riverfront Malecón to the CICOM Museum and then along the tree-lined Paseo Tabasco to Parque

La Venta before connecting again with MEX 186 east to Palenque for the
night.

Parque La Venta

*Blvd. Ruiz Cortines near Paseo Tabasco. Open daily, 8 a.m.-4:30 p.m.;
Fee.* • Olmec culture represents the initial flowering of civilization in
Mexico (1200-400 B.C.). Yet most sites of this first Mexican civilization lie hidden in the dense jungle surrounding the rivers of Tabasco
and Veracruz, remaining for all practical purposes inaccessible to tourists. La Venta is the exception, even though the road to these ruins
now leads to an oil camp that has destroyed much of the site. To protect the numerous and monumental La Venta sculptures, the Mexican
government transferred most of them from La Venta to this park,
which reproduces the original environment—even to crocodiles, deer,
and an artificial lake. (La Venta was built on an island of the Tonala
River.) Parque La Venta provides a unique opportunity to get as close
as convenience allows to visiting a site of this great and ancient civilization, so close, in fact, that you ought to bring along binoculars for
birdwatching and insect repellent. Painted footprints on the paths
lead you to the monuments, all of which have numbered plaques
keyed to a map available at the tourist kiosk.

La Venta was the second capital of the Olmecs, so the monuments
exhibited in the park date to the period of 900-400 B.C. Continuing
the artistic traditions of the first capital at San Lorenzo, the Olmecs at
La Venta created enormous stone sculptures from basalt hauled from
the mountains at Lake Catemaco 80 air miles away. Without metal
tools, these basalt boulders were carved into colossal heads, tremendous "altars," stelae, and other pieces representing both religious and
historical scenes.

Given the awesome effort required to create their monuments, it
shocks us to realize the Olmec ritually destroyed and buried them.
Archaeologist David Grove believes the monuments associated with a
ruler were destroyed or at least buried after his death to neutralize the
supernatural power associated with him. An even more baffling burial
custom of the Olmecs includes the construction of huge pits in which
were placed precious items—sometimes stylized jaguar mosaic masks
representing an Olmec deity (**Monuments 8** and **23**) and, in one
instance, 50 tons of polished green serpentine blocks. No bones have
been found in these pits (although bones rarely survived the centuries
in this destructive moist environment), so these precious, hidden
goods may have been offerings to the Olmec jaguar deity of the
Underworld. One burial, containing the bones of two juveniles surrounded by jade figurines and beads, was unlike the offering pits; this
burial was placed in a "hut" constructed of basalt columns (**Monument
24**) that was then buried in the platform of a building.

The Olmecs are often called the "Jaguar People" for the strange
beings they created called "were-jaguars," or human babies with jag-

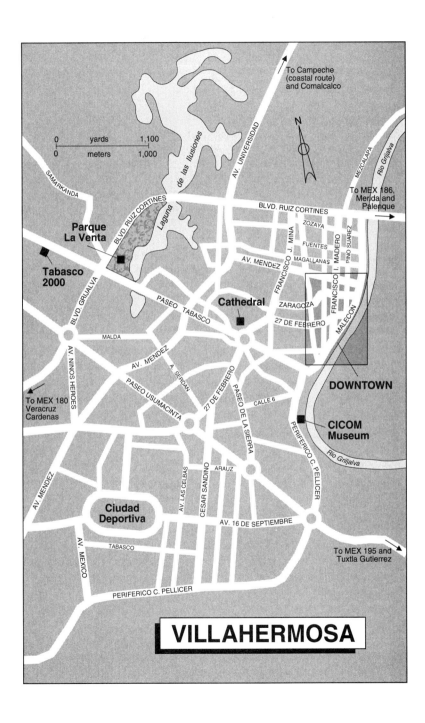

VILLAHERMOSA

uar facial features like a downturned, snarling mouth. These were jaguars symbolized the divine descent of the Olmec ruling class. On **Monument 29**, the ruler, holding a were-jaguar in his arms, emerges from a niche surrounded by symbols of the jaguar god. Although the park calls this monument the "altar of child sacrifice," David Grove believes it served as a throne and demonstrated the divine descent of the ruler and the were-jaguar held in his arms, who is being presented as the heir-apparent.

Not all Olmec art consists of abstract symbolism, for these people also produced some of the most realistic art from all of ancient Mexico. Colossal heads (**Monuments 11**, **25**, and **27**), found at all Olmec sites, are believed to be portraits of rulers. Since the largest head yet discovered is nearly 10 feet high and most of them weigh 20 tons, it is not surprising that these heads never had bodies. Each head wears a distinctive helmet, which may have clues to the ruler's name. **Monuments 10** and **21** remind us of the later Maya stelae tradition of important historical figures with fancy headdress carved on freestanding stones; the Olmec style, however, is less ornate and without hieroglyphic writing (although it often includes were-jaguar babies flying in the background). One stela, **Monument 22**, does have a few hieroglyphs on it—representing one of the earliest examples of writing found in the New World. The three symbols in front of this striding figure probably give his name, and the footprint behind him is used in later times to signify a journey. The less monumental art of the Olmec s—exquisitely polished jades and figurines—can be seen in the collection of the CICOM Museum.

CICOM Museum

Open daily, 9 a.m.-8 p.m.; fee • Located by the wide Grijalva river just west of the Paseo Malecón where it extends to the Periferico C. Pellicer, this anthropology museum is part of a new cultural center called Centro Investigaciones de Culturas Olmeca y Maya (or CICOM), which includes a crafts shop, offices, and Los Tulipanes Restaurant. Spacious and air-conditioned, this museum displays a superb collection of Mayan and Olmec art from the state of Tabasco, along with other pieces representative of all the cultures from ancient Mexico.

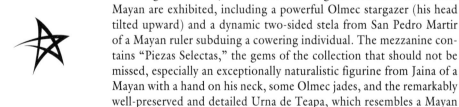

On the ground level, monumental carvings of both the Olmec and Mayan are exhibited, including a powerful Olmec stargazer (his head tilted upward) and a dynamic two-sided stela from San Pedro Martir of a Mayan ruler subduing a cowering individual. The mezzanine contains "Piezas Selectas," the gems of the collection that should not be missed, especially an exceptionally naturalistic figurine from Jaina of a Mayan with a hand on his neck, some Olmec jades, and the remarkably well-preserved and detailed Urna de Teapa, which resembles a Mayan stela executed in ceramic. The first floor (our second) displays mostly smaller Olmec and Mayan pieces, including jades and Jaina figures and some unusual Mayan urns. The second floor (our third) presents an overview of other ancient Mexican cultures with some Mixtec gold pieces, wonderful pre-classic figurines from central Mexico, and a handsome ceramic Nayarit couple. A wheeled Veracruz toy is also on display, showing the ancient Mexicans understood the principles of the wheel though they never used it for practical purposes.

Excursion To Comalcalco

About 60 km (37 m) northwest of Villahermosa and near the town of Comalcalco. Open daily, 9 a.m.-4 p.m.; fee. Refreshments. • The ruins of Comalcalco, once a province of the great Maya city of Palenque, can be visited by turning north off Blvd. Ruiz Cortines onto Av. Universidad and following signs for Comalcalco via Nacajuca. This tropical road, though laden with unannounced *topes*, gives you a sense of the continued presence of the Maya and it passes, after 42 1/2 km (26 m), the fabulous **Cupilco church** with its blue and yellow painted facade accented by flowers and kneeling angels as well as a mural of Guadalupe over the main door. The 1 km access road to the ruins is found 2 km beyond the town of Comalcalco toward Paraiso beach (16 km, 10 m). Buses drop you off within a block of the Paraiso road, where you can walk or taxi to the ruins; or just continue on the Paraiso bus to the access road.

RUINS

During the Late Classic period (A.D. 600-900), the region around Comalcalco experienced a population explosion probably due to the introduction of valuable cacao crops into the area. The area still cultivates these chocolate beans as well as tropical fruits, and Chontal Maya continue to live on the fertile land. The ruins show remarkable similarities to Palenque's architecture and stucco sculpture, even to having a tomb with carvings of the Nine Lords of the Underworld like the famous tomb of Pacal at Palenque. Since Comalcalco had no limestone with which to build its ceremonial buildings, it used fired bricks, the only major Mayan town to do so. Although the bricks were covered with layers of stucco and painted, they were first inscribed and even painted with hieroglyphs and animal designs, some very elaborate, that would never be seen. The **museum** displays some of these bricks, whose designs still baffle archaeologists.

The small, manicured ceremonial area of Comalcalco offers some tantalizing fragments of stucco sculptures. (The easiest way to locate carvings here is to look for the thatched shelters that protect them.) The first of such fragments—a captive held by the hair and presented to Palenque-style figures on a throne—can be seen at **Temple I** (to the left of the footpath as you enter the ruins). The remaining carvings are located in the **Acropolis** (farther along the footpath and to the right). At the base of the acropolis, an enormous mask of the sun god adorns Temple VI, and the elaborate staircase of Temple VII includes figures offering tribute. (The odd upside-down ceramic "column" is a burial urn.) Higher up on the acropolis is a small vaulted tomb with sadly deteriorated carvings of the Nine Lords of the Underworld. This tomb was plundered before archaeologists found it, and the sarcophagus has never been recovered.

WHERE TO STAY

Though several first-class hotels have opened on the outskirts of Villahermosa, commercial travelers keep them full. When we have failed to plan ahead for Villahermosa, we have been forced to stay in inexpensive, totally unacceptable hotels (with not only broken fans but broken toilets as well). To avoid adding such unpleasantness to your trip, reserve in advance by writing Villahermosa, Tabasco or by calling area code 931.

EXPENSIVE

Holiday Inn Tabasco Plaza

Paseo Tabasco 1407; ☎ *6-44-00; $143* • Located just east of Parque La Venta in the massive, starkly modern Tabasco 2000 complex, this large hotel is the best in town. The lobby is attractively tiled, the 270 rooms (a/c) are well-furnished and ample. Restaurant, popular lounge with live music. Shops (next door to mall). A large pool and garden; golf and tennis. Parking. For reservations, call, in the U.S., ☎ 800-465-4329.

MODERATE

Maya Tabasco

Blvd. Ruiz Cortines 907; ☎ *2-15-99; $77* • On the boulevard near Mina, this Mexican commercial hotel has a lively lobby and unusually pleasant service for Villahermosa. The 140 a/c rooms are decently maintained with small baths, and the preferred ones overlook the garden. Good restaurant, bar with entertainment, convenience shops. Large pool. Garage. Write apartado 131, or reserve in the U.S. at ☎ 800-528-1234.

Cencali

Calle Juarez at Paseo Tabasco; ☎ *5-19-96; $80* • This hacienda-style hotel has a tranquil setting overlooking Laguna de las Illusiones near the Parque La Venta. Some of the 120 a/c rooms have lagoon views; all have flagstone floors and wood detailing. Restaurant. Bar with entertainment. Pool. Parking.

INEXPENSIVE

Miraflores

Reforma 304; ☎ *2-00-22; $48* • Centrally located on a traffic-free street, this hotel is modern, immaculate, and plastic with 68 air-conditioned units. Restaurant and bar.

WHERE TO EAT

Club de Pesca (*27 de Febrero near Rayon*; a/c), just on the edge of downtown, is a local favorite for its seafood—and with good reason. Although
plain and neon-lighted, you'll stop noticing the plastic placemats by meal's
end. The offerings from the menu are extensive and very good, but the
daily specials—like the perch, or *mojarra en escabeche*—can be even better.
Whatever you eat will be sensibly priced for the quality and amount and
will be served with the motherly ministrations of the owner (*"Hija,* put
your crabmeat on a cracker!"). Afternoon is best here: open daily till 10
p.m.; moderately expensive. For more refined ambience, enjoy the river-
side location of **Los Tulipanes** (CICOM complex; a/c). The menu includes
steaks as well as decent seafood soups, a grilled whole snapper, and a mixed
salad. Piano music in the evening. Open noon-1 a.m.; expensive (double
check your bill). More for the pleasure of the cruise, consider dining afloat
the Grijalva on the riverboat **Capitain Beulo** (docked behind CICOM;
☎ 2-92-17; moderate). **Leo's** (Paseo Tabasco 429, between CICOM and
La Venta Park) is a Mexican fast-food restaurant, as plastic as such places
can be, yet with food terrific enough to attract great crowds in the evening.
The favorite order here is the beef *brocheta al carbon,* served with all the fix-
ings for making your own tacos. Then again, the *chuleta de cerdo* (pork)
was just as good—as are the hamburgers and french fries. (Inexpensive;
open 12:30 p.m.-1 a.m. except Wednesday.) Downtown there's the popular **Restaurant Madan** (Madero at Reforma), an immaculate, modern restaurant (a/c) with an all purpose menu (*antojitos* to salad, fish to banana
splits) capable of satisfying most appetites. Open 9 a.m.-9 p.m.; inexpensive. For just a snack or sandwich, stop at **La Baguette** (Juarez at 27 de Febrero).

GETTING TO AND FROM VILLAHERMOSA

AIR

Aeromexico and Mexicana connect Villahermosa to Mexico's major cities via Mexico City; Aeromexico also provides direct flights to Mérida. The
regional airline Aerocaribe offers service to Cancún and Huatulco; and
both Aerocaribe and Aviacsa fly to Tuxtla Gutierrez, Oaxaca, and Mérida;
Aerolitoral flies to Veracruz. The airport is 10 km (6 m) outside of town
on MEX 186. Price-controlled taxis are available into town.

CAR & BUS

MEX 180 and MEX 180D west connect this city with Veracruz. MEX
186 east leads past Palenque (and the Ocosingo road to San Cristobal) to
Escarcega and the crossroads to either Chetumal or Campeche and Mérida.
MEX 195 leads south to Tuxtla Gutierrez and San Cristobal de las Casas.
All these routes are well served by first-class ADO buses and deluxe Uno
service to Veracruz and Mérida. The roads around Villahermosa are heavily
traveled by trucks, often resulting in potholes and other conditions making
night travel particularly dangerous. For further information on these

routes, see the cities mentioned, particularly Palenque and San Cristobal de las Casas (in the Chiapas chapter).

DIRECTORY

Airlines • *Aeromexico,* in CICOM (☎ 2-15-28); *Mexicana,* in Tabasco 2000 complex (☎ 3-50-44); *Aerocaribe,* Fco. Javier Mina 901A (☎ 4-30-17); *Aviacsa* (☎ 4-57-70) and *Aerolitoral* (☎ 4-36-14), at airport.

American Express • *Turismo Nieves,* Sarlat 202 (☎ 4-18-18).

Bus Terminal • Central second-class terminal on Blvd. Ruiz Cortines opposite Madero; first-class buses at ADO terminal on Av. Mina 297 with colectivos to center and taxis.

Car Rentals • At airport and in town are a number of agencies, including *Hertz* (☎ 2-11-11) and *Dollar* (☎ 3-44-00 x739).

Post Office • Saenz 131 at Tejado.

Tour Agency • Tourismo Nieves, at Holiday Inn (☎ 6-03-15) and American Express (above), for tours to Comalcalco, Palenque, Yaxchilan, etc.

Tourist Office • Information kiosks in front of Parque La Venta and at the airport.

CHIAPAS

Maya Ruins of Palenque

> *Chiapa… in the opinion of the Spaniards beheld to be one of the poorest countries of America, because in it as yet there have been no mines discovered… if I may say, it exceedeth most provinces in the greatness and beauty of fair towns.*

Thomas Gage, 1648

HISTORY AND CULTURE

Chiapas is a state of overwhelming beauty. The mountains of the Sierra Madre de Chiapas fall off to the Pacific Coast on one side and

to the rift valley of Chiapas (Tuxtla Guticrrcz) on thc othcr, only to
rise again to form the Chiapas Plateau of San Cristobal de las Casas,
dropping off once more to the tropical rain forest of the Usumacinta
River and the magnificent sites of Maya civilization at Palenque,
Bonampak, and Yaxchilan. *Chiapas is a land rich in rivers and lakes,
highlands of pine and oak, and lowlands of wild orchids, exotic birds,
and howler monkeys.* The undulating mountains and dense jungle
form a terrain so rugged that only recently have paved roads penetrated the state, connecting the north with the south. It is not surprising that such a difficult land has been peripheral to history, with
the exception of the classic Maya cities, established as part of an unusual civilization that flowered in a most adverse environment. Because the isolation of Chiapas has protected the traditions of Indian
groups like the Tzotzil Maya in the Chiapas Plateau and the Lacandon Maya in the tropical rain forest, the state is a fascinating area for
observation of Indian customs.

ANCIENT MAYA

For many people, the art of the southern lowland Maya civilization
is the most graceful in the New World. The style reflects the shapes
of the luxuriant tropical environment of the Peten jungle in which it
evolved and, unlike much Yucatecan Maya art, it realistically portrays
the majestic figures of men and women from that civilization. This
great civilization flourished in the Peten jungle of Guatemala and
Belize and reached into Honduras to Copan on the east, and into
Chiapas on the west. During the Classic Maya period of A.D.
250-900, cities were built utilizing the pointed, corbel arch (not a
true arch, but the closest the ancient Mexicans came to this architectural accomplishment). And monuments were erected carved with
hieroglyphic writing and dates in a calendar more exact than the
Julian calendar used in Europe at the time. Most cities of the southern lowlands are not within Mexico's borders, but the ruined cities
in this region—Palenque, Comalcalco, Yaxchilan, Tonina, Chinkultic, and Bonampak—represent the western extension of this civilization. Although Chiapas sites are on the western edge of the Peten
civilization, they were in no way provincial. Studies by archaeologist
Joyce Marcus indicate that during the Late Classic period Palenque
and Yaxchilan may have been regional capitals of southern Maya
lowland civilization, sharing that distinction with only a few other
cities, such as Tikal in Guatemala and Copan in Honduras. The potential importance of the western sites for trade between the Gulf
Coast cultures and the Peten jungle and Guatemala highlands, via

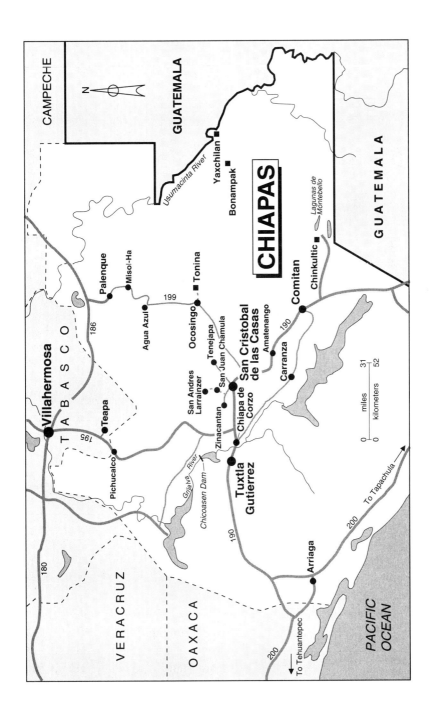

the Usumacinta and other navigable rivers, may account for their rapid growth and power during the 7th and 8th centuries. These Maya cities were no mere commercial centers, however. The cities, and the ceremonies performed there, had cosmic significance for the Maya. According to some archaeologists, *the pyramids symbolized sacred mountains that communicated with all layers of the cosmos, from the dreaded lords in the underworld to the beneficent deities in the heavens.* In the temples atop these pyramids and in the plazas before them, rituals were performed for the gods so that the life cycle could continue. Even the ball courts were part of the cosmology, permitting the reenactment of the creation of the earthly world by the Hero Twins, who in the *Popol Vuh*, the sacred book of the Maya, defeated the gods of the underworld in a ball game before being born as the sun and moon.

DECIPHERING MAYA WRITING

The importance of these Chiapas cities in ancient times is certainly no greater than their modern importance to archaeologists in their task of deciphering Maya writing. Carvings at both Yaxchilan and Palenque include extensive hieroglyphic texts that have enabled archaeologists to make enormous progress in translation. Their interpretation, by Tatiana Proskouriakoff at Yaxchilan and by Heinrich Berlin and others at Palenque, has led to a revolution in thinking about the ancient Maya. Before Proskouriakoff's work in the sixties, the only translatable hieroglyphs were calendrical, and the Maya were thought to have been ruled by a priestly class obsessed with the computation of time. Now it is known that these carvings represent rulers and other nobles, and that the texts tell us of their births, ancestry, accessions to power, conquests, and deaths. The texts tell us, too, of painful bloodletting rites that enabled the rulers, in their resultant hallucinatory state, to communicate directly with the gods. Now instead of nameless priests recording lunar events, we begin to understand the ancient Maya. Lord Pacal of Palenque and Lord Shield Jaguar of Yaxchilan are being rediscovered after more than a thousand years of mystery surrounding the Maya past.

Despite exciting progress in Maya studies, there are limits to how much the hieroglyphic texts on stone monuments can tell about any civilization. They do not tell us about daily life, what people ate, or whom they traded with. Apart from omitting much, the texts were official statements by the rulers and could be misleading (Pacal's texts indicate he lived to be 80, but analysis of his skeleton indicates he may have lived no more than 50 years). To date, these texts have not clarified the reasons for the collapse of this great civilization—certainly not a topic for rulers to boast about. According to one theory of the collapse (see the chapter on Yucatán), traders from the Gulf Coast, who had been middlemen between central Mexico and the Maya, took control for themselves. This becomes more credible with evidence that the collapse began closest to the Gulf Coast, for Palenque was the earliest city to fall (A.D. 800), and Yaxchilan fell soon after (A.D. 810). At Palenque, signs of terraced fortifications and of walled-up entrances indicate the city might have been in a state of seige. Tonina, further inland, didn't collapse until later—in fact, one monument is dated A.D. 909 in the Maya long count. Around this time, carvings of foreigners began to appear farther upstream on the Pasion River in Guatemala. No trace of great civilization appears again in the region until colonial times.

COLONIAL PERIOD

Spanish settlers with land grants in Chiapas preferred to live outside the area in more commodious towns. Indians failed to send tribute, however, and a special expedition was sent into the area of the rift valley and highland plateau. Although the victorious troops were instructed by Cortes to settle the area, once again they were eager to leave, necessitating yet another tribute-collecting expedition in 1527 under Mazariegos. Mazariegos founded the town now known as San Cristobal de las Casas. The southern part of Chiapas then, much as today, was not central to the political and social life of either Mexico or Guatemala, but in 1542 it was made a province of Guatemala.

The best-known figure in Chiapas' colonial history is the Bishop Bartolome de las Casas, who is commemorated in the name of the town of San Cristobal de las Casas where he became bishop in 1544. Las Casas, along with Vasco de Quiroga, was one of the few energetic protectors of Indians against the exploitative economic policies of colonialization. Although the absence of silver and gold mines in Chiapas may have accounted for the slow settlement of the area by the Spaniards, Las Casas' "interfering" policies may have contributed as well. Nearly a century later, Thomas Gage states there were no more than 400 Spaniards in the town, and the few churches were "mean."

The Dominican friars under Las Casas, finding little support in the town, went to the villages to convert Indians. Although their efforts resulted in some churches being built, many showing stylistic influence from nearby Guatemala, they failed to change the dispersed settlement patterns of the Indians, which continues even today.

MODERN CHIAPAS

During the Mexican Independence Movement, Chiapas declared itself independent of Spanish Guatemala and attached itself to Mexico. Because the town of San Cristobal was resistant to independence, it was punished in 1890 by being removed as the capital of the state, and indeed Tuxtla Gutierrez, the new capital, has proved to be a better location for development in the state. The rich coffee fincas on the mountain slopes, the cattle ranches and sugar cane haciendas on the coast, and the mahogany and gum of the jungle have made Chiapas important to the Mexican economy. Although the Spaniards were disappointed by their failure to discover silver and gold mines, the 20th century is delighted by the discovery of oil. This isolated and beautiful part of Mexico may soon be transformed by that discovery.

CONTEMPORARY INDIAN LIFE

The Maya have not vanished. They still populate the villages in Chiapas where they continue their ancient beliefs and practices, some with a touch of Spanish influence. A visit to Chamula or Zinacantan will bring you to Tzotzil-speaking Mayas who represent one of the largest Maya groups in the highlands. A visit to Palenque (or for the adventurous, a journey into the Lacandon tropical rain forest) may, if you are fortunate, be the opportunity to see some of the few remaining Lacandon Indians, a Maya group who come to Palenque to buy transistor radios and to sell a variety of hand-carved arrows in return.

THE CHAMULAS AND ZINACANTECOS

The remote ancestors of the Chamulas and Zinacantecos may have been part of the classic Maya civilization that flourished at Chinkultic or Yaxchilan. Later, they moved to the highlands, perhaps seeking safety after the collapse of the classic-period civilization. Today most live in hamlets surrounding their ceremonial centers of Chamula and Zinacantan, visiting these centers only on special occasions—for a religious ceremony, a market, or a dispute settlement. The centers have small permanent populations, but like the hamlets, are overwhelmingly Indian.

The customs of contemporary Chamulas and Zinacantecos provide anthropologists with data for speculation about the ancient Maya.

Perhaps the ancient sites like Bonampak and Yaxchilan, populated by their rulers and nobles, also served as centers for surrounding hamlets as do Chamula and Zinacantan. In Chamula one definite ancient practice continues—the use of a calendar that records a solar year with divisions from the ancient calendar—18 months of 20 days plus a 5-day special period. Used by the ordinary Chamula to date religious festivals and to schedule important agricultural activities, this calendar has survived for some 2500 years. This may not surprise you if you visit Chamula and see the power of tradition and the continued presence of ancient Maya religious concepts. The sun, one of the main deities in the past, is still the primary god for the Chamulas. Spanish influence is not entirely absent, as the sun god is identified with Christ.

THE CARGO SYSTEM

The cargo system—a very prestigious, religious hierarchy in charge of performing numerous and complex religious ceremonies in the centers—dominates life in the two villages. The one-year rotating cargo positions are treasured, yet costly. The cargos must leave work in their hamlets, move to the ceremonial center, and pay for the frequent ceremonies. For this reason, holding a cargo is viewed as bearing a burden for a year—an idea probably derived from the ancient Maya concept of year-bearer gods, divinities who carried the weighty divisions of time on their backs to insure its passage.

As you travel through this area you find the landscape dotted with apparent signs of Catholicism—churches and crosses abound. Crosses appear everywhere—on top of churches, outside homes, at the foot and the top of mountains, along quiet mountain trails, next to waterholes, and in caves. Your initial reaction may be that Catholicism has penetrated deeply into this remote Maya area. Yet the crosses are misleading.

CROSSES

In Zinacantan, crosses at the foot and top of mountains mark the homes of the ancestral gods. These are sacred mountains for the Zinacantecos just as the temple-pyramids were to their ancestors. Ancestral gods are the most important in their universe, just as they may have been for the ancient Maya. These gods are portrayed as elderly Zinacantecos who have lived in the mountains since far in the distant past. The crosses are viewed as "doorways" to the gods, places to bring offerings of black chickens, candles, incense, and rum. On occasion, you may find small pine trees tied to the crosses—the sign of a recent ceremony.

Nor are the crosses next to waterholes and inside caves Christian crosses. Rather they mark the second most important god, the Earth Owner who, according to anthropologist Evon Z. Vogt, "is pictured as a large, fat, Ladino (mestizo) living under the ground with piles of money, and with herds of cows, mules, horses, and flocks of chickens." Since this big, fat mestizo god owns all of the waterholes and products of the earth, and controls the clouds that emerge from the caves to produce rain for crops, the Zinacantecos must compensate him for the use of his land. This they do through offerings of liquor and candles at the waterholes and cross shrines at caves.

ANCESTRAL GODS

Beliefs about the soul serve to integrate the Zinacantecos with their environment, explain illness and death, and aid in social control. At birth, the ancestral gods place a soul in the infant and place the same soul in a wild animal cared for by the gods in a supernatural corral. An illness may be caused by angry ancestral gods inflicting punishment on a wayward Zinacanteco. The punishment may result in soul loss—one or more of the 13 parts of the soul will be removed from the sick person, or in serious cases, the animal companion will be released from its corral and allowed to roam helplessly in the forest. The pain and suffering of the animal will be felt by the Zinacanteco who shares its soul. The anger of the ancestral gods is aroused by violations of appropriate standards of conduct: fighting with kinsmen, not properly caring for maize fields, not washing regularly, or not helping pay for fiestas. Excessive wealth not shared with the community by the acceptance of a cargo may very well arouse the gods' anger. If so, the wealthy Zinacanteco will soon find himself paying for elaborate curing ceremonies that relieve him of both his illness and his wealth.

DEATH OF THE BODY

Death results from soul loss—the loss, this time, of all 13 parts. Next to the body of the deceased the Zinacantecos place charred tortillas. On its journey after the death of the body, the soul crosses a river on the back of a black dog, and the tortillas compensate the dog for his work. This vision of a dog carrying the deceased across a body of water was widely held throughout ancient Mesoamerica. In the Mayan area, excavations of ancient tombs have yielded skeletons of dogs apparently sacrificed for the journey. And depictions of dogs, perhaps these sacrificial ones, are found on some ancient Mayan bowls. Spanish reports about the burial practices of Indian lords in central Mexico at the time of the Conquest mention that a dog was cremated along with the lord in order to carry the ruler across a terrifying river on his journey through the Underworld in his afterlife. The modern Maya have retained this ancient belief but have kindly substituted offerings of tortillas for offerings of dogs.

The ancient Mayan belief in the Four-Corner gods persists in Zinacantan. These gods are still viewed as carrying our cubical world on their shoulders—an exhausting job even for a god. When one of the gods tires and shifts the weight from one shoulder to the other, an earthquake occurs. The earthquake subsides and quiet returns as soon as the weight is secured firmly on the other shoulder.

Catholic influence manifests itself in the association of the Sun with Christ and the Moon with the Virgin Mary and in the worshiping of numerous saints. The saints, like the ancestral gods, both expect and receive offerings, and they are objects of intense devotion. This reverence for some of the symbols of Catholicism does not appear to be transferred to priests—or, at least, not in Chamula. If you have the good fortune to visit the church in Chamula, you will see a highly charged scene suggestive of a religious marketplace— lighted candles, burning incense, intense chanting, and kneeling figures before images of saints. What is missing is a priest. Evon Z. Vogt explains this absence in his account of the attempt in 1968 by the Bishop of San Cristobal to build a Catholic chapel in a hamlet of Chamula.

> *The Chamula oligarchy mustered several hundred armed Chamulas to stop the construction. Furthermore, the resident Catholic priest in Chamula Center was warned in no uncertain terms by the Chamula leaders to stay at the Church of San Juan in the Center and not even to visit the hamlets. When he later tried to intervene against the performance of some of the traditional Chamula ceremonies inside the Church, he was evicted from Chamula entirely and now returns only to say Mass and perform baptisms.*

Thus, this area remains very much Maya.

THE LACANDON

Living amid the tropical rain forest in the Usumacinta drainage, men as well as women wearing shoulder-length, unkempt hair, their bodies covered by long white tunics, the Lacandon appear as people from another age and world. Until recently, they were the most unassimilated of the existing Mayan people, the most removed from the trappings of modern civilization. Their features are classically Mayan; their photographs often are placed next to those of rulers on Maya stela from Yaxchilan to show the remarkable similarity in appearance between the ancient and modern Maya. The Lacandon population, almost faced with extinction several years ago, is now on the rise, numbering about four hundred. This resurgence is fortunate for all of us for, according to Lacandon legend, when the last Lacandon dies, no one will remain with knowledge of the proper rituals to be performed in honor of the sun, moon, and other gods. As a result, all deities will fall to earth, causing an enormous earthquake that will destroy the world.

Despite numerous studies of the Lacandon, their ancestry remains clouded. Present-day Yucatec-speaking Lacandons most likely are descendants of Maya who moved late into Chiapas from the area around northern Guatemala and Campeche in the 17th and 18th centuries. Despite attempts by priests from the 17th through 19th centuries to convert them, the Lacandon remained far removed from Christianity—not even the veneer surrounded their lives. More recently, however, with the influx of cattle ranchers and farmers into the once isolated rain forest, missionaries have had greater success in obtaining Lacandon converts. Still, many Lacandons live primarily by farming, hunting, and fishing, and they are polygamous (necessitated today no doubt by their small numbers). They have survived extinction despite the diseases brought by the Spanish in the colonial period and more recent diseases contracted from mestizo lumbermen and crocodile hunters, as well as from ranchers and farmers who have penetrated into their homeland and decimated their environment.

As the tragedy unfolds and the rain forest becomes increasingly destroyed by outsiders, who bring with them the temptations of modern civilization, the contemporary Lacandon are in a delicate period of transition. On shopping trips to the town of Palenque, they present a startling and incongruous image—carrying hand-carved arrows for sale as they wander into local music stores to buy records and tapes. Later they may settle down in a local restaurant for a few beers, several cigarettes, and plenty of hearty laughs. Even the local Palencanos stop to stare.

TWO GEOGRAPHICAL GROUPS

The Lacandon presently are divided into two geographical groups—northern (Naja and Mensabak) and southern (Lacanja)—with slight differences in hairstyle and dress, but significant differences in religion. In the middle of this century, American missionaries succeeded in converting the southern Lacandon, who traded their Mayan gods and chants for Baptist hymns. Although some northern Lacandons have converted as well, those living in Naja continue to supplicate the Maya gods with offerings of balche, the drink made from tree bark and fermented sugar-cane juice, and tamales made from monkey meat. The men still carve dugout canoes from cedar or mahogany. And men, women, and children smoke large cigars, a practice rooted in antiquity. Tobacco undoubtedly played an important role in ancient Mayan life, since the Maya portrayed cigar-smoking gods and rulers on their carved stelae, frescoes, bowls, and in codices. The Spanish reported that they found the Lacandon making offerings of tobacco to their gods—a practice that the early 20th-century explorers of the area also encountered.

Some Lacandon today are still tied to ancient Mayan sites. The major "rediscovery" in 1946 of the spectacular Bonampak mural paintings was made possible by Jose Pepe Chan Bol, a Lacandon who led the photographer Giles B. Healey to the hidden site. Yaxchilan continues to be revered and, until recently, was the site of pilgrimages, for it is believed to be the home of the principal Lacandon gods, including the most important god, Hachakyum, who created the world and its first people from clay with teeth of corn. The sun god, too, is still worshiped. At sunset he descends into the Underworld where, carried on the shoulders of Hachakyum's older brother, he traverses the Underworld to rise again. Other natural phenomena have equally intriguing explanations. Wind occurs when a god waves the tail feather of a macaw, and lightning flashes when he strikes this feather against the edge of an axe. The Underworld is ruled by a rather nasty god, Cizin, who when angered shakes the poles of his house, causing earthquakes. Upon death, Lacandons are buried with their heads facing the sun. Usually included in a burial is a bone for the dog that will help the deceased cross a body of water to pass into the Underworld, where he or she remains until ready to move to the heaven of Hachakyum.

SAN CRISTOBAL DE LAS CASAS

Las Casas is charming but subdued, fascinating but aloof. Isolated since its abandonment as the state capital in 1890, Las Casas has preserved its simple colonial architecture and town plan with low buildings painted in soft pastels winding up hills with cobblestone streets. Pine-forested mountains dominate every view, bringing quiet to the valley. The chill from the altitude of this highland town completes the feeling of solitude.

The color and fascination of Las Casas is provided by the Maya Indians. Attracted by the market, Indians arrive from the mountain villages of San Juan Chamula, Zinacantan, and Tenejapa dressed in traditional costumes and displaying an independence from modern culture seldom encountered in increasingly industrialized Mexico. Their traditions are often startlingly old (the high-backed sandals worn by some of the men during fiestas duplicate those worn by the nobles depicted on ancient Maya sculptures at Palenque). Each village has its distinctive costume: Zinacantan is proclaimed by handsome men dressed in pink serapes; Chamula men are identified by their thick wool serapes; and Tenejapa is known for women in rich red brocaded *huipils* (blouses). This parade entices tourists to leave mestizo San Cristobal and follow the Maya home to their nearby villages. These brief excursions, especially during fiestas, are opportunities to observe social and religious traditions preserved from pre-Conquest times.

KEY TO SAN CRISTOBAL DE LAS CASAS

Sights • Las Casas is primarily atmospheric, with Maya Indians from surrounding villages providing most of its interest. For the amateur anthropologist, this is the best place in Mexico; for others, the spectacular scenery and local color are enough.

Shopping • Fine weavings and brocades as well as leather goods, amber and silver jewelry made in this region are sold in shops in the center of town.

Markets • Sunday in Chamula (on Friday during Lent) and Tenejapa. Every day but Sunday in Las Casas.

Sports • Excellent area for horseback riding and hiking.

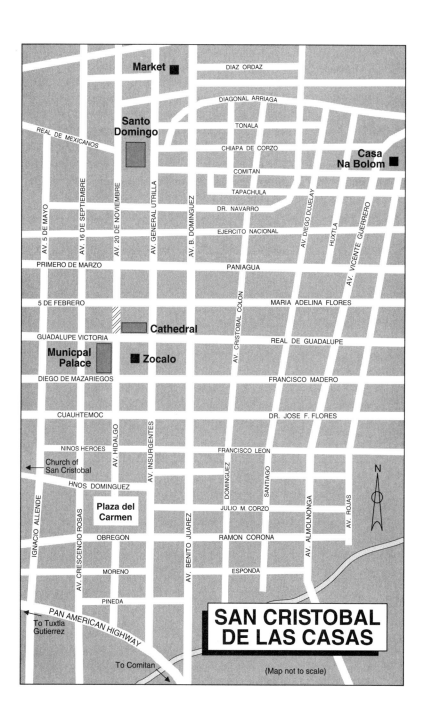

SAN CRISTOBAL
DE LAS CASAS

(Map not to scale)

Excursions • Maya villages and the National Park of Montebello Lakes and Lacandon Forest. Tonina and Chinkultic ruins in the vicinity; chartered flights go to Yaxchilan and Bonampak.

Fiestas • Exceptional fiestas occur in the region on January 20-22; Carnival and Holy Week; June 22-24; July 24-25; August 9-10; and December 30-January 1.

Where to Stay • No deluxe, but many comfortable, hotels at bargain prices. At fiesta time, reserve in advance.

Where to Eat • Restaurants basically cater to tourists, but the prices are good.

Entertainment • Best spent in front of a fireplace, enjoying your tranquillity, yet traditional music and jazz plentiful.

Getting Around • Las Casas is small and best explored on foot, though colectivos run from zócalo to market on Utrilla. For excursions, tours, taxis, and collective vans are available. Only one car rental agency in town. The main streets of Diego Mazariegos and Insurgentes divide the town at the zócalo, with smaller streets changing their names either side of them.

Practical Tips • It can be surprisingly cold. An extra sweater may prove critical to your enjoyment of this highland area. During the rainy season (June-October) and the frost season (December-January), you might prefer a room with fireplace. Offices and shops close between 2 and 4 p.m. Note: The altitude here is over 7000 feet.

Currency exchange can be difficult. Come with pesos or be prepared for long bank lines or poorer rates at the *cambios*.

WHAT TO SEE AND DO

Las Casas is a place to sleep late snuggled under many blankets, to take long, exhilarating walks or horseback rides to surrounding villages, and to observe the local Indian life at a respectful distance. A walk within town can be as aimless as you like, since it is the atmosphere of Las Casas that is so absorbing; but if you wish to walk with purpose, here are a few places to visit.

Zócalo

Plaza 31 de Marzo • The main square is a shady spot for a shoeshine or a refresco next to the kiosk. On Sunday evening everyone gathers here to be seen and to sip the traditional hot fruit punch bought from vendors by the cathedral. A number of 16th-century buildings surround the zócalo. On Calle Diego Mazariegos sits the former residence (now the Hotel Santa Clara) of Mazariegos, the founder of the town. On a corner of his house is a sculpture of a mermaid, much worn; turning the corner on Insurgentes you see a stone portal carved with silly columns surmounted by even sillier lions. On the opposite side of the zócalo is the **Cathedral,** with its baroque altarpiece of San Jose (at the head of the south aisle) and handsomely carved 16th-century wooden ceiling.

Church of Santo Domingo

Follow 20 de Noviembre from the zócalo • The intricately carved baroque facade of Santo Domingo displays influences from Antigua, Guatemala, which was the cultural capital of Chiapas during the colonial period. The church, established in 1528, was refurbished in the 17th and 18th centuries. The walls of the interior are covered with carved and gilded wood paneling; the pulpit in particular shows native exuberance with foliate patterns. The gilded decorations everywhere belie Thomas Gage's 1648 description of Las Casas as:

One of the meanest cities in all America...the Jesuits having got no footing there (who commonly live in the richest and wealthiest places and cities) is a sufficient argument of either the poverty of that city, or of want of gallant spirits and prodigality of the gentry.

Casa Na Bolom

Calle Vincente Guerrero 31, left off Real Guadalupe Museum and house tour daily at 4:30 p.m.; fee; Library open Tues.-Sat. 9 a.m.-1 p.m. • Once this was the home of Frans Blom, explorer and archaeologist. His widow Gertrude Duby, a photographer and anthropologist famous for her work on Lacandon culture and environment, still resides in Na Bolom providing spiritual and daily sustenance to those interested in the area. The tour includes the library, with Blom's memorabilia and an excellent collection of books on Mexican archaeology and ethnology. The museum displays a few finely engraved bowls and molded figurines from an excavation of the Classic Maya site of Moxviguil in the valley of San Cristobal. After the tour, you can opt to see a film on Sra. Blom's work in the Lacandon rain forest.

Church of San Cristobal

This yellow-trimmed white church is on a hilltop overlooking the town. A vigorous climb is rewarded by wonderful views of the small valley and town. Walk down Insurgentes to Calle Hnos. Dominguez, then persevere until you encounter an overwhelming number of steps climbing to the church.

THE MARKET AND SHOPPING

The **market** *(Av. Gen. Utrilla, 8 blocks north of the zócalo)* takes place every morning except Sunday. Once this market's walls were formed only by surrounding mountains; now a jumble of "supermarkets" and other structures scar that landscape. Although you will find nothing special to buy unless you are looking for produce or the delicious peanuts of this region, the market remains the best place to observe Maya from the surrounding villages.

For buying **regional crafts**—particularly the beautiful embroidery and brocades from Tenejapa and Larrainzar—visit **San Jolobil,** an Indian cooperative store selling the best-quality weavings in town, some of which are museum caliber. San Jolobil is located in the Convent of Santo Domingo on the side facing 20 de Noviembre (open daily, 9 a.m.-2 p.m. and 4-6 p.m.). In the plaza surrounding Santo Domingo, Maya women make and sell wool serapes, loosely woven belts, ceramic animals from Amatenango, and other odds and ends. Across 20 de Noviembre, the tiny shop **Ambar** sells amber jewelry. On nearby **Utrilla**, shops sell Guatemalan bags and San Cristobal leather belts. In addition to the Santo Domingo area, every shopper should head for the **Calle Real de Guadalupe**. One of the first stops on this street is the **Plaza de la Calle Real** (#5), a colonial "minimall" with "upscale boutiques" like **Citlali** (amber and silver jewelry). Continuing up the street, you can find almost anything, from bolts of Guatemalan tie-dyed textiles (#15), leather bags (#19), past the funky little shops with Lacandon pottery and Tenejapa wood sculpture, all the way up to #74 where **Tzontehuitz** has its looms and larger shop. Many other shops are scattered throughout town: **Casa de las Artesanias** (Ninos Heroes at Hidalgo) often has unusual pieces such as wood carved bowls and, managed by DIF, its proceeds go to charity.

HORSEBACK RIDING AND HIKING

There are many small villages for the intrepid tourist to visit, often as easily on horseback as otherwise. Popular riding trips include Chamula and Zinacantan as well as the pine forest around the caves called **Grutas San Cristobal** (10 km, 6 m south). Arrangements for horse rentals and guides can be made one day in advance at Casa Margarita, Real de Guadalupe 34, or at tour agencies. There are many lovely walks, from treks around the Lagunas Montebella (sponsored by Viajes Pakal), a hike over the mountain from Chamula to Zinacantan (Mercedes often includes this in her tour of the villages), to the 2-km nature trail of the **Huitepec Reserve** (Chamula Road 3.5 km; Tues.-Sun. 9 a.m.-5 p.m.; fee), an effort at education and forest conservation by Pro-nature Chiapas—sad to say, we saw poachers in the act of depleting the birdlife here.

EXCURSIONS

San Juan Chamula and Zinacantan

As you leave Las Casas on G. Victoria, follow signs for Chamula. After 8 km, the road forks, the left leading to Zinacantan, the right to Chamula. • A trip to these villages, only 10 km (6 m) from town, is a journey through areas sacred to the Zinacantecos and Chamulas. Triple crosses mark the spiritual entrances to these places, be they hills where the ancestral gods live or caves where the earth god creates clouds and sends them into the sky. (Sometimes when the clouds are so thick and so settled into the valleys, you can easily be convinced.) The crosses provide a veneer of Catholicism to beliefs that may be older than

Christianity. The daily life of these Maya is governed by rituals expressing their beliefs about the order of the universe and their relation with the supernatural. An outsider's visit to these tightly knit social and religious communities will be tolerated, but within limits.

PRACTICAL TIP

Ask for permission to enter churches; a small fee is required. Do not take photographs.

Collective vans now provide an indispensable alternative to the human cattle trucks formerly the only choice for public transportation to these villages. Both types of vehicles leave from the market area on Av. Utrillo. They are often crowded, and on Sundays do not seem to run at all. Since Sunday is market day in Chamula, you might want to arrange alternative transportation, a horse or taxi. We hired a taxi to Chamula and walked the six miles back to town along a well-worn path through hamlets and fields, passing girls spinning wool and watching sheep. It was a walk backward in time, so much more distant than six miles. Only our tired legs were pleased to return to the "bustle" of San Cristobal.

ZINACANTAN

The magnificent ride to Zinacantan goes through forested mountains, apple and peach orchards, and fertile fields of corn. The town, being the ceremonial center of the Zinacantecos rather than a true village, is quiet and usually nearly abandoned except for the guardians of the saints housed in the three chapels. Zinacantan is so quiet that the click of a camera echoes through the town's center, stopping the few people present dead in their tracks. Although the church (fee) has a more traditional Catholic veneer than Chamula's, the saints are dressed like Zinacantecos and the altar is delightfully adorned with Mexican candelabras. On Sundays, the mayordomos perform rituals in the chapel of Esquipulas (on right of plaza) but indigenous traditions overwhelm the main church only on major feast days and Holy Week. Unless it's a religious holiday, there's not much to see. You can contemplate this center of the Zinacanteco universe, feeling the presence of the ancestral gods from the mountains enclosing the town, and reflect upon the people whose lives are so integrated with their beautiful surroundings.

SAN JUAN CHAMULA

The political and ceremonial center of Chamula is defined by the church, municipal buildings, a few thatched huts, and the foothills of the Sierra Madres. Triple crosses mark its sacred places. The blue sky is its roof; the earth its pavement. Only the church disrupts nature's colors, proclaiming its importance by a facade of chalk-white festively adorned with painted designs. Inside shamans chant and burn candles while performing their curing rites with chickens, eggs, the traditional sugar cane liquor called "posh," and Coca Cola—a recent addition.

It's only when tour buses by the dozens arrive for festival or market days that much of this serenity is lost. Although the Chamulas gain by their sale of crafts and curios, the hustle brought by so much tourism can be an unpleasant surprise.

Sunday market is an opportunity for the Chamulas to visit the ceremonial center, not only to shop for subsistence goods, but to pray, to have disputes resolved by the Chamulan authorities, to acknowledge their resolution in the ritual drinking of posh, and, simply, to socialize. By eight in the morning, the church is lighted by candles, strewn with pine needles and boughs, and filled with incense and chanting. No priest presides. (Years ago we witnessed a couple who daringly entered the church—only to be carried bodily out the door by the Chamulas. Today you can enter *after* buying tickets at the Municipio across the street.) Civic officials stride importantly through the square with their staffs of office and incredible red tassels hanging from their hats. By nine o'clock, the officials are settled on their bench in front of the municipal building, hearing complaints and dispensing justice. Music blares through a loudspeaker system. The day is in full swing.

Ocosingo and Tonina Ruins

On MEX 190 and MEX 199 for 113 km (70 m) • The classic period Maya ruins at Tonina lie outside the town of Ocosingo on a dirt road that may be impassable during the rainy season. The road to Ocosingo (MEX 199) is occasionally repaved, then tropical downpours melt it away. But the road, even when rough, is scenic and passes small Mayan villages such as Abasolo and Oxchuc where the ruffled and beribboned blouses and the brightly striped *huipils* of the women flash against the verdant landscape.

If you are traveling to Palenque along this route, you might want to save the ruins till then. But you'll have a long day—and an impossible one if you plan to stop at Agua Azul, too. However, you can stay overnight in Ocosingo. Second-class buses (Autobuses Tuxtla) ply the road to Ocosingo; once there, you have to make costly arrangements for a taxi to and from the ruins.

OCOSINGO

12 km (7 m) south on Pan American Highway, then 87 km (54 m) on MEX 199 to left • Ocosingo has a shady zócalo and about six streets, some paved. The only real town along this road between San Cristobal and Palenque, most visitors are here to catch a bus or to eat. Given its isolated location, Ocosingo serves these functions well. A few restaurants surround the zócalo, but **La Montura** has some outdoor tables, a good breakfast, and a staff that also runs the **Hotel Central** (at the same location of Av. Central 1; ☎ (967) 300-24; $25). The hotel's rooms are basic, with ceiling fans.

TONINA RUINS

15 km (9 m) east of MEX 199; from Las Casas, turn at ruins sign just after the Pemex, but before the turn into Ocosingo; continue on well-marked, hard-packed dirt road for 1/2 hour. From the Ocosingo market, Guadalupe buses (every 2 hours) drop you 1 km from Tonina. After entering the site, continue 2 km to the museum shed. (Open 9 a.m.-4 p.m.; fee.) • Tonina's history spanned the centuries from A.D. 400-900, and judging from the number of mutilated monuments and carvings of captives found here, many of those years involved considerable turmoil. One

instance of warfare was uncovered by archaeologist Peter Mathews who deciphered the hieroglyphs on a panel, magnificently carved in the style of Palenque, only to discover that the bound captive shown was Kan-Xul, ruler of Palenque and builder of its famous tower. Although the Kan-Xul panel now is in the Tuxtla Gutierrez regional museum, a discovery here in 1991 of a fantastic stucco facade of life-size skeletons and mythic animals dancing around a decapitated head may indicate Kan-Xul's fate. In the **museum shed** are carvings from the site, some in Palenque style, others in Tonina's distinctive style, which includes stelae carved in the round, much like statuary.

The site, found over a stream and up a hill, is mostly covered with vegetation, despite the clearing of the rain forest here for a cattle ranch. But as you approach the site, the vast acropolis is exposed to your right, terraced into the hillside. At its foot you can find numerous carvings, including four round ball court markers and fragments of their accompanying stelae. From the area of the ball court, climb up the acropolis and you'll come to the **Quetzalcoatl Complex,** named for a throne with some stucco suggestive of serpent motifs. In the rooms about the throne are other stucco fragments, some retaining their original color. After working your way through this complex, you find a path at the top leading to the left and the **Plaza del Gobernador.** Here is a tomb of the "governor" with a stone sarcophagus and two stucco masks.

Comitan and Lagunas Montebello

Pan American Highway south for 140 km (87 m) • The multicolored lakes of Montebello are considered beautiful by some who believe they are worth the long drive to see them. However, you might want to delay your visit as Guatemalan refugee camps are located near the lakes and nearby is a sensitive part of the Guatemalan border. Roads are well paved, with the exception of some unpaved but serviceable roads around the lakes. Along the way, one can stop at the pottery-making village of **Amatenango** (37 km from San Cristobal), or take a brief excursion to the ruins of Chinkultic.

It is best to return to San Cristobal for the evening (although accommodations are available in Comitan), or include this excursion on the way to Guatemala. If you are traveling by bus, you have a choice between first-class (Cristobal Colon) and second-class (Autobuses

Tuxtla) scrvicc to Comitan. From Comitan, colectivos make several round trips daily to the lakes (Linea Comitan), but you may have difficulty visiting the more attractive lakes without a car or tour.

COMITAN

Approximately 87 km (54 m) from San Cristobal • A small town, but the major producer of sugar cane liquor (comitecho) for the region. Comitan is most important for its gas station, restaurants, and hotels. **Restaurant Nevelandia** (on a corner of the zócalo) is clean with decent food (inexpensive). In case you are detained, the best hotel is the ★ **Lagos de Montebello** (☎ (963)2-10-92; $28), on the highway. It has a dining room.

LAGUNAS MONTEBELLO AND LACANDON FOREST

About 15 km (9 m) south of Comitan at La Trinitaria, turn left onto a paved road and after continuing 36 km (22 m), you arrive at the entrance of this National Park. • There are 16 lakes of varying hues—emerald green, pale blue, deep violet—in the beautiful Lacandon Forest. But unless you have time to explore and hike this area you might be disappointed. The easiest visit is along the main, paved road (3 km) that passes the Laguna de Colores and ends at Laguna Bosque Azul along with all the buses and colectivos. Here, there is a map of the lakes, picnic tables, and swimming. The other lakes, quieter and more difficult to reach without a car or tour, are scattered off a 15 km (9 m) dirt road (often impassable in rainy season) that runs to the right near the entrance gate. Perhaps the easiest way to see all the lakes, if not to enjoy the forest, is to fly over them on one of the Yaxchilan tours leaving from San Cristobal.

CHINKULTIC

Off the road leading to the park entrance, 30 km from the Trinitaria turn-off, a dirt road on the left cuts through a hacienda for 1 km before arriving at the ruins. Open daily, 8 a.m.-5 p.m.; fee for parking. • Another way to get an aerial view of some of the lakes (as well as the encroaching farms that destroy the rain forest) is to visit the **acropolis** at the Maya ruins here (a 15-minute walk along a path found at the far end of the parking lot, left over a "bridge," then a steep climb up a dirt path that even sturdy shoes won't climb during the rainy season). On the platform of the acropolis there's a broken stela representing a ruler wearing a jaguar belt. Although this late classic site is only partially excavated, there are numerous carvings to be seen strewn near the **ball court.** (Return across parking lot to the guard's gate, turn right onto a path and walk for 7 minutes.) The stelae along the path, and just beyond the ball court, are eroded, but worth a look for their death heads and other symbols associated with sacrifice, including a decapitated ball player.

OTHER EXCURSIONS

Although collective vans and buses leave the market for early morning excursions to other Maya villages—among them **Tenejapa** *(27 km, 15 m to the northeast)* and **San Andres Larrainzar** *(36 km, 22 m on the Chamula road)*, travelers are more often interested in the charter flights to the ruins of **Yaxchilan** and **Bonampak** (see Palenque chapter). Such flights may cost well over $100 each person for a four-seater plane. Since reading John Lincoln's 1967 description of another small landing strip in the Chiapas jungle ("I could see two crashed planes at the end of the runway, an off-course American five-seater which had hit the top of the church tower when, to celebrate his engagement, the pilot had looped the loop too low."), we have preferred to travel by river and land. Yet safety conditions have improved since 1967 and remember, John Lincoln lived to tell the tale. Arrangements can be made through tour agencies in San Cristobal and Palenque, too, where you can also make the trip in a 4-wheel drive van for less than half the price (not recommended in the rainy season).

FIESTAS

Exceptional celebrations accompany various patron saint days and Carnival in Chamula and Zinacantan. Masked dancers perform to traditional music played on drums, flutes, and harps; farces are acted out ridiculing the forces of evil; and horse races and fireworks add to the general excitement. Although the villages are becoming accustomed to increasing numbers of tourists at their fiestas, you should remain cautious about taking photographs, especially of the saint figures. The major festivals are listed below, but always ask the tourist office whether others might be occurring during your visit.

January 20-22

Fiesta of San Sebastian is celebrated in Zinacantan. Ritual dances are performed on the feast day of the 20th and repeated on the 22nd. On the 21st, there is a fair, market, and other entertainment.

Carnival and Holy Week

In both Chamula and Zinacantan, this period is filled with processions and dances. **Martes** (Tuesday) **de Carnaval** in Chamula is famous for its performance of a purification ritual with masked dancers jumping over fire. By Holy Thursday, satirical Judas figures hang from church bell towers and homes. Fridays are also important during these holidays, and in Chamula the usual Sunday market is often held instead on Friday to coincide with the festivities. In Zinacantan, on the six Fridays in Lent, the saints are paraded through the church courtyard on flower-decorated platforms.

June 22-24

Chamula celebrates the festival of its patron saint, San Juan.

July 24-25

Las Casas has its own celebration in honor of its patron saint, San

Cristobal. At night, torches light the long and twisting path up the hill to the church.

August 9-10

The Fiesta of San Lorenzo, who became the patron saint of Zinacantan after his statue was discovered in the woods long ago, hungry and disheveled. It is said this San Lorenzo originally talked, but the elders did not like talking saints and threw hot water on him, silencing him forever. *Capitanes*, wearing feathered skullcaps and gold streaks on their faces, dance throughout the festival, demonstrating great endurance. On the 9th, huge crowds gather to see the dancing, ceremonies, and horse races. In the evening, the churchyard is lit with torches and the flares of *castillos* ("castles," handmade fireworks) and the crowd is rushed by *toritos* (men wearing "bull-shaped fireworks" with pinwheels and firecrackers). On the 10th, a mass where candles and flowers are brought as offerings to San Lorenzo follows the horse races.

December 30-January 1

Ceremonies for the annual change of officials and cargos in many villages, including Tenejapa, Chamula and Zinacantan.

WHERE TO STAY

The low cost of living in San Cristobal gives the tourist some of the best hotel buys in all of Mexico. Although none of these small hotels offers deluxe accommodations, all provide far more in atmosphere than their prices indicate. In the budget hotels, pesos may be the only acceptable form of payment (ask in advance so you can exchange your traveler's checks in good time). The night time chill in this highland town can sometimes go right to the marrow of your bones. If it is cool when you are visiting, check the blanket supply in your room or even try a hotel that has fireplaces (and ask if the wood costs extra). During major fiestas, reservations are recommended. For reservations, write San Cristobal de las Casas, Chiapas, Mexico, or ☎ area code 967.

MODERATE

Posada Diego de Mazariegos   ★★★

Ma. Adelina Flores 2; ☎ *8-05-13; $74* • Located one block north of the zócalo, this is the in-town full-service hotel. The service is good, the ambience warm, and the modernized colonial buildings attractive. Only the annex rooms, large and with fireplaces, merit the 3 stars, but all rooms, arranged around a scattering of courtyards and small gardens, are comfortable. Handsome restaurant. Patio and lounge with entertainment. Tour and car rental agency. Garage.

INEXPENSIVE

Na-Bolom   ★★

Vicente Guerrero 33; ☎ *8-14-18; $50* • This inn has long been favored by those studying the region and now is enjoyed by the serious traveler as well. Although not fancy and a bit out of the center, the setting in the home of Gertrude Blom is lovely. Classical music often fills the courtyard; Gertrude Blom herself usually presides at dinner. The 15 rooms are highly individualized, some in the park-like garden, others around the courtyard; all are decorated with paintings, photos, and crafts collected by the Bloms, and only one is without a fireplace. Meals are not required, but breakfast is recommended. 15% for service is added to the room rate. Reserve well in advance with 1 night's deposit.

Flamboyant
Primero de Marzo 15; ☎ *8-05-14; $65* • Formerly the Hotel Espanol, now completely redone, this centrally located colonial hotel offers 60 carpeted rooms, some with fireplaces (and TVs, in Las Casas, no less), a garden patio, restaurant, bar, travel agency, and parking.

Santa Clara
On zócalo; ☎ *8-11-40; $50* • Housed in the 16th-century residence of the founder of San Cristobal, Diego Marzariegos, this homey hotel offers a variety of rooms but all are large with basic baths, some with wood-beam ceilings. A courtyard serves as home to a number of scarlet macaws. Pleasant restaurant, bar, tour agency Pool.

Mansion del Valle ★★
Mazariegos 39; ☎ *8-25-82; $54* • Newer than most, and more bland in ambience as a result (for example, central heating, no fireplaces), the 45 large, carpeted rooms and helpful service might entice you instead. This neo-colonial hotel is located 3-1/2 blocks from the zócalo. Restaurant, bar with music.

BUDGET

Parador Mexicanos
5 de Mayo 38; ☎ *8-15-15; $30* • Three blocks north from the zócalo, then west, this motel with a sunny garden and kindly service offers a living room-style lobby with fireplace and 25 well-maintained, large rooms with basic baths. Breakfast room. Tennis. Parking. Reserve in advance for this bargain.

WHERE TO EAT

San Cristobal's restaurants reflect its popularity with Europeans as well as North Americans. Here you can find attempts at Italian and French cuisine, more successful efforts at health foods, and loads of coffee houses with everything from baguette sandwiches to *baba ghanoosh*. Even those spots serving regional cuisine cater to tourists and the local Chinese restaurant boasts of its vegetarian specials. Price categories are explained in the Introduction.

Despite the promise of so much variety, the food tends to be dull (but not bad) and the service can be painfully slow—problems certainly engendered by Mexican cooks not fully understanding what they're asked to prepare. There are exceptions—at Mexican restaurants. For example, the food is terrific at **Super Pollo** (*B. Dominguez 3 near Real de Guadalupe*; tiny entrance to left of roasting spits), a clean restaurant very popular with locals for its *pollo rotissado adobo* (roasted chicken adobo—not the much soupier house specialty called *barbipollo*), and for its turkey in a spicy mole sauce, as well as its tasty *lomo de puerco*, or stuffed pork. *(Open 7 a.m.-10 p.m. daily; budget prices)*; and the tacos are flavorful, whether *al pastor* (pork cooked on a spit) or with chicken and *nopalitos*, at **La Salsa Verde** (*20 de Noviembre #7*; budget).

More international restaurants are certainly worth trying, even if they become somewhat indistinguishable after a while. All are rustic with a bit of a cafe or artsy atmosphere. **El Faisan** (*a few steps from the zócalo on Madero*) is pleasant and features a more extensive menu than most that includes a decently priced breakfast and a satisfying *cochinita en asada*, roasted pork in sauce. *(Open daily till 10 p.m.; inexpensive but slightly higher than others.)* At **Madre Tierra** (*Insurgentes at Hermanos Dominguez; 9 a.m.-9 p.m.; inexpensive*) you can eat some of the best vegetarian food in San Cristobal in a cozy room or sunny patio (or take out muffins, loaves of whole grain breads, and slices of quiche from its bakery). The food is wholesome, the choice ranging from Greek spinach pies and chop suey to carrot cake. **Tuluc** (*Insurgentes 5; 6 a.m.-11 p.m.; inexpensive)* has some of the best bargain breakfasts and comidas and its service is relatively efficient.

Among the more upscale spots is **La Galeria** (*Hidalgo 3; 9 a.m.-9 p.m.; inexpensive plus*), a handsome two-tiered atrium restaurant around a garden in one of San Cristobal's oldest buildings. As tempting as the menu can be (paella on Sun.; fish on the comida corrida; steak with peppercorns), the food and service are just okay. There's a cafe here, too. Similarly disappointing is the French-Italian **El Teatro** (*1 de Marzo #8; noon-10 p.m.; almost moderate)*, with pizza, pasta, and Chateaubriand. More satisfying is **El Fogon de Jovel** (*16 de Septiembre; lunch and dinner; almost moderate*), catering to tourists, but nonetheless offering authentic Mexican cuisine, such as *sopa de chepilin* (a corn and green herb soup), chicken in pipian sauce, and a shot of *posh* (the ceremonial liquor of the Chamula).

ENTERTAINMENT

Just about every restaurant/cafe listed above usually has music in the evening. It is hard not to find some form of traditional entertainment in the hotel bars around cocktail hour (the patio at the **Diego Mazariegos** is especially pleasant) and the restaurants and coffee houses, too, offer jazz or Latino music. To find out what is happening, check for the musico vivo signs as you walk around town.

GETTING TO AND FROM SAN CRISTOBAL

AIR

The closest commercial airport is in Tuxtla Gutierrez (see "On the Road" below about fog warnings). From there the distance to San Cristobal is 90 km, 56 m on the Pan American Highway (MEX 190). The road climbs up 5000 feet and, though breathtaking in its beauty, must be driven slowly. Cristobal Colon runs first-class buses daily from Tuxtla to San Cristobal. If you arrive by plane in Tuxtla, it takes 2 hours to reach San Cristobal by rental car, and more time if you plan to take the collective van into Tuxtla to catch a bus. Try to share a taxi or rent a car—the price of a taxi between these two towns is almost the same as the rate of renting a car for one day. **Beware.** None of this applies to **Aviacsa** which uses the in-town military airport, closer to the bus terminal.

BUS

Tuxtla Gutierrez is the transportation hub for this region (see "Tuxtla Gutierrez"). However, first-class **Cristobal Colon** connects San Cristobal with Comitan and the Guatemalan border as well as with Oaxaca (one bus daily), Tuxtla and Chiapa de Corso. From Tuxtla, more buses leave for Oaxaca and other destinations. Second-class **Autotransportes Tuxtla** provides service from San Cristobal along both routes to Palenque (see below), the one via Villahermosa (10 hours) and the one via Ocosingo (6 hours). **Note:** Always reserve buses here; it's permitted even for second class, but only one day in advance.

CAR

Most travel to and from San Cristobal requires a trip to Tuxtla Gutierrez (see "Air" above). But there are direct routes to Palenque and the Guatemalan border. The **Guatemalan border** is approximately 170 km (105 m) from San Cristobal along the Pan American Highway (MEX 190) in the direction of Comitan and the Montebello Lakes. The nearest town in Guatemala for accommodations is Huehuetenango, another 85 km (53 m). Check U.S. travel advisories under "Driving Tips."

Palenque can be reached by MEX 199, the Ocosingo Road (south on the Pan American Highway for 12 km, then left toward Ocosingo), an exceptionally beautiful trip through mountains and jungle, along the San Cristobal excursion route to the ruins of Tonina and beyond to the great waterfalls of **Agua Azul** (see Palenque chapter). Although the Mexican government has been working on this road for a number of years, torrential downpours occasionally render it disastrous. Perhaps progress in such matters is best measured in centuries. In 1841, John L. Stephens described the "road" from Ocosingo to Palenque as:

> ...*necessary to follow sometimes on mules, sometimes on foot, sometimes on the shoulders of Indians, and sometimes in hammocks....After having experienced in the long [5 days] and painful journey every kind of fatigue and discomfort, we arrived, thank God, at the village of Palenque.*

Today the 207-km (128-m) trip can be made in five hours by car, usually with only a few rough stretches. Check conditions locally before setting out in rainy season.

MEX 195 to Teapa and Villahermosa provides an alternate route to Palenque. MEX 195 intersects with the Tuxtla Road (MEX 190) above

Chiapa de Corso, 56 km (35 m) from San Cristobal. Once the preferred route to Palenque, this 7-hour, 300 km (186 m) road to Villahermosa (then another 2 hours to Palenque) has deteriorated while the Ocosingo road has improved. Neither route, however, is without its bad spots. MEX 195 offers magnificently verdant mountains, often veiled in mist, and passes near hamlets of traditionally dressed Maya (along the first 90 km), who are particularly visible on Sunday market days. There are restaurants in Tapilula (190 km, 118 m). Fill up on gas before setting out.

DIRECTORY

Airlines • Main airport is in Tuxtla Gutierrez; charters for Yaxchilan and Bonampak leave from Ocosingo and near Comitan. Tour agencies reserve and reconfirm flights, and organize groups for charters.

Books in English • Libreria Soluna, Real Guadalupe 13, has a small selection.

Bus Terminal • Cristobal Colon/ADO: First-class service. At Insurgentes and Pan American Highway. Autobuses Tuxtla: Second-class service at Allende and Moreno.

Cambio • Lancantun, Real Guadalupe 12-A.

Car Rentals • Budget (Mazariegos 36; ☎ 8-18-71); or check Tuxtla Gutierrez.

Groceries • Commercial Jovel at Real Guadalupe 4.

Laundry • Lavorama (Guadalupe Victoria 20-A)

Post Office • Crescencio Rosas and Cuauhtemoc.

Taxis • On the zócalo.

Telegraph • Diego Mazariegos 19.

Tourist Office • A helpful display of information is at this office in the Municipal Palace on the zócalo. *Open Monday-Friday, 8 a.m.-8 p.m.; Sat. 9 a.m.-2 p.m., 3-8 p.m.; Sun. 9 a.m.-2 p.m.*

Tours • ATC (16 de Septiembre 1; ☎ 8-25-50); Posetur (Calle 5 de Febrero 1-A; ☎ 8-07-25) and Viajes Pakal (Hidalgo at Cuauhtemoc 6-B; ☎ 8-28-18) arrange charter flights to ruins, and horseback riding trips to villages, lakes, Chinkultic, and Tonina. For an enlightening tour of Chamula and Zinacantan, join Mercedes at the zócalo kiosk by 9 a.m. (daily).

ON THE ROAD

CHIAPA DE CORZO

Just 16 km (10 m) outside of Tuxtla Gutierrez on the road to San Cristobal is this picturesque colonial village. Founded in 1528, the town was built over an Indian one whose roots go back as far as 1500 B.C. (excavations can be seen to the southeast of town and on the highway). Today, the colonial architecture is more interesting than its pre-Hispanic ruins. The **Museo de la Laca** (on zócalo) displays the lacquered gourds for which this region is justly famous, many looking like flamboyant inspirations for the mural art of Diego Rivera (9 a.m.-7 p.m. except Mon. closed 1-4 p.m.) The museum shop and others around the plaza sell local crafts, but the high quality of the museum gourds may diminish your interest in these more contemporary items. Now that the Chicoasen Dam has been completed, you can take boat excursions on the Grijalva River through the **Sumidero Canyon**. This three-hour trip starts in Chiapa de Corzo and takes you past the awesome walls of the canyon, some towering 3000 feet above the river. Launches leave from the **Embarcadero** (one block down the street in front of the white church) where you can also enjoy the local shrimp and fried sunfish in the many tiny restaurants lining the riverfront.

TUXTLA GUTIERREZ

Tuxtla has little to detain you. As capital of the state of Chiapas, it is the major transportation center for the area. Its climate is uncomfortable, proving that no inland city should be within 2000 feet of sea level. Yet aficionados of pre-Columbian art will not want to miss the superb collection of the **Museo Regional** in the Parque Madero. All the works are from Chiapas, but that includes Olmec jades, Izapa carvings, and Maya carvings such as the Tonina panel of the captured ruler of Palenque, Kan-Xul (Open 9 a.m.-4 p.m.; closed Mon.; fee for parking). The Parque Madero is 10 blocks east of zócalo on Av. Central Ote. (colectivos run along here), then a 10-minute walk left on 11 Calle Ote.). Some might want to visit the **M. Alvarez de Toro Zoo** instead, a luxuriant park with everything Chiapan from peacocks and jaguars to scorpions. (Open 8:30 a.m.-5:30 p.m.; closed Mon.; taxis much faster than the Cerro Hueco bus on 1 Oriente near 7 Sur.) Also, you can visit nearby **Chiapa de Corzo** (colectivos at 3 Oriente at 3 Sur). **Tourist Information** is available in the excellent crafts store, **Casa de Artesanias** (B. Dominguez 2035 at 21 Poniente Sur; 9 a.m.- 2 p.m. and, except Sun., 5-8 p.m.)

WHERE TO STAY AND EAT

If you are detained in Tuxtla, then you'll want to head west from the zócalo on Central Pte. (by colectivo or taxi) until it turns into B. Dominguez. About 1 m from the zócalo is the ★★**Hotel Bonampak** (*Blvd. B. Dominguez 180*; ☎ [961] 3-21-01; $50) with 112 a/c units, most carpeted and motel-modern in a highrise, the rest older bungalows. Gardens, large pool, tennis, steam baths, a handsome restaurant, coffee shop, bar, and parking, make this a good choice. Another 1/2 m (turn right at Pemex for entrance) brings you to √★**La Hacienda** (*B. Dominguez 1197*; ☎ [961] 2-79-86; $29), a good buy for its nice service, 20 fresh a/c rooms around a shady lot with small pool, restaurant and parking. For those who prefer to stay near the bus station, the best choice is the **Gran Hotel Humberto** (Central Pte. 180; ☎ [961] 2-20-44; $38), a bit dreary, like all of the zócalo area, but adequate and with 119 a/c rooms and a restaurant. If you want to eat somewhere other than your hotel, the fancooled **La Selva** (*B. Dominguez 1360, just before La Hacienda*; ☎ 2-62-51; open breakfast–dinner; inexpensive) may have lost its thatched charm to modernization, but not its good chef. Try the regional antojitos, the sopa de chipilin, the pollo ajillo.

GETTING TO AND FROM TUXTLA

CAR

At San Juan airport and in town, **Budget** (☎ 2-55-06) and **Dollar** (☎ 2-89-32). *Bus Terminal:* First-class **Cristobal Colon** terminal (2 Norte at 2 Poniente), 3 blocks below Central Pte where *colectivos* run to B. Dominguez (to the right) and 2 blocks left is the zócalo. First-class buses run on the road routes below.

AIR

The main "San Juan" airport is 32 km (20m) west of the zócalo on the "libramiento;" colectivos available from Gran Hotel Humberto. (Check Nov.–Feb. on flight cancellations due to fog.) From here **Mexicana** (☎ 3-49-21) connects with Mexico City, the smaller jets **Aerocaribe** (☎ 2-20-32) with Oaxaca and Villahermosa. From the military airport **"Base Aero"** (7 km west of zócalo at B. Dominguez Pte 426; taxis and colectivos on Central Pte), **Aviacsa** (☎ 3-09-78) also flies Oaxaca, Villahermosa, and non-stop Huatulco.

ROAD

The Pan American Highway (MEX 190) passes by Tuxtla from Tehuantepec and Oaxaca (8 hours) before continuing to San Cristobal and Guatemala. From Tehuantepec, you can drive to the Pacific Coast and the resorts of Huatulco (7 hours) and Puerto Escondido. MEX 195 to Villahermosa (via Teapa) intersects the San Cristobal road (MEX 190) 34 km, 21 m north and takes 5-1/2 hours.

PALENQUE

The most exquisite ruins in Mexico lie just outside the small town of Palenque. These Maya ruins were once reachable only by river or horseback, then in the 1950s by train and small planes, and now by road from Villahermosa and San Cristobal de las Casas. The sleepy village, described by John L. Stephens as the most dead-and-alive place he had ever seen, has been awakened by growing tourism. In fact the town of Palenque is experiencing a boom, quadrupling in size if not in beauty. Really just an overgrown village, the new facilities are all for tourists, and like any resort, the prices tend to be high.

KEY TO PALENQUE

Sights • The most beautiful Maya ruins in Mexico.

Excursions • Majestic waterfalls of Agua Azul and Misol-Ha are easily reached by road, as are the museums of Villahermosa. Arrangements can be made for visiting the magnificent ruins of Yaxchilan and Bonampak.

Shopping • Curio shops, T-shirts, and plaster reproductions of Palenque sculptures.

Where to Stay • First-class to camping facilities available.

Where to Eat • Limited, if on the whole pricey, yet adequate restaurants.

Entertainment • Birdwatching at dawn.

Getting Around • While you can stay in town and visit the ruins by combi or taxi, a colectivo, tour, or car is necessary to explore some of the swimming spots and waterfalls.

Practical Tips • Palenque is in the tropics, so dress for hot weather. Bring insect repellent to ruins and swimming spots. Binoculars are handy for seeing details of carvings not at ground level of ruins. During school vacations reserve your hotel in advance.

RUINS OF PALENQUE

The ruins are 10 km (6 m) from town on well-paved road, by cab or combi van. Open 8 a.m.-5 p.m. Tomb open, 10-4. Soft-drink stand near entrance. Guides available. Museum, crafts shop, snack bar 1.5 km, 1m before ruins; open same hours. Admission fee.

The hauntingly beautiful ruins of Palenque, nestled in the lush green vegetation of a tropical rain forest and foothills of the Sierra Madre de Chiapas, are situated on a natural shelf overlooking vast fertile plains that stretch to the Gulf Coast. The architecture of the site is harmoniously incorporated into this natural setting. Here, the usual pre-Columbian plan of rectangular plazas bounded by buildings is often forsaken for the natural topography of streams, hills, and precipices. The result is a compelling arrangement, more graceful than monumental.

Today, only the central area, dating from Palenque's period of greatest power (A.D. 600-800) is exposed, its once-red buildings (yes, red all over, very red) now white from erosion. The finest structures of this center—the Temple of the Inscriptions with its famous tomb, the Group of the Cross, and most of the Palace—were constructed within approximately 80 years during the great reigns of Lord Pacal ("Shield") and Lord Chan-Bahlum ("Serpent-Jaguar"). Palenque's artists created new architectural forms of sloping mansard roofs on slender-walled temples and executed a multitude of masterful, yet delicate, low-relief carvings in stucco and stone. Such accomplishments in so brief a time represent a virtual explosion of innovative artistic activity and resulted in a legacy of hieroglyphic inscriptions enabling archaeologists to reconstruct some of the history of this once-great city.

Prior to Pacal's reign, Palenque was a minor site, with little monumental architecture, concentrated to the west of the present center. After Chan-Bahlum's rule, Palenque continued to expand politically and economically. Its stylistic impact is indisputable at the ruins of Comalcalco near the Gulf Coast, and its elaborate symbolism of rulership influenced even the great Maya city of Tikal in Guatemala. Palenque was abandoned earlier than most Classic lowland sites—the last dated work is from A.D. 799. However brief a role Palenque played in history, its artistic achievements remain monumental

TEMPLE OF THE INSCRIPTIONS AND TOMB

NOTE: *If you dislike climbing the steep stairs to the temple, a small path to the left and behind the pyramid can be used.*

Framed by luxuriant vegetation, this majestic temple rests on an nine-stepped pyramid, 75 feet above the plaza. The temple is dedicated to Lord Pacal, the great ruler who brought Palenque prominence and who guided its growth for almost 70 years (he was only 12-1/2 years old when he first came to the throne). The temple is named after the extensive hieroglyphic texts inside the portico that record Pacal's ancestry and accession to the throne in A.D. 615. The importance of Pacal's rule to this ancient city can best be judged by the statements of the texts that his accession to the throne was celebrated millions of years in the past (was his rule foreordained by the gods?) and thousands of years into the future. Only the carvings on the piers are not devoted to Pacal. They were added after his death by his successor and son, Chan-Bahlum, who had himself represented as the deified heir-apparent to Pacal (the "infant" with a serpent foot on each pier is Chan-Bahlum, identifiable by his six toes, represented as the god of rulership).

Tomb of Pacal

Reached by stairway inside the temple. The most unusual aspect of the Temple of Inscriptions is the tomb discovered deep inside the pyramid

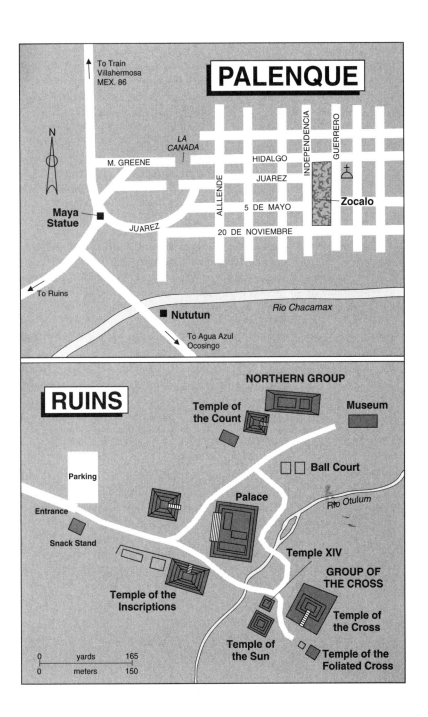

PALENQUE

To Train
Villahermosa
MEX. 86

N

LA
CANADA

M. GREENE

HIDALGO

JUAREZ

INDEPENDENCIA

GUERRERO

ALLLENDE

5 DE MAYO

Zocalo

20 DE NOVIEMBRE

**Maya
Statue**

JUAREZ

To Ruins

Nututun

Rio Chacamax

To Agua Azul
Ocosingo

RUINS

NORTHERN GROUP

**Temple of
the Count**

Museum

☐ ☐ **Ball Court**

Parking

Palace

Rio Otulum

Entrance

Temple XIV

Snack Stand

**GROUP OF
THE CROSS**

**Temple of the
Inscriptions**

**Temple of
the Cross**

**Temple of
the Sun**

**Temple of the
Foliated Cross**

| 0 | yards | 165 |
| 0 | meters | 150 |

base by archaeologist Alberto Ruz L'Huiller (whose own tomb is in front of this temple). In 1949, Ruz noticed that the temple walls continued beyond the floor and that one floor slab had holes on its edges. Lifting the slab, Ruz discovered an arched ceiling, a few stairs, and mounds of rubble. It took four field seasons for the stairway to be cleared. So much monotonous work in the airless stairwell was well rewarded in 1952 with the finding of the tomb. The first tomb found in any Maya pyramid, this discovery shocked the archaeological world. After years of fruitless searches for tombs, the belief had grown that ancient Americans, unlike the Egyptians, did not use their pyramids for burials. Even Ruz initially thought he had discovered an altar in a sacred chapel. Not until the 5-ton sarcophagus lid was lifted, exposing the jade-adorned skeleton of Pacal, did he know it was a tomb. Archaeologists now believe other Palenque rulers may be buried in still unexcavated pyramids.

The tomb is awesome, and certainly worth the somewhat eerie, difficult descent inside the pyramid. (The damp stairs are easier to descend barefoot.) The wall carvings and sarcophagus remain in the tomb, although the jades and smaller contents were removed to the National Museum of Anthropology in Mexico City. The carving of the sarcophagus lid is exquisitely executed—one of the finest works of art from ancient Mexico. Although Erich Von Daniken claims the human figure carved on the lid is driving a space ship, archaeologists believe otherwise, based on their understanding of Maya symbolism and beliefs. The central figure is Pacal against a background of the sacred tree of the universe. He is falling in death into the Underworld, represented by the skeletal face of the sun god beneath him. The wall carvings represent the Nine Lords of the Underworld. But the symbolism of the tomb is not only of death. The entire contents of the sarcophagus were awash with red cinnabar, a color associated by the Maya with the east, the rising sun, and rebirth. Pacal's jade death mask identifies him with the sun god. Like the sun, Pacal will rise again. As the sun, Pacal, too, is a god. Archaeologist Linda Schele reports seeing the setting sun during the winter solstice plunge into this temple, as if the sun were entering the Underworld through Pacal's tomb. A hollow "psychoduct" leads from the sarcophagus, up the stairs, on the right as you ascend, to the temple. Although other such psychoducts have been found at Maya sites, their meaning is unknown. Whether in this case it was to communicate with Pacal as a god or to provide him a link with the world of the living from the Underworld is also unknown.

GROUP OF THE CROSS

The three main temples of this harmonious group were built during the reign of Chan-Bahlum and dedicated in A.D. 692. Only the small Temple XIV, added later, intrudes on the perfection of the group. The three temples commemorate the accession to power of Pacal's son, Chan-Bahlum. In addition to the historical information carved inside these monuments, the texts establish a mythological relationship between the three gods of Palenque and Chan-Bahlum, claiming not only his legitimacy as a ruler, but his divinity as well. Pacal ruled for almost 70 years, yet required only the Temple of Inscriptions to describe his life, ancestry, and death. Chan-Bahlum ruled just 12 years but required an entire complex to elaborate on his ancestry and accession to the throne. We may know what he was trying to prove, but not why he had to try so hard. Was there some doubt about his legitimacy?

Each of the three temples originally had an interior panel carved with hieroglyphs, showing two figures flanking a central image. In two temples, the central image was thought to be a cross. These crosses are now identified as the sacred ceiba tree of the Maya that represented the three levels of the universe: the tree's roots grow into the Underworld, its main trunk is in the world of the living, and its top branches reach the heavens. Thanks to the work of Linda Schele, we now know that the small figure on each panel is Pacal, dead but deified offering the symbols of rulership to Chan-Bahlum. On the jambs of the inner sanctum, Chan-Bahlum stands, ruler of Palenque, holding the symbols of office received from his father.

Temple of the Cross

The temple has lost some of its facade but retains a good portion of its roof comb, which had a staircase leading to what must have been the most impressive view at the site. Linda Schele speculates that Chan-Bahlum may be buried under this temple, because much of the symbolism is similar to that on Pacal's sarcophagus lid. Current excavations, once completed, may decide the matter. The interior panel is no longer at the site, but the two carvings on the interior jambs are worth seeing. Chan-Bahlum stands to the left, holding his scepter of rulership, and God L of the Underworld is on the right smoking a cigar. According to Maya belief, the sun sets into the Underworld. During the winter solstice, the setting sun illuminates the carved figure of God L.

Temple of the Foliated Cross

The encroaching jungle around this temple makes you feel the entire site could easily disappear under its growth. The fallen facade exposes the architectural techniques of the Maya, including the keyhole design in the upper vaults that was used to lighten the weight the arches had to support. The interior panel with its particularly leafy sacred tree, topped by a bird deity and with ears of corn on the main branches, symbolizes the cycle of life and death. Here Pacal gives Chan-Bahlum a bloodletting tool for kingly rites of self-sacrifice that keep the lifecycle going.

Temple of the Sun

Only this temple retains its facade, roof comb, and most of its carvings, enabling us to imagine the original appearance of the other two temples. On the interior panel, the central image is a shield with the face of the Underworld jaguar god, a manifestation of the sun god and a symbol of the Palenque dynasty (Pacal means "shield"). Spears cross behind the shield, and two gods of the Underworld (including God L again, on the right) support the ceremonial bar of rulership. Since the Maya Underworld was associated with war and death, it is not surprising that Chan-Bahlum is presented as military ruler of Palenque on the jamb fragments.

Temple XIV

This small temple contains a lovely carved panel of a kneeling woman offering a small figure of the god of rulership to a "dancing" man. Although the man is Chan-Bahlum of Palenque (these name glyphs are the last two on the right), the hieroglyphs indicate the panel was carved after his death. A number of carvings from Palenque are of "dancing" men who are dead. These monuments may commemorate the ruler's resurrection. According to Linda Schele, Chan-Bahlum has just triumphed over the underworld and here is greeted in the afterlife by Lady Ahpo-Hel, his mother.

PALACE

NOTE: *Paths on the south side and rear provide access alternatives to the steep front steps.*

The Palace with its tower provides the unifying focus of the entire central area of Palenque. The structure may have been an administrative center as well as residence for the elite because steam baths and benches that may have been used for sleeping have been discovered in the southeastern section of the building. Constructed and renovated over a 200-year period, the Palace carvings and structures result from projects of Pacal as well as his successors. Much of the stucco decoration that covered the exterior and interior walls has disappeared, having disintegrated or been looted by explorers of the 18th and 19th centuries who camped in the shelter of the Palace galleries. Fortunately, carvings remain, scattered through the complex.

North Section

As you climb the stairs of the Palace, the complex on your left is the North Section, built by another son of Pacal and the successor to Chan-Bahlum, Lord Kan-Xul. The carved stuccos on the piers facing the stairs are believed to symbolize warfare themes. In fact, one pier with a carving of a figure standing with an axe held over a seated person is said to represent a decapitation. Another pier carving with a "dancing" figure may represent Kan-Xul's dead ancester, Pacal.

Although Kan-Xul's accession panel is in the museum (see "Museum" below), and his death as a prisoner is shown at the ruins of Tonina, the North Section still includes one of the most fascinating and strikingly unusual sets of carvings found at Palenque. Walk through the North Section toward the rear of the Palace until you come to the second, and northeastern, courtyard. Around two sides of the courtyard platform are figures in postures of submission. The western side includes a hieroglyphic staircase that has not been fully translated, but Pacal's birth and accession to the throne is mentioned as well as his allies at Yaxchilan who joined him in war.

The nine large figures across the courtyard from the hieroglyphic staircase are compelling yet lack the refinement of most Palenque carvings. Heads are enormous, and the bodies lack the human proportions found elsewhere at the site. The nine slab carvings were definitely not designed for their present location or designed to be a group. The headdresses have been cut off, in whole or in part, to create a uniform height and to fit the slabs into the platform. The slabs don't match each other in stone or human proportions. They may not even have been carved at Palenque.

Eight of the figures have their arms placed in a gesture of submission, and the upturned angles of their heads and kneeling postures make them seem cowering. Debates continue as to whether these figures represent captives about to be sacrificed or whether they symbolize tribute from subject towns. Some archaeologists speculate the slabs were made by conquered towns who were forced to give Palenque carvings of their humiliated rulers. The problem in deciding the issue is that most captives in Maya art are portrayed stripped of their jewelry and headdresses as a sign of debasement. Yet, eight of these slabs, plus the carvings on the opposite side of the courtyard, show well-dressed individuals. The ninth slab, on the extreme right, however, lacks any jewelry; and his hands, rather than making the gesture of submission, seem to be tied behind his back. Whichever interpretation is correct, this courtyard represents new emphasis on political power during Kan-Xul's reign.

Beyond this courtyard are carvings on the rear piers of the Palace, a kind of ancestral gallery for Kan-Xul, with both Pacal and Chan-Bahlum represented. On one pier, you can discern two kneeling persons with their arms in the gesture of submission to a more majestic standing individual.

Tower

The tower, unique in Maya architecture, was probably built by Kan-Xul. Why it was constructed remains unclear. Astronomical research indicates that it was not used as an observatory. Yet there is no doubt the tower provided an excellent view over the plain below, so perhaps it served as a watchtower. It may have served a cosmological function, too, because it provides the best view of the setting sun sinking into the Temple of the Inscriptions during the winter solstice. The staircase can still be climbed if you wish to explore the tower and the view, but the stairs start on the second story. Fortunately, a wall constructed later than the tower is convenient for reaching the second story. The ancient Maya probably used a ladder to reach the second floor, but archaeologists have no idea why.

After visiting the tower, look for the carving of the **Oval Tablet** in a well-preserved structure flanking the tower courtyard to the south. The Oval Tablet, the oldest carved panel from Palenque, represents the coronation of Pacal, who sits on a two-headed jaguar throne while being offered the headdress of rulership. But what is most unusual about the tablet is the figure on the left, who is Lady Zac-Kuk ("White Quetzal"), a woman ruler of Palenque. Her hair is cropped in a masculine style, perhaps due to the conventions of rulership. She offers the "drum-major" headdress to Pacal, an act performed in all other known cases by a man. Lady Zac-Kuk, Pacal's mother, ruled for the three years before his accession. Since he was only 12-1/2 when he became ruler, it would not be surprising if Lady Zac-Kuk continued to "influence" political matters beyond the official three years of her reign, making her one of the few known female rulers of the ancient Maya—another was Pacal's great grandmother! Later rulers placed their accession thrones under the Oval Tablet indicating their descent from this royal lineage. This is the only part of the Palace that was painted white, not red.

Other Sights

The Otulum River is guided in its course through the site by an ancient vaulted aqueduct, part of which can be seen behind the Palace. Just beyond the path continuing east of the ball court, the Otulum forms a lovely, tempting pool. Because the river is used for drinking water, swimming is prohibited (the former presence of a crocodile, even if it was tied up, cooled the most rebellious spirits). Few carvings survive in the north section of the site. The ball court, consisting of two unexcavated mounds thickly covered with jungle growth, is the oldest structure in the central area, dating from around A.D. 500. From here you can look back at the decorated north facade of the palace, surmounted by a magnificent stucco Maya head.

Museum

The museum contains many fine objects from Palenque, including examples of the portrait heads carved in stucco for which Palenque is famous. The accession panel of Kan-Xul found in the Palace (first large tablet) includes rare full-figured hieroglyphs (on the upper left side) so elaborate it is hard to believe they record only a date. The exquisite Tablet of the Slaves shows the pretentious Chac-Zutz, a nobleman but never a ruler, seated on a "throne" now thought to represent two war captives. This tablet was found outside the central part of the site.

OTHER SIGHTS AND EXCURSIONS
SPOTS TO COOL OFF

The only semi-public place to swim near Palenque is at the **Nututum Palenque**, (10 a.m.-6 p.m.) located where the powerful Chacamax River forms a natural pool. Small fee for dressing rooms unless you eat in the open-air restaurant. Reachable by car and about 3 km (almost 2 miles) on the road to Ocosingo.

Three **cascadas** (waterfalls)—Motiepa, Misol-Ha, and Agua Azul—provide opportunities to enjoy the beauty of the tropical rain forest while cooling off in their clear waters. They are described in order of increasing grandeur and distance from town. **Motiepa**, which can be visited on foot from the ruins (if you are still in shape after climbing the pyramid platforms), is only 1 km from the ruins on the road back to town (a sign on the left marks the short path leading to this pleasant waterfall surrounded by dense tropical vegetation). You might want to wade to cool off, but swimming is not feasible. The majestic 100-foot waterfall **Misol-Ha** (also spelled "Misola") can be observed after traveling 18 km (11 m) along the Ocosingo road and continuing to the right for 1 km (admission fee). If you're enchanted, there are 10 woodsy cabins here. **Agua Azul** requires a 58-km (36 m) drive along the Ocosingo road and a further 4-km trip to the right, but as bad as the road conditions can be at times, the trip takes you through the Sierra Madre de Chiapas and magnificent scenery with views of valleys patterned by the blue-green path of the Rio Tulija. Agua Azul won't disappoint you either, with its velvety aqua waters crashing from enormous heights only to form a safe and tranquil pool for swimming off to one side. Refreshments stands with limited food. Fee for camping and use of bathrooms. Small admission charge. For minibus tours to Misol-Ha and Agua Azul, the Cooperativo often has the lowest prices.

OFF THE BEATEN TRACK: YAXCHILAN AND BONAMPAK RUINS

These Maya ruins used to lie deep in the tropical rain forest, so deep that until recently they could be reached only by plane or by special river trips with camping on the banks of the Usumacinta. (Write Foundation for Latin American Research, Campus Box 2675, Rollins College, Winter Park, FL 32789 for information on river tours.) Both ruins can still be visited on charter flights from Palenque, San Cristobal, and Villahermosa (expect to pay about $130 per person on a four-seater plane). Groups to fill these planes are arranged by the tour agencies (see "Key"). Recently, however, land trips to these ruins and the Lacandon village of **Lacanja** have become available from Palenque for considerably less, usually less than half the charter price. These trips give you as much time at the ruins as the charter flights (2 hours at Yaxchilan; 1 hour at Bonampak), but more time is consumed traveling through the sadly diminishing forest. The seven-seater, four-wheel drive vans leave at 5 a.m. and don't return before 8 p.m. The Bonampak trip requires an 8-km (5 m) hike (one way); Yaxchilan involves a 45-minute boat trip and a somewhat difficult climb up a sand bank to the ruins. The best tour combines both ruins, and that requires an overnight in the rain forest. You should shop around, both for price and availability. If you plan to make one of these trips (not recommended and, often, not available during rainy season), come prepared with sturdy water repellant shoes or boots and rain ponchos (even during the "dry" season), with clothes to cover up against insects and scratches from branches and undergrowth.

Yaxchilan

Perched above the majestic Usumacinta River, Yaxchilan remains enshrouded by the tropical rain forest. Luxuriant vines and wild begonias cover its crumbling walls; the strident cries of howler monkeys fill its plazas in the deep of night. Romantically situated, Yaxchilan also rewards the visitor with its wealth of stone carvings and many reconstructed buildings. The monuments at Yaxchilan, although carved in a style distinctive from Palenque, are another superb example of Maya artistic achievement during the 7th and 8th centuries. Yaxchilan was the city of the rulers Shield Jaguar, founder of its greatest dynasty, and his son Bird Jaguar, ruler during its greatest growth. The stone monuments tell us of the dynastic history of Yaxchilan and of the political turbulence of the 8th century. Bird Jaguar often is seen in his quilted armor and one of his titles claims he was "lord of 20 captives"—each at least a noble, if not a ruler. More diplomatic efforts on his part to form political alliances may have resulted in his having four wives. The monuments also tell us about bloodletting, that painful ritual of self-sacrifice performed by the ruler and his wife to accompany important events.

Many of Yaxchilan's temples are built on steep, overgrown hills above the long, limestone shelf of the main plaza. Although the usual two-hour tour may not take you to the highest temples *(Temples 40 and 41 are 1 km above the plaza; the Temple 44 complex, with its eroded monuments dedicated to Shield Jaguar's military exploits, is closer, but up a steep path)*, they most certainly will take you up to the more accessible and richly adorned **Temple 33**. From the foot of this temple with its stalactite engraved with hieroglyphs to the roof comb above, you find sculpture. Under a protective roof on the top step are magnificent panels representing a ball game, perhaps a mythical game, judging from the ancient dates accompanying the scenes. Carved lintels are particularly distinctive of Yaxchilan and three well-preserved ones remain in each of the temple doors. These lintels were dedicated on the fifth anniversary of Bird Jaguar's rule, an occasion celebrated with him by his son, Shield Jaguar II, on the central lintel. The left lintel recalls Bird Jaguar's accession in A.D. 752 and shows Zero Skull, his wife, standing behind and holding a bundle for a bloodletting rite. Inside the temple is a sculpture of a seated man (Bird Jaguar?) that was unfortunately beheaded by lumberjacks in the 19th century.

Back down on the **Main Plaza** are numerous buildings with their associated altars (or thrones) and stelae as well as lintels, some still in place, others fallen and fragmented. If you descend near the center of the plaza, straight ahead you see some altars and **Stela 1**, commemorating Bird Jaguar's accession to the throne. Other interesting carvings are in the second temple to the right as you descend; this **Temple**

20 commemorated the birth of the heir to the throne, Shield Jaguar II. The fine lintel in the right doorway shows Bird Jaguar and his wife communicating with a god, after having performed bloodletting rites in honor of their son's birth. Across the plaza from this temple is **Stela 11**, under a protective roof. On the front, Shield Jaguar (left) designates his son, Bird Jaguar, as his successor. On the rear, Bird Jaguar apparently proves his readiness for rulership by showing himself fresh from battle with three captives at his feet. One senses that the sacrifice accompanying this event will not be performed on Bird Jaguar. His parents share in his victory from their seats above the scene. From here, you walk back through the plaza, past a ball court, to where you entered the site at the **Labyrinth**, a building with two carved altars in front.

Bonampak

This is a small site, famous for its frescoes, mural paintings rich in color and detail about the ancient Maya. Due to mineral deposits, the murals have become increasingly difficult to see and often disappoint those who visit the site. If you can, familiarize yourself with the reproductions in the National Museum of Anthropology in Mexico City before visting Bonampak. In room 1 is a procession with musicians and singers; room 2 contains the famous battle scene; and room 3 depicts a ceremony after the battle. The details of costume and customs revealed in these murals plunge you back into the 8th century. There are also some interesting carvings at Bonampak, most commissioned by Chaan-Muan, the ruler who commemorated his battle in the murals. Based on stylistic similarities, it has long been believed that Bonampak was a dependency of Yaxchilan. Now the archaeologist Peter Mathews has deciphered the glyphs on these monuments and they indicate that there was at least an alliance. On the central lintel of the mural building, Shield Jaguar II of Yaxchilan is shown capturing a prisoner; on Chaac-Muan's accession stela (far left on staircase), the wife standing behind him is named Yax-Rabbit, Lady of Yaxchilan.

WHERE TO SHOP

While Palenque is not a shopper's paradise, you can buy arrows from the Lacandon and dolls from Chamulas at the ruins. In town, T-shirts, sandals, and curios can be found at the **Plaza de las Artesanias** (*Juarez, 1 block before zócalo*), while plaster reproductions of Palenque carvings can be found here and there. Quality crafts from all over Mexico can be found at **Kolibri** (*Juarez 123*).

WHERE TO STAY

For reservations, write 29960 Palenque, Chiapas, or call area code 934.

MODERATE

Chan Kah Ruinas   ★★★

On the road to ruins, about 6 km (3.5 m) from town; ☎ *5-11-00; $75* • When functioning well, the Chan Kah is one of our favorite unpretentious hotels. Formed by 35 separate cottages surrounding gardens and common areas, the Chan Kah is landscaped so as to seem a part of its tropical rain forest setting. At dawn, you are awakened by the glorious chorus consisting of what must be all the birds in the universe. After visits to the ruins, you are refreshed by a swim in the several levels of its unusually lovely pool. Some of the cottages are on the edge of the forest overlooking a stream (preferred, but no a/c); others are set in gardens. All are spacious, simply decorated, and fronted by picture windows and terraces. Dining room with bar. Parking.

Mision Park Inn Palenque   ★★★

Rancho San Martin de Porres; ☎ *5-02-41; $115* • Located about 1 km (.6 m) east of the zócalo, this is the full service, modern hotel of Palenque. It offers 120 air-conditioned rooms with shared terraces, some with views of surrounding hills. The lobby often is bustling with tour groups. Restaurant and bar. Tour agency. Pool. Parking. Transport to town and ruins.

Nututun Palenque   ★★

Carretara Ocosingo Km 3.5. Car necessary; ☎ *5-01-61; $75* • Just a few miles along the Ocosingo road, you come to the beautiful, wooded location here next to a river. Decent accommodations complement the location with 60 ample rooms with large tiled baths—only these are recommended, not the bungalows. Pleasant restaurant by river. Bar. River swimming. Parking. Often full due to tour groups, so reserve in advance. Apartado 74.

INEXPENSIVE

La Canada   ★

Calle Merle Greene 14. Down dirt road to the left of Maya statue before entering town; ☎ *5-01-02; $40* • Near end of the dirt road, you come to the thatched-roof restaurant, La Chanampa, which serves as the reception area for the hotel. Within walking distance of town, this 36-unit "hotel" is in a lovely tree-shaded setting with both bungalows and room wings scattered about. Units are ample, with views of trees; some have a/c. Popular restaurant. Because archaeologists and tour groups use this hotel, it can be difficult to obtain rooms. Reserve in advance. Write Apartado 91.

Chan Kah Centro   ★

Juarez corner of Independencia; ☎ *5-03-18; $75* • Right on the zócalo, this is the most attractive hotel in the center and, since guests have access to the pool at the Chan Kah Ruinas, it also is a good buy. The 40 rooms are fan-cooled, with flagstone floors and nice baths. Restaurant.

Maya Tulipanes

Calle M. Greene 6; ☎ 5-02-01; $52 • In the same shady area near town as La Canada, this hotel has undergone some necessary upgrading. There are now 36 a/c rooms, with tiled baths, but they vary in quality from the 16 new ones to the smallest of the old ones. Small pool.

BUDGET

Kashlan

5 de Mayo 105; ☎ 5-02-97; $30 • Near the ADO terminal in town, this hotel has ample common areas and small, clean rooms with fans. One of the more acceptable budget hotels.

CAMPING

Maya Bell Camping and Trailer Park

On road to ruins, 8 km (5 m) from town on the left • Shelters for hammocks, tent, and RV spaces in the forest near the ruins. Restaurant. Write to Apartado 20.

Nututun Palenque Camping

On the road to ruins, turn left toward Ocosingo and continue 3.5 km (2 m) • A beautiful location on the river makes any visitor want to stay, but be prepared for no facilities.

WHERE TO EAT

For too many years eating in Palenque meant stringy chicken and canned everything else. Now a number of restaurants have sprung up offering the local *mojarra* fish, fresh fruit salads, *brochetas* (shish kebab), and decently prepared Mexican dishes. Most of these restaurants are thatch-roofed, clean, and completely geared to tourists—including their prices. One of the best, the attractive **Fogon de Pakal** (*end of M. Greene, next to La Canada; moderate*) also has the most regional food—chicken in *pipian* (a kind of mole), a delicious *sopa de chepilin*, tostadas—as well as salads and a few international items. Despite the hokey practice of dressing the staff in regional costumes, everything is made with high quality ingredients, the tortillas are house-made, and even the limeade is special. The priciest restaurant we found was **La Selva** (*near the Maya statue at the entrance to town; moderately expensive*), thatched yet polished and often with music—once we enjoyed tropical rhythms, another time "Strangers in the Night." The seafood here is reliable, the food tends to be international. We like the *brocheta de pollo* at the **Chan Kah Ruinas** (*moderately expensive*), a peaceful retreat after a visit to the ruins. The branch on the zócalo, **Chan Kah Centro**, has an inexpensive comida corrida in the afternoon. Nearby the **Restaurant Maya** (*on zócalo*) is a favorite budget spot for breakfast or whatever. But our favorite of the inexpensive spots remains **La**

Chanampa (*Hotel La Cañada*), one of the original thatched restaurants, with monkeys living in the surrounding trees, and one of the most relaxing for tostadas or *pollo ajillo*. Many evenings there's marimba music too.

GETTING TO AND FROM PALENQUE

AIR

Chartered planes fly from the Palenque airfield (3 km, 2 m north of town on road leading to MEX 186) to Yaxchilan and Bonampak. Regular air access available from Villahermosa airport followed by land travel to Palenque.

LAND

Palenque lies 28 km (17m) south of highway MEX 186 (from Villahermosa turn right after the Catazaja Pemex station). MEX 186—sometimes pocked with potholes large enough to remind you not to drive at night—connects Villahermosa with Escarcega where roads diverge to Mérida (558 km, 346 m), Campeche (363 km, 225 m) and Chetumal (490 km, 304 m). For the most part, the roads are two lanes and flat. **Tip:** Fill up with gas when you can, even if there is a line at the Pemex.

Palenque is 148 km (92m) from Villahermosa, 2 hours by rental car from the city, less from its airport; 2-1/2 hours by **ADO** bus. Many travelers arrive from Yucatán and the Caribbean and continue on to San Cristobal, never visiting the sights at nearby city of Villahermosa. Yet the bus service to Villahermosa and from there, to the rest of Mexico is superb. The bus service from Palenque is inferior and mostly second-class; the first-class ADO buses to Mérida and Chetumal run once a day only and often are full, so if you can't obtain a reservation, consider going to Villahermosa.

San Cristobal de las Casas is most directly reached by the Ocosingo Road (MEX 199), but the difficulties of maintaining this road under the excesses of tropical rain-forest weather usually result in some rough stretches along the way (see "San Cristobal de las Casas," above). Second-class **Transportes Tuxtla** and **Transportes Yucatán** buses run this trip daily.

RAIL

Pullman service from Mexico City to Mérida stops at Palenque. It took us exactly the scheduled 24 hours to reach Palenque from Mexico City, but others report much longer journeys. An estimated 13 hours is required between Mérida and Palenque (contrasted with 8 hours by bus). While the trip from Mexico City to Palenque passes through fascinating lush tropical areas, the time required makes it an option only for aficionados of trains.

Note: Thefts have been reported between Palenque and Campeche.

DIRECTORY

Airlines • For charters to Yaxchilan or Bonampak, check with the captain at the airport (hours uncertain) or tour agencies.

Buses • *First-class* **ADO** operates from an office right off the main street of Juarez, three blocks from the Maya statue. *Second-class* **Transportes Tuxtla** starts its San Cristobal trip from Juarez, one block from the Maya statue, and **Transportes Yucatán** is practically next door.

Combi Vans • The **Cooperativo de Transportes Chambola** starts its circuit run to the Palenque ruins from Allende just off Juarez.

Horseback Riding • **Turismo Mision** (see "Tours" below) offers 3-hour rides in the forest.

Post Office • Independencia, along left side of municipal palace.

Tourist Office • On east side of zócalo, across from Hotel Palenque. Open Mon.-Sat. 9 a.m.-2 p.m. and 3-8 p.m.; Sat. 9 a.m.-2 p.m.

Tours • The **Cooperativo** (see "Combi Vans") has colectivos for Misol Ha and Agua Azul; **ATC** (Allende at corner of Juarez; ☎ 5-02-10), **Turismo Mision** (Mision Park Inn; ☎ 5-04-44), and **Viajes Shivalva** (Hotel La Canada, ☎ 5-04-11) also make air and land arrangements to Yaxchilan and Bonampak, as well as other sites like Tikal in Guatemala (4-5 day tours available).

YUCATÁN AND CAMPECHE

Colonial fortifications, Campeche

> *If the number, grandeur and beauty of its buildings were to count to-*
> *ward the attainment of…reputation in the same way as gold, silver*
> *and riches have done for other parts of the Indies, Yucatán would have*
> *become as famous as Peru and New Spain.*
>
> **Diego de Landa, 1566**

HISTORY AND CULTURE

When the Spaniards discovered the Yucatán peninsula, they thought it an island separated from Mexico and surrounded by the Gulf of Mexico on its west and the Caribbean on its east. For its distinctive geography and independent traditions, this peninsula could in fact be considered an island. Instead of the usual mixed Mexican landscape with temperate highland valleys and rugged peaks, Yucatán is a huge, flat limestone plain lacking the altitude of the Sierra Madres to cool its tropical temperatures. In the south near Campeche, the *Candalaria* and *Champotan* rivers flow through a dense **tropical rain forest.** But in the state of Yucatán, the limestone bedrock has so little topsoil that Diego de Landa called it "the country with least earth that I have seen since all of it is one living rock." Here the limestone is so porous that rains seep through its crust, creating underground rivers. Only where the crust has broken over an underground cave, making a natural well called a *cenote,* is there any surface water. Wherever the land remains uncultivated, a low scrub jungle grows. Yet it is in this riverless environment that the ancient Yucatecan **Maya** built their grand cities and sustained their populations without the windmills and pumps of modern civilization. Today, the peninsula is divided into three states—**Quintana Roo** (see that chapter), **Campeche,** and **Yucatán**—and until recently these states shared a common history.

PREHISTORY

Yucatecan independence from most of Mexico reaches back to prehistoric times when its civilization evolved as part of the Maya region that extended through Chiapas in *Mexico, Belize,* most of *Guatemala,* and parts of *Honduras.* This region shared a common culture differing in many ways from the cultures of central Mexico (see the chapter on Ancient Mexico).

The Maya lowland and highland cultures interacted through trade, and sometimes warfare, as separate territories and considered each other foreigners. The **Aztecs** never controlled the Maya nor received tribute from them, but they did trade, conducting business not through Aztec merchants but through the Putun Maya, a seafaring group often referred to as the *Phoenicians of the New World.*

The Maya ruins of Yucatán will seem shockingly distinct if you have traveled to Palenque or to Maya ruins in Guatemala. Archaeologists found the difference so great they considered Yucatán cities a later Maya development. For decades, archaeologists believed Maya peoples from the southern tropical rain forest, mostly in Guatemala, migrated to a deserted Yucatán in about A.D. 900, founding a new culture after the collapse of their own cities. Since many Yucatec cities used a variant of the elaborate writing and dating system of the southern area, it was hard to determine when Yucatán flourished. The long count system of the southern area dated monuments in a manner more exact than the Julian calendar used in Europe until the 16th century, but in Yucatán dates were usually recorded in the so-called Short Count, an abbreviated system giving rise to multiple interpretations (just as '82 is confusing if we don't know the century in which it occurred). Only recently have decipherments revealed kings, such as Lord Chac at Uxmal and Kakupacal at Chichen Itza, both Late Classic rulers.

No one now believes Yucatán's culture began in **A.D. 900.** Excavations at the ruins of Dzibilchaltun have proved that Maya lived in Yucatán and built ceremonial centers there from as early as **800 B.C.,** thriving on salt trade from enormous flats in northern Yucatán. In fact, both Yucatán and Campeche shared the culture and architecture of the southern lowlands through the Early Classic era ending in **A.D. 600.** Thereafter, Yucatán developed a distinctive style of superior architecture and art more geometric than realistic. When the southern area began its decline and mysterious collapse, Yucatán continued to flourish, perhaps receiving refugees from the south.

THE LATE CLASSIC PERIOD
(A.D. 600-900)

The Late Classic Period represented a time of growth when many new cities flourished throughout ancient Mexico, a period of great exchange of cultural ideas—murals at Cacaxtla near Mexico City show extraordinary Maya influence, and in Yucatán the *phallic sculptures, columns, and masks of Tlaloc,* the rain god of the Valley of Mexico, show influences from various central Mexican areas. It is out of this "internationalism" and experimentation that the Yucatán art style evolved, creating the famous Puuc-style ruins of **Uxmal, Kabah, Edzna,** and so many other ancient cities that attract tourists to Yucatán today. Given the geography of the area and Maya dependence on agriculture, it is not surprising that buildings are adorned with endless carvings of the *rain god Chac.* Of course the cult of rulership, so important throughout the ancient Maya world, is present here, too, but often in more abstract designs so typical of the Puuc—such as the lattice pattern that probably is the simple woven mat symbolizing the ruler's throne.

With such an explosion of towns and cultures, demand grew at the end of the Late Classic period for cacao (**chocolate beans** used as currency as well as an elite drink), salt, obsidian, and cotton, yet no single power was in a position to control this trade. Into this vacuum movcd thc **Putun Maya** (known also as *Chontal Maya* and *Itzas*), a subgroup based along the *Campeche-Tabasco coast* who were great boatmen. By developing a sea route around the Yucatán peninsula and along the coast to Honduras, the Putun supplied the goods demanded, particularly cacao, and later, metals such as copper and gold, dominating trade until the Spanish Conquest. On the way to achieving their commercial success, the Putun probably cut off the southern, inland Maya area, perhaps conquering many of those cities, including Palenque and Yaxchilan, in the process. Many archaeologists believe the Putun conquered Chichen Itza in A.D. 918.

POST-CLASSIC PERIOD
(A.D. 900-1200)

In the early Post-Classic Period (A.D. 900-1200), **Chichen Itza** seems to stand alone as a great urban center, perhaps demonstrating the power concentrated in the Putun trade system. Earlier cities had been abandoned, including Dzibilchaltun near the valuable salt flats. Chichen Itza also stands alone in the Yucatecan Maya area for its remarkable use of *central Mexican art forms*, including depictions of warriors with *"non-Maya" features*—round heads and thick noses instead of the traditional Maya "Roman" noses and sloping foreheads (from deformation). An assumed conquest in **A.D. 989** by *Toltecs* from Tula near Mexico City has been used to explain these influences, but recent excavations have brought the theory into question (see "Chichen Itza" below). The internationalism of the Late Classic Period already had introduced foreign influences into Maya art before **A.D. 900**. If the Putun conquered Chichen Itza in **A.D. 918** and before the time of the Toltecs, they would have brought more Mexican traits and practices with them; for, although Mayas, they were strongly influenced by the central area as a result of their middle position in trade. The Yucatecan Maya even considered the Putun foreigners because they spoke a different dialect of Maya—and according to Yucatecans they were "stammerers and stutterers" and as foreigners brought new traditions that were "shameful." They actually may be the "non-Maya" represented at Chichen. With so many early sources of the central Mexican styles, it is unclear what the Toltecs could have added to Chichen's art or whether they ever invaded Yucatán at all. Whichever group or groups controlled the powerful city of Chichen Itza during its history, clearly they glorified their military might in carvings of warriors and murals of battles. Around **A.D. 1200,** however, their power faded and Chichen Itza became a deserted city, sacred to the Maya as a place of pilgrimage until at least the time of the Conquest.

THE CITY OF MAYAPAN
(A.D. 1200-1450)

Mayapan replaced Chichen Itza as the *center of power,* though the events leading to this shift in power are unclear. Some evidence exists that a branch of the Putun from the island of Cozumel founded Mayapan. Mayapan represents one of the largest and last cities built by a civilization that had been evolving since before the time of Christ. Mayapan's artistic achievements are poor copies of Chichen Itza, representing a **decline**, if not a decadence, in Maya art. Yet the city's political and military might is impressive, controlling as it did all 12 provinces of Yucatán with their elite residing in Mayapan. Many archaeologists believe Mayapan represents an evolution of Maya civilization away from great religious and administrative centers toward more secular control. To be sure, little architecture at Mayapan is devoted to religious functions—only 140 such buildings out of over 3600 total—and the finest architecture is found in residences of the elite.

A revolt against Mayapan's concentrated authority occurred in about **A.D. 1440,** ending that city's rule and the last of Maya investment in massive stone architecture. However, that civilization continued to evolve into a more **commercial society** (see chapter on **Quintana Roo**) and was thriving at the time of the Spanish Conquest. The Maya still worshiped their traditional gods and made their pilgrimages to the rain god at the sacred *cenote* of Chichen Itza, to the *creator god Itzamna* at Izamal, and to the *moon goddess Ix Chel* at Cozumel. They retained their ancient calendar, wrote histories of their people, and maintained their knowledge of astronomy. Though they no longer built great centers of stone for their rulers and gods, they still lived in towns large enough to cause the conquistadors to describe them as more impressive than Seville. Unfortunately, most of these towns now lie under later Spanish settlements.

Reports were made by Spanish observers, particularly *Diego de Landa,* about the daily life and appearances of the Maya at the time of the Conquest. According to Landa, the Maya often worked collectively in farming, hunting, and fishing. While the main occupation of the Maya was **farming,** "their favorite occupation was trading." *Corn, in various forms, was the staff of life,* but stews of vegetables, venison, or fowl also were eaten. Whatever they had, they shared, even if there was little for their own needs, for "the Yucatecans are very generous and hospitable." Often they would throw all their savings into a celebration that would be accompanied by music and dancing (never the men with the women).

Maya standards of beauty required definite effort and some pain to achieve, much like a modern facelift. Women filed their front teeth and both sexes **tatooed** their bodies. But that, Landa tells us, was not all:

> It was held as a grace to be cross-eyed, and this was artificially brought about by the mothers, who in infancy suspended a small plaster from their hair down between the eyebrows and reaching the eye.... They also had their heads and foreheads flattened from infancy.... Their ears were pierced for earrings.... They did not grow beards and say their mothers were used to burn their faces with hot cloths to prevent the growth. Nowadays, beards are grown, although they are very rough, like hogs' bristles.

In **war,** Maya men wore quilted cotton armor, which the Spaniards soon adopted for themselves, used bows and arrows, and hurled rocks and spears tipped with obsidian blades. While their weapons were no match for the Spaniards', the Maya must have been awesome as they advanced to a cacophony of conch trumpets and turtle-shell drums, with faces painted red and black, shoulders draped with jaguar skins. As the Spaniards learned, the Maya conducted war with great ferocity.

COLONIAL YUCATÁN

> But the Maya were not as effete as the Aztecs; it took three decades for the Spaniards to secure a permanent foothold on the peninsula. Three violent revolutions in the 1500s almost dislodged them in the early days.

E. Wyllys Andrews IV

The Spaniards encountered Yucatán before pursuing the gold of the Aztecs, but believing the area a lesser island and having been greeted by showers of arrows rather than gifts, they happily ignored it until *Francisco de Montejo,* one of **Cortes'** captains, decided to make his mark on history. In **1527,** Montejo mounted his first attempt to conquer Yucatán, and failed. In 1530, he did a little better by establishing a base in Campeche and, from there, another at the abandoned ruins of Chichen Itza. Lucky to escape with their lives, he and his troops were soon expelled by the Maya. By 1535, the Spaniards had been victorious in the Aztec capital for 14 years and already had conquered and settled Guatemala, yet there wasn't one Spaniard on the Yucatán peninsula. Despite their iron swords, guns, and crossbows, the Spaniards were unable to conquer the Maya until the Maya conquered themselves through an internal feud between the two most **powerful dynasties**, the **Cocoms** and **Xius.** When Montejo's son returned to Yucatán in 1541, he won a major battle over these divided Maya. Soon thereafter, Xiu, the leader of the largest Maya province, converted to Christianity, ending any possibility of unified Maya resistance. **Mérida,** the first permanent Spanish town in Yucatán, was founded in **1542.**

While the Maya continued to rebel (once by uprooting all the plants brought by the Spaniards from the Old World, as if to expunge all trace of foreign influence), they were crushed time and again. They were forced to congregate in Spanish towns where they could be better controlled and where they had no farmland. The Maya economic and social structure was destroyed. And in **1562,** their books on history, astronomy, and religion were burned by the then Friar Landa, who, not being able to read the books, nonetheless explained:

> *We found a great number of books in their letters, and since they contained nothing but superstitions and falsehoods of the devil we burned them all, which they took most grievously, and which gave them great pain.*

Some Maya escaped to hinterlands in Yucatán, areas not yet settled by the Spaniards. Others went to Tayasal in Guatemala where they weren't conquered until nearly the 18th century. Most died from disease. By **1700,** only 130,000 Maya remained in Yucatán, less than half of the population that survived the Conquest. Those who remained became serfs in the Spanish feudal system, quietly preserving their traditions as well as they could and understandably glorifying their past:

> *Then the Indians had no sickness; they had no aching bones; they had no burning chest. They had no abdominal pain; they had no consumption; they had no headache. At that time, the course of humanity was orderly. The foreigners made it otherwise.*

**The Book of Chilam Balam of Chumayel,
17th century**

From the Spanish point of view, Yucatán was a disappointment. No ready riches came to them—no gold, no silver, not even rich soil. The natural resources of the peninsula, such as the much-sought-after logwood of Campeche, were difficult to export due to a treacherous coast that was a stronghold for both English and French **pirates**. The Spaniards turned to their large landholdings to raise cattle and crops, and the area became a backwater of the Spanish Empire, neither part of New Spain (Mexico) nor of Guatemala. Only sections of the peninsula were settled by Spaniards: the northwest around Mérida, the area around the port of Campeche, and Valladolid. The entire East Coast, now called Quintana Roo, was practically abandoned except for the Spanish toehold at Lake Bacalar outside of Chctumal. Through these centuries of colonial rule, Yucatán remained a **feudal state**, entering the 19th century as a "social fossil," as *Nelson Reed* so aptly put it.

MODERN YUCATÁN

In 1821, without firing a shot, Yucatán found itself independent of Spain, a result of the bloody independence struggle in neighboring Mexico. Free of the commercial shackles of Spain, Yucatán changed quickly into a mercantile society, investing in plantations of export crops like **sugarcane** and **henequen.** (Henequen, an *agave* looking much like the century plant, is often called "*sisal.*" The plant flourishes in the poor soil of northern Yucatán and had been cultivated by the Maya in pre-Hispanic times for stringing their bows and making rope.) The area pursued such enterprises as cotton mills, stagecoach lines, and a printing press. A burst of commercial activity accompanied a population explosion—from 358,000 in 1800 to 580,000 in 1845. These two forces led to an increasing number of settlements in frontier regions to the south and east—areas in which Maya had formerly lived off the land independent of **European society**. The greed for land on which to grow valuable export crops went unchecked by the protective laws of Spain. Mayas, former hacienda owners, and the Church all often found themselves deprived of their property and access to water. Unlike the other losers in this land grab, the Maya were hard pressed to survive.

Along with independence came the issue of whether Yucatán should join Mexico. Used to being ignored, Yucatecans had an independent spirit yet still joined Mexico in 1823. Disliking the interference from Mexico City in Yucatecan affairs that resulted, but at times enjoying certain commercial advantages from the union, Yucatán seceded and joined, then seceded and fought over joining until 1849 when—as we shall see—**it had no choice but to be Mexican.**

THE CASTE WAR

The separatist movement in Yucatán, led by ladinos (or those of European stock) achieved success against Mexico by arming the numerous Maya and enticing them to fight with promises of better conditions. No matter how many times these promises were made and no matter how often the Maya fought the ladino battles, no land or tax reductions ever resulted. Mayas, now armed and experienced in **European war strategies,** grew increasingly angry. In 1847, while Mexico and the United States were fighting over Texas, Yucatáns fought each other over whether to be part of Mexico. During this

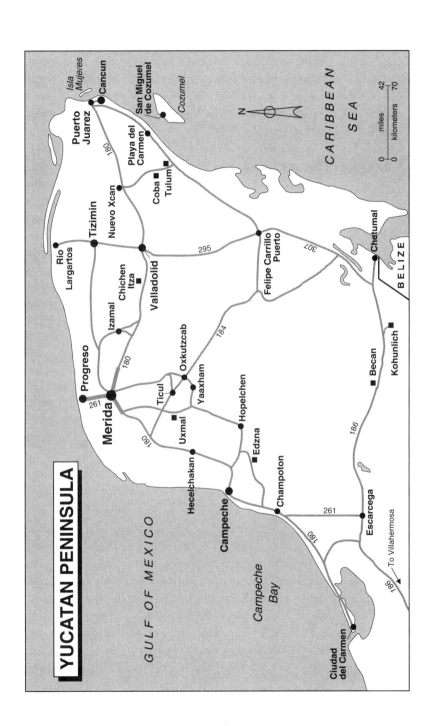

YUCATAN PENINSULA

turmoil, the Maya made their own demands for land. A political war grew, through misunderstandings and betrayals on both sides, into a devastating racial conflict, the Caste War of Yucatán.

The Maya from the frontier regions found little support from the assimilated Maya in the heavily settled areas of the northwest. Nonetheless, the first years of the Caste War saw the frontier Maya practically *pushing the ladinos into the sea.* By 1848, the **rebel Maya controlled** most of Yucatán. The ladinos had fled their outpost at Bacalar. Except for the few who remained trembling behind the fortified walls of the port of Campeche, the ladinos had abandoned the south and most had left Mérida. Then, at a time when the governor of Yucatán was composing his evacuation order for the remaining people in Mérida, the **Maya mysteriously disappeared** from the battlefields. They had seen **clouds of winged ants,** a traditional sign of the first rain, and had decided it was time to plant their fields in order not to offend their gods. As **Nelson Reed** says,

> *These people were masters of the tactics of the Yucatecan bush, but they had no concept of strategic demands.... They had beaten the Dzul [whites] and that was good; but now it was time to plant corn. The habits of a lifetime, the sense of religious duty and family responsibility commanded.... They were peasant farmers, not soldiers.*

THE REBEL MAYA

When the ladinos learned of their opportunity to regain Yucatán, they offered it as a colony to almost any country that could help them end the war—the **United States** (some Americans did volunteer to fight), **Cuba,** and **Spain.** But it was the Mexican government that provided the assistance in 1849 after the conclusion of the **Mexican-American War**. The Caste War continued off and on until 1855, when Yucatecans simply tired of it. The rebel Maya had been pushed back to the eastern part of the peninsula—where they congregated around their capital of Chan Santa Cruz and a speaking cross that promised them that God was with them. There they maintained a state separate from the rest of Yucatán and all of Mexico until the beginning of this century, when Federal troops finally took control of what is now called the state of Quintana Roo. The wars had taken their toll on Yucatán: its population had been reduced by half between 1846 and 1850, food was scarce, and the sugarcane plantations were destroyed forever.

The henequen industry survived to become the "**green gold**" of Yucatán, surpassing even silver in Mexico's foreign exchange and changing Yucatán from one of the poorest to one of the wealthiest states in Mexico. The world demand for the fine cordage produced from henequen increased throughout the end of the 19th century and reached its peak during **World War I.** Méridanos became *millionaires*, sending their children to universities in Europe, traveling abroad themselves, and affecting European customs. Even the Church regained some of its wealth, for the bishop took to riding in a jewel-encrusted carriage designed by a *Parisian* goldsmith. Nevertheless, the concentration of henequen displaced many people. Henequen was so valuable that little land was set aside for other crops such as corn, and food had to be imported for sale at expensive prices. Large numbers of landless individuals were held in debt peonage, or near slavery, by the henequen plantation owners. Henequen brought wealth, but it also set the stage in Yucatán for the **Revolution of 1910.**

The reforms of the Revolution for the first time created in Mexico the means for all its people—Indians, mestizos, and whites —to participate in the economy and to be citizens with rights in a modern state. Yucatán became more closely a part of larger Mexico as roads, trains, and air service firmly linked it for the first time to the rest of the country. But the revolution could do nothing about the decline that the henequen industry suffered after **World War II** because of new *synthetic fibers.*

Henequen remains one of the few plants to flourish in the harsh land of northwestern Yucatán, and 40% of the economically active population of the state depends on henequen for its livelihood. Mexican scientists have initiated intense research to find profitable new uses for the plant and hope that instead of just cordage this tough plant can be used to replace asbestos, cattle feed, or even become the basis of a cellulose industry. A new henequen carpeting now is selling quite well in Europe. More fortunate Campeche thrives from its Gulf Coast shipbuilding, fishing, and packing industry, and the entire Yucatán has profited from 20th-century tourism.

CONTEMPORARY MAYA LIFE

Maya culture…is still very much alive; one sees the present in the past and the past in the present.

J. Eric S. Thompson , 1970

Despite years of population loss suffered by the Yucatecan Maya from the Conquest and Caste War, their descendants today comprise the majority of the population in the state of Yucatán, populate the states of Campeche and Quintana Roo, and form one of the largest indigenous groups in all of Mexico. Despite devastating disruptions to their culture, the resilient and proud Maya have preserved important traditions from their ancient past, though some now have a Spanish veneer. They still speak Mayan, although most Yucatecan Maya are bilingual, speaking Spanish as well. And in housing, work, dress, diet, and religion, their pre-Hispanic past and colonial heritage continue to dominate.

THE MODERN MAYA HOME

The typical modern Maya home is the same *oval-shape hut* favored since before **100 B.C.** Its palm-thatched roof and whitewashed wattle-and-daub walls remain a familiar sight throughout Yucatán. Although *windowless,* the interiors of these homes are surprisingly cool due to the circulation created by the cracks between the wooden poles forming the walls. Wonderfully airy and comfortable hammocks replace beds to further combat the tropical heat; wisely, the smoky kitchens usually are set out in a rear yard.

Maya women dress in keeping with pre-Hispanic costumes, wearing *huipils,* a style of dress shown on many ancient Maya figurines from the island of **Jaina.** Made of spotlessly white cotton with red embroidery, these huipils are striking enough to have caught the attention of even **John L. Stephens,** the 19th-century explorer who had a great eye for ruins, but generally a poor one for costume. Stephens wrote that "they wore a picturesque costume of white, with a red border around the neck and shirt, and of that extraordinary cleanness which I had remarked as the characteristic of the poorest in Mérida."

As in pre-Hispanic times, the Maya economy is based primarily on agriculture; many farmers, like their ancestors, still subsist mainly by the cultivation of *maize,* with *beans, squash, and chile* comprising the other important crops. Since the Revolution of 1910, land has been reorganized primarily into communal *ejidos,* with the Maya farming collectively as they did before the Conquest. In many ways, farming techniques have not changed since pre-Hispanic times. Since the Yucatecan soil is not deep enough for plowing, farmers still plant by the laborious practice of making a hole in the ground with a stick and dropping a few grains into the hole by hand. **Ancient rituals** still are performed to gain favor from the gods who own the land and control the rain.

Some Maya received henequen lands after the Revolution, and they have suffered with the decreasing importance of henequen as a money crop. The alternative to a henequen-based agricultural economy for them appears to be migration to the cities and inevitable cultural loss. Ironically, whether these Maya maintain their traditions and language will be determined by the success of modern science in finding profitable uses for henequen.

Traces of the ancient Maya religion remain, but since the Maya absorbed parts of Christianity, their religion has become a fusion of **pre-Hispanic paganism and Catholicism.** Maya acceptance of Christianity was probably facilitated by similarities between the two religions. Both religions employed the cross as a major symbol, although for the Maya the cross was the stylized representation of the sacred *ceiba* tree that spanned the Underworld, the world of living, and the heavens. Both religions used incense, had altars, rituals for confession and baptism, and believed in fasting and continence. Both made ceremonial use of alcoholic drink.

REVERED GODS

Since the Maya are still tied to the soil, their ancient religion shines most brightly with the gods associated with agriculture. Not surprisingly, the most revered gods today are the ancient **Chacs,** the rain gods found adorning the temples at Uxmal and Chichen Itza. Next in importance are a collection of gods known as *Yuntzilob,* meaning "Worthy Lords," who guard villages against dangerous animals and evil winds, and protect farms from thieves and farmers from snakes. The principal god of the ancient Maya, *Itzamna,* the creator god, no longer appears in Maya religion, perhaps because he had no agricultural significance and was worshiped primarily by the ancient Maya elite.

From Catholicism the Maya have borrowed not Jesus but the numerous saints who are sometimes identified with ancient gods. The **Virgin Mary** receives prayer, but she has become identified with the Maya moon goddess *Ix Chel* (no virgin was she). As a result of Catholic influence, ancient idolatry has completely disappeared, with one important exception: the sacred *ceiba* tree is still worshiped. But Catholic influence is not totally absent even here since the sacred tree, represented as a cross by the ancient Maya, is now affectionately called "**our Lord Santa Cruz**."

Illness has many causes for the Maya, and many folk cures. Perhaps the most interesting example is evil eye or *mal de ojo,* which results from the gaze of certain people and afflicts children. While evil eye was introduced by the Spaniards, its cure is delightfully Maya. The person suspected of causing the disease must take the child in his arms and blow on its eyelids, the palms of its hands, the soles of its feet, and the crown of its head. What child (or adult) would not respond favorably to such treatment?

MÉRIDA

Yucatán may lack dramatic scenery, but it makes up this lack with an abundance of grand ruins (like Chichen Itza and Uxmal), provincial yet charming colonial towns, quiet coastal villages, and fine Maya towns, swept clean and full of oval, white, thatched houses in keeping with a tradition that has continued since before the time of Christ. Mérida, as the capital of this state and the gateway to Yucatán's pleasures for many travelers, provides an urban yet gracious setting for exploring the area.

The **"White City"** known as Mérida has become more variously hued with expansion, but the cool and chalk-white *guayaberas* (pleated shirts) of *mestizo* men and the white huipils embroidered with brilliant flowers of Maya women continue to give this capital city a distinctive atmosphere. The bustle of so tropical a city jars many who cannot believe that people can function so much and so well in weather so hot. Yet, when evening falls, traffic unsnarls, and the air cools, Mérida turns into a more romantic city, perfect for riding in a horse-drawn carriage to lighted colonial monuments and the tree-lined and elegant **Paseo de Montejo.**

While Mérida's accommodations and roads make it an excellent base for excursions to the many surrounding sights, the monuments reflecting its history, the kindliness of its people, and its cleanliness make the town itself worthwhile exploring. Try to spend at least a day visiting the zócalo and archaeology museum and shopping in the market area and boutiques.

KEY TO MÉRIDA

Sights • The sights of Mérida are overshadowed by its popular excursions; but its colonial and turn-of-the-century buildings, as well as its market and Maya life, make the city worthy of a visit.

Excursions • An area rich in Maya ruins (particularly Chichen Itza and Uxmal), colonial villages, and Gulf Coast towns.

Fiestas • Carnival is celebrated for five days with traditional dances and gaiety in Mérida and Gulf Coast villages. From September 28 to October 13, Mérida celebrates the Fiesta of the Christ of the Blisters ("Los Ampollas") with a carnival and parade along the Paseo de Montejo.

Sports • Swimming in the Gulf of Mexico or hotel pools; tennis at a few hotels; and golf just outside of Mérida.

Shopping • Mérida's shops and its daily market offer quality Panama and straw hats, fine hammocks, and huaraches (sandals). Guayabera shirts, gold filigree jewelry, and tortoiseshell knickknacks also are specialties of this region.

Where to Stay • Good hotels in all but super-deluxe categories. Reservations recommended.

Where to Eat • The distinctive cuisine of Yucatán should be tried, in addition to the seafood and Middle Eastern food.

Entertainment • Apart from the usual discos found in any city, Mérida offers some unusual nightspots with traditional dances and music and even a mock sacrifice.

Getting Around • The heart of the city is best walked, but taxis and calesas (horse-drawn carriages) abound for sightseeing and longer trips. Establish your fare for both in advance. Excursions are facilitated by car rentals, tours, and bus service to major sights.

The numbered streets in Mérida run north-south when they are even and west-east when they are odd.

Practical Tips • Mérida is hot all year, and particularly so from May to August. Air conditioning and a hotel with a pool can make all the difference in your comfort. A long siesta is in effect usually between 1-4 p.m., with shops opening again until 7 p.m.

THE ESSENTIAL MÉRIDA

WHAT TO SEE AND DO

Early morning and late afternoon are the best times to sightsee and shop, leaving the hottest part of the day to eat, nap, or take a swim. When you get tired, you can sit in a cafe with *Méridanos* or have your shoes shined while people-watching in the zócalo or town parks. You might consider a carriage ride for getting an overview of Mérida. Most rides begin near the Cathedral or Cepeda Park, continue north on Calle 60, and then take a turn on the *Paseo de Montejo* before returning via La Ermita.

Zócalo

Mérida's main square, its shrubs sculpted and formal and its *S-shaped love seats perfectly arranged for delicate tête-à-têtes*, sits on the location of the pre-Hispanic city of **Tiho,** which Diego de Landa described as "a squared site of great size, more than two runs of a horse." Here, the decisive battle between the Maya and Spaniards, led by Montejo the Younger, was fought in 1541, resulting in the conquest of Yucatán and the founding of Mérida. The Spanish victory can be seen in the colonial buildings surrounding the square, most of them constructed with stones quarried from Maya buildings. Nothing else remains of ancient Tiho.

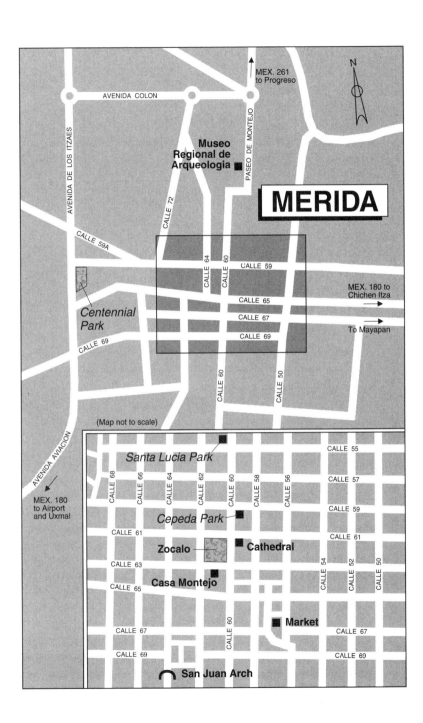

Montejo's Palace

South side of zócalo is a particularly strong reminder of the Conquest struggle: its carved facade shows two conquistadors standing on the heads of Maya Indians. This palace was built in 1549 by Maya artisans, and one can only wonder what they thought while carving the facade. The palace is now owned by a bank and is open to the public during banking hours.

The Cathedral

East side of zócalo built between 1561-1598 of stones from a Maya temple, is a ghost of its former splendid self, having been stripped of its interior furnishings during the Revolution of 1910. The shops and government offices next to it are housed in what originally was the Archbishop's Palace.

The Municipal Palace

West side dominates the square with its Moorish architecture and clock tower. The original municipal office sat atop a Maya pyramid that blocked the development of the western section of the city. Not until 1735 was this obstacle adequately overcome for the construction of the current building.

The Palacio de Gobierno (State House)

Northeast corner of the zócalo is a latecomer, being completed only in 1892. Murals depicting the history of Yucatán adorn its interior.

Calle 60, North of Zócalo

Clustered around Calles 59-55 are a number of small parks and buildings adequately noteworthy to make for a pleasant walk. **Cepeda Peraza Park** (formerly, and sometimes still, called Hidalgo Park) is a favorite Mérida spot for socializing. It is surrounded by a lovely ex-convent building, now a hotel, shops, and the **Church of the Third Order** (across Calle 59), built by the Jesuits in the 17th century before their expulsion from the Spanish empire. Walking just past the side of this church on Calle 59, you come to a restored colonial building that houses the **Pinacoteca del Estado,** with 19th-century portraits of the region's illustrious (closed Monday). On your way, notice the squiggle of a Maya carving embedded in the church wall. Continuing in front of the Church of the Third Order, on Calle 60, you will come to the tiny **Parque de la Madre,** named after its statue dedicated to motherhood. Opposite this park another small Maya carving can be seen in the rear wall of the **University of Yucatán.** Originally founded as a Jesuit university in 1618, the rebuilt Moorish building houses the state university.

Across Calle 60 from the university near Calle 57 is the **Teatro Peon Contreras,** a neoclassical gem restored and reopened in 1982 for performances and concerts. Established at the turn of the century during the period of enormous wealth from the henequen (sisal) trade, this theater was designed and built by imported Italian artists using Italian marble.

At Calles 55 and 60, you will come to **Santa Lucia Park** surrounded by a colonial arcade, the location of Thursday night concerts of traditional Yucatecan music. Originally, the area served as a stagecoach station; tethering hooks can still be seen on the columns. The small church was built in the 16th century and was the only church that could be attended by people "of color" until the following century.

Paseo de Montejo

Henequen, that spiked cactuslike plant seen ad infinitum to the north of Mérida, made the best rope available to the world until after World War II. The high demand for henequen products at the beginning of the 20th century made Mérida a place with more millionaires than any other city of comparable size in the world. Elegant mansions in French and Moorish style along the broad, treelined avenue of the *Paseo de Montejo* resulted from this affluence. The recent addition of sidewalk cafes makes this area even more enjoyable to visit.

Museo Regional de Arqueologia

Paseo Montejo at Calle 43; open Tues.-Sat., 8 a.m.-8 p.m., Sun. 8 a.m.-2 p.m.; admission fee • One of the most elegant, rococo mansions on the *Paseo de Montejo* houses the museum of archaeology. At the beginning of this century, this mansion served as the **Governor's Palace;** now its cool marble interior includes a fine collection of stone carvings, ceramics, and figurines from Chichen Itza and other Maya sites. Particularly interesting are the offerings of gold animal pieces and *jade* found in the sacred *cenote* at Chichen Itza.

Arches

At the end of the 17th century, Spaniards fortified their town with an encircling wall. Entrances to the town were defined by Moorish arches, three of which are still standing. Although not worth a special visit, you will spot them during your exploration of Mérida. The **Arco de San Juan,** to the south of the zócalo on Calles 64 and 69, just past the baroque Church of San Juan on Calle 62, is the arch most often seen, as traffic patterns take you through it on your return from La Ermita. To the east of town, the two remaining ones are within a block of each other on Calle 50: the **Arco de Dragones** at Calle 61 and the **Arco del Puente** at Calle 63.

La Ermita de Santa Isabela

Calles 66 and 77. • Originally outside the city walls, this 18th-century hermitage was a place to pray for a safe trip on the colonial road to Campeche. Today it possesses a beautiful garden with Maya statuary and a waterfall. At night, the dramatic lighting and waterfall are turned on upon request.

EXCURSIONS

Port of Progreso and Ruins of Dzibilchaltun

42 km (26 m) north of Mérida • If you find yourself wanting to get away from the crowd of tourists, *a day trip to the Gulf Coast for swimming and a visit to the ruins of Dzibilchaltun can be very pleasant,* although neither the beaches nor the ruins rival the better-known tourist spots. The beaches between **Progreso** and Chicxulub to the east, and Progreso and Chuburna to the west, are quite deserted in the winter season because, no matter how scorching the temperature may seem to us, Méridanos still consider it winter and keep their summer homes boarded up. Summers, especially weekends, are another matter and you'll be happy to move away from the center. Fortunately the beach stretches, seemingly endlessly, in both directions. Both Progreso and the new fishing port of Yucalpeten, several miles to the west, have dressing rooms for bathers. Fishing is very active in the area, and good seafood can be obtained at the small beach restaurants. Consider a *lunch* with a sea view at **Captain Marisco** (Malecón between 60 and 62; moderate), to the right of the main drag. If you would like to stay longer, there are some hotels including the new tourist development at Yucalpeten.

It is a 1/2-hour drive to Progreso, there is regular daily bus service leaving from the Calle 62 terminal in Mérida. If you are traveling by car tour, Dzibilchaltun can be visited easily; there is bus service, too, leaving from the Progreso terminal every day but Sunday.

Dzibilchaltun

15 km (9 m) north on Progreso Road turn right and continue 5 km (3 m) to Xcunya. The ruins are just south of town. Open 8 a.m.-5 p.m. Admission charge • Visiting these ruins you will find it hard to believe they represent the largest of Maya cities, a city whose wealth was based on trading salt from nearby coastal flats. Dzibilchaltun (zeeb-eel-chal-TOON) was occupied continuously from at least 800 B.C. until the Spaniards built a small chapel at the site in 1590. During its peak (A.D. 700-1000), the city covered an area larger than Washington, D.C. Today, only what archaeologist E. *Wyllys Andrews IV* described as the Pennsylvania Avenue of Dzibilchaltun reminds you of the grandeur once achieved with its paved 60-foot-wide causeway connecting the main buildings of the ceremonial center for a distance of 1-1/2 miles. Few of the buildings along the causeway could be restored because the cut stones of this ancient city were appropriated by builders of the Mérida-Progreso highway and nearby towns and henequen haciendas.

As you walk into the site, you may very well find workers busily sprucing up the ruins, and making more of them accessible. Usually you enter the site at the center of the causeway and at the natural well of the city, the **Cenote Xlacah.** The tranquil setting of the cenote makes it hard to imagine it was once the center of activity and surrounded by some of the largest Maya palaces ever discovered, one with 20 vaulted rooms. **Divers** exploring the cenote's more than **140-foot depth** discovered thousands and thousands of objects, mostly pieces of pottery and some interesting hairpins and rings carved with hieroglyphs. Also, bones were found—of Maya, of many cows that must have fallen in, and even those of a Spaniard. Based on the number of sea-fan offerings from coral reefs found in the cenote, archaeologists think the cenote played a part in the rituals of a sea cult. Some of the recovered objects can be seen in the small **Museum** near the guard's house.

The complex on the eastern end of the causeway, with its reconstructed **Temple of the Seven Dolls,** is the most interesting at the site. This temple with four stairways is aligned with three structures in front, an arrangement that indicates it was used as a solar observatory for making calendrical adjustments. Although the temple is ungraceful and its rare windows and small tower are awkward, it has a captivating history. The temple was constructed about A.D. 500 and later covered by a larger temple. Much later, in the 13th or 14th century, Maya cut through the larger temple into the Temple of the Seven Dolls and rededicated it by burying in the floor seven clay figurines (hence, the name of the temple) representing deformed individuals. A hollow tube, or psychoduct, was placed between the burial and temple floor for communication with the interred "spirits" during curing ceremonies. An altar painted with a medallion containing calendrical hieroglyphs, the only ones known from this later period, was constructed and repainted over time with new symbols, indicating continued use of the rededicated temple. The figurines are in the museum at the site.

Izamal

72 km (45 m) east of Mérida on MEX 180 or the toll road MEX 180D • Izamal charms you with its provincial atmosphere, colonial architecture, and horse-drawn carriages, and on-going restorations should make a visit even more worthwhile. Izamal reminds you of the early struggle for control between the proud Maya and determined Spaniards, because Izamal's *16th-century church and monastery* sit atop an earlier Maya pyramid. The church (closed 1-3 p.m.) was the seat of the Franciscan district administered by Diego de Landa, whose determination to convert the heathen Maya led to whippings and floggings. His zeal must have been intensified by knowing that Izamal formerly had been a Maya pilgrimage center dedicated to the god *Itzamna,* the creator of the universe. Few of the original **pyramids,** some dating from **A.D. 300-600** still exist, but one has been partially restored. Located 2-1/2 blocks north of the plaza (near the intersection of Calles 27 and 28) yet visible from the church, it is one of the *largest pyramids* from ancient Mexico and was dedicated to the **sun god.** Rumors persist that someone is buried inside; *perhaps excavations begun in 1993 will find evidence of a tomb.*

Izamal can be visited on a brief excursion from Mérida by bus or in combination with a longer trip to Chichen Itza, if you have a car. Follow the Valladolid-Cancún road to either Hoctun (30 m or 48 km) or Katunil (10 m farther)—there is only one exit from the toll road—and turn left onto a small paved road that reaches Izamal after 20 km (12 m).

Mayapan Ruins

(Banner of the Maya) 50 km (31 m) southeast of Mérida. Open 9 a.m.-5 p.m. An admission fee • Bring a picnic lunch. The little-visited ruins and villages along the road to Mayapan provide a pleasant half-day excursion for those who have already seen the more impressive ruins in Yucatán. Before reaching Mayapan, you pass remnants of an earlier Maya site (A.D. 250-600) intermingled with the present town and thatched houses of **Acanceh.** Although you can't miss the pyramid on the zócalo, the most interesting remains here are fragments of Teotihuacan-style carvings on a temple a few blocks from the main square. (To be taken to these ruins, visit the *encargado* at his home just to the right of the market, as you face it, at Calle 23 #94. Small fee.) As for Mayapan, its history is more interesting than its near-devastated physical remains, *but you probably will find yourself alone with the tumbled sculptures of feathered serpents scattered about the site.*

After the Conquest, Spanish chroniclers were told that Chichen Itza, Uxmal, and Mayapan formed a triumvirate controlling most of Yucatán. Yet excavations have shown that at the time of Mayapan (**A.D. 1200-1450**), Uxmal already had been abandoned for centuries and Chichen Itza's heyday too was over. In fact, Mayapan represents the last large city of Maya civilization. Mayapan was a true urban center, with an estimated 11,000-12,000 people concentrated within a small area of about two square miles. This **walled city** contained over 3600 structures, most of them houses, with a ceremonial district in its center. Like Tulum on the Caribbean coast, the city is enclosed by walls, although there is some controversy as to whether the walls could have effectively defended the cities. Unlike earlier Maya cities, Mayapan has no clear plan or arrangements of buildings, and paths among the houses are mazelike. The building techniques are crude, abandoning the fine-cut stones and veneer used during the Puuc period and at Chichen Itza. The scale, too, fails to be impressive. All this shoddy workmanship was covered with thick layers of stucco, which **J. Eric Thompson** called "heavy makeup to hide wrinkles."

While the decadence of the art of Mayapan is undisputed, its political achievements impress everyone who considers that this city singly ruled Yucatán and its estimated 12 provinces for at least 200 years. Mayapan's effective control was achieved by what has been variously described as a confederacy of provincial leaders or as their enforced residence in Mayapan. Militarism certainly lay behind such control. It was at Mayapan that the bow and arrow first was introduced in

Yucatán, supplementing the spear-thrower. The city, located in an agriculturally unproductive area, supported itself through tribute. The nobles, whether held against their wills or not, sent to their towns for what was needed, "such as birds, maize, honey, salt, fish, game, cloth, and other things" (**Landa**).

Around 1440, disgruntled Maya led by the Xiu rulers rose against Mayapan and destroyed it. The city was sacked and burned, its idols smashed. Today, the ruins stand in a poor state, though some of the ceremonial center has been partially restored. You can see many architectural features found at Chichen Itza and copied at Mayapan—colonnades, round structures (one like the *Caracol* was destroyed by lightning in the 19th century), and a platform with a carved serpent head at the top of its balustrades. The most important building at Mayapan, in the center of the ceremonial area, was a near duplicate of the Castillo at Chichen, but only half its size.

Regular bus service is not available to the Mayapan ruins. To arrive at Mayapan by car, leave Mérida on Calle 67 until it ends. Turn right, then angle right onto 4-lane Calle 69. Soon you'll cross MEX 180 and pass through Kanasin before coming to Acanceh (28 km, 17 m), where you turn right toward Oxkutzcab. Continue through the town of Telchaquillo and, after 2 km, turn right at the sign for the Mayapan ruins. *The paved and narrow road from Mérida to Mayapan and its continuation to Oxkutzcab (60 km, 37 m) reveals much of Yucatán's past. Rubble mounds of ancient ruins mark entrances to towns like Chumayel, while pyramids still stand in Acanceh; huge 16th-century mission churches dominate tidy Maya villages* like **Tecoh, Mama,** and **Mani;** abandoned colonial buildings at **Petectunich** speak to the former glory of the henequen trade. For all the drama and conflict these historic remains represent, the road provides a most tranquil alternative route to the Uxmal area. (See that chapter, "Crossroads: Oxkutzcab.") Note: Churches along this route close for a few hours around midday.

SHOPPING

Yucatecan hammocks, Panama hats, huipils, henequen and palm handbags, baskets and mats, gold and silver *filigree* jewelry, leather huaraches, pottery and *guayaberas* fill the market and shops of Mérida. Some of these crafts are of exceptionally high quality, particularly the **hammocks** and **Panama hats.** Yucatecan hammocks are far and away the *finest in Mexico,* and they are widely available in Mérida, even to being sold by street vendors in front of the first-class hotels. In the United States, they sell at exorbitant prices in exclusive boutiques. Used by the Maya in place of beds (and sofas and chairs!), these hammocks are extremely comfortable and ideal for sleeping or daydreaming in your backyard or porch. For the most comfort and support, you lie diagonally across them and hang them from ropes. The best ones are made from cotton, but more and more are now made from nylon—a material often preferred by the Maya for its durability.

The hammocks come in a variety of lengths and widths—the matrimonial size can sleep two Maya or one American football player fairly comfortably, and even larger widths are available. Sleep in a Yucatecan hammock and you may never return to your bed again.

Somewhat surprisingly, **Panama hats** are made in Yucatán. They received their familiar name when they gained constant use against the tropical sun during the construction of the Panama Canal. Known locally as *jipis* (hee-pees), they are woven from the fiber of the *guano* palm. Since this palm needs dampness to preserve its flexibility, the weaving traditionally is done in caves. The quality of the hats varies considerably, with the finest ones coming from the town of **Becal,** Campeche.

Look for the traditional *huipil,* the sacklike dress or long blouse still worn by the Maya women of Yucatán. The best huipils are of cotton with hand-embroidered flower designs around the neck; sleeves, and bottom. Inferior huipils have machine-made borders and often come in synthetic materials, but even these are cool and comfortable to wear in the tropical climate. For men, there are the popular **guayaberas**—those comfortable, pleated shirts which replace ties and jackets in the tropics. They abound in Mérida, where they are manufactured in a variety of styles, colors, and fabrics (they should contain some cotton to be cool).

Mérida offers an excellent selection of **huaraches**, which are comfortable but unfortunately not durable. Although the soles made from used tires last forever, the straps break easily. Try to find the huaraches with straps sewn directly into the soles rather than attached by metal rings. Since huaraches are inexpensive, you might want to buy an extra pair.

WHERE TO SHOP

You will find the best shopping in the market, the shops around the market area, and stores just beyond the zócalo around Calles 60 and 59. In the market and surrounding shops, bargaining is expected. Fixed prices generally are the order of the day in those shops close to the zócalo.

The bustling **market,** located a few blocks south of the zócalo, sprawls around Calles 56 and 67, and is filled with stalls selling food, crafts, clothing, and household items. Maya women in their white huipils appear everywhere, and vendors are low-keyed and friendly. The huaraches sold here (*Calle 67 at rear of indoor food market*) are as good as can be found anywhere, and the selection is enormous. Stalls are filled with henequen, straw, and palm goods, particularly hats and baskets. Other Yucatecan crafts are available in the **Mercado de las Artesanias** building. Even if you aren't buying, visit the market for its liveliness and local color.

Panama hats vary considerably in quality and price, as you'll notice surveying the stalls of *sombreristas (Calle 67 on left).* For some of the very finest Panamas you should walk out of the market to a nearby, tiny shop called **El Becaleno** *(Calle 65 #483, behind the post office).* Here you will find hats woven so finely that you will have difficulty seeing the weaving. Just ask for "los finos." These hats are so pliable they can be rolled into a tube and tied with a black hatband to fit into the smallest of suitcases. If you don't buy here, you can at least continue shopping in the market with a clearer idea of quality.

To find an excellent selection of hammocks head for **La Poblana** *(Calle 65 #492, near Calle 60)*. The owner will order his young employees to scurry after the hammocks you desire. Frequently, this requires acrobatic ability as they leap from banisters over boxes, performing death-defying feats to get to the hammock of your choice. The hammocks come in a variety of sizes, colors, and prices. Before buying, you should check the width and length to see if you will fit into it comfortably (remember, these hammocks are most comfortable when you lie in them diagonally, so the width is important). The length—excluding the hammock arms—should exceed your height. Check the arms to see that the strings are not twisted or tangled and give preference to a tightly woven hammock as it will have more resilience. There are lots of decisions to make, but the hammock you buy will be one of the finest in the world.

Other shops can be found in the area around the zócalo, particularly to the north. On the corner of Calle 60 at 59 is **Galeria Mexicana,** containing some decent silver jewelry. Next door is **El Paso,** with Escalera dresses alongside some curios. A few blocks away is **Boutique Maria Soleil** *(Calle 59 #511 at 62)* and **Fernando Huertas** *(Calle 62 #491)*, both with colorful designer clothes, some jewelry, and a few crafts. Guayaberas seem everywhere, but **Jack** *(Calle 59 #505)* and **Camiseria Canul** *(Calle 59 #496B)* have large selections. The **Museo de Arte Popular** *(Calle 59 between 48 and 50)* has a good crafts shop, well-stocked with items from all over Mexico. While here you might visit the costume and crafts exhibitions (open 8 a.m.-8 p.m., Sunday 9 a.m.-2 p.m., closed Monday; free). And lastly, the government-operated **Casa de la Cultura** *(Calle 63 between 64 and 66; closed weekends)* sells both crafts and curios from around Mexico. (On your way there, look into the chapel on the corner of Calle 64 for a glimpse of a finely hammered gold cross.)

WHERE TO STAY

Mérida has many hotels in all categories, but they are often full. Reserve in advance or be willing to hotel-hop looking for a room. When the temperature soars, particularly from May through August, air conditioning and a pool can be necessities for an enjoyable visit. For reservations write Mérida, Yucatán, 97000 Mexico or, call area code 99.

EXPENSIVE

Holiday Inn ★★★
Av. Colon 498 at Paseo de Montejo; ☎ *25-68-77; $165* • This modern hotel offers the most amenities in Mérida. Near the cafes and restaurants of the tranquil Paseo area, the hotel is just far enough out of center to require a taxi or car. Its 214 well-appointed, air-conditioned rooms are quiet, with views of the pool or fountain. Good service. Shops, coffee shop, restaurant, bar with evening entertainment, night-

club. Large pool with swim-up bar. Tennis. Parking. *For reservations, call, in the U.S.,* ☎ *800-465-4329.*

El Castellano

Calle 57 #513; ☎ *23-01-00; $95* • The centrally located, sleek, and modern El Castellano is a fine addition to Mérida's hotel offerings. Its lobby is large and airy; its 170 air-conditioned rooms are spacious and comfortable. Some rooms on upper stories have panoramic views of the city. Attractive restaurant and bar. Pool. Parking.

Los Aluxes

Calle 60 #444; ☎ *24-21-99; $95* • The polished common areas of this hotel along with its garden pool and good service, make it more than comfortable. The 109 air-conditioned rooms (some suites) are acceptable. Restaurants and lounges. Shops. Valet parking. *Write Apartado 1574-B.*

MODERATE

Casa del Balam

Calle 60 #488 at Calle 57; ☎ *24-88-44; $94* • Handsome and designed in contemporary colonial style with Mexican touches for color and warmth, this town hotel has six floors of rooms built around the lobby atrium and tranquil fountain. Some of the 56 large, sparely furnished, and air-conditioned rooms have exterior windows that can be noisy. Shops, dining room, and bar; intimate walled garden with shaded pool. Pay parking. In our view the most charming of the in-town hotels, but service needs improvement.

Calinda Panamericana

Calle 59 #455 at 54; ☎ *23-91-11; $88* • A 15-minute walk from the zócalo, this hotel offers enough ambience to be worth the slight inconvenience. The lobby is in a turn-of-the-century mansion decorated with stucco friezes and fountains. The 110 large and air-conditioned rooms are in more modern wings, but remain a bit old-fashioned. Restaurant, bar, and shops. Pleasant pool area. *For reservations call, in the U.S.,* ☎ *800-228-5151.*

Mérida Mision Park Inn

Calle 60 #491 at Calle 57; ☎ *23-95-00; $167* • This hotel remains one of the most popular in Mérida. Centrally located a few blocks from the zócalo, with 150 air-conditioned, somewhat plain rooms of good size, the Mision offers a large pool and garden, a restaurant, and bar with entertainment. *For reservations, call, in the U.S.,* ☎ *800-648-7818.*

INEXPENSIVE

Caribe

Calle 59 at 60; ☎ *24-90-22; $35-47* • Tucked away in a corner of the Parque Cepada, this converted convent offers a pleasant garden to relax in and a rooftop pool with view of church tops to cool off in. The

56 small rooms are brightly furnished and fairly well-maintained. Restaurant and bar. Some rooms are air-conditioned, others with fans.

Posada Toledo ★
Calle 58 #487 at Calle ☎ *57; 23-16-90; $42* • A lovely mansion, transformed into an intimate hotel around a garden. Most of the 22 rooms are large, if dark, and with a/c. No pool. Roof-garden lounge. Restaurant for breakfast only.

Colonial ★
Calle 62 #476; ☎ *23-64-44; $55* • This centrally located hotel may be a bit plastic, but it's well maintained. There are 52 small air-conditioned rooms. Small pool. Air-conditioned restaurant.

Colon ★
Calle 62 #483; ☎ *23-43-55; $59* • The tiled lobby and pool (steam baths too) are the best assets of this hotel. The 50 rooms are becoming precariously worn.

BUDGET

Dolores Alba √★
Calle 63 #464; ☎ *28-56-50; $30* • Three long blocks from the zócalo, you will find this small oasis of a hotel with 22 fresh and attractive rooms, a few air-conditioned. Decent pool. Dining room. A very good buy.

Montejo
Calle 57 #507; ☎ *28-02-77; $28* • Thirty monastic, clean rooms in a colonial building around a pleasant courtyard. Nice atmosphere in a good location. Most rooms with air conditioning.

WHERE TO EAT

A pig arrived...the cooking of which enlisted the warmest sympathies of all our heads of departments.... They had their own way of doing it, national, and derived from their forefathers.... They made an excavation on the terrace, kindled a large fire in it, and kept it burning until the pit was heated like an oven. Two clean stones were laid on the bottom, the pig (not alive) was laid upon them and covered with leaves and bushes, packed down with stones so close as barely to leave vent to the fire, and allow an escape for the smoke.

John L. Stephens

Stephens' mid-19th-century description of barbecued pig (*cochinita pibil*) would need few changes for present-day Yucatán. The distinctive traditional Yucatecan cuisine is kept alive in villages throughout the peninsula and, fortunately for the traveler, many of these intricate and tasty dishes are available in restaurants in Mérida.

YUCATECAN CUISINE

Two of the most flavorful dishes, *cochinita pibil* and *pollo pibil*, have similar cooking methods and sauces. **Pib** is the Maya word for the traditional oven described by Stephens—a pit with stones. Although in villages these dishes are still pit-cooked, in Mérida restaurants they steam them instead. Both are marinated for some 24 hours in a sauce with a variety of spices including achiote, a popular red spice made from the seed of the annatto tree. *Naranja agria* ("sour orange") helps to give these dishes their distinctive flavor. After marinating, the meat is wrapped in banana leaves and cooked for several hours. If you are a traveler with no love for hot food, you will be happy to learn there are no hot chiles in these or most other Yucatecan dishes.

OTHER TRADITIONAL DISHES

Other traditional dishes worth trying include *papadzules* (meaning "food for the lords"), wonderfully delicate in flavor, a creation of tortillas stuffed with chopped hard-boiled eggs covered with a pumpkinseed and tomato sauce and decorated with a green oil obtained from pressed pumpkinseeds. Although Yucatecans eat *papadzules* as an appetizer, you may find them perfectly adequate for a main dish. *Sopa de lima*, or lime soup, is the most popular Yucatecan soup, with good reason. Made from a rich chicken broth combined with sour lime juice, tomatoes, onions, spices, chicken pieces, and fried tortilla chips, the soup is memorable. Another set of dishes called *escabeche* come with chicken, turkey, or shrimp. *Escabeche* is a mild pickling marinade that often includes onions, vinegar, and a variety of spices. For breakfast, lunch, or any time of day, try the justly popular *huevos Motulenos,* named after the Yucatecan town of Motul where we can testify they do, somehow, make the best version of these eggs. Nevertheless, they are available all over Mérida. The dish consists of fried eggs on tortillas, piled high with everything in the house—refried beans, diced ham, peas, tomato sauce, and cheese. For a snack, try *panuchos,* small fried open-faced tortillas topped with beans, pickled onions, and either *cochinita pibil or pollo en escabeche. Venado* ("venison") in various forms is popular throughout the Yucatán peninsula, as are a variety of *pavo* (turkey) dishes. Perhaps the most popular turkey dish is *pavo en relleno negro,* made from a paste of burnt-black chile, which we find too bitter. If available, try the more delicately flavored *pavo en relleno blanco,* made with a rich, yet mild, white sauce with olives, capers, and almonds. Finally, look for *poc-chuc,* thin slices of very tasty pork grilled with spices, sour-orange juice, tomatoes, and onions.

Although Yucatecan cuisine is normally not hot, beware of the sauces served as side dishes. More often than not, they include the notorious Yucatecan *chile habanero*—pure fire—and reportedly the hottest of Mexico's chiles. If you like hot food as we do, the habanero is wonderful in small doses, that, no matter how small, still seem to pack a wallop.

Since Mérida is close to the Gulf Coast, fresh seafood is readily available. And due to the sizeable **Lebanese** community in Mérida, **Middle Eastern food** appears on many menus and in special restaurants. If all this does not provide enough choice for you, many restaurants serve **continental** and **American** dishes. Yucatán has its own **beers**. The more popular brands include *Montejo, Carta Clara,* and the dark *Leon Negra.* The locally made

Xtabentun, a liqueur flavored with anise and honey, may appeal to some tastes.

RESTAURANTS

Restaurants are casual, as they should be in this tropical town. Jackets are almost never required (or worn, for that matter). "Dressed-up" Yucatecan men will wear the popular guayabera shirts. Since many restaurants fall into the moderate and inexpensive categories, some fine meals can be had at very reasonable prices. Price categories are explained in the Introduction.

To try Yucatecan food head for **Los Almendros** *(Calle 50A #493 on the quiet Plaza Mejoroda between Calles 59 and 57)*, serving what we believe to be the finest, traditional Yucatecan dishes in a modest, yet comfortable, atmosphere. Only Yucatecan dishes are served, including *papadzules, sopa de lima, poc-chuc, pibil dishes*, and *pavo en relleno blanco*—all delicious, with our favorites being the pavo en escabeche and the cochinita pibil. Inexpensive to moderate. More centrally located, **El Patio** *(Calle 60 #496 at 59)* can be found through the wonderful old lobby of the Grand Hotel. This simple dining spot serves Yucatecan specialties at low prices.

CONTINENTAL

If you are in the mood for a bit more elegance and international cuisine, our number one choice is **Le Gourmet** *(Av. Perez Ponce 109A, extension of Av. Colon, running east off the Paseo Montejo;* ☎ *27-19-70)*, located in an old house with several comfortable dining rooms. Despite such bizarre features of the menu as egg rolls and shrimp chow mein, the food is mainly continental, with an emphasis on steak, shrimp, and fish dishes. Yucatecan businessmen flock here for lunch, and with good reason. The meal begins with a complimentary pumpkinseed dip and vegetables in a spicy marinade. Appetizers include oysters Rockefeller and a wonderful *congrejo relleno*, crab filled with tomato-flavored crabmeat. Le Gourmet's steaks are prized. We particularly like their thick filet in a green peppercorn sauce *(salsa pimienta verde)*. Among the shrimp dishes, you might want to try *camarones en chipotle*, shrimp in a spicy tomato sauce reminiscent of some Creole dishes. Service is leisurely. Since the restaurant is popular with locals and tourists are still scarce, the prices are quite reasonable given the quality. Moderate to moderately expensive. Open daily, noon-1 a.m. Closed Sun.

The pinnacle of elegance in Mérida, however, is **Chateau Valentin** *(Calle 58A #499, a few blocks from the Holiday Inn;* ☎ *25-56-90)*. The service is attentive; the setting is a turn-of-the-century mansion with chandeliers and piano music. The food includes some unusual seafood, such as oysters ajillo rather than shrimp, and flavorful, whole pompano. The crema de aguacate soup is tangy and cold, punctuated with coriander. Of course, there are many continental dishes, including Chateaubriand and oysters Rockefeller. Expensive (service added to bill).

CLOSER TO THE ZÓCALO

Near the zócalo are several restaurants featuring Middle Eastern food along with seafood as well as Yucatecan dishes. **Alberto's Continental Patio** *(Calles 64 and 57)* is a handsome restaurant around a shaded garden patio and decorated with antiques. You can choose either patio or air-conditioned dining. Alberto's specializes in Lebanese food. The tabouli—bulghar and parsley salad, served here with diced cucumbers and mint—is good and refreshing, as is the spiced lamb dish, *kafta*. International dishes are served, too, but stick with the rolled cabbage—it is the Lebanese food here that's best. Moderate to moderately expensive.

For intimate patio dining near the zócalo, we can recommend **Portico del Peregrino** *(Calle 57 #501 between 60 and 62)*. You enter through a narrow passageway to this attractive restaurant and can choose among international as well as a few Yucatecan dishes. Some seafood and shrimp is available. If the heat is too stifling, head for their air-conditioned dining rooms. Very moderate.

A restaurant we find ourselves returning to often is the conveniently located and comfortable **Restaurant and Cafe Express** *(Calles 60 and 59, facing Parque Cepeda)*. Méridanos sit for hours over coffee surveying the street scene outside and catching up on local gossip. We find the good breakfast selection (try the *huevos Motulenos* here), sandwiches, fruit salad, and *licuados* too convenient to pass up. Extensive menu with everything from snacks to Yucatecan entrees. Drop by any time of the day just to relax with a drink or snack. Can be a bit noisy since it opens onto a busy street. Inexpensive to moderate. During the steamy summer months a lot of Méridanos take their conversation to the plain but air-conditioned **Cafe Pop** *(Calle 57 #501 between 60 and 62; closed Sun. in summer)*. There's fudge cake and terrific coconut ice cream as well as an especially cheap breakfast and hot cakes, licuados, *pollo pibil....*

For light fare, more in the line of snacks, head for **Leo's** (*Paseo Montejo 56A, near Calle 37*), a branch of the Leo's in Villahermosa, serving delicious grilled meats that you can make into tacos. Very popular and inexpensive. Open daily 12:30 p.m.-1 a.m. Closed Wed.

SIDEWALK CAFES

A number of moderately priced sidewalk cafes line the elegant Paseo de Montejo. Most popular in the evening, these cafes offer a broad variety of specialties and a spot to relax in away from the noise and bustle of center city. **Los Arrecifes** *(#490, near Calle 43)* serves Mexican antojitos and charcoal-grilled meats. **La Gondola,** across from the Hotel Montejo Palace, specializes in pizza at night *(between Calles 39 and 37)* and just north, there are the tropical sherbets at **Dulceria y Neveria Colon** *(near Calle 39)*.

Back in town, juice and *licuado* stands seem to be on every block, with many concentrating around the zócalo. For some fine coconut, mango, or pitaya sherbet, stop by the **Dulceria Colon** located on the north side of the zócalo.

ENTERTAINMENT

In early evening the cheapest entertainment is sitting in the zócalo, perhaps splurging for a shoeshine, and watching the world of Mérida pass by. Another popular people-watching location is from a sidewalk cafe along the Paseo Montejo. Once 9 p.m. arrives, you can enjoy the free entertainment offered every night (except Sun.) in a different city park or patio, such as the *Yucatecan music* and dance in the **Plaza Santa Lucia** (Thurs.). Sundays (beginning 11 a.m.) usually bring a day-long festival on Calle 60. *(Check with the tourist office for the latest schedule on all these events.)*

Although there are discos and jazz clubs in Mérida, it is traditional music and dance that flourish. Melodious *serenata* music can be heard in many of the hotels such as the **Maya Bar** of the Holiday Inn (after 7 p.m.). These romantic songs also can be heard at the **Bar El Trovador Bohemio** *(Calle 55 #504; 9 p.m.-3 a.m.)* and at Los Tulipanes and El Faisan y El Venado, with their peculiarly local expressions of folk culture. **Los Tulipanes** offers the most unusual extravaganza—a dinner show (8:30 p.m.) with a cenote for mock Maya sacrifices. Difficult to find (except by taxi) at Calle 43 #462A, Los Tulipanes remains popular with tourists (☎ 27-20-09). For the simply funky, consider **El Faisan y El Venado** *(Calle 59 #617, at Calle 82).* The "Maya" atmosphere of this restaurant consists of a "zoo" with domesticated deer and a fake Maya temple. Occasionally the entertainment includes a performance of regional dances. The food is primarily Yucatecan. Open 24 hours. Our favorite of these local spots is **La Prosperidad** *(Calle 53 at 56),* which is earthy, entertaining, and inexpensive (despite the lack of posted prices). Too busy to be exactly clean, La Prosperidad is clean enough for a *típico* afternoon of Mexican torch singers and tropical and serenata music. The food is very regional, all venison and turkey in pibil or escabeche, but you can just opt for some of the *botanas*, or appetizers. *(Noon-7:30 p.m.;* ☎ *24-07-64.)*

GETTING TO AND FROM MÉRIDA

There is regular plane and bus service, and irregular train service, between Mérida and the rest of Mexico; and acceptable roads connect Mérida with the Caribbean, Gulf Coast, and the rest of Mexico.

AIR

International flights serve major cities throughout the United States and Canada. From Miami, the flight takes less than two hours. Mexicana and Aeromexico connect Mérida with Mexico City; Aeromexico only with Villahermosa and Cancún. Regional flights by Aerocaribe connect Chetumal, Villahermosa, and Cancún with Mérida daily. Bonanza Airlines has regular small-plane service to Chetumal. The Mérida airport is about 15 minutes from town. Controlled-price taxis are available. The "Aviacion" bus at the corner of Calles 60 and 67 takes you from town to the airport cheaply, 5 a.m.-8 p.m.

BUS

The busy terminal for first- and second-class buses is located on Calle 69 between 68 and 70, about a 15-minute walk or short taxi ride from the zócalo. Daily buses connect Mérida with the rest of Mexico, including Campeche *(via MEX 180)*, Mexico City, Palenque (second-class only), and Villahermosa. Buses also regularly run from Mérida to Caribbean towns such as Cancún, Puerto Morelos, Playa del Carmen, and Chetumal. If you are on a tight schedule use first-class service (or deluxe Oriente buses to Cancún; deluxe Uno buses to Villahermosa and Mexico City's TAPO bus terminal) and buy your ticket in advance (usually air-conditioned).

TRAIN

The station is located on Calles 55 and 48, about 9 blocks from the zócalo. In theory, you can get from Mérida to Campeche, Palenque, and Mexico City. The experience could be memorable. Unless you have lots of time, luck, or a passion for trains, take other transport.

CAR

Good roads connect Mérida to Cancún via Chichen Itza and Valladolid (MEX 180 D, the toll road, 4 1/2 hours or less, when completed) and to Chetumal (see "Chetumal"). Villahermosa via Campeche on the faster inland route covers 678 km (420 m). For a description of this route see below and Campeche.

DIRECTORY

Airlines • *Aeromexico*, Paseo Montejo 460 (☎ 24-85-54); *Mexicana*, Calle 58 #500 (☎ 24-66-33). *Aero caribe*, Paseo Montejo 476A (☎ 23-00-02), for regional service to Cancún and Chetumal. *Aerotaxis Bonanza*, at airport (☎ 28-04-96), for Chetumal.

Books in English • *Dante Books* (in Teatro Peon Contreras); El Paso (Calle 60 at 59) for used books.

British Consulate • Calle 58 at 53 #450 (☎ 21-67-99).

Buses • Central de Autobuses, Calles 68 and 69. First- and second-class service for excursions (except Progreso) and long-distance trips. At Calle 62 #524, between Calles 65 and 67, are the buses for Progreso.

Car Rentals • Major agencies at the airport, in hotels, and town such as *Avis* (☎ 23-96-12) and *Budget* (☎ 27-27-08).

Carriages • The horse-drawn variety, Cepeda and Centenario Parks and by the Archaeology Museum and Cathedral.

Golf • Club de Golf La Ceiba, just 9 km (5 1/2 m) out of Mérida on the Progreso Highway.

Groceries • *Isste*, Calle 60 between 47 & 49, or market.

Post Office • Near market at Calles 56 and 65.

Railroad Station • Calles 48 and 55.

Taxis • Cepeda Park on Calle 60 and near Municipal Palace on the zócalo.

Tour Agencies • They abound in most hotels and around town, with varying prices and services (limousine to bus-style). In case you get stuck, here are a few with established reputations: *Mérida Travel Service,* Hotel Casa del Balam (☎ 24-62-90); *Rutas del Mayab,* Calle 60 #491 (☎ 24-46-14); *Viajes Gonzales,* Calle 59 #476 and bus station (☎ 21-01-97), specializes in bus tours.

Tourist Office • Teatro Peon Contreras, Calle 60 near 57 (☎ 24-92-90); 9 a.m.-9 p.m., variable on weekends, and Palacio de Gobierno, zócalo and Calle 60; 8 a.m.-8 p.m. daily. Kiosks at airport and bus station.

U.S. Consulate • *Paseo Montejo* 453 at Colon (☎ 25-50-11; after-hours emergencies, ☎ 25-54-09). Open weekdays 7:30 a.m.-4 p.m.

ON THE ROAD

TO CAMPECHE

Two well-paved roads cut through scrub jungle to join Campeche and Mérida. The area abounds in iridescent motmot birds, and in July butterflies seem to breed in the millions, their yellow wings fluttering along the highways. MEX 180 north, also known as the short route, follows the colonial route called the Camino Real ("Royal Road") skirting villages with colonial churches built on foundations of ancient Maya ruins. Although **Helcelchakan** no longer has an archaeology museum, the town of **Becal**, *where world-renowned "Panama" hats are made* as well as less fine straw productions, remains a worthwhile detour. Centro Artesanal de Becal (on the highway) has many curios along with some fine sombreros. Or drive right through Becal, noting *the cement sombrero on the zócalo* and shopping at Artesanias Becalenos (main street, south of zócalo). The total distance between the two cities on MEX 180 is 195 km (121 m), a 2-1/2-hour drive.

MEX 261 north, the longer road, covers 245 km (152 m) but passes the ruins of Kabah and Uxmal along the way and is more convenient for visiting Edzna. Actually, it is quite feasible to visit all three ruins and arrive at your destination in one day. MEX 261 between Campeche and Bolonchen de Relon (120 km, 74 m) also takes you through numerous picturesque villages of the descendants of the ancient Maya, their thatched huts still oval-shaped and the women dressed in embroidered huipils. Many of the village names, such as Ich-Ek, are Mayan; some names indicate the only natural source of water in the area—wells deep below the surface in limestone caves, for example, **Hopelchen** ("five wells") and **Bolonchen** ("nine wells"). John L. Stephens visited the caves at Bolonchen de Relon in the

19th century and gave a harrowing description in *Incidents of Travel* in Yucatán of his exploration of wells a good 450 feet below the surface:

> *The cave was damp and the rock and ladder were wet and slippery....*
> *It was evident that the labor of exploring this cave was to be greatly increased by the state of the ladders and there might be some danger attending it, but, even after all that we had seen of caves, there was something so wild and grand in this that we could not bring ourselves to give up the attempt.*

It is said that guides can be arranged in the village for a visit to these caves, but after reading Stephens' account, we wouldn't dare.

CHICHEN ITZA

The most famous and extensive ruins of **Yucatán** can be visited in a one-day excursion from either Mérida or Cancún, but an overnight stay at one of the many pleasant hotels that have opened nearby is recommended. Not only is there much to see at this site, which encompasses an area 2 miles by 1-1/2 miles, but in addition there is the cave dedicated to the rain god to visit at *Balankanche* and a sound-and-light show at the ruins to enjoy most evenings. The intense afternoon sun at the ruins is more bearable after a swim in your hotel pool.

Chichen Itza (**Place of the Well of the Itza**) overpowers you with its massive structures, its warrior sculptures, feathered-serpent balustrades and columns, and ominous skull racks. It fascinates you with stories of its Well of Sacrifice and hints of conquest by the Toltecs from Tula near Mexico City. Chichen's fierce aspect may have resulted from the Toltecs, who brought highland Mexican influences to the more graceful art of the Maya region—the kind of influences most of us associate with gruesome stories about the Aztecs, the successors of the Toltecs.

Evidence for the Toltec conquest of Chichen Itza has consisted of two facts: the myth of **Quetzalcoatl,** known as Kulkulcan by the Maya, and the remarkable similarity between Chichen Itza's Temple of the Warriors and the Pyramid of Quetzalcoatl at the ruins of Tula. Quetzalcoatl, creator of the arts and learning, is represented frequently at Chichen as the feathered serpent. The Aztecs related the myth of Quetzalcoatl to the early Spaniards and seemed to provide a historical personage for this god. They said that Quetzalcoatl ruled Tula as a pure and chaste king, but he then was tempted by sin and expelled. In one version of the myth, Quetzalcoatl immolated himself and was reborn as the morning star; in another he sailed off to the east. This latter version has been interpreted to mean that King Quetzalcoatl left for Yucatán, where he conquered Chichen Itza in A.D. 987. The old Maya center of the south section was extended to the north for the creation of the new Toltec capital.

NEW ARCHAEOLOGICAL INFORMATION

The above reconstruction of Chichen's prehistory has been accepted by Mexican archaeology for a long time. It has been used to explain the unique blend of Maya and Toltec art in the north section, and to date that part of the site to the early Post-Classic period (A.D. 900-1200). The south section has been considered mostly pre-Toltec, belonging to the Late Classic Maya period (A.D. 600-900). Recently, however, the Toltec conquest and the sequence of Chichen's development has been *seriously challenged by new archaeological information.* There is evidence that Toltec traits existed at Chichen before Tula was even founded (see earlier background section "Yucatán and Campeche"). Some archaeologists now dare to suggest that Tula was a colony of Chichen, or that some exiles from Chichen built the structures at Tula, not the other way around. If the Toltec invasion cannot explain the unusual highland Mexican influences at Chichen that make it so distinctive from other Maya sites like Uxmal, then what did happen at this site over a thousand years ago? While there are attempts at explanation, for the moment you can enjoy your visit to Chichen knowing that it represents one of the greatest controversies in Mexican archaeology. Most things you hear about its past may very well be rejected within the decade.

KEY TO CHICHEN ITZA

Sights • The Maya ruins of Chichen Itza attract tourists from all over the world and, at least through 1994, they will provide the additional attraction of on-going excavations and restorations. The nearby Cave of Balankanche, used by the ancient Maya for worship, adds an extra attraction to your visit. There is nothing else here, but what more is needed?

Where to Stay • Attractive first-class hotels are within walking distance of the ruins; less expensive hotels are most easily found in Valladolid, 26 miles away.

Where to Eat • Acceptable, but limited.

Entertainment • Sound-and-light show in Spanish at 7 p.m. and in English at 9 p.m. at ruins. Getting Around Taxis are available at west entrance to ruins, and in the towns of Piste and Valladolid. Second-class long-distance buses will pick up and drop people at Valladolid and Piste.

Practical Tips • Bring your bathing suit—most hotels have pools, even in Valladolid, where you can also swim in the nearby Cenote Dzitnup for a small fee. Summer weather year-round but rains late in the afternoon during the summer.

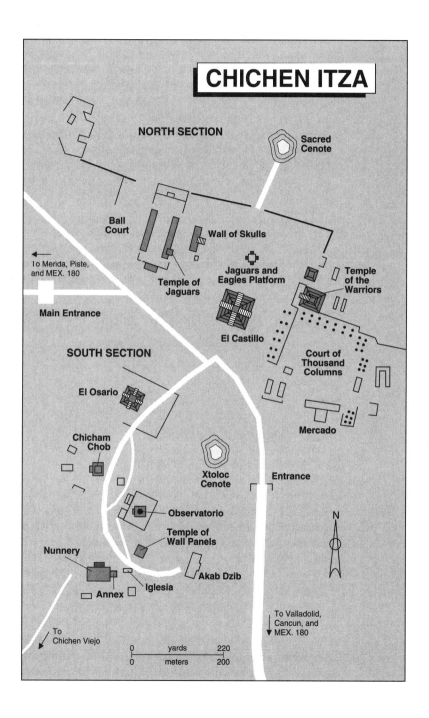

CHICHEN ITZA

NORTH SECTION

Sacred Cenote

Ball Court

Wall of Skulls

To Merida, Piste, and MEX. 180

Jaguars and Eagles Platform

Temple of the Warriors

Temple of Jaguars

Main Entrance

El Castillo

Court of Thousand Columns

SOUTH SECTION

El Osario

Mercado

Chicham Chob

Xtloc Cenote

Entrance

Observatorio

N

Nunnery

Temple of Wall Panels

Annex

Iglesia

Akab Dzib

To Valladolid, Cancun, and MEX. 180

To Chichen Viejo

| 0 | yards | 220 |
| 0 | meters | 200 |

RUINS

Open 8 a.m.-5 p.m. Admission fee. Additional fees for guides, parking, and sound-and-light show (cheaper Spanish version at 7 p.m.; English at 9 p.m.). Modern cultural center (small fee) at main entrance to ruins includes information desk, museum, video show, bookstore, restaurant, infirmary, currency exchange, long-distance telephones, and baggage check.

Practical tips: Hours for visting the interior temples of El Castillo, the Upper Temple of the Jaguars, and the Temple of the Warriors (if open, at all) should be checked at the cultural center. Refreshment stands and public bathrooms (small fee) are strategically placed around the ruins. Cool clothing, insect repellent, and comfortable climbing shoes are a must, as may be a hat, depending on your sensitivity to the sun.

The following walking tour of the ruins does not always agree with the version presented in the trilingual signs posted throughout the site. As explained earlier, there is a lot of controversy about these ruins. The signs reflect the older theory about the site while we have tried to incorporate more recent archaeological thought—especially in regard to the dates of the buildings.

NORTH SECTION: TOLTEC CHICHEN

The enormous northern plaza contains the most famous buildings of Chichen Itza. Standing in the center of the plaza you find the Ball Court to the west, the Castillo to the south, the Temple of Warriors to the east, and to the north the *sacbe* ("paved ancient causeway") leading to the **Sacred Cenote**. This area once was surrounded by a 6-foot-high wall and was the ceremonial center for the ancient city of 40,000. Although this section of Chichen is thought to show influences from the Toltecs of Tula (A.D. 900-1200), the art is more like a microcosm of ancient Mexico. The builders of Chichen seemed to experiment with a little of everything that had gone before them. The **Ball Court** carvings show similarities to Tajin in Veracruz, the columns may have been derived from Monte Alban in Oaxaca, the platform of the Temple of the Warriors shows Teotihuacan (near Mexico City) derivation, and many of the buildings use Puuc masonry like that of Uxmal, and corbel arches found only in the Maya area.

Some of the traits that are said to be most typically **Toltec** are the feathered serpents representing Quetzalcoatl, the skull rack, the low relief carvings of warriors with non-Maya or pugnacious features, eagles eating hearts, and chacmool sculptures. **Chacmool** sculptures are reclining, life-size stone figures with knees bent and hands holding a receptacle on the stomach. There are 14 found at Chichen, many placed in entranceways, with their heads carved to face out to the plaza. No one really knows what they signified or what their purpose was, although it has been suggested that hearts were placed in the receptacles during sacrificial ceremonies. Chacmools have been found in many places, including Costa Rica and Veracruz.

These Toltec features are found all over the northern section of Chichen as well as at Tula. Whether these art forms were developed at Chichen or at Tula is at the center of current controversy. Whatever is decided. Chichen is far more impressive than Tula. As art historian *George Kubler* said, "Chichen is like Rome, but Tula is like a frontier garrison."

El Castillo

Dominating Chichen Itza and actually the entire plain surrounding it, the Castillo, or **Templo de Kukulcan** as it is called here, gives the illusion of even greater height than its 75 feet because of the diminishing panel design on its nine terraces. There was a great staircase on each side of the pyramid, but only two have been restored, and only the one of the north side is carved with the feathered-serpent balustrades that led officials to name it after Kukulcan. In the ancient Maya world, platforms with four staircases usually were associated with the path of the sun, the calendar, and measurements of time. The Castillo is no exception, for the original number of steps with the one step of the temple platform add up to the 365 days of the solar year. *Twice a year, during the spring and autumn equinoxes, the setting sun casts shadows on the balustrade, making it appear like the body of an undulating serpent* with its head at the base of the balustrade bright with sunshine.

If you dare to **climb up the temple** (actually, climbing *down* is the difficult part), you will be rewarded with a magnificent view of the entire site. The temple itself is interesting, with serpent columns and carvings of warriors on its door jambs and inside pillars. On the south side of the temple is a hole penetrating the platform through which you can see jaguar carvings on the facade of an inner and earlier temple. The Castillo may have been built over the earlier pyramid and temple to commemorate the beginning of a new Maya 52-year cycle, an event similar to the beginning of a century for us.

Even if you do not climb the Castillo, you may want to climb the pyramid inside. (Open limited hours; not recommended for the claustrophobic.) An entrance at the base of the north stairway has been created so you can climb the steps, now internal, leading to the earlier temple. The temple has two chambers, and the rear one contains a magnificent red jaguar throne with jade for spots and eyes. The outer room contains a chacmool that puzzles archaeologists, since the temple was covered before Toltec times. The Castillo is one of the few structures at Chichen with a radiocarbon date providing a way of dating it independent of theories about styles and Toltec invasions. The outer structure probably was built by **A.D. 830,** well before the Toltecs. This makes the buried temple even earlier, though containing a "Toltec" chacmool. Maybe the invading Toltecs, like present-day archaeologists, found entry to the older temple and placed a chacmool there, little realizing the confusion they would create in the archaeological record. Or maybe chacmools just aren't Toltec.

Main Ball Court

Chichen's ball court is the largest in ancient Mexico, with the length of its playing field more than one and a half times the size of a modern football field. As impressive as the court is, it must have exhausted the players who had to run its length—keeping the heavy, solid-rubber ball continuously in the air while never using their hands. The target rings, 20 feet above the floor, could have provided few opportunities for the ball to pass through for a special victory, so special for the Aztecs that it was rewarded by the jewelry of all the spectators. This court, however, is so large that many believe it was purely ceremonial in function.

The carvings of the benches of this great playing field remind you of the religious, yet gruesome, **consequences of losing the game**—*sacrifice by decapitation.* Repeated along the court are low-reliefs of processions of two ballplayer teams converging upon a central disk representing the rubber ball (the central panels are preserved best). Flanking the disk, the captain of what was presumably the winning team stands with a flint knife in one hand, a head in another, having just decapitated the leader of the opposing team, who kneels on the opposite side of the ball. This unfortunate man has six serpents and a plant sprouting from where his head should be. The serpents symbolize blood, and the plant symbolizes the religious purpose of the ritual—fertility and renewal. Less riveting, but still interesting, are the ballplayers themselves, with their kneepads, thick playing belts, and two different kinds of shoes, one a sandal, and the other a closed shoe (but why, if they didn't kick?). The players, adorned with feathered headdresses, march against a background of vegetation and serpents.

Temples stand at both ends of the ball court. The northern one retains only traces of its formerly elaborate decorations that related to rituals of death and bloodletting. As you stand on its platform (via path to left) you can hear quite clearly what is being said 150 feet away at the opposite end of the court.

The most interesting ball-court structure is the **Upper Temple of the Jaguars,** on the east side and built on top of the Lower Temple of the Jaguars, which faces the main plaza of the Castillo (see below). Monumental serpent columns, 7-1/2 tons each, support the lintel of the temple. Two friezes decorate the facade, the upper one representing the feathered serpent and the lower one alternating prowling jaguars with round shields. The door jambs introduce the theme of the temple interior with carvings of warriors carrying spears. Inside (open only a few hours each day) the second chamber of the temple are rare fragments of paintings depicting battle scenes of spear-throwing warriors carrying round shields and attacking villages—the best-preserved painting fragment is just to the right, on your right, as you enter the chamber. These paintings have been said to represent the Toltec conquest of Chichen Itza, yet similar militaristic themes are found in

Yucatán at Uxmal and Kabah from Classic times, too early for an invasion from Toltec Tula. If these murals represent an early trend toward militarism in northern Yucatán, who is fighting and who is winning?

Lower Temple Of The Jaguars

Its entrance guarded by a jaguar throne, this temple has a richly decorated interior of low-relief carvings. Along the base run carvings of plants, birds, and fish, and at the very top are carvings of the sun disk. In the middle walk processions of individuals in full regalia. The lower-level processions seem to be Maya, but the upper bands of warriors with spear-throwers and long hair may be Toltecs or other foreigners. Like most ancient Mexican sculptures, these carvings were originally painted in bright colors of red, white, green, and yellow.

Platforms

Three platforms dedicated to religious rites are scattered in the area in front of the Lower Temple of the Jaguars and the Castillo. Spanish accounts describing comedies and other performances on two of these platforms seem incongruous with the gruesome theme of human sacrifice depicted in their friezes. The style and symbolism of these carvings are considered imports from the Toltecs of Tula.

The **Tzompantli** (Wall of Skulls) obviously received its name from the countless, highly individualized skulls carved on its base. When the Spanish arrived at the Aztec capital in present-day Mexico City, they discovered similar Tzompantli on which were displayed the real skulls of persons who had been sacrificed. On this Chichen structure are additional scenes of eagles devouring human hearts and warriors with writhing serpents projecting from their sides. Although no skeletons were found buried in this platform, two chacmool sculptures were.

Serpent heads project from the top of the four stairways of the **Platform of the Jaguars and Eagles**, and the platform itself is carved with jaguars and eagles clutching human hearts. Aztec warriors captured victims for sacrifice to the gods so the sun would continue its daily path across the heavens. A similar cult seems represented on this platform. The four stairways represent daily paths of the sun, and jaguars and eagles are emblems of the warrior caste. The goggle-eyed chacmool-type figure represents the rising sun.

The **Venus Platform** is part of the cult of the feathered serpent god Quetzalcoatl ("Kukulkan" in Mayan) in his identity of Venus, the morning star. Serpents mount the stairways, and carvings of Quetzalcoatl as the morning star (the man-bird-serpent motif) adorn the sunken sections of the platform. Venus and calendrical signs complete the design.

Sacred Cenote

Popularly known as "the well of sacrifices," this enormous natural well, formed by the collapse of the limestone plain into a subterranean cave, is reached by an ancient paved causeway from the main plaza.

The cenote, with its murky waters and precipitous walls, seems an appropriate place for the rituals first described by Diego de Landa in 1566:

Into this well they were and still are accustomed to throw men alive as a sacrifice to the gods in time of drought; they held that they did not die, even though they were not seen again. They also threw in many other offerings…so if there were gold in this country, this well would have received most of it, so devout were the Indians in this.

Although romantics later embellished Landa's account with stories of virgin sacrifices, no concrete evidence for any of these rituals came to light until the cenote was first dredged in 1923. Not only were skeletons of children, men, and women found along with the gold predicted by Landa, but also objects from all over ancient Mexico were recovered. Art historian Clemency Coggins recently studied these dredged-up objects and concluded that offerings began around **A.D. 800**, and that during Chichen's glory, they primarily were devoted to the warrior cult. Pilgrimages to the cenote after Chichen's abandonment deposited offerings to lots of different gods, including that of Mayapan's merchants. The European objects recovered show that cenote pilgrimages continued even after the Conquest.

Temple Of The Warriors

This famous Toltec temple is similar to one at Tula, near Mexico City. Both have colonnades at their base, and both have carved warrior columns. The colonnades and the temple were roofed, forming spacious and airy interiors unique in ancient Mexico. The ravages of time have erased the mural paintings that once decorated the temple at Chichen, but the sculptural remains are rich, including the highly individuated reliefs on the colonnades and the **finely carved friezes** found on the north and south sides of the platform (see "Thousand Columns" below).

Just as you reach the top of the stairs, you see figures above the serpents on the balustrades that served as standard-bearers, flying unknown kinds of flags. The temple facade itself is more Maya than Toltec, with carvings of Chac masks (the rain god) flanking sculptures of a human head emerging from an earth monster (Venus). The temple entrance is guarded by a chacmool statue and was once formed by the colossal columns of descending serpents, their voracious mouths painted red and their rattle tails holding the now-lost wooden lintel. The **carved warrior columns** in the interior supported a vaulted roof. In the inner chamber stands a throne carved with Atlantean figures. This throne may have originated in the earlier *Temple of the Chacmool*, now enclosed by the Temple of the Warriors (and presently closed to the public).

Court Of Thousand Columns

The large plaza beyond the colonnade to the right of the Temple of the Warriors is not often visited. Not in good repair, the plaza was originally surrounded on three sides by colonnaded halls and on the fourth by the so-called mercado (market) and a ball court. The colonnades, all **roofed**, must have provided an unusual amount of interior space. Since no palace buildings are found in the north section of Chichen, it is thought the colonnaded halls may have been the residences of the elite. Today you can walk along the north colonnade, past the frieze on the south wall of the Temple of the Warriors with its jaguars, eagles, and recumbent, chacmool-like figures representing the warrior sun cult already noted at the Jaguar and Eagles Platform. A bit further on is a platform, or dais, carved with processions. In front of it, at the end of a path leading across the plaza, is the **Mercado,** an area under excavation in 1993. Up the steps at the Mercado is another dais carved with two writhing serpents and, under them, individuals apparently watching a sacrifice. Down the path to the left, you soon come to what were **steam baths**.

SOUTH SECTION: MAYA CHICHEN

No archaeologist disputes the Maya origin of most buildings in the **Grupo Sur,** or south section. The Maya buildings are constructed in the Puuc style found at Uxmal and other Yucatecan sites dating from the Late Classic period of A.D. 600-900. It was believed that the center of Chichen shifted to the north plaza during Toltec times (A.D. 900-1200), but controversies over dating the "Toltec" section raise serious doubts about this assumption. Nonetheless, this section provides an interesting contrast in style to the north plaza area. Even the cenote here is different, having been a source of water rather than a place for ritual sacrifice.

Osario, or High Priest's Grave

The similarity of this pyramid and temple to the Castillo in the north plaza would be quite remarkable if it were reconstructed. In its present ruined state, you can try to discern its four stairways, and you still find **serpent columns** left from the temple with carvings similar to those on the Castillo. A paved causeway originally connected this building with the north plaza. Like Palenque's famous Temple of the Inscriptions, this pyramid covered a burial. If you climb to the top of the platform, you see a shaft that cuts down through the pyramid to ground level, where a natural cave is formed. Stone steps lead into the cave, which is 36 feet deep, where the "*High Priest*" burial was discovered. Above this cave were found other human skeletons and offerings of jade, copper bells, rock crystal, and shell.

El Chichan Chob

The path forks and only its right branch takes you to this temple, also called the "**Casa Colorada**" ("red house"). It poses a fascinating quandary for archaeology. The platform with rounded corners and plain temple surmounted by a decorated roof comb is dated to the Maya Late Classic through radiocarbon tests and style. Remains of a "Toltec" ball court at the base of the platform had been assumed to be added centuries later, because its carvings are like those on the great ball court in the north plaza. A recent exploration dramatically turned this comfortable theory inside out by demonstrating that the ball court is actually underneath, and therefore earlier than, the Chichan Chob. The so-called Toltec traits at Chichen seem to begin earlier than the presumed Toltec invasion. These **ball court** carvings flank the path at the base of the temple so that as you walk by, you actually are walking on the narrow court. A detour around this temple takes you to a plaza shared with the Temple of the Deer. If you climb up to the chambers of the Chichan Chob, you can see the **hieroglyphs** carved over the inner doorways where Mayanist David Kelley has deciphered the name of a 9th-century Chichen ruler called Kakupacal.

Observatorio

Better known as the **Caracol** ("Snail"), this is the earliest-known round structure in Yucatán, although there is controversy over its date of construction. The circular tower, a form associated in central Mexico with Quetzalcoatl but not found at Tula, has four outer doors facing the cardinal points, surmounted by Puuc-style rain-god masks. A small interior staircase winding like a snail to the upper level gave the building its name. In the remains of the upper chamber are three slit-like windows. The tower sits askew on two platforms where carvings dating to the Maya Classic period were found. The addition of a temple at the base made the overall proportions of the Caracol so awkward that archaeologist J. Eric Thompson wrote, "*It stands like a two-decker wedding cake on the square carton from which it came.*"

Many of the peculiarities of the building result from its being an astronomical observatory for solar, but especially Venus, sightings. The Maya concerned themselves with the setting and rising of **Venus** because they believed that once Venus disappeared from the sky, it traveled for a period through the evil Underworld, during which time it might have become contaminated. Its rising became a fearful event and often was marked by warfare. According to astronomer Anthony Aveni, the alignments of parts of the Caracol marked the most extreme north setting of *Venus,* enabling the Maya to calculate its rising as the morning star, which is also the celestial identity of Quetzalcoatl.

The Nunnery And Annex

For some reason, this complex reminded the Spaniards of their convents at home and so it received its name. The structure visible today is most definitely Late Classic Maya, and is the result of a number of building phases in which the platform was expanded and a second story and other rooms added. The mess to the right of the great staircase is the result of a 19th-century explorer blasting his way into the building. While fragments of paintings and hieroglyphic inscriptions can be found throughout the complex, the **eastern facade** of the Annex, the one-story wing, is unique at Chichen for its **Chenes-style facade.** Chenes style is a baroque form of Puuc in which the entire facade is covered in rain-god motifs. The door of the Annex forms the jaws of the earth monster, with the monster's teeth on its frame. Above the door is a carving of a seated Maya person. The hieroglyphs carved on the lintel have been associated with the Venus cycle.

La Iglesia

Next to the Annex is another Spanish-named building, "the church," a small one-room structure in Puuc style. The crudely cut stones and the heaviness of the decorations on the upper facade and roof comb make this building seem more an experiment than a success. Long-nosed rain-god masks decorate the upper part of the building, but the paired figures alternating with the masks represent the four Bacabs who, for the Maya, held up the sky.

Akab-Dzib

A palace-type of structure lies about 100 yards east of the Nunnery. The building is quite plain and in Classic Maya style. Its name means "obscure writing" in Mayan and results from the hieroglyphic text elegantly **carved** on a lintel over an inner doorway on the south side of the building. On the underside of the lintel is a carving of a person seated on a throne.

Templo De Los Paneles

Between the Iglesia and the Caracol is the **Temple of the Wall Panels,** with its remnants of columns and sculpture. Its name derives from the badly eroded carvings found on the exterior of the north and south walls. You can make out seated individuals, perhaps prisoners with their hands tied behind their backs, carved in an almost cartoonish style.

CHICHEN VIEJO

Chichen Viejo (Old Chichen) may look older than the southern section, but in fact it is simply unrestored. This overgrown section dates from the Late Classic Maya period but has some "Toltec" additions. If you enjoy exploring and have allowed yourself an overnight stay at Chichen, there are carvings and temples to be discovered on a walk through this southernmost section of Chichen.

Covered head to foot with insect repellent, take the narrow and overgrown path leading from the southwest corner of the Nunnery and continue walking for 15 minutes. It's so quiet here that you might be more comfortable accompanied by a friend or guide. Toward the end you find a chacmool to your right; to the left is the **Templo de la Fecha** (Temple of the Date), with a lintel carved with the only complete Maya date at Chichen. While the date has been translated as A.D. 879, it seems to be supported by later, Toltec Atlantean columns. These columns and lintel are freestanding because the rest of the building has collapsed. The path ends at the nearby House of the Phalli, named after the sculptures imbedded in the walls of its second room. Around the right of this house and to the rear are numerous carvings and Atlantean figures now deprived of their burdens. A path behind the **House of the Phalli** that led, after a hefty walk, to the Puuc **Temple of the Three Lintels** was so overgrown on our last visit that we no longer can recommend it.

BALANKANCHE CAVES

About 5 km (3 m) east of main entrance to ruins, where taxis are available. Admission fee. By guided tour only, with no less than 6 and no more than 30 visitors, on the hour from 9 a.m. to 4 p.m. A few tours given in English; check schedule with Chichen's information desk.

Although sealed for as much as a thousand years, local Maya tradition held that something hidden, but spectacular, lay behind the entrance to these caves (*Balankanche* means "hidden throne"). Not until 1959 were they proven correct. Squeezing through narrow tunnels, explorers discovered offerings left in ancient rituals to the central Mexican rain god, Tlaloc. Two groups of offerings were found in natural but awesome settings: the group of the "throne" in a large domed area with a pillar in its center of fused stalactites and stalagmites; and the group by the edge of a tranquil pool in which blind fish swim. Among the offerings were large incense burners embellished with the goggle-eyed Tlaloc and miniature corn grinders, small things being associated with this god. The access has been improved a bit and lighting has been provided so you can see these offerings just as they were found.

WHERE TO STAY

The hotels cluster in two areas: next to the ruins, and a bit over a mile to the west of them in the **village of Piste.** The MEX 180 bypass has isolated the hotels next to the ruins on an east access road without bus transportation. If you are traveling by bus, we recommend you get off in Piste and take a taxi to any of the hotels next to the ruins. If you stay in Piste, you probably will want to take a taxi the mile to and from the ruins, conserving your energy for climbing pyramids. It can be difficult to obtain a room near the ruins if you do not *reserve in advance.* Many visitors rely on the inexpensively priced hotels in Valladolid only 26 miles away (see "On the Road"). For reservations call area code 985.

EXPENSIVE

Mayaland   ★★★

East Access Road; ☎ *6-27-77; $105* • An attractive hotel containing some interesting antiques, which sits amid extensive gardens, beautifully landscaped. The main entrance frames the Caracol at the nearby ruins. Many of the 60 spacious units have views of the ruins; older rooms and cottages, looking onto the garden and fountains, are nostagically furnished in '30s style with burnished wood details; newer rooms have a/c, TV, and contemporary furnishings. Restaurants, snack bar and bar, evening entertainment, gift shops, and

25-meter pool. Pleasant service. AP sometimes required from December 15-April 16. *For reservations, call, in the U.S.,* ☎ *800-235-4079.*

MODERATE

Villa Arqueologica

East Access Road; ☎ *6-28-30; $99* • Like all the very modern Villas Arqueologica, the one at Chichen is highly recommended. Its 40 air-conditioned rooms are small, yet well-designed, with sleeping alcoves. As comfortable as we find this hotel, its service is too often devoid of Mexican warmth. Restaurant and bar. Plant-filled patio with pool; lighted tennis court. *For reservations, call, in the U.S.,* ☎ *800-258-2633.*

Mision Park Inn

Chichen Itza MEX 180, in Piste; ☎ *6-25-13; $93 MAP* • A modern hotel, its 42 comfortable and air-conditioned rooms are decorated in colonial style. Dining room, bar and pool in garden.

Hacienda Chichen

East Access Road; ☎ *6-27-77; $82* • Intimate 17th-century hacienda offers lovely gardens and extensive grounds containing parts of Chichen Viejo. Edward Thompson, who first dredged the Sacred Cenote, bought the hacienda and ruins of Chichen for $75 near the turn of the century. The 18 cottages built for the excavation team of the Carnegie Institute have been renovated into hotel rooms, and Thompson's original mansion is used for the common areas of the hotel. Dining room, bar, pool. Ceiling fans only. Reservations in U.S., same as the Mayaland. Open November to Easter only.

INEXPENSIVE

Piramide Inn

MEX 180, in Piste; ☎ *6-26-71 ext. 15* • This simple, motel-style inn has 45 large rooms with air conditioning, but not always hot water. Dining room, gardens, and large pool. **Temporarily closed.**

BUDGET

Dolores Alba

MEX 180, 2.5 km east of ruins; ☎ *(99) 28-56-50; $32* • A homey place with pool, cozy restaurant, and 16 basic rooms—the best have a/c. When owner is present, he takes you to ruins. Otherwise, a car is essential. *For reservations, write Calle 63 #464 in Mérida.*

WHERE TO EAT

For most visitors, lunch is the meal of concern after a hot morning at the ruins. Since you probably plan to return to the ruins later, you may not want to go any great distance just to eat. Your options are limited, though usually you can find an overpriced club sandwich as well as a hearty comida corrida. Closest to the ruins is the pricey restaurant in the **cultural center** (club sandwich, fried chicken, ice cream). A short walk away are the bland but acceptable comidas corridas at the Mayaland or Hacienda Chichen (moderate), and the air-conditioned **Villa Arqueologica** with probably the tastiest food (comida, moderate; à la carte, expensive.) Usually the hotel bars will serve you a club sandwich from 12:30 p.m. on; at the **Mayaland**, however, a pleasant à la carte lunch is served poolside (11 a.m.-4 p.m.) and the evening bar offerings include good Yucatec antojitos—try the salbutes (moderate). Lunch at the hotels also buys access to their bathrooms, lovely gardens, and, if you are lucky, refreshing swimming pools. In Piste, the air-conditioned **Xaybe** and the fan-cooled **La Fiesta** serve meals at a set price that includes the use of their pools. (Both are moderate and used by bus tours). More *típico* is the thatched-roof **Carousel**, clean and fan-cooled and serving some flavorful Yucatecan specialties, like *cochinita pibil* (inexpensive; 7 a.m.-9 p.m.).

Hotel meals are served during specific hours: Lunch 12:30-3:30 p.m. Dinner 7:30-9 p.m.

GETTING TO AND FROM CHICHEN ITZA

ROAD

Chichen is located 120 km (75 m) east of Mérida and 200 km (125 m) west of Cancún on MEX 180. An exit from the new toll road, MEX 180 D, is only 3 km from Piste, 5 km from the ruins, and is much faster. Tours for varying lengths of time can be arranged either from Mérida or Cancún (check "Directories" for these cities) or you can make your own car arrangements. A few first-class buses go to Chichen from Mérida (2 hours) and Cancún (3 hours); second-class buses between Mérida and Cancún are more frequent and stop at Chichen. Note: MEX 180 bypasses the center of the ruins so that you must enter the ruins by access roads to the east or west. While most buses take you right to the ruins, some drop you about a mile away in Piste, where taxis usually are available. *Tip:* An overnight is necessary to see the 9 p.m. sound-and-light show unless you have your own transportation or are willing to rely on flagging down a second-class bus at 10:30 p.m.

AIR

Flights to the ruins can be arranged through Aero Cozumel in Cancún and Cozumel, or Aerotaxi Bonanaza in Mérida. See "Directories" for those towns. The airport is located next to the MEX 180 bypass.

ON THE ROAD

VALLADOLID

Valladolid, only 42 km (26 m) east of Chichen, on MEX 180, has become popular with visitors to this area because of its bargain-priced hotels and restaurants. Taxis to the ruins are easy to arrange, and the second-class Cancún-Mérida bus stops in Valladolid and can drop you near the ruins.

On your way to or from Valladolid, consider a side trip to the **Cenote Dzit-nup** *(4 km, 2.5 m west of Valladolid on MEX 180, then 2 km south; small admission fee; open 8 a.m.-5 p.m.),* where stalactites and few rays of sun create an eerie setting for a swim in the coolest of cool, bluest of blue waters of this cave.

Valladolid was founded by one of the Montejo family in 1543 at the location of an older Maya settlement named Zaci. The Spanish residents were arrogant, valuing their pure European blood so much they banned Indians and mestizos from residing in their town. Not surprisingly, Valladolid was the first town attacked in the Caste War of 1847 and did not really recover until the 20th century. Few colonial buildings survived the war, but the 16th-century **San Bernadino Church** fortunately did *(Calles 41A and 50).* The **Cenote Zaci** also survived and remains a shady spot to visit, though swimming is no longer permitted (admission charged). The pleasant zócalo offers benches for prolonged negotiations with hammock vendors and a central spot from which to look over the surrounding hotels and restaurants.

WHERE TO STAY

To reserve by phone, call area code 985.

El Meson del Marquez
Calle 39 #203, on zócalo; ☎ 6-20-73; $40 • A charming colonial mansion converted into 27 hotel rooms, some with high ceilings, all with air conditioning. Some new rooms surround a swimming pool and garden. Good crafts shop. Restaurant and bar. Parking.

Don Luís
Calle 39 at 38; ☎ *6-20-08; $24* • Just a block from the zócalo, this modern, simply decorated hotel offers 20 air-conditioned rooms. Pool in garden.

San Clemente
Calle 41 #206, on zócalo; ☎ *6-22-08; $29* • The 64 air-conditioned rooms in this modern, colonial-style hotel are more attractive than those at the Don Luis, but we have yet to find the pool clean enough to be swimmable. Restaurant. Parking.

WHERE TO EAT

The open-air **Cenote Zaci,** three blocks from the zócalo near the intersection of Calles 36 and 39, serves both snacks and meals that include Yucatecan specialties from its scenic location overlooking the cenote (8 a.m.-7 p.m.; inexpensive). Less scenic, but comfortable and with more interesting menus are the very Yucatecan **Casa de los Arcos** *(Calle 39 between the zócalo and Hotel Don Luís; inexpensive)* and the handsome restaurant in the **Meson del Marquez**, with international and Yucatecan choices. (Moderately expensive.)

CROSSROADS

Valladolid is at the junction of MEX 295, which heads south to Felipe Carrillo Puerto in Quintana Roo (160 km, 99 m). Continuing east on MEX 180, or the faster autopista MEX 180 D when it is completed, for about 156 km (94 m) you reach the Caribbean coast of Mexico (see "Caribbean Resorts" and "Quintana Roo"). A road at Nuevo X-can *(80 km, 50 m east of Valladolid)* links MEX 180 directly with the ruins of Coba *(53 km, 33 m)* and Tulum *(an additional 43 km, 27 m from the Coba turnoff)*, and saves considerable time by bypassing Cancún.

OFF THE BEATEN PATH

MEX 295 north leads past the cattle and hammock-making region of **Tizimin** (on the zócalo, there is a good provincial restaurant called **Tres Reyes**) and continues to the odd, little fishing village of **Rio Lagartos** (105 km, 65 m). The main attraction in Lagartos are the thousands of flamingos nesting off its shores (November to March is the best season). The easiest way to see them is to make arrangements with the **Hotel Maria Nefertity** for one of their early-morning boat excursions. The hard way is to drive out to Las Coloradas, past the salt flats and then to get lost when the road ends and never locate the correct pier for pleasure boats. The Nefertity is the only hotel here; it was temporarily out of water and electricity on our visit, but its 40 spartan rooms had beds (Calle 14 #109; ☎ [986] 14-15; $30).

UXMAL AND NEIGHBORING RUINS

South of Mérida in the Puuc (pook) Hills cluster a tremendous number of ruins including the Maya masterpiece of Uxmal. While exploring this region on horseback in the 19th century, John L. Stephens found so many ruins he despaired of visiting them all. The area must have been densely populated from A.D. 600-900, but strangely there is no readily available supply of water, not even the cenotes, or natural wells, other ancient cities depended on. To sustain themselves during the dry season, the ancient Maya constructed cement-lined reservoirs and cisterns for collecting rainwater. By Stephens' time these techniques had been lost, and many villages located on the ancient sites suffered from drought. Today, the area is far from densely populated and many of the ruins have crumbled and disappeared, but together with Uxmal, the ruins of Kabah, Sayil, Xlapak, and Labna have been restored as monuments to the achievements and former grandeur of the Puuc region.

Most people visit Uxmal on a one-day trip from Mérida. It's feasible to make excursions to the surrounding ruins in one day if you have a car or take a tour. An overnight stay enables you to enjoy the sound-and-light show at Uxmal and to stop at the towns of Ticul and Mani and the Loltun Caves with their early Maya carvings and fabulous caverns.

KEY TO UXMAL AND NEIGHBORING RUINS

Sights • The famous ruins of Uxmal are near lesser known ones like Kabah, Sayil, and Labna. The Loltun Caves, containing ancient Maya artifacts, and the colonial towns of Mani and Ticul complete the attractions of this region.

Where to Stay • First-class hotels, located near the Uxmal ruins, are the only accommodations available.

Where to Eat • Rustic but good restaurants in Mani and Ticul supplement the limited options at Uxmal.

Entertainment • Sound-and-light shows in the evening at Uxmal.

Getting Around • To visit neighboring sights from Uxmal, you need a car, which should be arranged in Mérida, or a tour, which can be arranged in Mérida and, sometimes, at Uxmal cultural center.

Practical Tips • If you plan a two-day swing through this area, make sure you schedule your sightseeing around the limited visiting hours at the Loltun Caves. Bring sturdy shoes for pyramid-climbing and damp caves; a sun hat and bathing suit, if you want; and insect repellent.

UXMAL RUINS

Open 8 a.m.-5 p.m. Admission charge. Additional fees for guides, parking, and sound-and-light show (cheaper Spanish version at 7 p.m.; English at 9 p.m.) Modern cultural center at main entrance to ruins includes museum, video show, and restaurant.

Uxmal (oosh-MAHL) has been said to rival anything built in ancient Greece or Rome. Its architecture, called "Puuc" after the surrounding hills, is elegantly proportioned and finely finished, with small cut stones set into mosaics of geometric patterns across the upper facades of the buildings. Chac masks, representing the rain god so critical to this area, surmount the doors and corners of the buildings, their long snouts projecting into space like elephant trunks. The quality of this Puuc architecture was enhanced by the development of a local cement that enabled the Mayas to span large spaces with the corbel (pointed) arch and create large interiors, huge palace complexes, and impressive gateways.

As magnificent and as famous as Uxmal is, little is known about its past. Although monuments carved with hieroglyphs have been found at the site, the history they may preserve is just now being deciphered by archaeologists like Jeff Kowalski, who recently revealed the rule of a Lord Chac around A.D. 900. It is known that the city was occupied only during the Late Classic period (A.D. 600-900), a time of extensive growth in ancient Mexico and a time of intense interregional contact between the Maya and the cultures of highland Mexico. Despite its distinctive architectural style, Uxmal shows influences from central Mexico in its use of columns, mosaics, phallic symbols, and feathered serpent representations. Uxmal was the largest and most important city in the Puuc region, perhaps dominating other cities like Kabah (there is a 16-km paved causeway connecting the two). Its architectural style was adopted even by cities outside the Puuc area, like Chichen Itza and Dzibilchaltun. The reasons for Uxmal's flourishing and fall are unknown, but the prominence of Chichen Itza after A.D. 900 most likely had some role in depriving Uxmal and other Puuc cities of their importance.

Pirámide del Adivino

Pyramid of the Magician • As you enter the site, you will be confronted by the massive back of this pyramid, beautifully elliptical in shape and majestically rising in three stages to a temple. Although not the tallest Maya pyramid, the Magician is exceptionally steep and terrifies many people during the descent from the top. The pyramid receives its name from a legend that says it was built overnight by a dwarf with supernatural powers. More prosaic facts show that the pyramid is the result of many periods of construction extending over 300 years. Some of

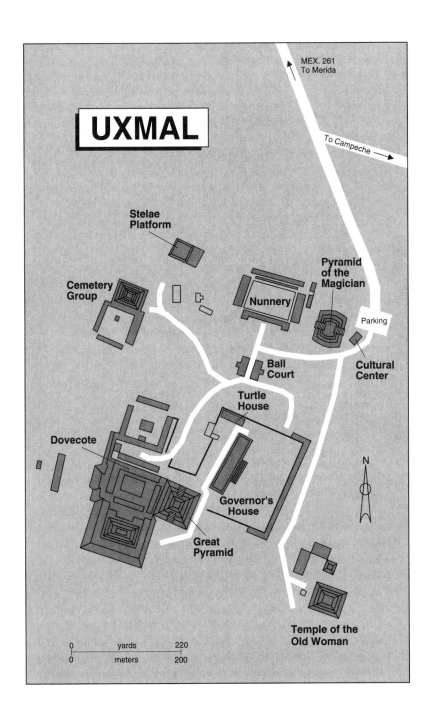

UXMAL

MEX. 261
To Merida

To Campeche →

Stelae
Platform

Cemetery
Group

Pyramid
of the
Magician

Nunnery

Parking

Ball
Court

Cultural
Center

Turtle
House

Dovecote

Governor's
House

N

Great
Pyramid

Temple of the
Old Woman

0   yards   220
0   meters   200

the stages of construction can be seen from the various temples incorporated into its structure. The hole excavated into the rear stairway leads to one of these earlier temples, but two others are more easily seen on the front, and west, side of the pyramid.

At the foot of the west stairway you can see the first phase of construction, a palace structure that belonged to a larger quadrangle complex like the adjacent so-called Nunnery. The pyramid covers most of the early complex, and the west stairway seemingly divides the original palace in half, yet much of its richly adorned facade can still be seen underneath the stairway, including some goggle-eyed rain gods from the highlands of Mexico. The next two stages of building are now enclosed by the pyramid, but the fourth stage is represented by the west stairway leading to a temple with its entire facade covered by a monster mask, the doorway forming its mouth. This Chenes-style of architecture is unusual at Uxmal, coming as it does from Campeche in the south, although another such building was found underneath the Governor's Palace at Uxmal. The west stairway is bordered by a series of chac masks and, just before reaching the temple, is interrupted by a throne shaped like another monster mask. Professor Kowalski believes Uxmal's rulers were coronated here, high above the populace. The last building phase included two staircases going around the Chenes temple to what is now the highest, and final, temple, decorated in a profusion of lattice designs.

Casa de las Monjas

Nunnery • Standing in the courtyard of this quadrangle of buildings you can see that each wing is at a different level and each facade different in decorative detail, yet the complex forms a harmonious whole. Uxmal architects were so concerned with visual effects that the upper walls slope outward to balance the long horizontal line of the buildings, and the arched entranceway provides a perfect frame for the ball court outside. Although this complex reminded the Spaniards of a nunnery, it was used by Uxmal's elite. In fact, Kowalski has noted many symbols of the rulers' cult here, from the lattice-design symbols for throne, the Venus and war symbols, and even the ceremonial bar of rulership and a carved stela.

The **North Building**, considered the oldest, is flanked by two temples at the foot of the stairs. The left temple, called the Venus Temple after some symbols on its frieze, uses columns supporting a lintel, which is rare at Uxmal but common at other Puuc sites. The stela on the stairs may name Lord Chac and is dated A.D. 895. The frieze of the upper building, interrupted by stacks of chac masks that project over the roof, includes small geometric pieces in a mosaic forming a lattice design. The niches are the doorways of stone representations of Maya thatched huts. These niches probably once held sculptures, and the hut design may represent the homes of ancestors and the lineages of the elite of Uxmal.

The **South Building**, built next, continues this stone-hut design. On the rear of the North Building are sculptures of nude prisoners.

The **East Building** is the least ornate, with chac masks only over the central doorway and corners. A background lattice mosaic adds texture to the primary design of inverted triangles composed of double-headed serpents, that may represent the ceremonial bar of rulership as well as the sky. The moldings represent serpents, their sculpted heads projecting at the corners of the building.

The **West Building** was the last constructed and the most ornate, with a profusion of geometric designs and three-dimensional sculpture. Winding its way through the design is the feathered serpent god Quetzalcoatl, usually thought to be introduced in Yucatán by the Toltecs from central Mexico during their conquest of Chichen Itza. Most evidence indicates Uxmal would have been abandoned at that time. Over the central doorway is a canopied throne containing a figure with the head of an old man and the body of a turtle, one of the Maya gods of the underworld.

Ball Court

As you walk through the arch of the Nunnery, through the ball court, and up to the large plaza to the House of the Turtles, the view of Uxmal is constantly changing with each level. Looking back on the Nunnery, it seems like a single building, the north wing forming a second story on the south wing. The ball court has been partially reconstructed. Lord Chac's name was written many different times in the hieroglyphs found here. The ball court ring with serpent at the bottom is dated A.D. 905.

Casa de las Tortugas

House of the Turtles • The central doorways of the House of the Turtles frame a magnificent view of the Nunnery. The House of the Turtles is a small gem of Puuc architecture, classic in its simplicity and restraint. Art historian George Kubler believes its colonnette design with three-part moldings imitates the wooden construction technique of Maya thatched houses. The building is named after the turtles carved on the upper molding, each with a distinctive pattern on its back. Maya traditions associate turtles with chac. When people suffered from drought, it was said the turtles grieved, and their eyes filling with tears brought on the rains.

Great Pyramid and the Dovecote Only

Only the north facade of this pyramid has been restored, so you can see the palace structure on top. This palace had its counterpart on each side of the pyramid that formed an unusual Nunnery-type quadrangle, but on the top of a pyramid. The palace was filled with rubble, and the pyramid was built up behind it, indicating the ancient Mayas were in the process of constructing yet another level, never completed. The palace is decorated with great chac masks and carvings of parrots (usually symbols of the sun). Inside, the huge snout of a chac mask serves as a step into a rear chamber. To the west of the Great Pyramid is the Dovecote, named after the **pigeon house** appearance of its lattice-design roof comb. The facade of the building has crumbled away, making it difficult to imagine its original appearance. It formed part of a quadrangle similar to the Nunnery, though earlier in date.

Palacio del Gobernador

Governor's Palace • This masterpiece of Uxmal and Puuc style, 340 feet long and composed of three wings connected by two corbel vaults, sits on an enormous artificial terrace about 50 feet above the other plazas. Despite the complexity of its frieze, with thousands of small cut stones fitted into mosaics of lattice and other geometric designs, chac masks, and serpents, the whole is remarkably harmonious. The **governor's palace** seems to have its back to the site, its orientation being unique at Uxmal. **Astronomer Anthony Aveni** explains the reason for this orientation in his discovery that the central door, lined up with the jaguar throne and uncarved column, or phallus, in the terrace, was used for sighting the exact point of **Venus** rising above the principal pyramid at the nearby site of Cehtzuc. The two corners of the north wall of the palace have been excavated to expose the cornice of an earlier, Chenes-style temple underneath, carved with symbols (a bar for 5 and 3 dots) relating to the period of 8 days when Venus disappeared into the Maya underworld. Because the Maya associated Venus with war, the astronomical importance of this building doesn't mean it wasn't in fact a palace. Kowalski believes it was the palace of Lord Chac, now the headless figure above the central door, because one of Uxmal's stelae shows him standing on a jaguar throne identical to the one here.

Other Sights

Paths to these other sights often are overgrown and difficult, particularly in the rainy season. To the south of the Governor's Palace a path runs to the **Casa de la Vieja,** or Temple of the Old Woman, now ruined. This temple continues the legend of the magician, for it is here that his mother, a sorceress, is said to have lived. Although there's really nothing to see, a visit makes a pleasant jungle walk. You can extend it by following the right prong of the fork (La Vieja is to the left) and climbing the mound of the **Templo de los Fallos,** where on the far side lie scattered some of the phallic stones. The entire walk is 1 km. There no longer is a path leading even further south to the **archway** that marks the beginning of the 16-km paved causeway that ends at the famous arch of Kabah.

To the west of the ball court, a path leads to several groups. The most interesting is the **Grupo del Cementerio** (Cemetery Group) named after the altars in the courtyard of the quadrangle complex with their carvings of skulls and crossbones and hieroglyphs, although there is no other evidence that it was used as a cemetery. A bit farther on, a path branches to the right, leading past the group of the columns. Usually you can't find the path to the **Stelae Platform** where 15 terribly eroded carved-stone monuments were discovered.

NEARBY SIGHTS

Kabah

About 22 km (14 m) south of Uxmal on 261. Open 8 a.m.- 5 p.m. Admission charge • The fabulous **Codz-Poop,** or **Palace of the Masks,** stands on the east side of the highway with its entire facade, from foundation to cornice, profusely, almost insanely, covered with rain-god masks. Sometimes the right angle of the sun restores balance to the facade, creating a rich texture of light and shade. Snouts of the chac masks are used as steps into some of the doorways on the facade and in the interior. A **hieroglyphic platform** in front of the *Codz-Poop* mentions Lord Chac of Uxmal, confirming the political ties long thought to have existed between the two sites. Across the highway is the freestanding arch where the paved causeway from Uxmal once entered Kabah. So little of Kabah has been explored that its actual size is unknown: aerial photographs indicate it might be larger than Uxmal. When *John L. Stephens* explored this site over a century ago, he discovered naturalistic carvings of individuals, some carrying weapons, similar to some of the door-jamb carvings at Chichen Itza.

Sayil

Continue 5 km (3 m) south on MEX 261 and turn left onto the paved road to Oxkutzcab for 4 km (2 m) to turnoff on right. Open 8 a.m.-5 p.m. Admission fee. Soft drinks available • The **Palace** at Sayil is magnificent; an accidental warm orange hue (from iron oxides in the soil) only adds to its attractiveness. Although the great size of the Palace—236 feet in length with 50 chambers—could have resulted in a bulky mass, the Maya architects achieved a building of lightness and harmony. The wide-portico doorways and rich decoration of the second story contrast with the restrained style of the other two levels. The frieze on the second story is decorated with typical Puuc designs of chac masks and colonnettes but also includes diving gods (figures most easily identified by their upside-down legs). **Diving gods** are found in the Maya area from Pre-Classic to Conquest times, but it is wondered if they have the same meaning throughout their history. In the earlier periods, the diving figures symbolize deified ancestors looking down from the heavens on worldly events, perhaps intervening on behalf of their lordly descendants. The symbolism, at Sayil and later at Tulum, is less certain. While there are several hundred buildings at Sayil, some with carved *stelae,* most remain covered by the jungle. Less than a quarter mile south of the Palace are the only other exposed buildings, which are in a somewhat ruined state. As you exit from the ruins, you can see a solitary building in the jungle across the main road.

Xlapak

At 7 km (4 m) from Sayil, turn right at sign. Open 8 a.m.-5 p.m. Admission charge • Xlapak (shla-pahk) means "old walls." On your way to Labna, you pass the sole building of old walls exposed on this ancient, but **unexplored site.** It is in Puuc style, with the upper facade adorned with chac masks and what is called a step-fret pattern. Columns are attached to the corners of the building.

Labna

At 4 km (2 m) east of Xlapak, turn right at sign and walk to entrance. Open 8 a.m.-5 p.m. Admission charge. Soft drinks available • Although Labna was a provincial center at the time of Uxmal, probably 3000 people lived in this center, sustained during the dry season by the 60 artificial cisterns for collecting rainwater. If you can find your way to the second story on the Palace near the entrance to the site, you can see one of these cisterns. The Palace has some similarity to the one at Sayil but is less sophisticated. On the lower and central section of this Palace, there is a massive chac mask. Nearby, projecting from a corner of this wing, is a fine sculpture of a human head emerging from the jaws of a crocodile. **Crocodiles** represent the Maya earth monster, its jaws the entrance to the Underworld. This sculpture may show the god Quetzalcoatl emerging from the Underworld as he rises to the sky as the morning star, a theme found also at Uxmal and Chichen Itza. The Palace is joined to the southern group by a raised causeway, now a mound of rubble. The southern group includes the famous **Labna arch,** which connected two small plazas. Although both facades of the arch are decorated, the west side mosaic is more elaborate and interesting with its representations of thatched huts above the doorways. Nearby is the pyramid and temple called El Mirador. Its 15-foot-high roof comb was once adorned with brightly painted carved figures of ballplayers and skulls, recalling the ceremonies depicted on Chichen Itza's ball court.

Grutas de Loltun (Caves of "Stone Flowers")

20 km (12 m) east of Labna, 7 km (4 m) south of Oxkutzcab at "intersection" of Yaaxcham and Oxkutzcab roads. From Oxkutzcab, turn right after visiting Loltun to pick up rest of loop tour. Open every day by tour only at 9:30 a.m., 11 a.m., 12:30 p.m., 2 p.m., and 3:30 p.m. On busy days extra tours scheduled. Tours (in English occasionally) last two hours. Admission fee. Caves artificially illuminated. Restaurant • These fascinating caverns contain not only impressive **stalactite** and **stalagmite** formations but also remnants of human use from at least 2500 B.C. through the Conquest. Mayas looking for water found Loltun generous, and left offerings, paintings, and carvings in the caves. The most important carving, of a Maya warrior, is perhaps the earliest of Yucatán, dating from around 300 B.C. Throughout the caves are stone troughs hollowed out to catch drops of "virgin" water from stalactites for religious ceremonies.

Crossroads: Oxkutzcab

At 7 km (4 m) north of Loltun Caves • At this point on your trip, you are 79 km (62.5 m) from Mérida via Ticul and Muna to the left. At Muna, another right takes you to MEX 261 and then Mérida. Straight ahead and north of Oxkutzcab, the road continues to the town of Mani and doubles back to Ticul, a detour of about 24 km (15 m). *Practical tip:* If you need sustenance at this point, you have two very Yucatecan choices: El Principe in Mani and Restaurant Los Almendros in Ticul.

Off the Beaten Track

If you have a car and some extra time, you can continue north from Mani for 52 km (32 m) and past numerous Maya villages and 16th-century churches to the ruins of Mayapan (see "Mérida Excursions"). Just beyond Mayapan, the road is easier until it reaches Mérida 50 km (31 m) farther on.

Mani

At 10 km (6 m) north of Oxkutzcab • The detour to Mani takes you along a road with shaded gardens and Mayas walking and bicycling to the *market at Oxkutzcab.* Mani is a pleasant small town, its large plaza surrounded with traditional oval and thatched Maya houses and dominated by one of the earliest (1548) and largest Franciscan churches in Yucatán. The church altars show a good deal of provincial skill and charm, with the "Corinthian" crowns of their columns looking somewhat like feathered headdresses. The town's cenote concludes the legend of the **magician from Uxmal,** for in this cenote lived the sorceress mother of the dwarf, after her departure from Uxmal.

Mani's unpresuming appearance belies its historical importance. The capital of the Xiu dynasty after the fall of Mayapan, Mani was the largest Maya city at the time of the Conquest. It became the second town established in Yucatán by the conquerors when its Xiu ruler capitulated to the Spaniards in Mérida and became the first Maya leader converted to Christianity, thereby facilitating the conquest of his people. Despite Mani's early conversion, its people continued practicing their former religion, which led to one of the most destructive events in colonial history—the *burning of Maya books by Diego de Landa.* The **auto-da-fe** in Mani was so thorough that no more than four Maya manuscripts exist today. Seeing the records of their history, science, and religion go up in flames, Landa wrote, the Maya "showed much sorrow." Some committed suicide. Today, a sign in the thatched, very Maya **El Principe Tutul Xiu Restaurant** *(Calle 26 #208)* recalls the *auto-da-fe* and says that "even after so many centuries the Indian still cries in the silence of the night." (This very clean, inexpensive restaurant serves fabulous *poc chuc* from its location on the right side of the entrance road from Oxkutzcab, a few hundred feet before the plaza. Open till 4 p.m.; closed Mon.)

Ticul

At 14 km (9 m) southwest of Mani or 17 km (10 m) west of Oxkutzcab •
Around Ticul's picturesque zócalo and on the outskirts of town are
craftmakers' shops. As a change from looking at buildings, you can
buy ceramic reproductions of ancient Maya bowls, straw hats, and
embroidered huipils. *John L. Stephens,* recuperating in Ticul's monastery from one of his many attacks of fever, described 19th-century
Ticul as:

*Altogether for appearance, society and conveniences of living, it is perhaps
the best village in Yucatán and famous for its bullfights and the beauty of its
Mestiza women.*

Unfortunately, the main street *(Calle 23)* leading off the zócalo
doesn't support his claim, but amid the hodgepodge of shops and
across the street from the Cine Ideal is **Restaurant Los Almendros**
(Calle 23 #207). This authentic Yucatecan restaurant serves excellent
traditional dishes at inexpensive prices in a comfortable atmosphere.
Even if you don't like exotic food, you will find the sopa de lima just
a very flavorful chicken soup and the papadzules (tortillas stuffed with
hardboiled eggs and topped with pumpkinseed sauce) quite tasty and
mild.

WHERE TO STAY AND EAT

Although the restaurant at the ruins is the most convenient, the
Nicte-Ha (across highway from ruins; 12:30-7 p.m.; moderate) is your best
bet for a light lunch (fruit salad, sandwiches, and a variety of main dishes)
at slightly lower prices. For a bit more, you can enjoy the hamburgers and
á la carte luncheon items in the lovelier setting of the poolside grill at the
Hacienda Uxmal (12:30-3 p.m.; moderately expensive). Otherwise, the
dining rooms in the hotels are the only places to eat. They all serve a comida corrida from 12:30-3:00 p.m. and at dinner for moderately expensive
prices. The **Villa Arqueologica** charges more for its à la carte continental
fare. Often you can negotiate an overpriced club sandwich (best price at
the **Misión**) at the hotel bars. *To call the hotels, dial area code 99.*

Hacienda Uxmal   ★★★

On highway across from ruins; ☎ *24-71-42; $97* • For a long time,
the lovely Hacienda provided the only accommodations at the ruins.
The hotel, with its extensive gardens and colonial decor, remains a
favorite. Its 82 rooms with ceiling fans open onto verandas furnished
with cane-back chairs. Dining room and bar; crafts shop. Pool. For
reservations, call, in U.S., ☎ 800-235-4079.

Villa Arqueologica   ★★★

At entrance to ruins; ☎ *24-70-53; $77* • A charming hotel with
attractive grounds, its 40 rooms are air-conditioned. Like other hotels
in this chain, it has a tennis court, pool, bar, and restaurant. For reservations, call, in the U.S., ☎ 800-528-3100.

Hotel Misión Uxmal

On highway 1.6 km (1 m) north of ruins; ☎ *24-73-08; $93 MAP* • A contemporary building with colonial decor on spacious grounds. Those of its 49 fan-cooled rooms with balconies and views of the ruins are especially recommended. Pool. Dining room and bar. For reservations, call, in the U.S., ☎ (800) 648-7818.

GETTING TO AND FROM UXMAL

ROAD

Uxmal lies 79 km (50 m) south of Mérida on MEX 261. Daily bus service from Mérida enables you to make an easy one-day trip to Uxmal with a return in the afternoon. The Ruta Puuc bus from Mérida visits Kabah, Sayil, and Labna in addition to Uxmal, all in just a few hours. Too few for most, since it departs 8 a.m. and returns at 3 p.m. It's best to arrange a car or tour for the sights along the loop. The trip from Mérida to Uxmal and then to Oxkutzcab covers 148 km (82 m). If you want to return to Mérida from Oxkutzcab by a new route, check the "Crossroads" section.

CAMPECHE

Dominated by the sea, open, breezy Campeche offers a **tropical climate** and important remnants from its rich history. A tour of this calm and handsome port takes you through narrow streets lined with colonial buildings and churches and to forts and ramparts— constant and vivid reminders of the conquistadors and **pirates** in Campeche's colorful past.

Although **Hernandez de Córdoba** arrived in Ah Kin Pech (as Campeche was then known) in 1517, and **Cortés** some two years later, it wasn't until 1540 that the present town was founded. In due time, Campeche flourished as the major port on the Yucatán peninsula, shipping timber, dye woods, and chicle to Europe. Its wealth and reputation soon attracted scores of pirates who made regular calls on the port to burn, loot, and plunder. Some of the pirates became legendary with names like **Pata de Palo** ("Pegleg") and **Diego the Mulatto.** The forts and walls you find throughout Campeche were built in the late 17th and early 18th centuries for protection against the marauding pirates. Once they sealed the city off from the sea, making Campeche the most fortified city in the New World. The walls are mostly gone now, but seven of the eight bulwarks remain as well as four forts; their cannons still point to the sea, and the pirates they took aim at still fill the lore and soul of Campeche.

Low-key Campeche is often overlooked by travelers since it is but a short hop of some 2-1/2 hours by land to its more famous neighbor, Mérida. Until recent European tours discovered it, this neglect resulted in few tourist facilities. Although there are some perceptible improvements, Campeche remains a very Mexican tropical city.

KEY TO CAMPECHE

Sights • Fortresses and the sea surround Campeche. Some archaeology museums, a market, a few colonial streets are the attractions here.

Excursions • The Maya ruins of Edzna are nearby.

Shopping • Campeche along with Mérida sells high-quality Panama hats. Maya huipils can be found.

Where to Stay • Limited choice, but both first-class and budget hotels.

Where to Eat • Too few good restaurants. Specialties of the area include stone crab and shrimp.

Entertainment • Not much. A few bars and a disco.

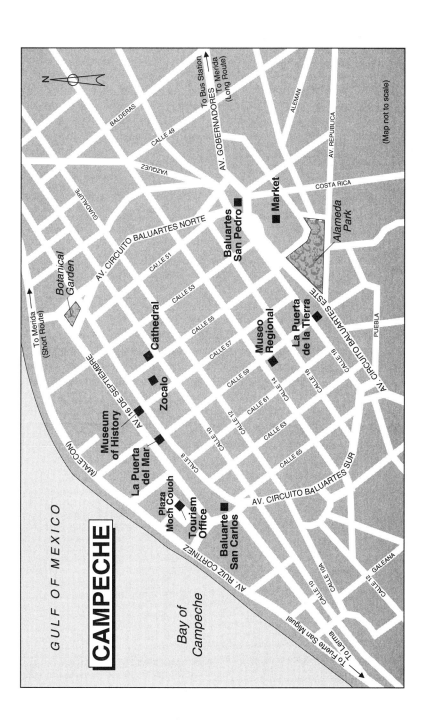

CAMPECHE

GULF OF MEXICO

Bay of Campeche

To Merida (Short Route)

To Merida (Long Route)

To Bus Station

(Map not to scale)

N

BALDERAS

CALLE 49

VAZQUEZ

AV. GOBERNADORES

ALEMAN

AV. REPUBLICA

COSTA RICA

GUADALUPE

AV. CIRCUITO BALUARTES NORTE

Botanical Garden

CALLE 51

CALLE 53

CALLE 55

CALLE 57

CALLE 59

CALLE 61

CALLE 63

CALLE 65

Cathedral

Zocalo

Museum of History

AV. 16 DE SEPTIEMBRE

La Puerta del Mar

(MALECON)

Plaza Moch Couoh

Tourism Office

Baluarte San Carlos

AV. RUIZ CORTINEZ

Baluartes San Pedro

Market

Alameda Park

Museo Regional

La Puerta de la Tierra

AV. CIRCUITO BALUARTES ESTE

PUEBLA

CALLE 18

CALLE 16

CALLE 14

CALLE 12

CALLE 10

CALLE 8

AV. CIRCUITO BALUARTES SUR

CALLE 10

CALLE 12

GALEANA

To Fuerte San Miguel
To Lerma

Getting Around • Go by foot around the center of the city; it's small and manageable. For some of the fortresses, churches, and museums you need a car, taxi (readily available), or city tour.

If you pretend that the Gulf is north, the odd numbered streets run north-south and the even numbered east-west.

Practical Tips • Campeche provides an interesting overnight for the leisurely traveler, but is not a major tourist destination.

Although located on the Gulf and subject to its breeze, Campeche is hot all year particularly from May to September. Air conditioning may be a necessity for some.

The long siesta takes place between 1 and 4 or 5 p.m. when a good deal of Campeche closes down.

WHAT TO SEE AND DO

Plaza

To get a feel of the sea, begin your exploration of Campeche with a walk or join the early morning joggers along the malecón (Av. Ruiz Cortinez) with its open vistas of the Gulf and shrimp boats. Until recently the massive eight-foot-thick walls that enclosed the city bordered on the sea. Now landfill separates them. One result of the landfill operation can be seen in the modern Plaza Moch Couoh (Av. Ruiz Cortinez between Av. 61 and 65), the site of the Tourist Office. Across the plaza, facing Av. 16 de Septiembre, are two modern buildings, the rectangular **Governor's Palace** and the fanciful "spaceship" **Congressional Building.**

Nearby across Av. 16 de Septiembre at Calle 59 you will find one of the two colonial entrances to the fortified city, **La Puerta del Mar** (Gate of the Sea); at the other end of Calle 59, about five blocks away, the other entrance, **La Puerta de la Tierra** (Gate of the Land), stands still surrounded by the late-17th-century city walls. The entrances and thick walls, along with the parapets, forts, cannons, drawbridges, and moats must have made Campeche a foreboding and imposing city— one that would make the likes of future Peglegs and Diego the Mulattos think twice before attacking.

Forts

Today the *baluartes*, or *bulwarks*, and *fuertes*, or forts, and several other colonial buildings have been converted into museums and galleries of arts and crafts. Although all are open to the public, you'll find that the two most important for archaeology are the **Museo Regional** and the **Baluarte Soledad**, and the most important for artesanias are the **Baluarte San Pedro** and the **ex-templo San Jose** (see "Shopping"). The most picturesque is the Fuerte San Miguel. As you walk to these sights, you'll be in the midst of colonial Campeche, along Calles 55, 57, 59, and the surrounding streets. On Calle 10, between 51 and 53, you can admire the later turn-of-the-century opulence of the Carvajal Mansion. Nearby is the **zócalo,** with flowers and benches and the old Cathedral to one side.

Museums

Of the three archaeological museums, the most extensive is the **Museo Regional** *(Calle 59 between 14 and 16),* in the restored governor's mansion. Although the fine collection is not dramatically displayed, it includes an unusual variety of ancient Maya sculpture from the ruins found throughout the state of Campeche—carved columns, immense stelae with narrative scenes, lovely Jaina figurines. A must for anyone interested in archaeology. The seond-floor exhibits are historical and include a model of the walled town. Open Tues.-Sat. 9 a.m.-8 p.m., Sun. 8 a.m.-1 p.m.; small fee. The **Baluarte Soledad** *(Calle 8 across from the zócalo)* contains the small but rewarding Museo de Estelas Mayas with Classic period Maya sculptures excavated by the National Institue of Anthropology and History (INAH). Here are some interesting stelaes from Edzna as well as a carved porch from Xcalumkin. Open daily 8 a.m.-8 p.m.; small fee. The **Fuerte San Miguel** *(4 km, 2-1/2 m west on malecón, turn left up hill at sign for "Camino Escenica")* has a tiny collection of pieces from all over ancient Mexico, but a trip is most worthwhile for its drawbridge entrance and view over the Gulf and city. Open Tues.-Sun. 8 a.m.-8 p.m.; small fee.

Church of San Francisco

About a mile northeast of the zócalo along the malecón (whose name changes from Ruiz Cortinez to Miguel Alemán), you will find the Church of San Francisco *(just before Calle Mariano Escobedo).* Founded in 1546, it is located on the site where in 1517 Córdoba and his party supposedly celebrated the first mass on the American continent. Córdoba's stay, however, was brief. Bernal Diaz del Castillo, who accompanied Córdoba, reported that their party received a rather unfriendly reception from the local Maya.

The warriors who were drawn up in battle array began to whistle and sound their trumpets and drums. When we perceived their menacing appearance and saw great squadrons of Indians bearing down on us ...we determined to retreat to the coast in good order.

The original font of the church still stands and has some historical interest, for it was used for the baptism of Cortés' grandson, Jerónimo. A few blocks from the Church of San Francisco near Av. Obregón is another reminder of the Spanish invaders, the **Pozo** ("well") **de los Conquistadores.** At this well the Córdoba party gathered water, which, according to Bernal Díaz, was the sole purpose of their innocent foray into Ah Kin Pech (Maya for "the place of serpents and ticks," the name derived from an idol in the area that had on its head a coiled serpent and, on the head of the serpent, a tick).

Beneath the city, but unfortunately now closed to the public, are interconnecting tunnels and caves first used by the ancient Maya for religious ceremonies and later as hiding places from the Spaniards. Ironically, the Spaniards in turn were forced to seek refuge in the tunnels and caves to escape the plunder of invading pirates.

EXCURSION TO EDZNA

A visit to the Maya ruins of Edzna can be part of your trip to Mérida or the Uxmal area from Campeche, as the distances are not great and the roads are good. Edzna can be reached **by car from Campeche.** Follow signs to the old road to Mérida (MEX 261) and turn right at the picturesque Maya village of Cayal after 46 km (29 m). Edzna lies 19 km (12 m) farther south. If you are bypassing Campeche on your way to Mérida, the Haltunchen turnoff just 16 km (10 m) north of Champoton will take you past Edzna (55 km, 34 m) on your way to Mérida.

Off the Beaten Track

If you have time to spend in the Campeche area, your own car, and the patience to ask directions in Spanish and to travel slowly on rough roads, you might want to track down the **Chenes ruins** in the area east of **Hopelchen** (modest restaurants available in this village). Chenes architecture dates from **A.D. 600-900** and represents a regional style of the Maya localized in this area, which sustained itself from the water of underground wells ("chen" means well). Chenes temples are covered with the long-nosed masks usually associated with the rain god. But their doors form the openings of the mouth of the earth monster, making them portals to the Maya Underworld where the gods of death and evil resided and required careful watching, ritual appeasement, and, sometimes, defeat. The road to a number of Chenes ruins leads off to the south of the zócalo of Hopelchen, and after 41 km (25 m) reaches the town of Dzibalchen. The fine ruins of **Hochob,** whose famous facade is reproduced in the National Museum of Anthropology in Mexico City, lie a short distance away (15 km, 9 m), but road conditions may make it inadvisable for you to visit. You can travel 6 m south on the rock road from Dzibalchen to Chencoh, then ask at that village about the conditions of the dirt road to Hochob. The ruins of **Dzibilnocac** can be reached by the rock road north to Iturbide (19 km, 12 m, from Dzibalchen), where they can be found on the eastern outskirts of that town.

EDZNA RUINS

Open 8 a.m.-5 p.m. Admission charged. Note: Current excavations may change visitor paths through the ruins; certainly they will reveal new sights. Today this ruined city may seem distant from any place of significance, but for the ancient Maya its location was on the trade route between northern Yucatán and the southern Maya area and the coastal town of **Ah Kin Pech** (Campeche). More important, perhaps, is its location in a valley that connects with the extensive drainage of the Rio Champoton. Occupied by 600 B.C. , Edzna grew to be one of the largest Maya cities in the Late Pre-Classic period (150 B.C.-A.D. 100). During this time its population constructed a massive hydraulic system that included nearly 14 miles of canals that were wide enough for canoe traffic. The system drained water from the region, creating new farmlands and reservoirs that could be used for dry season crops. Archaeologist Ray Matheny believes the system is without parallel and required an enormous population to construct it, all by about A.D. 100. Also at this time the Edzna observatory enabled the Maya to make their first predictions of solar eclipses.

Despite the early importance of Edzna, the ruins reflect its architecture during the Late Classic. Given its crossroads location, it's not surprising to find southern lowland Maya traits, (such as carved stelae with dates in the Long Count and hieroglyphic texts) alongside Puuc-style architecture. The Classic-period city covered an area at least 6 square km and then, like many Maya cities, was mostly abandoned around A.D. 900. Today most of the city still lies under jungle cover, but the **acropolis** with its *Cinco Pisos* ("five stories") main structure and the recent reconstruction of a few other complexes can be visited.

To the left of the ticket desk a shed protects a number of stelae carved with ruler portraits. One is eight feet high, another shows a ruler standing victorious over a prisoner, and most date from A.D. 672-810. Others are on display in Campeche. Beyond the ticket desk a short path leads to the main plaza, where you find the acropolis on the east (your left). Like all such complexes, this acropolis stands high on a series of platforms with limited access to its main buildings on the top. After climbing the one staircase to the top of the acropolis, you enter a large plaza with an altar in its center and buildings surrounding it on all sides. In front of you on the east side stands Cinco Pisos—a **pyramid-and-temple** structure—which has four levels of multichambered palace buildings forming the pyramid base rather than the usual solid, rubble-filled pyramid found elsewhere. In some ways, Cinco Pisos reminds us of the multilayered palace at Sayil, yet it is unique for having a temple atop its high-rise apartment complex, forming the fifth level. This temple dominates not only the acropolis group, but also all of Edzna, for it is the highest building at the site and could be seen clearly from a suburban area two miles to the west. Its platform steps are carved with hieroglyphs, some of which have been deciphered to give the date of A.D. 652, but excavations have proven that earlier, in the Pre-Classic, this already was the center of the city and 12 canals radiated out from here.

The south side of the main plaza was reconstructed in 1988. Walking through the ball court here (a sculpture of an Edzna ballplayer can be seen at the **Baluarte Soledad Museum** in Campeche), you enter another large plaza. The east side is the most interesting to explore. At the base of the temple here (with a throne or dais on the stairs?) are numerous fragments of sculptures. Judging from the size of the legs on a bottom stela fragment, some of the sculptures must have been more than life size and quite a number of them show rulers with their prisoners of war.

SHOPPING

The colorful **Municipal Market**—south of the zócalo, off Av. Circuito Baluartes Este between Alameda Park and **Baluarte San Pedro**—sells the usual household necessities and food. For crafts, however, you should visit the nearby Baluarte San Pedro (open 9 a.m.-1 p.m., 5-8 p.m. weekdays; 9 a.m.-1 p.m. Sat.). We found a few fine *jipis*, or so-called Panama hats (see "Shopping: Mérida") made in the village of Becal, lots of basketry, and white, embroidered Maya huipils—all items typical of the region. The **Museo de Campeche** *(Calle 63 at 10)* not only sponsors changing cultural exhibits (including artesanias from throughout Mexico) at its location in the restored ex-temple of San Jose, but it also has a crafts shop that sells local items.

WHERE TO STAY

In keeping with Campeche's low tourism profile, the choice of hotels is limited, but you can select from perfectly acceptable hotels in several price categories. For reservations write Campeche, Camp., Mexico, or call area code 981.

MODERATE

Ramada Inn Campeche
Av. Ruiz Cortinez 51, on the waterfront; ☎ *6-22-33; $110* • Located in the center of town, overlooking the Gulf of Mexico, the Ramada Inn is a totally modern, first-class hotel. The decent-sized 120 rooms are carpeted and air-conditioned with balconies overlooking the bay. There is a pleasant pool area, two restaurants, shops, and weekend disco. Service is good. The Ramada Inn offers the most luxury of any hotel in Campeche. For reservations, call, in the U.S., ☎ 800-228-2828.

Baluartes
Av. Ruiz Cortinez on the waterfront; ☎ *6-39-11; $59* • The stark white Baluartes, formerly the premier hotel in Campeche, now has been surpassed by its next-door neighbor the Ramada Inn. The renovated older Baluartes is a quite decent hotel, with 104 air-conditioned rooms. Those in front with a view of the Gulf are more desirable than the rear rooms with city and parking lot views. There are restaurants, bar, shops, and a large pool.

Alhambra
Av. Resurgimento 85; ☎ *6-68-22; $55* • Just 2 km west of the extension of the malecón toward Lerma, this modern motel sits across the road from the Gulf, but none of its 100 rooms have views. All are air-conditioned and carpeted. Restaurant. Bar. Pool in parking lot. Bus service into center. Although not in center, the Alhambra costs slightly less than others in this category.

INEXPENSIVE

Lopez   √

Calle 12 #189, between Calles 61 and 63; ☎ *6-33-44; $33* • A commercial-type hotel with panelled lobby and 39 air-conditioned rooms. Rooms are rather plain, but clean and acceptable. Good, attentive service.

OUTSIDE OF CAMPECHE

Si Ho Playa   ★ ★ ★

km 40 Carretera Campeche-Champoton, near town of Seybaplaya; ☎ *6-29-89; $30* • Drive 25 m southwest on MEX 180 to this hotel located right next to the Gulf of Mexico. The exterior looks like the facade of an old fort while the interior is a restored hacienda with 80 large, well-furnished, air-conditioned rooms. Restaurant, bar, pool, tennis, dock, and fishing facilities. Isolated. Write Apartado 275, Campeche.

WHERE TO EAT

Seafood and more seafood in many varieties! As you walk along the malecón, the fishing boats you see in the Gulf remind you that your meal will include the freshest of fish. Specialties of the area include *camarones* (shrimp), the wonderful sweet and succulent, if seasonal, *cangrejo moro* (stone crab), and a kind of shark taco called pan de cazon. Restaurant choices are limited, but it doesn't matter. Just return to your favorite again and again.

When in Campeche we head immediately to the **Restaurant Miramar** *(Calle 8 and 61).* The decor is modest, but the order of cold stone crabs here is the freshest and tastiest we've ever eaten. The menu is extensive, with numerous shrimp dishes, a good ceviche, and other seafood that attract the French tours when they're in town (and when a 15% service charge, in the European manner, is added to the bill). Moderate to moderately expensive. We've also enjoyed the crabs at **El Grill** of the Ramada Inn where they are served in air-conditioned comfort with finger bowls. Moderate to moderately expensive. Although the decor and low prices of **Del Parque** *(Calle 57 and 8)* make it popular with tourists, we were disappointed in the seafood. The fruit salad was more than ample. But for breakfasts and snacks, particularly an evening *merienda of tacos,* cheeseburgers, or desert, join all the locals at the bustling **Cafe Poquito** in the lobby of the Ramada Inn (inexpensive). Also very local and good is the afternoon comida at the **Restaurant 303** *(Calle 8 #303),* on the second floor of an attractive mansion across from the Congressional Building. Inexpensive.

ENTERTAINMENT

You won't find much night life in this quiet coastal town. You can take a stroll along the malecón to see the sunset over the Gulf or sit in the zócalo and dream of pirates and conquistadors. The lounges in the Baluartes and Ramada Inn sometimes provide live music, especially on weekends.

GETTING TO AND FROM CAMPECHE

AIR

No international flights are available to Campeche. Aeromexico flies daily between Mexico City and Campeche.

BUS

Frequent first-class bus service is available to Campeche from Mérida (via MEX 180), Villahermosa, and Chetumal. Buses also run along the ferry route between Villahermosa and Campeche via Ciudad del Carmen (see "On the Road").

CAR

Good roads link Campeche with **Villahermosa** and **Chetumal,** although near Villahermosa the road can be somewhat rough due to heavy truck traffic resulting from the oil boom. The total distance to Villahermosa via the longer, but faster, inland route is 483 km (about 300 m). To Chetumal the distance is 416 km (258 m). Take MEX 180 south of Campeche 64 km (40 m) to **Champoton** and the crossroads for MEX 261. On the way to Champoton, MEX 180 passes through congested Lerma, bustling from its fishing and boat-building industry, climbs over some local hills, and passes by the resort hotel of Si Ho Playa (see last page). Champoton, today a sleepy fishing village, once was one of the capitals of the seafaring Putun Maya and one of the first places the Spaniards landed in Mexico—only to be forced to retreat with their leader, Grijalva, fatally wounded. Between December 1 and December 8, Champoton comes alive with its fiesta in honor of the Virgin of the Immaculate Conception. After Champoton follow MEX 261 to Escarcega (83 km, 51 m). At Escarcega MEX 261 ends, and MEX 186 goes east to Chetumal (269 km, 168 m) and west past the Palenque turnoff (188 km, 117 m) and on to Villahermosa another 120 km (74 m).

DIRECTORY

Airlines • *Aeromexico*, at airport (☎ 6-66-56).

Buses • The Camionera Central is located outside the center of town at Av. Chile and Gobernadores.

Car Rentals • *Hertz* (☎ 6-48-55); *Auto-Rent* (☎ 6-22-33).

Post Office • 16 de Septiembre at Calle 53.

Taxis • Taxi stand at bus terminal, airport, and zócalo.

Tours • VIPS, Calle 59 near Ramada Inn, has city tours and excursions to Edzna.

Tourist Office • Located on the modern Plaza Moch Couoh near Calles 63 and Av. 16 de Septiembre (☎ 6-60-68). You can't miss the huge "Turismo" sign, but it's easy to miss the entrance, which requires some ingenuity and acrobatic ability to reach through the modernistic plaza. Open Mon.-Fri., 8:30 a.m.-3 p.m., 5-9 p.m.; weekends, 9 a.m.-1 p.m.

QUINTANA ROO:
THE CARIBBEAN

Cancún

> ... *the swaying, glowing magenta of the bougainvillea, and the fierce red outbursts of the poinsettia.*

> D. H. Lawrence

HISTORY AND CULTURE

An extensive Caribbean coastline, with abundant inlets, quiet lagoons, and submerged coral reefs has shaped Quintana Roo through both its prehistory and history. The area prospered only when oriented toward its magnificent coast, as with the ancient Maya sea trade or modern tourism. Quintana Roo, the eastern half of the Yucatán Peninsula, shares the same limestone crust as the state of Yucatán but is blessed by deeper soil and greater rainfall, resulting in a cover of tropical rain forest with mahogany and dyewood trees rather than scrub jungle. Quintana Roo also contains lakes, many of them remarkably beautiful. Laguna de Bacalar, or Lake of the Seven Colors—streaked with colors ranging from the deepest blue-black to the most flamboyant turquoise—was called by the Maya as the place "where heaven begins." The southern part of the state is marked by the Rio Hondo, which forms the border of the country of Belize. In this denser forest environment, it is not hard to find deer and wild turkeys or see flocks of parrots or toucans.

PREHISTORY

The entire Caribbean coast of Quintana Roo is dotted with structures dating from the very late period (A.D. 1200-Conquest), those at Tulum being the best known. These structures along the sea derive from a thriving commercial society that was based on extensive sea trade as well as "tourism" by indigenous people who made religious pilgrimages to the local shrines of the moon goddess, Ix Chel. Although many of these structures still standing were shrines to Ix Chel, archaeologist Arthur Miller believes others may have served as lighthouses. Perched prominently above the sea, with fires lit in them, these buildings could have served as navigational aids along this coast, which has few natural features to guide the way. Even today, the ruined buildings are used as navigation markers.

These late sea-trading Maya controlled trade from Tabasco on the Gulf Coast, around the Yucatán Peninsula to Honduras, and perhaps to Panama. They traded the salt and honey of Yucatán for cacao (used as money in the ancient world) and other goods. In 1502, Christopher Columbus himself encountered these Maya traders off the coast of Honduras. He describes seeing a boat, said to be from the province of Yucatán, with the owner or chief seated in the center under a canopy. The canoe was long as a galley and

eight feet wide. They had in it much clothing of the kind which they weave cotton in this land, such as cloth woven with many designs and colors...knives of flint...foodstuff of the country, copper hatchets, little bells, beans of cacao, and a fermented drink of maize.

As translated by Frans Blom

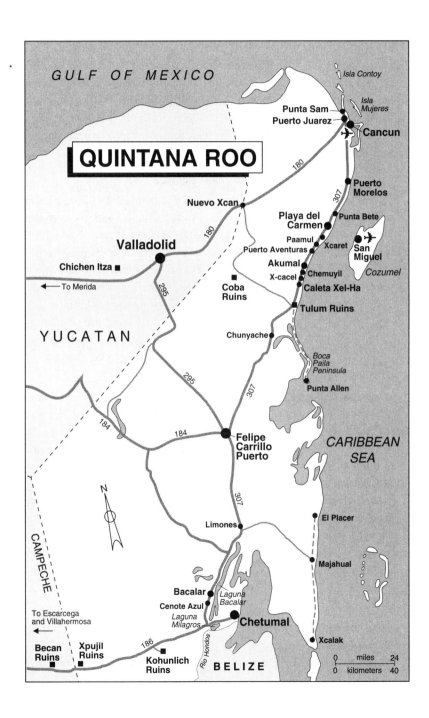

GULF OF MEXICO

Isla Contoy

Isla Mujeres

Punta Sam
Puerto Juarez

Cancun

QUINTANA ROO

180

Puerto Morelos

307

Nuevo Xcan

Playa del Carmen

Punta Bete

180

Paamul

Puerto Aventuras

Xcaret

San Miguel

Valladolid

Akumal

Chemuyil

Cozumel

Chichen Itza ■

X-cacel

295

← To Merida

Coba Ruins

Caleta Xel-Ha

Tulum Ruins

YUCATAN

Chunyache

Boca Paila Peninsula

295

Punta Allen

184

CARIBBEAN SEA

Felipe Carrillo Puerto

184

N

307

El Placer

Limones

Majahual

CAMPECHE

Bacalar

Cenote Azul

Laguna Bacalar

To Escarcega and Villahermosa

Laguna Milagros

Chetumal

Xcalak

186

Becan Ruins

Xpujil Ruins

Kohunlich Ruins

Rio Hondos

BELIZE

| 0 | miles | 24 |
| 0 | kilometers | 40 |

Before this Post-Classic period, Maya trade between Yucatán and Guatemala used overland routes. The two largest Quintana Roo sites from the earlier Classic period, Coba and Kohunlich, are both inland and probably played a role in overland trade. The shift to the sea routes and the shift of towns to the coast may have been accomplished by foreign Maya, called Putun, from Tabasco. The Putun are believed to have contributed to the collapse of the classic Maya civilization, and they may have been the conquerors of Chichen Itza. With the shift to the sea, the Classic period sites faded in importance, and their magnificent art and architecture was abandoned.

A MERCHANT SOCIETY

Until recently, archaeologists viewed the later Post-Classic period of sea traders as a time of cultural decadence, its art sad proof of the lowly state of the Maya after the Classic-period collapse. Now there is growing recognition that this society was vibrant and commercially successful. The ceramics were mass-produced, but that indicates a more efficient, merchant society rather than the ruler-elite society that characterized the Classic period. The public and religious buildings are not as impressive as those from the Classic era, but merchants invest most of their money in business, less in prestigious public buildings. What is lost in artistic merit is gained in growing wealth and greater egalitarianism.

This late culture is one that we of the industrial age may find familiar. But its religious beliefs are characteristically Maya. Ix Chel was the **goddess of procreation,** childbirth, medicine, and renewal. As the moon, she traveled each day through the Maya Underworld, struggling with its evil forces to be reborn in the heavens. Shrines to Ix Chel are found in the Caribbean area because it is here she rises from the sea at dusk, the sacred moment of rebirth. Pilgrimages to the area became extremely popular after 1400, probably increasing with the advent of the speaking idol, or **oracle,** of Ix Chel on the island of Cozumel, which became her major shrine. Red handprints found on buildings in this area may have been pre-Hispanic graffiti left by pilgrims from the Maya world, and perhaps even from as far away as central Mexico.

The combination of trade and religious tourism may seem odd, but archaeologist Jeremy Sabloff believes Cozumel became a neutral exchange point for merchants from competing and, perhaps, warring cultures. The oracle of Ix Chel sanctified the area, guaranteeing peace and safety for business negotiations. Indeed, Cozumel was one of the few places where the Spanish were not attacked. As Sabloff points out, not even when Cortes ordered their idols smashed did the people of Cozumel attack him. Rather they stated that a curse would fall on the Spaniards on the open seas away from their island. What new culture may have evolved from this commercial society will never be known, as the arrival of the Spaniards destroyed Maya civilization.

HISTORY

Such are the vicissitudes of history that in 1842, when John Lloyd Stephens visited the island of Cozumel, he found it uninhabited. After the Conquest, *disease and the disruption* of social and trade patterns took their toll on the Maya of Quintana Roo. Even during the centuries of the colonial period, the Spanish did little to develop the area, establishing only an outpost at Bacalar in an unsuccessful attempt to control French and English pirates who freely used the Caribbean coast as their land base.

The Maya who survived the centuries in Quintana Roo remained traditional and unacculturated. They played a key role in the **Caste War of 1847** (see "Yucatán"), angered by the encroachment of the increasing Spanish and mestizo populations on their lands. When the Caste War was over and the Maya defeated, many Indians retreated to Quintana Roo. No Spanish settlements remained in the area, and Quintana Roo, with **Chan Santa Cruz** (now Felipe Carrillo Puerto) as its capital, became an untouchable area dominated by rebel Maya. Although some control was established by the Mexican government in 1901, Quintana Roo continued to be isolated and became the "Siberia" of Mexico, a place of banishment as well as a refuge for outlaws and those escaping the political struggles of Mexico. Many renegades supported themselves by tapping zapote trees for *chicle* used to make chewing gum.

The beautiful Caribbean coast and lushness of Quintana Roo could not be ignored forever. In the middle of the 20th century, the Mexican government began a policy of resettlement and development. New roads linked it to the rest of Mexico, and the formerly isolated territory achieved statehood in 1974. Miles of beaches and coconut groves have now been transformed by multinational corporations into beach resorts. Crumbling, ancient Maya cities have been restored to their grandeur. And once again this Caribbean coast prospers from tourism.

CARIBBEAN RESORTS

The recent boom in tourism in Mexico's Caribbean is not without precedent. In the years before the arrival of the Spaniards, the ancient Maya flourished in this area because of tourism. Then as now, the green-blue of the Caribbean was considered precious; then as now, prosperity came from pilgrimages, not to the sun but to the **Maya moon goddess** whose temples adorn this coast. Although the Caribbean Coast became internationally well-known with the opening of the deluxe resort of Cancún, other islands have been popular vacation spots for some time. These resorts satisfy a diversity of tastes—**Cancún,** the ultramodern competitor of Acapulco; rustic, undeveloped **Isla Mujeres;** and beautiful **Cozumel** fits comfortably in between. Along the mainland coast, numerous isolated beaches and hotels attract those seeking tranquillity (see **"East Coast"**).

Each resort offers the pleasures of the Caribbean, palm tree-lined **white sandy beaches, good deep-sea fishing, snorkeling, and scuba diving.** In addition, impressive **Maya ruins** dot the mainland of the *Yucatán Peninsula*. Trips can be made from each resort to the ruins of *Tulum* or *Chichen Itza* (see "Yucatán"). A leisurely two-day excursion can be planned to the East Coast of *Quintana Roo*, which offers the ruins of *Tulum* and *Coba* and the lagoons of *Xel-Ha* and *Xcaret*.

PRACTICAL TIPS

The higher prices in the better hotels between **December 15-April 15** reflect not only the cold weather in much of the States and Canada, but also the excellent weather at these resorts. From April-August, the weather is hotter, with more rain, yet still pretty good. **September and October are risky months** because of tropical storms in the Caribbean. This is a very popular region; reservations recommended year-round.

In winter, many hotels require minimum stays, and some, particularly on the East Coast, require meal plans (American Plan, AP, with all meals; or Modified American Plan, MAP, with breakfast and dinner). Money-saving package deals are often available during the winter and summer months; check with your travel agent.

While Cancún, Chetumal and Cozumel are **free ports,** the prices are more impressive to Mexicans, who normally pay more for Planter's Peanuts, Dutch cheese and cookies, and the like than to Americans and Canadians who do not.

Even if you don't use a sun screen at home, you may need it in this intense tropical sun. Take in the sun slowly to avoid burns, and enjoy sun shelters on the beaches.

Under Mexican law, **all beaches are public,** so feel free to use beaches at hotels other than your own. *For a romantic vacation, plan your trip to avoid Mexican school vacations* (the week before Easter and the months of July and Aug.) when resorts become more family-oriented.

To date we have encountered only one restaurant at resorts requiring men to wear a tie and jacket. Bring casual clothes.

Note: *Accidents on rented mopeds aren't uncommon. Scuba diving requires skill; make sure your trainer is recommended. Leave valuables in your hotel, not unattended on the beach. Black coral and turtle products are in violation of U.S. wildlife protection laws and may be confiscated by customs.*

CANCÚN

With its ideal climate, gleaming white sandy beaches, warm, clear, turquoise Caribbean water, and convenient location, Cancún was a developer's dream. After careful study and computer analysis of the ideal location for the development of a new major resort, the Mexican government agency **FONATUR** selected the island of Cancún, formerly a virtually uninhabited jungle area. Cancún's average temperature is 80°F; most days are **pure sunshine;** rain is rare. The beaches are almost 100 percent limestone; the porous quality of the limestone makes for the **cool sand** under your feet even under the intense tropical sun. The **abundant Caribbean marine life** provides excellent snorkeling and scuba-diving opportunities. And the location is hard to beat, only **1 to 2 hours by air from Miami,** 1 to 6 from Mexico City, and *close to the major Maya ruins* of Chichen Itza, Tulum, and Coba. Judging from Cancún's popularity with both Mexican and foreign tourists, the computer's choice has become the people's choice.

Cancún's initial development since its opening in 1974 had been carefully controlled. Both the density of rooms per acre and the height of buildings (maximum 9 stories) were regulated to avoid congestion. Recently, however, the incredible popularity of Cancún has brought with it the construction of too many high-rise hotels and condominiums, and a profusion of shopping centers that have marred this once serene island. The resort is fresh, clean, but rather sterile and increasingly congested, with a number of luxury and first-class hotels on attractive beaches, a new mainland downtown business area with less expensive hotels, an abundance of restaurants, and a fairly active nightlife. Cancún's atmosphere is more luxurious and less quaint and intimate than neighboring Cozumel and Isla Mujeres. Compared with its rival, the older, bustling Acapulco, Cancún has a less authentic Mexican flavor and atmosphere, yet its newness and cleanliness may be more to your taste.

KEY TO CANCÚN

Sights • Mexico's most modern and luxurious Caribbean resort, with attractive beaches, fine hotels, excellent weather, and convenient location near Maya archaeological sites.

Excursions • One-day excursions can be made to the fascinating Maya ruins of Chichen Itza, Tulum, and Coba, to the islands of Cozumel and Isla Mujeres, to nearby lagoons and isolated Caribbean beaches.

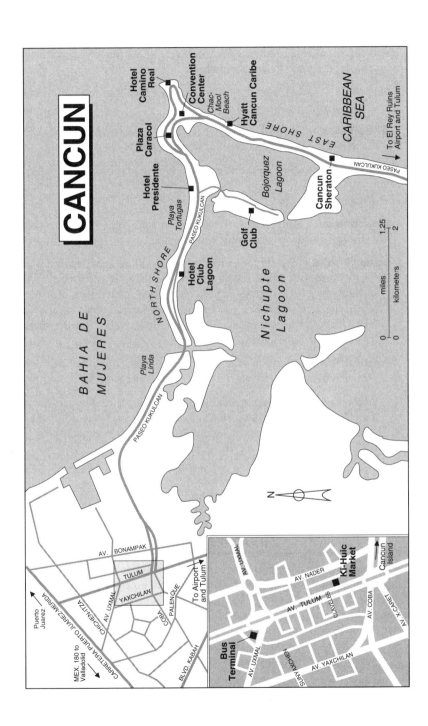

Sports • A haven for watersports—sailing, boating, waterskiing, snorkeling, scuba diving, and windsurfing. Bay fishing offers red snapper and bonefish; deep-sea fishing—especially in spring and summer—yields sailfish, marlin, and tuna. Fine 18-hole golf course. Tennis courts at most luxury and first-class hotels.

Shopping • Poor selection of quality crafts, but plenty of curios, T-shirts, and specialty boutiques.

Where To Stay • Good selection of luxury and first-class beachfront hotels and a fair number of moderate downtown hotels.

Where To Eat • Mainly steak and seafood, some good shrimp and lobster, with typical Mexican food harder to find. One restaurant serves fine traditional Yucatecan dishes.

Entertainment • Hotel bars with music; Mexican fiestas at hotels; some discos; bay cruises with music and dancing.

Getting Around • Av. Tulum is the main street running through Cancún City, lined with shops, restaurants, and banks. Since the streets intersecting Av. Tulum are U-shaped, you will encounter pairs of streets with the same name. Second class buses marked "Hoteles" run regularly between town and the hotel zone. Car rentals, moped rentals, and taxis also available.

Practical Tips • Cancún has the best year-round weather of all Mexican resorts, being very low on rainfall in the summer months.

Stores generally close for siesta between 2 and 5 p.m. Business hours are normally between 10 a.m.-2 p.m. and 5-9 p.m. Many stores close Sundays. Settle taxi fares in advance to avoid misunderstandings.

Prices in Cancún are some of the highest in Mexico. And car rental prices far exceed the cost in the U.S. Be prepared.

Cancún has become the college favorite for spring break, a time you may wish to avoid the cheaper package deals.

WHAT TO SEE AND DO

Cancún divides into two parts. The narrow 14-mile-long island section (Cancún Island) is lined with modern beachfront hotels surrounded by the Bahia de Mujeres (Bay of Women), the Caribbean Sea, and the Nichupte and Bojorquez lagoons. The mainland, downtown commercial section (Cancún City), connected to the island by a causeway, has broad avenues lined with whitewashed shops, restaurants, and hotels—a beach city in feeling, with a population of some 250,000 inhabitants.

If any of the following activities seem too demanding and exhausting for your Caribbean vacation, you can, of course, just collapse on the beach and enjoy the tropical sun. When you gather your energy you can stroll around the shops downtown or in the shopping plazas, or better yet, sit in one of the outdoor cafes downtown and think of your unfortunate friends at work back home.

BEACHES

The **East Shore,** on the Caribbean side of the island, has long, broad beaches, good surf, but some undertow. Before swimming, you need to check the danger warnings posted on the beaches. The **North Shore,** on the bay side, has calmer water, virtually no surf, and areas where the water is so shallow you need to walk hundreds of feet to reach a depth suitable for swimming. The area around **Punta Cancún** where the Camino Real, Hyatt Regency and Krystal hotels cluster, provides some of the best swimming. Since all beaches in Mexico—even those on which the luxury hotels are located—are public, you may use any one you like. If you are staying downtown and feel more comfortable at a beach away from a hotel, try the Playa Tortugas (popular with locals) located just beyond the Hotel Maya Caribe, the Playa Chac-Mool on the East Shore, or the Playa Caracol across from the Plaza Caracol.

WATERSPORTS

Watersports abound, primarily on the bay side. Snorkeling, especially off Playa Tortugas' dock and around Punta Cancún, is quite good. Scuba diving, boating, sailing, waterskiing, lagoon and deepsea fishing are popular. Stop by one of the many marinas for fishing guides and boats. For a different, delightful experience try windsurfing. After a few lessons you too will skim through the tropical waters on a surfboard with sail.

The Hotel Club Lagoon, just off Paseo Kukulcan on the lagoon, attracts many watersports enthusiasts, rents equipment, and provides instruction in sailing, waterskiing, snorkeling, and windsurfing.

GOLF

Golf addicts should be pleased by the 18-hole Pok-ta-Pok Club de Golf designed by Robert Trent Jones and located between the two lagoons. At the 12th hole, you encounter as **one of the hazards a genuine Maya ruin** that was uncovered during construction of the course. The Club also has two tennis courts and a pool. (For reservations call ☎ 3-08-71). Almost all the luxury and first-class hotels have tennis courts also.

RUINS

A visit to the jungle that once encompassed all of Cancún can be accomplished by a brief tour of the ruins of **El Rey** (The King). Actually, the birds are more interesting than the available ruins, but a number of platforms and a temple remain from this site dating to the same period as Tulum (A.D. 1200-Conquest). The stucco carved head giving its name to this site is in the museum at the Convention Center. Bring your insect repellent. To get to these ruins, take the Paseo Kukulcan toward Punta Nizuc. A sign on the right (beyond the Sheraton Hotel) for the ruins leads you to a well-packed dirt road, which after one kilometer arrives at El Rey. Open 8 a.m.-5 p.m.; fee.

The **Museo Arqueologico de Cancún** by the Convention Center was closed on our last visit due to hurricane damage. It contains a small but interesting collection of pre-Hispanic artifacts. You might want to check to see if it has reopened.

EXCURSIONS

Many people choose Cancún for their beach vacation because it can so easily be combined with a one-day excursion down the East Coast of the Yucatán Peninsula or to the great Maya ruins at **Chichen Itza.** The East Coast offers the ruins of **Tulum** and **Coba** as well as lagoons for snorkeling, such as **Xel-Ha**, and dolphin rides at **Xcaret**. Many hotels and travel agencies (see "Tour Agencies" in the Directory) offer tours to these sights, including some by air, or you can go on your own by renting a car or taking buses. (For details, see the East Coast and Chichen Itza chapters.) Buses leave Cancún from the terminal at Av. Tulum and Uxmal. Also Aero Cozumel flies small charter planes to Chichen Itza.

Other travelers opt for a visit to the resort islands of **Isla Mujeres** or **Cozumel.** Isla Mujeres is the most convenient and popular destination. Boat tours often include time snorkeling at El Garrafon at the tip of the island. Since the boats and schedules change frequently, you should check with your hotel or a local tour agency for the latest information on boat excursions. As an alternative just stop by the Terminal Playa Linda located next to the Hotel Calinda Cancún to check on some of the cruises. You can go on your own to Isla Mujeres by taking a town bus or a taxi the two miles to the passenger ferry at Puerto Juarez (see Isla Mujeres chapter). Cozumel is not quite as easy to explore without a car, but taxis and mopeds are available and the snorkeling at Chancanaab Lagoon is excellent. Cozumel can be reached in under a half-hour by Aero Cozumel's frequently scheduled flights.

SHOPPING

Although quality crafts are scarce, shopping malls are not. Mass-produced curios, an endless supply of T-shirts, and upscale designer clothing fill the stores and boutiques in the numerous shopping centers that sprout up regularly in fast-growing Cancún. Nevertheless, there are a few places that offer quality crafts and the boutiques do sell finely made Mexican clothing and accessories. Many stores close around 1 or 2 p.m. and then re-open at 5 p.m. for evening hours. Many stores are closed Sunday.

The recently opened **Flamingo Plaza** (East Shore, just past the Hyatt Cancún Caribe) has attracted some of the biggest names. Here you can find **Bally, Benetton, Gucci, Pelletier, Polo,** and other quality stores. If you are searching for anything from a bathing suit to a tent, you need look no farther than **Marti,** which contains a large selection of famous-name sporting goods and sportswear. And if too much lying on the beach has made you a bit flabby, head for **Gold's Gym,** a fitness center with weights that is also located in the Flamingo Plaza. After some vigorous exercise, your hunger may be satisfied by one of the many fast-food booths located in the center of the mall. The **Oyster Bar** had particularly fresh oysters, shrimps, and stone crabs on our last visit.

One of the original malls, the **Plaza Caracol** (near the Convention Center), still is worth visiting. Open late, it is best visited in the early evening when it is most attractive. In the marble arcades you can find the casual cotton clothing sold at **Aca Joe** and **Benetton,** handsome leather boots at **Nouveau,** tasteful jewelry at **Pelletier** and some books on Mexico, along with People magazine at **Farmacia Turistica.**

As you approach the Convention Center, you will come to **Victor,** operated by Victor Fosado, the son of the owner of the superb craft store of the same name in Mexico City. Victor sells reproductions of pre-Columbian works, particularly Maya bowls, nice cotton shirts designed by Victor, Indian jewelry, and some high-quality serapes. You never know what other interesting pieces he might have. Also near the Convention Center, in the otherwise undistinguished Mauna Loa shopping center, **Marcela** stands out for its selection of fine leather items and Oaxacan serapes.

The boutiques and stores at the Hotels Camino Real and Sheraton are often good for crafts. Downtown on Av. Tulum near San Francisco de Asis department store, the **Ki-Huic market** occupies a large area with stalls selling a variety of curios, serapes and blouses—not of the highest quality, but generally fine for souvenirs. The **Plaza Garibaldi** market, located at the corner of Av. Tulum and Uxmal, offers baskets, sweaters, and some nice Oaxacan serapes. Bargaining is expected at both of these markets. For additional shopping, just stroll along Av. Tulum which is lined with stores and boutiques catering to the traveler. **Polo** (Av. Tulum, near Coba), **Aca Joe** (Av. Tulum, corner of Tulipanes), and **Ocean Pacific** (Av. Tulum, corner of Azucenas) are especially popular for their tasteful and casual clothing.

WHERE TO STAY

Because Cancún has little rain, it retains its popularity year round. The extremely expensive beachfront hotels are heavily booked even during the "off season"—mid-April through mid-December and especially July, when prices drop by about a third and many visitors arrive on week-long package deals. If you plan a visit of a day or two, you will find Cancún **very expensive** unless you stay downtown in Cancún City—a bus ride to the beach. To get the most for your money at beachfront hotels, look for package tours, especially during the off season, advertized in your local newspaper. All the recommended hotels are air-conditioned. All of the large luxury and first-class hotels can arrange watersports, windsurfing being especially popular on the island. Hotel prices have skyrocketed, making Cancún's accommodations far costlier than hotels in other Mexican resorts. However, since Cancún has increased its number of hotel rooms to 21,000, travelers should benefit from this overbuilding by more vacancies and perhaps even somewhat lower prices. For reservations, write Cancún, Quintana Roo, Mexico or call area code 988.

RESORT EXPENSIVE

Camino Real   ★★★★★

Punta Cancún; ☎ *3-01-00; $245* • At the tip of Punta Cancún, this magnificent luxury hotel exemplifies the finest in modern hotel architecture. Low-lying, surrounded by sea and lagoon, the Camino Real spreads over several acres of exceptionally lush grounds and offers elegance in simplicity. Large, very attractive rooms (250) come with furnished terraces and either sea (better) or pool views. Room entrances surround handsome plant- and tree-filled courtyards. A new 85-unit tower should be open soon. Several restaurants and bars. Two tranquil beaches without surf; one has good snorkeling. Several pools, including a saltwater lagoon. Tennis and watersports. Arcade with a number of fine shops. Once here you may never want to leave to see the rest of Cancún. *For reservations, call, in the U.S.,* ☎ *800-722-6466.*

Hyatt Cancún Caribe   ★★★★

East Shore; ☎ *3-00-44; $209* • This crescent-shaped hotel provides a pleasant and calm contrast to the many bustling large hotel complexes that dominate much of Cancún. The main building of seven floors contains 139 attractive, light-filled rooms, all with balconies or terraces and sea views. The more expensive villas, especially those fronting the Caribbean, offer added comfort and privacy. Some units can be booked as Regency Club with its own breakfast room and cocktail lounge. Tasteful decor and warm, attentive service. Ample beach with some secluded spots. Several restaurants, bars, tennis courts, marina, putting green, and a good pool area. *For reservations, call, in the U.S.,* ☎ *800-228-9000.*

Ritz Carlton Cancún

East Shore; ☎ *5-08-08; $190-425* • Too new for us to have a chance to inspect and star-rate it, this Ritz-Carlton surely will provide the luxurious accommodations and polished service associated with its name. Located on the beach between the Sheraton and El Rey ruins, the Spanish-style hotel offers 370 rooms with patios or balconies; price varies with club location and view. Restaurants and bars. 2 pools. 3 tennis courts. Spa and fitness center. *In the U.S., reserve toll-free at* ☎ *800-241-3333.*

Cancún Sheraton   ★★★★

East Shore; ☎ *3-19-88; $220* • This huge hotel features an enormous, tastefully decorated lobby, lovely, plant-filled grounds, several bars, restaurants, and large pools. The Sheraton has participated in the Cancún building craze by adding over 400 rooms to its original 325, which may account for some complaints about service. Although all rooms are good-sized, not all have sea views. This massive complex can be overwhelming, but the facilities are good and the beach is long and beautiful. The Maya ruin next to the beach provides a special touch, and the climb to the top is rewarded with a dramatic view of the sea and lagoon. Tennis. Several good shops including one with a selection of books on Mexican art and archaeology. *For reservations, call, in the U.S.,* ☎ *800-325-3535.*

Fiesta Americana ★★★★

North Shore; ☎ *3-14-00; $242* • Built like an Italian hill town with differently shaped pastel-colored wings, this hotel provides 280 spacious rooms with balconies; pool; smallish beach with shallow water and no surf; restaurants, bars, shops, and nightclub. *For reservations, call, in the U.S.,* ☎ *800-223-2332.*

Crowne Plaza ★★★★

East Shore; ☎ *5-10-22; $198* • Located near El Rey ruins far out on the East Shore, this large, high-modern Holiday Inn opened in 1989 with a contemporary, stark lobby complete with atrium, several restaurants and bars, and four pools, including an immense one dramatically perched above the Caribbean. Decent-sized beach. Its 380 rooms are comfortable with small terraces and sea views. Tennis. *For reservations, call, in the U.S.,* ☎ *800-465-4329.*

Stouffer Presidente ★★★

North Shore; ☎ *3-02-00; $175* • This handsome hotel has attractive grounds and over 300 good-size rooms, most with views of ocean or bay (a few on the lower floors with terraces and garden views) and is across from the 18-hole golf course. Restaurant, bars with evening entertainment; two pools; Jacuzzi; tennis. Ample beach—but as at most North Shore hotels, shallow water and no surf. *For reservations, call, in the U.S.,* ☎ *800-468-3571.*

Hyatt Regency Cancún ★★★★

Punta Cancún; ☎ *3-09-66; $200* • This Hyatt's 14-story atrium with hanging garden balconies provides the dramatic setting for the 300 comfortable rooms, many with sea views and small balconies, several bars and restaurants. Although the pool is large and features a waterfall, the beach is minuscule. Nautilus, sauna, and access to tennis at Hyatt Cancún Caribe. *For reservations, call, in the U.S.,* ☎ *800-228-9000.*

Omni Cancún ★★★★

East Shore; ☎ *5-07-14; $198* • Another recent addition to Cancún, the 320-room Omni offers the usual amenities—several restaurants, pools, and tennis courts in a modern but not particularly distinctive setting. Rooms are large with marble floors and terraces. Some have sea views. The large pool area will be more attractive once the palm trees grow. Although the beach is fine, entry into the sea is rocky and can be difficult. *For reservations, call, in the U.S.,* ☎ *800-843-6664.*

Villas Tacul ★★★

North Shore; ☎ *3-00-00; $105-270* • Twenty-five quiet, very private villas, none smaller than two bedrooms and all in a garden environment. Restaurant, lovely pool, small beach cove, and tennis. Costs increase with size and whether the villa has an ocean view.

VERY EXPENSIVE

Playa Blanca ★★★

North Shore; ☎ *3-00-71; $130* • First-class accommodations in a friendly, tranquil environment. The 160 small, but fresh rooms have marble floors and balconies; most are without sea views. Pleasant strip of beach without palapas. Restaurant, bar, plant-filled pool area, and tennis. Shallow water, no surf. *For reservations, call, in the U.S.,* ☎ *800-528-1234.*

Club Lagoon ★★★

Paseo Kukulcan, km 5.8; ☎ *3-11-01; $140* • Overlooking the Nichupte Lagoon, the charming, whitewashed Club Lagoon provides 93 small but well-designed rooms—some with lagoon views and private patios, in a handsome architectural setting of two-story buildings. The suites occupy two floors, and all rooms are in white stucco and decorated with Mexican tiles. This very comfortable hotel offers a greater sense of privacy and a more human feeling than most of the high-rise hotels that abound in Cancún, yet its one drawback is that it is on a lagoon rather than the Caribbean. Restaurant, bar, pool, and marina. The Club Lagoon specializes in water sports and has sailing. Write Apartado 1036.

Calinda Viva ★★★

North Shore; ☎ *3-08-00; $140* • A large, modern, somewhat noisy hotel popular with families. The 212 rooms are on the small side, but all have small balconies and ocean view. The architecture is basic without any interesting touches. Small yet ample beach and shallow water; pool. Restaurant and popular bar with entertainment. Tennis. *For reservations, call in the U.S.* ☎ *800-228-5151.*

Maya Caribe ★★★

North Shore; ☎ *3-20-00; $75* • The Maya Caribe's smallness and quiet offer welcome relief from the large bustling beachfront hotels. Its appealing touches include flower-filled grounds, and simple, light-filled rooms with furnished balconies, some with ocean views. Beach, restaurant, bar and 2 pools are small. Tennis.

MODERATE

Downtown hotels, bus ride to beach:

Plaza Caribe ★★

Uxmal 36; ☎ *4-13-77; $74* • Located across the street from the bus station, the Plaza Caribe's interior is more pleasing than you might expect from the outside. It is modern with a decent-sized pool and poolside bar, an attractive garden restaurant, and bar with entertainment. The 112 rooms are comfortable.

Plaza del Sol ★★
Av. Yaxchilan 31; ☎ *4-38-88; $80* • This full-service modern, clean hotel provides comfortable carpeted rooms, a lobby bar, restaurant, and pool. Free bus service provided to beach at Maya Caribe Hotel. Warm service.

INEXPENSIVE

Maria de Lourdes √★★
Av. Yaxchilan near Av. Coba; ☎ *4-12-42; $55* • Small with a feeling of freshness; its hallways and rooms have white walls and red wall-to-wall carpeting. The best of the 51 rooms are those with pool views and the exteriors. Restaurant, bar, small pool, and gardens.

Antillano Hotel ★
Av. Tulum and Claveles, 37; ☎ *4-11-32; $50* • Above some shops is this small, inexpensive hotel with decent-size rooms, small pool, and cozy bar. No frills but cheery, and a good deal for downtown.

Novotel ★
Av. Tulum 2; ☎ *4-29-99; $55* • This hotel offers whitewashed walls, a plant-filled courtyard and 40 small, but fresh, clean rooms with tiled baths, some with AC. Restaurant. Pool.

Parador ★
Av. Tulum 26; ☎ *4-19-22; $44* • Clean, reasonably priced accommodations in a fresh atmosphere with smallish rooms around a plant-filled garden. Pool.

WHERE TO EAT

Cancún abounds in restaurants serving lobster, shrimp, and steak. With one notable exception, recommendable restaurants serving Yucatecan and traditional Mexican dishes are difficult to find. This is the place to indulge yourself in fresh seafood. Grouper (*mero*) and red snapper (*huachinango*) can be particularly good. Italian food is available at a few places. Restaurant prices are some of the highest in Mexico. Price categories are explained in the Introduction.

REGIONAL CUISINE

In Cancún City, **Los Almendros** (*Av. Bonampak Sur 60;* ☎ *4-08-07*) is a branch of the restaurants of the same name in Ticul and Mérida that specializes in Yucatecan dishes. It serves the finest traditional Mexican food in Cancún. The light and cheery dining room has high ceilings, a small aviary, and gaily painted chairs. Dishes include an excellent *sopa de lima* (a lime soup with chicken, tomatoes, onions, and fried tortillas), and such Yucatecan specialities as *papadzules, pollo pibil, cochinita* (a personal favorite), *poc-chuc,* and *pavo en relleno* (see "Mérida"). The *pavo en relleno blanco* is rather mild yet tasty, with a white sauce that includes turkey broth, capers, olives, and almonds. Prices are extremely reasonable. Service is friendly. Try it if you want to experiment with fine, hard-to-find Yucatecan cooking in a Mexican atmosphere. Inexpensive.

DOWNTOWN

Downtown Cancún is filled with numerous restaurants serving a variety of seafood and steak dishes. As you walk down Av. Tulum, you will probably be pestered by youngsters trying to entice you to eat in their restaurants. If you are in the mood for seafood, our recommendation is that you ignore the hustle and head directly for **El Pescador** (*Tulipanes, off Av. Tulum*), which serves, in our opinion, the finest seafood in Cancún City in a very casual atmosphere. Their 'shrimp angels on horseback' (*camarones angeles a caballo*)—large shrimp wrapped in cheese and bacon—is delicious and their grilled whole fish (*pescado parilla*) and spicy *ceviche de pescado* can be warmly recommended. Normally very crowded and deservedly so. Closed Mon. Moderately expensive. No reservations. Another good seafood choice is **Soberanis** (*Av. Coba 5, just off Tulum*), a branch of the popular Mérida restaurant. A variety of shrimp, lobster, and filet of fish dishes is served. Moderate-moderately expensive. **Blackbeard's** (*Av. Tulum, near Claveles;* ☎ *4-16-59*), provides a boisterous atmosphere—loud waiters shout above the loud music—and decent seafood including some ambitious, if not altogether successful, shrimp dishes, in addition to charcoal-broiled shish kebab and steak. Dining at a sidewalk cafe and indoors. Moderately expensive. For a quieter setting, and dinner by candlelight in a warm environment, try **Don Emiliano** (*Tulipanes;* ☎ *4-44-48*), for anything from a Yucatecan *sopa de lima* to *chiles rellenos*, shrimp, and steak. Moderately expensive.

Several popular restaurants are found on Claveles, just off Av. Tulum. Particularly recommendable is **Augustus Caesar** (☎ *4-12-61*), which serves a variety of pleasing Italian and seafood specialties. Their garlicky spaghetti with shellfish (*frutti di mare*) will perk up your taste buds and the tender and flavorful shrimp with garlic (*camarones al mojo de ajo*) should satisfy shrimp fans. For dessert, try the coconut ice cream. Moderately expensive. Nearby, **Chocko's and Tere's** (☎ *4-13-94*) has a thatched roof, graffiti on its walls, and provides lots of encouragement to shout and dance when you feel like it. Shrimp and lobster entrees are tasty but without much else on the plate. Moderately expensive. **Carrillo's Lobster House,** one of the original Cancún restaurants, serves turtle in addition to the usual lobster, shrimp, and steak at about the same prices as Chocko's and Tere's but with no encouragement to shout. Moderately expensive.

Wonderful Mexican ambience can be found at **Rosa Mexicano** (*Claveles 4, across from the Hotel Antillano*), gaily decorated with Mexican ceramics on white stucco walls, pinatas and paper cutouts hanging from the ceiling, and featuring live Mexican music. Even the menu is authentic, offering such traditional dishes as a cactus (*nopalitos*) salad, bean soup (*sopa de frijol*), *chiles rellenos, mole chicken* (*mole poblano*), and a host of other traditional dishes. Unfortunately, the food doesn't match the ambience and can be disappointing. On the whole, we've found the appetizers and soups more pleasing than the main dishes. Nevertheless, Rosa Mexicano is worth a visit for those seeking a more Mexican experience. Moderately expensive.

SNACKS

Pizza Rolandi *(Av. Coba 12)* tempts you with 15 varieties of pizza baked in a wood oven, many quite tasty, as well as several types of calzone and pasta dishes all at very reasonable prices. Inexpensive. For inexpensive breakfasts in the Av. Tulum area, head for **Cafeteria Pop** (*Tulum 26*), which offers a number of modestly priced Mexican and Yucatecan dishes in addition to the standard breakfast fare. The comfortable, air-conditioned **Pop** with its modern, plastic decor is very popular with local merchants who come here for coffee and lively conversation. And for fresh juice, fruit drinks and ice cream, try **La Flor de Michoacan** on Tulum, near Azucenas.

If you want to avoid the relatively high prices and hype of Av. Tulum and see a Cancún with a more authentic Mexican flavor, walk up Av. Coba, lined with taco stands and other cheap eateries. Turn right on Av. Yaxchilan, now populated with the overflow of restaurants from Av. Tulum. On a street without a name that runs next to the Hotel Plaza del Sol, you'll find **La Estancia,** a moderately priced, delightfully decorated restaurant offering the standard fish, shrimp, and lobster dishes as well as *fajitas*. Nearby, **La Placita** (Av. Yaxchilan, near Uxmal) is a good place for an evening snack with its outdoor grill featuring *carnes al carbon*, tasty grilled meats made into tacos and served at outdoor tables. Moderate. Across the street, **Ta Gueno** is a relaxing spot for a drink and some *queso fundido*.

IN THE HOTEL ZONE

On the island in the hotel zone there are numerous restaurants. **Chac-Mool Restaurant** (*next to Hotel Aristos Cancún on Chac-Mool Beach;* ☎ *3-11-07*) has the loveliest setting, and offers dining accompanied by the soothing sound of the surf and Vivaldi. A few pasta dishes are on the menu along with fine, if not memorable international seafood and beef dishes. We've eaten decent tournedos, a good caesar salad, a tasty, garlicky *langosta aioli*, and fairly flavorful *camarones San Francisco* (shrimp in sherry). Entrees are served with an assortment of vegetables. Front tables closest to the beach and surf are best. Romantic, warm, and relaxing atmosphere. The service at times can be pushy; more gracious service would better match the atmosphere and prices, which are quite high, even for this high-priced resort. Expensive.

Lorenzillo's (*East Shore across from the Hyatt Cancún Caribe Hotel*), overlooking the lagoon, is one of the few places where you can eat on the East Shore, outside of a hotel. Dining in this attractive restaurant is under an enormous, thatched-roof, and fish, shrimp and steak dishes are available at moderately expensive prices. Further along on the East Shore, **Captain's Cove** (*across from the Omni Cancún Hotel*) has an attractive setting overlooking the lagoon, and can be recommended for its dinner offerings. Limited menu available at lunch. Moderately expensive. **Carlos 'N Charlie's** (*Paseo Kukulcan by the Nichupte lagoon, across the road from Casa Maya;* ☎ *3-08-46*) is another branch of the popular restaurant chain that is loud and lively with an extensive menu, including many shrimp and steak dishes as well as a few traditional Mexican platters. Food is plentiful; prices are reasonable, and people always seem to enjoy themselves. Moderately expensive.

For a change of taste, try **Casa Rolandi** (*Plaza Caracol;* ☎ *3-18-17*), specializing in Italian food. Numerous spaghetti dishes are available, as well as manicotti, lasagne, ravioli stuffed with shrimp and a number of fish preparations. Moderately expensive.

Although we normally avoid hotel restaurants since they tend to be overpriced and not up to the quality of restaurants to be found elsewhere, the **Blue Bayou** (☎ *3-00-44*) at the Hotel Hyatt Cancún Caribe is a notable exception. Here we have found the finest food in Cancún served in handsome, intimate dining rooms set on several levels at competitive prices. Specializing in Cajun cuisine, the Blue Bayou features such Cajun specialties as blackened redfish and crawfish (*langostino*) etoufee. The succulent, large coconut beer-battered shrimps (*camarones rebosados con pasta de cerveza y coco rollado*) are delightful, and the blackened lobster (not always on the menu, but often available), although very expensive, is sublime. Attentive service and memorable dining. Well worth a special splurge. *Open for dinner only, 6:30-11 p.m.* Expensive.

Finally, if you have worked up an appetite by discoing till dawn, **Denny's** (*in Mayfair Galeria across from Fiesta Americana Cancún; also in Flamingo Plaza*) is open 24 hours and offers snacks and main dishes at moderate to moderately expensive prices.

ENTERTAINMENT

Cancún's nightlife is fairly active with enough variety to satisfy most tastes. Happy hours abound at the better hotels between 6-8 p.m., often with live music. For a different view with your drinks, try the **Palapa Bar,** overlooking the lagoon at the Hotel Club Lagoon. To up the beat, simply go over to the **Hotel Krystal's lobby bar** where pulsating music is featured nightly or to the wildly popular **Hard Rock Cafe** (Plaza Lagunas, next to the Mayfair Galeria) where you can get snacks or steaks to accompany the music.

Many hotels offer **Mexican Fiesta nights,** with floor shows of Mexican music and dance, one night each week. Moderately expensive prices include a buffet with the show. Check with your hotel for the current schedule. The Convention Center offers a more grandiose folklorico along with its dinner buffet Mon.-Sat. at 7 p.m. (☎ *3-01-99*), as does the **Cortijo Flamingo** (☎ *3-05-27*) in the Flamingo Plaza. The place for live salsa music and dancing is **Batacha,** in front of the Camino Real. Late-night discoing goes on at the Camino Real's Aquarius, with light show and ocean view, at Christine (*next to Hotel Krystal*), and at **La Boom** (*Paseo Kukulcan, on the lagoon*). For dancing in the downtown area try **Waves** (*Av. Tulum 37*).

GETTING TO AND FROM CANCÚN

AIR

Many U.S. airlines have direct flights from the U.S. to Cancún. Aeromexico and Mexicana also fly directly from the U.S. to Cancún. They also fly to Cancún from such major Mexican cities as Guadalajara, Mérida, and Mexico City. The smaller planes of Aerocaribe connect Cancún with Mérida, Villahermosa, and Oaxaca. Aero Cozumel offers airtaxi service from Cozumel and charters to Chichen Itza. Minibuses (*combis*) run from the Cancún airport to the hotels. If you rent a car at the airport, follow signs for "Zona Hoteleria" for the beachfront hotel area. The airport is a good distance away—about 19 km (12 m) to the first hotel. On our last visit, the money exchange booth (*casa de cambio*), located just outside the baggage area, was offering outrageously low exchange rates. For better rates simply go to the Banca Serfin booth located between Sala B and C.

CAR

Although an island, Cancún can be reached by car by the causeway from the mainland. MEX 180 connects Cancún with Mérida via the Maya ruins of Chichen Itza (4 1/2 hours). MEX 307 connects Cancún with Chetumal (5 hours). From Isla Mujeres, take the car ferry to Punta Sam, then MEX 307 to Cancún, only a few miles away.

BUS

There is regular bus service to Cancún from Mérida (via Chichen Itza), Tulum, Chetumal, Mexico City, and Playa del Carmen (where you can also catch the passenger ferry to Cozumel). The bus terminal in Cancún is located at Av. Tulum and Uxmal. For buses to Isla Mujeres, take the city bus that runs along Av. Tulum and goes to Puerto Juarez for the passenger boat and Punta Sam for the car ferry. The ferry ride takes about 40 minutes.

DIRECTORY

Airlines • *Aero Cozumel* ☎ (4-12-31) and *Aerocaribe* ☎ (4-21-11) both at Av, Tulum 29; *Aeromexico* ☎ (4-11-86); *Mexicana* ☎ (4-14-44); *American* ☎ (4-26-51); *Continental* ☎ (4-25-40); and *United* ☎ (4-25-28).

American Express • Hotel America, Av. Tulum at Brisas ☎ (4-19-99).

Banks • Several banks located on Av. Tulum; also bank in El Parian Convention Center and Flamingo Plaza.

Books and Magazines • Found at *Don Quijote* (Av. Uxmal, near corner of Tulum); Fama (Tulum near Tulipanes); and at luxury hotels and shopping malls.

Buses • Intersection of Av. Tulum and Uxmal.

Canadian Consul • Av. Tulum 200, local ☎ 312 (4-37-16); weekdays 10 a.m.-1 p.m.

Car Rentals • *Avis* ☎ (3-08-28); *Budget* ☎ (4-02-04); *Hertz* ☎ (4-13-26); *National* ☎ (4-12-22). Cheaper rates sometimes can be found at *Econorent*, Av. Tulipanes 16 ☎ (4-18-26) and *Rentautos Kankun* ☎ (4-11-75). *Viniegra*, next to Convention Center, rents mechanized 2- and 4-seater surreys.

Groceries • San Francisco de Asis and several small shops downtown on Av. Tulum; on the island small stores in shopping centers have basic supplies and liquor.

Laundromat • Av. Nader between Coba and Uxmal.

Moped Rentals • *Franky's*, Hotel Krystal; mopeds also at Hotel Aristos.

Newspapers • The English-language News is sold in most hotels and at the *Don Quijote* (Uxmal, near Tulum).

Post Office • Open Mon.-Sat., 8 a.m.-noon, 3-5 p.m. Av. Sunyachen about 4 blocks from intersection with Av. Yaxchilan.

Taxis • ☎ 3-04-37 in hotel zone.

Telegraph Office • Located in post office.

Tourist Office • Tourist booth on Av. Tulum near Tulipanes. State tourism office on Av. Coba at Nader, Fonatur Bldg. ☎ (4-32-38), Mon.-Fri., 10 a.m.-3 p.m.

Tour Agencies • Most luxury and first-class hotels often can arrange tour charters by air to Chichen Itza and Tulum; Wagon-Lits Tours at Hotel Camino Real and Av. Nader 21 downtown; Betanzos OK Tours, Av. Yaxchilan near Uxmal ☎ (4-31-94); and Avisa, Av. Yaxchilan 31-8, next to Hotel Plaza del Sol ☎ (4-02-38) arranges flights on small planes to Chichen Itza and Tikal (Guatemala).

U.S. Consul Av. Nader 40-31 ☎ (4-24-11). Weekdays 9 a.m.-1 p.m. and 2 p.m.-6 p.m.

Watersports Rentals • At most hotels, and especially at the Hotel Club Lagoon, Paseo Kukulcan, on the lagoon ☎ (3-11-11). Snorkeling, scuba diving, fishing gear, etc. for rent.

COZUMEL

Cozumel is enveloped by the blue of the sky and the Caribbean. It sparkles with sunshine and white sandy beaches. As soon as you arrive, your muscles relax and your mind adjusts to the pleasant, quiet pace of the island. It is hard to understand why Cortes and his troops decided to continue exploring Mexico when they landed here first. But, then, they were looking for glory and gold. You may be looking just for a spot on the beach under a palm tree, but Cozumel offers a lot more. It is a large enough island (28 m long, 11 m across) to have beaches and lagoons to explore and to provide excursions to the untamed east side dotted with small Maya shrines dating from about A.D. 1400. Cozumel is perfectly located for excellent snorkeling, scuba diving, and fishing. And its pleasant town of San Miguel, when it's not overwhelmed by day-trippers from cruise ships, is fine for browsing.

KEY TO COZUMEL

Sights • Mexico's largest and most typical Caribbean island, Cozumel offers the amenities of a good resort while maintaining the natural beauty of this mostly undeveloped island.

Excursions • Cozumel is the Caribbean resort closest to the ruins of Tulum and the lagoon of Xel-Ha. Visits to other East Coast sights and Chichen Itza are quite feasible.

Sports • The Palancar Reef is a mecca for scuba divers, and the waters near beaches are excellent for snorkeling and diving. Good deep-sea fishing and excellent angling for bonefish off the shores of Tulum and Boca Paila. Sandy beaches and beautiful swimming waters. Waterskiing, windsurfing, and tennis at many hotels.

Shopping • Decent craft selection from Mexico in town shops.

Where to Stay • Good selection of resort hotels and moderately priced town hotels. Reserve months in advance for high season, December 15-April 15.

Where to Eat • Excellent seafood, good international and Yucatecan fare.

Entertainment • A fair offering of discos and bars with evening shows.

Getting Around • To fully explore the island you need to rent a bike, moped, car, or use a taxi.

Practical Tips • The Mexican government has designated 20 miles of finest coral reefs an underwater national park. No spearfishing, black-coral diving, or shell collecting allowed within the limits of this park. Shops close from 1-4 p.m., but usually reopen until 8 or 9 p.m.

WHAT TO SEE AND DO

The better hotels are located on the beaches on the western part of the island not too far from town. As pleasant as these beaches are, the area about 9 miles south of town is worth exploring by launch or road. Here you find the **Parque Chankanaab** (8 a.m.-4:30 p.m.; fee), a natural underwater park and botanical garden located along a superb strip of beach. The snorkeling and scuba diving are excellent, with many caves to explore along the coast and the Chankanaab lagoon is a natural aquarium surrounded by nicely landscaped tropical gardens. There are dive shops, dressing rooms and a restaurant. After the park there's **San Francisco Beach,** so long that access roads divide it up into what seem to be numerous different beaches: some unnamed and deserted (except Sundays or when cruise ships are in); others, such as **Playa de Sol,** lively and with the conveniences of restaurants, dive shops, and taxi stands; and one fenced off for a hotel. Farther south, and off this shore (and visible only to the divers who flock to them) are the many reefs, including **Palancar,** one of the largest coral reefs in the world, with four different kinds of coral, including the rare black coral sold in town shops. Even if you're not a diver or snorkeler, you can glimpse the colorful underwater world of Cozumel on a glass-bottom boat tour.

ISLAND TOUR

The paved coastal road veers to the east on its continuation around the southern half of the island and takes you past some crumbling Maya temples and to the undeveloped east side where the sea is often rough and the wind strong (watch for tar on some of the beaches). Just as the road curves east, look for a 3 km (2 m) paved road on the left that leads to tiny **El Cedral,** the most accessible ruined Maya shrine on Cozumel. Then, as you approach the east coast, a right turn onto a dirt road toward the **Celerain Lighthouse** takes you past the minuscule Maya temple of **El Caracol** and along 5 km of dune-protected beach and rough surf. Back on the paved coastal road, head north along this windward stretch and stop at some of the calmer coves like **Punta Chiqueros** and **Punta Moreno** (both with small restaurants). At the crossroads, the paved road turns west for the final stretch back to town. Here you have some options. You might stop at **Mezcalito's,** probably the best restaurant (moderate) on the windward side, but not on the best beach.

Or if you have come prepared with a jeep, you might consider taking the wretched road north that was made even worse by Hurricane Gilbert. But if you avoid driving on the sand, you can make your way for about 10 km toward some of Cozumel's most magnificent beaches. **Playa Bonita** is definitely accessible, but not the **Castillo Ruin** and nearby **Playa Hanan** with its small off-shore reef. The road, when passable, ends at **Punta Molas Lighthouse** (1 hour for about 23 km, 14 m.). Without a jeep, you might

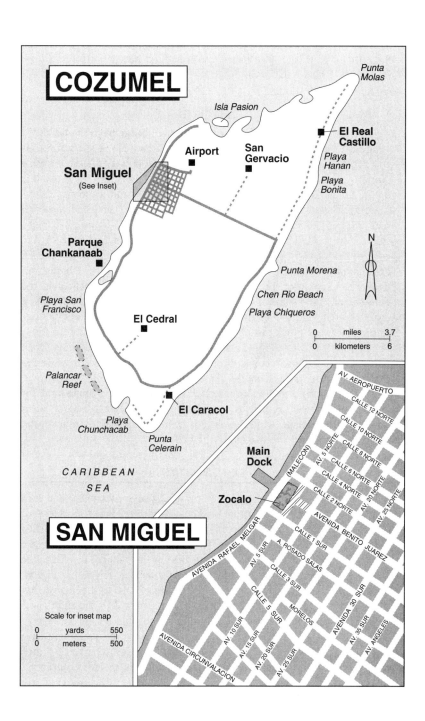

just turn at the crossroads, go about 6 km, 4 m, and turn right onto the unpaved, but slightly more accessible road to the ruins of **San Gervasio** about 7.5 km, 4 1/2 m away. San Gervasio, now sadly deteriorated, flourished as the Maya capital of Cozumel in the early 16th century, when the Spaniards visited it. If you haven't seen enough beaches, try one of the Robinson Crusoe day cruises; some take you to **Isla Pasion,** off Cozumel's north shore.

SAN MIGUEL

The only town on the island, provides a nice change from the beach. In addition to people-watching from the cafes located along the waterfront and zócalo, you can visit the attractive **Museo de la Isla** (*Melgar at Calle 4 Norte*). In a nicely restored 1937 building, the museum provides exhibits on the flora and fauna as well as the history of the island, from the earliest Maya periods to the present. The history rooms (upstairs) and the coral reef diorama are especially worthwhile (open 10 a.m.-2 p.m.; 4-8 p.m.; closed Sat.; fee). The museum also runs the **Archeological Park** on the edge of town (*4 km south on the Malecón at the cruise ship terminal, turn left and continue to Av. 65*), with replicas of 65 of Mexico's most famous pre-Columbian sculptures set in tropical park. (Bring insect repellent in the rainy season). And some of the island's best **shopping** is in San Miguel. You can't miss the countless shops selling curios, including **El Mercado de Artesanias,** located a block east of the zócalo on Calle 1 Sur. Numerous shops line Av. Melgar: Beginning to the north near Calle 8 Norte is **Los Cinco Soles** with an extensive collection of Mexican crafts and jewelry as well as designer cotton clothes from the likes of Girasol; around Calle 4 Norte you find **Ralph Lauren.** Just before the dock are **Van Cleef** and **Santa Cruz** for jewelry, including Taxco silver. On Melgar South, beyond Calle 1 Sur is **Boutique Urumbamba** with a variety of crafts, curios, and clothes. **Note:** Black coral products are banned in the U.S.

EXCURSIONS

The ruins of Tulum can be visited by small plane, by launch, and by a combined ferry-and-bus tour that includes a visit to the beautiful lagoon of Xel-Ha. Some tours include the ruins of Coba, which are certainly worth a visit even though they are slightly farther away. It is fairly easy to make these **East Coast** excursions (see that chapter) on your own. Take the morning waterjet to Playa del Carmen. At the ferry dock you'll find taxis for hire (prices posted on our last visit) and vans (for 6 to 8 persons). *Autotransportes del Oriente* (1 block up from dock, then 2 to the right) provides frequent enough second-class bus service to Tulum to make such an excursion easy. If you have problems returning, however, you might have to rely on a taxi—remember to check the time of the last ferry to Cozumel. For an overnight stay at Playa del Carmen, see the East Coast chapter.

Aero Cozumel (and tour agencies) can arrange a day trip to **Chichen Itza** by plane. When we last checked prices, the air tour was considerably cheaper than a ferry-and-taxi excursion. If you have a group of more than two, then the land trip is the better deal, if more time-consuming. The cheapest alternative is the Autotransportes del Oriente bus from Playa del Carmen, but you should plan on an overnight in Chichen to make it practical.

WHERE TO STAY

Cozumel is like most resorts in that the better and *more expensive hotels are on the beach and the inexpensive ones are in town.* Since the best beaches are 9 miles south of town or on the East Coast, and even the hotel beaches are at least one-half mile away, plans to stay in town should include the rental of a motorbike or bicycle. Although snorkeling can be found off the beaches of hotels to both the north and south, divers usually prefer the accommodations in town or to the south because of their proximity to the reefs. To stay at the hotel of your choice, make reservations in advance and write Cozumel, Quintana Roo, 77600 Mexico or call area code 987. Unless otherwise noted, hotels are air-conditioned.

RESORT EXPENSIVE

Stouffer Presidente   ★★★★

6-1/2 km (4 m) south of town; ☎ *2-03-22; $175* • This exceptionally attractive hotel has a fine beach and good snorkeling on its shoreline. Its 260 ample rooms are pleasantly decorated, most have a terrace, a few have no sea view—ask for a beachfront room. Restaurants and bars with entertainment. Pool, tennis courts, and complete rental facilities for watersports. Marina. *For reservations, call, in the U.S.,* ☎ *800-468-3571.*

VERY EXPENSIVE

Melia Mayan Cozumel   ★★★★

3-1/2 km (2 m) north of town; ☎ *2-04-11; $170-210* • Located on one of Cozumel's loveliest beaches, this hotel offers a total of 200 units. The large suites (more expensive) are in a 10-story tower and all have balconies and sea views (may be under renovation). The "villas" are standard rooms, yet ample, and situated in low-rise buildings; most have balconies and some have pool, not sea, views. Restaurants, bars, evening entertainment. Two pools. Excellent watersports facilities. *For reservations, call, in the U.S.,* ☎ *800-336-3542.*

Plaza Las Glorias   ★★★★

1 km (1/2 m) south of town; ☎ *2-20-00; $155-185* • This newest of Cozumel's hotels has a marble and carpeted lobby that overlooks the sea. Its 170 units are large and have furnished balconies—all with sea views. Suites include a balcony Jacuzzi. The rooms here are among the best, but the artificial beach terraces are a bit small. Restaurants, bars, and shops. Pool next to sea, windsurfing and other watersports. *For reservations, call, in the U.S.,* ☎ *800-342-Amigo.*

Sol Caribe   ★★★★

4 km (2 1/2 m) south of town; ☎ *2-07-00; $170-210* • This modern and massive hotel with Maya-inspired architectural details is focused around an extravaganza of a pool. Beach club lies across the road, yet is integrated with the hotel by a garden path. The large rooms, most with sea views, will number 350 with the completion of a new tower. Managed by Fiesta Americana, the hotel has many services: restaurants, bars, discos; shops; pool, tennis, and watersports. *For reservations, call, in the U.S.,* ☎ *800-223-2332.*

La Ceiba

4 km (2 1/2 m) south of town; ☎ *2-08-44; $135* • Without the extensive surrounding land of the pricier hotels, yet with handsome facilities on the beach, La Ceiba has 115 large rooms with balconies and views of the sea. Restaurants and bar with entertainment. Pool, tennis, jacuzzi, and watersports, particularly diving tours. *Write Apartado 184.*

Galapago Inn Dive Resort

1 1/2 km (1 m) south of town; ☎ *2-06-63; $150-200 AP* • A specialty hotel for diving excursions and instruction, with 50 rooms, many around a garden patio, some with sea views. Dining room and bar. Small beach, private dock with boats, dive shop. *Apartado 289; write for special diving packages or call, in U.S.,* ☎ *800-847-5708.*

EXPENSIVE

La Perla

Beach 2 km (2 m) south of town; ☎ *2-01-88; $100-110* • Run more like a condominium than a hotel, this tasteful 12-unit establishment offers very large rooms with balconies and views from its seaside location. Pool and swimming cove. Box 309. *Check to see if this hotel is still closed for renovations.*

Sol Cabanas del Caribe

3 km (2 m) north of town; ☎ *2-00-17; $125-160* • A variety of 50 smallish units—some, beach cabanas; others, garden units—are available at this very casual inn on a good beach. Restaurant and bar. Pool and watersports, including windsurfing. *For reservations, call, in the U.S.,* ☎ *800-336-3542.*

Cantarell

2 km (1 m) north of town; ☎ *2-01-44; $100-135* • This older beach hotel was renovated in the 80s and offers 75 smallish rooms with modern baths, most with sea views. Restaurants and bars. Dive shop and watersports. Pool. *Write Apartado 24.*

MODERATE

Villablanca

3 km (2 m) south of town; ☎ *2-07-30; $44* • A tranquil spot, set back from the road by a large lawn and with 48 rooms and suites. The units vary but many have sunken tubs and all are attractively appointed and set in gardens. Restaurants and bar, including ones on beach. Pool.

Tennis court (so-so surface). Tiny beach and dive shop across street. *Write Apartado 230.*

Mara ★★

2 km (1 m) north of town; ☎ *2-03-00; $87* • This unpretentious hotel on a small and quiet beach has 50 large and adequate rooms with balconies and sea views. Restaurant, bar. Pool and watersports. *Write Apartado 7.*

La Casa del Mar ★★★

3 1/2 km (2 m) south of town; ☎ *2-19-00; $90* • Despite this hotel's rather heavy architecture, its 100 rooms, especially those with balconies and sea views, are comfortable. The location near a growing shopping mall certainly is not for those dreaming of a quiet spot on the beach; nor is the pedestrian bridge that spans the road between the hotel and beach. But there are lots of facilities and the price is moderate. Restaurants and bar. Pool, dive shop. *Write Apartado 129.*

Bahia ★★

Av. Melgar at Calle 3 Sur; ☎ *2-02-09; $62* • A little pricey for an in-town hotel without many sea views, but the Bahia offers well-designed and nicely furnished junior suites that include money-saving kitchenettes. *Write Apartado 286.*

Barracuda ★

Melgar 628, 1 km (1/2 m) south of town; ☎ *2-00-02; $73* • The least expensive swimming beach hotel, with an accompanying lack of decor; 50 simply furnished and ample rooms with balconies overlooking water. Restaurant. Beach with dive shop and most watersports. *Write Apartado 163.*

INEXPENSIVE

Hotel Maya Cozumel ★

Calle 5 Sur #4; ☎ *2-00-11; $40* • Close to waterfront, this small, very pleasant hotel has 30 modernized rooms around a garden and pool.

Hotel Vista del Mar ★

Av. Melgar 45; ☎ *2-05-45; $42* • Across street from sea, this small hotel has 24 bright and ample rooms, many with balconies and good sea views. Pool (in parking area).

Hotel Mary Carmen ★

5 Avenida Sur #4; ☎ *2-05-81; $35* • A few steps from the zócalo, this well-maintained hotel has 28 clean, interior rooms around a pleasant garden.

WHERE TO EAT

During the day most vacationers stick to their hotels or favorite beaches. All of the west coast beaches and a few of the windward beaches have casual, open-air eateries. Although dining in town is mostly an evening experience, there are plenty of spots for a meal or snack. **Las Palmeras** is popular all day long, from breakfast through dinner and drinks. Its breezy location on Av. Melgar in front of the town pier, its moderately priced, extensive menu with everything on it from Yucatecan *cochinita pibil* to milkshakes, and its occasional live music, make for a bustling ambience (as a quieter alternative, see Del Museo, below). **Frutas Selectas** (*R. Salas between Av. 20 and Av. 15*) is really a fresh produce shop, but its counter is popular for fresh juices and coffee, for fruit salad and yogurt or even carrot cake. A good spot throughout the day for a snack, but not at lunch when it's closed. Inexpensive. The best place for a tasty Mexican meal at unbeatable prices is at the simple, thatched-roof **La Choza** (*10 Av. Sur & R. Salas; 1-5 p.m., with plans to stay open later*). A local favorite for its casual ambience is a bit south of town, the canopied and open-air restaurant **Mini-Lenny's** (*Melgar 601*) at the Costa Brava Hotel (not the Costa Brava Restaurant next door). The rather ordinary food ranges from the familiar seafood to Mexican items and even a slice of *pie de lima* for desert (*open breakfast to dinner; moderately expensive*).

For more elegance, you can select from a large number of restaurants that face the sea along Av. Melgar and serve a combination of seafood and steak items to please the North American palate. (For information on price categories see Introduction). One of the favorites is **Pepe's Grill** (*near R. Salas*) serving prime rib and flambe dishes, along with surf 'n 'turf, and what is probably the best salad bar in town (*expensive; open 5 p.m.-12 a.m.; reserve at ☎ 2-02-13*). With a few menu flourishes such as shrimp curry and chicken kiev, **El Acuario** (*overlooking the sea south of town next to the Hotel Barracuda*) serves its seafood, steak, and salad bar to tables set amid tanks of tropical fish (*expensive; noon to 11 p.m.; reserve at ☎ 2-10-97*). We especially enjoy the intimate and tranquil ambience of **Restaurant Del Museo** (*at Calle 4 Norte; second floor of museum*). On its breezy terrace overlooking the sea, you can enjoy a shrimp-stuffed avocado or tasty chicken fajitas. The service is pleasant (*moderate for lunch; moderately expensive for dinner; open for breakfast too*).

A Cozumel institution is **Carlos N' Charlie's** (*near Calle 2 Norte on Melgar*). Its moderately expensive prices bring ample portions to your table. The food is good, especially the ribs, but it is the frolicking ambience and loud, recorded rock music that has created so many imitators, none of whom carry it off quite so well. (Open lunch and dinner.) Another long-time favorite is **El Capi Navegante** (*Av. 10 Sur #312 near Calle 3 Sur; ☎ 2-17-30; moderate*), with no ambience but some of the best seafood on the island—for lunch, you might try their branch by the sea (just before Parque Chankanaab), with more ambience, but a more limited menu.

LESS COSTLY DINING

When seafood and steaks are no longer appealing or your budget just demands less costly dining, you still have options. **Pizza Rolandi** (*Melgar between Calle 8 and 6 Norte*) serves pizza, of course, as well as lasagne and salad, in a patio setting (*open 11:30 a.m.-11:30 p.m.; closed Sun.; inexpensive*). The tacos at **Las Tortugas** (*Av. 10 Norte at Calle 2 Norte; open lunch* *and dinner*) and **El Foco** (*5 Av. Sur #13; opens at 6 p.m.*) are flavorful options at modest prices.

For more regional food and Yucatecan ambience, there are a few places to try. A little Spanish might help, but goodwill and a few appropriate gestures will do just as well. **La Yucatequita** (*Av. 10 Sur 69 between Calle 6 and 8 Sur*) is a clean and simple, family-run restaurant. The daily specials change, of course, but they include such distinctive Yucatecan dishes (see "Mérida") as barbecued pork *cochinita* and an interesting turkey in a sauce of capers and almonds, called *relleno blanco*. Although not routinely open at night, you can arrange an evening dinner or a *merienda*—a casual meal of tamales, panucos, and the like—if you have a large enough group (*open 8 a.m.-6 p.m.; closed Sunday; 2-12-23; inexpensive*).

ENTERTAINMENT

Most restaurants and hotel bars serve you to the sound of live music ranging from the lovely melodies of *serenata trios* to more familiar rock and roll. On Sunday evenings (8 p.m.) you can hear a free concert on the zócalo and most evenings you can find a Fiesta Mexicana at one of the hotels, with traditional mariachi music and dancing accompanying elaborate buffets of Mexican food such as the elaborate one at the Sol Caribe on Wed. and Sat. nights. You might consider a cruise on the *Fiesta Pirata* that sails from the downtown pier several nights weekly and provides music, a beach buffet, and dancing. *The* disco on the island is the trendy **Scaramouche** on Av. Melgar near R. Salas.

GETTING TO AND FROM COZUMEL

AIR

There are international flights to Cozumel on Mexicana, Continental, and other U.S. airlines; and domestic flights from Mexico City on major carriers, from Mérida on Aerocaribe. Aero Cozumel makes the regularly scheduled short jumps to Cancún and Playa del Carmen as well as special tours to Chichen Itza. Combis can shuttle you to and from the airport (15 minutes from town); set-price tickets are sold inside airport.

LAND AND SEA

Buses along MEX 307 from Cancún and Chetumal connect with the **passenger ferry at Playa del Carmen** (69 km [43 m] south of Cancún and 310 km [192 m] north of Chetumal). The ferry takes just under an hour, but in half the time its first-class counterpart, the MV Mexico waterjet, makes the trip more smoothly with the added comforts of air conditioning and airplane-style seats. The waterjet costs more than the ferry, but still is inexpensive. The schedules of the two are almost identical early morning and late afternoon; between the two there are crossings from Cozumel to Playa del Carmen at 4 a.m., 6:30 a.m., 9 a.m., 11:30 a.m., 12:30 p.m., 2 p.m., 4 p.m., 6 p.m., and 6:30 p.m. and from Playa to Cozumel at 5:30 a.m., 7:30 a.m., 8 a.m., 10 a.m., 12:30 p.m., 2:30 p.m., 3 p.m., 5 p.m.,

5:30 p.m., and 7:30 p.m. *Always check for schedule changes!* While waiting for the ferry in Playa del Carmen, you can swim at the lovely beach near the dock, sit under palm trees, or eat at nearby restaurants. For more details, and especially if you are staying overnight, see "Playa del Carmen" on the East Coast.

A **car ferry leaves from Puerto Morelos** (*36 km [22 m] south of Cancún*) for which there is a monthly published schedule. Priority is given to cargo, so that even if you happen to hit the day of a departure, you might not get aboard. The crossing takes 2-1/2 hours. If you choose this route, you might need to spend the night in Puerto Morelos (see "East Coast" chapter).

DIRECTORY

Airlines • At the airport. *Aero Cozumel* ☎ (2-09-28) provides shuttle service on its small planes to Cancún. Charters to Chichen Itza and Tulum also available. Other airlines are *Mexicana*, Av. Melgar 17 Sur ☎ (2-01-57); and *Continental* ☎ (2-09-88).

American Express • Fiesta Cozumel, Melgar 27 ☎ (2-09-74).

Bicycle Rental • *Rentadora Cozumel* on Av. Sur at R. Salas ☎ (2-15-03) and many others.

Books in English • At the resort hotels.

Car Rental • There are many agencies located at the airport, zócalo, and resort hotels, including *Avis* ☎ (2-03-22) and *National* ☎ (2-15-15). Check *Aquila Rentacar* ☎ (2-00-11) at Hotel Maya Cozumel for low jeep prices.

Ferry • Playa del Carmen passenger ferry and the waterjet M.V. Mexico dock at the main pier near zócalo; car ferry docks south of town next to La Ceiba.

Fishing • *Club Nautico* ☎ (2-01-18) and tour agencies.

Gasoline • The one and only Pemex can be found at Juarez and Avenida 30.

Horseback Riding • Arranged through tour agencies.

Motorbikes Rentals • At Rentadora Cozumel ☎ (2-15-30) and at most hotels.

Post Office • Four blocks south of zócalo.

Supermarket • *Maxi's*, Av. 10 Norte at Calle 2 Norte.

Taxis • At main pier ☎ (2-02-36) and the Chankanaab Lagoon and hotels.

Tour Agencies • In resort hotels and Aviomar, Av. 5 Norte between 2 and 4 ☎ (2-04-77).

Tourist Office • East side of zócalo, on second floor overlooking patio of Mercado de Artesanias. Open weekday mornings.

Watersports Equipment • Diving and snorkeling equipment can be rented just about everywhere—at Dive Cozumel and Aqua Safari on Av. Melgar South, at Chankanaab Park, most resort hotels and west coast beaches. Some hotels specialize in diving equipment and tours, like Galapago Inn. Most beach hotels rent fishing gear, launches, and waterskiing equipment in addition to arranging tours. A number of hotels have sailing and windsurfing, such as the Presidente and the Melia Mayan.

ISLA MUJERES

Isla Mujeres was a Maya settlement in pre-Conquest times but received its name (Island of Women) from a brief encounter with the Cortes expedition of 1519. The wind swept the Spanish ships into the island's harbor and, as Bernal Diaz describes it: *"We lowered two boats and went on ashore …and there were four… houses of their Idols, and there were many Idols in them, nearly all of them figures of tall women, so that we called the place the Punta de las Mujeres."* Although these figures of the Maya moon goddess are no longer on the island, the name has endured. Except from pirates, the island received little attention after the Spanish landing, until modern tourism made it a favorite of those seeking simple pleasures under the sun. People who enjoy Isla Mujeres like feeling a part of the Mexican life on this unpretentious island while snorkeling, swimming, and eating the fresh seafood caught by local fishermen. Those who enjoy the luxuries of the fancier resorts like Cancún may enjoy a visit to Isla Mujeres for a day of snorkeling at El Garrafon and a stroll through the village.

KEY TO ISLA MUJERES

Sights • A resort island for those on limited budgets seeking the warm, green waters of the Caribbean.

Excursions • A one-day excursion by launch is easily arranged for a visit to the bird sanctuary on Contoy Island or to Cancún.

Sports • Excellent snorkeling off the south of the island at El Garrafon. Good deep-sea fishing for tuna and barracuda and, in the spring, marlin and sailfish. Calm swimming beaches at Norte and Lancheros. Good birdwatching.

Where To Stay • A variety of moderately priced and inexpensive hotels is available, along with a couple of fine, expensive hotels.

Where To Eat • Next to tourism, fishing is *the* local industry. The island is known for its lobster, turtle, shrimp, and other seafood. Preparation is simple.

Entertainment • Watching the sunset or strolling in town.

Getting Around • No car rentals available, so unless you bring your own on the ferry from Punta Sam, you might want to rent a bicycle, moped, or taxi for exploring the island. Hotels, the dock, and zócalo are within walking distance of each other. Street signs are virtually nonexistent.

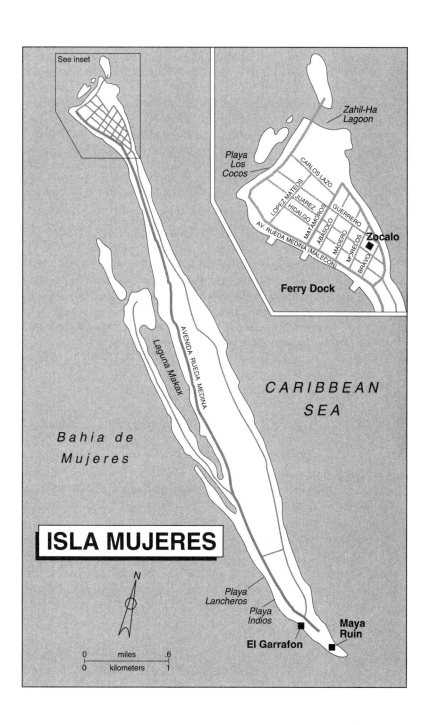

See inset

Zahil-Ha
Lagoon

Playa
Los
Cocos

CARLOS LAZO

LOPEZ MATEOS
JUAREZ
HIDALGO
MATAMOROS
ABASOLO
GUERRERO
MADERO
MORELOS
BRAVO
AV. RUEDA MEDINA (MALECON)

Zocalo

Ferry Dock

Laguna Makax

AVENIDA RUEDA MEDINA

*CARIBBEAN
SEA*

*Bahia de
Mujeres*

ISLA MUJERES

N

Playa
Lancheros
Playa
Indios

**Maya
Ruin**

El Garrafon

| 0 | miles | .6 |
| 0 | kilometers | 1 |

WHAT TO SEE AND DO

The small island, just 5 miles long and one-half mile wide, has a good swimming beach near town called **Playa Norte** (North Beach) and excellent snorkeling at the coral reef of **El Garrafon,** located at the southern tip of the island. (Admission fee to El Garrafon National Park and its facilities.) On the promontory above El Garrafon is a Maya temple to the moon goddess, which is also called "the lighthouse," perhaps recalling another pre-Conquest function of these buildings. North Beach is the most popular swimming spot, with calm waters but no shade except in the restaurants located on the beach. Although not as attractive as the beaches in Cancún and Cozumel, low-key Playa Norte attracts a loyal following. Another swimming beach is **Playa Lancheros,** located a few miles out of town with lots of shade trees on a beach not as long or wide as North Beach, but with good swimming and a swamp filled with empty beer bottles. Isla Mujeres has an export business in giant turtles, and visits can be made to the turtle pens at Lancheros.

One of the most pleasurable ways to see Isla Mujeres is by bicycle or motorbike. After you view the calm Caribbean side, make sure you continue past El Garrafon around to the rough, dramatic, windward side on your way back to town. In addition to arranging deep-sea fishing trips, you can take the justifiably popular launch tour from the main pier to the bird sanctuary on **Contoy Island,** where you will see flocks of pelicans, cormorants, flamingos, and red-pouched frigates among the 70 bird species found here. It takes 2-1/2 hours to get to the sanctuary, so this pleasing tour is an all-day excursion that often includes a snorkeling visit to a sunken pirate ship that can be seen just off Contoy Island.

Trips to the Maya ruins of **Chichen Itza** (see "Yucatán") and **Tulum** (see "East Coast") can be made via Cancún, where you have a choice of taking a tour, renting a car, or taking a bus to the ruins. It will be difficult to complete these trips in time to return to the island on the last ferry; an overnight stay on the mainland is recommended. An easy one-day excursion to **Cancún** can be made by the 40-minute ferry service.

Shopping other than for beachwear is limited, although vendors selling fine Yucatecan hammocks sometimes congregate around the main ferry pier, and **Rachat & Rome,** just across from the pier, sells quality jewelry. **La Loma** (on the zócalo), has by far the best selection of crafts in the area—and that includes Cancún. The store is especially strong in its mask collection which is one of the best we've seen in Mexico. La Loma also sells some fine ceramics and weavings. **La Sirena** (Morelos, just off the zócalo), a branch of La Loma, also has some quality crafts.

WHERE TO STAY

For reservations write Isla Mujeres, Quintana Roo, Mexico or call area code 987.

MODERATE

Na Balam ★★

Playa Norte; ☎ *7-02-79; $75-85* • The small and tranquil Na Balam is located right on North Beach, and in our opinion is the place to stay in Isla Mujeres. All of its ample rooms face the sea; some have balconies or terraces; some are air-conditioned. Its shady palm grove provides relief from the blazing sun. The large palapa with hammocks allows you to swing in the breeze while sipping a drink from the nearby bar. Restaurant.

Posada del Mar ★★

Rueda Medina 15 (Malecón); ☎ *7-02-12; $70* • Across from the beach and just four blocks from the main pier and three blocks from Playa Norte, this modern hotel has 50 fairly large, air-conditioned rooms, most with balconies overlooking the water. Attractive environment with gardens, pool, dining room, and bar. Air conditioning does not always work, nor is there always hot water, but service is efficient, even if without a smile. Rooms in main building are best. *Write Calle 50 #256, Mérida, Yucatán.*

Hotel Perla del Caribe ★★

Madero and Guerrero; ☎ *7-04-44; $70* • Located on the beach on the rough Caribbean side of the island, only a few blocks from the zócalo, the Perla del Caribe is a fresh, clean, and cheerful hotel—a bit too motel-like for our tastes—divided into two white-stucco wings. Although all rooms are ample and similarly decorated, one wing contains air-conditioned rooms, the other less expensive, fan-cooled rooms. Plans call for air conditioning all rooms. Many, but not all, rooms have terraces and sea views, but the ocean promenade has taken away any sense of seclusion. Pool and decent-sized beach, but the sea is unsafe for swimming on this side.

Cabanas Maria del Mar ★★

Playa Norte; Carlos Lazo #1; ☎ *7-01-79; $55-66* • Close to Na Balam with the same wonderful location on North Beach, the Cabanas Maria del Mar offers two types of accommodations—the older concrete bungalows, which are very basic and fan-cooled, and the newer and more desirable wings with air-conditioned rooms, terraces and sea views. Only the newer rooms get the 2-star rating. Due to its expansion, this hotel now feels a bit congested.

INEXPENSIVE

Rocamar ★

Bravo and Guerrero; ☎ *7-01-01; $54* • Located next to the zócalo and overlooking the sea, the popular Rocamar faces the rough windward side of the island. Many of the 31 clean and ample, simply furnished rooms have balconies with sea views and are recommended. Given the breezes on this side of Isla Mujeres, the ceiling fans provide adequate cooling and allow you to listen to the crashing of the waves.

Good beach feeling to this hotel. Rocky beach, and the water is too rough for swimming. Restaurant.

WHERE TO EAT

Fresh seafood, including several varieties of fish, as well as shrimp, lobster, and conch, is served in numerous restaurants throughout town. While the preparation is generally quite simple, the food is fresh, if not exciting. The restaurants are plain and informal, with prices well below those in most other resorts. Most restaurant meals will fall into the inexpensive to moderate categories, but if you choose to order lobster, expect an expensive meal. Most restaurants are open breakfast through dinner.

The finest food we've eaten on the island can be found at **El Cuba Ron** (*Guerrero 2, just off the zócalo*). Open for dinner only, 7 p.m.-midnight; closed Wednesday. Located in a simple wood-frame house, this tiny Cuban restaurant exudes the tropics while serving wonderfully fresh fish in its simple outdoor patio. The filet of fish (normally grouper or red snapper) or shrimp covered with the salsa cubana is tangy and full of flavor, but we'd recommend that you not pass up the delicate, extremely fresh, whitest of white *calamares* (squid)—a real treat. Chicken, pork and beef dishes also available. Good taped music in the background. Inexpensive to moderate. For breakfast with freshly baked whole grain bread or a lunch of seafood and salad, head over to North Beach to the Zazil-Ha, located at the Na Balam hotel.

POPULAR

Two of the more popular restaurants in town are **El Sombrero de Gomar** (*Hidalgo at Madero, 2nd floor*) and **Pizza Rolandi** (*Hidalgo between Abasolo and Madero*). The food at Gomar's is reasonably fresh and satisfying, and the prices moderate to moderately expensive. The enormously popular Pizza Rolandi serves decent pizza and pasta, as well as a very good tomato-and-onion (*dinamite*) salad, in this branch of the reliable Caribbean restaurant chain (*dinner nightly, lunch every day but Mon; inexpensive to moderate*). For other choices, you can try the seafood at **Guillermo's** (Juarez, one block from the ferry) with its inviting outdoor tables.

To get a feel of the sea, we find ourselves often returning to the basic and breezy **Miramar,** a small, open-air establishment on the Malecón, next to the pier and overlooking the water. While sipping a beer you can watch the activity at the ferry dock. In the evening, try the nearby **Brisas del Caribe** for a pre-dinner drink (but not for dinner). Overlooking the sea at **Playa Los Cocos**, the handsome **Nautibeach Club restaurant** seems a bit upscale for earthy Isla Mujeres, even offering a mixed salad to accompany its undistinguished fish and shrimp dishes. Prices are high for this island, with most dishes in the moderately expensive category.

Perhaps the cheapest lunch on the island is the flavorful fresh fish grilled over wood that is often available at **Playa Lancheros.**

ENTERTAINMENT

Nights are calm. If you are looking for some music you can try the **Tequila Video Bar** (*Hidalgo at Matamoros*) or the **Casablanca Nightclub** (*Hidalgo, just off the zócalo*). Or take a walk along the breezy ocean promenade which runs off the zócalo behind the Perla del Caribe hotel. Perhaps the best entertainment of all is simply to stroll through town where you can still see people making fishing nets, and where the everyday life of the island's residents spills out into the streets.

GETTING TO AND FROM ISLA MUJERES

Transportation routes for Isla Mujeres are the same as those for Cancún, which is only 1 mile from Puerto Juarez, the ferry port for Isla Mujeres. Buses and taxis connect Puerto Juarez and Punta Sam with downtown Cancún, so if you can get to Cancún, you can reach Isla Mujeres.

AIR

From the Cancún airport, a taxi can take you to the ferry landing at Puerto Juarez in about a half hour.

LAND AND SEA

Ferry service to Isla Mujeres leaves from two points, Puerto Juarez and Punta Sam, which is 3 miles north of Puerto Juarez. Only the ferries from Punta Sam carry vehicles in addition to passengers. There is parking at both landings. The crossing takes about 40 minutes. There are several departures and returns every day from both ports. Normally there are about **8 ferries** a day from **Puerto Juarez** and **6** from **Punta Sam.** Presently, the earliest departure from Puerto Juarez is at 5:30 a.m. and the latest 7:30 p.m., but the schedule frequently changes. Ferry irregularities and high demand mean you should arrive well in advance of a scheduled ferry. When demand is very high a human cattle boat is added to the Puerto Juarez schedule with chaotic boarding procedures that require perseverance and patience. At other times, the regularly scheduled ferry is reasonably comfortable and the trip pleasant. Taxis are available for shuttling between Puerto Juarez and Punta Sam. A simple hotel is near the pier at Puerto Juarez.

BUS

Service between Mérida and Cancún by ADO takes 4 1/2 hours. The local "Punta Sam" bus runs on Av. Tulum to the Isla Mujeres ferries. See above.

DIRECTORY

Banks • Juarez 3 and Rueda Medina near ferry.

Bicycle Rentals • Shops on Hidalgo, Madero, and Guerrero.

Launches • The main pier area (Malecón) is where to set up arrangements for a boat or tour.

Mopeds • On Madero, Juarez, Guerrero, and Hidalgo.

Post Office • Guerrero near Los Cocos Beach.

Supermarket • Super Mirtita, Juarez at Bravo.

Taxis • Next to the main pier.

Telegraph • Guerrero near Los Cocos Beach.

Tours • Trips to Contoy Island can be arranged at the piers along the Malecón.

Tourist Office • On zócalo, next to basketball courts ☎ (7-03-16). Open Mon.-Fri., 8 a.m.-2 p.m. and 5 p.m.-7 p.m.

Watersports • Fishing gear and boats can be rented off the Malecón. Several shops near the pier rent snorkeling and diving equipment. Snorkeling also can be arranged at El Garrafon.

EAST COAST

The flat, straight East Coast (see map of Yucatán) road, MEX 307, running south of Cancún to Chetumal, is mostly traveled by those on one-day visits to the **ruins of Tulum** and **Coba** and the crystal-clear waters of the **natural aquarium of Xel-Ha lagoon**. This road, surrounded by low-lying jungle so monotonous that farmers must mark their way with highly individualistic signposts—broken buckets or even a toilet-seat cover—cuts through an area rich in ruins and palm-lined beaches and lagoons requiring only a short trip down dirt roads to be enjoyed. The *lack of development* in this area makes the **virgin waters** excellent for snorkeling, scuba diving (Cancún to Tulum), and for deep-sea fishing (from Tulum down the Boca Paila Peninsula). A wonderland of beautiful beaches and lagoons, the East Coast warrants leisurely exploration.

MEX 307 has spanned the coast for decades, even during the years before Cancún existed. Then, the only accommodations were your sleeping bag placed next to the lagoons at Xel-Ha or your hammock hanging in one of the thatch-and-pole palapas on beaches owned by coconut *rancheros*. The temples at Coba were so entangled by jungle that only the caretaker could lead you to them. Today the road has been widened between Cancún and Tulum and you pay an admission fee to enter Xel-Ha. You have a wide choice of accommodations, most isolated on their own beaches, but ranging from Robinson Crusoe-style bungalows to private villas with hand-.painted tiled baths. More and more visitors spend their vacations here, learning to snorkel or scuba dive, or simply relaxing under the warm sun. There's some spillover of Cancún's booming success as real estate developers transform some of the landscape. Yet, the East Coast retains a feeling of isolation and tranquility. It's a place to **escape it all**—for both the better heeled traveler and the beachcomber, who can still find a palapa and, for a few bucks, can sling up a hammock on the beach for the night.

The clearest way to describe the sights along this coast is to provide a kind of trip-tik from which you can choose the sights you prefer according to your time and means of transportation. One-day tours can be arranged at either Cancún or Cozumel. But if you rent a car in Cancún, you can stay overnight in the area and provide yourself with a few days of exploring spots not often visited by travelers, or you might consider selecting one of the hotels and camping sites as your base for a week's vacation. Accommodations are listed under the appropriate town in the trip tik, and specific prices can be found in the "Hotel Quick-Reference Tables" under "East Coast." Not listed are the enticingly named beaches, such as Playa Secreto and Playa Paraiso, that are real estate developments of no interest to most travelers.

KEY TO EAST COAST

Sights • The East Coast offers the famous ruins of Tulum and Coba and exquisite, undeveloped Caribbean lagoons and beaches. While Cancún and Cozumel are good locations from which to begin a visit to these sights, the hotels along the coast are popular destinations, too.

Sports • The East Coast from Cancún to Chetumal has many beaches and lagoons, excellent for snorkeling, scuba diving, fishing, and swimming.

Shopping • There is a curio market at Tulum and Playa del Carmen, and shops here and there along the way.

Where To Stay • Along the East Coast are an increasing number of first-class hotels as well as some moderate and inexpensive ones. There's camping, too, and hammock palapas.

Where To Eat • Seafood is very good along the coast, but this area is too undeveloped to satisfy gourmets.

Entertainment • A beach walk by moonlight.

Getting Around • To properly explore the East Coast, you'll need a lot of time for second-class bus travel or a car rental or tour from Cancún or Cozumel. Given the high cost of car rentals, taxis provide a locally manageable alternative for those spending a week at a coast hotel and who want to make just one excursion or so. Buses between Cancún and Chetumal can drop you at Tulum and, of course, Playa del Carmen—the best place to make transportation arrangements.

Practical Tips • Always carry your bathing suit as well as insect repellent along this coast. The East Coast is at sea level so it's tropical and hot. June, September, and October are very rainy months. The off-season traveler can find bargain prices along the East Coast, even at the best hotels. Drivers should watch their gasoline gauge as there are few Pemex stations on MEX 307.

ON THE WAY TO TULUM
PUERTO MORELOS

36 km (22 m) south of Cancún. • Best known for its car ferry to Cozumel, Puerto Morelos has a fine, extensive beach and coral reefs for both snorkeling and scuba diving. The **Ojo de Agua** (turn left at Dona Zenaida's restaurant; formerly moderate in price; no details available) has partially rebuilt its simple but comfortable beachfront hotel after its devastation by Hurricane Gilbert. Otherwise there is not much reason to visit. The difficulties of arranging a car space on the ferry are such that only those planning a long-term stay on Cozumel should bother. Tourists should simply park their car in Playa del Carmen and cross on the passenger ferry. If you are taking the car ferry, however, the best rooms are at the Ojo de Agua and small nearby inns. For seafood, try **El Pelicano** (inexpensive) on the waterfront, a block from the zócalo.

PUNTA BETE

60 km (37 m) south of Cancún. • Two roads, separated by about a mile, lead to Punta Bete. The short 2-km roads arrive at this wonderful 5-mile stretch of secluded beaches. Two small hotels and campgrounds provide accommodations appropriate to these ideal beachcomber surroundings, and all can be reached from each other by walking on the beach. The first turnoff is marked by the sign for *Capitan Lafitte,* which is also the road to Kailuum.

WHERE TO STAY

Posada del Capitan Lafitte
☎ *(99) 23-04-85; $140 MAP* • Right on the beach, this hotel offers 28 small cabins with modern bathrooms, and ceiling fans. Each cabin has a terrace with sea views. MAP required in attractive restaurant; bar; pool; and dive shop with windsurfing rentals. Also, taxi tours and car rentals arranged. Reserve in U.S.: CVI Group, Box 2664, Evergreen, CO 80439; ☎ 800-538-6802.

Kailuum ★
$90 MAP Drive into the Lafitte, then follow the marked road to the left. • For those who dream of the beachcomber's lifestyle, but want some comforts, this tent-village is the ideal resort. There's no electricity, only candle- and kerosene-light, but your spartanly furnished tent at least has a real bed as well as daily maid service. Bathroom facilities are centrally located. The food in the thatched-roof restaurant is good (MAP required). Excellent crafts shop. Dive shop, car rentals at Capitan Lafitte. No children under 15. Reservation information same as Lafitte.

The second road (unpaved) to Punta Bete leads to some primitive cabins and hammock palapas on the not-too-scenic **Playa Xcalacoca.** No electricity.

Though not properly on Punta Bete, the following hotel is closest in spirit to the accommodations there. Go 7 km, 4 m south on MEX 307 until you come to the marked turnoff for the Shangri-La.

Shangri-La Caribe
$165 MAP • Down a 1-km dirt road is this beach resort of 50 stylishly thatched bungalows with fans and modern baths. A bit larger than its

cousin Capitan Lafittc, thc bungalows here all have terraces if not sea
views. The beautiful beach is long and sandy and stretches 1 km south
to Playa del Carmen. Bar and restaurant (MAP required). Car rental.
Dive shop. Pool. Same contact information as Lafitte.

PLAYA DEL CARMEN

69 km (43 m) south of Cancún. • This lively village is composed of a main
street leading from MEX 307 to the beach, maybe eight cross streets—
some paved, a zócalo, and a magnificent shoreline. There's a bank with a
money exchange (10 a.m.-12:30 p.m.) and a long-distance telephone. Despite being the main transportation crossroads on the East Coast with bus
"terminals," a dock for the Cozumel ferry and waterjet, taxis and even the
small airstrip, Playa del Carmen is a popular, offbeat place to stay. This
coast could be the ideal location for a vacation for those without a car.
Transportation is easily arranged for excursions; the beach is one of the finest and extends for some distance away from the activity near the ferry
dock. And unlike most of the more isolated beach hotels, you can socialize
in the village and meet some Mexicans as well as foreign residents.

WHERE TO STAY AND EAT

If you're here just for a while waiting for the ferry, you can spend some
pleasant time over a meal or snack. There are small **restaurants** on the
beach to the north (try the very reasonable **El Pirate** just two blocks beyond Juarez) and in town (**Nuestra Sra. del Carmen**, Av. 10 Near Juarez,
is very local and very good). Near the ferry dock is the terrace restaurant of
the **Hotel Molcas.** The food here is quite good, including some Mexican
specialties. Evenings bring serenata musicians to accompany your meal.
But watch out for the prices, especially for breakfast. The most popular
place for dinner is **Da Gabi** (Av. 10; moderate plus) with marimba music accompanying its Italian food. For snacks, **Sabor** (a few blocks beyond bus
station on Av. 5, turn left) has health food sandwiches and delicious coconut flan.

Accommodations include very casual camping and hammock facilities
(follow the road or beach running north of the dock), a CREA youth hos-
tel, a few inexpensive and budget hotels located along the 2.5-km length
of main street as well as some first-class establishments. The area code is
987.

Molcas   ★★

☎ *3-00-70; $90* • Facing the sea and ferry dock, but not on the beach,
the Molcas is a modern hotel with about 50 air-conditioned rooms,
the second floor holding most of the ample ones. Pleasant service and
pool area. Good restaurant and bar. Tour agency and car rentals.
Write Aparato 79, Playa del Carmen, Q.R.

Quinta Mija   ★★

5 Av. Norte at Calle 14; ☎ *3-01-11; $85* • Not far from the beach, the
11 fan-cooled condos and suites are large and comfortably furnished;

all have full kitchens, some separate bedrooms. Six regular hotel rooms by the same tranquil gardens, decks sea views, and small pool, but for a lower price. Pool bar. In U. S., reserve at ☎ 800-538-6802. Comfortable condos here include a kitchen and living room along with the usual bedroom and bath. Small pool. Very nice for the price. Write Apartado 54.

Costa del Mar ★★

☎ *2-02-31; $85* • Next to the Blue Parrot on the beach, but the rooms here are in motel-like wings without views. The 20 units vary from fan-cooled smaller ones to more modern air-conditioned ones. Beach palapa bar and restaurant. Small pool.

Copa Cabana

Av. 5 about 1 km from dock; ☎ *3-02-18; $40* • Not on the beach and not fancy, but the clean rooms are around a shady garden with hot tub. May very well be the best of cheapies. Write Apartado Postal 103.

XCARET

75 km (46-1/2 m) south of Cancún. Expensive fee except free for children under 12 • Several miles south of Playa del Carmen, this lovely cove of transparent Caribbean waters served as one of the pre-Hispanic embarkation points for pilgrimages to the shrine of the oracle of Ix Chel on the island of Cozumel. Its *ojos de agua*, or underground springs, make Xcaret (Shka-ret) special, because they have been dynamited to create an underground river (called "cenote water cave") where you can snorkel before resurfacing at a large lagoon (life preservers provided). Not only have cenotes been dynamited here and ruins reconstructed, but there is a dolphin swim (U. S. $50 above the entrance fee; not on Sat.), horseback riding (a bit less than the dolphin ride), restaurants with live music, beaches with giant inner tube rides—it's such an extravaganza that it should be called "Disney beach." To reach the "natural" park turn from the highway at Restaurant Xcaret (a good, unpretentious seafood restaurant; moderate) and drive 2 km to the entrance. There are special buses that leave the Cancún Convention Center (daily except Sun.) and make hotel pick ups before hitting the road for Xcaret. Taxis available at Xcaret.

PAAMUL

85 km (53 m) south of Cancún. • High tourism has yet to hit this beach cove. Still the 1/2-km hard-packed dirt road here may not be worth your while unless you have an RV (electricity available) or plan to stay in one of the run-down, budget-priced bungalows.

PUERTO AVENTURAS

90 km (56 m) south of Cancún • In a few years this will be the largest development on the coast. Unlike the unpretentious complexes that now line the beaches, the five hotels planned here will be deluxe, the condos and villas will number two thousand. Already the 9-hole golf course is growing to 18, the marina and its canals are dredged. The CEDAM **underwater archaeology museum** is open, exhibiting items recovered from the wreckage of an 18th-century galleon near Aventuras (open 10a.m.-4p.m.; fee). And **Carlos N' Charlie's** has opened a branch of its restaurant chain. The complex feels like a suburb—there's a tram to travel around the grounds and a daily ferry to Playa del Carmen in peak season. For our tastes, there are too many security officers. Of the hotels that have opened, we prefer:

Oasis Beach Club   ★ ★ ★

$135 • Built on a magnificent beach, this tasteful hotel offers 30 air-conditioned rooms, some with sea views. Open and breezy restaurant and bar. Car rental. Large pool. Fitness center with sauna. Dive shop. Airport transfers. *Write Box 1341, Cancún.*

YALCU

103 km (64 m) south of Cancún. • This wonderful, fish-filled lagoon has not yet been discovered by tour buses, so with or without your snorkeling equipment you can enjoy this spot in relative peace. The tranquil waters of the lagoon contrast with the rough waters and stony shore of the Caribbean just beyond. The short access road to Yalcu is not marked, so look for a small thatched-roof house with a long stone fence and flame trees and turn left.

AKUMAL

105 km (65 m) south of Cancún. • An extensive beach of white sand curves around the gentle waters of Akumal Bay. Once a private underwater explorers club, the beach now provides some of the most extensive resort facilities along this coast with three separate agencies providing accommodations and res-taurants (**Lol Ha** restaurant on the beach is said to be the best). Akumal does offer some choice in dining, tennis courts, an excellent dive shop, fishing boats, and windsurfing. Taxis, car rentals, a decent crafts boutique, and a small convenience store are available.

WHERE TO STAY

Las Casitas Akumal   ★ ★ ★

☎ *(987) 2-25-54; $140* • Isolated off to the quieter side of Akumal are these 14 luxurious villas overlooking the bay and with terraces for sunbathing. While not right on the sand, the location of these units, each with 2 bedrooms, 2 bathrooms, and a living room, is dramatic. All casitas include fans in each room and a refrigerator. Rates are for up to four persons per day. For reservations write Apartado 714, Cancún, Q.R.

Villas Akumal Hotel   ★ ★

☎ *(987) 2-25-32* • In the grove lining Akumal's beach, the Club offers two kinds of accommodations with a swimming pool. The 3-story ★ ★**Beachfront Hotel,** opened in 1987, has 21 large, air-conditioned rooms, some with kitchenettes and all with view of sea; $99. The **Villas Akumal** are 40 bungalows that we find too enclosed, but they are well-maintained, air-conditioned and more than adequate; $66-94. About 1/2 m away near Yalcu caleta is a complex of 4

2-bedroom, 2-bath villas. (Very expensive.) Reserve in U.S. at Akutrame, Box 1976, El Paso, TX 79950 or call ☎ 800-351-1622.

Hotel Akumal Cancún

☎ *(987) 2-24-53; $100* • A bit farther down the beach stands this more conventional hotel. Its 100 air-conditioned rooms are ample, with quarry tile floors and private balconies. Unfortunately, most rooms are in motel-like wings and do not have sea views. Like the other accommodations here, the hotel has restaurants and bars, but also a disco. Pool, fine beach and tennis courts. For reservations, write Apartado 28, Cancún, Q.R.

PLAYA AVENTURAS

108 km (67 m) south of Cancún. • There are two Aventura turnoffs. The first goes to the Hotel Aventuras Akumal, a "club" hotel that really doesn't welcome casual visitors and where everyone walks around with I.D. badges. The second turnoff continues down a 1-km road to a tranquil cove where a Spanish galleon was sunk during colonial times. Even today beads and other small items sometimes wash onto the shore. The wonderful beach here has been fenced off (not too effectively) by the DIF camp that serves as a vacation reward for children who do well in schools throughout the Yucatán peninsula. To the left of the camp is a beckoning strip of beach leading off somewhere unknown.

CHEMUYIL

109 km (67-1/2 m) south of Cancún. Small admission fee • A beautiful beach and cove with calm waters and some rock formations to explore while snorkeling. For good reason this is a favorite Mexican vacation spot during holidays when the hammock palapas right on the beach are full. (Hammock rentals available.) R.V. sites. Bath and shower facilities; no hot water. Restaurant. Beach closed to public at 6 p.m. on our last visit.

X-CACEL

112 km (69 1/2) south of Cancún. Small admission fee. • Yet another beautiful beach, X-Cacel (Shka-sell) is wilder than Chemuyil and has more surf. Tent camping, but no electricity. Also, the beach closed to the public at 6 p.m. Dressing rooms. Restaurant.

CALETA XEL-HA

115 km (71 m) south of Cancún. Admission charged and parking fee. Open 8 a.m.-5 p.m. • The waters of this beautiful inlet of the Caribbean used to be so magnificently clear that snorkling equipment was superfluous. They still are clear, but too many tourists have left a haze of suntan lotion. The coral reefs and lagoon of Caleta Xel-Ha (shell-HAH) surround a pre-Conquest temple and remain a popular spot to swim, snorkel (rental equipment available), and enjoy a meal at the restaurant. Dressing and shower facilities are available.

XEL-HA RUINS

116 km (72 m) south of Cancún. Admission fee. Open 8 a.m.-5 p.m. • Just past the entrance to the Caleta, on the opposite side of MEX 307, stand some restored ruins from ancient Xel-Ha. Unlike Tulum, Xel-Ha had an earlier, classic period flourishing when it may have been an outpost and, perhaps, even the port of Coba. The buildings you see now date from the post Classic period. One complex is in miniature; it is a 10-minute walk from the entrance (right at fork, left at houses) then just beyond a huge, inviting cenote of deepest blue (yes, you can swim!). As you approach the complex, you come to the **Casa del Jaguar,** a tiny temple named after a "diving" yellow jaguar (in the upside-down position of Tulum's diving god) painted inside the first door. Better preserved paintings can be seen in the **Templo de las Pajaros,** a crumbling building at the side of the highway. On one side of a wall, you can make out a flock of pajaros, or parrots; on the opposite side is frontally painted god, looking very idol-like.

TULUM

> *We followed the shore day and night, and the next day towards sunset we perceived a city and town so large that Seville would not have seemed more considerable nor better.*

Chaplain of Grijalva Expedition, 1518

Tulum is indeed dramatic, perched on a 40-foot cliff above the sea with the Caribbean as its backdrop. This ruined city was a major port for the late-Classic sea-trading Maya (A.D. 1200-Conquest). While the setting of Tulum is magnificent, its architecture lacks refinement and scale. Originally, the poor quality of the stone masonry at least was masked by many layers of stucco and paint. Yet, whatever the artistic failings of these late Maya, Tulum had great religious significance, its original name "Zama," meaning dawn, or more generally, rebirth and renewal. Until the middle of this century, the Maya continued to make pilgrimages to this ruined city, burning incense and candles here.

RUINS

Turnoff located 129 km (80 m) from Cancún; 250 km (155 m) from Chetumal. Open 8 a.m.-5 p.m. Admission fee. • The ancient town is surrounded on three sides by an 11- to 17-foot-high wall that originally had a walkway on top. The fourth side is naturally protected by its location above the sea. There is considerable controversy over whether the town was actually fortified. Many believe that Tulum and other sites on the East Coast were fortified against pirates from other parts of the Caribbean or even from other Maya groups (the coastal sites may have been settled by the foreign Putun Mayas from the Gulf Coast). Others believe that Tulum's wall could have been scaled too easily to serve a defensive purpose. Under this theory, it is suggested that the wall functioned to distinguish the ceremonial area within from the extensive suburban homes that once surrounded it. Within

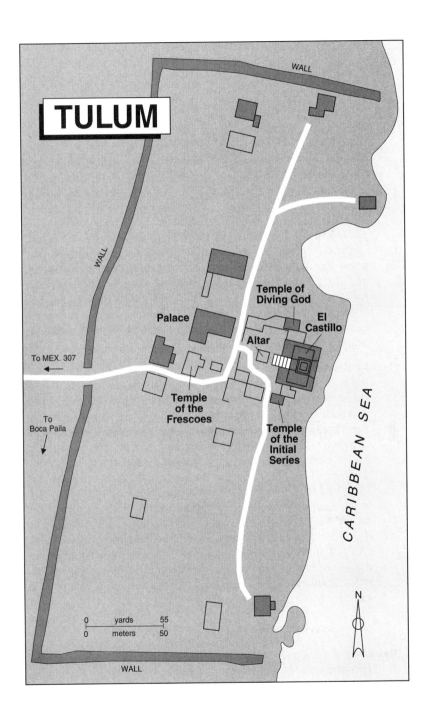

TULUM

WALL

WALL

Temple of
Diving God

Palace

El
Castillo

Altar

To MEX. 307

Temple
of the
Frescoes

To
Boca Paila

Temple
of the
Initial
Series

CARIBBEAN SEA

| 0 | yards | 55 |
| 0 | meters | 50 |

N

WALL

Tulum's walls there is another inner wall dividing the western, or outer, part from what was probably a more sacred area. In the western part, are some colonnaded buildings, mostly in ruins, that were residences for approximately 500 people.

Temple of the Frescoes

This is the best preserved and most interesting building in the western area. In front of this two-story structure stands a carved stela that is badly eroded. But archaeologists have been able to read some of the hieroglyphs and tentatively date it to **A.D. 1261.** The temple itself was constructed later, around **A.D. 1450.** The central niches on both stories of this temple retain carved remnants of the Diving God, a figure repeatedly represented at Tulum. The Diving God, so called because his feet are in the air and his head emerges in the lower part of the frame, has wings, a bird's tail, and holds a symbol for corn. A definite identification for this god is yet to be made. He may represent the planet Venus as the morning star (Quetzalcoatl) or a god with aspects of the diving bee. Since Yucatán was, and is, a major producer of **honey** (the only sweetener in pre-Hispanic times), the bee could have had special significance for this region. The corners of the west facade are carved with cartoonlike faces in low relief, with the eyes and nose between the moldings, the headdress above, and the chin and mouth below. These masks—originally painted orange, red, and black—are believed to represent the creator god Quetzalcoatl.

Mural Paintings

Inside the gallery of the Temple of the Frescoes are some well-preserved frescoes in a pictographic writing style believed to have evolved in central Mexico. Although these murals may have been painted by artists imported from central Mexico, their symbolism is characteristically Maya. One decently preserved mural can be seen through the bars in front of this temple. It is arranged in three rows, representing the levels of the Maya universe: the heavens, the middle world of the living, and the Underworld of darkness and death. In the top row, the creator god and rain god are crowned with symbols of corn. In the middle, the patron goddess of the East Coast, Ix Chel is portrayed on the right surrounded by vegetation and holding images of Chac, the rain god, in each hand. On the left is a detail of a god riding a four-legged creature that could have been inspired only by the **horseback-riding Spaniards.** The lower border contains a sea scene with fish and a manta ray. The **sea** often symbolized the Underworld for the Maya. The many positive symbols in this painting—of rain, creation, and corn—are in keeping with Tulum as a symbol of rebirth.

Castillo

The inner courtyard is dominated by the Castillo, the most imposing structure at Tulum. It represents a series of reconstructions starting with a palace at the base upon which was constructed the temple and staircase. The two small oratories at the base were added last. The niche carvings on the temple are partially destroyed, but a Diving God can be discerned in the center niche and a standing figure to the north. The serpent columns at the entrance to the temple, their rattler tails supporting the lintels and their heads resting on the temple platform, are reminiscent of the columns at the Temple of the Warriors at Chichen Itza.

Temple of the Initial Series
To the south of the Castillo is a well-preserved temple named for a stela that now is housed in the British Museum. The **stela** was carved with a Classic Period date of A.D. 564. Since Tulum was not constructed for another 600 years, it is believed this early carving was brought to Tulum from another site, most likely Coba, where there is a stela with some similarity to the one found here.

Temple of the Diving God
Although the Diving God is represented in a niche above the door, there is no particular reason for this temple to bear his name, because he appears on many Tulum buildings. Originally, there were wall paintings, similar to those you have already seen, but they have been weathered out of existence. The architecture of this temple is unique, its exterior walls sloping outward toward the cornice, its door reversing the slope.

SWIMMING
A path to the north of the Castillo leads down to the beach and the beckoning Caribbean for those who would like to swim after their visit to the ruins. Or you can go south on the road passing by the ruins searching for one of the many coves along this coast. A strong surf, and sometimes undertow, is characteristic of this area.

WHERE TO STAY AND EAT

A number of budget-priced restaurants are located in the curio market in front of the ruins: modest restaurants at the intersection of the highway with Tulum. **Motel Restaurant El Crucero** is our favorite of the intersection restaurants, with inexpensive to moderate prices on its typical Mexican menu. For first-class travelers, the food at nearby Akumal or the atmosphere at the Villa Arqueologica in Coba may be preferable to Tulum's spots (and more expensive). Akumal and Coba offer the best accommodations in this area, but Tulum has the cheapest places to stay. The road that passes in front of the ruins skirts the beach and sea south of Tulum. Along the way are rock-bottom facilities without electricity, such as **El Paraiso** (a paradise it's not). Of these spots (where you might want to sling up your hammock) the **Zazil Kin** at least offers the warmth of Don Armando and his family. Farther along (5 km, 3 m from ruins) is the internationally run **Osho Oasis** (moderate) with hot water and the best facilities, including a location by a lovely cove and some cabanas with king-size beds, private baths; others with hanging beds and communal baths. The restaurant (moderately expensive) has good vegetarian food. Write Apartado 99, Tulum, Q. R..

OFF THE BEATEN TRACK

The road running in front of Tulum ruins continues south past the Oceo Oasis, unpaved and bumpy for the most part, down the Boca Paila Peninsula. Miles of this peninsula have been protected as a natural habitat (not to be confused with a wilderness preserve, as humans are considered part of the ecosystem) called **Sian Ka'an.** If you have not found the East Coast adequately secluded and undeveloped for your taste, or if your interest lies in fishing or birdwatching rather than snorkeling, you might want to explore further (car required and preferably one with four-wheel drive; or arrange a boat from other points on the coast to take you to the lagoons and mangrove swamps where roseate spoonbills nest.) The area is famous for its deep-sea fishing, and the hotels scattered throughout the peninsula's length can help you make arrangements with boats and tours. Some hotels are exclusive fishing resorts like ★★★**Sol Pez Maya** where guests are flown in from Cancún. ($380 AP; rates include meals, boats, and guides. Adults only. No credit cards. For reservations, contact your travel agent.) Now a bridge connects the upper part of the peninsula with the lower part leading to Punta Allen (55 km, 34 m). For more information, contact Amigos of Sian Kaan in the Plaza America, in Cancún ☎ (4-22-01).

COBA

Drive 131 km (81 m) south of Cancún to turnoff on right and continue 47 km (29 m) to ruins on paved road. Admission fee. Open 8 a.m.-5 p.m. Snack stands. Nearby hotels and restaurants. • Coba is majestic; its towering pyramid temples reach above the treetops of the dense rain forest. Situated amid five lakes, its Maya name appropriately means "wind-ruffled water." Although Coba was explored at the turn of the century and was known to be one of the largest Late Classic period (A.D. 600-1000) Maya sites, with an estimated population of 55,000, only in recent years has it been cleared and restored.

Coba raises some fascinating questions. First, it is not in the northern Yucatán Maya style, but with its **high pyramid temples** and numerous **free-standing carvings** (stelae) of rulers, it is most like the great Maya site of *Tikal* in the Peten jungle of Guatemala. Why would Coba have a stronger resemblance to *Tikal*, a few hundred miles away, than to Chichen Itza only 60 miles to the north? Archaeologist Joyce Marcus suggests Coba flourished after a marriage alliance with the elite of Tikal. Some of the stelae of Coba depict women holding the ceremonial bar signifying rulership and standing on captives (which shows political control). Marcus says there is evidence to associate at least one of these women with *Tikal*. For *Tikal*, such a marriage alliance with Coba would have facilitated trade with the East Coast and northern Yucatán to obtain salt and honey. For Coba, it would have enhanced the prestige of its ruling elite.

Another baffling aspect of Coba is its numerous causeways, or *sacbes*. Other Maya sites have an occasional *sacbe*, but over 16 have been discovered at Coba. In fact, Coba is best described as the hub of these roads and settlements. Most of the roads run in straight lines connecting minor villages or zones to the main ceremonial grouping of Coba, and some may have originally crossed part of Lake Macanxoc. The most astounding *sacbe* connected Coba with Yaxuna, **62 miles** away near Chichen Itza. The Yaxuna causeway is over 30 feet wide, elevated 2 to 8 feet above ground, and constructed of stone rubble covered with a smooth facing of stucco. The function of these engineering feats is not known: the ancient Maya had no wheeled vehicles or beasts of burden to warrant such large and straight roads. Many archaeologists believe their function must have been ceremonial; others think they were trade routes. Some believe they had astronomical significance. Perhaps they were all three.

Coba's Classic-period fluorescence was brief, being confined to the 7th and 8th centuries. But remnants of paintings and temples in the style of Tulum indicate the site continued to be used beyond the Classic period until near the time of the Conquest. To date, only a small part of Coba has been cleared and restored.

RUINS

Practical Tips

Although the paths at the ruins are usually wide and well cleared, you should wear sturdy shoes to climb the pyramids or explore smaller, rocky paths.

Insect repellent and clothes to cover you are recommended, especially for the Macanxoc path.

Try to get to the ruins early (this may require an overnight at one of the hotels) when the birds (parrots and motmots) and butterflies are plentiful and the lush jungle is not yet too hot.

Coba Group

Located between Lake Coba and Lake Macanxoc is the central plaza area of Coba. Other architectural groupings of less importance, some of them over 3 miles away, are connected to the central area by sacbes. The main group is dominated by a pyramid of nine tiers and about 78 feet high. An entrance at the pyramid base takes you to where a **tomb** was discovered, but there is nothing left to see. A stela in the plaza is badly eroded, yet the outline of its **hieroglyphic** text can still be discerned. Following the path leading straight from the entrance, you pass the turnoff to the unrestored ball court and after about 5 minutes come to an "intersection." To the right (east) is a sign for Macanxoc, straight ahead a sign for Conjunto Las Pinturas, and to the left one for Nohoch Mul.

Grupo Macanxoc

The 10-minute walk on this narrow jungle path takes you to a number of stelae, some with decently preserved carvings representing a **woman ruler** (or rulers) standing on captives or flanked by kneeling and subservient figures. As you walk to the first carved stela, you will notice in the forest many unexcavated platforms covered with vegetation.

At the end of the path stands a platform surmounted by a large two-sided stela dating from around A.D. 675. Each side shows a woman holding a ceremonial bar signifying rulership and standing on captives with two subservient figures flanking her. Women can be identified by archaeologists through the hieroglyphic text, but another good, though not infallible, indicator is the wearing of a long skirt or robe as can be seen here

Given the absence of signs and well-cleared paths, you could easily think you have come to the end of the **Grupo Macanxoc,** but we found seven more stelae along small, overgrown paths in the area beyond. Continuing east past the double-sided stela is a clearing with a well-preserved carving in a niche to the right. The skirt of the woman represented is easily seen, and the text provides some evidence that she was connected with Tikal. She stands on a throne of two crouching, backto-back captives with a kneeling figure to one side. The glyphs near her feet may indicate a conquered town.

Most of the other stelae, all nearby, are badly eroded, with only an occasional face or some feet discernible. Two of the most interesting ones are reached by continuing east, then following the path to the left. A short detour off to the left leads to a stela with a very expressive remnant of someone standing on a prostrate captive. Back on the main path, but further along, a detour to the right takes you to a double-sided stela. On the first side of this stela, you can make out some hieroglyphs and one kneeling figure at the bottom; on the second side, the face of a ruler and two kneeling figures can be seen.

Conjunto De Las Pinturas

Within this group sits the **Temple of the Painted Lintel,** discovered in 1974. Named after paintings found both on the lintel and inside the temple, only traces of red, black, and Maya-blue paint on the lintel are now visible. Some look like hieroglyphs (it is actually easier to see the faint figures through binoculars from the plaza than close up). In the plaza in front of this temple are remnants of columns, indicating that both the paintings and architecture of this Conjunto are from the **Late Post-Classic Tulum period.**

Follow the path in front of the temple, past one stela, to an enormous one, perhaps 9 feet high. A standing figure holds a gigantic ceremonial bar of rulership and is flanked by two figures; the kneeling one looks as if his hands are bound behind his back. Although the bottom of this carving is eroded, you can just see two back-to-back captives forming a throne under the ruler's feet. Continue a few steps on this path and turn right. You are on your way to **Nohoch Mul.**

Nohoch Mul

About a mile from the Grupo Coba is the steep, more than 120-foot-high Castillo, built in a style resembling the monuments at Tikal in Guatemala. Its temple, in the style of Tulum, was added to this Classic-period pyramid at a much later date. If you are intrepid enough to **climb this pyramid,** you will see remnants of two temple carvings of the **Diving God,** that half-insect, half-human diety so important at Tulum. Near the Castillo is Structure X, which displays on its steps one of the best-preserved stela at Coba. This stela is carved in Mayan with the year A.D.. 780 and depicts a man holding the ceremonial bar and standing on what might have been a throne composed of captives such as you have seen on other carvings at Coba. Two smaller, and hence inferior, individuals with their hands bound stand next to him.

WHERE TO STAY AND EAT

While you may not choose to eat at the rustic establishments next to the ruins, at least look inside the *crafts shop* next to the ticket office. Here you might find the wooden jaguars, some snarling and others kittenish, carved by a local artisan. Both of the following hotels have *restaurants*: **El Bocadito** is thatched and inexpensive; the handsome **Villa Arqueologica** serves moderately expensive steak and seafood that seemed surprisingly mediocre given its excellent service and attractive surroundings. But the price of a meal may buy a swim in the pool, if you're lucky.

Hotel Villa Arqueologica

☎ *(985) 6-28-30; $68* • Flawless in its tasteful decor, this hotel is opposite the ruins, 1 km away, next to Lake Coba. The rooms are somewhat monastic yet comfortable, with interesting arches, white-washed walls, built-in furniture, and air conditioning. Magnificent gardens. Courtyard filled with tropical flowers and trees. Restaurant, bar, pool, tennis and parking. For reservations, call, in the U.S., ☎ 800-258-2633.

El Bocadito Hotel

$18 • *Near the Nuevo X-Can road, 2 km, 1 m from the ruins,* the tiny hotel here has a few simple, small rooms for those looking for a bargain. No hot water. Restaurant.

ON THE WAY TO CHETUMAL
CHUNYAXCHE

155 km (96 m) south of Cancún. • The ruins at Chunyaxche have yet to be adequately explored or excavated, but if it is the right moment to stretch your legs, you might want to look at the few still visible remains dating from the same time as Tulum. An open-air restaurant marks the turnoff on the left.

FELIPE CARRILLO PUERTO

226 km (140 m) south of Cancún. • This town is a major crossroads for those planning a car or bus trip to Valladolid (MEX 295) and, further west to Mérida (MEX 184), although the opening of the Nuevo X-can road to Coba from Valladolid might challenge Felipe Carrillo's status. The town was called Chan Santa Cruz ("Little Holy Cross") during the second half of the 19th century when it was capital of the rebel Maya after the Caste War. In its church stood the speaking cross, an oracle that directed the actions of the Maya. A number of small restaurants are clustered near the Pemex Station on the main road.

OFF THE BEATEN TRACK: XCALAK PENINSULA

310 km (192m) south of Cancún to Limones, soon after turn left onto paved road that leads to Majahual (55 km, 34 m) and the Caribbean. Fill up on gas at Felipe Carrillo Puerto. • This pristine stretch of coast is just off the Chichchorro reef. The diving, beachcombing, and birdwatching here are already attracting some small and simple hotels with only their private generators to keep them operational. A left onto a dirt road takes you along secluded beaches for 22 km to El Placer fishing lagoon, but there are no facilities available. A right onto a dirt road at Majahual to Xcalak leads past 50 km of deserted beaches. The best inn is **Costa de Cocos** in Xcalak with reliable divers, a cluster of simple rooms with mahogany floors and bathrooms, a restaurant, and a charter plane for excursions. If you book in the U. S. ☎ (800-538-6802), Cancún airport pick-up can be arranged.

BACALAR

343 km (213 m) south of Cancún. • If you are not planning to visit this area again (see "Chetumal"), you should at least get a view of the magnificent lake before continuing the last 36 km (22 m) or so into Chetumal, on MEX 186. Chetumal is a total of 379 km (235 m) from Cancún.

GETTING TO AND FROM THE EAST COAST

AIR

Cancún airport provides the most convenient entry to this coast. If you plan to stay on the coast, note that most hotels are 1 to 2 km from the buses on MEX 307. And the bus terminal is 16 km (10 m) from the airport. Buses to Playa del Carmen hotels are feasible; otherwise, you can arrange a car rental or taxi (negotiate the price) at the airport. Charter planes fly to Tulum from Cancún and Cozumel.

BUS

First-class buses running between Cancún and Chetumal (Autobuses del Caribe) will drop you at Tulum or Playa del Carmen, but they may have no room for your return when you try to flag them down. More than likely you'll find yourself returning on the second-class bus, at least to Playa del Carmen where you can try to transfer (all bus offices are clustered near a corner of the town plaza). At either Playa del Carmen or Tulum, you can arrange for cabs to other destinations on the coast, but if you plan to cover big distances, like to Coba, you may find a car rental not much more expensive but a lot more convenient. At Playa del Carmen you can check on the second-class **Autotransportes de Oriente** and its Ruta Corta bus that runs to Akumal, Xel-Ha, Tulum, and Coba crossing. From Coba crossing, the ruins are 2-1/2 km (1-1/2 m) away. Other Oriente buses go to Valladolid, Chichen Itza, and Mérida.

CAR

From Cancún, it is possible to spend a very full day visiting Tulum, Coba, and Xel-Ha and return to Cancún in the evening (178 km [110 m] one way to Coba). From Chetumal, a one-day round trip is exhausting, requiring a dawn departure and an unrecommended return at night (259 km [183 m] one way). A one-day trip is now feasible from Chichen Itza or Valladolid with the paving of an access road to Coba from Nuevo X-can (from Valladolid it is 175 km or109 m to Tulum).

Ferry to Cozumel See Cozumel chapter, "Getting To and From" section.

DIRECTORY

Airlines • Cancún airport serves this coast.

Buses • First-class *Autotransportes Caribe* buses run on the coastal road between Cancún and Chetumal. Playa del Carmen and Tulum are regular stops on these routes and modern mini-buses run between Cancún, Playa del Carmen and Tulum. Second-class *Autotransportes de Oriente*, based in Playa del Carmen, makes the same runs but more frequently and with more stops at tourist destinations along the way, including Coba.

Car Rentals • All major agencies, Cancún airport. A few at hotels on the coast and in Playa del Carmen.

Emergencies • Apart from Cancún, only Playa del Carmen and Akumal have telephones.

Ferries • Playa del Carmen is port for the waterjet and the passenger ferry to Cozumel. Puerto Morelos has the car ferry (not really convenient for tourists).

Groceries • In Playa del Carmen, and a convenience store at Akumal.

Taxis • Cancún airport to hotels; Playa del Carmen (at ferry dock), Tulum, and Akumal for more local service and day trips.

Telephones • Long-distance service at Hotel Playa del Carmen. (2-1/2 blocks from beach on main street of Playa. Open 8 a.m.-1 p.m., 3-7 p.m., except Sun. 8 a.m.-noon. No collect calls.)

Tours • Agencies in Cancún and Cozumel offer air charter, bus and small van tours here. On the coast, the dive shops, located near most hotels, arrange tours to different snorkeling and dive spots.

Watersport Rentals • Dive shops at most beaches and lagoons as well as at the first-class hotels.

CHETUMAL

Located on the Caribbean Coast next to the Bay of Chetumal and just over the border from Belize, the tropical capital of Quintana Roo has undergone rapid development while maintaining much of its funky charm. In pre-Hispanic times Chetumal ("Place of Hard Wood") was a key Maya port shipping cacao, gold, copper, and feathers to northern Yucatán. The present city is an outgrowth of Payo Obispo, the town founded in 1898 on the Bay of Chetumal by sailors under the command of Admiral Othon P. Blanco—fortunately for the residents, the town was not named after the Admiral. In 1936, the name changed to Chetumal; then in 1955 a tropical hurricane destroyed most of the city, making it necessary to build anew. Clean and relatively quiet, contemporary Chetumal combines wide boulevards lined with brilliant flame trees and low modern buildings housing a variety of small shops and restaurants. Unusual for Mexico are the small wood-frame houses, some on stilts, a style adapted from neighboring Belize. An intriguing mixture of people mingle in this hot and often steamy tropical port. Mexican tourists are attracted by its free-port status and abundance of foreign goods ranging from cameras to calculators, from Danish butter and Polish hams down to Planter's peanuts. Belizians cross the border to take advantage of Chetumal's cheaper gasoline prices and greater variety of goods. Other foreign tourists pass through on their way to snorkeling and scuba diving off the cays in Belize or exploring ruins of the ancient Maya. Some, with good reason, remain for a short stay in Chetumal to explore the interesting, nontouristy, nearby Maya ruins and to swim and savor the tropical sun at lovely surrounding lakes and watering spots.

KEY TO CHETUMAL

Sights • Chetumal is the only base for visiting Maya ruins like Kohunlich, Becan, and Chicanna and the colorful lakes of Milagros and Bacalar. It is not a resort.

Sports • Swimming and birdwatching.

Shopping • Chetumal is a free port selling imported cheese and cameras at prices that won't interest you, but it also sells Yucatecan hammocks.

Where to Stay • Chetumal has one first-class hotel and a few adequate hotels.

Where to Eat • A few modest but decent restaurants offer local seafood and, sometimes, venison.

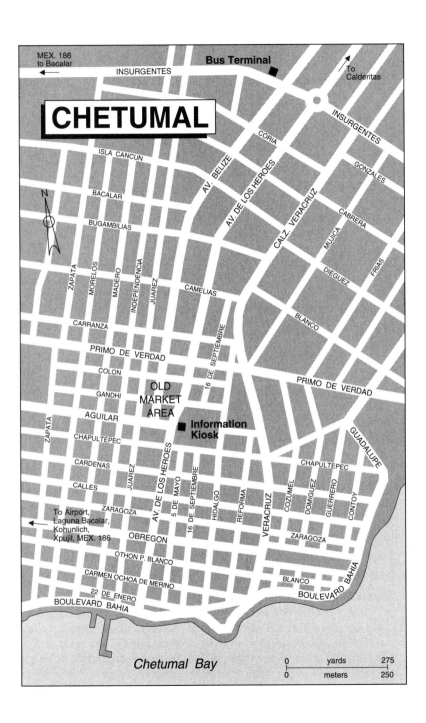

MEX. 186
to Bacalar

INSURGENTES

Bus Terminal

To
Calderitas

CHETUMAL

INSURGENTES

CORIA

ISLA CANCUN

GONZALES

BACALAR

AV. BELIZE

AV. DE LOS HEROES

CALZ. VERACRUZ

CABRERA

BUGAMBILIAS

MUJICA

FRIAS

N

ZAPATA

MORELOS

MADERO

INDEPENDENCIA

JUAREZ

CAMELIAS

DIEGUEZ

CARRANZA

BLANCO

16 DE SEPTIEMBRE

PRIMO DE VERDAD

COLON

PRIMO DE VERDAD

GANDHI

OLD
MARKET
AREA

AGUILAR

ZAPATA

CHAPULTEPEC

Information
Kiosk

CHAPULTEPEC

GUADALUPE

CARDENAS

JUAREZ

AV. DE LOS HEROES

5 DE MAYO

16 DE SEPTIEMBRE

HIDALGO

REFORMA

VERACRUZ

COZUMEL

DOMIGUEZ

GUERRERO

CONTOY

CALLES

ZARAGOZA

To Airport,
Laguna Bacalar,
Kohunlich,
Xpujil, MEX. 186

OBREGON

ZARAGOZA

OTHON P. BLANCO

CARMEN OCHOA DE MERINO

BLANCO

BOULEVARD BAHIA

22 DE ENERO

BOULEVARD BAHIA

Chetumal Bay

| 0 | yards | 275 |
| 0 | meters | 250 |

Entertainment • A few night spots are available.

Getting Around • There is good public transportation within town and to the waterspots on its outskirts. Excursions to the ruins require a car.

Practical Tips • This is the tropics. It's hot. June, September, and October can bring heavy rainstorms. Carry your bathing suit and insect repellent on excursions. And carry your tourist card, as there are "border" checks outside this free port.

WHAT TO SEE AND DO

Exploration of the town itself will take little of your time. The new high tech **Museo de la Antropologia** (*Av. de los Heroes near Aguilar*) should be open by your visit, however, with computer terminals used in interactive exhibits on ancient Maya civilization. To get a feel of this tropical city, take a walk down Avenida de los Heroes from the market (near Aguilar) to the bay, and peek into the shops. You may be amused to discover that whether a store is selling dresses or hardware, it will probably have few free-port items as well—radios or cans of Planter's peanuts. At the end of Av. de los Heroes is the pleasant waterfront and the lovely Boulevard Bahia that meanders around the bay leaving parks and restaurants in its wake.

Along your stroll in town, you might do some **shopping**. Fine Yucatecan **hammocks** can be found here. Vendors are normally located on **Av. de los Heroes** near the Hotel Del Prado or near the market. Bargaining is expected. Variety and prices are better in Mérida, so wait if you are heading there. The very finest Yucatecan hammocks we have ever seen are made by *Don Mario*, a Maya from Tizimin, now living in Huay Pix, a tiny village located outside Chetumal on

Laguna Milagros.Don Mario weaves rich, multicolored hammocks in a variety of innovative designs. To find him you need to go to Laguna Milagros and ask for directions. More than likely a child will be found to lead you to Don Mario's home—a 5-minute walk. A hammock takes three weeks to complete, so if you want to order one you may want to contact Valerie Searle (see "Directory") to help with the arrangements.

More interesting sights lie *outside of town*. They are easy to reach by car, bus (the "Bacalar" bus from terminal can drop you near Milagros and Cenote Azul as well), or collective vans (*combis*).

Laguna Milagros

14 km (9 m) on MEX 186 toward Escarcega. Make a left at sign and continue for a few hundred feet to the end of the road Combis marked "Huay Pix" to Laguna Milagros leave from combi terminal • The color of this lake is shockingly turquoise. When the wind is calm, it turns into a glimmering mirror that reflects the surrounding palm and lime trees. On weekends the many food stands attract great crowds. Wear your bathing suit because, at this writing, the facilities at the lake are closed, except on weekends.

Laguna Bacalar

36 km (22M) from Chetumal off MEX 307 toward Tulum Colectivos to Bacalar leave from combi terminal and drop you near the fort • This exquisite multicolor "**Lagoon of the Seven Colors**" with hues ranging from vivid turquoise to deep blue-black extends for some 50km. The lakeshore drive, or "costera," provides memorable vistas; the lake offers delightful swimming. A **fortress** on the west bank, built by the Spanish in 1733 for use against English pirates coming from British Honduras (Belize), still stands and can be visited. During the Caste War, the fortress was the scene of stormy battles between rebel Maya and Europeans. Control exchanged hands in 1848 and 1849, with the Maya finally gaining the upper hand in 1859 and holding on until the 20th century. From the fort and colectivo stop, walk to the waterfront and go to the left a few blocks for the community-owned **Balneario Ejidal** (fee for parking and dressing rooms) where you can swim in the lake or have a snack in *the* restaurant. However **La Esperanza** (1 block above fort, then 1 block right of zócalo; 9 a.m.-9:30 p.m.; inexpensive), the restaurant favored by locals, has no lake ambience. Instead you can enjoy a platter of good shrimp within its stone walls and finely-thatched roof. For hotels on the lake, see "Where to Eat."

Cenote Azul

35 km (22m) from Chetumal, just off MEX 307 and just before Laguna Bacalar • This swimming spot of velvety ink-blue, incredibly transparent water has a depth estimated between 200 and 500 feet. It offers you an invigorating and unforgettable swim. Enter the cenote by walking through the restaurant located on its bank. Weekdays are tranquil; on Sunday the cenote fills with celebrants. Dressing rooms available but not recommended. The popular, open air restaurant has friendly service.

Calderitas

9 km (6m) north of Chetumal. Follow Av. de los Heroes north past the market Colectivos leave from combi terminal. • Located on the Bay of Chetumal, this quiet, tiny village erupts on Saturday and Sunday, when Mexican families take their outings. Music blares from loudspeakers and transistors, small restaurants sell delicious fresh grilled and fried fish, and the bay becomes a scene of Mexican gaiety with many of the bathers jumping into the sea fully clothed.

EXCURSION TO RUINS OF KOHUNLICH

About 60 km (37 m) from Chetumal on the Escarcega road, turn left at sign and continue 9km. Small admission charge. Open 8 a.m.-5 p.m. • Named after the numerous date palms found at the site, these ruins are primarily from the Early Classic period (A.D. 250-600). Like the ruins of Coba, Kohunlich is in the tradition of the southern lowland Maya from the Peten Jungle of Guatemala. When Victor Segovia was excavating here not too long ago, a loudspeaker made Kohunlich the only site where a visit to the Maya past could be accompanied by Beethoven's Fifth Symphony. Today the ruins have resumed their overgrown, somewhat forlorn state of abandonment, but a visit is still worthwhile. Walking from the parking lot, you pass a plaza complex on your right and an impressive acropolis off to the left. A nball court is farther along to the right. But the special attraction of Kohunlich is the Pyramid of the masks at the end of the main avenue. Under small thatched covers, a row of three large masks borders each side of the stairs. Kohunlich was discovered by officials when thieves were caught trying to steal these masks. Awesome, they represent the Maya sun god, recognizable by the markings on the eyes and the "T"-shaped tooth.

EXCURSION TO RUINS OF XPUJIL, BECAN, AND CHICANNA

MEX 186, 130 km (81 m) on the Escarcega road from Chetumal • Just across the Campeche state line are many ruins, most unreachable and hidden by jungle. Fortunately, Xpujil, Becan, and Chicanna are near enough to the highway to be accessible to tourists. Chicanna is among our favorite ruins, partially because it has not been stripped of its beautiful tropical vegetation and partially because we are often its sole visitors, feeling like explorers into the past as we walk through jungle paths to discover isolated temples.

All three ruins can be visited in a one-day, round-trip, car excursion from Chetumal or on the way to Villahermosa or Palenque via the Escarcega road. All are open 8 a.m.-5 p.m. There are several thatched restaurants near Xpujil where once a day the ADO Villahermosa-Chetumal deposits visitors. Otherwise you might want to bring a snack and enough cool drinks to last you until you reach Bacalar or the Cenote Azul for a refreshing swim on your return to Chetumal. Because Chetumal is a free port, there is a "border" check along the way. Take your tourist papers with you as well as sturdy shoes for safe walks along jungle trails.

Xpujil
At km 152, or about 122km (76 m) from Chetumal Admission charge • One very impressive building of these extensive, mostly unrestored ruins (pronounced shpool-HEEL) stands to the right of the road about 1 m beyond the Pemex station. The Style, called **Rio Bec** and found only in this region, dates from A.D. 600-900. The Rio Bec style is famous, if not notorious, for its fakery, Towering temples have no inner chambers and no special function, and pyramid steps are so steep and narrow that they are mere etchings on the facade. The constructions are there only to impress—and that they do quite well. The **Xpujil Complex** has three **fake** towering temples that add grandeur to the one-story functional temples at their base. (One tower here is highly unusual for the practical staircase it contains.) The style is accompanied by elaborate carvings of "**dragon**" or sky-monster masks, some of which can still be seen at this site. The finest remaining mask

is on the rear of the middle tower, where fresh green ferns sprout above it like a feathered headdress.

Off The Beaten Track: Ruins of Rio Bec

The namesake of the Rio Bec style is not too far from Xpujil, across the road from the Pemex station and 35 km (22 m) into the rain forest. The ruins of Rio Bec were rediscovered recently after being **lost in the jungle for over 50 years** (lost to archaeologists if not to the local people). Their rediscovery, with the assistance of Juan Briceno, guard at Becan, was the subject of a television documentary. While there are plans to restore Rio Bec and a nearby site called Hormiguero, the present road conditions require a jeep, a guide, and a lot of time. Check to see if the rumored restoration has included an improved road. If not, Juan Briceno or the caretaker at Xpujil may be able to help you obtain a guide for the trip to these ruins.

Becan

At km 146 Admission fee a bit steep for so brief a visit • Becan is the largest of the three sites, with the most monumental buildings. Since it has been extensively excavated, more is known about its history than just the Rio Bec-style buildings still seen at the site today. Becan was occupied from at least 550 B.C. until about A.D. 1000. Sometime around A.D. 250, the site was fortified by a ditch, or dry "**moat**," 10 meters deep and 2 kilometers in circumference. It is estimated that the ditch would have taken 350,000 worker days to construct. Evidence of such early fortification is unusual in the ancient Maya world. Another unusual find at Becan is a building with stylistic influences from the great highland Mexican city of Teotihacan in which was buried a Teotihuacan vase and figurines. Whether Teotihuacan traders had a base here (obsidian from central Mexico is found at Becan) or briefly controlled the site is unknown. All other aspects of Becan are Maya.

Restorations in 1984 revealed the awesome scale of the buildings surrounding the main plaza. The building facing you upon entering the plaza was crowned with what may have been elite residences. By climbing this building (*access is less steep at the rear*), you can see these elite residences surrounding a small plaza on top. Some remnants of carvings remain as well as benches that would have served as sleeping areas. A sweat bath has been identified nearby. A path off the northwest corner of the plaza leads through the jungle and past other complexes; some still shrouded in vegetation, others partially and tantalizingly restored. The path ends at a restored temple decorated with a monster mask.

Chicanna

At km 144, turn left at sign for ruins Admission charge • Chicanna is small, but elegant, with many well preserved carvings. It is contemporary with Becan, yet so close as to make you wonder what their relationship could have been. So many ruins in this small region suggest a stupendous population during the Late Classic Maya period (A.D. 600-900). (In fact, archaeological surveys of the area around Becan support this casual impression. The studies indicate that a minimum of **2.7 million Maya** lived in a 10,000 square kilometer area, and less conservative estimates would give this area a population density greater than modern Massachusetts.) Today, the area is only sparsely settled, and the jungle has reclaimed the land to such an extent that most of the ruins remain unexplored and some may still await discovery. Chicanna was discovered only in 1967, and **Temple XX,** just 300 yards from the main plaza, was not discovered until 1970. The only major plaza is bordered by a Rio Bec structure on the west (**Structure I**) and a magnificent Chenes-style (see Index) temple on the east (**Structure II**). The nature of the buildings on the other two sides is not known although the serpent steps on one are visible. It is Structure II that fascinates. The center building represents an open-mouth reptile, **its entrance forming the monster's mouth.** On the lintel are the monster's teeth; just above are its snout and eyes. The temple platform is slightly raised to form the lower jaw. The monster motif is repeated in a large profile at the sides of the entrance and then in verticle rows of miniature profiles. On the right you can see remnants of hieroglyphs, painted red. The monster probably represents the entrance to the Maya Underworld. To the left of the monster temple is a well-preserved facade of a symbolic thatched house, the temple entrance representing its door.

A short walk along the path behind Structure II leads to **Structure VI,** which has a well-preserved roof comb and a panel of monster masks. A path to the north passes by Structure I before turning right and leading to **Structure XX,** which is simply beautiful—with stone carvings of the monster mask and corners adorned with verticle rows of long-nosed masks. A monster-jaw step leads you into this building with benches.

WHERE TO STAY

Chetumal has some modern, air-conditioned hotels along with several plain, bare-and-basic ones. Finding hotel space, especially in the cheaper hotels, can often be a problem, so if possible reserve in advance. Chetumal can get very hot and steamy; although ceiling fans can work wonders, for some people air conditioning may be a necessity. If you want to bypass Chetumal on your way to the ruins or beaches, check the listing for Bacalar where there also is the Trailer Park Cenote Azul, just off MEX 307 and right across from the cenote. *For reservations in the city, write Chetumal, Q.R., Mexico or call area code 983.*

MODERATE

Los Cocos   ★★★
Av. de los Heroes 138, near Chapultepec; ☎ *2-05-44; $80* • The best

hotel in Chetumal is a refreshing relief from the numerous, somewhat depressing, budget hotels. Located about 2 blocks south of the old market, this modern structure has a welcoming garden and pool. The ample rooms are air-conditioned, carpeted, and cheery. Bathrooms are fresh and clean. Restaurant bar with entertainment. Parking. Luxurious by Chetumal standards.

Rancho Encantado

Laguna Bacalar, 5 km off MEX 307; $120 MAP • Just beyond the checkpoint on the road to Cancún, a right turn will lead you to this lakeside retreat. The attractively decorated and well-maintained 5 garden cottages each include a dining/sitting area, kitchenette, ample bedroom, tiled bath, and terrace. Swimming dock, windsurfing, boats, some excursions. During winter season 3 night stay required; no children under 12. Contact Box 1644 in Taos, NM. ☎ (505-758-3065) or Apartado 233 in Chetumal.

INEXPENSIVE

Laguna

Costera of Bacalar; $37 • This hotel is right on the edge of Lake Bacalar and most of its 35 fan-cooled, clean and simple rooms have balconies and lake views. A tranquil spot for swimming in the lake or pool; a convenient one for those with cars visiting the sights between Palenque and Cancún, but not requiring a Chetumal stop. Restaurant and bar. Parking.

El Cedro

Heroes 105 at Calles; ☎ *2-68-78; $29* • Above a row of shops right in the center, this modern and plain hotel offers 18 large, clean rooms with a/c.

Principe

Av. Heroes 326; ☎ *2-47-99; $32* • About two blocks before Insurgentes and one mile from the bay is this modern hotel with 50 ample rooms with tiled baths and air conditioning.

WHERE TO EAT

Although Chetumal is no mecca for food, you won't die of starvation here either, and on occasion you will be pleasantly surprised. Seafood, including *caracol*, one of the specialties of the area, is widely available. Small restaurants specializing in tacos come and go, yet with persistence you can find some tasty ones. Venison (*venado*) appears on some menus, and pizza has arrived in Chetumal. Yucatecan beer is available. Popular with some locals is the native drink *aguardiente*, distilled from sugarcane and affectionally called "*el fuerte*" (the strong one). Actually, it is not as strong as tequila and is pleasant tasting—if a bit rough. Price categories are explained in the Introduction.

Cafeteria Los Milagros

Zaragoza between Heroes and 5 de Mayo • A good place to stop any time of the day. Popular with Chetumalenos as well as the local foreign community, the outdoor tables here are full of locals catching up on town news. The menu is extensive and includes options for breakfast, lunch (try the special *torta milagros,* a hearty sandwich with milanesa, cheese, and much more), dinner (fish filet and numerous Mexican specialities like the spicy *puntas de filete Milagros*), or just a snack or refreshing fruit *licuado.* The food is good, the owners are friendly, and the prices inexpensive. Open 7 a.m.-10 p.m.; Sunday till noon.

Sergio's Pizzas

Av. Obregon 182 • Unlikely, but true, there is good pizza in Chetumal, and it is served by Sergio in an attractive setting. The restaurant has rapidly become one of the most popular evening dining places, and with good reason. The pizza will satisfy most tastes, but you pay for the quality (moderate). A variety of additional toppings available. Spaghetti (inexpensive) and flavorful steaks (moderately expensive) are also served. There is a salad bar. Near the lighthouse on the Boulevard Bahia, you can enjoy the evening breezes with the *Chetumalenos* by dining on the seafood at **Paco's** or the beef *brocheta* and *queso fundido* at **El Patio.** Both often have music at night; both are moderate.

For more portable dining, consider taking out one of the tasty chickens roasted on a spit at **Pollo Brujo** (*Obregon 208*). For tacos, walk over to Av. Carmen Ochoa de Merino near the corner of Juarez (across from Veterinaria del Caribe, a reliable place for having your animals cared for) where you will find a blue shed housing a small restaurant that serves tasty tacos at inexpensive prices.

GETTING TO AND FROM CHETUMAL

There is some plane service to Chetumal, regular bus service, and fairly good roads linking Chetumal with Mérida, Cancún, and Villahermosa. At this writing, there is one agency for car rentals in Chetumal; otherwise, if you plan excursions by rental car (the only way to see most of the sights outside of Chetumal) make arrangements in Mérida or Cancún.

AIR

Few choices here. Aerocaribe flies turbojets to Flores, Guatemala, Cancún, Villahermosa, and Cozumel; Aviacsa, non-stop to Mexico City. Smaller airlines operate out of airport; only Bonanza flies non-stop to Mérida. Collective vans and taxis are available at the airport.

BUS

Daily, regular bus service connects Chetumal with Mexico City, Veracruz, and Villahermosa. Many buses a day run from Chetumal to Tulum, Playa del Carmen, and Cancún, and buses travel frequently between Chetumal and Mérida as well as to Belize City via Corozal and Orange Walk. Deluxe, non-stop buses run to Cancún and Mérida.

CAR

Decent roads connect Chetumal with Cancún, Mérida, and Palenque-Villahermosa. To Cancún, follow MEX 186 to MEX 307 (5 hours); to Mérida, take MEX 186 to 307 to 184. MEX 184 passes through a number of attractive Maya villages with traditional white Maya huts (6 hours). To Palenque-Villahermosa, follow MEX 186 via Escarcega. The scenery is not particularly interesting, but you will pass the archaeological sites of Xpujil, Becan, Chicanna, and Kohunlich (see "Excursions"). For Palenque, you need to make a left off MEX 186; for Villahermosa, continue on 186 (Palenque, 6 hours; Villahermosa, 7 hours).

DIRECTORY

Airlines • *Air Caribe*, Airport ☎ (2-66-75); and *Aviacsa*, Hotel del Prado ☎ (2-76-76).

Bus Terminal • *Terminal Autotransportes del Caribe*, Insurgentes near Av. de los Heroes, on periphery of town.

Car Rentals • *Hertz*, in Hotel Del Prado ☎ (2-05-44)—maybe. You can rent in Mérida or Cancún.

Combi Terminal • Hidalgo at Primo Verdad, near old market.

Consulates • *Belize*, Obregon 10 ("notario publico"); *Guatemala*, Obregon 342 ☎ (2-13-65).

Groceries • Market; *Blanco*, next to bus terminal.

Post Office • Av. Plutarco Calles 2A at 5 de Mayo.

Telegrams • See Post Office.

Tourist Office • Information kiosk, Heroes at Aguilar.

Travel Advice • For information about Chetumal and the surrounding area including Belize, you can contact Valerie Searle, an English-speaking resident, near Bacalar at the Trailer Park Cenote Azul, just off MEX 307. Valerie has a wealth of information about roads, sights, swimming, restaurants, shopping—you name it. Over the years, she has helped many travelers with sage advice and incredible warmth.

PACIFIC COAST RESORTS

Acapulco Bay

The western Sierra Madre mountains create a dramatic backdrop for the ribbon of beaches and resorts that stretch from Mazatlán through Puerto Vallarta, Manzanillo, Ixtapa/Zihuatanejo, and Acapulco and all the way to Puerto Escondido and Huatulco, about a thousand miles south of Mazatlán. Where these Sierras, covered with lush tropical vegetation, tumble right into the sea, they create scenic bays at Acapulco, Puerto Vallarta, and Zihuatanejo. And tucked away off the Pacific Coast highways (MEX 15 and MEX 200) are less developed areas for the adventurous beach lover to explore, from fishing villages such as San Blas and isolated resort hotels along the Costa de Oro to lonely coves like Destiladeras. (See index.)

The variety offered by the large resorts allows you to choose a spot for your winter vacation that best suits your tastes. Urban Acapulco can't be matched for chic restaurants and nightclubs; Mazatlán is the favorite for deep-sea fishing. Puerto Vallarta may not have Acapulco's chic, but its nightclubs swing just the same and its shopping is the best of all. Zihuatanejo, with its first-class companion at Ixtapa, is the most tranquil, offering a retreat in a splendid setting. Manzanillo is best for those wanting self-contained resort hotels rather than a resort town; and little Puerto Escondido is favored by surfers and beachcombers, while Huatulco is targeted for major development.

With the exception of Puerto Escondido, these resorts offer you luxuries you might not be able to afford at home. The best hotels have waiter service at your pool (and often on the beach) and provide live entertainment around sunset. Some pools have a "swim-up bar." Watersports abound. Parachute rides over the bays, golf, tennis, and even horseback riding are available, and usually cruises with dancing and entertainment, deep-sea fishing trips, and excursions to paradisical beaches. Evenings feature all sorts of entertainments, but you are *never required to dress formally.* So alert to your needs are these resort hotels that even the bellhops speak a bit of English (though a "gracias" here and there is always appreciated).

PRACTICAL TIPS

For peak season (December 15-April 15), when resort prices are highest, *reservations should be booked months in advance.*

So good is the winter weather that some hotels boast they will refund your money for any day spoiled by rain. June, September, and October are the rainiest months at these resorts and the worst time to plan a visit. Other summer months have decent weather—hotter and more humid than the winter and with occasional rain, but good enough for you to enjoy the considerably cheaper prices. Even in July and August you should reserve in advance, as Mexican families take their vacations then.

Check with your travel agent for packaged tours in both winter and summer for less expensive rates.

Be cautious with the tropical sun (bring strong sunscreen lotion with you). Use the palapas, or thatched umbrellas, provided for shade on the beaches.

Under Mexican law, all beaches are public.

Accommodations in the chapters that follow are listed by high winter rates. There is no set policy for reductions during the summer. Usually only the inexpensive hotels have the same rates year-round; most others offer reductions from 10-50%.

Note: *Leave your valuables in the hotel, not unattended on the beach. Accidents on rented mopeds and parachute rides are not uncommon.*

ACAPULCO

Acapulco, the reigning queen of Pacific resorts, is justly famous for its magnificent bay surrounded by mountains, its ultramodern, deluxe high-rise hotels, and its fabulous night life that can keep you entertained from sunset to dawn. Critics say it lacks Mexican atmosphere, but you can find Mexican touches: Regional bark paintings and ceramics are for sale, Mexican food is available along with international cuisines, and Caleta and Puerto Marques beaches are full of **Mexican ambience.** Yet as the oldest Mexican resort, Acapulco's appearance and atmosphere remind you of established urban resorts everywhere from those on the French Riviera to Miami. Being urban has defects and assets. Most of the beaches are crowded, most hotels cluster together, and the bay is not quite clean; the main drag of **Costera Aleman** is as congested as most city streets. Yet congestion is what makes Acapulco exciting, for it results in countless good restaurants, nightclubs, and discos and creates a stimulating, vibrant atmosphere that each year attracts thousands upon thousands of tourists from around the world.

While Acapulco is the *oldest Mexican resort,* it is far from decaying. The Mexican government continues to renovate the water system, roads, and infrastructure of Acapulco to prepare this resort for the **21st century.** New parks have been added, and the old town zócalo area has been pleasantly refurbished. As Acapulco looks increasingly to the future, it leaves far behind the pre-Hispanic Indian village named Acapulco (meaning "Place where the reeds were destroyed") and the Spanish port that traded with the Orient and was besieged by pirates like Sir Francis Drake. Such pieces of history can be found only in books because Acapulco belongs totally to the jet age.

KEY TO ACAPULCO

Sights • This ultramodern, sophisticated resort has many beaches and coves apart from strikingly scenic Acapulco Bay. The Sea World-style aquarium, Spanish fort, and small archaeology museum offer some diversion from resort activity.

Excursions • A day trip to colonial Taxco for silver shopping and sightseeing is popular; due to excellent air connections with Mexico City, Acapulco can be easily combined with a visit to other sections of Mexico.

Sports • Swimming; tennis; golf; deep-sea fishing for sailfish, marlin, and tuna from December to March, and red snapper all year; freshwater

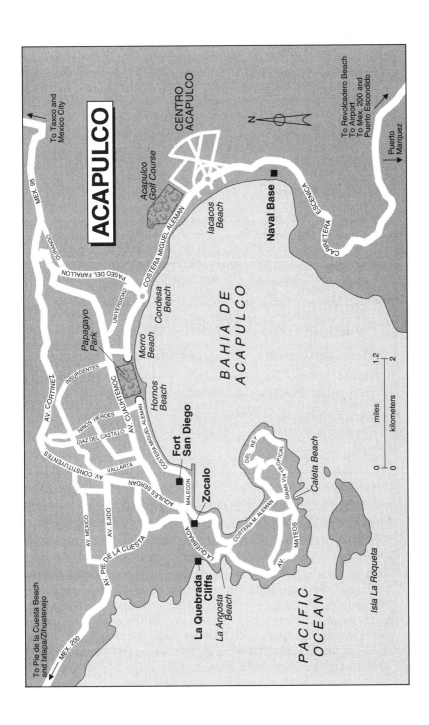

fishing in nearby lagoons; sailing; waterskiing; parachute rides over the bay and horseback riding at the Princess Hotel beach.

Shopping • Not particularly good for quality crafts, but lots of clothing and specialty boutiques.

Where to Stay • Countless modern deluxe and first-class resort hotels and surprisingly numerous moderate and inexpensive hotels. Camping, too.

Where to Eat • Acapulco has all kinds of food in many price ranges; like all coastal resorts, it has excellent seafood, too.

Entertainment • From noon to dawn, you can dance, listen to music, choose all kinds of shows in what must be one of the great night spots of the world.

Getting Around • Acapulco sprawls, so exploring it on foot is none too easy. Buses run all the way from Caleta to Puerto Marques and from the zócalo to Pie de la Cuesta; horse-drawn carriages ply the central Costera Aleman area; car rentals and taxis are plentiful. Good maps are posted in the bus stops along the Costera.

Practical Tips • Acapulco dress is casual, but any kind of trendy dress is much appreciated though shorts and jeans are banned in the evening by many restaurants and discos.

Shops close between 1-4 p.m. but often reopen until 8 or 9 p.m.

Check the taxi rates posted in front of major hotels and restaurants and pay the driver just that amount.

A recent bay clean-up improved swimming conditions; some bathers, however, still prefer to confine themselves to pools.

WHAT TO SEE AND DO

Getting around Acapulco's beaches and visiting town or the fine museum at the old fort require some means of transportation other than your legs. Or you can just stay put at your hotel enjoying the abundant watersports.

BEACHES

Acapulco is large and sprawling, curving around numerous bays and fronting on the open Pacific. Centrally located playas (beaches) are lively, filled with beach chairs, sunbathers, vendors of mangos, and watersports facilities from inner tubes to parachute rides. Beach chairs usually belong to a restaurant, hotel, or some other enterprise, and there may be a small rental fee for their use. Far-flung beaches are quieter but usually have much stronger surf requiring extreme caution.

Acapulco's most famous beaches stretch along Acapulco Bay to form a broad, continuous expanse of sand from town to the east at the naval station. Beach names vary along this stretch, but the wide avenue of Costera

Miguel Aleman—lined with shops, hotels, restaurants, and most of Acapulco's tourist attractions—runs its complete length. The most swinging
part of the Acapulco scene is along **Condesa Beach,** where afternoon dancing is not unheard of and where tourists flock to chic boutiques and trendy
restaurants. Condesa's influence has spilled east (beyond the Centro Acapulco to the Naval Base) along **Icacos Beach,** where an increasing number
of high-rise hotels appear each year; and west (past the Diana Circle) to the
broad expanse of **El Morro Beach,** which is rapidly becoming indistinguishable from its more famous neighbor. Farther west, toward town (where the
Costera Aleman emerges from the underpass), there's a less fanciful section
with numerous good swimming beaches. Collectively called **Hornos Beach**
this stretch of sand is officially designated a "public" beach, which seems
to mean only that no hotels are built on it since all beaches in Mexico are
public. There are good and bad days for cleanliness in this bay, just as there
are for strong undertow. Look for red flags warning of dangerous swimming conditions.

If you follow the Costera Aleman through town you will pass the dock
area, or **Malecón,** where you can stroll along **Fisherman's Walk** or continue
west to old Acapulco nestled about **Caleta Beach.** In the early years when
Acapulco was first discovered as a vacation wonderland, it was to this section that tourists came. No longer fashionable but undergoing a revival,
Caleta is more a beach for families, with the giant waterslides of its **Magic
Marine World** (8 a.m.-7 p.m.; fee). From Caleta boats provide a 10-minute
shuttle service to **Roqueta Island** with its beach and tangled trails leading
to lookout points. Or you can simply rent your own paddle or sail boat to
make the trip. The murkiness of the bay should lessen the appeal of snorkeling equipment or the glass-bottom boats ("fondo de cristal"). When
there are enough people, you can arrange a boat to take you to Puerto
Marques (see below).

AND MORE BEACHES

The Costera Aleman, or some such continuation of it, curves past Caleta
Beach and starts climbing rocky cliffs above the Pacific. It passes the small
cove called **La Angosta** and continues to the **Quebrada Cliffs,** where divers
plunge into the Pacific 156 feet below every day at 1, 7:30, 9:30, and
10:30 p.m. Down Quebrada's main street, you'll drive through town and
back to the Malecón. But if you follow MEX 200 north for 13 km (8 m),
you'll come to the **Pie de la Cuesta Beach,** a favorite spot for sunset watch-
ers (its rough surf makes swimming forbidden). As you enter la Cuesta,
drive the length of the 2-km road to pick out your favorite restaurant, be
it on the oceanside or along the tranquil **Coyuca Lagoon.** This freshwater
lagoon once was a birdwatcher's paradise, but it now is the favorite spot for
waterskiing. Also, there are boat tours and rentals.

Taking Costera Aleman in the opposite direction from town toward Icacos Beach, you pass the naval station and drive along the scenic road (Carretera Escenica) toward the airport. As you pass Las Brisas Hotel and
descend a hill, watch for a turnoff to **Puerto Marques,** a most Mexican and
tropical cove so continuously lined with food stands that you can barely

find the beach. Once there, you can collapse in a beach chair and order a song from a musician or rent a sailboat. Our next beach is **Revolcadero.** Revolcadero is a long expanse of sand with rough open surf. The public portion is reached by turning right off the airport road just beyond Puerto Marques near the Pemex station and continuing along the lagoon to the beach. Here there's a pool (fee), chairs, and a restaurant. Farther along this beach you can rent horses for a ride in front of the Pierre Marques and Princess hotels.

OTHER SIGHTS

If the beach gets to you, consider deep-sea fishing, golf, tennis, or even a bullfight during the winter season (uneven in quality). Or take a yacht cruise with live music, dancing, food, and drinks while you tour the bay and stop at one of its beaches, like the Puerto Marques, for a swim. The Bonanza yacht even has a stern that lowers to the sea for swimming. A tour of the city, on your own or through an agency, should include not only a walk around the pleasant zócalo that opens to the Malecón, it should definitely also include nearby **El Fuerte San Diego,** the old Spanish fort now handsomely renovated into a museum of the city with displays emphasizing the epoque of the Manila galleon and Acapulco's trade with the Orient. (Open Tuesday-Sunday 10:30 a.m.-5 p.m.; fee). If you have children, take them to CICI. **CICI** (toward Icacos Beach) has dolphin shows, an aquarium of sharks, "crazy" whales, a freshwater pool with artificially created waves, waterslides, and more (10 a.m.-6 p.m.; fee). If you're curious about Acapulco's most ancient past, visit the small **archaeology museum** and art gallery at the Centro Cultural (open 10 a.m.-2 p.m., 5-8 p.m.; closed Sunday) on the Costera, just past the Centro Acapulco. You might like to take a day off from Acapulco entirely and visit picturesque **Taxco** (see "Mexico City Excursions"), 3-1/2 hours away by tour, car, or bus.

SHOPPING

Some of the most ardent shoppers used to stay right on the beach and bargain the day away with vendors of jewelry, T-shirts, and the occasional craft item, like baskets or Guerrero masks. Since 1990, itinerant vendors have been banned, but you can find more of the same at curio markets like **Artesanias Finas Acapulco** (*Av. Horacio Nelson near Baby-O's*) where onyx souvenirs and charro hats also can be bought. Unfortunately, we couldn't find any shops offering the more sublime examples of Mexican folk art.

While crafts shopping is noticeably poor in Acapulco, you will find more than enough resorts and designer clothing, quality leather and silver often at prices considerably lower than at home. Many of the best shops can be found along the Costera from Condesa to El Morro Beach. **Armando,** in the Torre Acapulco, carries his own designs as well as the beribboned and colorful clothes of Josefa; across the street is **Fiorucci.** Toward the Diana Circle, around the Presidente hotel, are the casual clothes of **Ruben Torres** in addition to the youthful sports clothes of **Ocean Pacific.** Just before the Diana Circle, you find Girasol and **Sergio Bustamante's** art gallery across from **Polo Ralph Lauren, Aca Joe,** and the **Marti** sporting goods complex, unmissable with its statue of a hurdler. Next door is the Marbella shopping complex, with a branch of **Piaget/Pelletier** jewelers. Crossing the Diana Circle you come to the multileveled mall at the **Acapulco Plaza,** with branches of many of the above shops plus the fine silver of **Emi Fors.** For those homesick for a real American mall, the **Plaza Bahia** next door might do the trick. Completely air-conditioned and enclosed, the mall offers everything from chocolate chip cookie kiosks to Acapulco's most chic boutiques.

WHERE TO STAY

Acapulco has hundreds of hotels from in-town budget ones to inexpensive ones scattered about the coves of Caleta beach, to moderate and very expensive hotels clustered about the main strip of Costera Aleman, to super-deluxe resorts located outside of the congestion near Revolcadero Beach. Your selection of a hotel determines not only the cost, however, but also which Acapulco you'll experience the most—the village atmosphere of Caleta, the bustle of the Costera high-rises, or the quiet of the isolated resort hotels. Buses run west from town to Caleta and, of course, along the Costera Aleman. The fanciest remote hotels provide their own transportation into the Costera Aleman area. While the highest prices occur from **December 15 to April 15,** around the end of February some hotels increase rates for George Washington's birthday. A few hotels require meal plans during the winter season. Below are listed hotels in each category according to their highest winter rates; only inexpensive hotels with a pool, sea view, or some beach amenity are recommended. Unless otherwise noted, hotels are air-conditioned and charge fees for tennis, golf, and the like. For reservations, address your letter to Acapulco, Guerrero, Mexico, or call area code 74.

RESORT EXPENSIVE

Las Brisas ★★★★★

Carretera Escenica 5255; ☎ *84-15-80; $237* • A picturesque complex of 300 villas built into the mountainside, on hundreds of acres overlooking the Pacific, about 11 km (7 m) from town toward the airport. Each duplex villa, or suite, has either a semiprivate or private pool; the price varies according to which you choose as well as its location on the mountain. No tipping allowed; instead you pay a set service fee. Remarkable for its luxury and privacy, this hotel has restaurants and elegant disco, free membership in La Concha Beach Club, two saltwater pools, a beach, watersports, a health spa, and tennis and jeeps. Golf nearby. For reservations, call, in the U.S., ☎ *800-722-6466.*

Acapulco Princess ★★★★★

Airport Highway; ☎ *84-31-00; $300 MAP* • On the wide ocean expanse of Revolcadero Beach and amid hundreds of acres, this luxurious hotel is 17 km (10-1/2 m) from town. The lobby of its famous pyramid-shape main building is open on its sides, framing a magnificent oceanfront and allowing fresh tropical breezes to sweep through. Its tropical ambience is enhanced by trees growing right in the lobby and the sound of waterfalls everywhere. Outside, one magnificent pool is designed to look like a natural, forested river, with rock slides, a suspended bridge, and a swim-up bar under a waterfall. With over 1000 rooms (not all with sea views), this immense hotel also shares facilities with the Pierre Marques (see below). At the Princess are nine restaurants, bars, a nightclub, boutiques, many tennis courts, five pools, an 18-hole golf course, all watersports, and horseback riding on the beach. Transportation around grounds provided. MAP required in winter. For reservations, call, in the U.S., ☎ *800-223-1818.*

Pierre Marques

Airport Highway; ☎ *84-20-00; $212* • CP On Revolcadero Beach and surrounded by 240 acres of gardens and a championship golf course, this country-club-style hotel is adjacent to the Princess. Smaller than the Princess and with less elaborate architecture and facilities, the Pierre Marques combines a club atmosphere with an attractive beach setting. Its 340 units of suites, villas, and bungalows, many with terraces and views of the beach, are spread about its extensive grounds. In addition to its three restaurants, bar, pools, tennis courts, 18-hole golf course, and sauna, you can use the facilities of the Princess Hotel (connected by regular bus service). MAP required in winter. Closed off season. For reservations, call, in the U.S., ☎ *800-223-1818.*

Villa Vera Racquet Club

Loma del Mar 35; ☎ *84-03-33; $205-320* • In the foothills and within walking distance of Condesa Beach, this chic and exclusive enclave may lack sand and surf but certainly not anything else. The 95 units are tastefully placed amid vast gardens and vary from villas with enormous terraces, bars, sunken bathtubs, and private pools to sumptuous suites sharing pools and simpler "superior" rooms the size of most junior suites. The main pool, bar, and restaurant overlook Acapulco Bay. Clay tennis courts; fitness center; Jacuzzis, sauna, and massage. Beach club with watersports. No children under 16 permitted; 10% surcharge for service. The hotel can be located by turning off Costera at Prado, then turning left onto Loma del Mar. Write Apartado 560.

Exelaris Hyatt Regency

Costera Aleman 1; ☎ *84-28-88; $175-205* • On Icacos Beach next to the naval base, this large high-rise hotel has an extensive and elegant lobby, six restaurants, coffee shop, bars, nightclub, and fine shops, but lacks the atmosphere of the beach. What its formal lobbies lack, its 649 exceptionally large rooms have in abundance: sliding-glass doors and balconies offer fabulous views of Acapulco Bay. Large pool with swim-up bar; sauna, tennis, and access to watersports. Golf nearby. Parking. For reservations, call in the U.S., ☎ *800-228-9000.*

Acapulco Plaza ★★★★

Costera Aleman 123 on El Morro Beach; *85-80-50; $185* • This deluxe Holiday Inn is exceptionally well maintained, with an open breezy lobby and sunken garden with macaws and peacocks providing the focus for the 1000 rooms and suites here. Rooms are ample and comfortable, with angled views of the sea. Many restaurants and bars with entertainment, including one in the lobby, where live and loud rock music captivates many and drives others mad (especially those with rooms overlooking the main pool). Shops. Two pools next to beach, others in the health club along with saunas and steam baths. Tennis courts. Watersports. Parking. For reservations, call, in the U.S., ☎ *800-238-8000.*

VERY EXPENSIVE

Fiesta Americana Condesa ★★★★

Costera Aleman on Condesa Beach; *84-23-55; $193* • One of Acapulco's first high-rise beach hotels, the Condesa was modernized recently. It's located in the heart of Acapulco's tourist zone and has a spectacular pool that seems suspended right over the sea. Its 500 large rooms and suites all have sea views. Two restaurants and bars; a rooftop supper club with dancing. Shops. Two pools and watersports. Pleasant service. For reservations, call, in the U.S., ☎ *800-223-2332.*

EXPENSIVE

Acapulco Ritz ★★★

Costera Aleman on El Morro Beach *85-73-36; $120* • This delightful hotel is most Mexican in ambience, decorated as it is with crafts and vibrating pinks and soft blues. Its lobby and common areas are breezy and comfortable, many of them overlook the broad beach and sea. With 225 rooms, those with balconies are very large, well furnished, and with fabulous ocean views. Shops, restaurants, bars, and nightclub. Pool and watersports. Parking. Write Apartado 259.

La Palapa ★★★

Fragata Yucatán 210; *84-53-63; $110* • At Icacos Beach across from the Centro Acapulco, this 30-story hotel has a large open lobby with plants and wicker chairs adding informality. Its 340 units are all junior suites, many with terraces overlooking the ocean. Three restaurants, bar, disco, two freeform pools, watersports on beach. Arrangements for tennis.

Calinda Acapulco ★★★

Costera Aleman on Condesa Beach; ☎ *84-04-10; $135* • Another white tower in the thick of the Acapulco "scene," this Mexican branch of Quality Inns has a breezy lobby and bar area, a somewhat congested pool, palapas on the beach, and 358 rooms, most with bay views. 2 restaurants, 2 lounges, and 2 pools. Parking. For reservations, call in the U.S. ☎ *800-228-5151.*

Maralisa

Enrique el Esclavo; ☎ *85-66-77; $120* • On El Morro Beach, this refreshingly small hotel is a relief from its high-rise neighbors. Modern, unpretentious, and well-maintained, the Maralisa has 100 pleasant rooms around its tranquil pools and sunning terraces. Restaurant and bar overlooking beach. Two pools, watersports, and sauna. Parking. Write Apartado 721.

Royal Elcano

Av. del Parque and Palmas; ☎ *84-19-50; 125* • Tucked away on a tranquil part of Icacos Beach and with good swimming waters, this 10-story hotel has been a good buy for those avoiding Acapulco's glitzy side. We can only hope recent remodeling will improve the 140 rooms without raising prices. All the rooms have terrific balconies with views of the sea, and the pool sits amid a lovely garden. Restaurant next to beach. Parking. Write Apartado 430.

Copacabana

Tabachines 2 on Icacos Beach; ☎ *84-31-55; $135* • This 16-story tower may be without some of the sybaritic touches of other beachfront hotels, but it is quite decent and functional. The 480 rooms have small furnished balconies with sea views. Shops. Restaurants and bars with entertainment. A good beach with pools and Jacuzzi. Parking.

MODERATE

Boca Chica

Caletilla Beach; ☎ *82-60-14; $150 MAP* • On a promontory overlooking Roqueta Island and Caleta Beach, this attractive and well-maintained hotel, built on a series of terraces, has 45 plain, yet fresh rooms with views of the ocean. Restaurant, bar, and pool overlook the bay. The private swimming cove is said to be good for snorkeling. MAP required during winter. Write Apartado 1211.

Majestic

Av. Pozo del Rey 73 in Caleta; ☎ *82-49-50; $85* • On the hill overlooking the bay, this hotel may have no beach (there are free van runs to Caleta Beach) but its 250 rooms are ample, and some have sea views, but they are pricier than the annex rooms in this price category. Two restaurants and lounges, one poolside. Tennis. To arrive, turn left at La Jolla Motel.

INEXPENSIVE

Belmar

Gran Via Tropical; ☎ *83-80-98; $67* • As you enter the area of Caleta Beach, turn left up the hill in front of the Hotel del Playa for about 1 1/2 blocks. The Belmar is a quiet hotel amid attractive gardens. Its 68 rooms are plain, clean, and quite spacious, all with large furnished terraces overlooking gardens. Restaurant, two small pools. Within walking distance of Caleta Beach. Parking. A good buy.

Versalles √★

Gran Via Tropical; ☎ *82-60-02; $42* • Next to the Belmar, this clean hotel has 50 fresh, air-conditioned rooms with balconies and many with views back into town over Acapulco Bay. Dining room. Small pool, and within walking distance of Caleta Beach. Parking.

Doral Playa ★

Costera Aleman 265; ☎ *85-02-32; $55* • Across the street from Hornos Beach, this is an older hotel, but the 143 rooms are adequate, some with ocean views and balconies. Restaurant, a small rooftop pool, and sunning terrace.

BUDGET

Lindavista

Caleta Beach; ☎ *82-27-83; $50* • A few steps from Caleta Beach, the Lindavista is a very plain but bright hotel quite popular with Mexican families. The 45 rooms vary; some have small balconies. Tiny pool. Parking.

WHERE TO EAT

You can't possibly starve in Acapulco. Dozing on the beach and feeling slight hunger pangs, you need only open your eyes and gesture to the nearest waiter or buy a mango from a passing beach vendor. Sudden cravings for fettucine Alfredo, lobster, or even a bowl of American chili con carne are satisfied only too easily. Waking in the middle of the night with thoughts of food, you can go to the **24-hour Vips** overlooking Condesa Beach, or even have breakfast at an all-night disco. Food at various prices in a variety of cuisines and settings abounds everywhere. Price categories are explained in the Introduction.

LUNCH ON THE BEACH

Considering lunch, you might want to stay put in your swim clothes and eat at your hotel's terrace restaurant or visit the **Chula Vista** at the Acapulco Princess for an excellent salad (expensive) and a view of Revolcadero Beach. Most popular for late-afternoon meals and festivities is Condesa Beach. Many establishments line Condesa Beach with both restaurants open to the sea and palapa dining right on the beach. **Beto's** is our favorite. It manages to serve consistently good grilled red snapper and shrimp to the dance tunes of its salsa band, and at only moderately expensive prices. Lively, but not noisy, it's recommended from noon to midnight. Upstairs, overlooking the beach, but not on it, is **Mimi's Chili Saloon** (open noon-midnight), with moderately priced chili, hamburgers, nachos, and home fries. Or if the prices at Condesa are too high or the ambience not Mexican enough, try one of the shady beach restaurants at Caleta and Los Hornos, where the food is more moderately priced, especially a caldo de camaron (shrimp soup). At Puerto Marques, the beachcomber-style shacks offer an even more rustic atmosphere in which to try a decently priced mojarra (sea bass) or shrimp.

CHEAP MEXICAN EATS

Like cities around the world, Acapulco has many pricey restaurants and hotels charging more than you like to pay for breakfast or a club sandwich. Unlike many resorts, it also has many modest alternatives. One of the best is the chain **100% Natural**. The green awnings of its branches dot the Costera from Hornos beach to Icacos—one is even near the Princess. Many remain open 24 hours. The breakfasts are good (the toast is whole wheat), the salads and exotic fruit drinks delicious (all prepared with purified water), and the sandwiches hearty. Many other affordable establishments can be found for breakfast, snacks, or even a tasty main meal. Apart from the air-conditioned plastic splendor of **Vips** (a deal for breakfast), a good rule of thumb for locating these spots is to look for plain Mexican establishments that wouldn't know about that gringo specialty called a "combination plate." Fortunately, these clean and unpretentious restaurants can be found even in the Condesa Beach area, such as **La Tortuga**, in a garden a few steps up the side street marked by Denny's, with its reasonably priced huevos rancheros for breakfast and chiles rellenos. The Costera between the Acapulco Plaza and the Ritz, however, is a bonanza for such spots, with **El Zorrito** among the most popular with Mexicans for antojitos—pozole (hominy soup heaped with goodies), enchiladas, and the like. In the Icacos Beach area, there's another cluster of eateries near La Palapa as well as the northern Mexican restaurant, **El Cabrito**, a bit of a disappointment for its cabrito (roasted kid), but with less expensive items like queso asado, machaca estilo nortena (eggs with jerked beef), delicious charro beans, and guacamole. All these restaurants have items within the inexpensive range and serve breakfast through dinner.

In town are more inexpensive and budget restaurants than one could ever count. Our favorite for people-watching is the outdoor cafe at **La Flor de Acapulco**, right on the zócalo (breakfast till 2 a.m.) and a good place to sip coffee or enjoy Mexican snacks. A few blocks away, following Juarez off the zócalo, is our favorite seafood spot, the plain but clean **Nacho's** (*Jose Azueta at Juarez; 10 a.m.- 8 p.m.*). Lobster here runs the price of the red snapper at Condesa beach restaurants. We favor the even cheaper ceviche followed by a platter of shrimp. Then we round the corner for a slice of New York-style cheese cake or struedel at the **Fat Farm** (*Juarez 10; breakfast-10 p.m.*), a cafe run by and for the Acapulco Children's Home.

DINNER WITH AMBIENCE

Restaurants in Acapulco not only serve some sophisticated food, but they also usually have remarkable views or fabulous decors. While most establishments open between 6 and 7 p.m., the more elegant spots are busiest around 9 p.m.

In the expensive category, many of the restaurants seem to vie with each other for the best view over the bay or the most beautiful decor when they should be more concerned about the quality of their food. Among those that we found to have both good food and dramatic settings, **Madeiras** stands out as exceptional. Not only does it have a spectacular view over the bay and Acapulco, it serves imaginatively prepared food in a romantic, candlelit setting. Dinner here is a four-course, fixed-price meal in which you have plenty of choice with items such as huitlacoche crepes, with their rich, mushroomy flavor, for an appetizer, a cold guava soup, a wonderful fruit-and-nut- stuffed quail or Southwestern-flavored red snapper for an entree, with a chocolate torte for dessert. Located on the Carretera Escenica just beyond the Extravaganza disco, Madeiras is closed Sunday. (*Reserve as far in advance as possible;* ☎ *84-69-21.*) Nearby, across from Extravaganza, with superb views over the bay and city is the **Miramar**. Though a beautiful restaurant, the Miramar disappointed us on our last visit with tasteless, apparently long-frozen seafood. But those in the tour groups seemed better satisfied with their Chateaubriand. (*Open dinner only; reserve at* ☎ *84-78-74).* **Villa Demo's** (*Av. del Prado 6 off the Costera near La Torre Acapulco*) is away from the bay but beautiful nonetheless. Around a lush palm garden and fountain, this intimate restaurant serves decent Italian food—fine salads, fresh pastas (try the cannelloni), as well as seafood and veal dishes. Good service and highly recommended (☎ *84-20-40; closed Monday off-scason*). In a category all its own for both price and ambience is **Coyuca 22** (*at Av. Coyuca 22 in the Caleta area; follow signs off the Malecón; closed during the off season;* ☎ *82-34-68*). This elegant outdoor restaurant is a series of terraces floating off a mountainside with Acapulco Bay on one side and the Pacific on the other. Polished tableware, flickering candles, and Italianate columns and fountains spotlighted against the sky add romantic touches to what is already breathtaking. The prices rival those of very expensive restaurants in the U.S. and are double those of the preceding restaurants. Somehow, we don't think you're paying for the food—prime rib of beef, lobster—on the very limited menu here. **Casa Nova** (*Carretera Escenica near Las Brisas; closed Monday off season;* ☎ *84-68-15*), a new enterprise of the Coyuca owners, has a far more ambitious menu with many northern Italian specialties such as ravioli in lobster sauce and trout with artichoke hearts. We found, however, that the food (except for a lovely cappellini alla primavera) wasn't up to the celestial level of the prices. The setting, although beautiful, didn't quite elevate the glitz into more enjoyable kitsch. Maybe time will improve it. For all these restaurants, make reservations.

If you would like to enjoy some of Acapulco's restaurant ambience at more affordable prices, there are some moderately expensive restaurants to try. **Los Rancheros** (*out on the Carretera Escenica before La Vista Shopping Center*) is a casual Mexican restaurant with striking views of Acapulco Bay. While the English menu here offers a combination plate, you can also sample less costly chiles rellenos or more exotic items from the Spanish menu like a tasty sopa medula (bone marrow soup) or chicken mole. (*Open for lunch, too;* ☎ *84-19-08.*) You can keep to moderate prices at the very Japanese restaurant **Suntory** (*Costera Aleman near Hotel La Palapa*) by sitting in the handsome bar and enjoying fresh sushi and sashimi (☎ *84-80-88*). And don't forget the dancing and seafood at **Beto's** ("Lunch on the Beach").

Also in this category are two restaurants that are the best of those specializing in period decors—from the roaring twenties or scenes from Robert Louis Stevenson's novels. All these restaurants are noisy, lively, and extremely popular. **Carlos 'N Charlie's** (*Costera 999 near Condesa Beach*) serves the best food in the least overwhelming environment. Its extensive menu includes a variety of seafood and steak dishes, salads, and excellent ribs. (Open 6:30 p.m.-1 a.m. No reservations.) The lines might not be any shorter, but the views over the bay are superb at **Sr. Frog's**, a branch just down the hillside from the Miramar on the Carretara Escenica (open lunch, too). In our opinion, the **Embarcadero** (*on the Costera near the Hotel La Palapa;* ☎ *84-87-87; closed Monday off season*) is the nicest of the Sunshine Boys restaurants. (Others include **Blackbeard's** overlooking Condesa Beach.) Decorated with their usual attention to atmosphere, this one is designed as a wharf with crates as tables and a bridge over a crocodile-infested canal. International and Polynesian specialties.

DINNER WITH ENTERTAINMENT

A number of the resort hotels have supper clubs with music. Two to consider are the elegant **Bella Vista** (☎ *84-15-80; reservations required*) at Las Brisas, serving continental specialties to the accompaniment of music and superb bay views (*expensive; reservations required*; ☎ *84-15-80*); and the rooftop **Techo del Mar** (☎ *83-15-50; closed Sunday*) at the Fiesta Americana Condesa, with stunning panoramic views, music for dancing, and prime ribs, lobster, and flaming desserts. Both are expensive, the Bella Vista more so.

ENTERTAINMENT

As you've probably found out by reading the eating section, entertainment in Acapulco starts pretty early in the day. Yet we still have to cover cocktails and activities from late night to dawn. Sunset watching over a drink is the best way to finish your day in the sun. If you're energetic, you can taxi over to **Pie de la Cuesta Beach**, sit in a beach chair, order a drink, and watch the crashing surf and setting sun at this ideal viewing spot. Also, the stupendous views from the bar at **El Campanario** make a trip to the hilltop location of this restaurant worthwhile; you might even want to stay for dancing under the stars. (Located on the highest point above Condesa Beach.) If you've started your lunch late on **Condesa Beach**, you might just continue through the sunset. Or if dancing, not sunset watching, is your thing, check out the hotel lobbies where often you can dance to live rock music starting with 5 p.m. cocktails.

DISCOS AND NIGHTS SPOTS

There are so many discos and night spots with entertainment that we cannot possibly list them all. Better, we will try to give you a sense of the diversity available here. Most such entertainment is subject to cover charges. Hotels have their own discos and evening entertainment—like the rooftop **Numero Uno** at the Exelaris Hyatt Regency, with major performers like the Supremes—but to give you an idea of the extent of Acapulco's night life we will mention mostly clubs outside of hotels. For nightclubs, La Perla Restaurant (*in Plaza Las Glorias hotel;* ☎ *82-11-11*) has ringside seats for the **Quebrada cliff divers**. (You can watch the divers more cheaply by sitting at the terrace bar of the hotel or joining the public outside. Show times can vary, but usually performances occur at 7:30, 9:30, and 10:30 p.m. **El Fuerte**, across from Hornos Beach at Costera 239, offers two shows nightly (*10 and 11:30 of flamenco music and dancing. Closed Sunday;* ☎ *82-61-61*). Less traditional, but popular, is the **Gallery Show Bar**, a disco with shows performed by female impersonators (*Av. Deportes 11, a block off Costera near D'Joint*). Shows are at 11:30 p.m. and 1:30 a.m. And you can head out to sea on the yacht **Fiesta Cabaret** for a moonlight cruise with Mexican entertainment and floor show (*7:30-10:30 p.m. except Sundays;* ☎ *83-15-50*). Or check out the big show entertainment often available at the **Acapulco International Center**.

Discos don't start up until 11:00 p.m.; some don't even open before then, and many remain open until dawn. All are sleek and sophisticated, varying in their decor and, sometimes, their clientele. **Baby-O**, near the Centro Acapulco, has a very young crowd sustained by videos and rock music; while **Disco 9** (*Av. de los Deportes 9*) caters to gays. If you don't particularly fit into those categories or if you want to experience more places, try these very popular spots: The unmissable neon club called **Extravaganza** and **Fantasy**, both with dramatic bay views from their Carretera Escenica locations; **The News** (*across from Icacas Beach*), with its great tree of lights, large dance floor, and light show. Just in case all these options aren't earthy enough for you, there's a **red light district** for which you are on your own.

GETTING TO AND FROM ACAPULCO

AIR

Acapulco's airport is busy with jumbo jets landing from all over the United States. There's frequent service from Mexico City on both Mexicana and Aeromexico; and many international flights stop in Mexico City on their way to and from Acapulco, making it easy to include that city on your itinerary. Mexicana and Aeromexico flights also connect Acapulco directly with Guadalajara.

The airport is located 20 km (12 m) from the town, with a choice of air-conditioned limo, colectivo van, or bus transport into town. Buy tickets at the sidewalk desk (prices posted).

BUS

Estrella de Oro runs nearly hourly first-class buses to Mexico City (6-1/2 hours) as well as deluxe, non-stop service; reserve in advance. Some of these buses stop at Taxco and Cuernavaca. There's frequent service to Zihuantanejo, too. Second-class Flecha Roja runs buses to Puerto Escondido as well as Taxco, and the like. You might reserve your ticket in advance, especially on weekends. The trip to Mexico City takes a good 6-1/2 hours because of the climb through the mountains to the highland area. In Mexico City, Acapulco buses depart from the Terminal Central de Autobuses del Sur near the Metro Tasquena.

CAR

MEX 95 winds its way through the mountains to **Taxco** 270 km (167 m) away. Although the four-lane bypass of Iguala expedites this trip, it can take over 3 hours due to delays caused by the widening of the rest of the road. Beyond Taxco MEX 95D is a toll road to Cuernavaca, then on to Mexico City. Total distance: 438 km or 272 m, or under 6 hours. For more information on sights along this route see "Mexico City Excursions." The completion of MEX 95 D, the superhighway to Mexico City, is expected soon. Although it may reduce the travel time to 4 hours, it's also said the tolls might be equivalent to a Mexicana flight. Check on details locally.

The coastal road MEX 200 runs north along the Pacific for 230 km (145 m) before reaching the resort of **Ixtapa/Zihuatanejo,** in 4 hours. At Papanoa, 153 km (95 m) outside of Acapulco, begin magnificent stretches of beach that continue for 30 km to the palapa eateries at La Barrita. (Better yet is the food at Club Papanoa, at Km 155, north of Papanoa. Moderate.) MEX 200 south (turn left at Puerto Marquez intersection) takes you to **Puerto Escondido** (see "On the Road," below), 429 km (266 m) away and **Huatulco** (another 100 km, 60 m).

DIRECTORY

Airlines • *Aeromexico* ☎ (84-70-49) and *Mexicana* ☎ (84-81-92), both at Costera 1252 at Condesa Beach; *American* ☎ (84-12-44); *Continental* ☎ (84-69-00); and *Delta* ☎ (84-07-16).

American Express • Costera Aleman 709-1, Condesa Beach near Diana Circle ☎ (84-55-50).

Boats • Sailboats at Puerto Marquez and Caleta; fishing boats through hotels or at Malecón.

Books in English • Deluxe hotel shops; Sanborn's on Costera Aleman in town and at Condesa Beach.

Bullfights • October through Easter, at Cajetilla Stadium (quality variable). Reserve through hotel.

Buses • First-class Estrella de Oro ☎ (85-87-05), Cuauhtemoc at Massieu near Parque Papagayo; second-class Flecha Roja ☎ (83-30-70), Av. Ejido, downtown.

Consulates • *British* ☎ (84-66-05); *Canadian* ☎ (85-66-21; weekdays 9 a.m.-1 p.m.); *U.S. consul* ☎ (85-66-00 x273; weekdays 10 a.m.-2 p.m.).

Car Rentals • *Hertz* ☎ (85-68-89); *National* ☎ (84-56-08); SAAD ☎ (84-50-70) for safari jeeps. Many more agencies located at airport and in hotels.

Cruises • Yachts like the *Fiesta* and *Bonanza* ☎ (82-20-55) and the cata-maran *Aca Tiki* ☎ (84-61-40) leave from Malecón in town.

Fishing • Malecón at downtown pier has a yacht club for arrangements for deep-sea and lagoon fishing. Also, you can reserve through your hotel.

Groceries • In hotels; along Costera Aleman; in particular, Gigante across from Hornos Beach near underpass, Super Super across from Cici.

Golf • Nine-hole municipal course in front of Hotel Elcano and two 18-hole courses at the Princess and Pierre Marques hotels.

Horseback Riding • Revolcadero Beach; arrange through hotels.

Post Office • Costera Aleman in town near Sanborn's at 209.

Telegraph • See post office.

Tennis • *Club de Tenis Alfredo*, Prado 29 ☎ (84-00-24); *Villa Vera Racquet Club* at hotel of same name, and other deluxe hotels.

Tourist Office • Centro International Acapulco ☎ (84-70-50, ext. 165).

Tours • Located in major hotels for town tours, cruises, bullfights, and trips to Taxco.

Watersports • Beaches on Acapulco Bay have all facilities for parachuting, sailing, boating, and waterskiing. Caleta Beach best for renting small boats; Puerto Marques for sailing; Pie de la Cuesta for waterskiing.

ON THE ROAD

MEX 200 south (turn left at Puerto Marquez intersection) takes you to Puerto Escondido (429 km, 266 m) and Bahias de Huatulco (another 100 km, 60 m south). Although the road is dull driving, the region it passes through has a rich history. It skirts **Ometepec**, the former gold-mining town, now the decaying center of the Amusgo region where strong traditions have been protected by years of isolation. The Amusgos make fine cotton weavings, especially their wedding *huipils* with exquisite flower patterns woven into them. Other Indian groups, Mixtec and Chatino, live farther to the south. On the edge of the Amusgo region is **Cuaji** (234 km, 145 m), a village founded in colonial times by Bantu slaves, who escaped from a ship taking them to Acapulco (illegally, for slave trading was banned by Spain). Settling along this coast, they were later ruled by Johann Schmidt, a German-American tyrant who happened along here at the end of the 19th century. With no official authorization, he established his own kingdom and was deposed only with the Mexican Revolution of 1910. The combination of ethnic and racial groups along this coast is remarkable, and most easily seen at the Sunday market at **Pinotepa Nacional** (286 km, 178 m), in the heart of the Mixtec region. (Your best bet for food and lodging is here, at the Hotel Cremona, on the right as you enter town.) While the pre-Hispanic history is a mystery due to lack of excavations, ruins have been found along the coast (such as those on the hill overlooking **Tutepec**, 74 km, 46 m south of Pinotepa for turnoff). There is a lively but illicit international trade in antiquities originating from the interior of Guerrero. Many fine green stone Mezcalan figurines have reached art galleries in the U.S. and Europe from this region that also "exports" marijuana. Continuing on from Pinotepa Nacional, you pass the access road for the **Chacahua Lagoon** (at Zapotalito, not Chacahua, about 84 km) and **Manialtepec Lagoon** (on the road at Las Hamacas, about 128 km), both described under Puerto Escondido (143 km, 89 m) excursions, later in this chapter.

NOTE: Removing antiquities from Mexico is illegal.

PUERTO VALLARTA

When John Huston brought his movie crew to Puerto Vallarta (vah-YAR-tah) to film *Night of the Iguana*, very few tourists had discovered this then inaccessible fishing village. True, the few flights arriving did carry such famous individuals as Richard Burton and Elizabeth Taylor. With Hollywood stars enjoying the pleasures of this Pacific paradise, others were soon to follow. Hotel after hotel rushed to open in this once-rustic town, transforming it into the well-known resort it is today. While the *Libramiento*, the bypass road, has relieved some traffic congestion in town, the airport road continues to be scarred by unbridled construction. Until these development projects are completed, you must seek quiet on your beach, or on the Isla Cuale, or along the still magnificent stretch of road south toward Mismaloya.

Despite the congestion, Puerto Vallarta combines the beauty of the Pacific Coast and the luxury of resort beach hotels with the charm of a lively town. Pelicans fly low over the green waters of the Pacific while you relax on beaches that range from broad open expanses of sand with crashing surf to small coves dramatically formed by the Sierra Madre mountains tumbling into the ocean—coves so quiet that crabs sunbathe on nearby rocks. When the sun sets, the Pacific turns fiery, so wondrous that it demands all movement stop for one breathtaking moment. Into this magnificent setting on the **Bay of Banderas,** enters the modern resort with its luxurious resort hotels with beachfront locations, tropical gardens, and sybaritic swim-up bars. Then there is the busy town with its cobblestone streets and tiled-roof villas climbing up cliffsides, its breezy Malecón along the oceanfront and bustling town beach, its boutiques and art galleries and restaurants galore.

KEY TO PUERTO VALLARTA

Sights • One of Mexico's three most popular urban resorts, Puerto Vallarta offers a combination of natural beauty and luxury centered on a bustling town.

Excursions • Visits to Yelapa and other remote beaches like Quimixto and Las Animas can be made by leisurely boat trips. Lively Mismaloya can be visited by land or sea. The city of Guadalajara is only a half-hour away by plane.

Sports • Waterskiing, parasailing (parachute ride); snorkeling and scuba diving at Los Arcos and Quimixto; golf, tennis, fishing for sailfish and marlin (Nov.-May), and snapper, bass, tuna, and bonito; horseback riding and even donkey polo for laughs on the beach.

Shopping • Excellent shopping in town boutiques and galleries selling quality Mexican-designer clothes, crafts, and even paintings and prints by local artists. Plenty of souvenirs and curios available at town market.

Where to Stay • A very good choice of deluxe resort hotels and more moderate and inexpensive ones. Camping. Reserve months in advance for December 15-April 15.

Where to Eat • A multitude of attractive restaurants offering seafood, steaks, continental cuisine, and even, occasionally, Mexican food.

Entertainment • Plenty of options ranging from fiestas Mexicanas, to bars with music and dancing, to nightclubs and discos.

Getting Around • Car rentals, taxis, and maxi-buses can get you to and from most outlying beach hotels and town. If driving, you can avoid the Malecón traffic by taking the Libramiento from the airport road to the exit near Playa Los Muertos. Once in town, only walking will enable you to enjoy it, but a taxi or "Hoteles" bus (out to Marina on Juarez; in to Playa Los Muertos on Morelos) is possible.

Practical Tips • Puerto Vallarta is casual in dress, requiring no ties or jackets or formal gowns.

Most shops close between 2-4 p.m. or even 5 p.m., but stay open until 8 or 9 p.m.

Weather is typical of other resorts, usually perfect in winter, more humid and hot in the summer with some brief showers, and best avoided Sept.-Oct.

Construction along the airport road has brought unpleasant congestion that has gone on too long.

WHAT TO SEE AND DO

BEACHES

Puerto Vallarta's Bay of Banderas, shaped like an enormous horseshoe, has a broad, flat expanse of beach along its north shore lined by most of the resort hotels. Along its south shore, villas and a few fortunate resort hotels are located amid scenic mountains and next to small coves like **Playa Punta Negra.** In the center of these two wings is the town itself, divided into north and south by the Rio Cuale. On the south side of town is **Playa Los Muertos,** or Deadmen's Beach, supposedly named after a pirate's raid on the town, and often called by the more inviting name Playa del Sol ("sun") instead. Far from reminding anyone of its pirate past, this town beach is full of life, a bit honky-tonk, and lined with numerous thatch-covered restaurants filled with aficionados of local color and backgammon. (Unfortunately, the sea here is not always the cleanest.) Enterprising locals visit all

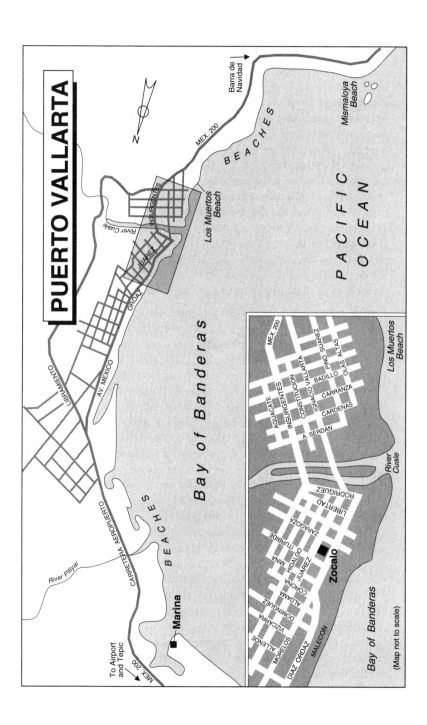

PUERTO VALLARTA

the beaches, giving you an opportunity to parasail (a parachute ride over the ocean), water-ski, and even to play burro (donkey) polo on the beach.

Trips to nearby beaches that must resemble the old Puerto Vallarta can be made most leisurely on boats that sail from the marina each day. One of the most beautiful spots is **Yelapa,** a tropical village lined with a slip of a beach that would have pleased Gauguin. There you can horseback ride along mountain trails or walk to a waterfall with a 150-foot drop. Some Americans have homes here, and a few shops have opened. The *Serape and Vagabundo* are among the boats with bars, tropical music, and dancing that leave each morning from the marina for this day trip. At Yelapa, you can try a *sopa de marisco* full of shrimp at one of the thatched-roof eateries. Or take along a box lunch from your hotel. Other cruises are available; some going nearby to **Mismaloya beach** with snorkeling at **Los Arcos** rock formation, and others for the horseback ride to the waterfalls at **Quixmito.** The trimaran *Bora-Bora* leaves from the marina each morning on its way to **Las Animas beach;** along the way you can fish, enjoy an open bar, and have lunch. Or you can take a tour or Pacifico bus to Nayarit in the north, where the **Punta Mita** peninsula juts into the sea. (See "On the Road".) For reservation on all these trips, check with your hotel.

Mismaloya Beach can be reached by road as well, by taking Calle Badillo to Insurgentes then following MEX 200 south out of Puerto Vallarta (12 km, 7 m). The location of *The Night of the Iguana* (and other less famous movies), Mismaloya beach is nestled at the foot of tropical, lush mountains, but it has been visited by too many tourists to have retained its pristine beauty untouched. In fact, a new hotel complex has risen next to the lively stalls selling food and drink. Boats will take you to the nearby rock formation, Los Arcos, for snorkeling. You can continue farther along the road to the crumbling set from *Night of the Iguana.* In the vicinity of Mismaloya beach are numerous restaurants with dramatic water views and tropical-jungle ambience. New ones seem to open each year, but the original and the funkiest is **Chino's Paradise,** which looks just like a location for Tarzan movies at its inland location (2 km) along the Mismaloya River. Getting to Chino's is part of the adventure. From town, take first left after La Jolla hotel, pass by the thatched roofs of Mismaloya village, and then follow the river and its increasingly luxuriant vegetation along a bumpy dirt road into the mountains. Chino's is built into a cliff next to a natural pool formed by a waterfall. Daring children jump off high rocks into the pool while you sip a rum punch served in a pineapple, or join in the swimming yourself (*open 10 a.m. to 6 p.m. daily; moderate*). Most of the others can be found south of Mismaloya on MEX 200. The most elegant is **El Kliff** (4 km, 2-1/2 m), a multilevel restaurant and bar, terraced down a cliff to the sea, that seems to float over the ocean (open 11 a.m.-10 p.m.; expensive). **Chico's Paradise** is the farthest away (10 km, 6 m south). Overlooking the rapids of Los Horcones River and with huge rocks for sunbathing as well as acceptable food, Chico's is perhaps the most popular. Just don't swim here; some have died trying (10 a.m.-6 p.m.; moderate). Tours take you to some of these restaurants, but you can also take the 02 colectivo to Hotel La Jolla at Mismaloya, then hire a cab for your excursion.

TOWN SIGHTS AND SHOPPING

Puerto Vallarta provides the best shopping of any resort in Mexico. Both sides of the Rio Cuale sport a multitude of boutiques and shops offering resort clothing, quality crafts, and some art galleries featuring the work of the local artist Manuel Lepe, now deceased, who captured the fantasy and color of Mexico life in his paintings. As you cross the river between the north and south sections of town, consider strolling through the tropical gardens of the **Isla Cuale,** an island with a number of shops and cafes and the small **Museo del Cuale** (near Calle Morelos; 9 a.m.-3 p.m.; small fee) with art exhibits, both contemporary and pre-Columbian. On Insurgentes near the river is a **market** with endless stalls of inexpensive souvenirs and curios.

North Side

In the north area of town around the Malecón are more shops than you could ever visit. Along the Malecón are numerous designer boutiques specializing in sportswear, from **Polo Ralph Lauren** (*Aldama at Malecón*) to **Aca Joe** (*D. Ordaz 588*). There is even a greater density of shops beginning at Corona and Molelos. Here **Galeria Uno** (*Morelos and Corona*) offers work of Manuel Lepe as well as other Mexican artists. **Designer's Bazaar** (*Morelos 500*) sells Vercellino cotton resort clothes. **El Patio Antigues** (*Corona 169*) has fine Tonala ceramics and good-quality serapes along with other superior Mexican crafts and **Majolica** (*Corona 191*) sells handsome Talavera ceramics from Guanajuato and Puebla. **El Aquila Descalza** (*Corona 179*) sells Mexican designer clothes for women, fine beribboned and embroidered cottons, while **Boni** (*Juarez 524*) sells dresses made of silk-screened fabric designed by Escalera. **Galeria Pacifico** (*Juarez 519*) is a fine gallery, with Tamayo and Zuniga prints as well as paintings by younger Mexican artists. **Huaracheria Lety** (*Juarez 472*) features a good selection of sandals and **Ole** (*Juarez 500*) has lots of sweaters and serapes, if you can get yourself to think of what winter in northern climes is like. The main square, at Zaragoza and Juarez, is bordered by the municipio on its north side. In the patio inside, on the second floor, is a Manuel Lepe mural. Back on Juarez, toward Guererro, are the surreal sculptures of the Mexican artist **Sergio Bustamante**. At the corner is the silver jewelry of **La Azteca** (*Morelos at Guerrero*), and down Guerrero is **Galeria Lepe**, with posters by the master and his brother Rodrigo. At the corner of Morelos and Libertad, **Nebaj** sells quality Guatemalan crafts and **Nabu** some designer clothes and jewelry.

South Side

On the south side of the Rio Cuale toward Los Muertos beach (along Venustiana Carranza and Lazaro Cardenas near Pino Suarez), the shops are just starting to sprout as this section of town becomes fashionable. Here is Vallarta's most fabulous crafts shop, **Olinala** (*Cardenas*

274). The collection of masks from all over the world, but particularly Guererro in Mexico, is superb. Also very fine are the Huichol beadwork and the hand-painted laquerware from Guerrero. **Galeria de Indias** (*Madero 268*) is a branch of Olinala. Its emphasis is more on interior decoration, however, than folkart. **Viva** (*Vallarta 579 near Madero*) has handsome furnishings and Tonala ceramics.

WHERE TO STAY

While price will certainly be a consideration in your selection of a hotel, you also may want to consider its location. In the north section along the congested road to the airport (Carretera Aeropuerto), the beach is long and continuous with rough surf that is often unswimmable but the marina and golf course are conveniently near. In the south (Mismaloya Road), hotels have fabulous views of the mountains, and beaches seem more private because each hotel is located on a cove and the ocean is calmer and swimmable. Unfortunately, there are few hotels in the south section, but to us it is the **most beautiful area of Puerto Vallarta** and worth the effort of even seeking out a condo or villa rental (*Rentas CAPSA, Apartado 56* (☎ *2-06-26*), is one such agent and *Puerto Vallarta Villas*, ☎ *800-322-3133* in U.S is another; see also "Practical Travel Information.") In between these two luxury areas in the north and south lies the town, with a few hotels on the beach and the most inexpensive ones set back from, but within walking distance of, the water. As usual with inexpensive hotels, we will try to recommend only those that give you some appropriate feeling of being at a resort—a sea view, a good pool, or a location close to the beach. Price categories are based on high-season or winter prices, and you will find them considerably lower during the summer—when you can often get fabulous package deals from your travel agent. All hotels are air-conditioned unless otherwise noted. For reservations, include in the address Puerto Vallarta, Jalisco, Mexico or call area code 322.

RESORT EXPENSIVE

Camino Real ★★★★
3 km (2 m) south on Mismaloya Road; ☎ *3-01-23; $185* • An elegant modern high-rise on magnificent Estacas beach, with dramatic views of bay and mountains, this hotel sits amid lush gardens. Its 250 rooms and suites, all with ocean views, are very large and well decorated and soon will be supplemented with 75 deluxe suites, many with their own terraces and pools. The excellent service includes such fine touches as a tropical flower placed on your pillow each night. Restaurants, bars (including a swim-up bar in the largest pool), and boutiques. Tennis, watersports, and health club under construction. For reservations, call, in the U.S., ☎ *800-722-6466.*

Hyatt Coral Grand ★★★★
8-1/2 km (5 m) south on Mismaloya Road; ☎ *3-07-07; $198* • Opened in 1988, this contemporary hotel on a quiet beach offers only suites—150 of them. All are huge, with sitting areas and furnished

balconies, but the superior ones also have private Jacuzzis with sea views. Two restaurants, bars, and shops. Pool, 1 tennis court, watersports, and gym. For reservations, call, in the U.S., ☎ *800-722-6466.*

Fiesta Americana ★★★★

3 km (2 m) north on Carretera Aeropuerto; ☎ *4-20-10; $231* • This large beachfront hotel has a dramatic thatched-roof lobby that is breezy, busy, but attractive—with marble floors and waterfall. Its 282 large, well-appointed rooms have balconies and ocean views and soon are to be joined with a new tower of suites. Numerous shops, restaurants, and bars, and a disco. Large pool with swim-up bar; Club de Tenis with instruction available; sauna, Jacuzzi, and massage. Watersports. For reservations, call, in the U.S., ☎ *800-223-2332.*

VERY EXPENSIVE

La Jolla de Mismaloya ★★★★

1 km (6-1/2 m) south on Mismaloya Rd.; ☎ *3-06-60; $165* • Opened in 1987, this immense condo complex offers glorious sea views from every unit at its location on Mismaloya beach. The 450 condos are tastefully furnished, all with terraces and views and complete kitchens and some with 2 bedrooms and 2 baths. A bit far from the center, but colectivos and taxis available. Restaurants and bars, disco, and shops. Four pools (one for laps); watersports; tennis. Jacuzzi; gym. Write Apartado 186.

Buganvilias Sheraton ★★★★

2 km (1 m) north at Carretera Aeropuerto 999; ☎ *3-04-04; $180* • On Las Glorias beach, this enormous modern hotel has a very handsome lobby decorated with plants and palms. The 500 rooms and suites are ample, with ocean views. Numerous restaurants, and bars; nightclub and shops. Huge pool with swim-up bar. Somewhat narrow beach. Tennis and watersports. For reservations, call, in the U.S., ☎ *800-325-3535.*

EXPENSIVE

Quinta Maria Coretez ★★★

2-1/2 km (1-1/2 m) south on Mismaloya Rd.; ☎ *2-11-84; $70-145* • In the villa section overlooking Playa Conchas Chinas and just a short walk to the beach, are these seven suites. Each is elaborately and quite distinctively furnished with brass beds, overstuffed sofas, and the like. All have whimsical touches, especially in the baths, and all have large furnished terraces and kitchenettes. Breakfast available. Tiny pool. To reach, turn right off Mismaloya Rd. at Rentas CAPSA and down cobbled path, half-way to beach. Closed some summer months. Write Apartado 356 well in advance.

Las Palmas ★★★

2-1/2 km (1-1/2 m) north on Carretera Aeropuerto; ☎ *4-06-50; $129* • On a narrow beach, Las Palmas is as close as you can get to the luxury resorts without paying their prices. Its lobby is smaller and more intimate than the Fiesta Americana's, but it's just as thatched and romantic. All 150 rooms are around pool or palm-shaded beach. Quiet and pleasant, these rooms have shared balconies or terraces with views. Restaurants, bar. Write Apartado 55.

MODERATE

Playa Conchas Chinas
2-1/2 km (1-1/2 m) south on Mismaloya Road; ☎ *2-01-56; $70-85*
• Located on a hillside overlooking a series of tiny beach coves, with excellent views of bay and mountains, this small hotel has limited common areas, but its 32 rooms are ample and simply, yet decently, furnished. Restaurant and bar on beach; El Set restaurant is popular for sunset watching. Jacuzzi, Roman bath, no pool, but here the ocean is swimmable. A good buy for this exclusive location. Apartado 346.

Pelicanos
2-1/2 km (1-1/2 m) north on Carretera Aeropuerto; ☎ *2-21-07; $75*
• Next to Las Palmas, but not directly on the beach, the Pelicanos is a modern, friendly, unpretentious hotel. Half its 193 rooms face the pool, the others look out on some plants. Rooms are plain, clean, and pleasant. Restaurant and bar. Beach with bar only a few hundred feet away. Apartado 199.

Playa Los Arcos
Olas Altas 380; ☎ *2-15-83; $70* • On the town beach Los Muertos, this popular modern hotel surrounds a large pool and has 120 fresh, bright, and ample rooms, many with private balconies and good views. The few unrecommendable rooms can be avoided by requesting a private balcony. Restaurants, one overlooking beach, bar. Pool and rooftop tennis court.

Molino de Agua
Aquiles Serdan and Vallarta; ☎ *2-19-07; $61* • With a beautiful setting among gardens and shade trees, its pleasant, quiet atmosphere is filled with bird songs; 53 comfortable, small bungalows with porches or terraces, a few more modern and expensive ones with ocean views over a not very special beach. Restaurant and bar next to Rio Cuale. Two pools. Parking. Write Apartado 54.

Suites Esmeralda del Mar
6 km (4 m) south on Mismaloya Road; ☎ *2-04-95; $82* • On a hillside above the bay, with dramatic views from some rooms, this condo hotel rents out suites for short or long stays (discounts available). To us, the suites seemed furnished out of someone's attic, and the elevator looked a bit run-down, but for a family or a group needing space, this could be a good buy. Small suites have one bedroom, living room, kitchen, and large terrace. Directly on beach; small pool. Write Apartado 596.

INEXPENSIVE

Tropicana

Calle Amapas 214; ☎ *2-09-12; $45* • Conveniently located on Los Muertos beach, this large hotel is a bit plastic in our opinion, but for the price and location on the beach it's worth a stay. Its 200 rooms are ample, if plain, and many have ocean views. Restaurant and bar. Pool and tennis. Write Apartado 31.

Fontana del Mar

Manuel M. Dieguez 171; ☎ *2-05-83; $55* • Sharing facilities with the Hotel Playa Los Arcos, this nearby hostelry looks more like an apartment house than a hotel. Its 40 rooms are fresh and clean and only one block from Los Muertos beach. Restaurant; rooftop pool and bar with good views of mountains and ocean.

Rosita

Diaz Ordaz 901; ☎ *2-10-33; $40* • This informal town hotel on the Malecón is recommendable for those of its 100 rooms that have bay views and some quiet. These rooms are clean, simply furnished, ample, and with fans. Restaurant and bar. Pool. Write Apartado 32.

BUDGET

Posada de Roger

Badillo 237; ☎ *2-08-36; $29* • Given the price of the 52 clean rooms surrounding quiet courtyards, it is understandable that a loyal following makes it hard to book a room in peak season. Restaurant and bar. Small pool. Near Playa Los Muertos.

Rio

Morelos 170; ☎ *2-32-35; $33* • A modern, informal hotel. A condo complex has blocked this hotel's view of the ocean, but its pool provides some compensation. Not near a swimming beach; 48 simple, clean rooms. Restaurant and bar. Write Apartado 23.

WHERE TO EAT

Puerto Vallarta specializes in seafood and steak houses with a Mexican dish or two for accent, which is not surprising given the excellent local supply of fresh seafood and the tourists' demand for steak. The food is good, if not great, and it is almost always served in pleasant surroundings. During the afternoon, some people manage to leave their hotel beach and wander about sampling shish-kebab chased with a rum-filled pineapple at **Chino's Paradise** or an avocado stuffed with shrimp at **Le Kliff** (*for directions see* *"What to See and Do"*). Or, if shopping in town, they might stop for breakfast or lunch at one of the open-air restuarants such as **Las Palomas** (*near Aldama; moderate*). Most tourists stay comfortably close to the sea and eat at terrace restaurants around the beach or pool at their hotel. Often the hotel restaurants serve excellent food, particularly the **Camino Real,** where a sumptuous buffet is served Sunday afternoons to the accompaniment of excellent mariachi music. It is in the evening that people exchange their swimsuits for casual clothes and head out to a restaurant, usually in town. Restaurant price categories are explained in the Introduction.

Dining on a filet of red snapper, a steak, or lobster and shrimp is only too easy. Many of the most popular restaurants offer these basics with so little variation that they try to distinguish themselves by finding the most dramatic location—usually one positioned for the sunset. The one to have outlived most contenders is **El Set** (*in Hotel Playa Conchas Chinas;* ☎ 2-03-03), terraced low enough on a cliff to give you a sense of the surf. With a more panoramic view is the trendier, more sophisticated **Capriccio** (*Pulpito 172;* ☎ 2-15-93) at its location above Playa Los Muertos. (*Reached by steps from Pulpito or by car off Mismaloya Rd.*) Both restaurants are very expensive.

When your palate craves something different, there are a number of restaurants to choose from that still provide plenty of ambience. **Daiquiri Dick's** (*Olas Atlas 246;* ☎ 2-05-66) is right by the sea at Playa Los Muertos. With the surf as background music and candles for light, you can enjoy the interesting, California treatment of seafood and vegetables offered here. Usually there are daily specials, including a good seasonal salad, but the tuna carpaccio with salsa Mexicana, the tuna steak with cilantro sauce, and the dramatically presented whole huachinango are satisfying standbys found on the menu. The key lime pie is decent too. Moderately expensive. **Le Gourmet,** at the Posada Rio Culale, (*Aquiles Serdan 242;* ☎ 2-04-50) offers a pleasant poolside terrace near the river for dining (except during the rainy season, when most are forced inside). Much of the food here is prepared at tableside, be it a very good Caesar salad, shrimp al mojo de ajo, steak Diane, or crepe Suzettes. **Le Bistro** (*Isla Cuale near Insurgentes; no reservations; closed Sun.*), set in a lush garden by the river, is one of Vallarta's handsomest restaurants. The jazz played over the superb sound system is alone a reason to visit, if just for a drink in the bar. The continental cuisine is very popular, though we found it heavy and recommend the lighter brochetas or grilled seafood. Expensive, unless you choose the crepes (shrimp and spinach among them) or Mexican dishes that are far more moderate.

Three special places with completely different cuisines should be noted. **Moby Dick** (*31 de Octubre #182;* ☎ 2-06-55) has the best seafood in town, in our opinion. The environment is bright and cheerful, the shrimp Moby Dick (wrapped in cheese and bacon) delicious, the lobster fresh, and the offerings varied—a good cream of lobster soup, tostadas de jaiba (crab), whole red snapper (not just a filet), and octopus. Open for lunch too. Expensive. **Pietro's** (*Hidalgo at Zaragoza*) may not be the most elegant Italian restaurant in Vallarta, but its food is among the best. Its ambience is casual yet pleasant all the way down to its red-checkered tablecloths. Its pizza comes out of a brick oven, the ravioli and canneloni are homemade, and the rigatoni alla Bruno is very flavorful. Moderate. **Las Cazuelas** (*Badillo 479;* ☎ 2-16-58) has been nourishing tourists on Mexican food for years and although it has moved to more elegant surroundings it still promises "home cooking." The food is limited to each evening's specialties. Moderate. *6:30-11 p.m. Closed Mondays and all summer. Reservations required.*

For moderately expensive prices, there are a number of restaurants to try in the center of town on or near the Malecón. **La Margarita** (*Juarez 512;* ☎ *2-12-15*) has good, set-priced meals at dinner, with several choices of entree from seafood to Mexican specialties. This attractive restaurant, with tables arranged around a courtyard, is enjoyable in the evening when (starting at 8 p.m.) a seranata trio and mariachis provide free entertainment. **Carlos O'Brian's** (*Diaz Ordaz 786;* ☎ *2-14-44*) has an extensive menu offering all kinds of seafood, steak dishes, and salads. The quantity and quality of the food makes it worth the price, but you have to put up with loud recorded rock music in this lively and popular restaurant. Open for lunch and dinner. **Brazz Bar and Restaurant** (*Morelos and Galeano*) specializes in prime ribs and offers giant shrimp and lobster. Its large, handsome bar, with mariachis nightly starting at 9:30 p.m., is open noon to midnight.

Some inexpensive restaurants provide the atmosphere of the old fishing village of Puerto Vallarta. Head for Los Muertos beach and walk down Calle Pulpito to find the thatched-roof, **El Dorado** (*open till 8:30 p.m. only*) where the ocean almost laps the legs of your table. Mariachis sometimes drop in to play for the price of a song. If the prices are too high, you can continue to the beach and one of the vendors cooking up fresh fish. Or look around the Playa Los Muertos area for other spots like **Los Pinquinos** (*Olas Altas 397*), clean and with an extensive menu from seafood to queso fundido. Toward the river is **Senor Pancho's** (*Madero near Vallarta*), a tipico spot with good prices for seafood as well as its Mexican specialties.

For cheap breakfasts and snacks from juices, licuados, and sandwiches, look for **Tutifruti** (*Morelos 552*), or **Malibu** (*Morelos and Guerrero*). Lovers of American breakfasts should seek out **Pancake House** (*Badillo 289; closed Mon.*). It's a favorite for pancakes, waffles, and French toast—all served through lunch. Lovers of ice cream should head for **Helados Bing** (*Juarez 280*), with lots of tropical fruit flavors to choose from like pineapple, coconut, and mango.

ENTERTAINMENT

Certainly the most popular form of entertainment in Puerto Vallarta is a relaxing meal to the accompaniment of music. Many restaurants with entertainment have been mentioned already, but you might want to try one of the Fiestas Mexicanas—elaborate buffets with Mexican specialties, live music, and traditional dances. **La Iguana** (*Lazaro Cardenas 167;* ☎ *2-01-05*), a restaurant serving an odd assortment of Chinese, Mexican, and international dishes, bursts with gaiety during its Fiestas Mexicanas on Thursday and Sunday nights. Most first-class hotels offer these fiestas at least one night weekly.

Another favorite pastime is positioning yourself for this resort's awesome sunsets at the bar of your choice. Our choice is **El Nido**, the rooftop terrace at the Restaurant Chez Elena (*Matamoros 520 in the vicinity of Corona*), with breathtaking views out over the cathedral and orange-tiled roofs of town to the open expanse of water. (*Closed during rainy season.*) Some of the resort hotel lobby bars, like those at the **Fiesta Americana** or El Set at the **Hotel Playa Conchas Chinas**, provide fine views as do the terraces at **Felipe's** and **Sr. Chico's** in Altavista. **Daiquiri Dick's** (*Olas Altas 246*) and **La Palapa** on Los Muertos beach as well as **Franzi's Cafe** on Isla Cuale are but a few of the other popular sunset-watching spots you have to choose from. Or you can outdo any of these spots by checking out a sunset cruise to Mismaloya.

Later in the evening the disco scene begins. Three of the most popular are **Capriccio**, with its tongue-in-cheek decor at the restaurant above Playa Los Muertos; **Christine** (*3-1/2 km, 2 m north on Carretera Aeropuerto*) has the latest in sound and video equipment for its elegant disco; **Friday Lopez** (*Carretera Aeropuerto at Fiesta Americana Hotel*) has live music. These late-night spots don't get started before 10 p.m. and usually stay open until 3 or 4 a.m. Often there's an admission charge. If you're still awake, check out the earthier scene around Playa Los Muertos where some restaurants, like **La Cabana de Pancho Villa** (*Carranza 248*), just get going around midnight and stay open till 5 a.m.

GETTING TO AND FROM PUERTO VALLARTA

AIR

International jets fly directly to Puerto Vallarta or make one stop on the way there at Guadalajara or Mexico City. Domestic flights on Aeromexico or Mexicana connect this resort with Guadalajara several times a day (half-hour flight) and Mexico City, Mazatlán, and border cities. The airport lies approximately 6 km (4 m) north of town; car-rental agencies and fixed-price collective vans available. Town buses run on adjacent highway.

BUS

There's first-class service south to Manzanillo and north to Tepic (3 hours) and Guadalajara (6 hours). To reach Mazatlán only Tres Estrella de Oro (1 bus daily) doesn't require a Tepic transfer.

CAR

MEX 200 runs along the Pacific 270 km (167 m). The resorts closest to Puerto Vallarta on this road to the south are along the Costa de Oro (175 km, 109 m to Careyes) and at Manzanillo (270 km, 167 m), or 6-1/2 hours. Mazatlán, 468 km (290 m) and San Blas, 243 km (151 m) lie to the north on MEX 200, then MEX 15 beyond Tepic. The fastest route to Guadalajara is north on MEX 200 for 135 km, 84 m to Compostela and the tollroad bypass (MEX 68D) to MEX 15 (see "On the Road"). Total distance: 340 km (211 m) or 5 hours.

DIRECTORY

Airlines • At airport: *Aeromexico,* (☎ 1-10-55); *Mexicana,* (☎ 2-61-55); *American* (☎ 2-37-88); *Continental;* and others.

American Express • Centro Comercial Villa Vallarta (☎ 2-68-76).

Books in English • Franzi Cafe on Isla Cuale will exchange used books (one of theirs for two of yours).

Buses • *Tres Estrellas de Oro,* for first-class buses, Insurgentes 210 (☎ 2-10-19); second-class buses clustered nearby. Town Buses: Bus service around town, out to the airport, and combis to Mismaloya, starts at the plaza on Pino Suarez and Cardenas (6 a.m. until 9 p.m.).

Canadian Consul • Hidalgo 226 (☎ 2-53-98); weekdays 9 a.m.-1 p.m.

Car Rentals • Numerous agencies are at airport and in-town hotels. Some are: Avis (☎ 2-11-12); Budget (☎ 2-29-80); and the less costly Rent-Mar (☎ 2-14-56).

Fishing • Boats Arrangements at the Marina (see below) and pier on north end of Malecón.

Golf • Club de Golf Los Flamingos, 18 holes, 10 km (6 m) north of airport (☎ 2-09-59); Marina Vallarta Club de Golf (☎ 1-01-71), 18 holes.

Groceries • Super Market Max (Insurgentes and Cardenas).

Horseback Riding • At Yelapa and Los Muertos, and through hotel tour agencies.

Laundry • Lavanderia Roger, Olas Altas south of Badillo.

Marina • Carretera Aeropuerto near Hotel Playa del Oro, 5 km (3 m) north.

Post Office • Morelos 444.

Taxi Stands • Along Malecón and in front of resort hotels.

Telegraph • Hidalgo 582, near Aldama.

Tennis • Clubs open to nonmembers: *John Newcombe Tennis Club* at Fiesta Americana Hotel and *Tennis Club Vallarta* near Krystal Hotel, both on airport road.

Tourist Office • Municipal Palace at Juarez and Independencia (☎ 2-02-42). Open 8:30 a.m.-8 p.m. Monday-Friday; 9 a.m.-1 p.m. Saturday.

Tours • Hotel tour agencies arrange city bus tours, including Mismaloya, tropical tours, horseback riding, etc.

U.S. Consul • Insurgentes at Libertad, local 12A (☎ 2-00-69); weekdays 9 a.m.-2 p.m.

Watersports • Watersports can be arranged at most hotel beaches and Chico's Dive Shop at Mismaloya as well as in town at Diaz Ordaz 772 (☎ 2-18-95) offers snorkeling, diving equipment, instruction, and special excursions. Closed Sunday.

ON THE ROAD

North of Puerto Vallarta, MEX 200 winds its way past the residential development of Nueva Vallarta (10 km, 6 m) and the Flamingos Golf Club and stretches deeper into the state of Nayarit where you might consider turning off to some undeveloped beach areas. The loveliest area to explore can be found just 30 km (18-1/2 m) from the center of Puerto Vallarta. Turning off the highway at the sign for Punta Mita, you travel on a peninsular road that runs near the sea and passes the fishing village of **La Cruz de Huanacaxtla** as well as tempting lanes down to isolated beach coves. After 8 km, 5 m, you come to the fine-grained beach and magnificent sea at **Destiladeras**. Here there are at least a few facilities if you wish to spend the day—a rustic restaurant and an outhouse where two billy goats had taken up residence on our last visit. It's 14 more kilometers (9 m) down the peninsula to **Punta Mita**, but we didn't have a chance to explore them. Back on MEX 200 the tropical vegetation becomes even denser with mango and banana groves until 44 km (27 m) later you come to **Rincon de Guayabitos**, a long and narrow curve of a beach next to a thatched town and a very Mexican resort of bungalows, small hotels, and RVs. MEX 200 becomes curvier as it climbs through the foothills toward Compostela and the toll road turnoff to Guadalajara. It continues to wind its way to the regional town of **Tepic** (175 km, 109 m from Vallarta) where there are overnight facilities (see index).

IXTAPA/ ZIHUATANEJO

As recently as 1972, Zihuatanejo (zee-whah-tah-NAY-ho) was a tropical paradise explored by tourists who didn't mind its lack of paved streets and air-conditioned hotels. Bumping along a dirt road from Acapulco or flying cheek by jowl with the pilot in a small plane from Mexico City, these adventurers were rewarded with the seclusion and beauty of a fishing village on a dramatic bay formed by the rugged Sierra Madre mountains and surrounded by luxuriant tropical vegetation. Soon Zihuatanejo's excellent beaches and Polynesian beauty attracted developers who saw its potential as a major Pacific resort. Today jets fly into a new airport, paved roads connect with Acapulco and other towns, and Zihuatanejo itself sports modern touches. Formerly dirt streets now are cobblestoned, and hardware stores have been replaced by restaurants and boutiques. Still, it remains **a picturesque fishing village**—with boys playing soccer on the beach in the late afternoon, women buying regional mangos, payapas, and coconuts in the market, and fishermen bringing in oysters and lobsters to the town dock. Zihuatanejo's natural beauty has been preserved because the Mexican government wisely created the deluxe resort of Ixtapa four miles away.

Ixtapa (ish-TAH-pah) sits on Palmar Bay, a broad expanse of beach and open surf perfect for sunset watching even if it lacks the spectacular mountain formations and intimacy of Zihuatanajo Bay. Here, you find the totally modern and deluxe amenities expected of a first-class resort, including a golf course designed by Robert Trent Jones, internationally known hotels, numerous restaurants, lively discos, and a tangle of small shopping malls, their number increasing with each year. Although created out of virgin jungle, Ixtapa is quite suburban in appearance with its row of hotels set amid groomed lawns along a single, immaculate boulevard. But it is a suburbia wedged between mountain and sea.

By itself, Ixtapa is too small to make for a perfect vacation, but with the "new" Zihuatanejo nearby you have a charming town, many lively beaches, restaurants, and boutiques to add diversity to your vacation. Many travelers prefer the rustic charm and dramatic scenery of Zihuatanejo, and stay in the simpler and older hotels on the hills above La Madera and La Ropa beaches.

KEY TO IXTAPA/ZIHUATANEJO

Sights • Small first-class and ultramodern resort of Ixtapa combined with the enchanting rustic village resort of Zihuatanejo. Fine beaches and dramatic scenery.

Sports • Good swimming, water-skiing, windsurfing, snorkeling, and scuba diving; deep-sea fishing for marlin, bonito, and other Pacific fish; golf and tennis. Parachute rides. Horseback riding.

Excursions • Acapulco is 4 hours away by road. Regular one-hour flights to Mexico City make this resort easily combined with a sightseeing visit to the capital.

Shopping • Good-quality Mexican crafts, handcrafted jewelry, plus many spots for beachwear.

Where to Stay • Deluxe to first-class in Ixtapa; mostly moderate and charming in Zihuatanejo, which also has inexpensive hotels. Some camping.

Where to Eat • Decent seafood and international and Mexican food in both Ixtapa and Zihuatanejo.

Entertainment • A number of discos and bars with live entertainment.

Getting Around • Ixtapa and Zihuatanejo are small enough to explore on foot, and minibuses connect them frequently from 7 a.m.-8 p.m., running along Blvd. Ixtapa to Morelos at Juarez in Zihuatanejo. Taxis, car rentals, mopeds, and tours available. Many of Zihuatanejo's streets are closed to traffic so it's best to park your car and walk.

Practical Tips • If your international flight has a stopover in Mexico City or Guadalajara, you might arrange a few days there in addition to your time at the beach at little additional traveling cost.

If you want to stay in Zihuatanejo, you may have to emphasize this fact to your travel agent, as they most often book into Ixtapa hotels. The atmosphere and accommodations in these neighboring spots are quite distinctive.

Most shops close between 2-4 p.m. and stay open in the evening.

Ixtapa has become a collegiate favorite at spring break, when you might prefer to avoid the cheaper package deals.

WHAT TO SEE AND DO

For a relatively small resort, Ixtapa/Zihuatanejo offers quite a number of different beaches and islands to visit, many with their own specialties of snorkeling, windsurfing, and even wildlife sanctuaries. Seafood and Mexican dishes can be enjoyed at these beaches in simple, thatched-roof restaurants that also provide beach chairs and shade to their patrons.

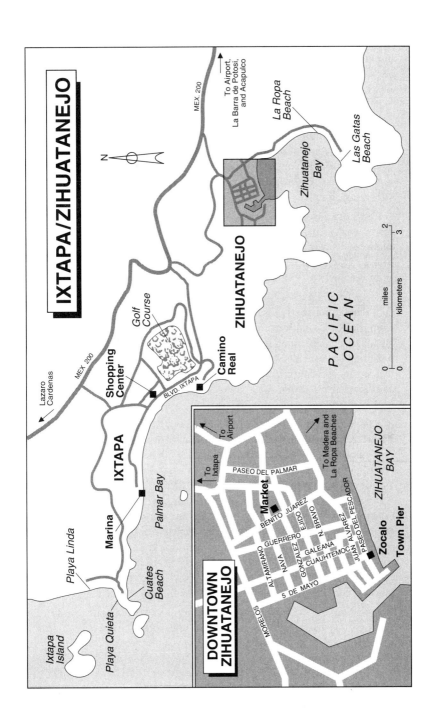

IXTAPA/ZIHUATANEJO

To Airport,
La Barra de Potosi,
and Acapulco

MEX 200

La Ropa
Beach

Las Gatas
Beach

Zihuatanejo
Bay

ZIHUATANEJO

N

PACIFIC
OCEAN

Golf
Course

Shopping
Center

Camino
Real

BLVD. IXTAPA

MEX 200

Lazaro
Cardenas

IXTAPA

Marina

Palmar Bay

Playa Linda

Cuates
Beach

Playa Quieta

Ixtapa
Island

miles
kilometers

2
3

0
0

DOWNTOWN ZIHUATANEJO

To Airport

To Ixtapa

PASEO DEL PALMAR

To Madera and
La Ropa Beaches

Market

BENITO JUAREZ

ALTAMIRANO

GUERRERO

NAVA

GONZALEZ

EJIDO

GALEANA

N. BRAVO

CUAUHTEMOC

JUAN ALVAREZ

PASEO DEL PESCADOR

MORELOS

5 DE MAYO

ZIHUATANEJO
BAY

Zocalo

Town Pier

Zihuatanejo Bay has several beaches, including the town beach, **Playa Principal** (palm-lined, convenient, and full of local color) and others to the south at the base of the hills jutting into the Pacific (follow signs to Zona Hotelera). The first of these is **La Madera beach**, a tiny strip of brown sand about a 15-minute walk from town, followed by **La Ropa**, a white sandy expanse along excellent swimming waters. La Ropa is not only a beautiful beach, it also is the center of the Zihuatanejo scene, offering thatched-roof eateries, hotels, and windsurfing and water-skiing. At the tip of the bay is **Las Gatas**, approached by a rocky path at the end of La Ropa or, more easily, by a 10-minute boat ride from the town dock. The coral reefs at this beach make it a favorite for scuba diving and snorkeling. However, if it is isolation you're looking for, consider renting a boat here or from the town dock for an excursion to nearby **La Manzanilla** or **Majahua,** both beaches stretching along the rough open sea (no facilities).

A favorite day trip is to **Ixtapa Island**, 10 miles from the coast with protected beaches facing inland. These wonderful swimming and snorkeling spots border a wildlife sanctuary that provides good bird-watching. Make tour arrangements in Ixtapa hotels, or negotiate your own transportation from the docks at Zihuatanejo or Playa Quieta.

Away from Ixtapa's hotel front are other beautiful, quiet beaches. In fact, **Palmar beach** itself is lovely as it stretches a half mile northward, away from the hotels and toward the marina complex. Ten minutes north of Ixtapa, past the bird-filled Laguna de Ixtapa, is the snorkeling cove of **Cuates beach** and the neighboring mountain-dominated cove of **Playa Quieta**, where Club Mediterranee has opened. Ixtapa Island is close to this beach, and boats are available for a visit. Nearby is **Playa Linda**, with horses to rent.

A favorite excursion south of Zihuatanejo is to the village of **La Barra de Potosi** (22 km, 14 m), located on the isolated beach expanse of Playa Blanca. Countryside tours take you to the village, but if you want a day of adventure in the tropics, you can try this yourself. Leave Zihuatanejo on the airport road and continue for 12 km on MEX 200 until the sign for Puente Los Achotes. (Petatlan minibuses from Juarez near Bravo in Zihuatanejo can stop here). After the sign, turn right and decide whether you want to take a "bus" (four-wheel drive, human cattle truck) or drive the 10-km (6-m) dirt road that passes by coconut and mango ranches, primitive huts, and a bird-filled lagoon, before reaching the beach lined with thatched restaurants, and La Barra de Postosi. The "bus" is recommended in the rainy season when the road becomes badly eroded, if not flooded.

Excursions to Acapulco or Mexico City can be arranged through tour agencies, or you can just go on your own using other chapters in this book as your guide.

SHOPPING

Although Ixtapa/Zihuatanejo offer only a few of the designer shops that so dominate the Acapulco shopping scene, the crafts sold here are far superior and the number of sportswear, T-shirt emporiums, and silver jewelry shops are more than enough. We like shopping in Zihuatanejo best, where we head straight for **Coco Cabana** (*Guerrero, next to Coconuts restaurant*), with its superb collection of folk art—signed Oaxacan ceramic figures by Josefina Aguilar, exquisitely painted Guanajuato majorlica ceramics, and Huichol bead work. Less pricey but good are the cluster of shops in the Casa Marina (*Paseo Pescador and 5 de Mayo*) where you can choose from the Oaxacan rugs of **La Zapoteca**, the masks of **El Jumil,** the delightful assortment of wooden and straw whatnots at **La Tzotzil**, and the contemporary clothes made from handwoven textiles at **El Embarcadero** (*facing Alvarez*). Up Cuauhtemoc from the beach, you soon pass **Explora** with its Naturebrand T-shirts, and then around Bravo you find **Alberto's** fine silver jewelry amid other silver shops. Then, continue to Ejido for the colorful and quality cotton designer clothes at **La Fuente**.

In Ixtapa, you might first try the shops at the end across from the Presidente hotel. In the two-story Los Patios complex you'll find some of the more interesting clothing shops, such as **Girasol,** and the handscreened T-shirts of **Coco** (upstairs). Also here are Taxco jewelry shops and some designer boutiques, like **Ellesse**, as well as the small crafts shop, **Laddi Guichi**, with Oaxacan wooden animals and serapes. Behind Los Patios is Centro Ixpamar with a similar variety of shops, including the fascinating traditional masks sold in **El Huizteco** and the odd assortment at **El Amanecer** of fine crafts amid some curios and Swatch watches.

WHERE TO STAY

Just as there are two locations to this resort, two very different sets of hotel options exist. Along broad Palmar beach of Ixtapa are modern first-class hotels. A golf club is within walking distance of this hotel district. Most packages for Ixtapa/Zihuatanejo entail stays only at these first-class, air-conditioned hotels. (**Note**: The undertow at Palmar beach allows frolicking, but not always swimming.) In Zihuatanejo, on the other hand, you find more moderately priced hotels along the good swimming beaches of Madera and La Ropa, some with air conditioning, but more often with an older, open form of architecture allowing rooms to be cooled adequately by fans and sea breezes. If you seek a vacation with the simpler pleasures, such as hearing the crashing surf rather than an air conditioner, these are the places for you. Some of Zihuatanejo's beach hotels require modified American plan during the winter season. Inexpensive hotels within a block of the Playa Principal in Zihuatanejo at least offer access to the beach. In our opinion, the best deals are the cottages at La Ropa and Madera beaches or the smaller rooms at the Sotavento-Catalina.

Rooms are air-conditioned unless specified otherwise. For reservations, address letter to either Ixtapa or Zihuatanejo 40880, Guerrero, Mexico or, call area code 743.

RESORT EXPENSIVE

Westin Resort   ★★★★★
Playa Vista Hermosa; ☎ *3-21-21; $198* • The spare architecture of
this modern hotel is its strength, enhancing the dramatic views framed
by open walls and enriching the colors and textures of the decor. As if
the architecture weren't enough, the hotel is situated on an isolated
hillside above the sea, surrounded by the lush tropics. Each of the 450
units has a sea view, terrace, and sunning area; their prices decrease as
the rooms and suites descend the hill. A walk through the tropical forest brings you to a series of pools joined by aqueducts and waterfalls,
or you can take the special elevator to the private beach. Five restaurants; bar with entertainment; and shops. Jeeps for rent; free transportation around grounds—still, there can be a lot of walking here. Pools;
tennis courts; access to fishing, golf, and watersports. Parking. Turnoff to hotel is located south of Ixtapa center, in Ixtapa. *For reservations, call, in the U.S.,* ☎ *800-722-6466.*

Villa del Sol   ★★★★
Playa La Ropa; ☎ *4-22-39; $253 MAP* • The Westin Resort is palatial
and formal in contrast to the romantic intimacy of the Villa del Sol.
This small inn has La Ropa beach for its lobby and 25 suites arranged
around gardens and courtyards. The ambience is casual, with hammocks slung on terraces and ceiling fans an option in addition to the
a/c. The suites vary in size (some two bedrooms, two baths; some
more like studios; some duplex casitas; others in two-story wings),
location (very few on beach), and price, but all are tastefully decorated
a la mexicana, with beds canopied in mosquito netting, bathrooms
with handpainted tiles, and living rooms enlivened with folk art. Service is good, but never intrusive. While MAP is required in high season, the food is very good. No children under 14 during winter
season. Restaurant, palapa bar, shop, and beauty salon. Small pools,
tennis, watersports. Parking. Write Apartado 84.

Omni Ixtapa;   ★★★★
☎ *3-00-03; $176* • Opened in 1990, this addition to Ixtapa's beach-
front hotels has colorful folkloric decorator touches throughout, even
in the lobby with its geodesic-style hi-tech ceiling. The 300 comfortable rooms include furnished balconies and most have sea views. Restaurants and lounges. Shops. Pool with small waterfall. Access to
watersports and tennis.

VERY EXPENSIVE

Ixtapa Sheraton   √★★★★
Ixtapa; ☎ *3-18-58; $170* • This 358-room Sheraton has captured a
lovely corner of Palmar beach. A striking 12-story lobby with glass
elevators is surrounded by handsome rooms with small well-furnished
balconies (half of which overlook the sea; half the mountains). Three
restaurants; snack bar; three bars and entertainment. Pool; tennis

courts; watersports including sailing; and arrangements for fishing.
Parking. *For reservations, call, in the U.S.,* ☎ *800-325-3535.*

Stouffer Presidente

Ixtapa; ☎ *3-00-18; $174* • The comfortable and attractive garden
complex of this hotel on Palmar beach has been supplemented by a
modern tower with glass elevators riding the outside and offering
views of the surrounding area. With a total of 400 rooms, the tower
rooms are ample, most with views of the sea; the garden rooms all
have furnished terraces, a few on the beach, most in lush gardens.
Three restaurants, bar, and disco. Two pools, tennis courts, and access
to watersports. Parking. *For reservations, call, in the U.S.,*
☎ *800-468-3571.*

Dorado Pacifico

Ixtapa; ☎ *3-20-25; $160* • On Palmar beach, this modern high-rise
has several fountains in the lobby and glass elevators riding the walls
of the multistoried lobby atrium. Most of the 300 smallish rooms have
sea views, balconies, and marbled bathrooms. Restaurants and bars;
pool with big slides; tennis, and access to watersports. Parking.

EXPENSIVE

Posada Real

Ixtapa; ☎ *3-16-25; $102* • This unpretentious hotel on Palmar beach
is surrounded by gardens and offers 110 small, well-maintained
rooms, some with sea view. Restaurant and bar on the beach. Pool,
beach club, a tennis court, and access to fishing and watersports. Parking.

MODERATE

Sotavento and Catalina Hotels   √★★★

Playa La Ropa; ☎ *4-20-74; $90-110 MAP* • The Sotavento and Cata-
lina not only share the same management, but recent building projects
have actually joined them. Terraced into the hillside above the beach,
with stairs wandering down to the Pacific, this complex of 115 rooms
is large for Zihuatanejo. Only some of the rooms are worthy of three
stars, however, and they are called terraza suites (floors 3-8). These
units have enormous terraces with furniture and hammocks for enjoying sea breezes and striking views of the Bay; the rooms themselves are
large, fan-cooled, and quite decent, if rather plain. Those in the Catalina are a bit smaller and cheaper. The Catalina also has 26 bungalows
(variable size, quality, and price; all functional) that attract a loyal following. Several restaurants, including one on the beach—unfortunately MAP required during high season. Lounges. Access to
watersports. Parking. *Write Apartado 2.*

Villas Miramar   ★★

Playa Madera; ☎ *4-21-06; $65-75* • For those who can't quite afford
the Villa del Sol, this tranquil inn might be perfect. On a hill above the

beach, few rooms have sea views, but all 20 are handsomely decorated junior suites, with sitting rooms, tiled bath, and either a patio or balcony. Restaurants and bar. Two small pools. *Write Apartado 211.*

Fiesta Mexicana ★★

Playa La Ropa; ☎ *4-37-76; $78* • The lobby of this complex is the beach, arranged with beach chairs and plants, a restaurant and bar. The 35 small rooms are almost spartan, but with tiled baths and small balconies overlooking gardens. Small pool. Access to watersports. Frequent transportation to Hotel Irma on Madera Beach. *Write Apartado 4.*

Irma ★★

Playa Madera; ☎ *4-20-25; $78* • On hill overlooking Madera beach, which is reached by walking down steep stairs, this well-run, quiet hotel is set in gardens. Its 80 rooms are clean and modest, some with views of sea. Open-air dining, bar. Two small pools, scuba diving instruction, and access to other watersports. Transportation to La Ropa beach. Parking. *Write Apartado 4.*

Las Urracas ★

Playa La Ropa; ☎ *4-20-49; $65* • This bungalow complex consists of 16 separate casitas with porches, all set in a shady garden area—only a few face the beach. They are especially large; plain, yet well-maintained. *Write well in advance to Apartado 141.*

INEXPENSIVE

Bungalows Vepao ★

Playa La Ropa; $55 • 12 modern double-decker units (a few facing the sea) in a garden setting next to the beach. Each unit has a kitchenette, plain bath, and balcony. *Reserve in Mexico City at* ☎ *(5) 670-7572.*

Bungalows Allec ★

Playa Madera; ☎ *4-20-02; $55* • CP The ten bungalows here climb the hillside overlooking Madera beach so that all units have sea views, though only a few are right on the beach. Only a few units are designed just for 2 people. Most accommodate 4 persons (and if the price is divided by that number, the category is inexpensive) and have two bedrooms and a sitting area. All units have kitchenettes, terraces, and fans. Friendly management. Breakfast included. Boat takes you to other beaches. Access to watersports. Write Apartado 220.

Susy

Guerrero y Juan Alvarez; ☎ *4-23-39; $40* • Located a block from the Zihuatanejo town beach, this simple, clean and modern hotel has 14 airy rooms, some of which have balconies and garden views. Fans only.

Posada Citlali   √

Guerrero 3; ☎ *4-20-43; $37* • Next door to the Susy, this pleasant hotel has 15 clean rooms, most with small windows overlooking interior garden. Ceiling fans.

WHERE TO EAT

Whether you're staying in Ixtapa or Zihuatanejo, you'll want to explore restaurants in both places just to see what's going on four miles away. Zihuatanejo has the most nonhotel restaurants. During the winter season, dinner reservations are recommended. Restaurant price categories are explained in the Introduction.

With all the seafood available from the Pacific, you won't have any difficulty finding lobster (always expensive, of course), shrimp, and red snapper. If you're spending an afternoon at Las Gatas or La Ropa beach, or even Ixtapa Island, rustic, thatched restaurants will be near at hand to serve local seafood and some Mexican specialties. Also in the area are Mexican restaurants, plenty of steak houses, and a restaurant here and there adds an Italian or Japanese touch to its menu.

IXTAPA

If you're visiting for the afternoon, you might select a spot on Palmar beach for your lunch—on the tranquil stretch of beach beyond Carlos 'N Charlies, there are thatched eateries where modestly priced seafood can precede a soothing snooze in a hammock. If the beach isn't in your luncheon plans, the shopping complex offers great variety. Our favorite here is **Le Montmartre** (across from Omni hotel; breakfast through dinner; moderate and up). The French food at this pleasant second-story terrace restaurant is consistently good; at lunchtime, it includes some of the tastier offerings in Ixtapa—pâté maison, salade tomate, and quiche, along with choices of fish and even an individual, savory pizza. Across from the Presidente hotel is the popular and inexpensive **La Hacienda**, a good choice for breakfast and snacks.

In the evening, there is a variety of cuisine and ambience to choose from among restaurants that charge U.S.-style prices. The **Villa de la Selva** *(Westin Resort access road; reserve at* ☎ *3-03-62)*, nestled amid tropical vegetation, with terraces overlooking the rocky cliffs and the Pacific far below (illuminated at night), offers spectacular sunsets over cocktails and candlelight dining for its international cuisine (filet mignon, Caesar salad, seafood). The villa of a former Mexican president, the restaurant is now one of the most romantic in Ixtapa. On the opposite side of this mountain is **El Faro** *(Westin Resort access road or funicular from east end of Palmar beach; 6-11 p.m., closed Sunday; reserve at* ☎ *3-06-85)*, with dramatic views over Palmar beach, piano music, and steak and seafood. At sea level, you might try the **Villa Sakura** *(shopping complex across from Krystal hotel; 6 p.m.-1 a.m.;* ☎ *3-02-72)*. This Japanese restaurant is set amid gardens with fountains and waterfalls and serves seafood in many styles—sashimi, sushi, tempura, and teppanyaki among them. Here, too, is **El Sombrero** *(Ixpamar mall;*

dinner only, closed Sunday; no reservations), cheerful and Mexican in ambience, if not romantic. You can order a good steak or even red snapper, but what is special is the sophisticated Mexican food, made with the freshest ingredients—try the sopa de medula or mole. Surprisingly, the prices are as high as any in Ixtapa. There are less expensive options in the shopping center. **Le Montmartre** *(across from Dorado Pacifico; moderately expensive)* serves its fish poached and with hollandaise in the evening, while neighboring **Da Raffaello** *(lunch and dinner; 3-23-86; moderate)* serves decent manicotti and other Italian specialties.

ZIHUATANEJO

If you are just visiting for the day, you might head for La Ropa beach. The **Villa del Sol** lets non-guests use its terrific beach terrace for the price of a lunch (moderately set minimum), while down the beach, almost to the end, you can enjoy the surf and food at the locally popular **La Perla** *(9 a.m.-9 p.m.)* where the prices remain modest despite the new sports bar. Breakfast is inexpensive here, as are the good ceviche and fried oysters. In town, **La Bocana** *(Alvarez 14)* is a pleasant, typical Mexican restaurant near the beach that serves a good, inexpensive breakfast, a budget comida corrida, and evening antojitos like tostadas and hearty pozole (hominy soup). On the Playa Principal are food stands serving up inexpensive grilled, whole fish and ceviches; fronting the beach along the Paseo del Pescador, restaurants, like the old favorite **Elvira's**, offer fuller menu options, including breakfast, at similarly inexpensive prices. For exotic fruit drinks, sandwiches, and salads, head for **100% Natural** *(Gonzalez at Cuauhtemoc; inexpensive).*

In the evening, Zihuatanejo has its share of finer restaurants. They tend to be less expensive than in Ixtapa, more intimate, but also less heavy on the ambience. **The Bay Club** *(road above Madera beach; closed Sunday and parts of summer;* ☎ *4-38-44; expensive)* offers lovely views over Zihuatanejo Bay and a tranquil indoor restaurant with continental cuisine. There's also a mesquite grill on the outside terrace and dancing in the evening. The **Villa del Sol** *(see hotels; expensive)* offers a very limited, set price menu, but the food is good, the location is La Ropa beach. Back in the center of town, there are a number of popular restaurants within a few blocks of the town beach. **Coconuts Bar and Restaurant** *(Guerrero near Alvarez)* offers a garden setting with candlelit tables for enjoying a good house salad or lobster bisque, chateaubriand, and a slice of American pie. The menu is varied, the food quite decent, just avoid the pasta. *(Noon-4:30, 6:30-10 p.m.; reserve at* ☎ *4-25-18; expensive.)* More moderate, but with less variation on the menu is the smaller, candlelit **El Castillo** *(Ejido 25)* where we had a fine meal of filet maitre d'hotel, red snapper, and mixed salad. *(Open for dinner Wednesday- Monday;* ☎ *4-34-19).* Despite its location six blocks from the beach, **Chili's** *(Altamirano 46; closed off season,* ☎ *4-37-67; moderately expensive),* has become a favorite for expertly prepared Mexican dishes, such as its chiles rellenos, and an attractive setting. **Las Cascadas** *(Cuauhtemoc, between Ejido and Bravo; moderate)* is simple in ambience, yet popular for its Italian cuisine—we can only vouch for its pizza.

ENTERTAINMENT

Not many years ago, when Zihuatanejo's streets weren't yet paved, it nonetheless had a disco. Today, the town's streets are cobblestoned and there are all of two discos. If you want to dance, you surely will visit the hotels in Ixtapa. You might want to take in Ixtapa around early evening anyway, because the most spectacular sunsets can be seen from its beach and the hotel lobby bars, like the one at the Westin Resort, offer live music. Later in the evening, many hotels have Fiesta Mexicana nights with live music, folk dances, and buffets of Mexican food. (For the ever changing schedule of the fiestas, check with the tour agency in your hotel). Among Ixtapa's discos are: **Christine** at the Krystal and, practically across from it, the **Magic Circus**. If dancing on the beach sounds better, then head for **Carlos 'N Charlie's,** beyond the Posada Real. In Zihuatanejo, **Ibiza** (on hillside above Madera beach) is the long-time favorite of many of the town's devotees. Apart from checking out the basketball game on the town square with the ocean as a backdrop, join the local foreign community in the bar scene at **Coconuts** (open later than the restaurant).

GETTING TO AND FROM IXTAPA/ZIHUATANEJO

AIR

Many international flights have stopovers in Mexico City or Guadalajara and domestic flights connect Zihuatanejo directly with these two cities, making this resort a convenient complement to a sightseeing vacation in either city.

The airport is about 20 minutes from Ixtapa and a bit closer to Zihuatanejo. Buses (to Ixtapa only) and collective vans provide public transportation to your destination, and there are car rental agencies at the airport.

BUS

First-class Estrella de Oro buses run several times a day to Acapulco (4 hours), Mexico City via Toluca (7-1/2 hours), and to Lazaro Cardenas (Playa Azul); and Uruapan (7 hours). From the Central de Camiones, Estrella Blanca also runs first-class buses to Acapulco.

CAR

Acapulco is 230 km (143 m) south on MEX 200, a good 4 hours away. MEX 200 north runs through a remote area until it reaches the dams of the great Balsas River and the industrial congestion of Lazaro Cardenas (110 km, 68 m). Just beyond the road skims Playa Azul (a wide, not especially attractive beach and town), before beginning its mountainous climb to Michoacan (see "Uruapan") or continuing to Manzanillo (see that chapter).

Mex 134, the 332-km (206-m), 7-hour mountain road to Toluca is too remote to be an attractive alternate route to Mexico City, Taxco (turnoff at Altamirano) or Morelia (via Zitacuaro). If you go this way, be prepared for limited facilities.

DIRECTORY

Airlines • *Aeromexico*, Juan Alvarez 34 (☎ 4-20-18); Mexicana, Dorado Pacific in Ixtapa (☎ 3-22-08); and Delta (☎ 4-33-86).

Banks • *Bancomer*, behind Villa Sakura in Ixtapa, offers good exchange rates (10 a.m.-1 p.m.); in Zihuatanejo, check Banamex at Cuauhtemoc 4 (9 a.m.-noon), and others.

Boat Rentals • At Zihuatanejo town pier, Playa Quieta, or through tours.

Books in English • Shops at Westin Resort, El Presidente, and other Ixtapa hotels; Byblos (Alvarez near Guerrero) in Zihuatanejo.

Buses • *Estrella de Oro*, Paseo del Palmar near Morelos; Central de Camiones, Morelos 2 km east of Juarez.

Car Rentals • At airport and in both towns; there are several agencies, among them Avis (☎ 4-22-75) and Hertz (☎ 4-25-90).

Fishing • Through Ixtapa hotels or docks in Zihuatanejo and Playa Quieta.

Golf • Palma Real Golf and Tennis Club in Ixtapa near hotels; 18-hole course (☎ 4-22-80).

Groceries • Mini-Super in La Puerta Center in Ixtapa; the market for produce around Paseo Benito Juarez, and *La Surtida*, 1 block from beach on Cuauhtemoc in Zihuatanejo.

Horseback Riding • Horse rentals behind La Ropa beach and north of Ixtapa at Playa Linda.

Mopeds • La Puerta Shopping Center, Ixtapa.

Post Office • Left off Guerrero in Zihuatanejo, 6 blocks from beach.

Scuba Diving & Snorkeling • *Oliverio* at Las Gatas and Ixtapa Island, for equipment and instruction; also *Zihuatanejo Scuba Center*, near town dock; others on Cuates Beach.

Taxis • At hotels (prices often posted in lobbies), along streets, and stand at Juarez and Bravo (☎ 4-28-16) in Zihuatanejo.

Telegraphs • Altamirano near Cuauhtemoc in Zihuatanejo.

Tennis • At Palma Real Golf Club (☎ 4-22-80) in Ixtapa; at La Ceiba (above Playa Madera; ☎ 4-49-77 Zihuatanejo; and many hotels.

Tours • Hotels; Ixtapa Shopping Center travel agencies; and Zihuatanejo dock for fishing and beach-hopping.

Tourist Office • Paseo del Pescador, near town hall (☎ 4-22-07; weekdays 9 a.m.-2 p.m. and 5-7 p.m.); in Ixtapa, Kiosk at La Puerta Shopping Center (weekdays 10 a.m.-3 p.m.).

Watersports • Windsurfing and waterskiing at La Ropa, Las Gatas, and Ixtapa.

MAZATLAN

This modern city thrives on fishing. Originally established as a port for shipping the gold and silver pouring out of inland mines, Mazatlan's sailfish and marlin now attract deep-sea anglers from California, and its commercial facilities for catching and packing shrimp are the largest in Mexico. Here, the Sierra Madre mountains retreat inland, and only three hills break up the immediate landscape of the city, making Mazatlan the least picturesque of Mexico's Pacific resorts. Yet, Mazatlan's excellent sports-fishing facilities (the best season is Jan.-May), and its convenience to the western United States attract thousands of tourists each year.

KEY TO MAZATLAN

Sights • Not stunningly beautiful or offering the best Pacific beaches, but modern, comfortable, and convenient for travelers from the western U.S. Short day trips can be arranged to former silver-mining towns or into the tropical rain forest around San Blas.

Sports • The place for deep-sea fishing for marlin and sailfish; other watersports, golf, and tennis at hotels.

Shopping • While this is not a major crafts region, a number of good boutiques bring Mexican specialties to Mazatlan.

Fiestas • Carnival has long been celebrated in Mazatlan, and the festivities grow with every year. These five days of gaiety occur before Lent.

Where to Stay • Many hotels in all categories, and camping too. Reservations required months in advance of Carnival celebrations.

Where to Eat • Seafood, especially shrimp.

Entertainment • Sunday bullfight and evening discos.

Getting Around • If rental cars and mopeds, cabs, and buses don't please you, flag down a golf-cart-style pulmonia. The Sabalo bus runs from town to the beaches and better hotels, and Playa Sur buses go to ferry dock area. (There's service from 8 a.m.-midnight.)

The Malecón, or coast drive, changes its name often during its 25 km (15-1/2 m) sweep from the docks to the northern beaches. Around Gaviotas Beach is the Zona Dorada, or "Golden Zone," the tourism center of Mazatlan.

Practical Tips • Mazatlan is subject to some cool gusts from the north during the winter season. Its average annual temperature is 16° cooler than Acapulco.

Most of touristic Mexico is on central time, but Mazatlan is on mountain time.

Most shops keep American hours (10 a.m.-6 p.m.) Mon.-Sat.

WHAT TO SEE AND DO

Most important to the sun worshipers are the beaches, and Mazatlan has a wide variety of them. At the foot of the Mirador, the Malecón begins its handsome broad sweep around the city at **Olas Altas Beach**. The beach here is good for sunset watching and strolls rather than swimming, especially farther north at the rocky coast of **Los Pinos** (also known as "The Cannon" because of its location near the Spanish Fort). Even farther north, near the Monument to the Fisherman, is the wide and beckoning beach at Avenida del Mar called **North Beach**. Both Olas Altas and North Beach, edging the downtown area, are modest resorts of considerable character. Olas Altas has started to renovate some of its handsome colonial buildings (most in the few blocks just off the Malecón). And mid-morning at North Beach, fishermen bring their boats ashore so that pelicans and shoppers alike can look over the day's catch (Malecón near Juarez). As you continue north on the Malecón, passing the landmark disco Valentino's, you enter the more modern resort zone. Here the beaches hide behind hotel facades at **Camaron** and **Las Gaviotas** only to reemerge farther north at **Sabalo Beach** and the lovely, palm-lined, not yet totally developed (but occasionally scarred by ungainly condominiums), **Playa Escondida**, which stretches for miles out to Cerritos Point. Wherever you choose to swim or waterski, you'll find yourself in the area of Las Gaviotas Beach for shopping, eating, and entertainment. Called the **Zona Dorada**, or Golden Zone, the name must refer to the profits dreamed of by the owners of the many shops, restaurants, moped rental agencies, and fast-food emporiums that have collected here in too random a manner.

ISLANDS

Launches and cruises take you to other beaches and tour the harbor. **Isla de la Piedra** has a small village and a good beach; a ferry near the northern end of the freighter docks will take you there. The amphibious Super Pato can take you to another island, **Isla Venado**, for swimming, snorkeling, and scuba diving *(departures from the beach next to El Cid)*. Or better yet, sail yourself to Isla Venado or the other two small islands just offshore near El Cid and the Holiday Inn. Leaving from the docks on the south side of town near the lighthouse are two cruise ships, the *Mazatlan Fiesta Cruise and Sinaloa Fiesta Yacht*. In addition to a harbor tour, they stop at a beach for swimming and sometimes offer a moonlight cruise with entertainment.

MUSEUMS & EXCURSIONS

For land touring, you can get panoramic views from **El Mirador**, just beyond Olas Atlas at the top of the zigzagging coastal road, and then descend

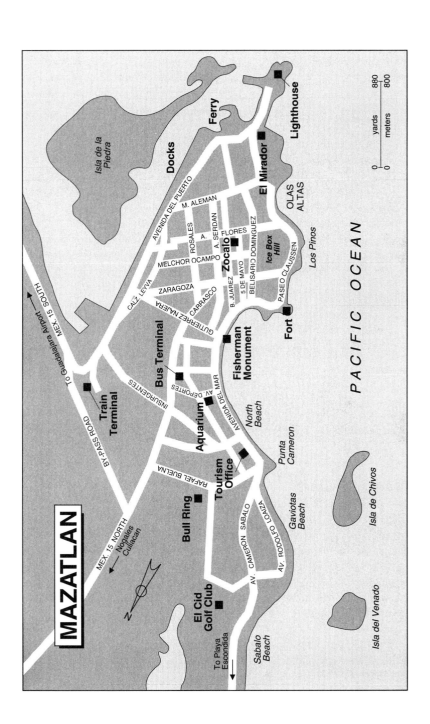

MAZATLAN

Isla de la Piedra

Ferry

Docks

Lighthouse

El Mirador

OLAS ALTAS

AVENIDA DEL PUERTO

M. ALEMAN

A. SERDAN

A. FLORES

ROSALES

MELCHOR OCAMPO

Zocalo

BELISARIO DOMINGUEZ

Ice Box Hill

Los Pinos

CALZ. LEYVA

ZARAGOZA

B. JUAREZ

5 DE MAYO

PASEO CLAUSSEN

GUTIERREZ NAJERA

CARRASCO

To Guadalajara Airport

MEX. 15 SOUTH

Fort

PACIFIC OCEAN

Bus Terminal

INSURGENTES

Fisherman Monument

Train Terminal

BY-PASS ROAD

AV. DEPORTES

Aquarium

AVENIDA DEL MAR

North Beach

Punta Cameron

RAFAEL BUELNA

Tourism Office

Isla de Chivos

MEX. 15 NORTH

Nogales
Culiacan

Bull Ring

SABALO

Gaviotas Beach

AV. CAMERON

AV. RODOLFO LOAIZA

N

El Cid Golf Club

Sabalo Beach

Isla del Venado

To Playa Escondida

yards 880
meters 800

0
0

to the area of the lighthouse and the bustling harbor. The old downtown around the zócalo and Olas Altas has been revitalized. The tiny **Museo Regional** *(Sixto Osuno 76; weekdays, free)*, is situated in a colonial building just a half block off Olas Altas. And 3 blocks farther away is the 1860 opera house, the **Teatro Angela Peralta** *(Sixto Osuno; open for concerts and during Carnaval)*. Also, there is the **Acuario Mazatlan** *(Av. de los Deportes 111)* with 250 species of fish from all over the world. *(Tuesday-Sunday, 10 a.m.- 6 p.m.; fee.)* The place to go for colonial architecture and the ambience of traditional Mexico is the 16th-century mining town of **Copala**, just over an hour away. The drive through the foothills of the Sierra Madres is scenic and as you wind your way to Copala on MEX 40, you pass **Concordia**, a furniture and pottery-making village. At tiny Copala, it doesn't take long to walk about the cobblestone lanes and check out the church, so plan on having lunch to break up your trip. The Posada San Jose, a restored colonial building on the zócalo, will be visited no matter what, so you might also check out its restaurant, with decent Mexican food and moderate prices. (If you drive, take MEX 15 south through Villa Union and turn left at the Pemex onto MEX 40 in the direction of Durango.) Another excursion is the **Jungle Trip** offered by tour agencies. A day is spent visiting a few sights around San Blas and boating through the tropical rain forest. You can make your own arrangements by traveling along the coast to San Blas (see "On the Road" below) and then bargain for a launch up the river. *Practical tip:* Bring insect repellent.

SHOPPING

The easiest place to shop is right on the beach, where vendors most certainly will find you to hawk everything from costume jewelry to wool sweaters. Many of the same items, as well as attractive polished huaraches, or sandals, can be obtained more cheaply in the town **mercado** *(Juarez, 2 blocks before zócalo)*. Bargain at beach and market. Boutiques can be found in every hotel and they dot the Malecón, but the greatest number and choice can be found in the Golden Zone, the loop formed by Av. Cameron Sabalo and Rudolfo Loaiza as it brushes past Gaviotas beach. As you head up Av. Cameron Sabalo from town, you'll see the cotton sports clothes of **Polo Ralph Lauren** and **Aca Joe**. Then swing left onto Loaiza (also called Gaviotas) and you'll come to the **Mazatlan Arts and Crafts Center**, with numerous clothing shops and a large crafts store with paper flowers and hand-blown glassware. Next door is **Sea Shell City**, then **Tequila Tree Mall**, with resort clothing boutiques and a shop with handwoven cotton tablecloths. After passing a large curio market at the corner of Las Garces, you come to the fine shops in Hotel Playa Mazatlan, including **Casa Roberto**, with charming tinware, lacquer trays and other Mexican crafts. Farther along Av. Loaiza you pass the main store of **Designer's Bazaar,** with Vercellino's resort clothes and Sergio Bustamente's sculptures in the upstairs galleries. A few steps away is **El Baul**, with giant charro sombreros. As you finally complete the loop with Av. Camaron Sabalo, you arrive at leather heaven with several shops selling finely tooled pieces as well as cowboy boots.

WHERE TO STAY

Buses connect the zócalo in town with Sabalo and Escondida beaches in the north so that even without a car you have means of traveling from the downtown area to the north beaches where most of the better hotels are. Unless stated otherwise, rooms are air-conditioned. The winter season (December 15-April 15), especially during Carnival celebrations, requires reservations in advance. Write Mazatlan, Sinaloa, or, call area code 69.

VERY EXPENSIVE

Camino Real

11-1/2 km (7 m) north at Punta del Sabalo; ☎ *83-11-11; $140* • On a rocky promontory overlooking the sea and a lagoon, this three-story, intimate hotel is surrounded by gardens and terraced down to the beach level. The 162 large rooms are tastefully decorated and those with lagoon, not sea, views are less costly. Restaurants, bars, and shops. Pool, watersports, and two tennis courts. Golf and deep-sea fishing arranged. *For reservations, call, in the U.S.,* ☎ *800-722-6466.*

EXPENSIVE

El Cid Tourist Resort

9 km (5-1/2 m) north on Av. Camaron-Sabalo; ☎ *83-33-33; $129* • An enormous pool that meanders under bridges and past waterfalls is the set piece for this 1000-unit resort club and convention hotel on Sabalo beach. Two high-rises, along with lower structures (some right on beach) share facilities and 140 acres of land with a condominium complex across the street. (The higher priced units are on the beach side of the street.) Seven restaurants and bars, supper club, and disco. Pools, a sauna, 18-hole golf course, 17 tennis courts, squash, and watersports including sailing and scuba diving. *Write Apartado 813.*

Los Sabalos

6-1/2 km (4 m) on Av. R. Loaiza; ☎ *83-53-33, $107* • On a fine section of Gaviotas beach, this stark white and ultramodern complex has 10-story towers with 180 units, many with sea views. The rooms are large and well-decorated and have small marble bathrooms; some have balconies. Restaurants and bar. Zigzagging pool, tennis, and health club with Jacuzzi and sauna. *Write Apartado 944.*

Holiday Inn

8-1/2 km (5 m) north at Av. Camaron-Sabalo 696; ☎ *83-22-22; $95* • This well-maintained hotel has 200 comfortable units (half with sea views) in a six-story complex on Sabalo beach. Restaurants and disco. Decently landscaped pool area (sea difficult for swimming); tennis and arrangements for watersports and golf. *For reservations, call, in the U.S.,* ☎ *800-465-4329.*

MODERATE

Suites Las Flores

7 km (4 m) on Av. R. Loaiza; ☎ *83-51-00; $70* • On Las Gaviotas beach, this nine-story tower is bustling and efficient. It offers some well-decorated, large suites with kitchenettes and balconies with sea views. (Less costly regular rooms available as well among the 122 units.) Restaurant and bar. Shops. Small pool and access to other sports. *Write Apartado 583.*

Oceano Palace

10-1/2 km (6 1/2 m) on Av. Camaron-Sabalo; ☎ *83-06-66; $60* • The lobby area of this slightly older hotel on Sabalo beach struck us as undistinguished, but the 200 rooms in this six-story complex are modern and well designed, most with pool or ocean views. Restaurants, bars, and disco. Shops. Pool, dive club, and arrangements for golf and tennis. *Write Apartado 411.*

Playa Mazatlan

7 km (4 m) north on Av. R. Loaiza; ☎ *83-44-44; $75* • On Las Gaviotas beach, this sprawling, bustling, and convenient hotel has so grown over the years that its 355 units vary greatly in size and view as well as whether they are in older, hacienda-style units or modern towers. Though our star-rating is for the better rooms, all are adequate. Restaurants, bar with entertainment, and many shops. Pool and arrangements for watersports, tennis, and golf. *Write Apartado 207.*

Hacienda Mazatlan

3 km (2 m) on Av. del Mar at Flamingos; ☎ *82-70-00; $60* • Located in the unpretentious and enjoyable North Beach area, the hotel and its terrace rocking chairs look across the Malecón to the beach. All 100 rooms are well furnished and large, with balconies and sea views. Restaurants, bar with entertainment, and night club. Pool, underground passage to beach, and arrangements for other sports. Apartado 135.

Motel Los Arcos

7 km (4 m) on Av. R. Loaiza; ☎ *83-50-66; $60* • On Las Gaviotas beach, this "motel" really is nothing more than 20 modern and large suites (a/c in bedroom only) all cozily arranged around a pleasant beachfront terrace. Most, not all, units with sea view. *Write Apartado 132.*

Aqua Marina Best Western

3 km (2 m) at Av. del Mar 110; ☎ *81-70-80; $60 CP* • Without the charm of the Hacienda, but on the North Beach road, this motel has 150 decently appointed rooms. Restaurant. Pool. Parking. *For reservations, call, in the U.S.,* ☎ *800-528-1234.*

Tropicana

6-1/2 km (4 m) at Av. R. Loaiza 27; ☎ *83-80-00; $48* • Across from Los Sabalos Hotel, this modern hotel is centrally located in the Zona Dorada. Half of the 80 rooms have balconies and sea views (from across the street); all are large with modern baths. Restaurant, bar, and shops. Small pool, access to beach. Parking. Rates increase Dec., Feb., and Mar.; otherwise a bargain. *Write Apartado 501.*

BUDGET

Posada de la Mision   √★

10-1/2 km (6 1/2 m) on Calz. Camaron Sabalo; 83-24-44; $30 • Across from Sabalo beach, this hacienda-style hotel wraps around a very pleasant garden and offers 69 clean and adequate rooms with ceiling fans. Restaurants and pool. *Write Apartado 546.*

La Siesta

Olas Altas 11; ☎ *81-26-40; $29* • On the Malecón, this hotel has three stories of 60 fresh and brightly furnished rooms around a courtyard containing the popular El Shrimp Bucket restaurant. Though the music stops at 10 p.m., those sensitive to noise should beware.

Belmar

Olas Altas 166; ☎ *85-11-11; $34* • On the Malecón, the 200 rooms may not have sea views, but they are better furnished than the age of this hotel would suggest. Older bathrooms, though. Restaurants nearby. Pool.

Joncol's

B. Dominguez Norte 149; ☎ *81-21-31; $20* • Near the beginning of North Beach, this hotel (37 rooms) is nothing fancy, but the front rooms are ample and have balconies, with glimpses of the sea. May be closed for renovations.

WHERE TO EAT

Shrimp, shrimp, and more *camarones* cooked *natural* and served cold, fried, or grilled and spiced a *la diablo*, or with bacon and cheese, or just good old garlic. When you tire of shrimp, try an appetizer of smoked marlin or switch to *langosta* or oysters Rockefeller or even share a feast called *parrillada de mariscos* (mixed seafood grill). Some of the very popular places for enjoying these specialties are **El Shrimp Bucket** *(Olas Altas 11;* ☎ *82-80-19)* and **El Marinero** *(Paseo Claussen at 5 de Mayo;* ☎ *81-76-82),* both lively spots with traditional music to accompany your dinner; and **Tres Islas**, right on the beach beyond the Holiday Inn, where you can have a tranquil lunch or dinner *(*☎ *83-59-32).* All these spots are moderately expensive to expensive (price categories are explained in the Introduction).

More elegant dining can be found at two spots. **Sr. Pepper's** *(Av. Camaron Sabalo across from Camino Real;* ☎ *84-01-01)* is smartly decorated with polished brass, mirrors, and candlelight. There's mellow music and dancing in the bar and set-price meals of mesquite grilled seafood or steak. Dinner only; very expensive. **Casa de Tony** *(Mariano Escobedo 111, 1-1/2 blocks behind the Shrimp Bucket;* ☎ *85-12-62)* is a handsomely renovated colonial mansion, with a piano bar, several formal dining rooms and, in good weather, an outdoor garden. The cuisine is continental—shrimp in white wine, beef medallions in bordelaise—with a Mexican inspiration here and there. Open lunch and dinner; expensive, but not much considering the ambience and fare.

There are other variations on the seafood theme. At **Sr. Frog's** (Av. del Mar; no reservations), a branch of the popular Carlos 'N Charlie's chain (so is El Shrimp Bucket, above), a variety of beef and chicken entrees are added onto the seafood and served up in ample portions at moderately expensive prices. The good food and roar of recorded rock attracts the young. And there are numerous Italian restaurants around town, but by far the most interesting one is **Anifanti** *(Av. Camaron Sabalo 550;* ☎ *84-20-00)*, where your shrimp or oysters are served with fettuccine and entrees include a salad bar. Open lunch and dinner. Moderate-moderately expensive.

LESS COSTLY MEALS

For less costly meals, you might try **Mamucas** *(S. Bolivar 73)*, just 2 blocks behind El Marinero restaurant. Justifiably popular with locals, this plain, air-conditioned restaurant offers its fresh seafood at some of the lowest prices in town. Come here to enjoy not just shrimp (ask for the *especiales*, or larger ones not on the menu), but also a pate of smoked marlin or *albondigas* (fishballs), a whole grilled red snapper, or turtle stew. Open 11 a.m.-10:30 p.m. Moderate. **Los Nortenos** *(Av. del Mar near turnoff for bus terminal)* has a decent price on shrimp as well as regional dishes from northern Mexico like machaca (jerked beef) and queso fundido at inexpensive prices. Overlooking the Malecón at Olas Altas are several sidewalk cafes, like **El Farol** (#33), open all day with modest prices on seafood and a wide choice of inexpensive *anto-jitos*. Near the zócalo is the popular family restaurant **Doney's** *(Escobedo at 5 de Mayo; 8 a.m.-10 p.m.)* decorated with historic photos and serving a budget-priced comida corrida. On the opposite side of town try **Jungle Juices** *(Laguna y Los Garces in the loop area off Camaron Sabalo near R. Loaiza.)*, with good fruit plates and eggs for breakfast, sandwiches and salads for lunch (inexpensive), as well as ribs and other platters (some pricey) for dinner. **Tip:** Mazatlan brews Pacifico beer, which costs less here than other brands.

ENTERTAINMENT

The place to check out for a Sunday afternoon in the winter is the **Plaza de Toros** if you are a bullfight fan. In the summer you might check to see if a rodeo is taking place. In addition to the finer restaurants, fancier resort hotels provide live music in their lobby bars during happy hour and later in the evening as well. The **Hotel Playa Mazatlan** offers a Fiesta Mexicana a number of times each week with a floor show of folk dance and music accompanying its extensive buffet (☎ 83-44-44). El Cid offers **La Cava**, its supper club with floor shows and dancing. Discos abound, but **Valentino's**

is the most inviting, a Moorish palace perched by the sea at Punta Camaron, and the posh **El Caracol Tango Palace** (at El Cid) is very popular with
the young. Perhaps you'll be intrigued by the *espectaculo* promised at **Plaza
Maya** (Av. Loaiza near Sea Shell City—you can't miss the "Maya" pyramids), where a buffet dinner is accompaneid by prehispanic dances of "fire
and the human sacrifice." (Closed Sun.)

GETTING TO AND FROM MAZATLAN

AIR

International (from western U.S.A.) direct flights and domestic flights
on Aeromexico and Mexicana. Daily flights to Mexico City, Guadalajara,
Puerto Vallarta, Zihuatanejo, Monterrey, and other cities. Aviles Bros. offers charter flights if you have something more local in mind, such as San
Blas. The airport lies 23 km (14 m) from town on MEX 15 south and has
car rentals, taxis, and colectivos for getting to your destination. (If you're
renting a car, get explicit directions to your hotel, as the road signs may
mislead you.)

SEA

A ferry connects Mazatlan overnight with La Paz and can take both you
and your car on its 16-hour trip. While there are plans for a tourist ferry,
now it can be difficult to obtain tickets as commercial traffic has priority.
Reserve a month in advance—even then you can be bounced. (In La Paz,
[682] 2-94-85; Mazatlan, 82-21-59).

BUS

The pullman service from Nogales to Mexico City passes through Mazatlan and Guadalajara, so this resort is well connected to both the U.S. border and the rest of Mexico. But there is only one daily through bus (Tres
Estrellas de Oro) to Puerto Vallarta, otherwise reachable only via Tepic.

TRAIN

Special first-class ("Estrella"), but not pullman, service is available on
Del Pacifico from Mexicali (22 hours), Nogales, and Guadalajara (11
hours).

CAR

MEX 15 starts at Nogales and passes through Mazatlan after 1230 km
(763 m). For travel warnings and places to overnight on this trip, see
"Land Routes into Mexico." After 269 km (167 m) south, MEX 15 arrives
at Tepic, where you can continue south on MEX 200 to other Pacific resorts, like Puerto Vallarta (6-1/2 hours from Mazatlan)—or head inland
on MEX 15 for the 4-hour drive to Guadalajara. Total distance to Guadalajara: 525 km (326 m).

DIRECTORY

Airlines • *Aeromexico*, Av. Camaron-Sabalo 310 (☎ 84-11-11); *Mexicana*, Paseo Claussen 101-B (☎ 82-77-22); *Aviles Bros.* for charters (81-37-28).

American Express • Av. Camaron-Sabalo, across from Lyni's (☎ 83-06-00).

Books in English • Mazatlan Arts and Crafts Center on Av. R. Loaiza and better hotels.

Buses • Central de Autobuses, a few blocks inland from North Beach.

Canadian Consulate • Hotel Playa Mazatlan (☎ 83-73-20). Weekdays 9 a.m.-noon

Car Rentals • At airport and "Golden Zone": *Avis* (☎ 82-05-33); *Budget* (☎ 83-20-00); and *National* (☎ 82-03-22).

Cruises • Through hotels or on south side of town near lighthouse.

Ferry • *Sematur* to La Paz, terminal at port, on south side of town (☎ 82-21-59).

Fishing • Charter boats docked south side of town and reservations can be made through hotels or *Aviles Bros.* (☎ 81-37-28).

Mopeds Rentals • everywhere along Av. Camaron-Sabalo in the "Golden Zone."

Post Office • On Juarez at Zócalo.

Railway Station • Beyond docks on south side of town.

Sailboats Rentals • at Hobbie Cat on beach just beyond Holiday Inn and at Agua Sports, next to El Cid.

Tennis • *Las Gaviotas Racquet Club*, North Beach; at resort hotels.

Tourist Office • Federal office on second floor at Olas Altas 1300 (☎ 85-12-22).

Tours • Check hotel agencies for fishing, jungle, and town tours.

Watersports • Sailing, scuba diving, waterskiing, and other sports at many beaches and Agua Sports Center next to El Cid (☎ 83-33-33) and Playa Mazatlan.

ON THE ROAD

SAN BLAS

The small tropical town of San Blas lies 4 hours south of Mazatlan (234 km, 145 m) on a congested stretch of MEX 15, then 36 km (22 m) along a turnoff before Tepic. Once an important Spanish port that supplied the frontier colony of California, San Blas boasts a fort and customs house, both in ruins. In fact, everything in this quiet fishing village seems to be crumbling. Perhaps San Blas' appeal, in addition to low prices, is that it just keeps going on despite the centuries of change around it. The beaches are located a bit inconveniently: the town beach of **Playa Borrega** lies 1 m from the zócalo, and Matachen and Las Islitas a good 3 m. (Take a second-class Santa Cruz bus or drive 4 km, 2-1/2 m, from zócalo on Tepic road, then turn right. After 3 km, the enormous, shadeless expanse of **Matachen** will be off the road to the left; **Las Islitas** down a gravel road straight ahead.) One of the great attractions here is a boat trip to **La Tovara Spring**, situated in the rain forest filled with hundreds of species of birds. Birdlife is best in the morning, so make your arrangements for the tour the night before at the dock near the entrance to town, or in Matachen.

WHERE TO STAY

No deluxe or even beachfront hotels exist here, but the following ones are at least within walking distance of Playa Borrega. For reservations, call area code 321.

Las Brisas ★
Cuauhtemoc 160 Sur; *5-01-12; $77* • Located down a tranquil lane and amid shady gardens, this well-maintained hotel offers 34 large and fresh rooms, some with a/c. Helpful management. Pleasant restaurant and pool. Parking.

Mision San Blas ★
Cuauhtemoc 197 Sur; ☎ *5-00-23; $55* • Just across the lane from Las Brisas, the Mision actually affords some views over the inlet. Basically clean, the 20 rooms here are fan-cooled and cheerful. Restaurant. Write Apartado 14, San Blas, Nayarit.

WHERE TO EAT

Until you spend an afternoon at Borrega Beach sipping a Tecate and eating a budget-priced shrimp or whole fish while the surf thunders nearby, you won't really have experienced San Blas. There must be hundreds of small eateries lining the beach with thatched ramadas for shelter and the beach for a floor; we particularly like **Si Simon**, near the beginning of the line. In town, there's the colonial style **La Familia** *(Batallon 18; 8 a.m.-10 p.m.)* • with jazz background music and international influences in its seafood based cuisine, as well as the more local **La Isla** (Paredes and Mercado;

2 p.m.-10 p.m. closed Sun.) with tablecloths, and shell decorations on the walls, and large platters of seafood (and chicken)—both are a bit upscale for this town, but remain inexpensive.

San Blas requires insect repellant to survive the buggy assaults in early morning and evening. Aeromar flies from Mexico City to Tepic (☎ 2-42-19), where buses connect with San Blas.

TEPIC

Just 35km (22 m) • Beyond the turnoff for San Blas on MEX 15 is the capital of the state of Nayarit but too long isolated from Mexican events to have much historical interest. Two of the most interesting Mexican Indian tribes, the Tarascans and Huichols, live in the mountains of this state, and the local **Museo Regional** (Av. Mexico 91; closed Monday; free) has exhibits on these two groups (see chapter on Michoacan and Guadalajara). By taking the first exit for Tepic (or the one after the bypass, if you're driving from the south), you enter town on Independencia, which, after 4 km, 2-1/2 m, passes La Loma Park, where you can find a number of restaurants, like the clean and airy **Beachcomber** with good, moderately priced seafood (closed Monday) and, just beyond, accommodations:

Motel La Loma   ★
Paseo de la Loma 301; ☎ *(321) 2-29-37; $52* • Has 52 clean rooms with either fan or a/c, a pool, restaurant, and bar for an inexpensive fee.

MANZANILLO: THE COSTA DE ORO

When the Spaniards discovered Manzanillo in 1531, they set about using it for shipbuilding and as a port to launch explorations of Baja California and the Philippines. Today Manzanillo has grown into a major freighting port for commerce with the Orient and has expanded so much that it has absorbed the neighboring town of Santiago. Although Manzanillo's appeal as a commercial port is unmistakable, its reputation as a resort is due to its placement at the beginning of the numerous bays and far-flung beaches along what has become known as the Costa de Oro. Anchored by the facilities of Manzanillo and the world-renowned Las Hadas resort, the gold coast stretches north past golf resorts and broad beaches like the Playa de Oro until, after 60 km (37 m), it arrives at Bahia de Navidad, with its lively villages of Barra de Navidad and San Patricio. Then, along another 60 km, the coast continues past a slowly developing region with numerous beach coves hidden down dirt paths as well as isolated resort hotels at Los Angeles Locos, El Tecuan, and the Costa de Careyes. Many visit the area to collapse in one of the self-contained resort clubs, others prefer the unpretentious atmosphere of Navidad Bay or Las Brisas in Manzanillo, and yet others enjoy resort hopping along the coast, perhaps even ending their explorations at Puerto Vallarta to the north. But if you really want the concentrated diversity and wide choice of an urban resort, such as Puerto Vallarta, this region might disappoint you. Because the Costa de Oro covers 120 km along MEX 200, we present its sights and facilities in the form of a triptik.

KEY TO THE COSTA DE ORO

Sights • The commercial port of Manzanillo marks the beginning of miles of beaches stretching north to Barra de Navidad and beyond to Careyes. A good area for exploration, for deep-sea fishing, and for self-contained resort clubs like Las Hadas.

Sports • Swimming, golf, and tennis at hotels. Deep-sea fishing. Horseback riding.

Where to Stay • From deluxe resort clubs to camping.

Where to Eat • Excellent local seafood.

Entertainment • Quite limited.

Getting Around • In Manzanillo and around Navidad Bay there is local bus service, but if you plan to explore the coast, it's best to rent a car in Manzanillo or hire a taxi. One-day trips on the coast and to Colima can be arranged with tour agencies in Manzanillo.

Practical Tip • Most resort hotels have security guards at the entrance, so when resort hopping be prepared to give your reason for visiting, be it eating in a restaurant, talking to reception personnel, or whatever.

MANZANILLO

Manzanillo can be any variety of places depending on your preferences. At Las Hadas, Manzanillo turns into its most beautiful with dramatic vistas over a town that glitters by night. At nearby Santiago village, it is at its most touristy, with services for patrons of villas and golf clubs. At Las Brisas, it becomes a most pleasant beach area dotted with small hotels and within easy striking distance of downtown (bus service available for these 8 km, 5 m). On the sea, it is a favorite for deep-sea fishing, offering plentiful marlin and sailfish, red snapper and yellowtail, as well as international tournaments in November and February. In town and along the Costera it is far from pretty: Highway blight blocks the 15 miles of coastline around the bay; railroad tracks run next to the center of all social activity, the zócalo. Yet the containerized port bustles with commerce and the zócalo is surrounded with lively cafes. On one corner is the earthy but friendly cantina called the Bar Social; nearby is the old-fashioned Hotel Colonial, its restaurant frequented by stately ladies and uniformed ships' officers. Manzanillo may not have the best beaches in Mexico and it may not satisfy all tastes, but its diverse offerings attract their own loyal following.

WHERE TO STAY

There are many motels along the highway strip as well as other resort and golf hotels in the northern area near Santiago Bay, but we think the following offer the most attractive accommodations for their price category. Rooms are air-conditioned unless otherwise specified. For reservations, write Manzanillo, Colima, or call area code 333.

Las Hadas ★★★★★

turnoff 12 km (7 m) north of Manzanillo, 37 km south of airport; ☎ *3-00-00; $275* • This stark-white resort village designed in fantasy-style architecture with domes, Moorish arches, and Disneyland turrets is terraced into 15 acres of a hillside that descends to the good swimming waters of the bay and a decent 500-yard private beach. Under night lights, Las Hadas dazzles the eye and easily becomes the most remarkable sight along the coast. Its 203 villas and rooms are incredibly spacious and most come with balconies, scenic views, and wall-to-wall white marble floors. Electric carts provide transport around this estate; 3 year-round restaurants, 5 in winter; many bars, one with entertainment, one a disco, and one the Arabian tent of the

Oasis beach bar with cushions for lounging in the most indulgent manner. Fine shops. Two pools, one with its own island, suspension bridge, and waterfalls; sports fishing, and lots of watersports; 10 tennis courts; 18-hole golf course; arrangements for horseback riding. All this, plus the shops and restaurants at the marina next door. *For reservations, call, in the U.S.,* ☎ *800-722-6466.*

Roca del Mar   ★★★

8 km, 5 m north in Las Brisas; ☎ *3-29-50; $135* • This condominium development on one of Manzanillo's nicest beaches offers 40 handsomely and fully furnished units complete with 2 bedrooms, kitchen, and lovely tiled baths. Apart from the snack bar in the club house, you have to find restaurants elsewhere, which are conveniently nearby as are arrangements for most sports. Small pool. 2-night minimum. *Write Apartado 7.*

Hotel La Posada   ★★

8 km (5 m) north in Las Brisas; ☎ *3-18-99; $73 CP•* This charming, American-run inn is right on the beach and next to Roca del Mar. Intimate and tranquil, the inn has only 24 units, each pleasantly rustic, yet comfortable, and fan-cooled. Some restaurant services, bar. Small pool and access to fishing, boating, and other sports. *Write Apartado 135.*

WHERE TO EAT

Manzanillo not only offers plenty of seafood, it dares to serve the tourist sea bass (robalo in Spanish) and mahi mahi (dorado), not just red snapper and shrimp. All usually can be found at the handsome palapa restaurant, **Manolo's** *(Costera, 1 km south of Las Hadas access road; open 6-11 p.m., closed Sunday;* ☎ *3-04-75; moderately expensive),* where the mahi mahi Veracruzano and the pork loin Manolo alike are accompanied with vegetables and salad bar. And try the pecan pie, too. The fish at **Willy's** *(Las Brisas, turn right after Crucero; dinner only; no reservations; moderately expensive)* is excellent and the French chef's onion soup and other specialties can be very good, though the sauces, like mango and ginger, can be heavy to those accustomed to nouvelle cuisine. Stick to the simpler preparations and enjoy the terrific location next to the sea. At the crucero is **El Vaquero** *(1 p.m.-1 a.m.; moderately expensive).* Despite the silly looking chuckwagon on its facade, El Vaquero is an authentic northern Mexican steak house that serves grilled quail and roasted kid, too—often to the accompaniment of traditional music. The spot for romantic dining and sunset watching is **L'Recif** *(Club Vida del Mar, 8 km north of Las Hadas access road, then 1-1/2 km to left;* ☎ *3-06-04; expensive).* The food is continental with mango mousse for dessert; the cliffside views of the sea are lovely. And after lunch you can stay for an afternoon by the pool.

There are plenty of more modest spots. The Hermosa Cove marina next to Las Hadas has several waterfront restaurants, including **100% Natural**, for salads, fruit drinks, and sandwiches. A breezy spot by the sea is the thatched and simple, but clean **Playa de Oro** *(Costera just north of Santiago; till 5 p.m.; moderate)*, serving ceviche and grilled fish. And in town the **Bar Social** *(21 de Marzo)* on the zócalo serves a "free lunch" of guacamole and ceviche for the price of a beer (starting at 1 p.m.) and inexpensive snacks in the early evening when musicians ply their trade under the tropical fans.

BAHIA DE NAVIDAD

North of Manzanillo center, 60 km (37 m).

Following MEX 200, you arrive at crescent-shaped Navidad Bay, edged by one continuous beach stretching a few miles from **Barra de Navidad** to **San Patricio-Melaque** (also known simply as Melaque or San Patricio). Both villages are popular with those seeking an inexpensive vacation along the Pacific Coast, particularly those who aren't too demanding about amenities. Barra de Navidad is where the action is: Along a narrow strip of land lapped on one side by the bay and on the other by a lagoon are the beaches, paralleled by the main street called Legazpi. Here, the surf is too rough for novices, and the entire length of Legazpi seems a bit honky-tonk. Yet, when the sun sets behind the mountains over in San Patricio to the accompaniment of pounding surf, Barra is at its best. Then, as the crowds disappear from the beachfront restaurants, a peace settles over the village and house doors open to cobblestone lanes for breezes and sociability. Over in San Patricio, the sea is much gentler, but the town sprawls, without the appeal of Barra. Minibuses connect the two towns.

The *Tourist Office* is in Barra, Av. Veracruz 206, 1/2 block off Legazpi near Hotel Tropical (☎ 7-01-00).

WHERE TO STAY

With the exception of the Cabo Blanco, you may find the local hotels often lack hot water and scrupulous maintenance. Yet their prices are exceptionally low for a beach area. For reservations in peak season, address correspondence to either Barra de Navidad, Jal. 46930 or San Patricio Melaque, Jal. 48980, or call area code 333.

Cabo Blanco ★★
Pueblo Nuevo in Barra de Navidad; ☎ *7-63-82; $90* • With none of the local ambience and located a quarter-mile from its private beach club (transportation provided), this hotel does offer some of the frills lacking at others, particularly that valuable summer commodity called air conditioning. Built around canals and a marina, the suburban-style facilities include 120 large rooms, many with kitchenettes. Good service. Restaurants and bar. Disco at beach club. 2 pools, tennis, boat rentals, and fishing. Taxi service. To reach, turn off MEX 200 for Barra de Navidad, then turn left just before town. Write Apartado 31

Barra de Navidad ★
Legazpi 333 in Barra de Navidad; ☎ *7-01-22; $42* • On a better part

of the town beach, this hotel has 60 clean and basic fan-cooled rooms, half with sea views. Restaurant and bar. Pool.

Hotel de Legazpi   ★

Extension of P. Sanchez in Melaque; ☎ *7-38-97; $38* • Located at the north edge of town, the Legazpi has one of the best swimming beaches on the bay. The small, friendly hotel is set off the beach with 14 plain, fan-cooled rooms, a pool, and beach palapa. Parking. Write Apartado 15.

Playa Trailer Park

G. Farias in the center of Melaque • 45 sites with hookups and showers on the beach.

WHERE TO EAT

The favorite place to eat local seafood is anywhere overlooking the water in Barra de Navidad. Along Legazpi you find any number of rustic, open-air beachfront restaurants that fill to capacity in late afternoon. The favorite place among the favorites is **Pancho's**, jammed full at 4:30 p.m. with people savoring their shrimp *al mojo de ajo* or their *ceviche campechano*. (Open 8 a.m. to sunset or till the food runs out which might be earlier; inexpensive.) **Eloy's**, down a side street and with a terrace overlooking the lagoon, also is popular for its inexpensive seafood. (Open breakfast to sunset.) If it's dinner you want, then **Corales** (open till 10:30 p.m.; inexpensive) may be the only place along Legazpi still open for enjoying the sunset over a pleasant meal of sopa de mariscos and red snapper. Upscale for the neighborhood, this clean restaurant has tablecloths, no less. Among the long string of beach restaurants in Melaque, we particularly enjoyed the seafood and cleanliness of **Los Pelicanos** (beyond Legazpi hotel; inexpensive).

NORTH ALONG MEX 200

TENACATITA BAY

North of Manzanillo center 84 km (52 m).

Turn off the highway at the Los Angeles Locos exit for Tenacatita Bay and you'll find yourself following a paved road through exceptional tropical scenery and past soaring coconut trees. After 4 km you arrive at a first-class hotel, next to the broad expanse of Los Angeles Locos beach.

Hotel Fiesta Americana   ★★★★

Los Angeles Locos; ☎ *(333) 7-02-20; $210 AP* • This enormous, earth-toned resort complex functions as an all-inclusive resort. The lobby and restaurant areas are open and breezy, the 221 air-conditioned rooms are a bit spartan with sitting areas and private balconies, most with sea views. 2 restaurants (try the creamy and rich avocado soup), bars. Shops and tour agency. Fixed price includes not only all meals but aerobics, tennis, horseback riding, snorkeling and other sports, and, of course, the pool. Secured entrance. Taxi service. One week minimum stay.

For a small fee plus lunch, you can have access to the facilities here—the swimming is good. But Tenacatita Bay is quite large, with other beaches and even a few tiny villages, all reachable by dirt roads found further north on MEX 200.

EL TECUAN

North of Manzanillo center, 98 km (61 m).

The paved access road to El Tecuan (10 km, 6 m) curves its way through the hills to a lagoon lined with mango trees. The hotel here is simpler than most isolated resort hotels and overlooks the open coast, where treacherous surf pounds shadeless expanses of beach. Fortunately, the lagoon is nearby for boating and an inlet by a river for swimming.

El Tecuan Hotel ★★★

Carretara; ☎ *(333) 7-01-32; $75* • High above the sea, this hotel offers great panoramic views. While the facilities are not fancy, the Tecuan offers a lot for the money. Its 35 units are modern and decent-sized, with sea or lagoon views. Restaurant and bar. Pool, tennis, canoeing, waterskiing, bicycling, horseback riding, and shady beach club. Secured entrance. Private airfield. Write Garibaldi 1676, Guadalajara, 44680 Jalisco.

COSTA CAREYES

North of Manzanillo Center, 119 km (74 m).

The Costa Careyes (Turtle Coast) covers 3700 acres of verdant hillsides rimmed by small coves and 15 beaches. While most of this area remains merely slotted for development, some fabulous Mediterranean-style casitas cluster near the two resort hotels here. Only by staying in these hotels can you arrange the horseback riding or boat trips that enable you to explore this coast. After turning off MEX 200, you come to a fork in the road where one prong leads to the **Club Med Playa Blanca** and the other leads to the hotel (2-1/2 km) and private casitas managed by the Careyes developers:

Plaza Careyes ★★★★

☎ *(333) 7-00-10; $135* • Located on one of the most picturesque swimming coves we've seen, the hotel offers 100 rooms, suites, and condos built in Spanish hacienda style around a "plaza" of palm trees. The setting is sublime, the architecture romantic, and the facilities plentiful. 3 restaurants, 2 bars, and shops. 2 beach coves, pool, and tennis. Dive club, boat rentals, windsurfing, and excursions for horseback riding, nature watching, and fishing. Secured entrance and taxi service. You might want to splurge for one of the slightly pricier suites or magnificent casitas. In the U.S., call ☎ 800-543-3760.

OTHER

Farther north is the nondescript town of **Chamela** (9 km, 5 m from Careyes turnoff) that anchors the camping resort, **La Villa Polinesia**, found a few miles away on the beach. Chamela simply offers highway relief with a few restaurants to sustain you. Another 10 km (6 m) north brings you to a Pemex station. These facilities are the only ones along the remaining 130 km (81 m) stretch to the edge of Puerto Vallarata. And after the access road to what is said to be the lovely beach of **Mezcales** (7 km beyond the Pemex), MEX 200 veers inland and becomes monotonous.

GETTING TO AND FROM COSTA DE ORO

AIR

Manzanillo has a few international flights, as well as direct daily flights from Guadalajara and Mexico City. The airport is located down a 4 km access road 39 km (24 m) north of Manzanillo and 24 km (14-1/2 m) south of Barra de Navidad. Car rentals and taxis available for entire coast; combis available for Barra de Navidad and Manzanillo.

BUS

Numerous first- and second-class buses leave the Manzanillo bus terminal every day for Guadalajara via Barra de Navidad (1-1/2 hours) for this trip that takes about 5 hours. But service to Guadalajara is faster via Colima. Other buses head north to Puerto Vallarta, south to Playa Azul (see below).

TRAIN

Once a day, Servico Estrella ("star service") on El Colimese between Manzanillo and Guadalajara via the capital city of Colima. The trip is scheduled to take 7 hours.

CAR

Highway construction around Manzanillo already enables you to bypass much of the port area on new toll roads; when MEX 200D is completed, you will be able to bypass the congested Costera, too, from north of Santiago to the south at Tecoman. This will greatly facilitate travel to **Colima** (MEX 200 to MEX 110D at Tecoman, a total of 105 km, 65 m) and Guadalajara (MEX 54D and MEX 15), which will be only 270 km, 167 m, and about 3-1/2 hours from Manzanillo when MEX 54D is completed. In fact, progress on the new highways already makes it quite feasible to travel from Barra de Navidad to Guadalajara in a day that includes a worthwhile detour to Colima's **Museo de la Cultura** (on MEX 110D at entrance to Colima, follow signs to P. Galvan; in 5 minutes the museum will be on your left at the end of a government complex; open 9 a.m.-7 p.m., closed Sunday; free). The collection of Colima dogs, musicians, and other archaeological materials (see Michoacan background) is delightful. (After visiting, continue in the same direction on P. Galvan and soon you'll pick up MEX 54D to **Guadalajara**, just after you pass an area of decent hotels and restaurants.) The old MEX 80 route to Guadalajara may be tempting to those staying at Barra de Navidad or along the northern Costa de Oro; it does have the advantage of being free. But even from Barra, the 295 km take a bit longer than the toll highways, especially when summer rains cause damage.

The Manzanillo bypass also will speed you on your way **south**, beyond the Tecoman turnoff for Colima, taking you parallel to the Pacific Coast on MEX 200. Along the way are many turnoffs to **popular beaches**, such as **Boca de Pascuales** near Tecoman and **Faro de Buceria,** farther south. However, from here, there is a 200-km stretch of MEX 200 to **Playa Azul** that can be blocked and/or washed away during the rainy season. We unfortunately drove here in the summer recently. Although the first 100 km from Playa Azul were most scenic and easy, the remainder took 2-1/2 wretched hours to negotiate the landslides. Although the most direct and scenic route to highland Morelia and points south, the road is remote, with limited facilities, and should not be traversed without first inquiring about conditions locally. The alternative route is via MEX 110.

To reach **Puerto Vallarta** (*270 km, 167 m*), follow MEX 200 north along the Costa de Oro.

MANZANILLO DIRECTORY

Airlines • *Aeromexico*, in Santiago Center (☎ 2-12-67); *Mexicana*, Av. Mexico 382 (☎ 2-19-72).

American Express • Agencia Bahia Gemelas, at Las Hadas (☎ 3-10-53).

Boats • Charters arranged through hotels.

Bus Terminal • Central Camionera, Hidalgo and Galeana.

Car Rentals • At airport and in Manzanillo: *National* (☎ 3-06-11); and *Avis* (☎ 3-01-94).

Groceries • Mini-supers along Costera.

Post Office • 5 de Mayo at Juarez.

Railroad Station • At end of Juarez near Fiscal Pier.

Tour Agencies • RTM Tours (☎ 3-04-34); see American Express, too.

Tourist Office • Juarez 244 (2 blocks past Bar Social), 4th floor walk up; weekdays 9 a.m.-3 p.m. (☎ 2-00-00).

PUERTO ESCONDIDO

A longtime haunt of surfers following the big waves, Puerto Escondido is slowly being discovered by others attracted by the ease of combining a vacation by the Pacific Ocean with a sightseeing visit to Oaxaca. Although Puerto Escondido has long anticipated the region's touristic development with the opening of a few first-class hotels, its main street was paved only recently. Whether the development of nearby Huatulco will further yuppify this small village is unclear. For the moment, it seems to be going in three directions at the same time, with the rather sterile Bacocho Beach development to the north, the international surfers' shelters along Zicatela beach, and the more Mexican village in the center.

KEY TO PUERTO ESCONDIDO

Sights • A small fishing village with beaches and good surf, and a relaxed atmosphere that leaves you feeling free enough to walk through town barefoot.

Excursions • Daily flights to Oaxaca make this a good sunning spot after a sightseeing tour there. Less developed Puerto Angel and bird sanctuaries are nearby; Huatulco is in striking distance.

Sports • Horseback riding on Zicatela beach, surfing, and swimming.

Shopping • T-shirts galore plus curio markets here and there.

Where to Stay • To date, there are some first-class and a few pleasant moderate hotels, and quite a few surfers' specials.

Where to Eat • Good seafood and international restaurants.

Entertainment • Hanging out on the Andador Turistico.

Getting Around • You can certainly walk this village, especially along the shortest route, which is the beach. Boats and taxis help you to reach some of the isolated beaches more easily. Buses, tour agencies, car rentals, and taxis for excursions farther afield.

Avenida Perez Gasca, the paved main street, is closed to traffic in its center (where it is called the "Andador Turistico"), so you can enter town from the west or east, but you cannot drive through.

WHAT TO SEE AND DO

Fishing boats and many town activities make the main beach a fascinating hub of activity, especially when the fishing boats return. Here, too, is the most popular swimming beach. On the northern edge of town, there is good swimming at lovely **Puerto Angelito Beach** and the even more isolat-

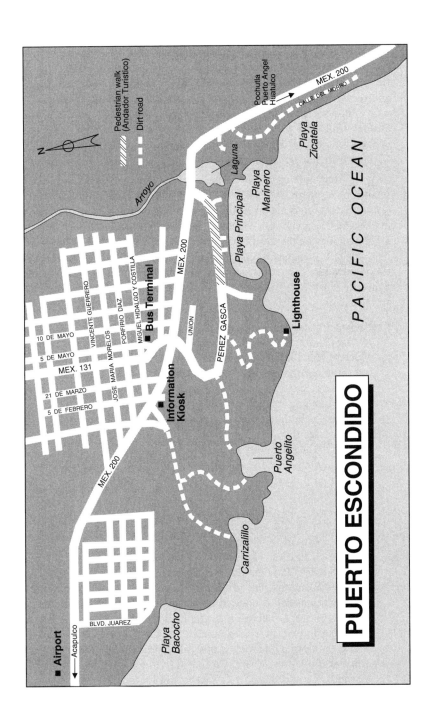

N

Pedestrian walk
(Andador Turístico)
Dirt road

Arroyo

MEX. 200

Laguna

Pochutla
Puerto Angel
Huatulco

CALLE DEL MORRO

*Playa
Zicatela*

*Playa
Principal*

*Playa
Marinero*

PACIFIC OCEAN

MEX. 200

Bus Terminal

MIGUEL HIDALGO Y COSTILLA

PORFIRIO DIAZ

VINCENTE GUERRERO

10 DE MAYO

5 DE MAYO

MEX. 131

JOSE MARIA MORELOS

21 DE MARZO

5 DE FEBRERO

UNION

PEREZ GASCA

Lighthouse

Information
Kiosk

*Puerto
Angelito*

Carrizalillo

MEX. 200

■ Airport

Acapulco

BLVD. JUAREZ

*Playa
Bacocho*

PUERTO ESCONDIDO

ed **Carrizalillo** (path near Puerto Escondido Trailer Park). Both beaches are at the foot of cliffs, though a "road" leads to Angelito and its thatched restaurants. Boats can take you to both beaches. A bit farther north is the long, but difficult for swimming, **Bacocho beach**, now more pleasant with the umbrellas, pool, and restaurant of Cocos Beach Club. South from town the main beach makes a broad sweep, before coming to **Marinero beach** and rocks. Beyond the rocks begins **Zicatela beach**, stretching for over a mile to Punta Zicatela and often as populated by joggers as surfers. Known as one of the four great surfing beaches in the world, Zicatela has a very dangerous undertow in addition to its huge waves. In fact, you may notice that there are few safe swimming spots.

Apart from walking the beaches, or even trying to find some of the smaller ones, there isn't a lot to do in Puerto Escondido. Main street (Perez Gasca) offers a number of T-shirt emporiums as well as small curio markets on either end of the **Andador Turistico**. Or buy fish from the boats as they come in on the town beach around 8 a.m. and 5 p.m.—or just relax. Nothing else is happening. Farther afield, there are other beaches and coves to explore. Tour agencies offer trips to these spots as well as to the Bahias de Huatulco (110 km, 66 m southeast), or you can make your own arrangements.

Puerto Angel Excursion

82 km (51 m) southeast on MEX 200 • A quiet hideaway in the tropics, Puerto Angel is located on a small cove with rocky promontories blocking out the rough sea and protecting the two little beaches that form the focus of the town. Several miles away by dirt road begins the long, white stretch of Zipolite beach (strong undertow), and 1/4 mile towards Pochutla, the good snorkeling waters of Playa Estacahuite (right at sign then 10-minute walk). In this sleepy fishing village, you can watch the maneuvers at the navy base, shop for crafts at La Posada (below). Or you can snack in the beachfront restaurants (**Leyvis y Vicente** on Playa del Panteon also rents boats and snorkeling gear in addition to serving food; between the town beaches is the slightly more upscale Beto's, open 4-11 p.m., with inexpensive seafood). If this sounds like the vacation spot for you, there are a few inexpensive accommodations in town, our favorite being √★**La Posada Cañon Devata**, which is only for those who can enjoy its simplicity and intimacy (8 rooms and 6 bungalows, the latter with patios; fans; $22-26). Within walking distance of tiny Playa Pantheon, this inn is set amid shady gardens and decorated in a monastic sort of way with hand-carved furniture. There's a chapel in the hills; a shop with owner Mateo's paintings as well as Amusco weavings, wood carvings, hammocks, and other fine local crafts. Family-style meals, vegetarian and some seafood, are served. Closed May-June. Write Apartado 74, Pochutla, Oax. 70900. If you want to visit for the day, take a minibus from Puerto Escondido for the 70 km (43 m), nearly hour trip to Pochutla, then transfer for the remaining 12 km (7 m) to Puerto Angel.

Wildlife Preserves

Not far north of Puerto Escondido are two coastal areas that are reminiscent of the Florida Everglades, with their lagoons and mangrove swamps surrounded by jungle and filled with wildlife. Boat trips through these lagoons take you near nesting pelicans, egrets, roseate spoonbills, and many other species of magnificent wading birds. The **Manialtepec Lagoon** (13 km, 8 m north on MEX 200) is closest and arrangements can be made at La Alejandria or Las Hamacas, two spots right on the road. The **Lagunas de Chacahua** (60 km, 37 m north on MEX 200 to Zapotalito turnoff) are larger and part of a national park. Boats can be arranged through a cooperativo at the end of the Zapotalito turnoff. You can make these excursions on your own, in a rental car; plan on two hours at Manialtepec and four, if you want, at Chacahua. Mornings are best, of course, for birdwatching. There are restaurants, but you might want to take a picnic lunch. Tour agencies also offer these excursions.

WHERE TO STAY

Puerto Escondido is undergoing considerable development along its fringes, so that new hotels and hostels should be opening. Those on Zicatela beach, now accessible by the dirt road Calle del Morro, are typical of the surfers' Escondido. Those in the surburban "hotel zone" of Bacocho are isolated from town, about 1-1/2 miles north on MEX 200. Several hotels have opened here, but we list the only ones with beach views. If you don't like Escondido, you might want to check out Bacocho. For reservations, write Puerto Escondido, Oaxaca, Mexico, or call area code 958.

EXPENSIVE

Posada Real Best Western ★★★

Blvd. Benito Juarez; *2-01-33; $90* • Overlooking the sea and near the treacherous waters of Bacocho beach, about 1-1/2 m from town, this 100-room air-conditioned hotel is the best of many superior accommodations planned for the area. (Unused roads now crisscross this "hotel zone" awaiting their hotels.) The grounds, gardens, and large pools (one by the sea at their Cocos Beach Club) can make a stay pleasant. Restaurants. Bar with entertainment. Shops. Location requires taxi into town. *For reservations, call, in U.S.,* *800-528-1234.*

MODERATE

Santa Fe √★★

Calle del Morro; ☎ *2-01-70; $68* • Just a 10-minute walk east of town at the beginning of Zicatela beach, this charming hotel is designed like a set for Romeo and Juliet, complete with balconies and an occasional turret. The 40 units vary in size (some are enormous); all are decorated with Mexican crafts and have air-conditioning and terraces (some with sea views, others look over the shady gardens). Next door, they offer the 8 suites called "Bungalows Santa Cruz," pricier and no a/c but with capacity for 4 people; all with views and kitchenettes, and handsomely decorated with Mexican crafts. Good restaurant, bar, both with ocean view. Crafts shop. Small pool. Reserve in advance at Apartado 96. To reach by car, from town turn right off MEX 200 south at the paved road marked "Zicatela." At beach, turn left.

INEXPENSIVE

Paraiso Escondido

Calle Union, 1/2 block off Perez Gasca West; ☎ *2-04-44; $55* • On a hill overlooking the sea, the well-maintained Paraiso is lovingly cared for, from its tiny chapel and its tranquil gardens to its folkloric wallpaintings and Spanish-style architecture. Half of its 20 comfortable rooms have sea views, all have balconies and a/c; the baths are simple and adequate. Terrace restaurant; pool; parking.

Arco Iris √★

Calle del Morro; ☎ *2-04-32; $31-40* • On Zicatela beach, just 5 minutes farther along than the Santa Fe, this well-run hotel is the most substantial of the surfing establishments, and appealing to all looking for a modestly priced room. The 20 rooms are large enough to hold 2 double beds comfortably and the best have balconies to ease the watch for the big wave. Fans only. Top floor restaurant and bar with panoramic views of sea, and magazines and books in English to browse through. Pool, garden. Parking. *Reserve in advance at Apartado 105.*

Las Palmas ★

Av. Perez Gasca; pedestrian walk; ☎ *2-02-30; $40* • The 35 fan-cooled rooms here have floor-to-ceiling windows and open onto a junglelike garden facing the town beach. Private beach chairs and attractive restaurant.

BUDGET

Acali

Calle de Morro; ☎ *2-07-54; $34* • When the beachcombing urge becomes too strong to resist, consider this Polynesian-style enclave, seemingly constructed of varnished sticks. For a bargain price you can have a casita (ask for the larger bungalows) just off Zicatela beach (near the Santa Fe) with mosquito netting, private bath with hot water, fan and a kitchenette. Pool, garden. Write Apartado 11.

WHERE TO EAT

The days of the cheap thatched seafood huts on the town beach are fast disappearing. Increasingly tipico are places like the **Cabo Blanco** (*Zicatela beach near the Santa Fe; inexpensive*) with its vegetarian stir fry. But don't despair. You can still enjoy a good meal of the local *sopa de mariscos* (spicy seafood soup) and grilled whole red snapper; it's just that the thatching is disappearing and the dirt has been pretty much swept away. Our favorite of these places is **Los Crotos** (*moderate*), right on the town beach, clean, and with very fresh seafood—sweet shrimp tostadas, large portions of red snapper prepared in many ways, but good even when simply grilled a *la plancha*—at reasonable prices. Nearby is **Nautilus** (*west end of Andador; moderate*) with a second-floor breezy terrace overlooking the beach. Owned by a German-Italian couple, the food, primarily seafood, is surprisingly sophisticated and good; for example, grilled Sicilian eggplant (maybe ask for the yoghurt a parte) and tuna steak in greenpepper and wine sauce. Then there is the restaurant at the **Hotel Santa Fe** (*moderately expensive*) with its mesmerizing location on a breezy terrace overlooking the rocks and waves of Zicatela beach. Popular breakfast through snacks, drinks, and dinner, the Santa Fe offers a wide choice of vegetarian and health foods, some Mexican (our favorite is the fish a la Veracruzana with tomatoes, peppers, and olives) and Italian (the lasagne is good)—all prepared with good ingredients, if a bit too timidly with the spices.

Given our choice, we would just alternate among the Nautilus and the Crotos for huachinango, and the Santa Fe for everything else. Maybe you demand more variety. Well, for pizza and salad, try the **Osteria del Viandante** (*Andador Turistico; evenings only; inexpensive*). **El Cappuccino** and **Bananas** (*both on Andador Turistico*) are good spots for a sandwich, fruit licuado, or dessert; Bananas is a bit cheaper and with an outdoor terrace. And for breakfast in town, perhaps the gentlest place to wake up is the palm court restaurant of the **Hotel Las Palmas** (*town beach; inexpensive*), where the eggs *Oaxquenos* are very good.

GETTING TO AND FROM PUERTO ESCONDIDO

AIR

Mexicana flies daily to Mexico City; regional airlines to Oaxaca.

CAR

The paved and scenic road (MEX 175) leaves Oaxaca (see "On the Road" for Oaxaca) and reaches Puerto Escondido (310 km, 192 m) via Pochutla (near Puerto Angel) after 6 hours.

Acapulco lies 429 km (266 m) or 6 hours to the northwest on MEX 200. For a description of that road, see "On the Road" in the Acapulco section. MEX 200 continues southeast past the Pochutla turnoff for Puerto Angel and on to Santa Cruz Huatulco Bay (110 km, 66 m), then Salina Cruz (250 km, 155 m), near Tehuantepec.

BUS

There is now express bus service from Oaxaca to Puerto Escondido. The trip takes 7 hours. Check with a local travel agent for the time and place of departure. Second-class Flecha Roja buses also provide service to Oaxaca (via MEX 175 and Pochutla) and Acapulco. These trips take about 8 hours. Mini-buses shuttle to P;aaochutla and Huatulco. And at Pochutla, you can reserve for the single Cristobal Colon 1st-class bus to San Cristobal de las Casas.

DIRECTORY

Airlines • Airport, 3 km north on MEX 200 with taxi and colectivos (for return arrange through travel agencies) to center; at airport, *Mexicana* (☎ 2-03-02), *Aviacsa* (at airport), and *Aeromorelos* (☎ 2-07-34).

Boat Rentals • On town beach near Las Palmas.

Bus Station • Just across MEX 200 at Perez Gasca West.

Car Rentals • Budget, Posada Real (☎ 2-03-15), at airport, too.

Taxis • At two ends of pedestrian Perez Gasca.

Telephone • Long-distance calls can be made from Telefonos, west end of pedestrian Perez Gasca.

Tours • *Viajes Garcia Rendon* (☎ 2-01-14) on Andador Turistico near Telefonos, and in Posada Real.

Tourist Office • Just off MEX 200, at access road to Playa Angelita; at airport.

BAHIAS DE HUATULCO

Not too long ago, you could visit the tiny village of Santa Cruz Huatulco, sling up your hammock for the night, and spend your days on a fisherman's boat, exploring the 33 beaches and 9 tranquil bays that define the surrounding 18 miles of Pacific Coast. In recent years your beachcomber's serenity would have been disturbed by bulldozers and construction crews busily creating a brand-new resort sponsored by the Mexican government and called Bahias (bays) de Huatulco.

By 2018, Bahias de Huatulco is supposed to be as large as Cancún, with an estimated 2 million visitors annually. The several thousand Mexican residents of the villages will swell to 200,000. Huatulco's location certainly warrants such optimism. The mountains and rocky coastline provide a dramatic setting for exquisite beaches and tranquil swimming and snorkeling coves. Most encouraging is that much of this natural beauty will be left untouched, with many bays and beaches reachable only by boat. For day excursions, there are flights to the colonial city of Oaxaca and its surrounding pre-Hispanic ruins. Up the coast a bit are the more traditional beach towns of Puerto Escondido and Puerto Angel.

Today Huatulco is nearing the completion of its second phase of development. A 2-1/2-mile coastal boulevard connects the three main bays of Santa Cruz, Chahue, and Tangolunda. Boats from Santa Cruz Bay and the resort hotels take you to La Entrega for morning snorkeling or remote beaches such as Maguey y Organo or beautiful San Agustin. The marina on Tangolunda for deep-sea fishing and the Joe Finger-designed golf course are ready. And the brand-new town of La Crucecita, just inland from Santa Cruz bay, is taking shape with shops, restaurants and hotels; its plaza principal already has a band kiosk, but still lacks its church. And the condos and apartments, the boutiques and cafes are filling up their allocated spaces at Bahia Santa Cruz (where there's a curio market) and Punta Tangolunda, too. This chapter will surely grow in length over the next few years. For now it stands merely as an announcement: Bahias de Huatulco is receiving guests.

KEY TO HUATULCO

Sights • A new beach resort more planned than realized.

Excursions • The lovely city of Oaxaca and its ancient ruins and craft villages are easily reached by air; nearby beach villages of Puerto Angel and Puerto Escondido, by land.

Sports • Watersports, including snorkeling. Marina for sports fishing and golf course. Horseback riding. Tennis at hotels.

Where to Stay • Several deluxe hotels and more modest ones away from the beach have inaugurated the new resort.

Where to Eat • Limited at this early phase of development.

Entertainment • In hotels.

WHERE TO STAY

Given the newness of Huatulco, check with your travel agent for the latest information. The area code for Huatulco is 958; postal code 70989.

Club Med ★★★★
Bahia de Tangolunda; ☎ *1-00-33;* • All-inclusive With an exceptional location along three coves of Tangolunda Bay, this total resort club has tastefully divided its 500 bungalow-style units into four small, Mexican "pueblos." Each unit is air-conditioned and has a private, furnished terrace. The extensive grounds are crossed by shuttle cars and the sports activities seem unlimited: 1 Olympic-size pool plus 2 other pools; 12 tennis and 3 squash courts; driving range, fitness center and aerobics; windsurfing; sailing; kayaking, snorkeling; deep sea fishing; and more. There are numerous restaurants with a variety of cuisines, and a disco. Rates vary since the price includes the flight and everything else except bar drinks and excursions. *Call, in the U.S.,* ☎ *800-Club-Med.*

Sheraton Huatulco ★★★★
Bahia de Tangolunda; ☎ *1-00-55; $165* • One of the three first-class hotels sharing the beach around this bay, the Sheraton is the most elegant and the only one not functioning as an all-inclusive. Those of its 346 rooms with ocean views are the most dramatic. Several restaurants and lounges. Pool, fitness center, tennis with instruction and, of course, watersports, especially snorkeling. Access to golf. *Call, in the U.S.,* ☎ *800-325-3535.*

Royal Maeva ★★★★
Bahia de Tangolunda; ☎ *1-00-00; $284 AP* • This hotel is a handsome facility on the Tangolunda beach next to the Sheraton. Like the Club Med, it is an all-inclusive resort, but it provides little escape from the constant noise and hubbub of organized activities, many of them oriented to children. The set price includes not only meals but unlimited cocktails (up till 9 p.m.), sports and fitness activities (some fees

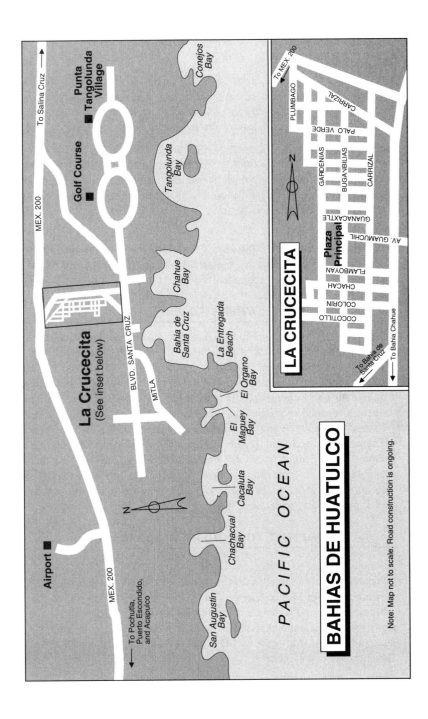

BAHIAS DE HUATULCO

Note: Map not to scale. Road construction is ongoing.

LA CRUCECITA

for golf and fishing), as well as evening entertainment. There are 300 rooms with sea views from their terraces. Restaurants, bars, discos. Pools, tennis courts, snorkeling, kayaking, sailing, windsurfing, aerobics, gym, and even bingo. Write Apartado 227.

Posada Binniguenda

Juarez 5 in Santa Cruz; ☎ *7-00-77; $84* • A block away from the commercial activities of Santa Cruz Bay, this hacienda-style hotel offers tranquil gardens and 100 large, air-conditioned rooms with tiled baths. Airport transport, restaurant, bar. Pool and garden.

Suites Buganbilias

Plaza Principal; ☎ *7-00-18; $50* • In the center of La Crucecita, there's not much of a lobby here, but the 14 junior suites are decently appointed and offer fans, servibars in addition to two double beds. Restaurant. Write Apartado 289.

Grifer

Guamucil s/n; ☎ *7-00-48; $34* • Near the main square of La Crucecita, the Grifer has a pleasant lobby and 20 fan-cooled rooms. Sidewalk cafe. Write Apartado 159.

WHERE TO EAT

A number of pleasant restaurants have opened around the Plaza Principal and in the evening cool, their tables spill out onto the sidewalk. The snappiest is **Maria Sabina** *(Flamboyan on Plaza Principal; 5 p.m.-11 p.m.; moderate)* with its charcoal grilled fish and shish kebab. A block away **Rancho El Padrino** *(Guamuchil; lunch and dinner; inexpensive-moderate)* serves authentic regional specialties, such as the amarillo and verde moles (see "Oaxaca" chapter). Or you can opt for a late afternoon feast of "botanas," platters of tamales, tostadas, and other antojitos. To prove that Huatulco is almost a full-fledged resort, **1/2 Carlos N' Charlies** *(Carrizal at Flamboyans; 5 p.m.-11 p.m., closed Sun.; moderately expensive)*, a small branch of the well-known chain, has opened with its usual lively ambience and international menu of fish, meats, and salads.

GETTING TO AND FROM HUATULCO

AIR

Between the two domestic airlines, Mexicana and Aeromexico, Huatulco is connected with Mexico City by daily flights. The small jets of Aeromorelos connect with Oaxaca; Aviacsa with Tuxtla Gutierrez. Eventually, international carriers are expected to provide more direct service from the U.S. and Canada. Airport is on MEX 200, 16 km (10 m) from Huatulco. Hotel transport provided.

LAND

Huatulco lies 40 km, 25 m south of Pochutla on MEX 200 then 4 km (2-1/2 m) toward the sea. Pochutla is the crossroads for buses on the coast, situated as it is at the intersection of MEX 200 and MEX 175, the five-hour road to Oaxaca. Puerto Angel is only a few miles from Pochutla and Puerto Escondido is 70 km, 43 m further along MEX 200. From Pochutla, second-class buses can be arranged to Santa Cruz.

DIRECTORY

Airlines • Airport, 16 km (10 m) north, off MEX 200, with colectivos to hotels; *Mexicana* (☎ 7-02-23), *Aeromexico* (☎ 4-03-28), *Aeromorelos* (☎ 1-00-55), *Aviacsa* (☎ 4-85-90), all at airport.

Banks • *Banamex*, Blvd. Santa Cruz near market, with cirrus ATM.

Boat Rentals • Bahia Santa Cruz

Bus Station • In Pochutla, 40 km north on MEX 200; minibuses to Huatulco.

Car Rentals • *Dollar* (☎ 4-03-06), in various hotels and with moped rentals.

Golf • Punta Tangalunda

Horseback Riding • Rancho Caballo del Mar, with mountain and beach rides; arrange through hotels.

Taxis • Bahia Santa Cruz, Punta Tangolunda, and Crucecita plaza.

Tours • *Servicios Turisticos del Sur*, Blvd. Santa Cruz at turn to La Crucecita, and in hotels, with trips to 9 bays, Puerto Escondido, and air tours to Oaxaca.

Tourist Office • La Crucecita, Guamuchil near Plaza Principal.

BOOKS ON MEXICO

READINGS

ANCIENT CIVILIZATIONS
The Maya, Michael D. Coe
Mexico, Michael D. Coe
The Art of Mesoamerica, Mary Ellen Miller

THE CONQUEST
History of the Conquest of Mexico, William H. Prescott
The Broken Spears, Miguel Leon-Portilla, editor

EXPLORATION AND ADVENTURE
Incidents of Travel in Central America, Chiapas & Yucatán, John L.
 Stephens
Incidents of Travel in Yucatán, John L. Stephens

HISTORY AND POLITICS
A History of Mexico, Henry Bamford Parkes
Limits to Friendship, Robert A. Pastor and Jorge G. Castenada
Distant Neighbors, Alan Riding

NOVELS
The Underdogs, Mariano Azuela
The Death of Artemio Cruz, Carlos Fuentes
The Power and the Glory, Graham Greene
The Plumed Serpent, D. H. Lawrence
The Bridge in the Jungle, B. Traven

PEOPLE AND CULTURE
Idols Behind Altars, Anita Brenner
Five Families, Oscar Lewis
A Treasury of Mexican Folkways, Frances Toor

REFERENCES AND FURTHER READINGS

Quotations in this book are from the following sources (which also offer excellent reading).

E. Wyllys Andrews IV, "The Development of Maya Civilization after Abandonment of the Southern Cities," In *The Classic Maya Collapse*, ed. T. Patrick Culbert. University of New Mexico Press, 1973.

Anthony F. Aveni, *Skywatchers of Ancient Mexico*, University of Texas Press, 1980.

Joseph Armstrong Baird, *The Churches of Mexico*, University of California Press, 1962.

Ralph Beals, "Gifting, Reciprocity, Savings, and Credits." *Southwestern Journal of Anthropology*, Vol. 26, 1970.

Frans Blom, *Conquest of Yucatán*, Houghton Mifflin, 1936.

Frances E. I. Calderon de la Barca, *Life in Mexico* (1840), E. P. Dutton, 1931.

Bernal Diaz del Castillo, *The Discovery and Conquest of Mexico 1517-1521*, The Mexican Press, 1928.

Hernan Cortes, *Five Letters*, W. W. Norton & Co., 1962.

Charles C. Cumberland, *Mexico: The Struggle for Modernity*, Oxford University Press, 1968.

Fray Diego Duran, *Book of the Gods & Rites & the Ancient Calendar*, University of Oklahoma Press, 1971.

Thomas Gage, *A New Survey of the West Indies* (1648), Robert M. McBride & Co. (abridged), 1929.

Angel M. Garibay, *Historia de la literatura Nahuatl*, Mexico, 1953.

——, *La litertura de los Aztecas*, Mexico, 1964.

George Kubler, *The Art and Architecture of Ancient America*, Penguin Books, 1975.

Diego de Landa, *Yucatán: Before & After the Conquest* (1566), Dover Publications, 1978.

D. H. Lawrence, *Mornings in Mexico*, Alfred A. Knopf, 1927.

Miguel Leon-Portilla, editor, *The Broken Spears: The Aztec Account of the Conquest of Mexico*, Beacon Press, 1962.

John Lincoln, *One Man's Mexico: A Record of Travels & Encounters.* Harcourt, Brace & World, 1967.

Michael C. Meyer and William L. Sherman, *The Course of Mexican History*, Oxford University Press, 1979.

Martin C. Needler, *Politics & Society in Mexico*, University of New Mexico Press, 1971.

Henry Bamford Parkes, *A History of Mexico*, Houghton Mifflin, 1969.

Octavio Paz, *Labyrinth of Solitude: Life and Thought in Mexico*, Grove Press, 1961.

John Reed, *Insurgent Mexico* (1914), Simon & Schuster, 1969.

Nelson Reed, *The Caste War of Yucatán*, Stanford University Press, 1964.

Ralph L. Roys, ed., *The Book of Chilam Balam of Chumayel*, University of Oklahoma Press, 1967.

Fray Bernadino de Sahagun, *A History of Ancient Mexico: 1547-1577: The Religion & the Ceremonies of the Aztec Indians*, Rio Grande Press, 1976.

Stanley J. Stein and Barbara H. Stein, *The Colonial Heritage of Latin America: Essays on Economic Dependence in Perspective*, Oxford University Press, 1970.

John L. Stephens, *Incidents of Travel in Central America, Chiapas & Yucatán* (1841), 2 vols., Dover Publishing, 1969.

——, *Incidents of Travel in Yucatán* (1843), 2 volumes, Dover Publications, 1963.

J. Eric S. Thompson, *Maya History & Religion*, Oklahoma University Press, 1970.

——, *The Rise & Fall of Maya Civilization*, University of Oklahoma Press, 1954.

Evon Z. Vogt, "God and Politics in Zinacantan and Chamula." *Ethnology*, Vol. 12, 1973.

——, *The Zinacantecos of Mexico: A Modern Maya Way of Life*, Holt, Rinehart & Winston, 1990.

Elizabeth W. Weismann, *Mexico in Sculpture: 1521-1821*, Harvard University Press, 1950.

John Womack, *Zapata & the Mexican Revolution*, Random House, 1968.

ROAD SIGNS

Arena suelta	Loose gravel
Camino angosto	Narrow road
Carril izquierda solo para rebasar	Left lane for passing only
Caseta de cobra	Toll booth
Cuidado	Caution
Cuota	Toll
Curva peligrosa	Dangerous curve
Curva resbalosa	Slippery curve
Despacio	Slow
Desviación	Detour
Dirección única	One way
Hombres trabajando	Men working
No pavimento	Unpaved
Peligro	Danger
Puente angosto	Narrow (one-lane) bridge
Rebasar	To pass
Topes	Road bumps
Tramo en reparación	Road under repair
Túmulos	Road bumps
Una vía	One way
Un solo carril	One lane only
Vibradores	Road bumps

Slippery Road
Loose Gravel

Narrow Bridge

Two-way Traffic

No Left Turn

No U Turn

No Parking

Keep Right

Do Not Enter

Steep Hill

Bumps

Yield Right-of-Way

Dip

Parking

Stop

Do Not Pass

Use Right Lane

SPANISH GLOSSARY

PRONUNCIATION

Although it is often said that Spanish is spoken just as you would expect, there are a number of exceptions. While we recommend you buy a phrase book or dictionary to help you speak Spanish, the following phonetic alphabet includes some of the most obvious pitfalls for you to avoid.

VOWELS

a *ah*, except before u, when it becomes more like *ouch*. Other vowels can also transform this vowel.

e *eh*

i *ee*

o *oh*

u *oo*, except in qui, que, gue, etc., when it is silent.

TROUBLESOME CONSONANTS		
cu	before a, o, and u	
qu	before i or e	are pronounced like k
k		
c	before i, e	
z		are pronounced like s
s		
ch		is close to choo choo

743

TROUBLESOME CONSONANTS

g j	before i, e	are like the h in "hero"
g gu	before a, o before e, i	are pronounced hard like "go"
h		is silent
ll		is pronounced like y ("yes")
r		is often closest to a "d" in sound
rr		is rolled
v b		are pronounced like "baby"
x		is most often like an "s", especially before consonants; sometimes before vowels it's like "h" as in Mexico; other times it's impossible.

VOCABULARY

GREETINGS

Buenos días	Good morning
Buenas tardes	Good afternoon, good evening
Buenas noches	Good night
¿Como está?	How are you?
Bien, gracias	Well, thank you
Hasta luego	So long
Adiós	good-bye

BASIC EXPRESSIONS

No hablo español	I don't speak Spanish
¿Habla usted inglés?	Do you speak English?
No entiendo	I don't understand
Escríbalo, por favor	Please write it
Estoy enfermo	I'm sick
Necesito un médico	I need a doctor
¿Cuando?	When?
Ahora	Now

Ayer	Yesterday
Mañana	Tomorrow
Hoy	Today
¿Cuanto cuesta?	How much does it cost?
¿Cuanto cuesta un timbre?	How much does one stamp cost?
Gracias	Thank you
De nada	You're welcome
Por favor	Please
Perdón	Excuse me
Más	More
Menos	Less
Sin	Without
Con	With
Bastante	Enough
Caliente	Hot
Frío	Cold

DIRECTIONS

¿Donde está el museo?	Where is the museum?
el camión?	the local bus?
la calle Juarez?	Juarez street?
el correo?	the post office?

NUMBERS

uno	1	once	11	treinta	30
dos	2	doce	12	quarenta	40
tres	3	trece	13	cincuenta	50
cuatro	4	quatorce	14	sesenta	60
cinco	5	quince	15	setenta	70
seis	6	dieciseis	16	ochenta	80
siete	7	diecisiete	17	noventa	90
ocho	8	dieciocho	18	ciento, cien	100
nueve	9	diecinueve	19	quinientos	500
diez	10	veinte	20	mil	1000

SHOPPING

Algodón	Cotton
Aretes	Earrings
Artesania	Handcrafts
Baúl	A wooden chest, often laquered
Bolsa	Bag
Camisa	Shirt
Cerámica	Ceramics
Cinturón	Belt
Cobre	Copper
Collar	Necklace
Flores	Flowers
Guantes	Gloves
Guayabera	A pleated skirt, popular in Yucatán
Hamaca	Hammock
Huaraches	Sandals
Huipil	A woman's long blouse, sometimes worn as a dress
Jícara	Gourd
Jorongo	Serape or poncho
Joyas	Jewelry
Laca	Lacquer
Lana	Wool
Madera	Wood
Máscara	Mask
Mercado	Market
Milagro	A silver ex-voto offering
Oro	Gold
Piñata	A papier-mâché figure with a ceramic jar interior, often filled with sweets and broken during the Christmas posadas.
Plata	Silver
Piel	Leather
Quexquemetl	A sleeveless shoulder cape
Rebozo	Shawl
Retablo	A painting recounting a miracle

Serape	A poncho or blanket; can also be used as a rug
Sombrero	Hat
Tapete	Rug or carpet
Vela	Candle
Vidrio	Glass
Zapatos	Shoes

EATING OUT

MEALS

Almuerzo	Midmorning breakfast
Antojitos	Mexican snack or appetizers, like tacos
Botana	Snack
Cena	Dinner
Comida	Midday meal
Comida corrida	Fixed-price meal
Menu turístico	Fixed-price meal

COOKING METHODS

Ahumado	Smoked
A la mantequilla	In butter
A la plancha	Grilled
A mojo de ajo	In garlic
Asado	Roasted
Cocido	Boiled
Empanizado	Breaded
Frito	Fried
Guisado	Stew
Milanesa	Fried in batter
Picado	Minced
Revuelto	Scrambled
Tibio	Soft boiled
Veracruzano	In tomatoes, capers, onions, and chiles

MEATS (CARNES)

Biftek	Steak

Cabrito	Kid
Carne	Beef
Carnitas	Roasted pork pieces
Cerdo	Pork
Cordero	Lamb, mutton
Jamón	Ham
Puerco	Pork
Ternera	Veal
Tocino	Bacon

POULTRY (AVES)

Pato	Duck
Pavo	Turkey
Pollo	Chicken

SEAFOOD (PESCADOS AND MARISCOS)

Almejas	Clams
Camarones	Shrimp
Cangrejo moro	Stone crab
Caracol	Conch
Cerviche	Marinated raw-fish cocktail
Dorado	Mahi Mahi
Huachinango	Red snapper
Jaiba	Crab
Langosta	Lobster
Mariscos	Shellfish
Mero	Grouper
Ostiones	Oysters
Pargo	Gray Snapper
Pescado	Fish
Pulpo	Squid
Róbalo	Bass
Trucha	Trout

VEGETABLES (LEGUMBRES)

Aguacate	Avocado
Arroz	Rice
Berro	Watercress
Calabaza	Squash
Cebolla	Onion
Ensalada	Salad
Frijoles	Beans
Jitomates	Tomatoes
Lechuga	Lettuce
Nopalitos	Cactus
Papas	Potatoes
Papas a la francesca	French fries
Papas fritas	Potato chips
Sopa de arroz	Rice soup

FRUITS (FRUTAS)

Durazno	Peach
Fresas	Strawberries
Manzana	Apple
Naranja	Orange
Piña	Pineapple
Sandía	Watermelon
Toronja	Grapefruit
Tuna	Prickly pear

DRINKS (BEBIDAS)

Agua mineral	Mineral water
con gas	with carbonation
sin gas	without carbonation
Café	Coffee
Cerveza	Beer
Ginebra	Gin
Jugo	Juice
Leche	Milk

Licuado	Fruit drink
Refresco	Soft drink
Ron	Rum
Té	Tea
Vino blanco	White wine
Vino tinto	Red wine

MISCELLANEOUS

Azúcar	Sugar
Caldo	Soup
Hielo	Ice
Huevos	Eggs
a la Mexicana	Scambled with tomatoes, onions and chiles
rancheros	Fried with green or red chile sauce
Mantequilla	Butter
Mayonesa	Mayonnaise
Mermelada	Jam
Miel	Honey
Mostaza	Mustard
Pan	Bread
Queso	Cheese
Sal	Salt
Salsa Mexicana	Hot tomato sauce
Sopa	Soup

DESSERTS (POSTRES)

Flan	Caramel custard
Galleta	Cookie, cracker
Gelatina	Gelatin, Jell-O
Helado	Ice cream
Pastel	Cake

USEFUL PHRASES

| *Bien cocida* | Well done |
| *Media cocoda or rosa* | Medium rare |

Casi cruda or roja	Rare
En lata	Canned
Bien frío	Very cold
Bien caliente	Very hot
¿Pica?	Is it spicy hot?
No picante, por favor	Not spicy, please
Sin chile	Without chiles
La propina	Tip
La cuenta, por favor	The check, please
Mesero	Waiter
Joven	Waiter (literally, "young man")
Señorita	Waitress

HOTEL QUICK-REFERENCE CHARTS

Prices given below are in U.S. dollars. Although they are as accurate as we could make them at press time, they are not guaranteed—prices are not government controlled. It is best to consider them estimates that will vary due to inflation, peso-value, seasonal demand and whim.

Except as otherwise noted, rates include tax and are for an average double on the European Plan, without meals. Where CP (Continental Plan) is indicated, breakfast is included; AP (American Plan) includes breakfast, lunch and dinner; MAP (Modified American Plan) includes breakfast and either lunch or dinner.

HOTEL	PHONE	RATE
LAND ROUTES INTO MEXICO		
CREEL (Area Code 145)		
Cascada Inn	6-01-51	118
Copper Canyon Lodge	15-82-14 (in Chihuahua)	130AP
Parador de la Montana	6-00-75	60-65

HOTEL	PHONE	RATE
DIVISADERO		
Cabanas Divisadero Barrancas	10-33-30 (in Chihuahua)	140AP
CEROCAHUI		
Hotel Mision	N/A	150AP
CHIHUAHUA (Area Code 14)		
San Francisco	16-75-55	80
Victoria	N/A	60
LOS MOCHIS (Area Code 681)		
El Dorado	5-11-11	52-64
Santa Anita	5-70-46	84

MEXICO CITY

MEXICO CITY (Area Code 5)		
Antillas	526-5674	29
Aristos	211-0112	119
Bamer	521-9060	60
Bristol	208-1717	75
Camino Real	203-2121	209
Casa Blanca	566-3211	85
Casa Gonzalez	514-3302	22-26
Century	584-7111	119
De Cortes	218-2181	89
Doral	592-2866	51
Fiesta Americana Aeropuerto	571-6753	165
Fiesta Americana Reforma	705-1515	183
Fleming	510-4530	40
Galeria Plaza	211-0014	171
Gillow	518-1440	40
Gran Hotel Howard Johnson	510-4040	88
Imperial	566-3118	155
Krystal Zona Rosa	211-0092	171
Majestic	521-8600	77

HOTEL	PHONE	RATE
Marco Polo	511-1839	168
Maria Cristina	566-9688	65
Maria Isabel Sheraton	207-3933	256
Nikko Mexico	280-1111	231
Ramada Airport	785-8522	138-154
Ritz	518-1340	66
Sevilla	566-1866	30
Stouffer Presidente	327-7700	253
Suites Amberes	533-1306	90
Vasco de Quiroga	546-2614	50

MEXICO CITY EXCURSIONS

TEOTIHUACAN (Area Code 595)

Hotel Villa Arqueologica	6-02-44	77

TAXCO (Area Code 762)

Hacienda del Solar	2-03-23	170
Los Arcos	2-18-36	29
Montetaxco	2-13-00	95
Posada de la Mision	2-00-63	70-85
Posada de Los Castillo	2-13-96	30
Rancho Taxco-Victoria	2-02-10	55-75
Santa Prisca	2-00-80	46

CUERNAVACA (Area Code 73)

Cadis	18-92-04	30
Cuernavaca Racquet Club	11-20-67	130
La Posada de Xochiquetzal	18-69-84	70-75
Las Mananitas Hotel	12-46-46	90-300

TEPOZTLAN (Area Code 739)

Tepoztlan	5-05-22	70

PUEBLA (Area Code 22)

Aristos	32-05-99	90
Colonial	46-41-99	44

HOTEL	PHONE	RATE
Lastra	35-97-55	81
Palacio San Leonardo	46-05-55	74
Posada San Pedro	46-50-77	78
CHOLULA (Area Code 22)		
Calli Quetzacoatl	47-15-33	50
Villa Arqueologica	47-19-66	70
TLAXCALA (Area Code 246)		
Albergue de la Loma	2-04-24	32
Mision Park Plaza	2-01-78	80
CUETZALAN (Area Code 233)		
Posada Cuetzalan	1-02-95	55
SAN JUAN DEL RIO (Area Code 467)		
Antigua Hacienda Galindo	2-00-50	100
La Mansion de Andrea	2-01-20	130
ALTACOMULCO (Area Code 73)		
Hacienda de Cortes	15-88-44	194
COCOYOC (Area Code 735)		
Hacienda Cocoyoc	6-22-11	86
IXTAPAN DE LA SAL (Area Code 724)		
Ixtapan	566-2855	149AP
Kiss	3-09-49	95AP

SILVER CITIES

SAN MIGUEL DE ALLENDE (Area Code 465)		
Aristos San Miguel	2-26-99	41
Casa de Sierra Nevada	2-04-15	98-218
Hacienda de las Flores	2-18-08	115-136
Hacienda Hotel Taboada	2-08-50	208AP
Mansion del Bosque	2-02-77	65-70MAP

HOTEL	PHONE	RATE
Posada Carmina	2-04-58	42
Posada de la Aldea	2-12-96	55
Posada de las Monjas	2-01-71	40
Posada de San Francisco	2-14-66	55
Quinta Loreto	2-00-42	32
Rancho El Atascadero	2-02-06	95
Villa Jacaranda	2-10-15	95-120
Villa Santa Monica	2-04-51	145 CP

QUERETARO (Area Code 42)

El Meson de Santa Rosa	14-57-81	85-105
Mirabel	14-35-35	40-50

GUANAJUATO (Area Code 473)

Casa Kloster	2-00-88	27
Castillo Santa Cecilia	2-04-85	100
El Carruaje	2-21-40	48
El Socavon	2-48-85	40
Ex-Hacienda San Gabriel	2-39-80	69-75
Hosteria del Frayle	2-01-85	48
Parador San Javier	2-06-26	82
Posada Santa Fe	2-00-84	80
Real de Minas	2-14-60	80
San Diego	2-14-99	85

ZACATECAS (Area Code 492)

Aristos Zacatecas	2-17-88	80
Gallery	2-33-11	72
Paraiso Radisson Zacatecas	2-61-83	156
Posada de la Moneda	2-08-81	40
Quinta Real	2-91-04	180-205

SAN LUIS POTOSI (Area Code 48)

Cactus	12-18-71	57
Filher	12-15-62	24
Panorama	12-17-77	70
Real Plaza	14-69-69	70

HOTEL	PHONE	RATE
TEQUISQUIAPAN (Area Code 467)		
Balneario El Relox	3-00-06	89

MICHOACAN AND GUADALAJARA

MORELIA (Area Code 451)		
Calinda Quality Morelia	4-57-05	92
Casino	3-10-03	46
Catedral	3-07-83	57 CP
de la Soledad	2-18-88	67
Mansion Acueducto	2-33-01	37
Villa Montana	4-02-31	123
Virrey de Mendoza	2-06-33	88
SAN JOSE PURUA		
Spa San Jose Purua	510-49-49	150AP
	(in Mexico City)	
ANGANGUEO (Area Code 725)		
Albergue Don Bruno	512-4918	33
	(in Mexico City)	
VALLE DE BRAVO (Area Code 726)		
Avandaro Golf Club & Spa	2-00-03	120
Los Arcos	2-00-42	90
TOLUCA (Area Code 72)		
Castel Plaza Las Fuentes	16-28-56	100
PATZCUARO (Area Code 454)		
Hosteria de San Felipe	2-12-98	42
Los Escudos	2-01-38	34
Mansion Iturbe	2-03-68	37
Meson del Gallo	2-14-74	28-30
Mision San Manuel	2-13-13	35
Posada de la Basilica	2-11-08	30
Posada Don Vasco	2-02-27	63

HOTEL	PHONE	RATE
URUAPAN (Area Code 452)		
Mansion del Cupatitzio	3-21-00	63-87
Motel Pie de la Sierra	4-25-10	38
Plaza Uruapan	3-34-38	54
Villa de las Flores	4-28-00	27
GUADALAJARA (Area Code 36)		
Calinda Roma	14-86-50	77
Camino Real	47-80-00	189
Hotel de Mendoza	13-46-46	81
Fenix	14-57-14	85
Fiesta Americana	25-34-34	209
Frances	13-11-90	55
Crowne Plaza Holiday Inn	34-10-34	190
Hyatt Regency	22-77-78	154-160
Posada Regis	13-30-26	34
Quinta Real	52-00-00	209
Universo	13-28-15	33-40
Vista Aranzazu	13-32-32	81
Vista Plaza del Sol	47-88-90	96
AJIJIC (Area Code 376)		
Danza del Sol	5-25-05	85
La Nueva Posada	5-33-95	60CP
Real de Chapala	5-24-68	89
CHAPALA (Area Code 376)		
Nido	5-21-16	27

OAXACA

HOTEL	PHONE	RATE
OAXACA (Area Code 951)		
Fortin Plaza	5-77-77	85
Gala	4-22-51	55
Las Golondrinas	6-87-26	30
Marques del Valle	6-32-95	50
Mision do los Angeles	5-15-00	98

HOTEL	PHONE	RATE
Posada San Pablo	6-49-14	24
Presidente	6-06-11	150
Principal	6-25-35	30
Senorial	6-39-33	50
Victoria	5-26-33	100-150
Villa de Leon	6-19-77	45
TEHUACAN (Area Code 238)		
Mexico	2-00-19	47
TEHUANTEPEC (Area Code 971)		
Calli	5-00-85	
ARRIAGA (Area Code 966)		
Auto Hotel El Parador	2-01-35	59
TAPACHULA (Area Code 962)		
Lomo Real	6-14-40	125
Motel Kamico	6-26-40	99

CENTRAL GULF COAST

JALAPA (Area Code 281)		
Xalapa	8-22-22	130
COATEPEC (Area Code 281)		
Posada Coatepec	6-05-44	105
VERACRUZ (Area Code 29)		
Baluarte	36-08-44	32
Colonial	32-01-92	37-42
Emporio	32-00-20	106
Hostal de Cortes	32-00-65	93
Mocambo	37-16-61	90
Veracruz	31-22-33	90
Villa del Mar	31-33-66	51

HOTEL	PHONE	RATE
FORTIN DE LAS FLORES (Area Code 271)		
Fortin de las Flores	3-00-55	48
Posada Loma	3-07-53	37
CATEMACO (Area Code 294)		
La Finca	3-03-22	58
Posada Koniapan	3-00-63	24
Playa Azul	3-00-01	24
SANTIAGO TUXTLA (Area Code 294)		
Castellanos	7-02-00	33
PAPANTLA (Area Code 784)		
Tajin	2-01-21	28-35
POZA RICA (Area Code 782)		
Poza Rica Inn	3-19-22	60
TECOLUTLA (Area Code 784)		
Balneario Tecolutla	5-09-01	47
XICOTEPAC DE JUAREZ (Area Code 776)		
Mi Ranchito	4-02-12	60
PAHUATLAN		
San Carlos	551-3859 (in Mexico City)	36
VILLAHERMOSA (Area Code 931)		
Cencali	5-19-96	80
Holiday Inn Tabasco Plaza	6-44-00	143
Maya Tabasco Hotel	2-15-99	77
Miraflores	2-00-22	48

CHIAPAS

OCOSINGO (Area Code 967)		
Central	3-00-24	35

HOTEL	PHONE	RATE
SAN CHRISTOBAL DE LAS CASAS (Area Code 967)		
Flamboyant	8-05-14	65
Mansion del Valle	8-25-82	54
Parador Mexicanos	8-00-55	30
Posada Diego de Mazariegos	8-05-13	74
Santa Clara	8-11-40	50
Na-Bolom	8-14-18	50
TUXTLA GUTIERREZ (Area Code 961)		
Bonampak	3-21-01	71
La Hacienda	2-79-86	50
Gran Hotel Humberto	2-25-04	54
PALENQUE (Area Code 934)		
Chan Kah Centro	5-03-18	44
Chan Kah Ruinas	5-11-00	75
Kashlan	5-02-97	30
La Canada	5-01-02	40
Maya Tulipanes	5-02-01	52
Mision Palenque	5-02-41	115
Nututun Palenque	5-01-61	75

YUCATÁN AND CAMPECHE

MÉRIDA (Area Code 99)		
Calinda Panamericana	23-91-11	88
Caribe	24-90-22	35-47
Casa del Balam	24-88-44	94
Colon	23-43-55	59
Colonial	23-64-44	55
Dolores Alba	28-56-50	30
El Castellano	23-01-00	95
Holiday Inn	25-68-77	165
Los Aluxes	24-21-99	95
Mérida Mision	23-95-00	167
Montejo	28-02-77	28
Posada Toledo	23-16-90	42

HOTEL	PHONE	RATE
CHICHEN ITZA (Area Code 985)		
Dolores Alba	28-56-50 (in Mérida)	32
Hacienda Chichen	6-24-62	82
Mayaland	6-27-77	105
Mision Park Inn Chichen Itza	6-25-13	93MAP
Piramide Inn	6-26-71x15	temporarily closed
Villa Arqueologica	6-28-30	99
VALLADOLID (Area Code 985)		
Don Luis	6-20-08	24
El Meson del Marquez	6-20-73	40
San Clemente	6-22-08	29
RIO LAGARTOS (Area Code 986)		
Maria Nefertity	14-15	30
UXMAL (Area Code 99)		
Hacienda Uxmal	24-71-42	97
Mision Uxmal	24-73-08	93 MAP
Villa Arqueologica	24-70-53	77
CAMPECHE (Area Code 981)		
Alhambra	6-68-22	55
Baluartes	6-39-11	59
Lopez	6-33-44	33
Ramada Inn Campeche	6-22-33	110
Si Ho Playa	6-29-89 (in Seybaplaya)	30

QUINTANA ROO: THE CARIBBEAN

CANCÚN (Area Code 988)		
Antillano	4-11-32	55
Calinda Viva	3-08-00	140
Camino Real	3-01-00	248
Cancún Sheraton	3-19-88	220

HOTEL	PHONE	RATE
Club Lagoon	3-11-01	140
Crowne Plaza	5-10-22	198
Fiesta Americana	3-14-00	242
Hyatt Cancún Caribe	3-00-44	209
Hyatt Regency Cancún	3-09-66	200
Maria de Lourdes	4-12-42	55
Maya Caribe	3-20-00	75
Novotel	4-29-99	55
Omni Cancún	5-07-14	198
Parador	4-19-22	44
Playa Blanca	3-00-71	130
Plaza Caribe	4-13-77	74
Plaza del Sol	4-38-88	80
Ritz Carlton	5-08-08	190-425
Stouffer Presidente	3-02-00	175
Villas Tacul	3-00-00	105-270

COZUMEL (Area Code 987)		
Bahia	2-02-09	62
Barracuda	2-00-02	73
Cantarell	2-01-44	100-135
Galapago Inn Dive Resort	2-06-63	200AP
La Casa del Mar	2-19-00	90
La Ceiba	2-08-44	135
La Perla Beach Hotel	2-01-88	100-110
Mara	2-03-00	87
Mary Carmen	2-05-81	35
Maya Cozumel	2-00-11	40
Melia Mayan Cozumel	2-04-11	170-210
Plaza Las Glorias	2-20-00	155-185
Sol Cabanas del Caribe	2-00-17	125-160
Sol Caribe	2-07-00	170-210
Stouffer Presidente	2-03-22	175
Villablanca	2-07-30	44
Vista del Mar	2-05-45	42

HOTEL	PHONE	RATE
ISLA MUJERES (Area Code 987)		
Cabanas Maria del Mar	7-01-79	55-66
Na Balam	7-02-79	75-85
Perla del Caribe	7-04-44	70
Posada del Mar	7-02-12	70
Rocamar	7-01-01	54
EAST COAST (Area Code 987)		
Akumal Cancún	2-24-53	100
Copa Cabana	3-02-18	40-45
Costa de Cocos	no phone	50CP
Costa del Mar	2-02-31	85
El Bocadito	no phone	18
Kailuum	no phone	90MAP
Las Casitas Akumal	2-25-54	140
Molcas	3-00-70	90
Osho Oasis	no phone	55
Posada del Capitan Lafitte	23-04-85 (in Mérida)	140MAP
Puerto Aventuras	3-22-66 (in Cancún)	168AP
Quinta Mija	3-01-11	85
Shangri-La Caribe	23-04-85 (in Mérida)	165MAP
Sol Pez Maya Fishing Camp (Boca Paila)	2-00-72 (in Cozumel)	116
Villa Arqueologica Coba	6-28-30 (in Chichen Itza)	68
Villas Akumal Bungalows	2-25-32	66-94
Villas Akumal Hotel	2-25-32	99
CHETUMAL (Area Code 983)		
El Cedro	2-68-78	29
Laguna	2-35-17	37
Los Cocos	2-05-44	55
Principe	2-47-99	32
Rancho Encantado	no phone	120MAP

HOTEL	PHONE	RATE
PACIFIC COAST RESORTS		

ACAPULCO (Area Code 74)

Hotel	Phone	Rate
Acapulco Plaza	85-80-50	185
Acapulco Princess	84-31-00	300MAP
Acapulco Ritz	85-73-36	120
Belmar	82-15-25	67
Boca Chica	83-66-01	150MAP
Calinda Acapulco	84-04-10	135
Copacabana	84-32-64	135
Doral Playa	85-02-32	55
Exelaris Hyatt Regency	84-28-88	175-205
Fiesta Americana Condesa	84-23-55	193
La Palapa	84-53-63	110
Las Brisas	84-15-80	237
Lindavista	82-27-83	50
Majestic	83-47-10	85
Maralisa	85-66-77	120
Pierre Marques	84-20-00	212CP
Royal Elcano	84-19-50	125
Versalles	82-60-02	42
Villa Vera Racquet Club	84-03-33	205

PUERTO VALLARTA (Area Code 322)

Hotel	Phone	Rate
Buganvilias Sheraton	3-04-04	180
Camino Real	3-01-23	185
Fiesta Americana	4-20-10	231
Fontana del Mar	2-05-83	55
Hyatt Coral Grand	3-07-07	198
La Jolla de Mismaloya	3-06-60	165
Las Palmas	4-06-50	129
Molino de Agua	2-19-07	61
Pelicanos	2-21-07	75
Playa Conchas Chinas	2-01-56	70-85
Playa Los Arcos	2-15-83	70
Posada de Roger	2-08-36	29
Quinta Maria Cortes	2-13-17	70-145

HOTEL	PHONE	RATE
Rio	2-32-35	33
Rosita	2-10-33	40
Suites Esmeralda	2-04-95	82
Tropicana	2-09-12	45

IXTAPA/ZIHUATANEJO (Area Code 743)

Bungalows Allec	4-20-02	55
Bungalows Vepao	670-7572 (in Mexico City)	55
Dorado Pacifico	3-20-25	160
Fiesta Mexicana	4-37-76	78
Irma	4-20-25	78
Ixtapa Sheraton	3-18-58	170
Krystal Ixtapa	3-03-33	174
Las Urracas	4-20-49	65
Omni	3-00-03	176
Posada Citlali	4-20-43	37
Posada Real	3-16-25	102
Sotavento and Catalina Hotels	4-20-74	90-110MAP
Stouffer Presidente	3-00-18	174
Susy	4-23-39	40
Villa del Sol	4-22-39	253MAP
Villas Miramar	4-21-06	65-75
Westin Reosrt Ixtapa	3-21-21	198

MAZATLAN (Area Code 69)

Aqua Marina	81-70-80	67CP
Belmar	85-11-11	34
Camino Real	83-11-11	140
El Cid Tourist Resort	83-33-33	129
Hacienda Mazatlan	82-70-00	60
Holiday Inn	83-22-22	95
Joncol's	81-21-31	20
La Siesta	81-26-40	29
Los Sabalos	83-53-33	107
Motel Los Arcos	83-50-66	60
Oceano Palace	83-06-66	60
Playa Mazatlan	83-44-44	75

HOTEL	PHONE	RATE
Posada de la Mision	83-24-44	30
Suites Las Flores	83-51-00	70
Tropicana	83-80-00	48
SAN BLAS (Area Code 321)		
Las Brisas	5-01-12	77CP
Mision San Blas	5-00-23	55
TEPIC (Area Code 321)		
Motel La Loma	3-22-22	52
MANZANILLO (Area Code 333)		
La Posada	3-18-99	73CP
Las Hadas	3-00-00	275
Roca del Mar	3-29-50	135
BARRA DE NAVIDAD (Area Code 333)		
Barra de Navidad	7-01-22	42
Cabo Blanco	7-01-03	90
SAN PATRICIO MELAQUE (Area Code 333)		
de Legazpi	7-03-97	38
COSTA DE ORO (Area Code 333)		
El Tecuan	7-01-32	75
Fiesta Americana	7-02-20	210AP
Plaza Careyes	7-00-10	135
PUERTO ESCONDIDO (Area Code 958)		
Acali	2-07-54	34
Arco Iris	2-04-32	31-40
Las Palmas	2-02-30	40
Paraiso Escondido	2-04-44	55
Posada Real	2-01-33	90
Santa Fe	2-01-70	68
PUERTO ANGEL		
La Posada Canon Devata	no phone	25-29

HOTEL	PHONE	RATE
BAHIAS DE HUATULCO (Area Code 958)		
Club Med	1-00-33	NA
Grifer	7-00-48	34
Posada Binneguenda	7-00-77	84
Royal Maeva	1-00-00	284AP
Sheraton Huatulco	1-00-55	165
Suites Buganbilias	7-00-18	50

INDEX

Introducing the 1994 Fielding Travel Guides— fresh, fascinating and fun!

The travel guide series that started truth in travel is back.

An incisive new attitude and an exciting new look! All-new design and format. In-depth reviews. Fielding delivers travel information the way frequent travelers demand it—written with sparkle, style and humor. Candid insights, sage advice, insider tips. No fluff, no filler, only fresh information that makes the journey more fun, more fascinating, more Fielding.

Australia 1994	**$16.95**
Belgium 1994	**$16.95**
Bermuda/Bahamas 1994	**$16.95**
Brazil 1994	**$16.95**
Britain 1994	**$16.95**
Budget Europe 1994	**$16.95**
Caribbean 1994	**$16.95**
Europe 1994	**$16.95**
Far East 1994	**$16.95**
France 1994	**$16.95**
The Great Sights of Europe 1994	**$16.95**
Hawaii 1994	**$16.95**
Holland 1994	**$16.95**
Italy 1994	**$16.95**
Mexico 1994	**$16.95**
New Zealand 1994	**$16.95**
Scandinavia 1994	**$16.95**
Spain & Portugal 1994	**$16.95**
Switzerland & the Alpine Region 1994	**$16.95**
Worldwide Cruises 1994	**$16.95**
Shopping Europe	**$12.95**

To place an order: call toll-free
1-800-FW-2-GUIDE
add $2.00 shipping & handling, allow 2-6 weeks.

For Travel Insiders Only!

FIELDING'S
TRAVEL
SECRETS

FIELDING'S TRAVEL SECRETS is the insider's travel guide, available only to travel professionals and a very limited number of Fielding Travel Guide readers. Created by Fielding's experienced staff of writers and released in six bi-monthly installments per year, the insider's report is packed with timely travel information, trends, news, tips and reviews. Enroll now and you will also receive a variety of significant discounts and special preview information.

Due to the sensitive nature of the information contained in these reports, subscriptions available to non-travel industry individuals are limited to the first 10,000 subscribers. The annual price for all six installments is $60. This offer also comes with an unconditional money-back guarantee if you are not fully satisfied.

To Reserve Your Subscription
1-800-FW-2-GUIDE

Favorite People, Places & Experiences

ADDRESS:	NOTES:
Name	
Address	
Telephone	
Name	
Address	
Telephone	
Name	
Address	
Telephone	
Name	
Address	
Telephone	
Name	
Address	
Telephone	
Name	
Address	
Telephone	
Name	
Address	
Telephone	

Favorite People, Places & Experiences

ADDRESS:	NOTES:

Name

Address

Telephone

Name

Address

Telephone

Name

Address

Telephone

Name

Address

Telephone

Name

Address

Telephone

Name

Address

Telephone

Name

Address

Telephone

Favorite People, Places & Experiences

ADDRESS:	NOTES:

Name

Address

Telephone

Name

Address

Telephone

Name

Address

Telephone

Name

Address

Telephone

Name

Address

Telephone

Name

Address

Telephone

Name

Address

Telephone

Favorite People, Places & Experiences

ADDRESS:	NOTES:

Name

Address

Telephone

Name

Address

Telephone

Name

Address

Telephone

Name

Address

Telephone

Name

Address

Telephone

Name

Address

Telephone

Name

Address

Telephone

Favorite People, Places & Experiences

ADDRESS:	NOTES:

Name

Address

Telephone

Name

Address

Telephone

Name

Address

Telephone

Name

Address

Telephone

Name

Address

Telephone

Name

Address

Telephone

Name

Address

Telephone

Favorite People, Places & Experiences

ADDRESS:	NOTES:

Name

Address

Telephone

Name

Address

Telephone

Name

Address

Telephone

Name

Address

Telephone

Name

Address

Telephone

Name

Address

Telephone

Name

Address

Telephone

Favorite People, Places & Experiences

ADDRESS:	NOTES:

Name

Address

Telephone

Name

Address

Telephone

Name

Address

Telephone

Name

Address

Telephone

Name

Address

Telephone

Name

Address

Telephone

Name

Address

Telephone